Understanding Business Ethics

Third Edition

To Casey and Olive, Sarah, Olivia, John, and Bill,
who have given me invaluable ethical guidance in my role as son,
husband, father, and brother.
—PAS

To Peter, Olivia, and John—the three most important reasons
for staying on an ethical track, and to my family, especially my mother,
and special friends, those who are here and those no longer with me,
who have provided inspiration and taught me through example
that ethics really do matter.
—SDS

SAGE was founded in 1965 by Sara Miller McCune to support the dissemination of usable knowledge by publishing innovative and high-quality research and teaching content. Today, we publish more than 850 journals, including those of more than 300 learned societies, more than 800 new books per year, and a growing range of library products including archives, data, case studies, reports, and video. SAGE remains majority-owned by our founder, and after Sara's lifetime will become owned by a charitable trust that secures our continued independence.

Los Angeles | London | New Delhi | Singapore | Washington DC

Understanding Business Ethics

Third Edition

Peter A. Stanwick
Auburn University

Sarah D. Stanwick
Auburn University

Los Angeles | London | New Delhi
Singapore | Washington DC

Los Angeles | London | New Delhi
Singapore | Washington DC

FOR INFORMATION:

SAGE Publications, Inc.
2455 Teller Road
Thousand Oaks, California 91320
E-mail: order@sagepub.com

SAGE Publications Ltd.
1 Oliver's Yard
55 City Road
London EC1Y 1SP
United Kingdom

SAGE Publications India Pvt. Ltd.
B 1/I 1 Mohan Cooperative Industrial Area
Mathura Road, New Delhi 110 044
India

SAGE Publications Asia-Pacific Pte. Ltd.
3 Church Street
#10-04 Samsung Hub
Singapore 049483

Acquisitions Editor: Maggie Stanley
eLearning Editor: Katie Bierach
Editorial Assistant: Nicole Mangona
Production Editor: Bennie Clark Allen
Copy Editor: Diana Breti
Typesetter: C&M Digitals (P) Ltd.
Proofreader: Wendy Jo Dymond
Indexer: Karen Wiley
Cover Designer: Candice Harman
Marketing Manager: Liz Thornton

Copyright © 2016 by SAGE Publications, Inc.

Printed in the United States of America

Library of Congress Cataloging-in-Publication Data
Stanwick, Peter Allen, author.

Understanding business ethics / Peter A. Stanwick, Sarah D. Stanwick. — Third edition.

pages cm
Includes index.

ISBN 978-1-5063-0323-9 (pbk. : alk. paper)

1. Business ethics. I. Stanwick, Sarah D. (Sarah Dunn), author. II. Title.

HF5387.S675 2016

174'.4—dc23   2015028462

This book is printed on acid-free paper.

Certified Chain of Custody
SUSTAINABLE FORESTRY INITIATIVE
Promoting Sustainable Forestry
www.sfiprogram.org
SFI-01268

SFI label applies to text stock

18 19 10 9 8 7 6 5 4 3

• Brief Contents •

• Detailed Contents •

PART II • INTERNAL FOCUS ON ETHICAL ISSUES   67

PART V • CASES   277

• Preface to the Third Edition •

A s the second decade of the new millennium moves forward, businesses around the world continue to address the ethical behavior of their employees. Whether you consider Charles Ponzi in the 1920s, Kenneth Lay in the 1990s, or Bernard Madoff in current times, unethical behavior is as old as commerce itself. Greed is part of human nature, and as long as there are finite amounts of goods of value, some people will try to obtain those items by whatever means possible.

In the movie *Wall Street,* trader Gordon Gekko, portrayed by Michael Douglas, highlights in his "Greed Is Good" speech that there is a fine line between using self-interests to motivate and using those same interests to obtain riches through unethical and greedy actions.

Our Philosophy

The philosophy of this textbook is to serve as an integration tool in the classroom to highlight the positive consequences of ethical behavior and the negative consequences of unethical behavior. The primary focus of the chapters is to present potential ethical dilemmas that decision makers may face pertaining to a number of different decision-making areas. Of the 26 cases in the textbook, 20 of the cases highlight the negative consequences for the company's stakeholders when managers pursue unethical decision making. Our challenge was to write a textbook that covers the necessary issues related to business ethics so that students will be better prepared for the ethical dilemmas they will face in their chosen careers. In addition, the presentation of six organizations that have a positive ethical focus also highlights that companies can be a positive force in supporting the needs of society.

We have found through our experiences in the classroom over the past 20 years that students need to be exposed to ethical situations. We believe that business students prefer a real-world approach. Today's business students like to discuss companies they are familiar with and those companies whose products and services create a familiar surrounding for them in their daily lives. Our goal was to use real-world scenarios in examples and cases that provide students with a basic understanding of the issues surrounding business ethics and that demonstrate that ethics really matter. Our textbook presents a broad and comprehensive perspective of ethics that includes chapters on information technology, financial management, marketing, human resources, natural environment, strategy, and the developing world. In addition, we also present information related to the Association to Advance Collegiate Schools of Business (AACSB)'s recommended topics of the responsibility of business in society, ethical decision making, ethical leadership, and corporate governance.

One of the benefits of this textbook is the flexibility it gives instructors for presenting the material. This textbook can be used at both the undergraduate and graduate levels. We believe that case discussions will differ significantly at each level. At the undergraduate level, we expect that students will focus on the most concrete ideas in the cases. However, at the graduate level, we expect that students will evaluate the cases by integrating their own experiences into the discussions, as well as recognize the more subtle aspects of the chapters and cases. The cases in the text are designed to stimulate class discussion on a variety of ethical issues.

Our goal was to write a textbook that differs from other ethics textbooks on four dimensions: (1) global perspective, (2) real-world business ethics cases, (3) comprehensive and diverse selection of ethics topics, and (4) a central theme linking each chapter. Each of these dimensions is expanded in the following discussion.

Key Dimension 1: Global Perspective

Seven ethics cases discuss organizations that are headquartered outside the United States, which demonstrates that ethical issues in business are both global and domestic in nature. Our textbook integrates a global focus within each of the 13 chapters in the textbook, and it includes one chapter (Chapter 11) that focuses on ethical issues related to developing countries. This allows the student to see the global impact of ethical decisions, and it allows the instructor the freedom to integrate ethical topics from a global perspective.

Key Dimension 2: Real-World Business Ethics Cases

The cases highlight a number of different ethical issues, including defective products, inaccurate financial statements, illegal investor trading, and top management misconduct. The majority of the cases included in our textbook are current and ongoing. This gives the instructor and the students the ability to update the case and analyze how the case is progressing.

The number of cases included in our textbook is greater than in other textbooks. We believe that professors need an adequate number of cases to make the course interesting and to eliminate the need to supplement the cases presented in textbooks. The quantity of cases presented allows instructors flexibility in adapting to various time formats for the class.

Our approach in writing this textbook was a practical and applied approach. We believe that students want real-world connections when studying in today's business environment. Business students today are more connected to the current issues than were the students of 20, or even 10, years ago. Today's students have access to immediate information and are computer literate. Given this, our textbook focuses on real-world examples and avoids fictional scenarios.

In addition, each chapter contains an opening ethical vignette and closing real-life ethical dilemma, which enhance the opportunity to develop discussion among the class members during the lecture period.

Key Dimension 3:
Comprehensive and Diverse Selection of Ethics Topics (Better Coverage and Content)

With 13 chapters and 26 cases, we believe this is one of the most comprehensive business ethics textbooks in the marketplace. In addition to a comprehensive presentation of the ethical issues in the cases, our textbook has chapters on financial reporting, information technology, strategy, and the developing world that are not included in many of the other business ethics textbooks. Furthermore, we have comprehensive topic areas within each chapter that have been developed based on real business scenarios. This allows for a more focused, yet still comprehensive, presentation of the material in the chapters.

Key Dimension 4:
A Central Theme Linking Each Chapter

We believe that it is necessary to have a central theme that is recurrent in each chapter. When reading textbooks, students often view each chapter as unrelated to the next. Therefore, our goal was to link each chapter with one common theme that focused primarily on the interaction of the firm with its various stakeholders. We stressed in each chapter that facing ethical dilemmas is a challenge and that there are consequences attached to each decision that is made in the business world. Our purpose was to present ethical challenges that students will face and help them see the consequences of their decisions. The challenges are discussed in the chapter material, and the consequences of actions/decisions are emphasized in the cases.

Structure of the Chapters

We believe that the 13 chapters in the textbook cover, in a comprehensive nature, the most relevant topics related to business ethics. A major topic of each of the chapters is introduced in the beginning of the chapter with a real ethical scenario. These scenarios are a good starting point in any lecture pertaining to that particular chapter. In addition, there are thought-provoking questions at the end of each chapter to also allow the instructor to facilitate discussion in the classroom. Furthermore, the end of each chapter includes a real-life ethical dilemma that will also enhance the discussion during the class period.

Chapter 1 introduces the student to the theoretical background of ethics by answering the critical question of why studying business ethics is important. By drawing on the teachings and beliefs of ancient philosophers, Chapter 1 provides business students with a strong theoretical support from a philosophical perspective. Chapter 1 also discusses how the legendary seven deadly sins are linked with unethical actions by individuals.

Chapter 2 addresses the evolving complexities related to business ethics. The chapter includes a discussion on the global issues related to business ethics. Chapter 2 continues by presenting a history of the study of ethics and discusses how integrity plays a role in ethical decision making. Chapter 2 also highlights the cheating culture and how cheating is perceived by different generational demographics.

In one of the cornerstone chapters, Chapter 3 presents the relationship between businesses and their stakeholders. Stakeholder theory is one of the integrating tools used to link the different chapters by identifying management's responsibility to others when a firm makes a decision. In addition, Chapter 3 highlights that the firm's responsibility is to be aware of its global social commitment to others and includes the role of triple-line reporting. Chapter 3 also discusses issues related to corporate reputation and corporate philanthropy.

Chapter 4 is devoted to the ethical issues related to financial reporting. Chapter 4 presents financial concepts such as creative accounting, insider trading, and Ponzi schemes. Chapter 4 also discusses the role of external auditors, who are responsible for verifying the accuracy of the financial statements and the components of the Sarbanes-Oxley Act. Chapter 4 also presents some common ways in which management can manipulate the financial statements to present desired but inaccurate financial data.

Chapter 5 addresses the issues of transformational and transactional ethical leadership and the role of corporate governance in protecting the rights of the firm's stakeholders. Chapter 5 also addresses issues related to the board of directors' actions.

Chapter 6 discusses strategic planning, corporate culture, and corporate compliance. Chapter 6 highlights the impact trust and power can have on how ethical and unethical decisions are made by management. Chapter 6 also addresses how decisions are made during an ethical crisis and disaster. The chapter presents the argument that ethical leadership links the ethical issues related to strategic planning and corporate culture. Chapter 6 also addresses the role of corruption in the operations of businesses globally.

Chapter 7 discusses ethical decision making and human resources. The chapter highlights Lawrence Kohlberg's model of moral development as well as two classic obedience-based studies developed at Yale and Stanford. Chapter 7 also discusses human resource issues such as workplace diversity, employee misbehavior, extreme jobs, sexual harassment and discrimination, office bullying, and employee monitoring.

Chapter 8 addresses ethical issues relating to the firm's interaction with the natural environment. This chapter presents a topic that is missing from many other ethics textbooks. Chapter 8 discusses how firms need to address the different environmental demands of various stakeholders. In addition, Chapter 8 also presents how firms can use the natural environment as an opportunity to enhance their competitive advantage. Furthermore, Chapter 8 addresses current topics such as environmental sustainability, climate change, and a firm's carbon footprint.

Chapter 9 also addresses a topic not discussed in many other ethics textbooks, which is the ethical issues relating to information technology. As today's students become more technologically savvy, they need to understand that new ethical issues are created with every technological advancement. Topics covered in Chapter 9 include privacy issues related to various stakeholders, the role of government regulations, big data, and the control of personal information.

Chapter 10 discusses ethical issues related to marketing and advertising. Topics for this chapter include green marketing, relationship marketing, consumer boycotts, social media, product recalls, false and misleading advertising, the role of marketing in the tobacco industry, and advertising aimed at children.

Chapter 11 addresses another ethical focus not common in other business ethics textbooks: ethical issues related to the developing world. Topics for Chapter 11 include the bottom of the pyramid market, social entrepreneurship, human rights, poverty, hunger, and the UN Millennium Development Goals.

Chapter 12 examines the role of a code of ethics and the establishment of ethical guidelines to assist decision makers in making the correct ethical decisions. Chapter 12 examines the benefits of a firm having a strong code of ethics and also presents content areas that should be considered in a code of ethics. Chapter 12 also presents some global ideas that firms could integrate into their own ethics philosophy.

Chapter 13 concludes the chapters in the textbook by examining how firms can evaluate their ethical commitment. Chapter 13 highlights the importance of a strong ethical commitment by presenting data pertaining to cases of fraud that occur globally. The chapter also addresses the establishment of a comprehensive ethical training program to ensure that employees understand their responsibilities. Chapter 13 addresses the importance of having a corporate ethics officer who is ultimately accountable for the ethical conduct of the employees. Also addressed is the issue of firms developing opportunities for employees to be whistle-blowers when they suspect unethical activities are occurring within the firm.

Structure of the Cases

The cases were selected based on their relevance, timeliness, and the representation of a broad range of ethical issues globally. Seven of the 26 cases deal with firms headquartered outside the United States. The locations of these cases are Germany (Siemens), Italy (World Food Programme), England (Rupert Murdoch and News Corporation and BP), South Africa (De Beers), and Japan (TEPCO and Olympus). Furthermore, two cases, Apple and Mattel, address the issue of outsourcing their manufacturing operations to companies located in China. In addition, the companies in the cases represent a number of diverse industries, including telecommunications, food and food distribution, financial services, aerospace and defense, automobiles, toys, mining, media, energy, durable goods, pharmaceuticals, music, and retailing. Furthermore, the cases highlight a number of ethical issues, including financial and wire fraud, bribery, lack of corporate governance, manipulation of data, perjury, Ponzi schemes, obstruction of justice, lying to government officials, violations of government regulations, product recalls, and the death and mutilation of employees and customers.

The authors believe that this textbook represents a comprehensive review of current ethical issues from a global perspective. The 13 chapters and 26 cases will allow any instructor the ability to fully integrate current ethical issues in the classroom in an effective manner. Using *Understanding Business Ethics: Third Edition* in the classroom will enlighten students to the complex ethical issues they will face in the business world.

What Is New for the Third Edition

1. **An update of all 13 chapters and 26 cases**.
2. **The addition of opening vignettes** including Sir Nicholas Winton, money laundering at HSBC, "nut rage" and Korean Airlines, environmentally sustainable billboards in Peru, *The Interview* movie and North Korea, Samsung and child labor, and the Hillsborough soccer disaster.
3. **The addition of cases** on Disney's CSR and the GM ignition recall issue.
4. **The addition of a section on barriers to an ethical organization** reflecting challenges organizations must address to ensure the ethical behavior of their employees.
5. **The addition of a section on NGOs as stakeholders** and an expansion of the discussion on CSR including a global approach, the presentation of different models of CSR, implementation of CSR, and the role of employee engagement and CSR.
6. **The addition of a section on insider trading**.
7. **The addition of a section on extreme jobs**.
8. **The addition of a section on ethical issues related to big data and social media**.

• Acknowledgments •

SAGE Publications gratefully acknowledges the following reviewers:

Volker Brecht, Southern University at New Orleans

Biruk Alemayehu, Southern University at New Orleans

Shelagh Campbell, University of Regina

Alberto Costa, Universidade De Aveiro

Epameinondas Katsikas, University of Kent

Jolaine Jackson, Yavapai College-Prescott

Christine Grant, Coventry University

Chapters and Corresponding Cases Matrix

Case #	Name	Part I				Part II				Part III			Part IV	
		Chapter 1 Individual Ethical Duty	Chapter 2 Individual Ethical Behavior	Chapter 3 Stakeholder Corporate Social Resp.	Chapter 4 Financial Reporting	Chapter 5 Leadership Corporate Governance	Chapter 6 Strategic Planning Culture	Chapter 7 Decision Making Human Resources	Chapter 8 Environment Sustainability	Chapter 9 Information Technology	Chapter 10 Marketing Advertising	Chapter 11 Developing Countries	Chapter 12 Code of Ethics	Chapter 13 Evaluating Ethics
1	Bernie Madoff	X	Z	Z	Z	Z	X	Z						Z
2	Siemens	X	X	Z	Z	Z	Z	X					X	X
3	TOMS Shoes	Z	Z	Z		X	Z	X	Z		Z	Z	X	X
4	Disney	Z	Z	Z		Z	Z	X	Z	X	Z		Z	Z
5	World Food Programme	Z		Z		Z	Z	X	Z			Z		
6	News Corporation	Z	Z	Z		Z	Z	Z		Z	Z		Z	Z
7	Enron	Z	Z	Z	Z	Z	Z	Z					Z	Z
8	Google	Z	X	Z		Z	Z	X		Z	Z		X	X
9	HealthSouth	Z	Z	Z	Z	Z	Z	Z			X		Z	Z
10	De Beers	Z	Z	Z		Z	Z	Z	X		Z	Z	X	X
11	Interface	Z	Z	Z		Z	Z	Z	Z		Z		**Z**	Z
12	Facebook	Z	Z	Z		Z	Z	Z		Z	Z		Z	Z
13	Mattel	X	X	Z	Z	Z	Z	Z	X		Z	Z	Z	Z
14	GM	Z	Z	Z		Z	Z	Z	Z		Z		Z	Z
15	McWane	Z	Z	Z		Z	Z	Z	Z				Z	Z
16	Merck	Z	Z	Z		Z	Z	Z		Z	Z		X	X
17	Music Industry	Z	Z	Z		Z	Z	Z		Z	Z		X	X
18	Apple	Z	Z	Z		Z	Z	Z	Z		Z	Z	X	X
19	Patagonia	Z	Z	Z		Z	Z	Z	Z		Z	Z	Z	Z
20	Tokyo Electric Power	Z	Z	Z		Z	Z	Z	Z				Z	Z
21	Tyco	Z	Z	Z	Z	Z	Z	Z					Z	Z
22	Olympus	Z	Z	Z	Z	Z	Z	Z					Z	Z
23	Wal-Mart	Z	Z	Z		Z	Z	Z	X		Z	Z	Z	Z
24	WorldCom	Z	Z	Z	Z	Z	Z	Z		X			Z	Z
25	BP	Z	Z	Z		Z	Z	Z	Z		Z		Z	Z
26	Greyston Bakery	Z	Z	Z		Z	Z	Z			Z		Z	Z

Legend

Z = Primary Topic
X = Secondary Topic

FROM ETHICAL FOUNDATION TO ADDRESSING STAKEHOLDER NEEDS

The Foundation of Ethical Thought

The biggest corporation, like the humblest citizen, must be held to strict compliance with the will of the people.

—Theodore Roosevelt

We demand that big business give people a square deal; in return we must insist when anyone engaged in big business honestly endeavors to do right, he shall himself be given a square deal.

—Theodore Roosevelt

Chapter Objectives

After reading and studying Chapter 1, students should be able to

1. Define the terms *ethics* and *business ethics.*
2. Describe the different types of ethical examinations and frameworks.
3. Explain the seven deadly sins and their relationship to ethical behavior.
4. Discuss the Global Business Standards Codex with respect to a company's responsibility.

Panera Cares Community Cafés: A Loaf in Every Arm

The foundation arm of Panera Bread has established the "Panera Cares community café" program. A Panera Cares café is a café in which the customers decide how much to pay for their meal. The menu is consistent with a regular Panera Bread café, and for those customers with limited financial resources, the café will exchange one hour of volunteer work for a meal. Panera Bread's philosophy is that "at the end of the day, this café isn't about offering a handout. It's about offering a hand up to those who need it."[1] Located in Portland, Oregon; Clayton, Missouri; Chicago, Illinois; Boston, Massachusetts; and Dearborn, Michigan, the Panera Cares locations are strategically selected based on the needs of the local community and infrastructure variables such as easy access via public transportation. There are no prices or cash registers; there are only suggested donation levels and donation bins. Panera Cares café is run by the Panera Bread Foundation, a registered charitable organization. With the identification of a broad customer target market, Panera Cares states that its mission is to "make a difference by offering the Panera Bread experience with dignity to all—those who can afford it, those who need a hand up, and everyone in between."[2] Customers who have the means to pay for the meal like the option of deciding how much to contribute. For example, one day the customer may be generous and pay above what the price of the meal would cost in a traditional Panera Bread, but other times the customer may only have a few dollars on hand to pay for the food. In fact, the majority of the customers pay the retail value of the food or more. Panera Bread has calculated that approximately 60% of the customers pay the retail value, 20% pay more than the retail value, and 20% pay less than the retail value. Panera Bread has found that the communities surrounding the Panera Cares cafés have embraced the concept that this café will ultimately survive because of shared responsibility. The average Panera Cares café will generate revenue of $100,000 monthly and yield a "profit" of $3,000 to $4,000 a month. The profits are used to fund job training programs for high-risk young people. The graduates of the job training programs are offered work at other traditional Panera Bread cafés. Panera Bread founder Ronald Shaich stated that there are a few people that abuse the system but that "More people are fundamentally good. . . . People step up and they do the right thing."[3]

Introduction

As human beings, we are accountable for our actions. Our day-to-day interactions in every activity we participate in affect both the human and the nonhuman elements of our world. As a result, as employees of a business organization, we take on the additional burden of also being responsible for the actions of the business organization. An underlying component in guiding our behavior both inside and outside a business setting is the role of ethics.

Ethics can be defined as the values that an individual uses to interpret whether any particular action or behavior is considered acceptable and appropriate. Some questions that could be asked to help identify the values needed to interpret the particular action or behavior could be the following:

1. Is the behavior or action consistent with the overall basic duties of the individual in question?
2. Does the behavior or action acknowledge and respect the underlying rights of all the individuals who will be affected by the action?
3. Would the behavior or action be considered the best practice in that specific set of circumstances?
4. Does the behavior or action match the overall entrenched beliefs of the individual?[4]

Business ethics can be defined as the collective values of a business organization that can be used to evaluate whether the behaviors of the organization's collective members are considered acceptable and appropriate. To understand what is acceptable and appropriate for individuals, their moral values must be identified and supported.

The Role of Morals

The moral values of an individual comprise three components, which are the individual's principles, the individual's character, and the consequences of a particular action. Although each of these components is distinctive, there are also numerous interactions among the components.[5] Individuals rely on their own principles and standards of conduct to determine what course of action to take. Through various sources, such as religious affiliations, individuals are "taught" to determine "right" from "wrong." In addition, being a member of society "teaches" individuals what are acceptable principles or moral standards based on the moral values of the society. The moral values of the individual are based on his or her character. This component includes the strength of character, virtue, and integrity. Strength of character is based on adhering to one's moral beliefs even if it will result in a great cost for the individual. *Virtue* embodies characteristics such as prudence, fairness, trustworthiness, and courage. *Integrity* can be described as the ability to have a clear conscience and be at peace with your actions. The consequences of the individual's actions focus on the moral importance to the "ends" as well as the "means." You have to strive for a morally positive outcome and not just have positive moral actions. The result is as important as the avenue taken to reach that result.[6] The ends and the means are critical issues related to business ethics as they are incorporated into a free enterprise society.

Is Greed Good?

The point is, ladies and gentleman, that greed—for lack of a better word—is good. Greed is right. Greed works. Greed clarifies, cuts through, and captures the essence of the evolutionary spirit. Greed, in all of its forms—greed for life, for money, for love, knowledge—has marked the upward surge of mankind. And greed—you mark my words—will not only save Teldar Paper, but that other malfunctioning corporation called the USA.[7]

—Gordon Gekko, *Wall Street*, 1987

In the movie *Wall Street*, Michael Douglas plays the role of Gordon Gekko, who is a corporate raider. A corporate raider such as Gekko buys a majority of stock in underperforming companies in which the total market capitalization of the company is below the value of the assets. This means that the asset value of the company is higher than the total value of outstanding stock of the company. Gekko, like other corporate raiders of the time, would buy a controlling interest in the company and then break up the company by selling the assets separately and would capture the arbitrage difference between the higher asset price and the total market capitalization. While attending the annual meeting of a company in which he had just become the majority shareholder, Teldar Paper, Gekko presented this speech to the stockholders about the virtues of greed. This section of the speech, which lasts less than 45 seconds on screen, identifies the true underlying conflict that is inherent in a capitalistic economy and is the basis of any discussion related to the value of business ethics. The free enterprise system is based on motivating individuals to be productive. The more productive they are, the more resources they are able to accumulate. Thus, according to Gekko, individual self-interests and greed are integral for the success of a capitalistic society. Individuals must understand and agree to the rewards of their actions to meet the expectations of their jobs. As Gekko states, people are rewarded for their efforts through this competition of being better than others. As with any competition, however, there are both winners and losers. The ideals of business ethics attempt to address this distinction of "winners" and the rest of society. Although everyone has the right and freedom to accumulated resources based on their efforts, there is a line at which the self-interests of the individual do not supersede the interests of society. The establishment of laws and regulations control this type of behavior. Furthermore, as free will can be used to accumulate resources, it can also be used to determine what is perceived to be ethical or not. For example, it may be legal to have young girls sew shirts together for the equivalent of one dollar a day in developing countries such as Bangladesh and India; however, the question each company that considers this option must also ask is whether this action is ethical.

The study of business ethics is not always a black-and-white or a yes-or-no decision. The complexity of the issue must be considered by each decision maker as he or she makes decisions that affect the company and other stakeholders in society. For example, the opening vignette on the Panera Cares community cafés highlights how one company has addressed hunger in the community by allowing the customers to determine how much they would pay for the meal or provide one hour of volunteer work in exchange for the meal. Therefore, Panera Bread determined that the "cost" of offering these meals at below the traditional retail cost is more than offset by the company's outreach commitment to local communities. This is an example of the complexity surrounding the concept of business ethics and underlies why studying ethics is important.

Why Is Studying Ethics Important?

Business ethics can be described as having many shades of gray rather than being black and white. Within a corporate environment, individuals are always being tested to determine the direction of their moral compasses. In a highly completive global environment, there are many Gordon Gekkos who will do whatever it takes to win, even if it includes unethical actions. For many individuals, the ends rather than the means are important. As long as they "win" the competition, they do not care what means they use to obtain the "victory."

As a result, each individual decision maker is vulnerable to pressures, both from peers and superiors, that may not coincide with his or her ethical beliefs. A 2012 study by Ernst & Young (E&Y)[8] demonstrates how entrenched unethical behavior can be within corporations. More than 1,700 executives from 43 countries were surveyed by E&Y. Fifteen percent of the respondents stated that they would be willing to make cash payments in the form of a bribe to obtain business from a customer. In addition, 39% of the executives responded that bribery and corruption are common in doing business in their countries. Furthermore, 24% of the executives stated that bribery and corruption had increased due to the global economic downturn. Five percent of the executives admitted that they would be willing to misstate financial performance to achieve the company's objectives, which was an increase from 3% in the previous study. The results of the study also show that executives from numerous companies have little if any control systems in place to stop unethical behavior. Of the respondents, 13% stated their firms did not perform regular internal audits, 23% of the respondents stated their company does not have a regular audit from an external auditor, and 44% of the respondents worked for companies that did not have a whistle-blower hotline. Furthermore, 81% of the executives stated that their companies had corporate policies addressing corruption issues, yet only 42% of the executives had received training on the anticorruption policies. Each individual must know his or her own ethical beliefs, as well as those of his or her employer. To understand how ethics play a role in an individual decision-making process, it is important to understand that there are different types of ethical examinations. Information pertaining to ethical issues can be classified as descriptive, analytical, and normative.

The Foundation of Ethical Theory

Types of Ethical Examinations

Descriptive ethics is the presentation of facts related to the specific ethical actions of an individual or organization. Descriptive ethics is used when an observer wants to understand the course of events that generated the ethical issue. Within the descriptive ethics context, there is no interpretation of the facts or assumptions concerning why certain courses of action took place.

The second way in which ethics can be examined is through an analytical lens. *Analytical ethics* can be described as understanding the reasons a course of action that may have an ethical impact took place. Analytical ethics, or metaethics, moves from the how and when inquiry, which is the basis of the descriptive ethics viewpoint, to inquiring why something is happening. Hypotheses can be developed from analytical ethics to help us understand the relationship between different variables affecting ethical behavior. From a legal standpoint, analytical ethics would address the "motive" behind the actions instead of just being satisfied with a description of the actions.

The third approach to view ethics is from a normative perspective. *Normative ethics* can be defined as a prescribed course of action that attempts to ensure that ethical behavior will be followed in the future. Normative ethics moves the evaluation of the ethical behavior from a past to a future tense. Normative ethics presents information on what should be done in the future rather than what was done in the past, which are both part of descriptive and analytical ethics. This prescriptive approach allows employees and managers to address potential ethical issues before they occur.[9]

An Example of Ethical Examinations Using Enron Executives

The use of descriptive, analytical, and normative ethical examinations can be used to describe the actions of the two former CEOs of Enron Corporation, Kenneth Lay and Jeffrey Skilling.

Descriptive The descriptive examination is the presentation of the facts of the unethical behavior at Enron. These facts include having Enron manipulate the financial statements of the company using complex off–balance sheet transactions. Lay and Skilling sold Enron stock after they knew the company was going to collapse, yet they told its stockholders that the stock would continue to go up in price. The harassment by Enron executives of the whistle-blower, Sherron Watkins, who was trying to help the company and the employees, is another example of the facts of the case.

Analytical The analytical ethical examination of the Enron collapse includes, in part, trying to understand why Lay and Skilling acted unethically. Through their individual cognitive lenses, Lay and Skilling stated (and did even after their convictions) that they had done nothing wrong. They were the CEOs; they received agreement from their external auditor, Arthur Andersen, about their off–balance sheet accounting; and were allowed to sell stock when they wanted to but still stated that the stock price was going to go up. Alternatively, it could be argued that Lay and Skilling knew their actions were unethical, yet they thought they were too smart or too clever to be caught. One of the many creeds at Enron was that the employees were always the best and brightest and can out-negotiate and outthink anyone—whether it was a company, the state of California, or the U.S. Department of Justice.

Normative There has been a direct normative response to the Enron collapse. The design of the Sarbanes-Oxley (SOX) Act was, in part, a direct response to the unethical activities at Enron. Government regulations from SOX now impose limits on how long external auditors can work for the same client, barred having the external auditor also provide consulting advice (which occurred between Arthur Andersen and Enron), forced top executives including the CEO to disclose stock transactions within 2 days of the event, and strengthened the power of the board of directors to challenge the actions of the CEO. SOX reinforces the belief that every cloud has a silver lining. Even though many companies initially complained about the cost and red tape associated with SOX, more than 12 years after its passage, SOX has fortified the image and belief that the United States has the strongest due diligence and protection of investor rights in the world.

Teleological Frameworks

Although types of ethical examinations focus on information and how decision makers use information, teleological ethical frameworks focus on explaining the conduct of the individual from a philosophical perspective. Teleological frameworks focus on the results of the conduct of the individual. Derived from the Greek word for fulfillment, *telos*, these frameworks focus on the ramifications, positive and negative, resulting from the actions and conduct of individuals. The three teleological frameworks are ethical egoism, utilitarianism, and Sidgwick's dualism.[10]

Ethical Egoism

Although Thomas Hobbes has been credited with the development of ethical egoism, it can be said that Plato may have actually been the father of the ideas that have evolved into this framework. Contemporary writers such as Ayn Rand have embraced the concept of focusing on each individual's self-interest. Ethical egoism is based on the belief that every individual should act in a way to promote himself or herself if the net result will generate, on balance, positive rather than negative results.

Derived from the Latin word *ego*, which is defined as one's self, ethical egoism allows self-interests to play a role in the actions of the individual as long as there are also positive benefits for others. Of course, individuals who abide by the philosophy of ethical egoism may have different interpretations about what would be considered, on balance, an action that is good for others as well as themselves. Some ethical egoists may argue that based on their own perceptions, all of their actions, on balance, generate more positive than negative benefits. This level of rationalization may evolve into the justification that pursuing a person's self-interest is necessary to generate a positive outcome for others.

The supporters of ethical egoism argue that this framework is the only ethical model that captures the essence of motivation within individuals. Without self-interest, ethical egoists argue, why would someone do anything? As a result, ethical egoists argue that their philosophy supports a "win-win" proposition. An individual will reward his or her self-interest while yielding benefits for the rest of society. Those who argue against ethical egoism state that part of the connection of the actions that motivate an individual also require certain obligations of an individual.[11]

Utilitarianism

The utilitarianism movement started in England in the 18th century. Originally developed by Jeremy Bentham in his *Introduction to the Principles of Morals and Legislation* in 1789 and John Stuart Mill's *Utilitarianism* in 1863, utilitarianism holds the belief that any action of an individual will be based on providing the greatest good for the greatest number of people. Derived from the word *utility*, utilitarianism is based on the principle of utility: Each person's actions add to the overall utility of the community affected by his or her actions. As a result, utilitarians focus on the net result of their actions instead of the means or motives that generated the reason for their actions.

Utilitarianism can be based on single acts of individuals (act utilitarianism) or on guiding behavior indirectly through an evaluation of ethical conduct via rules and procedures (rule utilitarianism).[12] Those who support utilitarianism state that this theory is the only one that captures the essence of benevolent behavior. Without utilitarianism as a framework, supporters argue, people will not act to help others if the actions don't benefit the self-interests of the individuals. Those who oppose the utilitarian viewpoint state that it is difficult to ever properly evaluate the effectiveness of utilitarianism because it is practically impossible to determine what would be the greatest good for the greatest number. These people also argue that there will be some inherent contradictions with this theory. Stating that the actions support the greatest good for the greatest number begs the question whether the minority that does not receive the greatest good would be treated unfairly.[13]

Sidgwick's Dualism

First published in 1874, *The Methods of Ethics* by Henry Sidgwick attempted to bridge the gap between the two competing ethical frameworks of ethical egoism and utilitarianism. Sidgwick argued that a common ground could be found between the two theories. Hence, Sidgwick's dualism was developed. At the core of the argument is that both previous theories had elements of using cost–benefit analysis to help analyze the actions of individuals. Sidgwick's dualism attempted to resolve the fundamental difference of whether the actions for one's self-benefit affect just the individual or others. Sidgwick argued that utilitarianism is a foundation component of any ethical framework, which he called *rational benevolence*. However, he also argued that the self-interest of ethical egoism must be included in the ethical framework he called *prudence*. He argued that rational benevolence is necessary in an individual's actions, but he also stated that prudence is necessary because the happiness of the individual is the common goal of the action and it would not be logical for an individual to sacrifice his or her own happiness to help others. Therefore, he argued that a harmony can exist among rational benevolence and prudence viewpoints to have a rational ethical model. He concluded by stating that there had to be some reconciliation between the two theories to explain how individuals act in their self-interest as well as in the interests of others.[14]

These frameworks can be used to present different arguments from a business perspective. The supporters of the ethical egoism theory argue that businesses should focus solely on their self-interests and maximize their level of profitability by developing a strong competitive advantage. Those who support the utilitarianism theory accept government intervention as a way to protect the interests of the majority against the decisions of the minority within any given business. In his book *An Inquiry into the Nature and Causes of the Wealth of Nations* (1776), Adam Smith presented an argument that could support Sidgwick's dualism. Smith argues that the greatest good for the greatest number is achieved by individuals pursuing their self-interests in the marketplace.[15]

An Example of Teleological Frameworks Using Panera Cares

The opening vignette describes how Panera Bread is making a commitment to the local community by offering meals through its Panera Cares programs for those individuals that cannot afford to pay the full price for a meal. The actions by Panera Bread would be different based on the teleological frameworks.

Ethical Egoism The simple response to Panera Bread based on ethical egoism is that it would not have established Panera Cares programs if the company followed an ethical egoism approach. By solely focusing on the self-interests of the individuals, the self-interests would not support "giving away" food and profit without maximizing the potential financial return of the meal. Therefore, Panera Cares would not be considered a viable use of the resources of Panera Bread because they are not maximizing their financial investment.

Utilitarianism It could be argued that Panera Cares is a utilitarian-focused program. Many more members of the local community are being fed because of the availability of the Panera Cares program. In addition, the ability to trade one hour of volunteer work for a meal allows underproductive people in the community to be used to the benefit of Panera Bread and the individual. However, it could also be argued that Panera Cares is not a "pure" utilitarian project because Panera Bread expects people to pay for their food and expects that the payments will be close to the actual cost of the food.

Sidgwick's Dualism Therefore, it could be argued that Panera Cares most resembles a project that matches the middle ground between ethical egoism and utilitarianism, Sidgwick's dualism. Under Sidgwick's dualism, there are benefits of both serving self-interests and providing the greatest good to the greatest number. Panera Cares seems to be a better fit with Sidgwick's dualism. It is utilitarian in that it is serving the needs of many who would otherwise not be served, yet Panera Bread still collects money from the customers with the subtle peer pressure to give close to the actual food amount if the customer is able. Therefore, projects such as Panera Cares serve as a reminder that firms can use various methods to serve others as well as themselves. Although the teleological frameworks focus on how the decisions made by the individual achieve the desired results, an alternative philosophical framework focuses on the duty of the individual.

Deontological Frameworks

As opposed to teleological frameworks, which focus on whether the results are favorable or not, deontological frameworks focus on the duty or obligation in determining whether the actions are right or wrong. The term *deontological* is derived from the Greek word *deon*, which means *duty*. There are three deontological frameworks: existentialism, contractarianism, and Kant's ethics.[16]

Existentialism

Existentialism is based on the underlying belief that the only person who can determine right and wrong is based on the free will of the person making the decisions. Each individual determines his or her actions and is ultimately responsible for the consequences of those actions. Philosophers such as Søren Kierkegaard, Friedrich Nietzsche, and Jean-Paul Sartre have all embraced existentialism as the most viable way to connect duty with actions. Through authenticity of their actions, individuals are able to develop their own sense of personal virtue. Existentialism does not use universal principles because each individual determines acceptance of his or her actions.[17] As Polonius advises his son, Laertes, in William Shakespeare's *Hamlet*, "This above all: to thine own self be true, and it must follow, as the night the day, Thou canst not be false to any man."[18]

Contractarianism

Contractarianism, or social contract theory, is based on the belief that all individuals agree to social contracts to be a member within a society. This theory is based on the work of John Locke's 1690 book, *Two Treatises on Government*; Jean-Jacques Rousseau's *The Social Contract, or Principles of Political Right*, published in 1762; and, more recently Garrett Hardin's 1968 book, *The Tragedy of the Commons*, and John Rawls's 1971 book, *A Theory of Justice*.

Contractarianists hold the view that membership in society comes with certain duties and responsibilities. Individuals agree to the norms of society by establishing a social contract with the other members of the society. The underlying principle of contractarianism is to have guided principles that are fair to everyone. If the principles are fair, everyone in the society should agree to abide by the principles. Rawls proposed that individuals in a society contract freely to have economic and political components that help guide our day-to-day living. Rawls argued that everyone should have equal rights and duties. Furthermore, he stated that if there are social and economic inequalities, it would be acceptable to the society only if these inequalities were able to generate benefits for everyone in society. Rawls challenged the utilitarianism philosophy by stating that it would not be acceptable to focus on actions for the greater good if the minorities do not also benefit from the decision.[19]

Kant's Ethics

In his book *Foundations of the Metaphysics of Morals* (1785), Immanuel Kant discusses ethical decisions based on the free will of the individual. Kant argues that the free will to make decisions that were considered rational needed to be converted into a universal will. Kant's ethical view is considered a dualism because it attempts to bridge the gap between the existentialist and contractarian points of view. The linkage Kant made was to consider his principle pertaining to free will based on the philosophy that an individual should act in a way in which one would expect everyone to act if it were a universal will and to treat other individuals as the end, not the means to an end. As a result, Kant rejects the view of using heuristics of "gut feelings" as a justification for a decision because these findings are not always predictable nor are they acceptable. In addition, the rationale for not committing an illegal act such as dumping dangerous chemicals into a water source should not be based on the legal requirements or the potential negative image that would be created for the company. Kant would argue that the manager should consider only whether his free will action to dump the toxic waste would be acceptable as a universal will in which any company or individual could dump any chemical he or she wanted into any water supply. Kant argues that this should be the only way in which managers should consider their decisions.[20]

Using WorldCom as an Example of Deontological Frameworks

Existentialism Former WorldCom CEO Bernie Ebbers claimed that he did nothing wrong. Even after his conviction, he stated that he did not know what type of fraudulent activities were occurring at WorldCom. From an existentialist perspective, Ebbers is justifying his actions based on his individual interpretation of the value of his actions. Ebbers's interpretation was that he did not do anything wrong; therefore, he did nothing wrong.

Contractarianism By becoming a publicly traded company, WorldCom agreed to certain social norms. Those norms included being truthful when disclosing the financial performance and identifying any actual or potential problems to the owners and employees of WorldCom. This norm of transparency assures society that the information that was presented by WorldCom is accurate and timely. Of course, WorldCom broke that trust by violating this norm by not being transparent.

Kant's Ethics Cynthia Cooper is a good example of someone who used Kant's ethics. By ignoring the requests of her superiors, Ms. Cooper began an investigation into financial transactions occurring at WorldCom. She uncovered the massive fraud that was occurring at WorldCom. This is a Kant's ethics approach because she believed that her actions to discover the fraud would be done by others as part of a universal will under the same set of circumstances.

Seven Guiding Principles to Support Ethical Actions

As with anyone trying to do what is right and ethical, it helps if there are guiding principles to help direct our actions. In his book *The Right and the Good* (1930), W. D. Ross argued that individuals should follow certain principles that are considered part of the prima facie obligation an individual has to society. Ross identified in his book that there could be a conflict between the duties and obligations of specific circumstances and that actions may override an individual's actual duty. For example, Ross explained that telling a lie or breaking a promise to an individual may be acceptable in certain circumstances. The circumstances help develop the distinction between a prima facie duty based on that specific set of circumstances and an actual or absolute duty.

Ross presented seven basic principles to support his ethical philosophy. By following these principles, individuals develop a level of intuition that becomes incorporated in their decision-making process. The seven guiding principles are as follows:

1. **Fidelity:** An individual needs to keep explicit and implicit promises.
2. **Reparation:** An individual must act on repairing the consequences for previous wrongful acts.
3. **Gratitude:** An individual must be able to show gratitude for the kindnesses that others have given him or her.
4. **Justice:** An individual should try to see that any goods are fairly distributed.
5. **Beneficence:** An individual should focus on trying to improve the lives of others.
6. **Self-improvement:** An individual should improve oneself by focusing on virtue and intelligence.
7. **Noninjury:** An individual should not cause any harm to others.

Ross draws on the work from previous theories. Ethical egoism is represented in self-improvement, and utilitarianism is represented in beneficence and noninjury. Furthermore, existentialism is represented in fidelity, and self-improvement and contractarianism are represented in fidelity and justice.[21] One of the founding areas of guidance for those unsure about their ethical standing is referred to in the seven deadly sins.

The Seven Deadly Sins

For centuries, human behavior has been evaluated based on seven deadly sins. The seven deadly sins are lust, gluttony, greed, sloth, wrath, envy, and pride.

Lust

Lust can be defined as the trait of an individual who has obsessive and compulsive continuous thoughts of sexual desire. The thoughts of sexual drive overtake all other functions of the individual in the attempt to satisfy the individual's sexual appetite. Dante referred to lust as the "excessive love of others."[22] This excessive love is considered a sin because it supersedes the love and devotion the individual should have with God.[23] In Dante's *Inferno*, lust is included within the second circle of Hell, and the individuals are sinful because "they subordinate reason to desire."[24]

Gluttony

Gluttony is overindulgence and overconsumption of anything good to the point that the good is wasted when it is consumed. The sin related to gluttony is the rationale that someone who is not as well off would have received a much larger positive benefit had the good not been wasted. For example, a person who drinks 10 glasses of wine could have generated a benefit for nine other people if he or she had drunk just one glass. In addition, gluttony allows animal instincts such as appetite to control the behavior of the individual. The net result is that the individual who is gluttonous is one who puts himself before others with his or her actions, which is considered sinful and a distraction from a spiritual life.[25]

Greed

Greed, or avarice, is also considered a sin of excess like lust and gluttony. *Greed* is an excessive desire by the individual to obtain wealth, status, and power. In addition, greed can be considered the continuous accumulation of material wealth without regard for the methods used to obtain such wealth. Furthermore, miserliness and unethical business practices are considered part of the sin of greed. Greed drives the individual to "worship" material goods instead of spiritual goods. The worshiping of "false idols" allows the individual to focus only his or her self-interests with no consideration of alternative paths that would help others in society.[26] Dante, who identifies greed in the fourth circle of hell, criticizes individuals who are driven by greed, or other misers who spend their material wealth too freely. Dante explains that both are excessive behaviors, and the individual ignores the value of moderation.[27]

Sloth

By far the least familiar of the seven deadly sins, the definition of *sloth* as a sin has evolved over time. Initially, the term *sloth* was described as an individual's apathy, sadness, and lack of joy in his or her everyday life. The definition was refined to include when individuals fail to use their full potential of talents and gifts they were given as humans. However, a more modern definition of *sloth* includes being lazy and indifferent about one's actions.[28]

Wrath

Wrath can be defined as an uncontrollable level of anger or rage. Anger can lead to actions such as impatience, revenge, and vigilantism. Without forgiveness, wrath can dominate the actions of the individuals for the rest of their lives. To focus on revenge means that the individual is not satisfied with the current set of circumstances and will not rest until those circumstances have changed. Dante referred to wrath as "love of justice perverted to revenge and spite."[29]

Envy

The sin of envy or jealousy relates to focusing on one's self-interests in the desire to obtain qualities or possessions of another person. Dante describes envy as the "love of one's own good perverted to a desire to deprive other men of theirs."[30]

Pride

Pride, vanity, and *hubris* refer to competitively measuring one person's characteristics or actions based on the characteristics or actions of another person. The sin of pride relates to being considered above or "superior" to another person. It is considered the most serious of the seven deadly sins because it is the source of the other six sins. By having a desire to be superior and more important than others, the individual focuses solely on his or her self-interests and fails to acknowledge the good work of other people.

Although the seven deadly sins have been a traditional measure of the virtue of human beings based on their actions, the moral values of an individual can be identified in numerous ways. Philippe Foot believed that virtues could be measured and compared objectively from one person to another. The measurement of the virtue of the individual decision maker is the basis of the "trolley problem."

The Trolley Problem

A runaway trolley is speeding out of control down a hill. The brakes do not work, so it cannot be slowed down. At the end of the track are five people who will be killed if the trolley hits them. The only choices the driver of the trolley has are (1) do nothing and kill the five people or (2) pull a lever that would result in the trolley shifting to another set of tracks in which one person who is unaware of the runaway trolley would be killed. As the driver, what would you do?

If you decided that killing one was better than killing five people, then Judith Jarvis Thomson has an alternative scenario that may yield alternative results. A surgeon has been attempting to help five people who all need a different organ transplant. A patient comes in for a routine checkup, and the surgeon realizes that the patient's organs would be compatible with all five of the patients who need the organ transplants. In this scenario, would it be morally correct to save five people by killing one person? Of course, the distinction is that in the trolley example, the driver has to decide between two negative duties, while the surgeon has to decide between a negative and positive duty.

Thomson added two additional scenarios pertaining to the trolley problem. Another scenario is based on having a bystander observe the trolley going down the tracks and having to make the decision to either doing nothing and five people end up dead or diverting the trolley and assume that he or she would be responsible for the death of the one person. The other scenario is based on the circumstance in which a bystander from a bridge observes the trolley going down the track and realizes that only a large heavy object could stop the trolley if it is thrown in front of the trolley. The bystander looks around the bridge and the only object big enough to stop the trolley is an overweight man also standing on the bridge near him. Would the bystander try to throw the overweight man over the bridge to stop the trolley?[31] These are the types of ethical dilemmas that individuals must address throughout their lives. As a result, individuals can benefit by having different ethical principles to help guide them during their lifetimes.

Global Business Standards Codex

In a study to develop a framework to evaluate the conduct of companies around the world, the Global Business Standards Codex was established.[32] This codex captures the eight major underlying principles in which ethical behavior can be interpreted and evaluated. The eight ethical principles are fiduciary, property, reliability, transparency, dignity, fairness, citizenship, and responsiveness.

Fiduciary Principle

As part of the legal structure of a business organization, each officer and director of a company has a legal fiduciary duty to act in the best interests of the stakeholders and other employees within the firm. Furthermore, there is also an implied fiduciary duty for every employee within the organization to act in a way that generates positive benefits for the firm. The traditional components of fiduciary duty include ensuring that there are no actual or potential conflicts of interest given the actions of the employee. It also is implied that each employee will not put his or her self-interests above the overall interests of the firm. Additionally, it is assumed that employees will perform good-faith efforts in carrying out each of their responsibilities, will be prudent with the company's resources, and will exercise due diligence regarding the quality of their work. Specifically, *due diligence* includes ensuring that the employee actively promotes the interests of the company in a diligent and professional manner. The employee is also expected to develop a sense of loyalty to the firm. From a loyalty perspective, the employee is expected to use his or her job title and the company resources available to him or her for company purposes only. A loyal employee is expected to report any ethical violations and conflicts between the employee's own interests and the company's interests. A loyal employee is expected to refuse any type of gift that could be considered excessive within a business relationship context.[33]

Property Principle

The property principle is based on the belief that every employee should respect property and the rights of the owners of the property. Traditional examples of violations of this principle include theft, misappropriation of funds, and wasting resources. This principle has been expanded to intangible property and now includes the misappropriation of intellectual property or other types of information. An employee is expected to protect the tangible and intangible assets of the firm. In addition, the employee is expected to be a good steward to the resources the employee has access to. As a result, it is the duty of the employee not to damage or steal any assets or allow a third party to take any of the company's tangible or intangible assets or steal the assets of another firm. Therefore, it is the employee's responsibility to prohibit any misappropriation of company funds, to not allow the firm's proprietary information to become available to a competitor, or to obtain access to a competitor's proprietary information.[34]

Reliability Principle

The reliability principle is based on the belief that it is the employee's responsibility to honor the commitments he or she has made to the firm. Employees are expected to follow through with the promises and commitments that have been made between the employees and the firm. Traditional violations of the reliability principle include breaching a promise or contract or not fulfilling a promised action. Employees are expected to do their best to make a good-faith effort to fulfill all the commitments that the employee has promised. The reliability principle also includes ensuring that suppliers and other business partners are paid in a timely manner.[35]

Transparency Principle

The transparency principle is based on the belief that every employee should conduct business in a truthful and open manner. It is expected that the employees will not make decisions based on personal agendas. As a result, employees are expected not to act in deceptive manners and to keep accurate and current records of all the business obligations that are currently the responsibility of the employee. Employees should allow any other interested party to understand how the pattern of behavior was justified based on his or her actions. Traditional violations of this principle include fraudulent and deceptive actions of the employee.

Transparency also incorporates how the employee deals with information. Transparent actions include accurate and up-to-date records of the information related to the actions and the decision-making process. This also guarantees that the financial information presented to investors is truthful and accurate and that the information is developed within the guidelines of auditing and financial reporting standards. Furthermore, transparency guides the employees in ensuring that the relationship between the company and its suppliers and partners is done in an honest manner. Transparency also ensures that the firm's marketing focus does not mislead or misinform its current and potential customers. Transparency ensures that firms present accurate and truthful customer warnings for any health and safety issues that could affect the customer's use of a product.

Transparency makes it clear to the employees that the acquisition of proprietary information from competitors is not acceptable. The benefits of following the transparency principle include the ability to make better-informed decisions, the ability to ensure that the truth is always presented to others in the organization, and an allowance for improved cooperation within the firm through the development of trust among the employees.[36]

Dignity Principle

The dignity principle is based on the belief that each employee needs to respect the dignity of all individuals. Protecting the dignity of people in society includes ensuring the human rights of health, safety, and privacy. Furthermore, the dignity principle encourages the enhancement of human development within the company, in the marketplace, and in society at large. Therefore, any type of humiliation, coercion, or other type of human offenses directly violates the dignity principle. The dignity principle involves making affirmative efforts for those individuals who need help in their personal pursuits, and it helps protect those individuals who are vulnerable to unethical actions. Those vulnerable could be employees who potentially face harassment or other factors that could create a hostile work environment. Under the dignity principle, the company is responsible for ensuring that employees do not face unnecessary physical risks as they perform their work responsibilities.

Furthermore, the company is responsible for respecting employees' and customers' privacy and for protecting confidential information. The company should not accept any labor opportunities in which child labor would be directly or indirectly involved in the manufacturing of the firm's products. The firm should allow the employees to form a union and permit collective bargaining to take place pertaining to labor issues. Moreover, the dignity principle highlights the sensitivity employees should have as they interact with people from other cultures and other countries.[37]

Fairness Principle

The fairness principle is based on the belief that stakeholders who have a vested interest in the firm should be treated fairly. There are four types of fairness: reciprocal fairness, distributive fairness, fair competition, and procedural fairness. *Reciprocal fairness* addresses the issues of treating another party fairly and having the other party treat the firm fairly. *Distributive fairness* is based on the assumption that the allocation of finite resources within the firm will be distributed fairly based on maximizing the benefits of those allocations. *Fair competition* focuses on the fair treatment given by the firm as it interacts with its existing and potential competitors. This includes ensuring that collusion does not occur between the firm and its competitors pertaining to factors such as price, number of products produced in geographical locations, and market share. It also includes ensuring that bribes or any other illegal financial incentives are not given to interested parties in exchange for a favorable relationship with those parties. *Procedural fairness* deals with ensuring that parties that interact with the firm are treated fairly from a due process perspective. This also includes ensuring that employees would not experience retaliation if they notify government officials of any illegal violations.[38]

Citizenship Principle

The citizenship principle is based on the belief that every employee should act as a responsible citizen in the community. Employees should respect the laws of the community. This includes criminal laws, as well as competition, environmental, and corporate social responsibility laws. Employees are expected to protect and preserve public goods available to the community. This includes sustainability and other environmental issues, public space issues, and legitimate government. Employees should also be cooperative with community officials. This includes notifying the proper authorities if there are health and safety issues that relate to the goods and services provided by the firm. Employees should be cognizant of unacceptable involvement in political or government issues, including illegal financial involvement or other illegal use of resources to support a political official. The employees should contribute to the general well-being of the community by volunteering to help the community through charitable organizations or other community-based programs.[39]

Responsiveness Principle

The responsiveness principle is based on the belief that employees have a responsibility to respond to requests for information about the operations from the various stakeholders. As a result, employees must reply to stakeholders' requests for information and must be responsive to ideas presented by the stakeholders to help improve the operations of the firm. From a customer perspective, a responsive firm is one in which the goods and services offered at least meet, if not exceed, the expectations of the customers. A timely response to any complaints from the customers concerning the firm's products should also occur. Responsiveness is expected with the firm's interaction with its employees. A responsive firm is expected to react in a timely manner to resolve any outstanding issues that have been raised by the employees, interest groups, suppliers, the local community, and any other stakeholder that has a vested interest in the company.[40]

In summary, this chapter exposed the complex nature of business ethics. From frameworks to guiding principles, business ethics is a multifaceted concept that has many dimensions.

Questions for Thought

1. Which of the teleological frameworks most closely match your ethical beliefs? Under what circumstances would you shift toward another of the frameworks? For example, if you were trapped in downtown New Orleans during Hurricane Katrina, what would you do to stay alive and provide for your family?

2. Do you think "Greed Is Good"? Can a free market economic system survive without human greed?

3. Which of the seven deadly sins do you believe is the most serious to commit? Which of the seven deadly sins do you believe is the least serious to commit? Do you think certain sins have gained or been reduced in importance over time?

4. Using the principles set forth in the Global Business Standards Codex, find an example of a company that does or did not follow one of the principles. Discuss the implications of the company's actions.

Real-Life Ethical Dilemma Exercise

Sir Nicholas Winton: A True Humanitarian

In 1938, a 29-year-old English stockholder was invited by a friend to visit Prague when their planned skiing trip to Switzerland was cancelled. Instead, Sir Winton visited refugee camps in Sudetenland, which was a German-speaking part of Czechoslovakia. Sir Winton realized that it would be very difficult for the refugees to be able to leave Czechoslovakia, and therefore, he focused on trying to transfer some the children, mostly Jewish, from Czechoslovakia to England. He took the letterhead from an existing organization called the British Committee for Refugees from Czechoslovakia and added "Children's Section" to the heading. He became the "chairman" of this new division and sought English families to adopt the orphans from the refugee camps. Sir Winton would forge travel documents for the orphans when the proper documents did not come quickly enough from the British government. He would reserve a train and the orphans would travel from Prague through Holland and then eventually reach London. A total of eight trains carrying 669 orphans reached London. A ninth train was scheduled to depart carrying 250 children on September 1, 1939, but it was stopped at the train depot when war was declared.[41,42,43]

Questions for the Real-Life Ethical Dilemma Exercise

1. Discuss how this issue would be addressed using each of the teleological frameworks.

2. Explain why Sir Winton is considered a humanitarian.

3. Winton saved many children on his orphan trains. Discuss the ethical implications of what Winton accomplished.

Student Study Site

Visit the Student Study Site at **study.sagepub.com/stanwick3e** to access the following resources:

- Video Links
- SAGE Journal Articles
- Web Resources
- Web Quizzes

The Evolving Complexities of Business Ethics

Ethical decision making isn't an option today. It's an obligation—in business, in education, in government, in our daily lives.

—Willard C. Butcher,
retired chairman of the Chase Manhattan Corporation

Chapter Objectives

After reading and studying Chapter 2, students should be able to

1. Explain the global complexity of business ethics.
2. Describe the historical development of business ethics.
3. Define *integrity*. Explain the role of integrity in the corporation.
4. Describe some of the tests used for measuring integrity.
5. Describe the three ethical tests used in corporate decision making.
6. Explain the methods people use to rationalize their unethical behaviors.
7. Discuss the elements of a cheating culture.
8. Explain generational differences in cheating.

Bono: I Still Haven't Found the Tax Rate That I'm Looking For

Located in a building where slave traders and spice merchants made business trans-actions 400 years ago, a company called Promogroup has its corporate headquarters. Promogroup helps individuals and companies with high levels of income "shelter" the tax exposure of their income. Clients include the three members of the Rolling Stones—Mick Jagger, Keith Richards, and Charlie Watts—the record label EMI; CORE Media Group, the company that owns the rights to *American Idol*; and Elvis Presley's estate. Promogroup was able to reduce the total tax paid by the three Rolling Stones members to $7.2 million on income of $450 million, resulting in an aggregated tax rate of 1.5%.

Another client of Promogroup is Bono and the rest of U2. Bono is well known for his stance on many global causes, including AIDS awareness, reducing global poverty, and helping developing countries reduce their level of foreign debt. He also wrote the foreword to the book *The End of Poverty*, written by Jeffrey Sachs in 2005.

The tax shelter established by Promogroup is based on the simple flow of royalties that go into and leave the Netherlands. A Dutch holding company was established for Promogroup's clients, and the revenue from the royalties of any other intellectual property sent to the holding company is exempt from taxes. The clients are then allowed to withdraw the royalties with the tax being "paid." A tax consultant in Rotterdam, the Netherlands, Ton Smit, stated that for the vast majority of clients who set up these holding companies, the sole motivation is to achieve either tax minimization or tax avoidance. The Dutch tax shelters are available only to artists who are not U.S. citizens. The U.S. Department of the Treasury charges the standard corporate income tax rate on any revenue that is transferred into the United States from a Dutch company.

U2 has accumulated an estimated net worth of more than $900 million, and band members felt that they needed to move their royalty revenues because Ireland was going to greatly reduce the tax incentives given to musicians and other artists living in Ireland. In June 2006, U2 moved its song publishing catalog to the Netherlands via Promogroup. A research group in the Netherlands, SOMO, the Centre for Research on Multinational Corporations, concluded that the tax haven given to individuals and corporations through the use of holding companies was having a negative impact on the capacity of developing countries to be able to provide essential services to their citizens and on the ability of developed countries to reduce or forgive their outstanding debt agreements with developing countries. One of the authors of the SOMO report, Richard Murphy, who runs a tax research institute in England, stated that Bono's tax agreements through U2 Ltd. in the Netherlands is completely inconsistent with Bono's stance on helping developing countries move from poverty conditions. Murphy continued, stating that Bono cannot demand that resources be given to antipoverty campaigns because he is not giving the resources to the governments so they can implement antipoverty campaigns.

In commenting on Bono's shifting his tax burden to the Netherlands, a spokesperson of the Irish Labour Party, Joan Burton, stated that Bono should be applauded for being an advocate for improvements in developing countries. However, those improvements come from taxes, and it would be difficult to ask other people to pay taxes to improve economic development if he is not paying taxes himself.

U2's business manager, Paul McGuinness, stated that U2 is a global business and pays global taxes. In addition, approximately 95% of U2's revenue, which includes concert ticket sales and record sales, is earned outside Ireland. The band pays taxes all over the world on its worldwide income and abides with all Irish tax laws. However, McGuinness continued by stating that unique tax solutions are common in Ireland and that U2 runs its business in the most tax-efficient way possible.[1]

In 2011 at the Glastonbury Music Festival, when U2 took the stage, activists from the organization Art Uncut inflated a 20-foot balloon that stated "U Pay Your Tax 2."[2]

The Global Complexity of Business Ethics

We no longer live in a world of nations and ideologies, Mr. Beale. The world is a collage of corporations, inexorably determined by the immutable bylaws of business. The world is a business, Mr. Beale. It has been since man crawled out of the slime. And our children will live, Mr. Beale, to see that perfect world in which there's no war or famine, oppression or brutality—one vast and ecumenical holding company, for whom all men will work to serve a common profit, in which all men will hold a share of stock, all necessities provided, all anxieties tranquilized, all boredom amused.[3]

—Arthur Jensen, *Network*, 1976

In the movie *Network*, a television show host, Howard Beale, convinced his viewers to complain and cancel a deal made by the corporation that owned the television network Beale works for. The CEO of the corporation, Arthur Jensen, summoned Beale up to the boardroom to convince him that what he had done was wrong. Although this speech is more than 35 years old, it could be argued that it is more relevant today than in 1976 when *Network* was made. The power of corporations has grown phenomenally during the past three decades as corporations have become more global and new markets have emerged. From China to India, from Eastern Europe to South America—countries that were difficult if not impossible to penetrate by multinational corporations are now just one more market in the global competitive marketplace. As a result, as companies increase in size and geographic representation, they also increase in power. From global marketing to global political lobbying, corporations use these resources to enhance their ability to become financially stronger. As a result, it could be argued that corporations have become more powerful in many areas as compared with governments.

A simple example showing how powerful corporations have become can be demonstrated in the trade policies of the U.S. government and corporations. Even though there are sanctions and trade embargoes established by the U.S. government with certain countries, corporations are still allowed to sell products to customers in blacklisted nations. The Office of Foreign Assets Control in the Department of the Treasury has allowed companies such as Pepsi and Kraft Foods to do business with countries that are barred from doing business with the U.S. corporations. The exceptions allowed by the Department of the Treasury are based on specific agricultural and medical humanitarian needs. These needs have been interpreted broadly enough to include cigarettes, gum, hot sauce, weight loss products, body supplements, and sports rehabilitation equipment. Some of the companies that have been granted exemption licenses include Bank of America, Bayer, Boeing, Bristol-Myers Squibb, Chiquita Brands, Citigroup, Coca-Cola, ConAgra Foods, Del Monte, Eastman Kodak, Eli Lilly, ExxonMobil, General Mills, Johnson & Johnson, JPMorgan Chase, Lockheed Martin, Mars, MCI, Merck, Motorola, Occidental Petroleum, Oracle, PepsiCo, Pfizer, Philips Electronics, 3M, and Wells Fargo Bank. A listing of blacklisted nations that were involved in the trade transactions include Burma, Cuba, Iran, Iraq, Kosovo, Liberia, Libya, North Korea, and Sudan. Some companies have considered the costs and benefits of the decision to trade with blacklisted nations and have decided that trade is not the optimal solution. General Electric, which was one of the leaders applying for exemption licenses, decided that it would stop all but true humanitarian businesses and would donate its profits from Iran to charity. Another company, a small player called Anndorll, had second thoughts after its license to sell in Iran had been approved. Owner Joshua Kamens decided not to complete the authorized deal, stating, "I'm an American . . . Even though it's legal to sell that type of product, I didn't want to have any trade with a country like Iran."[4] As Arthur Jensen stated, the role of corporations and the influence they have over individuals are not new but are as old as commerce itself.

History of Business Ethics

Derived from the Greek word for character, *ethos*, ethics have been debated for centuries. Ethics need to be given even higher consideration in today's corporate environment. Ethical climates are created by individual judgments. But knowing the corporate stand on certain aspects can contribute to management's creation of a strong ethical culture. The discovery of ethics began many centuries ago with discussions initiated by Aristotle, Socrates, and Plato. In fact, Aristotle stated that a person is not complete until that person is a contributing member of society. In addition, Aristotle explained that a true friend would tell another friend when he or she is acting selfishly and foolhardily.[5]

As long as there has been commerce, there have been ethical issues about how business is conducted. In the 17th century, the United Kingdom offered companies such as the Hudson Bay Company, the East India Company, and the Massachusetts Bay Company monopolistic charters so "English" settlements could be established in different countries.

The climate of today's business ethics has seen a real change from those initial discussions that were made centuries ago.[6] During each decade, we have been faced with turbulent ethical times. In the 1960s, the climate of business ethics was more of a period of social unrest. Employees and employers began to have an adversarial relationship, casting aside the earlier values of loyalty with management created in the 1950s. Issues such as the environment and drug use among employees began to be dilemmas for employers. This era showed the birth of the corporate social responsibility movement, with corporations beginning to establish codes of conduct to help deal with these newfound problems.

The economy of the 1970s suffered a recession, and the unemployment rate rose dramatically. Several scandals involving defense contractors and corporations led to a mood of value-centered ethics. Human rights issues began to come to light, and environmental issues continued to be a major focal point for corporations. This was when companies began to cover up their wrongdoings rather than deal with the issues head-on.

In the 1980s, financial fraud surfaced through the savings and loan scandal. Loyalty to employers decreased dramatically. The Ethics Resource Center helped form the first business ethics office at General Dynamics in 1985.

The 1990s saw an outgrowth of global opportunities for companies, but they were not without concerns. Unsafe work practices, child labor issues, and environmental issues gained prominence. The significant outgrowth of companies gave rise to financial mismanagement.

At the new millennium, unethical companies began to surface, wrought with financial mismanagement problems. Intellectual property theft, cybercrime, and personal privacy issues surfaced. The most significant event in the United States was the passage of the Sarbanes-Oxley Act in 2002, which attempted to control the financial mismanagement issues eroding the integrity and confidence of corporations and their stakeholders. Companies continue to use unethical practices to become more competitive and to increase their level of profitability.

Who Are the Dead Peasants?

Corporate-owned life insurance (COLI), commonly called dead-peasant policies, allow corporations to establish life insurance policies on any employee within the firm. The corporation pays the premium and receives the full amount of the payout when the employee dies. Although it was designed to be used to ensure top-level executives "protect" the firm, dead-peasant policies are routinely issued for rank-and-file employees. The net result is that if an employee dies prematurely while working as an employee at the company, the company is under no obligation to give the grieving family any monies that are obtained from the policy. The company receives the death benefits and uses the proceeds to pay for various company expenses. In 2008, the Bank of America had $17.3 billion in such policies, and other financial institutions were not far behind: Wachovia Corp, $12 billion; JPMorgan Chase, $11.1 billion; and Wells Fargo, $5.7 billion. A total of $122.3 billion of insurance policies have been "invested" by banks and will yield an estimated $400 billion in death benefits. In regulatory filings, these insurance policies are referred to as "mortality dividends" or "yields." Banks have used the payouts to help fund bonuses for their employees. In 2006, Congress passed regulations that allowed companies to set up insurance policies only for the top third earners of their employees and the employee must provide consent. The regulations were not retroactive, so there are still millions of insurance policies that are on the books for numerous corporations.[7]

The dead-peasant policy was spotlighted in Michael Moore's *Capitalism: A Love Story* when a 26-year-old female employee who was a cake decorator for Wal-Mart passed away. Wal-Mart received a $81,000 payout from the dead-peasant insurance policy. The family was faced with $100,000 in medical bills and $6,000 for the funeral. Wal-Mart did not offer to pay any part of the outstanding debt. In fact, the Moore documentary explained that young women are the "best" people for corporations to insure: They will give the largest payouts because they have the longest life expectancy.[8]

This is not the only time Wal-Mart has been part of a media report related to COLI policies. In 2009, Wal-Mart settled a lawsuit that charged that Wal-Mart COLI policies violated Texas law. Texas law stated that a corporation can only have an insurance policy issued to an employee who has an "insurable interest" for the corporation. In other words, Wal-Mart was allowed to insure only top-level executives, not the rank-and-file employees in Texas. Wal-Mart was estimated to have 350,000 employees who were covered with COLI policies. The standard insurance rate for the rank-and-file Wal-Mart employees was between $60,000 and $80,000. Wal-Mart claimed it stopped its COLI program in 2000.[9]

The Role of Integrity

Integrity is derived from the Latin word *integri*, which means *wholeness*. The term *integrity* is defined by *Merriam-Webster Dictionary* as "a firm adherence to a code of especially moral or artistic values."[10] The underlying assumption of the role of employees within the organization is a deeply rooted level of organizational commitment. That commitment generates an attitude in which the employees can be passionate about their effort and the overall commitment of the firm. After they leave the firm, the employees want to believe that there is a legacy of their contribution to the success of the firm. This commitment, passion, and dedication drives employees to a high level of integrity within their work settings. Integrity is based on employees' continuous efforts to balance their personal values with the requirements for performing their jobs effectively throughout their careers. Integrity could include understanding and fulfilling the duties of their jobs, as well as admitting when errors have been made and making corrections when needed. One of the greatest dangers to an employee's integrity is to have his or her integrity compromised over time. Having an employee's individual integrity erode allows potential negative consequences that could include unethical and illegal behavior as well as dysfunction within the professional and personal relationships the individual has with others.[11]

An individual could evaluate the integrity of his or her actions based on some simple rules of thumb or heuristics in the form of different tests. The *publicity test* asks whether the individual would be comfortable if his or her actions were publicized in a newspaper or on television. The *trusted friend* test asks whether the individual would be comfortable in telling his or her best friend or a close family member about his or her actions. The *reciprocity test*, also known as the *Golden Rule*, asks whether the individual treats others as he or she would like to be treated. The *universality test* asks whether the individual would consider it acceptable behavior if anyone in the world did the same action. The *obituary test* asks the individual to look back on one's previous actions during one's career and ask if he or she is comfortable with the evaluation.[12]

Specific Behaviors of High Integrity

As shown previously, testing is one method in which the interpretation of behavior of high integrity can be determined. An alternative method is a listing of specific behaviors that would support a high level of integrity with the opposite behavior considered a low level of integrity. Donald Zauderer listed 13 specific behaviors that can help identify the level of integrity in individual actions: possessing humility, maintaining the ability to be concerned about the greater good, being truthful, fulfilling commitments, striving for fairness, taking responsibility, having respect for the individual, celebrating the good fortune of others, developing others, reproaching unjust acts, being forgiving, and extending oneself for others.[13]

Possess Humility

An individual should be humble in his or her actions when interacting with others. There is no value added in being arrogant or in exaggerating one's individual contribution to the success of the firm.

Maintain Concern for the Greater Good

An individual should always make decisions that benefit the firm overall. The individual should never make decisions where the individual's self-interests supersede the interests of the firm.

Be Truthful

An individual should always be truthful in his or her statements and in his or her actions. An individual should never make untrue statements or take credit for the efforts of others.

Fulfill Commitments

An individual should always make a good-faith effort to fulfill all the commitments the individual promised to complete. An individual should never breach an agreement or deliver a required project late or not at all.

Strive for Fairness

An individual should make decisions that are fair to everyone who can be affected by the decision. An individual should never be biased in decisions, including making judgments without all the relevant documents or assigning employees based on subjective criteria that discriminates against other employees.

Take Responsibility

An individual should always take full responsibility for one's own actions. An individual should not shift the blame to others or falsely accuse others of actions that are not accurate.

Have Respect for the Individual

An individual should respect the interests and actions of others. An individual should not reduce the level of respect for other employees by not acknowledging recognition when it is warranted. An individual should also not refuse the input of other employees and should not display rude behavior toward other employees.

Celebrate the Good Fortune of Others

An individual should share the joy in another person's accomplishments. An individual should not be envious of the success of a colleague.

Develop Others

An individual should be able to support the employee development of other employees within the organization. An individual should make a good-faith effort in helping coach and train others and give effective, constructive performance evaluations of his or her subordinates.

Reproach Unjust Acts

An individual should refuse to perform any act that he or she would consider to be unjust. In addition, the individual should stand up and defend his or her principles.

Be Forgiving

An individual should let go of past actions that have had a negative impact. An individual should let go of the previous ill will and release any grudges that developed between the individual and others within the organization.

Extend Self for Others

An individual should help and provide assistance to others in a time of need. In addition, an individual should be generous with rewards to others when it is warranted.[14]

An Example of High Integrity

In March 2012, the ethical conduct at Goldman Sachs was in the spotlight when a senior broker for the company, Greg Smith, wrote a letter to *The New York Times* titled "Why I Am Leaving Goldman Sachs." In the letter, Smith, who had worked for Goldman Sachs for 12 years, stated the culture at Goldman Sachs was toxic and destructive. He described the culture in the past as based on teamwork, integrity, humility, and always doing the right things, but now the client is second to the interest of Goldman Sachs. He continued by stating that the decline in the moral fiber of the company represents the most serious threat to the long-term survival of the company. In addition, he cited examples when the Goldman Sachs managing directors called their clients "Muppets," and he said the most common question asked by the junior analysts is, "How much money did we make off the client?"[15]

Is Everyone Unethical?[16]

One of the underlying assumptions that is made pertaining to ethical behavior is that people are always aware of their own behavior. Under certain circumstances, people can act in an unethical manner and not even realize it. Unintentional unethical behavior can take place, in part, because of the illusion of objectivity. The illusion of objectivity occurs when a decision maker believes that his or her decisions are free of biases, but biases are actually part of the decision-making process. The biases may be undetected because they are not congruent with the explicitly held beliefs of the decision maker. Bono may be dealing with an illusion of objectivity in the example that was given at the beginning of the chapter. It appears that he does not see any contradiction in asking others to pay to improve the standard of living of citizens in developing countries while he is trying to pay as little income tax as possible. There are four avenues along which unintentional unethical behavior may be developed: (1) implicit forms of prejudice, (2) a bias that is favorable to the decision maker's own "group," (3) the tendency of the decision maker to claim credit for other people's actions, and (4) actual and potential conflicts of interest.

Implicit Prejudice

This is a bias that occurs based on unconscious beliefs. A common bias occurs when a decision maker supports the decision pertaining to a person by relying on unconscious stereotypes or the unconscious comparison of past behavior to a person in the past that had similar characteristics with a person currently working for the organization. Gender and ethnic biases can be common implicit prejudices.

In-Group Favoritism

In-group favoritism occurs when the decision maker forms a bias toward individuals in the same "group" as the decision maker. For example, a manager may be more helpful to subordinates who have a good personal relationship with the boss. A principal reason that a close, personal relationship could have developed between the boss and the subordinate is that they share the same interests or ethnic background. As a result, managers may give more "help" to subordinates in their own groups rather than to other subordinates while not realizing that a bias has occurred.

Claiming Credit for Others' Actions

Claiming credit for others' actions occurs when the decision makers believe that they are above average in their job duties, responsibilities, and general intellect, which results in above average performance. In a study at Harvard, MBA students were asked to determine what percentage their individual contribution was to a group project. The overall average percentage for each group was 139%, clearly indicating some individuals were claiming more than their fair share.[17]

Conflicts of Interest

A bias occurs when there is a conflict of interest and the decision maker favors a solution in which there would be personal benefits. A conflict of interest can unintentionally shift the focus as to what course of action should be considered. An example of how conflicts of interest can skew the decision-making process relates to the ability of physicians to accept compensation when they refer patients to be viable participants in a clinical trial. A simple rationalization that it is in the best interest of the patient and that no harm is done by receiving money for it could become entrenched in the physician's mind-set.

Decision makers must be aware that potential unrealized biases can become part of their decision-making pattern. As a result, decision makers must make themselves aware of the potential unconscious biases that could affect their "objective" decision making. The objectivity of the decision making can also be clouded by a society where cheating is tolerated.

Five Barriers to an Ethical Organization[18]

Max Bazerman and Ann Tenbrunsel argue that good managers can often let bad things happen due to not fully understanding the consequences of their actions. They state that there are five barriers erected by managers that can hinder the ability of an organization to be ethical: ill-conceived goals, motivated blindness, indirect blindness, the slippery slope, and overvaluing outcomes.

Ill-Conceived Goals Ill-conceived goals occur when goals are set to promote a positive behavior but they actually encourage a negative behavior. An example is evaluating an employee on the basis of his or her billable hours. Although the objective is to motivate the employee to work harder, in fact, the employee may focus on unethical actions to artificially increase the number of billable hours.

Motivated Blindness Motivated blindness occurs when managers "overlook" the unethical behavior of employees if it is in the best interest of the managers to not be aware of the actions of the employees. Similar to a "Don't Ask, Don't Tell" philosophy, motivated blindness "allows" the manager to plead ignorance about the unethical actions of others once these actions have been discovered by other employees within the organization.

Indirect Blindness Indirect blindness refers to not applying the same level of ethical accountability when a third party is involved in the questionable actions within the organization. An example of "transferring" the questionable ethical actions to another party occurs when a drug company sells the rights to a drug to another company and that company raises the price. The drug company still manufactures the drug on a contract basis, so it would benefit from the price increase, yet the increase is "officially" an act of the third party. Therefore, the drug company is "protected" by the decision of the third party.

The Slippery Slope The slippery slope refers to the inability of managers to see the unethical actions of others if these behaviors develop slowly over time. If a manager accepts minor questionable actions, over time it will be more difficult to identify unethical behavior as the actions increase in unethical severity.

Overvaluing Outcomes Managers are more likely to accept unethical behavior if the final outcome is positive. This barrier reinforces the "ends justify the means" philosophy of managing. As a result, from the managers' perspective, the outcome supersedes the actions that took place in order to achieve the outcome.

The Cheating Culture

In his book *The Cheating Culture: Why More Americans Are Doing Wrong to Get Ahead*, David Callahan argues that cheating has become integrated into today's society as an acceptable activity. Individuals will accept cheating because they rationalize that "everyone does it," which creates a culture that supports cheating.[19] Callahan defines *cheating* as any action in which an individual breaks the rules to benefit his or her self-interests, whether it is academically, professionally, or financially. Breaking the rules does not necessarily mean breaking the law, but it does refer to actions that give an unfair advantage to those who do not follow the rules established by society.[20] Callahan warns that the laissez-faire attitude toward government regulations in the marketplace incorrectly assumes that businesses can voluntarily regulate themselves. Callahan states that the "hidden hand" or market competition will not enforce moral and fair decisions by decision makers in corporations.[21] The cheating culture is supported by a "Winner Takes All" attitude. Each individual will do "whatever it takes" to get ahead and "win" at every opportunity he or she has in life. Whether it is the most billable hours for a lawyer or the largest amount of stock options by a CEO, the competitive spirit of the cheating culture supports winning instead of playing the game of life. Furthermore, the increased emphasis on material wealth enhances the motivation of individuals to succeed to get their just rewards. The cheating culture also glamorizes the wealthy and powerful and increases the temptation of all members of society to also aspire for the top of the "material pinnacle." In addition, once you have reached the "winning class," the incentives to cheat increase because the rewards are larger and the enforcement of the rules is weak or nonexistent.[22]

Some business schools have developed honor oaths to emphasize the level of ethical commitment of their students. Columbia's Business School's honor code states, "As a life-long member of the Columbia Business School community, I adhere to the principles of truth, integrity, and respect. I will not lie, cheat, steal, or tolerate those who do."[23] Even former Enron CEO Jeffrey Skilling's alma mater, Harvard Business School, has developed an MBA oath that focuses on serving the greater good by acting responsibly and ethically and refraining from advancing their self-interests above those of others. In May 2009, 160 students out of a class of 800 Harvard MBA graduates signed the voluntary oath.[24]

In a global study measuring different components of cheating, it was discovered that the cheating culture is not just occurring in the United States but is a worldwide phenomenon. Cheating occurred regardless of the level of corruption within the country. The results showed that the moral character was the same in corrupt versus non-corrupt countries. However, the survey also found that corruption within countries will lead to more corruption by the citizens of that country. They also found that female respondents were less likely to act upon and support cheating behavior than male respondents were.[25]

I'll Take Cheating for $200

Apparently no one is immune to the temptations of cheating. The Federal Communications Commission (FCC) investigated whether the producers of the planned Fox television game show titled *Our Little Genius* had given potential contestants for the program the answers before they competed on the show. It was alleged that a few days before the child was going to go on the show, one of the program's staff reviewed potential topics for the show as well as specific answers to questions for which the child did not initially know the correct response. The premise of the show was to showcase the intellect of children between the ages of 6 and 12 years old with the prizes being potentially "life-changing money." The creator and producer of the show was Mark Burnett, who is famous for producing such shows as *Survivor,*

Celebrity Apprentice, Shark Tank, and *Are You Smarter Than a 5th Grader?* The FCC started the investigation when a parent of one of the potential contestants wrote the agency and complained about the tactics used by the Fox representative. The program was withdrawn from the Fox schedule 6 days before the premiere was supposed to air. The official explanation from Fox was that there were some questions pertaining to "how some information was relayed to contestants during the preproduction . . . [and that] there can be no question about the integrity of our shows."[26]

But, I Did Graduate . . . Or Did I?

Cheating and lying in all its forms can appear to be harmless and victimless but the consequences can be very real and very severe. The former CEO of Yahoo, Scott Thompson, knows the impact of lying firsthand. Thompson had claimed he had received a bachelor's degree in accounting and computer science from Stonehill College. In actuality, Thompson had received a bachelor of science degree in business administration with a major in accounting from Stonehill College. By falsifying his credentials by stating he had obtained a degree in computer science, he apparently assumed that this additional degree would "fit" more comfortably with the expectations of a Web-based technology company such as Yahoo!. The error was not discovered by anyone within Yahoo but by one of Yahoo's investors, Daniel Loeb. Loeb did a simple Google search and discovered the error in Thompson's resume. Yahoo did not use a background-checking firm before hiring Thompson. Thompson initially still had the support of the board after the disclosure was made, but that support quickly evaporated when Thompson blamed others, including his previous employer PayPal and the executive recruiting firm, for adding the second degree to his credentials. Thompson had only been employed by Yahoo for 4 months and was expected to be the person to correct the declining financial performance of the firm. Thompson had to forfeit $22.5 million in potential stock options and a $1.5 million cash bonus and $1 million salary, but he did leave Yahoo with $6.5 million from his exit package.[27]

Thompson follows a long list of top executives who misrepresented themselves by lying about the credentials. In 2002, Bausch & Lomb CEO Ronald Zarrella falsely claimed that he had received a Master of Business Administration (MBA) from New York University. He offered to resign, but the board did not accept his resignation. They did, however, take away his bonus for the year. In 2006, RadioShack CEO David Edmondson had to resign when he stated he had a Bachelor of Science from Pacific Coast Baptist College when he had only a certificate, which had fewer requirements than a bachelor degree. In 2008, Herbalife president and chief operating officer Gregory Probert resigned when it was discovered that he did not graduate from California State University, Los Angeles, with an MBA. He never completed all the requirements of the program yet claimed this credential on at least 19 different regulatory filings.[28] Misleading others pertaining to one's accomplishments is just one of the many avenues available to people to use their own unethical behavior for their own personal gain.

Cheating and the Job Market

Many retail stores require job applicants to take a personality test as part of the hiring process. The test, given by many retailers, uses 130 statements in which the applicants must decide whether they strongly agree or disagree with each statement. The only problem is that an unauthorized answer sheet was posted on the Internet that gives the "correct" responses for the applicant. The correct responses are based on determining what the retailers want the applicant to answer as the correct response. For example, one statement is "You have to give up on some things that you start," for which the correct answer is "strongly disagree," and another statement is "Any trouble you have is your own fault," for which the correct answer is "strongly agree." The creator of the test called "Unicru" commented that there is a low incidence of cheating because there is no decline in the benefit the test generates, which is lower employee turnover and better financial performance. Of course, this is an indirect evaluation of this test because a more accurate objective to measure it would be the decrease in ethical or unethical behavior by the employees since the test was released on the Internet. The applicants are graded as green, yellow, or red based on their responses. Green applicants will be hired, but yellow and red applicants are less likely to be hired. Friends who did well on the test helped others in explaining what answers were needed, and other applicants went to retailers that the applicants knew would have the test so the applicants could experiment with the answers and then apply for the jobs they really wanted.[29]

Grade Inflation and the Institutional Pressure to Cheat

The Loyola Law School in Los Angeles wanted to make its students more attractive in the highly competitive job market for lawyers. A simple solution was to adjust their grades. The law school added 0.333 points to every grade of their students for a few years to increase students' overall grade point average. The Loyola Law School is not alone in this action. At least 10 law schools in the past 3 years have adjusted the grades of the students to increase their grade point averages. Those law schools included New York University, Georgetown, and Tulane University. There is also another incentive for the law schools to raise the grade averages of their students. Grade point averages are a factor in the calculation of how law schools are ranked against each other in major publications.[30]

In the spring of 2010, an elementary school near Houston was ready to announce the results of the state achievement tests. The stakes were high because high scores meant a positive boost for the careers of the principal and vice principal and a potential bonus of $2,850 for fifth-grade math and science teachers. The results showed high scores that were suspicious in nature. The result was that the principal, assistant principal, and three teachers were forced to resign after it was discovered that they had tampered with the administration of the test. The educators "tubed" the state science test booklet by squeezing it so that the questions could be read without having to break the paper seal. After examining the questions, the educators created a detailed study guide to be used to "help" the students perform well on the test.[31]

In another case, the principal of a charter school in Springfield, Massachusetts, ordered the teachers to look over the shoulder of the students and point out wrong answers that needed to be corrected on a 2009 state test. In Georgia, an investigation of 191 schools in February 2010 showed that the number of erasures on the form from the wrong to the right answers was far outside logical statistical probability. It was determined that the teachers were erasing the wrong answers and bubbling in the correct answers. Additional pressure for the students to perform well on the tests came from many states using standardized tests for teaching evaluation purposes in making decisions such as tenure, dismissal raises, and bonuses. In addition, the No Child Left Behind law mandates that all public schools have their students up to their grade level in reading and math by 2014.[32] Technology has broadened the scope and depth of cheating by individuals by its convenience and disconnect from the physical world.

The Role of Technology and Cheating

The use of digital technology can blur the distinction between plagiarism and one's own work. Trip Gabriel gives examples where college students that copy and paste from a frequently asked questions page on a website were not considered to be plagiarizing because no author was cited. Another example is a student who copied from Wikipedia and did not cite the source because the information was considered "common knowledge." The ease in which pages of ideas can be quickly transferred from one text to another can eliminate the moment of reflection by the "authors" about the legal and ethical validity of their actions. A survey done by the Center of Academic Integrity found that from 2006 to 2010, approximately 40% of the 14,000 students who responded to the survey admitted that they copied text without properly referencing the material. In the same study, only 29% of the respondents believed that copying text from the Internet was considered "serious cheating."[33] Some students will rationalize that cutting and pasting someone else's thoughts is not considered cheating but rather another skill set for developing their careers. It seems that the skills developed when getting a college education are moving away from focusing on insightful thought and development of intellect and instead focusing on practical training in which any action is justified to obtain the desired result. Of course, the underlying educational issue concerns ethical issues and the development of knowledge by the student. Today's students have always had the Internet to rely on and view writing not as a development of individual thought but as a "collage" of ideas that have been developed by others and are available to copy.[34]

Generational Differences Pertaining to Ethics

In its 2011 National Business Ethics Survey,[35] the Ethics Resource Center (ERC) found a number of interesting results when comparing the ethical values of Millennial, Generation X, and Baby Boomer employees. Table 2.1 highlights the characteristics of these three demographic groups. Of the respondents in the study, 8% of the Baby Boomers, 10% of the Generation X, and 7% of the Millennials felt pressure to commit unethical acts in the workplace. This study also showed that significantly more employees experienced retaliation after they reported misconduct to company officials. Fifteen percent of Baby Boomers, 14% of Generation X, and 16% of Millennial respondents reported that they faced some type of retaliation for whistle-blowing. The results also showed differences in whether employees have observed unethical misconduct. Approximately 56% of Millennials observed unethical misconduct, whereas 49% of Generation X employees and 48% of Baby Boomers also observed this type of behavior.[36] In addition, the study also demonstrated that Millennials had a less positive view of the company's ethical culture and were less likely to report unethical activities. Table 2.2 presents the results of this study. In addition, Millennials were more likely to consider it acceptable behavior to comment negatively on social media about their employers, and because of their belief of "free information flow," they are more likely to obtain copies of confidential information to keep.[37] An underlying issue of unethical conduct relates to the lack of trust between the employee and the employer.

TABLE 2.1 ● Three Primary Generations in the U.S. Workforce: 2009

	Baby Boomers	Generation X	Millennials
Other Names for Generations	Boomers "Me Generation"	Baby Busters Slacker Generation X-ers	Generation Y Echo Boomers Generation Next
Range of Birth Years	1946–1964	1965–1980	1981–2000
Significant World Events During Their Lifetimes	Born after World War II Economic prosperity Assassinations of John F. Kennedy, Robert F. Kennedy, and Martin Luther King Jr. Civil rights movement Vietnam War	Baby bust Latchkey kids Rise in divorce rate Personal computers Economic uncertainty	Internet Terrorism Globalization
Positive Traits	Hardworking Idealistic Committed to harmony	Entrepreneurial Flexible and creative Comfortable with technology	Tech-savvy Accept diversity Skilled multitaskers
Negative Traits	Sense of entitlement Workaholics Self-centered	Skeptical and cynical Lazy, slackers Question authority figures	Lacking literacy fundamentals Very short attention spans Not loyal to any organization
Workplace Attributes	Belief that hard work equals long hours Long-term commitment to employing organization Self-motivated Does not like feedback	Desire for work-life balance Prefer flexible structures Expect to have multiple employers	Excellent in integrating technology in the workplace Demand immediate feedback and recognition Expect to have multiple employers
Motivators	Salary	Security	Be able to maintain a full personal life

Source: Adopted from *Generational Differences in Workplace Ethics. A Supplemental Report of the 2011 National Business Ethics Survey* (Arlington, VA: Ethics Resource Center 2013).

TABLE 2.2 ● A Comparison of Unethical Observations of Other Employees by Three Primary Generations in the U.S. Workforce: 2009 and 2011			
Misconduct	Millennials 2009/2011	Generation X 2009/2011	Baby Boomers 2009/2011
Sexual Harassment	8%/15%	7%/11%	7%/8%
Abusive Behavior	21%/21%	22%/20%	24%/22%
Accepting Gifts/Kickbacks	4%/9%	4%/6%	3%/3%
Discrimination	18%/18%	13%/14%	14%/13%
Health/Safety Violations	14%/13%	10%/13%	10%/12%
Conflict of Interest	17%/18%	17%/15%	15%/15%
Improper Hiring Practices	12%/12%	9%/10%	9%/9%
Lying to Customers, Vendors, or the Public	13%/14%	12%/13%	11%/10%
Lying to Employees	21%/22%	20%/20%	18%/20%
Stealing or Theft	12%/16%	10%/12%	7%/9%
Internet Abuse	16%/17%	20%/17%	17%/14%
Employee Benefits Violations	15%/17%	11%/12%	9%/10%
Company Resource Abuse	26%/21%	23%/21%	22%20%
Employee Privacy Breach	8%/13%	12%/11%	11%/11%

Source: Adopted from *Millennials, Gen X and Baby Boomers: Who's Working at Your Company and What Do They Think About Ethics?*, Supplemental Research Brief, 2009 National Business Ethics Survey (Arlington, VA: Ethics Resource Center 2010) and *Generational Differences in Workplace Ethics: A Supplemental Report of the 2011 National Business Ethics Survey* (Arlington, VA: Ethics Resource Center 2013).

The Role of Trust in Ethical Conduct

Trust is an important component of supporting cooperation throughout the organization. If the employees believe that there is a high level of trust within the organization, it will reduce the employees' level of uncertainty and anxiety.[38] As positive actions by the employees are supported by the organization, employees' level of trust increases. Therefore, as the level of trust increases, the employees feel more confident that following high ethical standards will be rewarded and those who do not follow the ethical standards of the firm will be punished. Furthermore, trust allows the employee to believe that he or she will be able to blow the whistle on other employees who are performing unethical acts without being punished for doing so. Pablo Cardona and Helen Wilkinson proposed that trust allows a virtuous circle to develop between the manager and the subordinates.[39] Managers can demonstrate their commitment to developing a trusting relationship with their subordinates by their actions, which include being consistent and predictable, having integrity, sharing information with the subordinates, delegating decision-making responsibilities, showing concern for others, and standing by the employees. This pattern of behavior by the manager strengthens the level of trust the subordinates have for the manager, which may result in the employees being more likely to take the initiative to solve problems, help colleagues support the firm, go beyond the minimum requirements of the job, and enhance the level of loyalty they have toward the firm.[40]

Questions for Thought

1. Why do you think that Bono fails to see the inconsistencies of his actions? What could Bono do now to help correct this perceived hypocritical behavior?

2. Do you agree with the argument that corporations are more powerful than governments? Do you expect corporations to become weaker or more powerful in the future?

3. Do you think how people view what is ethical has changed over time? How have the ethical values changed from your grandparents' era? Explain.

4. Do you believe we live in a cheating culture? Explain your answer.

Real-Life Ethical Dilemma Exercise

Can He Still Cheer for NYU?[41]

In October 2010, a U.S. district judge upheld a decision made by the New York University Stern School of Business to deny an MBA degree to a student who had withheld that he or she had been convicted of insider trading. Ayal Rosenthal had pleaded guilty to conspiracy to commit securities fraud in 2007 when he told his brother insider information obtained when he was working at PricewaterhouseCoopers in 2005.

He was in the part-time MBA program at Stern at the time of the conviction and served 60 days in prison. Rosenthal had completed the requirements at Stern but was denied the degree after it was decided that he had violated Stern's honor code and code of conduct. The judge ruled that Rosenthal had completed the degree requirements only by concealing that he had been convicted, and the question of whether he should receive the degree should rest in the hands of the MBA faculty. The president and CEO of the Association to Advance Collegiate Schools of Business (AACSB), the national accrediting association for business schools, stated it was the first time a business school had decided whether to award a degree based not on behavior within the program but on a student's external professional dealings. Rosenthal's defense attorney said the verdict was creating a "dangerous slippery slope," giving the faculty full power to determine who receives an MBA degree. The underlying ethics question is whether the actions of a student outside the realm of academic requirements and behavior can supersede the actions and efforts of the student in completing his or her degree.

Questions for the Real-Life Ethical Dilemma Exercise

1. Do you think the correct decision was made? Why or why not?

2. If the student had been convicted before he started the MBA program, would that

change the decision to deny his degree? Explain.

3. If the conviction occurred after he had graduated, should NYU have the power to revoke the MBA by citing the same violation of code of ethics? Explain.

Student Study Site

Visit the Student Study Site at **study.sagepub.com/stanwick3e** to access the following resources:

- Video Links
- SAGE Journal Articles
- Web Resources
- Web Quizzes

3

Stakeholders and Corporate Social Responsibility

A business that makes nothing but
money is a poor kind of business.

—Henry Ford, founder of Ford Motor Company

Chapter Objectives

After reading and studying Chapter 3, students should be able to

1. Explain the concept of *stakeholders*.
2. Describe the difference between immoral, amoral, and moral managers.
3. Define *power, urgency,* and *legitimacy* with respect to stakeholder theory.
4. Describe the concept of trust with stakeholder groups.
5. Define *triple bottom line reporting*.
6. Define a *benefit corporation* and the criteria to be classified as a B corporation.
7. Explain the concept of suppliers as stakeholders and its relationship to outsourcing.
8. Identify the different stakeholders that could exist for a company.
9. Define *corporate social responsibility* and discuss its components.
10. Explain the role of corporate reputation in an organization.
11. Explain the role of corporate philanthropy in an organization.

When Is Fair Trade Not Fair?

The "Fair Trade" logo on numerous food products, including coffee, is an indication that the farmers at the company received a "fair wage" for their work through the higher prices that are charged for the product. By 2006, 35,000 retailers and restaurants in the United States, including McDonalds and Dunkin Donuts, distributed products that have "Fair Trade" labels. From 1999 to the beginning of 2006, more than 100 million pounds of food products, including coffee, cocoa, tea, rice, sugar, and various fruits, have been certified as fair trade products.[1] Globally, in 2013, there were 12,000 fair trade certified products worldwide.[2] A major supporter of fair trade products, Green Mountain Coffee Roasters, is the largest purchaser of fair trade coffee in the world. The company imported approximately 50.3 million pounds in 2011, or 24% of its raw coffee purchases.[3]

In the United States, Fair Trade USA is the organization that certifies companies that can have the "Fair Trade" logo on their products. Fair Trade USA is one of 25 nonprofit organizations around the globe that certify fair trade products and collect licensing for each product that uses the "Fair Trade" logo. The 25 organizations are controlled by the Fairtrade Labelling Organizations International (FLO), which is headquartered in Bonn, Germany. FLO is responsible for setting international fair trade standards, organizing support for producers around the world, developing global fair trade strategy, and promoting trade justice internationally.[4]

The CEO of Fair Trade USA, Paul Rice, stated in 2006 that the program allows the farmers to deal directly with the wholesaler, eliminating as many as five different intermediaries that could include a local buyer, a miller, an exporter, a shipper, and an importer.[5]

However, the underlying question remains: Where does that additional money for every pound of Mountain People's coffee go? Critics of the fair trade program state that the farmers are not the beneficiaries of the additional profit; rather, the distributors and the retailers receive the additional revenue. Lawrence Solomon, who analyzed trade and consumer issues for the Canadian Energy Probe Research Foundation, stated that the fair trade "premium" is captured by the distributors with very little, if anything, trickling down to the farmers. Furthermore, fair trade labels do not identify how much money the farmers are paid for their products. From information available at Fair Trade USA in 2006 (when the organization was called TransFair), it was calculated that coca farmers received 3 cents from the $3.49 spent on an "organic fair trade"–labeled 3.5-ounce chocolate bar sold at Target. For one pound of fair trade sugar sold at Whole Foods for $3.79, the farmers received 24 cents. The $10 for a pound of coffee sold at Mountain People's Co-Op netted the farmer $1.26 compared to $1.10 for non–fair trade coffee. The $1.26 rate was fixed, so the farmer would continue to get that rate regardless whether the coffee sold for $10 or $15.[6]

A company that took advantage of the fair trade image was Costa Coffee, one of the largest coffee retailers in Great Britain. When Costa Coffee started using fair trade coffee, it added 18 cents to each cup of coffee brewed, even though the fair trade coffee cost them only between 1 and 2 cents extra per cup. Once this information was released to the public, Costa Coffee reduced its price on the fair trade coffee. At the other end of the continuum, Starbucks Coffee Company bought 11.5 million pounds of fair trade coffee in 2005 and established a buying program called Coffee and Farmer

> Equity Practices (C.A.F.E.) to ensure that the farmers are compensated fairly. To be able to participate in the program, all suppliers to Starbucks must give Starbucks' external monitor, Scientific Certification Systems, written receipts that verify how much each party in the supply chain was paid for the coffee.[7]

What Is a Stakeholder?

The beginning of stakeholder theory was first presented by A. A. Berle in the *Harvard Law Review* in 1931. Berle stated that all of the powers that are given to a corporation are to be used to create benefits in the interest of the shareholders. Berle argued that managers within a corporation should consider themselves trustees and guardians of the investments made by the shareholders.[8]

In a rebuttal to Berle, the following year E. Merrick Dodd stated in the *Harvard Law Review* that the interests of the shareholders should be considered but that corporations need to recognize their obligations to the community, to their workers, and to the consumers. Dodd argued that corporations are allowed to become legal entities because they serve a purpose to the community instead of just providing opportunities for financial gain by their owners. Dodd cited in his article the CEO of General Electric, Owen D. Young, who stated that, as a CEO, it makes a big difference in his attitude whether he is considered a trustee of the company or an attorney for the interests of the investors. If a CEO is considered a trustee, then the decisions made by the company should consider the effect it would have on the shareholders and on the employees and the customers.[9]

In 1970, Milton Friedman picked up the gauntlet that Berle had thrown down by reiterating the sole importance to the shareholder in the decisions made by managers. The title of the article in the *New York Times Magazine* explains the thrust of his argument: "The Social Responsibility of Business Is to Increase Its Profits." Friedman argued that in a free market system in which people are allowed to own property, the executives of the company need to be considered as the employees hired by the shareholders. The managers also have a responsibility to their employees, but that responsibility entails trying to help the employees achieve their desires, which are to make as much money as possible within the legal rules and ethical customs of society. Friedman argued that social responsibility is a fundamentally subversive ideal and that the only social responsibility a manager has is to ensure that the company's resources are optimized to enhance the level of profitability of the firm.[10]

A comprehensive definition of a stakeholder presented by the Stanford Research Institute in 1963 is a member of a group whose support is necessary for the firm to continue to exist. Edward Freeman believed that stakeholders were any individuals or groups that can affect or be affected by the actions of the firm.[11]

Freeman built on the original work of Dodd by broadening the definition of stakeholders to encompass any individuals or groups that have a vested interest in the operations of the firm.

The multitude of stakeholders in today's business operations make the shareholder just one of many groups interested in ethical behaviors of the business. In the past, many companies looked after only the stockholders, but this sense of constituencies has changed in recent years. Corporations now look toward a stakeholder approach.

FIGURE 3.1 ● **Stakeholder Model**

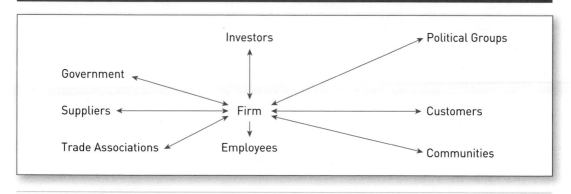

Source: Thomas Donaldson and Lee E. Preston, "The Stakeholder Theory of the Corporation: Concepts, Evidence, and Implications," *Academy of Management Review* (1995): 69.

Stakeholders are defined as any group or individual that has a vested interest in the operations of the firm. Traditional stakeholders for a firm include employees, suppliers, stockholders, customers, the government, local communities, and society as a whole. Employees must be encouraged to relay relevant information pertaining to ethical conduct to the management of the firm. This information flow is critical to ensure that the needs of all the firm's stakeholders are satisfied. A model showing the relationship between stakeholders and the firm is shown in Figure 3.1.

Management's Response to Stakeholders

Moral Management and Stakeholders[12]

A manager's response to stakeholders depends, in part, on the level of morality of the manager. As Archie Carroll states in his 1991 *Business Horizons* article, "The Pyramid of Corporate Social Responsibility: Toward the Moral Management of Organizational Stakeholders," managers can be classified based on three types of moral values: immoral, amoral, and moral. An immoral manager is one who does not care how his or her decisions affect the stakeholders, but the actions are actively counterintuitive to what is the right and ethical thing to do. These managers focus only on their own goals and the goals of the company and consider legal requirements as constants or barriers that are ignored when their corporate actions are implemented. Recent examples of Kenneth Lay, Bernie Ebbers, and Dennis Kozlowski demonstrate that immoral managers can reach the pinnacle of a company and are able to disperse their immoral viewpoints throughout the company.

An amoral manager is a manager who could be considered ethically neutral. An amoral manager does not focus proactively on ethical issues, nor does he or she try to purposely go against the social and legal norms that are expected of the firm by society. The danger with an amoral manager is that because ethical considerations are not contemplated in the decision-making process, the manager may unintentionally commit unethical acts and not realize the impact the decision had on various stakeholders.

An example of unintentional amorality could occur when a police or fire department has stringent height and weight requirements for potential applicants. Although the reason for the restriction is to ensure that the applicant will be able to physically cope with the demands of the job, the height and weight restrictions could unintentionally exclude otherwise viable candidates such as women and certain ethnic groups.

Moral managers are those decision makers who understand the importance and relevance of considering ethical issues when they are making decisions. Moral managers meet the minimum legal standards and are proactive in presenting ethical leadership to the firm's employees and other stakeholders.

How these three types of managers react with various stakeholders highlights the difference in their management styles. Table 3.1 highlights the various interactions that the three types of managers have with the various stakeholders.

TABLE 3.1 ● Moral Management Style and Stakeholders

Immoral Manager

Interaction With Stockholders

Shareholders are given minimum attention. The focus is on increasing personal compensation for the managers. Managers' self-interest supersedes the interests of the stockholders. Immoral managers will conceal their actions, if necessary, so the stockholders are not aware of what management is doing.

Interaction With Employees

From an immoral manager's perspective, employees are considered just a means of production that can be treated at a minimum level. Immoral managers use negative reinforcement and controlling tools to ensure that employees meet their production standards.

Interaction With Customers

Immoral managers view customers as current and potential opportunities in that they can be exploited by the firm for the manager's personal gain or for the gain of the firm. The goal of immoral managers is to generate revenue by any means possible, including cheating, deceiving, and misleading the customers into purchasing their goods and services. The maximum level of exploitation continues with decisions on the advertised pricing and distribution of the products and services.

Interaction With the Local Community

Immoral managers consider the local community as just another avenue in which their interests and the interests of the company supersede the interests of others. As a result, immoral managers justify polluting the natural environment, massive firings of company employees, and taking advantage of all the resources of the community as justifiable means for the managers and firm to achieve their own financial objectives.

Amoral Manager

Interaction With Stockholders

Amoral managers do not view stockholders as more important than any other group. Amoral managers acknowledge their existence and realize that they have to have at least a minimal level of accommodation for their needs. Amoral managers understand that profitability of the firm is the reward for stockholders but will communicate only what is legally required for the stakeholder group.

Interaction With Employees

Amoral managers treat employees based on the legal and government requirements that have been established. Amoral managers motivate their employees by trying to enhance the level of productivity, but the employees are still considered a means of production.

Interaction With Customers

Amoral managers view customers as purely a revenue generator in which the firm is obligated to follow legal and government regulations pertaining to the products and services that are offered to the customers as well as how the customers are treated.

Interaction With the Local Community

Amoral managers do not consider factors related to the community when they make decisions. Amoral managers view the community like the employees, as just another means of production. Amoral managers have minimal contact with the community and follow the legal standard when interacting with the community.

Moral Manager

Interaction With Stockholders

Moral managers view both the short- and long-term interests as a critical factor in the decision-making process. Moral managers treat stockholders fairly and justly, as they do with any of their stakeholders. To ensure that ethical standards are established within the firm, an ethics committee could be formed by the board of directors. In addition, moral managers would ensure that a code of ethics is developed and is incorporated in the decision-making process of all the employees within the firm.

Interaction With Employees

Moral managers treat employees as human resources, not just a means of production. Moral managers treat employees with dignity and respect and ask that they make a physical contribution and actively participate in the strategic decision-making process within the firm. Moral managers treat the employees fairly and respect their rights, privacy, and freedoms.

Interaction With Customers

Moral managers view customers as equal partners in any transaction between the two parties. Moral managers present customers with safe products that give the customers fair value for the price. In addition, the firm gives customers access to full disclosure of the products as well as a full guarantee of customer satisfaction.

Interaction With the Local Community

Moral managers view the local community as a valuable asset to be protected by the firm. As a result, moral managers take a leadership role in being actively involved in helping promote the best interests of the local community. Moral managers would lead the way to promote the arts, education, environmental initiatives, recreational groups, and philanthropic groups.

Source: Archie Carroll, "The Pyramid of Corporate Social Responsibility: Toward the Moral Management of Organizational Stakeholders," *Business Horizons* (July–August, 1991): 46–47.

Which Stakeholders Are More "Important"?

Another issue with stakeholder theory is the determination of which groups the corporation must be directly accountable to. One way of identifying the importance of stakeholders is to examine the attributes of power, legitimacy, and urgency of the stakeholder group. *Power* is the extent to which the organization can influence or impose its will on the stakeholder group. *Legitimacy* is the assumption that the actions of the corporation are desirable, proper, or appropriate within the limits of the corporation. *Urgency* is the degree to which the issues raised by the stakeholder must be dealt with in a time-sensitive manner. When all three of these attributes are present, that stakeholder must be considered a high-priority stakeholder.[13] By using this attribute approach, corporations may be better able to determine which stakeholder groups have the highest priority in their day-to-day operations.

Stakeholders affect organizations through four roles:

- Stakeholders establish expectations (explicit or implicit) about corporate performance.
- Stakeholders experience the effects of corporate behaviors.
- Stakeholders evaluate the effects of corporate behaviors on their interests or reconcile the effects of those behaviors with their expectations.
- Stakeholders act upon their interests, expectations, experiences, and evaluations.[14]

The Ability to Build Trust With the Stakeholders

There is an inherent need to build and maintain a relationship of trust between the firm and the stakeholders. Just as managers are expected to be trustworthy agent managers of the financial resources of the stockholders, managers are also expected to manage the interests of the various stakeholders who have a vested interest in the firm's operations. Trust can be considered a moral exchange between the stakeholders and the managers of the firm. Three elements of trust affect the relationship between stakeholders and the firms: rational prediction of outcomes, emotion, and a clear moral element. Stakeholders enhance their trust in a firm if they become more optimistic that the results of the actions of the firm will have a positive impact on their needs and expectations. Stakeholders will also strengthen their level of trust the more they become vulnerable by the actions of the firm and become more emotional than rational.

Stakeholders also have faith that their trustworthy relationship with the firm is based on mutual moral and ethical commitment.[15] In addition, a high level of trust allows less stringent corporate governance structures to be developed to monitor the actions of the top-level managers, which reduces costs and enhances the firm's competitive advantage. A relationship between the stakeholders and the firm built on trust strengthens both parties' level of cooperative behavior. Four dimensions can enhance the level of trust between the stakeholders and the firms: ability, benevolence, integrity, and information quality. *Ability* is based on the firm's level of expertise, competence, and product development in the economic success of the firm. *Benevolence* is based on the level of the firm's corporate social responsibility and amount of information that is dispersed from the firm. *Integrity* is based on perception of how the firm is performing in its function of keeping its promises and the ability to demonstrate to the stakeholders its law-abiding behavior. *Information quality* is evaluated based on the level of objectivity and intelligibility.[16]

The ambiguity pertaining to the Fair Trade products discussed in the opening vignette demonstrates that stakeholders must be well informed and diligent to ensure their expectations are met by the actions of others. From the farmer in the co-op to the distribution of the products to the retailer to the customers who buy the product, each stakeholder must ask the questions that demand that their beliefs pertaining to a fair trade program coincide with the actual actions of the various other stakeholders throughout the fair trade program. For example, if the customers ask for proof of the validity of the fair trade program, it could create a ripple effect throughout the supply chain all the way back to the farmer of the product.

The Role of Stakeholder Communications

One major area to consider is stakeholder communications. If management must be concerned with the needs of all legitimate stakeholders and, to a certain degree, derivative stakeholders, then how should management communicate necessary information to the groups? The concept of stakeholder communications must be viewed from the perspective of both management and the stakeholders. How should information be communicated? For instance, some companies explicitly mention stakeholders in their vision or mission statement. These companies might want to open lines of communication with these stakeholders. Methods such as open houses, public service announcements, and public newsletters all distribute information about company issues. Another way to open dialogue is to offer a town meeting to discuss relevant issues about the corporation. Management needs to be open to the informational needs of stakeholders, and stakeholders need to express their comments and concerns in a nonthreatening manner.

Triple Bottom Line Reporting

Triple bottom line reporting is a concept that is receiving momentum as a way of satisfying the reporting and disclosure needs of various stakeholder groups, although many companies refer to the concept as an *accountability report*. A concept that was first introduced in 1998 by John Elkington in his book *Cannibals with Forks: The Triple Bottom Line of Twenty-First Century Business*, the concept of the triple bottom line expands traditional financial reporting to include environmental and social reporting. Elkington purports looking beyond just the financial numbers and including the environmental performance and social performance of the company in an all-inclusive company report. The triple bottom line is also known as 3BL or by the phrase "People, Planet, Profit."[17] As a result, a triple bottom line centers on the vested interests of all the stakeholders instead of focusing solely on the interest of the shareholders. Focusing on the environmental and social impacts as well as the financial impacts encourages a firm to establish social and environmental objectives and benchmarking goals. With these goals in place, it may be easier for firms to justify their focus on social and environmental issues that would result in long-term financial rewards for the firm. It is necessary to establish metrics for nonfinancial objectives to properly evaluate the effectiveness of the firm in achieving these goals. In addition, the establishment of these objectives increases the level of transparency of the actions of the firm that can be effectively evaluated by its stakeholders. Environmental performance is generally focused on the amount of resources used in operations in areas such as energy, land, and water. The environmental performance evaluation also focuses on by-products of the production process such as waste, air emissions, and chemical materials and measures their long-term impacts. Social performance is usually based on how the firm and its suppliers both positively and negatively affect the local communities in which they operate.[18]

In addition, triple bottom line reporting allows a quicker response by management because these objectives are being monitored and allows a closer matching of the firm's actions and stakeholders' expectations.[19]

For example, the Canadian Imperial Bank of Commerce (CIBC) has published an accountability report that bank officials feel encompasses the triple bottom line. In this report, the CIBC refers to a balanced scorecard that tries to balance financial and non-financial measures. The report discusses the objectives CIBC officials have set for society, clients, employees, community, environment, suppliers, and corporate governance, all areas that they feel help them achieve the triple bottom line approach.[20]

In actuality, the triple bottom line is not just a link between the stakeholders and the firm but is also a valuable tool the firm uses to enhance its long-term sustainability from both a financial and a nonfinancial perspective. Both the Paris and Johannesburg stock exchanges require all companies listed on these exchanges to produce sustainability reports. Therefore, triple bottom line companies focus on long-term business sustainability, which can be viewed as a firm that meets not only the long-term needs of its own operation but also the long-term needs of its stakeholders.[21]

The Benefit Corporation

A benefit corporation (B Corp) is a new type of corporation that addresses issues related to financial, social, and environmental objectives. B Corps must have three criteria that are not mandated in traditional corporations: (1) They must meet comprehensive and transparent social and environmental performance standards, (2) they must meet higher legal accountability standards than traditional corporations do, and (3) they must build business constituencies for public policies that support sustainable business.[22] The underlying motivation of the B Corp concept is that corporations can both focus on shareholder value and provide social and environmental goods to society. In addition, the concept can "protect" the beliefs and values of top executives of current companies who focus on the triple bottom line but want to ensure those beliefs continue in the future. When California allowed the creation of B Corps beginning on January 1, 2012, Patagonia, a sports clothing and gear retailer, was the first corporation to register as a B Corp. Patagonia CEO Casey Sheahan stated the purpose for Patagonia: "We're trying to preserve for the long term the way our company is run."[23] Patagonia's founder, Yvon Chouinard, also supported the B Corp registration by stating, "Patagonia is trying to build a company that could last 100 years . . . Benefit corporation legislation creates the legal framework to enable mission-driven companies like Patagonia to stay mission-driven through succession, capital raises, and even changes in ownership by institutionalizing the values, culture, processes, and high standards put in place by founding entrepreneurs."[24] The president of Greyston Bakery, Mike Brady, stated that benefit corporations are important because they "add another level of accountability and transparency"[25] to the actions of the firm. Case studies of both Patagonia and Greyston Bakery are located in the second half of this textbook.

B Corps are certified by the nonprofit organization B Lab. To become certified by B Lab, a corporation must successfully complete a stakeholder impact assessment, incorporate its social and environmental objectives into the mission and legal frame-work of the firm, and sign a "Declaration of Interdependence" that acknowledges its interdependence with its stakeholders.[26] The B Corp must also publish an annual ben-efit report that evaluates how well the corporation achieved its financial, social, and environmental goals. By April 2015, there were 1,237 B Corp firms from 121 industries located in 38 countries.[27] In the *B Corporation 2011 Annual Report*, the top five reasons why it would be beneficial for the firm to become B Corp certified were the ability to increase profits, attract more investors, generate positive press, preserve the mission of the firm, and build a movement to enhance political commitment to the values and ideals established by B Corps.[28]

Suppliers as Stakeholders

It is necessary to begin requiring social responsibility and ethical behavior in the rela-tionship between firms and their suppliers. As the fair trade example demonstrated at the beginning of the chapter, the ethical relationship between suppliers and their partners can be difficult and complex to understand. Many companies want those they do business with to demonstrate the same commitment to do the right thing that the company itself is displaying. For example, several computer companies have devel-oped electronics industry codes of conduct to use in conjunction with their suppliers. In 2004, Hewlett-Packard, Dell Computers, and IBM used an electronics industry code of ethics as part of the validation process for corporate social responsibility. This code is seen as collaboration for these companies to demand socially responsible business practices from companies in their supply chains. The code covers issues such as labor (child labor practices, wages and benefits, etc.), health and safety (occupational injury, occupational safety, industrial hygiene, etc.), environment (hazardous substances handling, air emissions, permits and reporting, etc.), management systems (company commitment, training measures, risk assessment and management, etc.), and ethics (disclosure of information, business integrity, protection of identity, etc.).

An example of a framework companies could use to ensure that the relationship between suppliers and the firm is based on ethical values. This is summarized in Intel's Supplier Ethics Expectations.[29] The relationship between suppliers and the firm should be based on three components:

1. The supplier must be in strict compliance with the law.
2. The supplier must have respect for competition.
3. The supplier must not have any actual or perceived conflicts of interest with any other party.

Outsourcing is defined as assigning a function or task that was previously done within a company to an external third party. As companies continue to try to identify areas to reduce costs, outsourcing has become a global issue. Outsourcing traditionally focuses on transferring a manufacturing or service function to an area or a country in which the labor costs are lower. The net reduction in labor costs results in an increased level of profitability for the firm. However, working conditions in those countries that have lower labor rates have been accused of exploiting the workers by having low wage rates, having poor working conditions, using child labor, and indulging in physical and verbal abuse.

An independent nonprofit organization called Verité focuses on social auditing and research programs to examine the working conditions of people around the world. Verité officials reviewed working standards in 27 countries and presented *BusinessWeek* with a summary of working conditions in nine of the top countries in which "sweatshop" conditions can take place. Each of the countries was evaluated based on its use of child labor, forced labor, freedom of association, gender equality, health and safety, and hours and wages.[30]

China

Requiring excess overtime and paying below the minimum wage rate are common in some Chinese factories. The workers are not allowed to form an independent trade union. China has very high rates of health and safety violations. In the mining industry, the death rate of Chinese workers is 10 times that of the rate in the United States.

Brazil

Brazil has a number of labor concerns including forced labor, unequal pay for women, and safety issues in the workplace. Thousands of workers are employed basically without any pay because they are required to pay off debt bondage or were abducted, which results in de facto slavery conditions. Male wages are significantly higher, with women receiving only 54% to 67% of male wages. Numerous work-site accidents occur and are especially prevalent in mining, logging, construction, and oil refining work sites.

India

Child labor is very common in India's non-export industries. There are also numerous violations of worker safety, overtime, and fair pay issues in export factories. Based on an audit done by Verité in 2004, 60% of the audited firms were in violation of minimum wage rules and 83% of the factories were in violation of overtime rules. An estimated 100 million children between the ages of 4 and 14 work at least part-time in a factory, with an estimated 12.6 million children working full-time. Furthermore, an estimated 65 million people work in slavery or bondage conditions. Most of the 65 million who are permanently bonded to their owners come from the Dalit caste, which is the lowest level of the Hindu caste hierarchy. Dalit are considered outcasts and untouchables and are usually assigned only the most menial tasks in India.

Indonesia

Millions of children work in Indonesia in such diverse industries as construction, fishing, mining, and domestic services. Work hazards are high in the mining and fishing industries. The government standards for minimum wages are not enforced well in export manufacturing factories.

Mexico

Child labor is common in non-export oriented industries. A major concern is workers in various industries lack the freedom to organize a union. Many facilities have sweatshop-like conditions for the workers throughout the country, especially in export assembly plants near the U.S. border.

Peru

An estimated 21% of the workers in Peru receive a wage rate that is below the minimum standard. Temporary workers receive even less. Peru is rated as having poor compliance with wage rates and overtime standards.

The Philippines

More than one third of all the garment factories in the Philippines are estimated to be violating wage and work-hour standards. Some of the factory owners can avoid paying even the minimum wage by classifying the workers as "apprentices" or having a facility employ less than 10 workers. Under those two scenarios, factory owners are exempted from paying the minimum wage based on the government exception. Men are paid at twice the rate of women. In addition, 4 million children between the ages of 5 and 17 work, and 2 million of those are working in dangerous conditions.

South Africa

It is estimated that 36% of the children in South Africa work in non-export-oriented industries such as agriculture, cleaning, and family businesses. In the agriculture sector, violations for safety and overtime issues were common.

Sri Lanka

In audits done in 2003 and 2004, Verité found numerous safety violations in a number of facilities. The violations included blocked exits, extremely loud noise, and lack of personal safety. One study of the grain and spice mill industry found that 60% of the workers lost either a finger or contracted skin diseases while working in the facilities. In addition, work was mandatory on Sundays and holidays, and compensation was below the minimum wage.

Customers as Stakeholders

It is critical for any company to understand the role customers have on the ultimate survival of the firm. Customers must have a high level of trust with the firms they are buying goods and services from, or the customers will seek those goods and services from companies they feel they can trust. Ethical behavior must be the norm in four critical areas in the relationship between the firm and the customers:

1. The manufacturing process
2. Sales and quotes
3. Distribution
4. Customer service[31]

The Manufacturing Process

The customers expect and demand products that are safe to use and are of at least reasonable quality. As a result, customers trust the firms to manufacture products that are dependable and are not a safety hazard to the public. In addition, customers expect that the products and services used in advertising represent the same products and services that are sold to the customers. Furthermore, customers expect that the firm has developed its own products and services and has not illegally copied or counterfeited the products from another company.

Sales and Quotes

Customers expect that salespeople will be honest and ethical in dealing with them. Customers also expect that the features and prices quoted by salespersons are valid. Furthermore, customers expect that the company will not mislead the customer by presenting information that misrepresents its product. An example of potentially misleading information is the use of stealth marketing. *Stealth marketing* is having a company give financial incentives to "agents" who, through word of mouth, explain why the product should be bought. It is considered stealth marketing because the customers may not realize that they are receiving purchasing advice from a paid endorser of the product. In addition, customers do not tolerate unethical practices, such as baiting the customer with one product then switching to another product. In the United States, firms that do business in other countries must abide by the Foreign Corrupt Practices Act (FCPA) of 1977. Under this act, it is illegal for any company to make illegal payments in the form of bribes to secure business contracts in other countries.

Distribution

Customers expect that the items they order will be exactly the same items that will be delivered. Customers also expect to be informed of any adjustments that have been made to the order once the distribution of the order takes place.

Customer Service

The firm is expected to honor any guarantees or other promises given to the customer at time of purchase. As a result, customers trust the firm to fulfill the obligation that was agreed upon when the customer purchased the goods or used the services.

Government as a Stakeholder

The government's role as a stakeholder is primarily based on compliance issues. The government establishes and implements laws that require firms to comply with the rules and regulations of the laws. If a firm does not comply with the law, the government has the authority to punish the firm through fines and possible prison terms for employees within the firm.

NGOs as Stakeholders

Nongovernmental organizations (NGOs) can play a significant role in the decision-making process of firms. Focusing on a specific cause, such as human rights, the natural environment, or individual freedoms, NGOs use their resources to bring these issues to the attention of various stakeholders, including employees, customers, governments, and society. NGOs will usually target large corporations, if possible, for information dissemination and activism, to capture attention by the media and other interested stakeholders. The common goal of most NGO campaigns is to use customer and public pressure to force the corporation to adjust its strategic focus. There are three factors for firms to consider when addressing the issues related to NGOs: transaction costs, brand impact, and competitive position. Transaction costs refer to the costs to the firm to adjust its strategy in order to address the issues identified by the NGOs. This could include manufacturing costs, plant costs, and equipment costs. Brand impact refers to how much of a threat a public protest would be to brand reputation and sales of the firm's products and the threat of the consumers shifting to a competitor's brand. Competitive position refers to the threat that a firm's competitive advantage may weaken if its competitors do not have a strategic focus that concerns the NGOs.[32] Some of the most famous NGOs are Amnesty International, Care International, Greenpeace, Civil Society and Governance, Human Rights Watch, Oxfam International, and World Vision International.[33]

Local Community and Society as Stakeholders

The interest of local communities and society as a whole primarily focuses on issues in which "quality of life" can be negatively affected. For example, firms that release high levels of pollution into the air or into the water are of concern to the local communities. In addition, health and safety issues that could affect the well-being of the people living in the community also would raise concerns. A firm's action may have the most significant effect on the day-to-day operations of the firm's local facility in the local community.

Every firm should consider its stakeholders in any decision process. A formalized tool to aid in this evaluation is the Stakeholder Analysis Tool.[34] This five-step process incorporates the expected impact the action taken by the firm will have on various stakeholders. Step 1 is to identify the specifics of the firm's project or activity and identify key goals and milestones. Step 2 involves identifying all vested stakeholders who would be affected by the project and could affect the firm's success of completing the project. Step 3 involves identifying both interests and expectations of the stakeholders. The project is evaluated as having either a positive or negative impact on the needs of each stakeholder. Step 4 involves rating the level of importance of each stakeholder relative to the success of the project. And finally, step 5 involves identifying the actions needed to satisfy the interests and expectations of the stakeholders.[35]

From a stakeholder's perspective, a number of interests and expectations need to be addressed by the firm[36] include accessibility to communicate with the firm's ability to get information in a timely manner, forthrightness and honesty of the firm, being treated in a welcoming manner and with warmth by the firm, being accommodating and reasonable to the needs of the stakeholders, and receiving accurate and transparent information.[37]

The Role of Corporate Social Responsibility

Although components of corporate social responsibility can been seen in the 1930s with the interchange between Berle and Dodd (mentioned earlier in this chapter), many scholars consider the book *Social Responsibilities of the Businessman* by Howard Bowen to be the first comprehensive attempt to develop and interpret the concept of corporate social responsibility.[38] Corporate social responsibility is the obligation companies have to develop and implement courses of action that aid in social issues that affect society. As a result, the term *corporate social responsibility* is used by corporations to signify several topics for corporations, including legal responsibility, fiduciary duty, legitimacy, and charitable contributions.[39]

Carroll presented a three-dimensional model of corporate performance based on answering three questions:[40]

1. What components should be included in the definition of *corporate social responsibility*?
2. What are the overall external social issues that the firm must acknowledge?
3. How will the firm address the social issues that affect its operations?

The Competitive Advantage of Corporate Social Responsibility

In the past, the perception of corporate social responsibility (CSR) was based on the belief that CSR would be a cost that would be higher than the perceived benefits. By financially supporting "charity"-based initiatives, firms are not performing their fiduciary duty to their shareholders. CSR yields a positive cost-benefit evaluation, and it can greatly enhance the firm's competitive advantage.[41] The four arguments in support of firms focusing on CSR as part of their strategic focus are the following: moral obligation, sustainability, license to operate, and reputation. *Moral obligation* refers to the firm being a good corporate citizen whose actions are the "right thing to do." *Sustainability* refers to the ability of the firm to provide environmental and community stewardship. *License to operate* refers to the "permission" given by the government, the community, and other stakeholders to operate their business. Corporate reputation can enhance the relationship between the firm and the stakeholders and can enhance the firm's competitive advantage.[42] *Reputation* is the establishment of a corporate image in which stakeholders develop perceptions related to their commitment to CSR issues.

Components of CSR

Carroll argued that to understand the role CSR plays in the decision-making process of the manager, there must be a clear, comprehensive definition based on a number of components. Carroll argued that total corporate social responsibilities are based on economic, legal, ethical, and discretionary responsibilities. He argued that the four components are not necessarily mutually exclusive but, rather, represent a continuum in which CSR can be examined.

Economic Responsibilities Economic responsibilities are based on the underlying foundation of why a firm has been created, normally to develop economic value. Economic responsibilities are based on the belief that the firm has a responsibility to use the resources available to produce goods and services for society. The economic responsibilities lay the foundation for the firm to be able to support its other three responsibilities. As a result, some specific components of a firm's economic responsibilities could include maximizing earnings per share, generating a high and consistent level of profitability, establishing and maintaining a strong competitive position, and operating the firm at a high efficiency level.[43]

Legal Responsibilities Legal responsibilities are the laws and regulations that all firms are expected to abide by as they perform their daily functions. Firms are expected to be able to fulfill their economic responsibilities while following the legal requirements that have been established by society. Some specific components of a firm's legal responsibilities could include having the firm perform in a way that is consistent with government and legal expectations; displaying complete compliance with all local, state, federal, and international regulations; and being a good, law-abiding corporate citizen. It is important that a definition of a successful firm be one in which all of its legal obligations are fulfilled so that all the goods and services produced by the firm meet at least the minimum legal standards.[44]

Ethical Responsibilities Ethical responsibilities are difficult to define and can change over time because they are based on the expectations of society. As society changes over time, its expectations of what is considered ethical by firms also changes. However, one constant is that society expects that a firm should have ethical responsibilities that are beyond just meeting the legal requirements established by society. Some components of the ethical responsibilities of the firm include (1) making sure the firm performs in a manner that meets or exceeds the expectations of both social and ethical norms, (2) having an ability to adapt to new or evolving ethical and moral norms within society, (3) ensuring that ethical norms are not ignored or compromised so that the firm can achieve its objective, (4) behaving in a manner commensurate with being a good corporate citizen based on its ethical and moral conduct, and (5) realizing that corporate integrity and ethical behavior go beyond the minimum legal and governmental standards.[45]

Discretionary Responsibilities Discretionary responsibilities are those responsibilities in which society does not have a clear message to present to businesses what their courses of action should be. These responsibilities are left in the hands of the managers to exercise the proper judgment. Some examples of discretionary responsibilities include having firms give to charity organizations, providing programs to help people who are drug dependent, or providing day care centers to help families cope in a work environment. These actions are considered discretionary, so if a firm does not want to participate in these programs, the firm's lack of commitment would not be considered unethical. Philanthropic components of a firm's CSR could include ensuring that the firm performs in a manner that is consistent with charitable and philanthropic expectations from society, helping support causes such the fine arts and the performing arts to enrich the cultural basis of society, ensuring that managers and other employees also become involved by volunteering at various charitable organizations, providing financial and nonfinancial assistance to educational institutions, and volunteering to support community projects that enhance the overall quality of life for the community.[46]

Carroll concludes that CSR can be defined as how well a company meets its economic, legal, ethical, and discretionary responsibilities. Carroll also presents a CSR pyramid in which the profitability of the firm is the foundation that becomes

FIGURE 3.2 ● The Pyramid of Corporate Social Responsibility

Source: Archie Carroll, "The Pyramid of Corporate Social Responsibility: Toward the Moral Management of Organizational Stakeholders," *Business Horizons* (July–August 1991): 42.

intertwined with the firm's legal responsibilities. Those two components allow the firm to develop its ethical responsibilities, which could lead to discretionary responsibilities in the form of philanthropic responsibilities. The pyramid is shown in Figure 3.2.

A Global Approach to CSR

In his pyramid of Global Corporate Social Responsibility, Carroll extends his CSR model of economic, legal, ethical, and philanthropic responsibilities from a global perspective.[47]

Global Economic Responsibility

At the base of the pyramid, global economic responsibility is represented by the firm doing what is required by global capitalism. It is expected that any global firm, like any domestic firm, must be profitable in order to guarantee its long-term sustainability. However, within a global setting, there could be a wide variance of what is an acceptable financial performance of a firm's foreign-based divisions, based on the economic conditions of the country.

Global Legal Responsibility

At this level of the pyramid, firms address the issues related to doing what is required of them by global stakeholders. As is the case with the firm's global economic responsibility, the firm's global legal responsibility must address the issues related to differences in the legal environment in different countries. Different laws and different perspectives related to acceptable actions by individuals in other countries make it imperative for any global company to understand the differences and levels of complexity in countries that have a different legal system. In addition, governments of countries may always enforce the laws to protect the rights of the firms and the employees.

Global Ethical Responsibility

At this level of the pyramid, firms address the issues related to doing what is expected by their global stakeholders. As was stated in the global legal responsibility component of the framework, the global ethical responsibility of the firm is critical because governments and legal systems may not be consistent in enforcing the laws, and those laws may not be consistent with the legal system of the United States. The firm's ethical responsibilities include ensuring that the ethical norms, standards, and expectations are consistent globally. Because the home and host countries' ethical standards may not match, the firm needs to reconcile this misalignment in order to present and enforce a global ethical vision.

Global Philanthropic Responsibility

At the top of the pyramid, firms address the issues related to the needs of the global stakeholders. At this level, firms are expected to be involved in socially responsible activities that have not been mandated by various stakeholders. The desired perception is to be proactive and anticipate what the future needs of the stakeholders will be before they present them to the firm. As is the case in all the levels of the pyramid, the expected socially responsiveness can vary significantly from one country to another. For example, in Finland the expected level of philanthropic responsibility is low because the Finnish people are taxed at a relatively high rate, and, therefore, it is expected that the social needs of the individuals in Finland will be addressed through government programs.[48]

Models of CSR[49]

There are three different models firms can use to develop a perspective related to CSR: business case model, social values–led model, and syncretic stewardship model.

Business Case Model

Firms that use the business case model view CSR as a means to generate financial results. The philosophy is based on the belief that because firms are driven to perform financially in the short term, the only justifiable investments in CSR occur when there are also short-term financial benefits for the investment. The value of CSR is the enhancement of the firm's competitive advantage, which results in higher financial performance. In this model, the firm's competitive advantage could be enhanced by using CSR to broaden the appeal of their products and/or using CSR to address external threats such as the threat of government intervention and the threat of activists publicly demonstrating against the firm's lack of concern related to CSR issues.

Social Values-Led Model

Firms that adopt the social values-led model use CSR as a tool to address a specific CSR issue. The firm's commitment to CSR is based on using the specific CSR issue as a critical factor in the decision-making process of the managers of the firm. These would be types of firms in which a social policy entrepreneur is a dominant driving force. In these firms, a triple bottom line approach to performance is used to evaluate the overall performance of the firm. The firm evaluates its financial, social, and environmental performance in order to determine whether it has reached its goals.

Syncretic Stewardship Model

Firms that use a syncretic stewardship model view CSR from a comprehensive stakeholder perspective. Syncretic stewardship model firms encourage feedback and information flow between the firm and all their stakeholders. For these firms, CSR is more than a program or an activity; it is an underlying management philosophy that is intertwined in their day-to-day operations. This philosophy included using CSR in the development and revision of the firm's mission, values, goals, and processes.

Employee Engagement and CSR

One of the underlying benefits of a strong CSR commitment is the impact CSR can have on employee engagement. The first benefit is that the values and vision developed within the firm's CSR program can be transferred to a strong positive culture that supports the employees in their performance. The second benefit is that a strong CSR commitment can be the foundation of a strong positive firm reputation, which enhances the pride and commitment of the employees. The third benefit is that CSR enables employees to capture and incorporate their individual social values to help society by participating in CSR programs that impact external stakeholders.

It is through these benefits that firms are developing different models to serve the needs of the employees and the firms. There are three traditional models of engagement: transactional approach, relational approach, and developmental approach

Transactional Approach

The transactional approach is based on the development of firm programs to serve the needs and interests of the employees who have an interest in participating in CSR programs. It is considered transactional because it serves the short-term interests of the employees, which can evolve and change over time. This approach increases employee engagement by satisfying higher level self-esteem needs of the employees. This approach focuses on addressing the employee issues related to the question, "What do I want from my job?"

Relational Approach

The relational approach is based on the CSR programs mutually agreed upon between the firms and the employees. The approach focuses on entrenching the commitment by the employees by developing mutual trust and developing a shared interest in the programs between the firms and the employees. This approach will help the firm develop a socially responsive culture and can support a more positive identity and image. This approach increases employee engagement by enhancing the employee's identity within the workplace, focusing on the "whole self" instead of just the working interests of the employee. This approach focuses on addressing the employee issues related to the question, "Who am I as a person?"

Developmental Approach

The developmental approach is based on a philosophy of being more proactive related to CSR issues and having a more comprehensive commitment of both the firms and the employees in development and participation in CSR programs. This approach will help the firm implement its commitment to facilitate the positive impacts of CSR on the firm and its employees and to make improvements to society. This approach increases employee engagement by supporting the employees' need for self-actualization. This approach focuses on addressing the employee issues related to the question, "Who do I want to be as a person?"[50]

How Firms Implement CSR

Martinuzzi and Krumay present a model that links the implementation of the firm's CSR vision to four major components: project-oriented CSR, quality-oriented CSR, strategic CSR, and transformational CSR.

Project-Oriented CSR

Many firms focus on the development and execution of a social and/or environmental project with the objective of "doing good." The project may address the need of specific internal and/or external stakeholders. Sponsoring a 5k run or allowing employees to volunteer at a homeless shelter one day a month are examples of a firm using a "project management" approach to implement their CSR philosophy.

Quality-Oriented CSR

Firms can show their CSR commitment by the implementation of quality control systems, which creates not only cost efficiencies but can reduce the environmental impact of their operations. This philosophy supports the belief of avoiding doing "bad things." The use of Total Quality Management (TQM) and International Organization of Standardization (ISO) certifications integrates CSR in the production and manufacturing process. In addition, a quality-oriented focus can also address working conditions and human rights issues as it relates to the firm's global operations.

Strategic CSR

The strategic CSR perspective is based on the belief that the needs of society can be converted into opportunities for the firm, which may require the firm to rethink its business model. The goal is for the firm to integrate its CSR philosophy into the decision-making process of the firm. This integration could be in the form of new and innovative approaches to the traditional issues the firm must address. It is through this innovative approach that firms can differentiate their products and services from their competitors'. An example would be the introduction of a micro-credit initiative by Muhammad Yunus, who used the CSR vision of helping the poor to create a financially self-sustaining financial operation.

Transformational CSR

Firms that focus on a transformational CSR view CSR as not only an avenue to develop a competitive advantage but an opportunity to transform the firm. Within this framework, firms use organizational learning in order to reevaluate the perspective pertaining to their interactions with their stakeholders. This transformational process will aid the firm as it seeks to develop a long-term sustainable competitive advantage based on alignment of its future needs with the needs of its stakeholders.[51]

Alternative Firm Configurations to Address Stakeholder Issues

Firms can take very different approaches to how they address the needs of the stakeholders. There are four alternative firm configurations based on the values and beliefs of the firm.[52] The two dimensions proposed in the framework are normative and instrumental. The normative dimension is based on Kantianism and fairness. When a firm has a normative perspective of stakeholders, the benefit is that all stakeholders, regardless of importance, will be treated in the same manner and be treated equally. Firms with a normative perspective interact with all stakeholders based on respect, dignity, and just consideration. Furthermore, a normative model guides the firm with the "expected" actions, now and in the future, for each decision so that there is consistency and fairness in addressing the needs of the stakeholders. A highly *normative stakeholder firm* is one in which universal principles and standards are applied fairly and equitably across all stakeholders regardless of importance. In addition, a highly normative stakeholder firm welcomes the input of the stakeholders and encourages a close relationship to ensure that their needs have been met completely. A firm with a low normative belief related to stakeholders views the interaction of stakeholders as an obligation that the firm must fulfill. In addition, such firms believe the focal point of the firm is to address the needs of the shareholders and owners before addressing the needs of the other stakeholders.

Instrumental stakeholders are those whose support is required so the firm can achieve its objectives. As a result, high participation of the stakeholders is not based on fairness or equality but is considered a means to get to results for the firm. Therefore, the influence of the stakeholders is needed so the firm can perform its corporate responsibilities. High *instrumental stakeholder firms* are those in which stakeholder interaction is encouraged for those having existing or future benefits from the

FIGURE 3.3 ● Stakeholder Orientation Framework		
	Low Normative	**High Normative**
High Instrumental	Pragmatic	Engaged
Low Instrumental	Skeptical	Idealistic

Source: Thomas Donaldson and Lee E. Preston, "The Stakeholder Theory of the Corporation: Concepts, Evidence, and Implications," *Academy of Management Review* (1995): 69.

achievement of the firm's goals. Stakeholder relationships are based on issues of power and urgency. Stakeholders can be used to influence the outcomes of the firm. Firms with low instrumental stakeholder relationships believe that stakeholder interest and interaction should not be based on the level of influence they have on the firm's operations. The four types of firms are described and are shown in Figure 3.3.

Skeptical Firm

The skeptical firm is based on the view that shareholders, not stakeholders, are the dominant focal point. Skeptical firms do not consider the interests and needs of other stakeholders, per se, in their strategic decisions. Skeptical firms only consider other stakeholders when they are forced to by law. Examples of skeptical firms are those companies in industries that have had controversial reputations such as tobacco, gaming, and oil.

Pragmatic Firm

The pragmatic firm recognizes the current and future benefits of interactions with various stakeholders. Through these relationships, firms can use influence and power to help achieve their financial goals. These "active" stakeholders are needed so the firm can navigate its way through a complex dynamic competitive environment. The focal point of pragmatic firms is maximizing the financial performance of the firm to serve the needs of stakeholders. However, pragmatic firms understand that to achieve this goal, they must also interact with influential stakeholders. An example of a pragmatic firm is Coca-Cola. Coca-Cola focuses on financial objectives and addresses stakeholder issues on an ad hoc basis. When there are compliance issues related to water depletion and the generation of pollution in developing countries, Coca-Cola will address the specific needs of specific stakeholders that company officials believe are necessary to eliminate all obstacles related to financial growth and prosperity.

Engaged Firm

An engaged firm focuses on the long-term sustainability of its operations. Engaged firms believe that complete stakeholder commitment will greatly enhance their ability to survive in the long term regardless of the environmental conditions. An engaged firm believes that each stakeholder—like spokes in a wheel—can contribute to the financial success of the firm and rejects the belief that serving the stakeholders and shareholders are mutually exclusive goals.

Idealistic Firm

Idealistic firms believe that serving stakeholders and society are the primary goals of the organization. As a result, the purpose of the firm is to serve the needs and interests of the stakeholders. The financial success of the firm allows it to focus on social needs of the stakeholders. Idealistic firms are usually founded by social entrepreneurs. Some examples of idealistic firms are Ben & Jerry's and The Body Shop.[53]

The Role of Corporate Reputation

In his seminal work on corporate reputation, *Reputation: Realizing Value From the Corporate Image,* Charles Fombrun argues that corporate reputation is not just "nice" to have but can add overall value to the corporation. Fombrun argues that everyday decisions are based on reputation, whether it is the company you buy products from or the plumber you need to fix the sink. Most people ask friends, neighbors, colleagues, and experts from whom or where they should buy their products and services. This referral system is based on the reputation that has been established by the firm. Fombrun explains that if we have the choice between someone who is well regarded in the industry and another company for which we have no information, we would more likely use the company in which we are assured of its service based on its reputation. A reputation is valuable to a company because it communicates the expectations of the company to the buyer. As a result, a reputation has strong strategic value because it identifies why the individual should buy products and use the services of one company rather than those of another, enhancing the level of differentiation of the products and services. Fombrun argues that intangible assets such as the firm's corporate reputation can potentially provide a firm with a long-term competitive advantage by continuing to support the positive reputation.[54]

From a corporate perspective, a firm's corporate reputation is valuable because it helps stakeholders determine which companies will best serve their needs, and that may include dependable products, a positive work environment, and succeeding in their corporate financial and nonfinancial objectives. As a result, a firm's reputation is an intangible asset that can enhance the value of the firm and strengthen the firm's competitive advantage.[55] For example, Sir Richard Branson, founder of the Virgin Group, develops strategies for his various businesses around Virgin's reputation instead of specific products and services. Grahame Dowling defines *corporate reputation* as "an overall evaluation that reflects the extent to which people see the firm as substantially 'good' or 'bad.'"[56] Firms with good reputations can foster trust and confidence with their stakeholders, but firms with bad reputations do not create these positive attributes. In addition, a firm with a positive reputation can develop a halo effect with its stakeholders. A *halo effect* refers to when, because of the positive reputation of the firm, stakeholders will judge negative actions less harshly than if the firm had a neutral or negative corporate reputation. This benefit of a doubt allows the firm to explain its actions before the stakeholders have concluded their judgment on the action. The halo effect is valuable to a firm because it allows the firm time and gives officers the ability to explain their actions before the consumers jump to a negative conclusion. A negative halo effect occurs when the firm has a negative corporate reputation and the negative actions reinforce customers' negative belief about the firm. In this scenario, the halo effect is not desirable because the firm does not have a chance to justify its actions to the public.

The firm's corporate identity refers to what characteristics would be used by the stakeholders to describe the firm. As a result, a firm's corporate reputation reflects the integration of the firm's strategy, corporate culture, and values as perceived by its stakeholders. With a positive corporate reputation, a firm is given the opportunity to build trust and enhance its credibility with its stakeholders.[57] A positive corporate reputation can dissolve quickly, as we can see in Case 7, which tells the story of Enron, the former natural gas pipeline company whose top-ranking officers inflated the value of the company to keep stock prices artificially high. Ranked as one of the most admired firms in 2001, by December 2001, Enron was bankrupt and the name became synonymous with fraud and deceit. To use its reputation effectively to its competitive advantage, a firm must identify what is needed for a strong positive reputation and how it can be used to separate the firm from its rivals. In addition, the firm must consider how the reputation is validated over time and determine what specific activities are needed within the firm to support the competitive advantage.

Corporate image answers the question, "What are the public's perceptions and beliefs about the firm?" The firm's corporate identity is based on the description or attitudes that are used to describe the firm. Corporate identity asks the question, Who are you as an entity? Dowling argues that there are four major components of corporate image and identity: character, ability, products and services, and behavior. Factors that can affect the character of the firm include the organizational culture and the level of competitiveness within the industry. The ability of the firm is based on the drive and commitment of the CEO and employees and the availability of resources that are needed to develop and execute the firm's overall strategy. The factors to be considered for the firm's products and services include the quality, value, and range of products available to sell to the customers. The behavior of the firm is based on the managers' leadership capabilities and the level of drive the managers have toward maximizing profitability levels. The corporate image and identity of the firm focus on the stakeholder values that yield the firm's corporate reputation. The firm's corporate image is based on the perceived level of esteem, respect, trust, and confidence the public has related to interactions with the firm. The validation of the firm's corporate reputation is based on (1) the feedback given to the firm by its customers, (2) the evaluation given by investors, (3) financial analysts and the media, (4) the linkage between its corporate reputation and its business model, (5) the establishment of a code of ethics, and (6) the willingness to be evaluated based on the triple bottom line (social, environmental, financial) perspective.

A critical aspect related to corporate reputation is to ensure the corporate reputation is communicated to various stakeholders. For external communications, the firm must ensure that the information presented increases the level of awareness and support for the reputation and actions of the company. In addition, effective communication is critical when the company has to defend or explain its actions that may be controversial or may not meet the expectations of various stakeholders. For internal communications, the firms must be consistent with their message as they explain their actions to their employees. Dowling argues that a firm can effectively enhance its reputation by presenting an effective reputation story. The story comprises the beliefs of the firm, including the firm's mission, morality, and modes of acceptable behavior. These beliefs are presented in a story format using actual facts and figures that support and reinforce the beliefs of the stakeholders, generating a strong, firmly entrenched positive corporate reputation.[58] A firmly entrenched positive corporate reputation can enhance the competitive advantage of the firm because it is difficult to develop and maintain. The difficulty of developing and maintaining a positive corporate reputation increases its value to the firm because the reputation allows the firm to differentiate itself from its competitors in the marketplace. The management of the employees within the firm is critical for the long-term sustainability of the corporate reputation because ultimately the employees' actions will either enhance or weaken the firm's corporate reputation.

Having a strong positive reputation can produce three major benefits for the strategic focus of the firm. The first benefit is that stakeholders prefer to do business with firms that have a positive corporate reputation. When a customer is unfamiliar with attributes of one product versus another, the reputation of the firm is considered. If the firm has a positive reputation, this could determine which item the customer will purchase. In addition, if the customer has already bought a different product from the firm, the customer will be more likely to purchase the additional product from the same firm because of its corporate reputation. The second major benefit is that a strong positive corporate reputation can greatly aid a company during a crisis. The third major benefit is that a strong positive corporate reputation can increase the financial performance of the firm because of the firm's superior competitive advantage.[59]

The Role of Corporate Philanthropy

Back where I come from, there are men who do nothing all day but good deeds. They are called phila-, er, er, philanth-er, yes, er, good-deed doers.[60]

—The Wizard, from *The Wizard of Oz*

An underlying question is whether the "good deeds" done by the firm can help improve the corporate reputation of the firm. One study found that firms that had a number of Environmental Protection Agency (EPA) and Occupational Safety and Health Administration (OSHA) violations were able to improve their corporate reputation through their corporate giving programs. Although the firms' positive reputations diminished because of the violations, they were able to preserve a positive reputation by financially supporting numerous causes that affected their stakeholders.[61] Michael Porter and Mark Kramer[62] warn that corporations must understand the true meaning of strategic philanthropy. Placing the firm's support toward a single philanthropic cause via public relations or advertising is not strategic philanthropy. In fact, this "cause-related" marketing can backfire and lead to mistrust and suspicion about the true motives of the firm. Porter and Kramer argue that true strategic philanthropy is based on the belief that the actions of the firm can benefit society and the firm through the firm's development of unique assets and expertise. As a result, firms can use their philanthropic focus to enhance their competitive advantage. For example, Cisco Systems has developed the Cisco Networking Academy to train computer network administrators. This is beneficial to society because the individuals going through the academy have developed computer network skills, and it is beneficial to Cisco Systems because the company now has a larger selection pool from which to hire new employees.[63]

The Competitive Value of Corporate Philanthropy

A 2011 study of 311 senior executives of companies with sales over $500 million demonstrated the competitive value of corporate philanthropy. The results of the study showed that 64% of the respondents stated that having a corporate philanthropy and community involvement program improves employee relations. In addition, 59% of the respondents stated it increased employee skills/leadership, and 53% stated it helped differentiate the company from its competitors. In addition, 72% of the respondents believed that philanthropy and volunteerism were critical in helping the company recruit younger qualified employees.[64]

Strategic Configurations of Corporate Philanthropy

Heike Bruch and Frank Walter argue that the type of commitment firms have will be based on their level of corporate philanthropy related to market and competence orientation.[65] Market orientation is based on using corporate philanthropy to address the external demands on the firm through its stakeholders. Corporate philanthropy is used to improve the image and reputation of the firm, and the result will be an enhanced competitive advantage. This competitive advantage will occur because the positive image and reputation will improve marketing and selling capabilities, attract a larger labor pool, and improve relations with the government and local communities. Market-oriented companies address the needs of the stakeholders through their philanthropic activities.

Competence-oriented firms use corporate philanthropy to address internal goals. These firms align their corporate philanthropic programs to their own abilities and core competences. An example is the consulting firm McKinsey & Company, which offers free consulting services to nonprofit organizations. This benefits the nonprofit organizations, and it motivates and enhances the skill sets of the McKinsey employees.

Four Types of Corporate Philanthropy

Based on the level of market and competence orientation, four strategic configurations are related to corporate philanthropy: peripheral philanthropy, constricted philanthropy, dispersed philanthropy, and strategic philanthropy. These are shown in Figure 3.4.

Peripheral Philanthropy A company with a high market orientation and low competence orientation is described as having a peripheral philanthropy configuration. *Peripheral philanthropy organizations* use stakeholder demands and expectations as the core of the corporate philanthropy. This type of philanthropy is not usually related to the

FIGURE 3.4 ● Four Types of Corporate Philanthropy

	Low Competence Orientation	High Competence Orientation
High Market Orientation	Peripheral Philanthropy	Strategic Philanthropy
Low Market Orientation	Dispersed Philanthropy	Constricted Philanthropy

Source: Heike Bruch and Frank Walter, "The Keys to Rethinking Corporate Philanthropy," *MIT Sloan Management Review* 47, no. 1 (Fall 2005): 51.

company's core activities but is used to enhance its image and reputation. Companies do not link their philanthropic activities to their core competences, so there is a danger that skeptics could consider their actions superficial and lacking sincerity and creditability.

Constricted Philanthropy A firm whose philanthropy focus is high for competence orientation and low for market orientation is described as a *constricted philanthropy configuration*. Constricted philanthropy uses the potential synergies that can be created between their operational activities and their philanthropic activities. These firms use their core competences for social activities. In addition to potentially improving their core competences, this strategic focus can also allow an evolution of the firm's corporate culture and employees' beliefs by connecting their business and philanthropic activities. The risk with this strategic configuration is that it could potentially alienate stakeholders because they may believe their needs and expectations are not being addressed. Hilti Corporation, a construction tool manufacturer, is an example of a company using constricted philanthropy when it donated several containers of construction materials to help in the cleanup efforts at Ground Zero after the terrorist attacks on September 1, 2001.

Dispersed Philanthropy A *dispersed philanthropy configuration* is based on a firm having both a low-market and low-competence orientation. A dispersed philanthropy configuration lacks focus on the strategic direction of the philanthropy efforts. Philanthropy programs are usually uncoordinated, and there are no specific criteria to determine what social programs and causes should be supported. As a result, the firm usually supports numerous small programs that do not specifically address the firm's core competences or the needs and expectations of its stakeholders. In addition, a lack of strategic focus raises concerns about the creditability and motive of the philanthropic contributions by the firm.

Strategic Philanthropy A firm that has a high level of commitment from both a market and competence orientation is described as having a *strategic philanthropy configuration*. This is considered the most effective approach because it addresses both internal and external issues. These firms align their philanthropic actions with their core competences and address the needs and expectations of their stakeholders. The firms are able to capture sustainable results internally by enhancing their competitive advantage and externally by satisfying the needs of their external stakeholders. The net result is that the firms are able to create new market opportunities, develop and maintain highly motivated workforces, stimulate customer demand for their products, and attract highly skilled potential employees.[66]

Questions for Thought

1. Why is fair trade an ethical issue? What are the competitive advantages of fair trade? What are the potential problems with fair trade?

2. Identify all of the different stakeholder groups and comment on their roles in corporations.

3. Why is a firm's corporate reputation important? Explain how a company can quickly lose its positive corporate reputation.

Real-Life Ethical Dilemma Exercise

The Partial Sinking of the *Costa Concordia*:
Is "Women and Children First" an Antiquated Notion?

In January 2012, the *Costa Concordia* started its voyage off the coast of Tuscany in Italy. While there are different accounts of the facts and events leading up to the crash and Captain Francesco Schettino's actions concerning the evacuation and rescue efforts, some accounts have alleged that the actions of the captain may have caused to the boat carrying more than 4,200 passengers and crew members to crash into a reef and end up resting on its side. Once the ship had crashed, it appeared that the crew members were left to evacuate the ship. When the Italian Coast Guard tried to contact the captain onboard, there was no answer. When the Coast Guard finally contacted the captain by phone, his response was, "I'm not on board because the bows of the ship are coming up. We've abandoned her." The Coast Guard responded by stating, "What do you mean? You've abandoned ship?" The captain responded with, "No. No way have I abandoned ship. I'm here." The final call made by the Coast Guard went as follows: First the Coast Guard stated, "Schettino? Listen, Schettino. There are people trapped on board," to which the captain responded by stating "Commander, please . . .," with the response of the Coast Guard being, "No, please, . . . You go on board, this is an order . . . There are already dead bodies." The captain responded by asking, "How many?," to which the Coast Guard responded by stating, "I do not know. One I know. One I heard. You are the one who has to tell me how many there are . . ." The captain responded by stating, "But you realize that it's dark and here we see nothing . . .," which drew the response "Do you want to go home, Schettino? It's dark and you want to go home? Go up on the bow of the ship on a rope ladder and tell me what you can do, how many people are there, and what they need. Now!" "All right," Mr. Schettino said. "I'm going."[67] A total of 32 people lost their lives as a result the crash, and another 64 were injured. After the crash, there was mass confusion on board as crew members tried to regain order to get the maximum number of passengers on each lifeboat. Maritime safety procedures were established in 1914 with the adoption of the Safety of Life at Sea (SOLAS) convention, which was a direct response to the *Titanic* disaster. Although not explicitly stated in SOLAS, the captain must be the last person to leave a sinking ship. There is a provision that the captain must exercise "prudent seamanship," referring to ensuring the safety of the crew and passengers. After the crash, the owner of the cruise ship, Carnival Corporation of Miami, saw its stock price decrease by nearly 20%.[68]

In July 2014, two-and-a-half years after it was partially submerged, the Costa Concordia was removed from its resting place. It is considered to be the largest passenger shipwreck in history, based on tonnage. The *Costa Concordia* is twice the size of the *Titanic*.[69] On January 26, 2015, Italian prosecutors asked the court to convict Francesco Schettino and sentence him to 26 years in jail for his role in the disaster. Schettino was accused of committing manslaughter, causing the shipwreck, and abandoning the ship while many passengers and crew members were still on board.[70] On February 11, 2015, Francesco Schettino was convicted of multiple counts of manslaughter and abandoning ship for his actions related to the sinking of the *Costa Concordia*. He was sentenced to 16 years 1 month in prison. Captain Schettino and Costa Crociere, a division of Carnival Corporation, were ordered to pay $34,000 in damages to every passenger on the ship as well as several millions of euros to both local and the Italian government for the environmental damage caused by the sinking. The salvage operation has cost Costa Crociere over $1.2 billion, and the final cost including dismantling the *Costa Concordia* is estimated to be up to $2 billion.[71,72]

(Continued)

(Continued)

Questions for the Real-Life Ethical Dilemma Exercise

1. Which stakeholder(s) did the captain of the *Costa Concordia* consider, based on the alleged actions described?

2. How were the different stakeholders affected by this disaster?

3. What role should Carnival Corporation have in resolving the needs of the various stakeholders impacted by this disaster?

Student Study Site

Visit the Student Study Site at **study.sagepub.com/stanwick3e** to access the following resources:

- Video Links
- SAGE Journal Articles
- Web Resources
- Web Quizzes

INTERNAL FOCUS ON ETHICAL ISSUES

PART II

4

Ethics and Financial Reporting

When money speaks, the truth keeps silent.

—Russian proverb

A firm's income statement may be likened
to a bikini—what it reveals is interesting,
but what it conceals is vital.

—Burton G. Malkiel, *A Random Walk Down Wall Street*

Chapter Objectives

After reading and studying Chapter 4, students should be able to

1. Explain the concept of "creative" accounting.

2. Describe the specifics of Ponzi schemes.

3. Describe potential conflicts of interest that could occur in financial reporting.

4. Explain what the responsibilities of management, auditors, and audit committees are with respect to financial reporting.

5. Explain how heuristics affects accounting.

6. Describe the accounting "tricks of the trade."

7. Explain the concept of off–balance sheet arrangements.

HSBC: Products for Tax Evasion and Money Laundering, but No Free Toaster

In 2007, Hervé Falciani stole a large number of data files from his employer, HSBC. Headquartered in Geneva, Switzerland, HSBC was well known to accommodate the needs of nontraditional clients. A former computer security specialist, Falciani acquired files that listed more than 100,000 names of people who had accounts at HSBC who used the accounts to evade taxes, to launder money, and to commit other illegal activities.[1] The clients on the list included firms that were linked with selling arms to child soldiers in Africa, Third World dictators, and blood diamond traffickers.[2]

Under the umbrella of secrecy, HSBC had protected these transactions from scrutiny from various governments. HSBC would offer their clients products such as the creation of shell corporations, trusts, and other methods to shield the money. It was estimated that more than 4,000 of the clients had a connection to the United States, with more than $13 billion in HSBC accounts. The files showed one New Jersey client insisted that she got assurances from the HSBC that the IRS would not have access to her account. It is a felony in the United States for any bank, regardless of location, to assist a United States citizen in evading United States federal taxes.

After he stole the files, he fled to France and turned over eight DVDs of encrypted data to French authorities. It took approximately one year to decipher the files, and the French government was able to reclaim between $250 and $300 million from penalties related to tax evasion.

In 2012, HSBC had to pay a $1.9 billion settlement in the United States for their involvement in laundering money for a drug cartel.

The man at the center of the scandal, Hervé Falciani, is still on the run from Swiss authorizes. The Swiss government considers him a thief, yet he believes he is a whistleblower. His ex-girlfriend stated that the real motive of Falciani was to sell the files and make millions of dollars. She claimed he attempted to sell the files in Lebanon before he gave them to the French authorities.[3]

HSBC's response was "[We] have undergone a radical transformation . . . [and] . . . We have taken significant steps over the past several years to implement reforms and exit clients who did not meet strict new HSBC standards, including those where we had concerns in relation to tax compliance."[4]

Ethics and Financial Reporting

Accounting is a critical tool used by managers in the decision-making process. The financial statements of a firm show how well the organization has performed in the past and help indicate what course of action the company can take in the future. Of course, the value of the firm's financial statements is only as good as the numbers presented in the statements. If the numbers are false or erroneous, whether intentionally or not, the value of the financial statements has been voided.

The Role of Creative Accounting

In a parody of the Nobel Prize awards, the organization Improbable Research presented the 2002 IgNobel Prize in Economics to the CEOs, corporate directors, and auditors of a number of firms that were involved in corporate accounting scandals. The managers and auditors of such firms as Adelphia Communications, Arthur Andersen, Enron, Global Crossing, Rite-Aid, Sunbeam, Tyco, and WorldCom won the award for their development of the mathematical concept of "imaginary numbers" used in the business world.[5] Although the award was supposed to be a humorous way to address accounting fraud, the actual consequences of this unethical behavior are much more real. A common phrase related to misrepresented financial statements is "cooking the books." Although the exact origin of the term is still debated, a common citation used is from the 1806 book *Adventures of Peregrine Pickle. Plays and Poems* by Tobias Smollett. In the book, Smollett refers to inaccurate financial information as "some falsified printed accounts, artfully cooked up, on purpose to mislead and deceive."[6] These imaginary numbers were the driving focus behind the concept of creative accounting. *Creative accounting* can be defined as the deviation from the traditional methods used to interpret an accounting rule or standard.

Critic David Ehrenstein claims that the term *creative accounting* came from the Mel Brooks film *The Producers*, which eventually became a Broadway musical.[7] In *The Producers*, the director and the producer of the play sold "shares" of ownership to multiple partners. They sold more than 100% of the rights of the show, with the assumption that they would never have to pay out the profits to the investors. The director and the producer purposely produced the "worst" show on Broadway so it would be closed after one performance, and therefore, they would no longer have a financial obligation to any of these "little old lady" owners. With songs such as "Springtime for Hitler," they thought for sure the play was going to be a flop. Much to their surprise, the show was a hit, and the financial troubles started. Although the original film was released in 1968, the story line appears eerily familiar to a number of the accounting scandals that were taking place 30 years later. Firms such as WorldCom and Enron artificially propped up their financial statements to convince their stockholders that they still had viable companies, which actually fell like houses of cards. Creative accounting quite often walks the fine line between legal and illegal activities. Within the standards set by professional accounting organizations such as the Accounting Standards Board in the United Kingdom and the Financial Accounting Standards Board in the United States, there is always some room for interpretation of the accounting standards. However, sometimes it is hard to see where "aggressive" accounting stops and "fraudulent" accounting starts. The rationality and objectivity of accounting is based on the level of rationality and objectivity of the people who interpret the rules.[8]

The History of Ponzi Schemes

I do not anticipate that another Charles Ponzi will ever appear in the financial world.[9]

—William H. McMasters, Charles Ponzi's publicist, 1920

The offer seemed too good to be true, and of course it was. Italian immigrant Charles Ponzi promised investors that they would receive an increase in their investments by 50% in just 45 days. Born in 1882, he arrived in Boston and eventually moved to Montreal, where he served 3 years in prison for check forgery. He moved back to Boston and developed his "scheme" to make money. At that time, different countries issued prepaid coupons that were used to send mail back to the country. The scheme involved Ponzi buying the coupons at a fixed rate and then selling them for a profit because of the fluctuating exchange rates between countries. However, Ponzi never made any significant investment in the prepaid coupons. He used the purchasing and selling of the coupons to "explain" to the customers how he was making his money. In reality, he was taking money from one investor and then paying off another investor.[10] Ponzi started his scheme in December 1919 and by April 1920 had received more than $140,000 in payments from his customers. The amount grew quickly to more than $440,000 by May 1920, to more than $2.5 million by June 1920, and to almost $6.5 million in July 1920. Ponzi took in $10 million, but he owed his customers $15 million. He was arrested in August 1920 and was convicted of a number of federal and state offenses. He was deported back to Italy in 1934. Ponzi died a poor man living in a charity ward in Brazil in 1949. He was 66.[11]

The fundamental flaw of a Ponzi scheme is that it never ends until the person committing the fraud is caught or disappears. More and more new investors are always needed to pay off the previous investors in a never-ending cycle. The cascading flow of money is similar to the shape of a pyramid, and hence, Ponzi schemes have also been called pyramid schemes. For example, if the person committing the fraud promises to double the investors' money within one month, the Ponzi player obtains $100 each from two investors in the first month. In the second month, the Ponzi player needs four investors of $100 each to pay off the first set of investors, who are expecting $200 each. In the third month, the Ponzi player needs eight investors to pay off the previous four investors, and so on. By the 10th month, the Ponzi player needs 1,024 investors, and by the 18th month, the Ponzi player needs more than 250,000 investors.[12]

The Role of Insider Trading as an Ethical Issue

In general terms, insider trading occurs when an employee breaches his or her fiduciary duty by using material nonpublic information to make decisions based on the employee's self-interest instead of the best interests of the firm. The underlying basis of the illegality of insider trading can be traced to Rule 10b-5 of the Securities and Exchange Act. This rule states that it is "'unlawful for any person, directly or indirectly,' to 'employ any device, scheme, or artifice to defraud.' Or to 'engage in any act, practice, or course of business which operates or would operate as a fraud or deceit upon any person . . . in connection with the purchase or sale of any security.'"[13] The SEC focuses on a two-part evaluation of whether insider trading has taken place. The first part is the determination of whether a relationship has been created in which information has been obtained that is available only from within the corporation. The second component is whether there is an inherent unfairness to taking advantage of the information that is not available to the public. There are three major categories of insider trading: traditional theory, temporary insiders, and tippers and tippees.

Traditional Theory

The traditional theory focuses on the acquisition of insider information based on the position of the individual. Traditional insiders include officers, directors, employees, and stockholders. It is their connection to the information flow within the firm that allows them to obtain insider information.

Temporary Insiders

Temporary insiders are those individuals who do not have a permanent positon with the firm but are still privy to insider information. Temporary insiders can include accountants, lawyers, and consultants. Again, based on their temporary position within the firm, they are able to obtain insider information.

Tippers and Tippees

A tipper is someone who has obtained insider information and has disclosed that information to another person who is the tippee. Both the tipper and the tippee are subject to prosecution if insider information was used by the tippee.[14]

Ethical Philosophies and Accounting Issues

At least 10 different ethical perspectives can be directly applied to the decision-making process of accountants.[15] These philosophical perspectives can lead to a better understanding of why so many firms can produce inaccurate financial statements for an extended period. Table 4.1 highlights how different ethical perspectives affect accounting-based decisions.

The Role of Financial Reporting

There are three primary objectives of financial reporting. Accurate financial reporting is needed to provide investors and other interested parties with the ability to (1) make investment, credit, and financial decisions that relate to the firm; (2) help the reader determine the level of cash flows for the firm; and (3) identify the economic resources and obligations to the firm, as identified by the Financial Accounting Standards Board.[16]

Brian Shapiro argues that to understand how accountants can interpret financial reporting in a different manner, you must understand the general philosophical presuppositions that affect financial reports.[17] A summary of the five general philosophical presuppositions is shown in Table 4.2.

As a result, two accountants with the exact same information may make two completely different decisions based on their own cognitive lenses. Therefore, the inherent subjective nature of developing and interpreting financial information opens the door for different interpretations that could lead to both unethical and illegal interpretations.

The Objectives of Financial Reporting

Not since the Securities Acts of 1933 and 1934 has the financial reporting environment changed as it has with the passage of the Sarbanes-Oxley Act of 2002. This act established new regulations for public companies following the ethical scandals that have arisen in the past few years. Although most would like to think that companies operate in an ethical manner, it is difficult for users of financial reports to believe this in the wake of these financial scandals.

TABLE 4.1 ● How Different Ethical Perspectives Affect Accounting-Based Decisions

Ethical Perspective	Summary of Ideas	Driving Value	Accounting Application
Self-Interest	Everyone in society would be better off if each individual could pursue his self-interests	Personal self-interest	Self-serving bias drove the scandals at Enron and WorldCom
Utilitarian Beliefs	A law is "right" if the benefits to society are greater than the harm	Greatest good for the greatest number	Could be a huge gap between short-term and long-term benefits
Personal Virtues	Individuals must adopt a set of values that support virtuous behavior	Other people should be given acceptable treatment	Virtues of courage and integrity protect accounting's credibility
Religious Injunctions	Individuals need compassion and kindness as well as truthfulness and temperance	Need to have reciprocity and compassion	Apply the Golden Rule to accounting decisions
Government Requirements	Fundamental rules are developed from agreed-on central authorities	Laws represent the minimum standards of morality for society	Government regulations and accounting standards set the rules for accounting
Universal Rules	Inspired rules dictate action for the greater good	Rules will be used to eliminate the self-interests of those making the decisions	Rules and principles must be integrated to control self-interests
Individual Rights	A summary of rights that can be agreed on to guarantee freedoms	Protect each individual's guaranteed rights and freedoms	Focus on stakeholders' rights when making accounting decisions
Economic Efficiency	Maximize output and level of profitability	Economic efficiency	Accountants must understand the cost of inaccurate financial statements
Distributive Justice	Never implement a course of action that harms the less powerful	Those individuals who are disadvantaged should be guaranteed a social contract	Inaccurate financial statements can harm society
Contributing Liberty	Do not try to obtain self-fulfillment that results in the disruption of the rights of others	Follow the rights of liberty within the limitations established by laws	Accountants need to protect the interests of the public by their actions so the rights of the public are not violated

Source: David Satava, Cam Caldwell, and Linda Richards, "Ethics and the Auditing Culture: Rethinking the Foundation of Accounting and Auditing," *Journal of Business Ethics* 64 (2006): 275.

TABLE 4.2 ● **Five Philosophical Presuppositions of External Financial Reporting**

External Realism—The financial statements are independent of the actual items they represent.

Representational Faithfulness—The financial representation of the firm shown in the financial statements is true only if it corresponds with the underlying economic reality it is attempting to represent.

Conceptual Relativism of Financial Reporting Schemes—All conceptual frameworks are based on a human perspective and, therefore, are socially constructed. Alternative frameworks can be used to represent the same reality. The difficulty is that the objectives of financial reporting are based on values that are normative that cannot be accurately verified or validated from an empirical evaluation.

Subjective Judgment—The accountants' ability to make valid judgments about the economic reality of the financial statements are influenced by cultural, economic, political, and psychological factors. As a result, absolute epistemological objectivity is not feasible in the accounting profession because every individual makes a judgment of economic reality based on individual perspective.

Commitment to Rationalism—Information and knowledge is epistemologically objective only to the point where society can agree on both the criteria to evaluate the justification or evidence for the assertions made by the decision maker.

Source: Brian Shapiro, "Objectivity, Relativism, and Truth in External Financial Reporting: What's Really at Stake in the Disputes?," *Accounting, Organizations, and Society* 22 (1997): 167.

Where Were the Auditors?

With the tidal wave of accounting scandals that occurred during the past 15 years, a question that many stakeholders asked was, "Where were the auditors?" How could firms continue to make up "imaginary numbers" year after year without the internal and, especially, the external auditors identifying the problems and raising huge red flags?

An audit is required to be conducted each fiscal year for companies that are publicly traded. An audit consists of an inspection of the accounting records and other information deemed necessary to express an opinion on the fairness and adequacy of the financial statements. In many cases, specific procedures and tests are not required, but judgment must be used by the auditors. The culmination of the audit process is the issuance of the auditors' report, which states the auditors' opinion about the fairness of the financial statements, expressed in compliance with generally accepted accounting principles and performed using generally accepted auditing standards.

Auditors are considered the gatekeepers for the stakeholders.[18] The auditors are responsible for ensuring the integrity of the financial reporting by the firm. One potential problem is the disproportionate power the companies have over their auditing firms. Because the company pays to be audited by the accounting firm, there is also the possibility that the external auditors will accept "overaggressive" accounting if the result is that the accounting firm retains the client. As a result, if the auditors do compromise their level of independence from the firm and are not willing to challenge key information that may upset the client, then both the objectivity of the auditor and the accuracy of financial statements that are approved by the auditor have to be questioned.

Three potential conflicts of interest can take place during the auditing process: auditor–firm, shareholders–management, and self-interests–professional standards.[19]

Auditor–Firm Conflicts of Interest

The firm will always want the financial statements to show how well the executives at the top are managing the firm. As a result, the firm could potentially put pressure on the auditor to sign a "clean audit" regardless of any concerns the auditor has with the statements. As was stated previously, the auditor has a financial incentive to please the firm because the firm is a revenue-producing client for the auditing firm. However, the auditor has to abide by all the accounting standards and guidelines when he or she makes the overall evaluation of the integrity of the financial statements.

Shareholder–Management Conflicts of Interest

The firm wants its external stakeholders and especially its shareholders to be given the financial statements of the firm without any conditional issues having been raised by the auditors. Because the shareholders do not want any negative issues related to the firm's financial statements, the managers of the firm want to present "clean" financial statements to the shareholders. However, the auditor also has a duty to the shareholders to review objectively the financial transactions of the firm because the shareholders, via the board of directors, have selected and pay the external auditors.

Self-Interest–Professional Standards Conflicts of Interest

The auditor may face a situation where he or she can benefit by violating the professional standards established by accounting organizations. For example, if an auditor has a financial interest in the firm, there would be a self-interest incentive to disregard financial transactions that have a negative impact on the firm.

Responsibilities of Management

Management has the ultimate responsibility for the accuracy and transparency of the firm's financial statements:

1. Ensure the proper tone at the top with an expectation that only the highest-quality financial reporting is acceptable.
2. Review all elements of the company's internal control—control environment, risk assessment, control activities, information and communication, and monitoring—in light of changes in the company's business environment and with particular attention to significant financial statement areas.
3. Ensure that appropriate levels of management involvement and review exist over key accounting policy and financial reporting decisions.
4. Establish a framework for open, timely communication with the auditors and the audit committee on all significant matters.
5. Strive for the highest-quality, most transparent accounting and disclosure— not just what is acceptable—in both financial statements and management discussion and analysis (MD&A).
6. Make sure estimates and judgments are supported by reliable information and the most reasonable assumptions in the circumstances and that processes are in place to ensure consistent application from period to period.

7. Record identified audit differences.
8. Base business decisions on economic reality rather than on accounting goals.
9. Expand the depth and disclosure surrounding subjective measurements used in preparing the financial statements, including the likelihood and ramifications of subsequent changes.
10. When faced with a gray area, consult with others, consider the need for SEC clearance, and focus on the transparency of financial reporting.

The Use of Heuristics in Auditing

Flawed auditing of the financial statements of a firm might not always be the result of dishonesty. Don Moore and colleagues argue that due to the inherent potential conflict of interest between the auditor self-interests and the responsibilities of the auditor, the auditor is more likely to use certain heuristics that would bias the evaluation of the financial statements.[20] The heuristics are these: selective perception, plausible deniability, and escalation of commitment. *Selective perception* occurs when an individual is selective pertaining to the information given him or her when a decision needs to be made. Auditors are "hoping" for "clean audits" so that their clients will be happy. Therefore, implicitly or explicitly, auditors may be more likely to select information that supports the conclusion that the financial statements are accurate. *Plausible deniability* occurs when the individual is hesitant to reject a biased proposal from someone else. From an auditor's perspective, auditors are more likely to agree with what the managers have presented as a proposal than if the proposal were developed by the auditor. *Escalation of commitment* is based on the belief that additional commitment is needed for a course of action even if this is not the correct course of action. If the auditors had allowed "aggressive" accounting methods in the previous year's audits, it would be difficult to now conclude that these methods are no longer valid. As a result, the auditors become committed to the methods presented by the managers.[21]

Responsibilities of Auditors

The auditors are responsible for verifying the accuracy of the firm's financial statements in accordance with Generally Accepted Auditing Standards. Auditors who address each of the following responsibilities will heighten their objectivity regarding their clients' financials by reducing the likelihood that they will be influenced by selective perception, plausible deniability, and escalation of commitment:

1. Understand how a company is affected by changes in the current business environment.
2. Understand the stresses on the company's internal control regarding financial reporting and how these stresses may affect its effectiveness.
3. Identify key risk areas, particularly those involving significant estimates and judgments.
4. Approach the audit with objectivity and skepticism, notwithstanding prior experiences with or belief in management's integrity.

5. Pay special attention to complex transactions, especially those presenting difficult issues of form versus substance.
6. Consider whether additional specialized knowledge is needed on the audit team.
7. Make management aware of identified audit differences in a timely manner.
8. Question the unusual and challenge anything that doesn't make sense.
9. Foster open, ongoing communications with management and the audit committee, including discussions about the quality of financial reporting and any pressure to accept less than high-quality financial reporting.
10. When faced with a gray area, perform appropriate procedures to test and corroborate management's explanations and representations, and consult with others as needed.

Responsibilities of Audit Committees

The audit committee is responsible for oversight of the auditing procedures and the control procedures. Addressing each of the following responsibilities will help auditor committees heighten their objectivity regarding their clients' financials by reducing the likelihood that they will be influenced by selective perception, plausible deniability, and escalation of commitment:

1. Evaluate whether management exhibits the proper tone at the top and fosters a culture and environment that promotes high-quality financial reporting, including addressing internal control issues.
2. Question management and auditors about how they assess the risk of material misstatement, what the major risk areas are, and how they respond to identified risks.
3. Challenge management and the auditors to identify the difficult areas (e.g., significant estimates and judgments) and explain fully how they each made their judgments in those areas.
4. Probe how management and the auditors have reacted to changes in the company's business environment.
5. Understand why critical accounting principles were chosen and how they were applied and changed, and consider the quality of financial reporting and the transparency of disclosures about accounting principles.
6. Challenge management for explanations of any identified audit differences not recorded.
7. Understand the extent to which related parties exist, and consider the transparency of the related disclosures.
8. Read the financial statements and MD&A to see if anything is inconsistent with your own knowledge.
9. Consider whether the readers of the financial statements and MD&A will be able to understand the disclosures and risks of the company without the access to management that the committee enjoys.
10. Ask the auditors about pressure by management to accept less than high-quality financial reporting.
11. When faced with a gray area, increase the level of communication with management and the auditors.

AICPA Code of Professional Conduct

The American Institute of Certified Public Accountants (AICPA) established its current professional code of conduct in 1988 based on six principles: responsibilities, the public interest, integrity, objectivity and independence, due care, and scope and nature of services:[22]

1. Responsibilities: "In carrying out their responsibilities as professionals, members should exercise sensitive professional and moral judgments in all their activities."[23]
2. The Public Interest: "Members should accept the obligation to act in a way that will serve the public interest, honor the public trust, and demonstrate commitment to professionalism."[24]
3. Integrity: "To maintain and broaden public confidence, members should perform all professional responsibilities with the highest sense of integrity."[25]
4. Objectivity and Independence: "A member should maintain objectivity and be free of conflicts of interest in discharging professional responsibilities. A member in public practice should be independent in fact and appearance when providing auditing and other attestation services."[26]
5. Due Care: "A member should observe the profession's technical and ethical standards, strive continually to improve competence and the quality of services, and discharge professional responsibility to the best of the member's ability."[27]
6. Scope and Nature of Services: "A member in public practice should observe the Principles of the Code of Professional Conduct in determining the scope and nature of services to be provided."[28]

Components of the Sarbanes-Oxley Act

In direct response to the corporate scandals of Enron and WorldCom, the U.S. Congress passed the Sarbanes-Oxley Act (SOX) in 2002. When it passed, many corporations were vocally opposed to it and claimed that it was just an additional set of government regulations that would cost more time and money, which they could not afford in an increasingly competitive global marketplace. However, by 2004, the viewpoint had changed significantly for a majority of firms. In a 2003 survey of 153 boards of directors' members by *Corporate Board Member* magazine, 60% of those surveyed thought the Sarbanes-Oxley Act had a positive effect on the firms. In addition, 70% of the directors thought that SOX had a positive effect on the actions of boards of directors.[29]

The Sarbanes-Oxley Act is geared toward public companies. Established to help increase transparency, integrity, and accountability of public companies, it has been touted as the biggest reform in corporate America since the 1933 Securities and Exchange Act. A number of provisions in SOX have both immediate and long-term impacts on how firms are monitored in the United States. These include the following:

- The Sarbanes-Oxley Act established the Public Company Accounting Oversight Board, composed of five members who are considered to be "financially literate." Of the five members, two must be certified public accountants (CPAs). The oversight board creates and approves the guidelines used to audit companies.

- The Sarbanes-Oxley Act requires that the external (independent) auditors who review the financial statements of the firms be restricted to performing audit-based functions. Contrary to what was acceptable in the past, external auditors are no longer allowed to perform bookkeeping functions, nor are they allowed to do non-audit-based consulting on companies that they audit.
- The firm's audit committee must preapprove all the services provided by the external auditors.
- For each client, the lead audit partner and the partner responsible for the audit must change at least once every 5 years.
- The firm's CEO and CFO must certify all annual and quarterly reports sent to the SEC. This means that the CEO can no longer plead ignorance as a defense for inaccurate financial statements. This provision states that the CEO and CFO are guilty of fraud if they certify inaccurate financial results, regardless of whether they knew the results were false or not. In addition, the CEO and the CFO are required to forfeit any financial gain that has occurred through bonuses or profits based on inaccurate financial results.
- All of the board members and the top executives of the firm must report all stock transactions to the SEC within 2 business days.
- It is the fiduciary duty of the firm's lawyers to report to the board of directors any violations of securities fraud. The issuing of personal loans to any director or top executive by the firm is no longer allowed.
- Every publicly traded company must include in its annual report a description of the firm's internal controls. Although not explicitly stated, the requirement has been interpreted to mean operational and information technology controls as well as financial controls.
- The external auditor must review the internal control procedures of the firm.
- Each firm must develop and make available a corporate code of ethics applicable to the firm's top executives at a minimum.
- Firms are required to hold separate directors meetings where the CEO is not present. This allows for a more explicit separation of the influence the CEO has on the agenda and the direction of the board meetings.
- In direct response to Enron's manipulation of financial statements, the act requires the firm to report, in detail, all off–balance sheet transactions.

Through SOX developments, top management and board members will no longer be able to use the excuse that they didn't know what was happening when a company is caught conducting itself unethically. It will mean that top management and the board of directors must show more involvement and be responsible for this involvement. For example, top management must know what is going on with their subordinates by asking questions and being involved in a more direct manner with the day-to-day operations of the company. It may mean that the bottom line, once thought to be the driving point for top management decisions, is no longer the most important aspect.

In addition to having to deal with internal control requirements of the SOX, companies will also place greater reliance on the information provided by their service providers. This means that anywhere in the supply chain, the information provided to the SEC under SOX must be accurate. The companies will be responsible for any inaccuracies in the data. It is extremely important to choose service providers wisely in this age of the new internal control reporting environment under SOX.

Public Company Accounting Oversight Board

One of the major additions to corporate governance that came with the Sarbanes-Oxley Act was the establishment of the Public Company Accounting Oversight Board (PCAOB). As a result, the accounting profession now has direct government regulations to monitor the business practices.

Section 404—Internal Controls

Most important, companies are required to test internal controls on a regular basis, and these tests must be done by an accounting firm different from the company's outside auditor. This requirement attempts to eliminate any possible conflicts of interest that may exist. Section 404 of the Sarbanes-Oxley Act requires companies to document and test their financial accounting controls. Through this act, they would be increasing the assurance that the reports are accurate. This increase in the documentation of financial controls will surely benefit investors.

The less expensive aspects of SOX that companies adopt include the following:[30]

- Having CEOs and CFOs certify financial statements
- Developing an internal code of ethics
- Appointing independent board members and an audit committee
- Creating processes for reporting concerns and protecting informants from retaliation for complaints made in good faith
- Insisting on true independence for outside professionals
- More clearly defining the client of the attorney or accountant for the organization as a whole
- Splitting audit and non-audit services between separate accounting firms

A Comprehensive Model of Top Management Fraud[31]

One of the underlying issues related to corporate fraud is to understand why top managers commit fraud by misrepresenting the financial statements of the firm. What set of circumstances supports, in the minds of the top-level managers, that it is "acceptable" to falsify the financial position of the firm? To understand how a manager would arrive at this conclusion, it is necessary to understand the antecedent factors and the moderating factors that can influence this decision. Top management fraud can be separated into individual and corporate-level types of fraud decisions. *Occupational management fraud* refers to fraud that benefits the individual, and *corporate-level fraud* focuses on making materially misleading information pertaining to the financial status of the firm. In this comprehensive framework, the antecedents of the fraud are based on societal issues, industry-based issues, and organizational issues (see Figure 4.1).

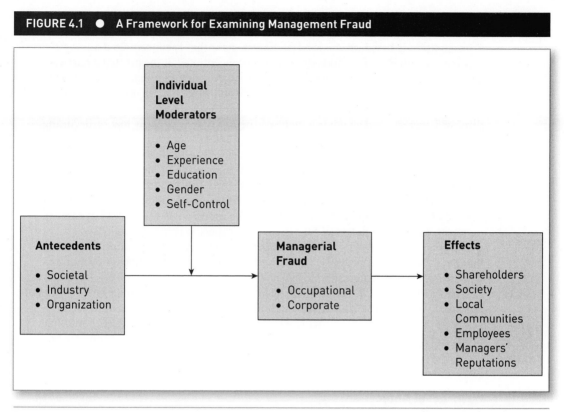

FIGURE 4.1   ● A Framework for Examining Management Fraud

Source: Shaker A. Zahra, Richard L. Priem, and Abdul A. Rasheed, "The Antecedents and Consequences of Top Management Fraud," *Journal of Management* 31 (2005): 803–828.

Societal-Level Issues

The societal-level issues are first based on the role of "cultural deviance" or how the activity is measured based on the accepted norms of society. The second societal-level issue relates to what the aspirations of the decision makers are based on their need for material goods and success.

Industry-Based Issues

The industry-based issues relate to the industry in which the company competes. Factors that can play a role include the cultures, norms, and histories of the industry. These are the foundation characteristics that help shape the type of behavior that is considered acceptable by firms in the industry.

A second set of industry factors includes industry investment horizons, payback periods, and financial returns. The benchmark for financial expectation of the firm based on the standards set in the industry can influence the type of benchmarking measure the firm must address with its financial performance. If the industry expects short-term quick financial returns, there will be increased pressure on each firm in the industry to perform at the same standards as the rest of the industry.

The third factor is the level of industry concentration. As the industry increases in concentration, the chances increase that collusion will take place in the industry. Concentration is based on the level of market share that is concentrated among the firms in the industry. If the industry is hugely concentrated, it means that a relatively few firms have a large percentage or concentration of the market share of the industry.

The fourth factor is the level of environmental hostility. *Environmental hostility* refers to the competitive environment of the industry. For example, the level of hostility will increase in the environment of the industry if there is low or declining demand, very stringent government regulations, intense competition, low profit margins, and a low rate of long-term survival of firms. The more hostile the environment of the industry, the more likely that top-level managers will engage in fraudulent activities to "improve" the financial status of the firm through misrepresentation.

The fifth factor is the level of environmental dynamism, which refers to the rate of speed and unpredictability of change within the industry. As the level of dynamism increases, so does the potential for top-level managers to commit fraud. The level of dynamism can have a direct impact on the rate of return on investments and may hamper short-term profitability, which would entice top-level managers to manipulate the financial statements to "cover" up the short-term investment loses.

The sixth factor is the level of environmental heterogeneity, which refers to the level of diversity of the markets and customers that must be addressed by the firm. The level of diversity leads to increased levels of complexity in dealing with multiple markets and customers. Therefore, the higher level of complexity allows top management more opportunities to hide fraudulent behavior without believing they would be caught.

Firm-Level Antecedents

The third antecedent of top-level fraud relates to the characteristics of the organization. The board composition is the first characteristic of the organization. The more that the board of directors comprises insider board members, the higher the probability that top-level managers will be enticed to commit fraud because there is an assumption that the check and balances of the board are not as stringent as in the case of a board dominated by board members who are outside the company.

The second firm-based factor is the level of senior leadership. The senior leaders set the ethical example for the rest of the company. By "talking the talk" and "walking the walk," senior leaders lead by example and have a positive ethical vision to help guide the organization. Alternatively, if senior managers are not ethical leaders, they give their implicit and sometimes explicit support for unethical activities by the rest of the employees of the firm.

The third firm-based factor is the organizational culture of the firm. Related to the ethical vision of the top-level managers, the organizational culture must also support the positive ethical climate of the firm. The organizational culture aids in the employees determining what is acceptable and not acceptable in business operations within the firm. The culture can support a positive ethical climate if that is developed by the top-level managers, or the culture can support unethical behavior of the employees if that type of behavior is condoned and even observed by the top-level decision makers.

Individual-Level Moderators

The individual characteristics of the top-level managers also play a role in the ability of the top-level executives to commit fraud. Age is the first characteristic to consider as a moderator. As the top-level managers get older, they are less likely to take risks and are not as concerned about short-term gratification. Therefore, some believe that as the top-level managers mature, they are less likely to consider committing fraud within the corporation.

The second individual moderator is the level of experience by the top-level manager. As the level of experience of the top-level managers increases, the likelihood of the top-level managers committing fraud decreases. The experience in the workplace creates potential resistance to change or do things differently plus the more experience the top-level managers have, the more likely they have seen struggling condition in the past in which they will not panic in trying to resolve the problem through misrepresenting financial statements.

The third individual moderator is the level of education. The higher the level of formal education of the top-level executive, the higher the level of moral development by the executives. As a result, it is expected that the level of education is inversely related with the probability the top-level managers will commit fraud.

The fourth individual moderator is the gender of the top-level executive. Previous research has shown that male decision makers are more likely to commit unethical behavior than female decision makers are.

The fifth individual moderator is the level of self-control by the top-level executives. The higher the level of self-control, the lower the likelihood that the executive will commit unethical actions. High self-control enables the executive to discount immediate gratification as a necessary "reward" of the decision-making process.

Depending on the antecedents and moderators, top-level managers may be more likely to commit occupational- and corporate-level fraud. The consequences of the fraudulent actions affect the critical stakeholders of the firm including shareholders, society, local communities, and employees, as well as the reputations of the managers.

Accounting Shenanigans or Tricks of the Trade

It is an ongoing challenge to ensure that firms produce accurate and reliable financial statements. There will always be potential problems when the self-interests of the managers supersede the interests of the firm's stakeholders.

In an effort to understand financial statements, it is necessary to understand where companies may practice aggressive accounting methods. It is difficult to supply a comprehensive list of all of the ways management can manipulate financial statements or manage earnings. However, following are some examples of where many tricks can occur on a company's books.

Revenue Recognition

Revenue recognition is one of the four major principles of Generally Accepted Accounting Principles (GAAP). If a customer pays in cash, the revenue or sale is recognized when the cash is given to the firm. However, revenue recognition becomes harder to determine and, therefore, open to abuse when cash is not paid. This is called an accrual payment, which means the customer will pay the money at a future point in time. The determination of the future point in time can lead to unethical manipulation of this concept. The revenue recognition principle states that if accrued, revenue should not be recognized until it is realized or realizable and earned. SEC Staff Accounting Bulletin No. 101 identifies four criteria that must be met for revenue to be realized or realizable and earned: (1) persuasive evidence of an arrangement, (2) delivery occurred or services rendered, (3) price fixed or readily determinable, and (4) collectability reasonably ensured. This provides an easy way for managers to either record the revenue before it is earned or to record revenue that may not even exist. It may be necessary to compare cash flows to net income using the statement of cash flows. The numbers may need to be investigated in more depth if the amount of net income consistently exceeds the cash flows for the period. Remember, accrual accounting basically says that income should be recorded when earned and expenses should be recorded when incurred. Payment of cash or collection of cash does not factor in recording these items under accrual-basis accounting. Cash is probably one of the most difficult items to manipulate on financial statements because the figure should be reconciled with the bank balance, but it is an asset that can be easily stolen without thinking about this reconciliation. Earnings are estimated for the period, using many different types of methods, but cash flow can be verified or reconciled with the bank records.

Onetime Charges

Sometimes companies take expenses in one year that they know will not necessarily be recurring yearly. Firms can manipulate their expenses by classifying events as onetime charges when that is not actually the case. Investors will discount the impact of onetime charges when they evaluate a firm's financial performance because it is a nonrecurring event.[32] This means that firms include the amounts as separate and sometimes as extraordinary charges on the income statement. The amount is recognized in a single reporting period. Although they may be legitimate, these special charges are being used to cover up some other expenditures or to help the company's earnings look better than before because the onetime charge is used to explain a onetime event that management says it does not expect again.

Restructuring charges may fall into this category as well. Sometimes companies begin to take restructuring charges when times are going bad. It may be that these companies are using these charges to artificially improve their net income.

Raiding the Reserves/Cookie Jar Accounting

Cookie jar accounting comes from the concept that management can manipulate the financial results of a company by adding or taking away reserves (cookies) from a "jar" depending on the circumstances. Under the cookie jar system, management will build up financial reserves in profitable years. When the firm has unprofitable years, the reserves are "released" into the financial statements so it appears that the firm was much more profitable than it really was based on its operations. The releasing of the reserves allows the firm to smooth the peaks and valleys of its financial performance.[33]

This concept gives rise to income smoothing because the companies will be understating their earnings in good years and overstating their earnings in bad years. One example that describes a company using reserves to inflate earnings was noted in the Enron trial in 2006. A former accountant in Enron's trading division, Wesley Colwell, admitted in court that he reduced reserves by $14 million in 2000. Because this amount was added to income for the period, Enron reported earnings per share at 2 cents greater than what analysts were predicting for the period. Colwell said in court that while Jeffrey Skilling didn't directly tell him to use the reserves for this purpose, Colwell knew that Skilling favored beating the analysts' expectations. Colwell, agreeing to cooperate with prosecutors for immunity, paid the SEC $500,000 to settle charges against him.[34]

Lease Accounting

In 2004, many companies in the retail, restaurant, and wireless tower industries (among others) had to deal with errors made in their lease accounting. It seems that many companies had failed to follow the lease accounting rules that had guided the treatment of leases for years. Many companies were expensing leasehold improvements over the expected life of the property, rather than for the duration of the lease. This created an error in the amount of depreciation the companies were recording, effectively causing less depreciation to be expensed for the leasehold improvement.

Off-Balance Sheet Items

Off-balance sheet financing creates separate legal entities from the parent company. These entities are not wholly owned subsidiaries and can be hidden from the investors by keeping the entities off the financial statements. However, they are legal entities. The SEC has identified that the definition of *off-balance sheet arrangements* includes (1) certain guarantee contracts, (2) retained or contingent interests in assets transferred to an unconsolidated entity, (3) derivative instruments that are classified as equity, and (4) material variable interests in unconsolidated entities that conduct certain activities. The entities are used to provide financing for new or existing ventures, and liquidity or credit support for the parent company. In addition, the arrangements could provide leasing, hedging, or research and development services.[35] These arrangements are intended to shift assets or liabilities off the balance sheet but should be disclosed in the company's footnotes to the financial statements. In effect, the arrangements shift risk from the parent company to the new company. A good example of a company that violated the use of off-balance sheet arrangements is Enron. Enron attempted to make the company look better through these special arrangements rather than providing a legitimate business operation.

Earnings Management

In recent years, companies have been employing earnings management techniques. Larry Bitner and Robert Dolan refer to *earnings management* or *income smoothing* as the purposeful intervention in the process of reporting income numbers with the objective of dampening the fluctuations of those numbers around their trend.[36] The reasons for income smoothing vary, but most financial professionals will agree that it exists mainly to overstate corporate earnings.

Managers may be under pressure from their boards to increase earnings, or they may need higher earnings to earn a bigger bonus at year-end. One thing is clear: The public scandals that have resulted from earnings management have caused the public to lose confidence in the financial reporting process.

Questions for Thought

1. Swiss banks have had a long tradition of keeping information about their clients confidential. Is this still the correct strategic focus to take in the 21st century? Should the United States government have the right to demand information pertaining to United States citizens who have bank accounts in countries other than the United States?

2. Why is earnings management considered a trick of the trade? Explain.

3. In all of the accounting scandals of the past decade, where were the auditors? Explain.

4. Why do Ponzi schemes continue to work time after time?

Real-Life Ethical Dilemma Exercise

Tales From Lehman's Crypt[37]

At the peak of the financial crisis in September 2008, one of the oldest and most established brokerage firms in the world, Lehman Brothers, declared bankruptcy. The collapse of this well-established financial institution demonstrated how serious the crisis was and how the financial service industry had lost touch with the delicate balance of risk and return. For many at Lehman Brothers, it was not just the loss of a job but also the loss of one's identity. Although Lehman brokers admitted they were partially to blame for the collapse, they also pointed out that there were many guilty parties, including government regulators, senior executives at Lehman Brothers, competitors, and their colleagues who also had faith in computer algorithms. These algorithms had become an important part of the trading "decision making" at all the Wall Street brokerage firms. Brokerage firms, such as Lehman Brothers, would bundle, trade, or sell "packages" for mortgages, auto loans, and other types of financial products. These packages were then sold to investors based on the "calculated" risk from the algorithms. Lehman Brothers did it because all its competitors did it, and the competitors did it because the investors wanted to invest in those packages that could yield "premium" returns. Lehman Brothers managers knew as early 2007 that there were problems with its risk models. The brokers saw that the models displayed warnings that started showing higher levels of delinquencies and defaults. Colleagues started to ask each other about the loan quality of these packages. However, the warning signs were discounted or ignored because Lehman Brothers was ranked as the top loan originator on Wall Street. In addition, senior executives wanted rapid growth from the company, and they had targeted these investors as a viable way to grow quickly. As a result, there was no incentive to disclose these warnings, and employees were considered troublemakers if they raised questions related to these loans, stopping their climb up the corporate ladder.

Questions for the Real-Life Ethical Dilemma Exercise

1. What role should government regulators have in the brokerage industry? Why do you think the regulators were not more active before the 2008 financial crisis?

2. What would you do if you knew these "packages" were going to fail in the future?

3. Would you be a whistle-blower if you warned investors about the danger of these packages? If you did blow the whistle, who would you contact?

Student Study Site

Visit the Student Study Site at **study.sagepub.com/stanwick3e** to access the following resources:

- Video Links
- SAGE Journal Articles
- Web Resources
- Web Quizzes

5

Ethical Leadership and Corporate Governance

At this moment, America's highest economic need is higher ethical standards—standards enforced by strict laws and upheld by responsible business leaders.

—George W. Bush

Corporate governance is concerned with holding the balance between economic and social goals and between individual and communal goals. The corporate governance framework is there to encourage the efficient use of resources and equally to require accountability for the stewardship of those resources. The aim is to align as nearly as possible the interests of individuals, corporations, and society.

—Sir Adrian Cadbury

Chapter Objectives

After reading and studying Chapter 5, students should be able to

1. Define *ethical leadership.*

2. Distinguish between transformational leadership and transactional leadership.

3. Describe the transformation of a moral person to an ethical leader, citing examples of leadership styles.

4. Define *corporate governance* and the role of ethics in corporate governance matters.

5. Describe the purpose of the board of directors and the core ethical values that should guide them.

6. Identify some of the decisions made by the board of directors.

"Nut Rage" on the Tarmac at JFK: It's a Good Thing She Didn't Ask to See the Wine List

On December 5, 2014, on a Korean Air plane that was on the tarmac at the John F. Kennedy airport in New York, the daughter of Korean Air's Chairman, Cho Hyun-ah, was given an unopened bag of macadamia nuts. Ms. Cho was sitting in the first class cabin and told the flight attendant that she should have first asked Ms. Cho whether she wanted the nuts and that the flight attendant was required to serve the nuts on a plate and not in a bag. Ms. Cho "scolded" the flight attendant and asked to speak to the purser, who was in charge of the in-flight administration. After discussing the proper procedure for food service, Ms. Cho was not satisfied with the responses given by the purser. She demanded that the plane return to the gate and the purser be forced to leave the aircraft. As a result, the plane was delayed by approximately 20 minutes while it returned to the gate to drop off the purser.

Korean Air's initial response to the incident was to apologize but point out that because Ms. Cho was a vice-president in charge of Korean Air's in-flight services, she had a responsibility to inspect cabin service and monitor aircraft safety. Korean Air also stated that the purser had not followed the proper procedures and regulations on the flight, and therefore, Ms. Cho questioned his capability to perform the proper procedures on the flight. South Korean aviation regulations state that the only situation in which a plane should return to the gate is if the pilot determines that there is an emergency.[1] The controversy has led to a significant increase in macadamia nut sales. In the week after the incident was reported, one of the largest South Korean online marketplaces saw an increase of sales by 139%.[2]

On December 12, 2014, the chairman of Korean Air announced that his daughter would be stripped of all her titles and duties at Korean Air due to her "foolish" behavior. Cho Yang-ho admitted, "I failed to raise her properly."[3]

On December 16, the South Korean transport ministry announced that Korean Air will face sanctions in its attempt to cover up the "nut rage" of Ms. Cho. Korean Air was accused of pressuring some of its employees to lie during a government investigation into the incident. The purser who was forced to leave the aircraft, Park Chang-jin, said that Korean Air officials pressured him to alter his story for government officials.[4] In addition, it was revealed that Ms. Cho's actions on the flight included yelling at the flight attendants who kneeled before her, pushing one flight attendant, and throwing an object at the cabin wall.

On January 7, 2015, Ms. Cho was indicted on charges of assault, changing the flight plans of an aircraft, coercion, and obstruction of justice.[5] In addition, it was announced that a Korean Air executive only identified by his surname, Yeo, was charged with obstruction of justice, destruction of evidence, and coercion for his role in trying to cover up the incident by pressuring the employees to alter their stories to government investigators.[6]

On February 2, 2015, South Korean prosecutors announced that they were requesting that Ms. Cho be sentenced to three years in prison for her "nut rage."[7] On February 12, 2015, Ms. Cho was sentenced to one year in prison. The court ruled that Ms. Cho had illegally forced the plane to change its route by demanding that the plane return to its gate, which subjected the passengers on the plane to potential danger. The judge commented that "it is doubtful that the way the nuts were served was so wrong. . . . She forced the plane to turn around as if it were her own private plane."[8]

Ethical Leadership

Ethical leadership can be defined as "the demonstration of normatively appropriate conduct through personal actions and interpersonal relationship, and the promotion of such conduct to followers through two-way communication, reinforcement, and decision making."[9] Ethical leadership is the driving force for a firm to have a positive ethical climate with its employees. With a positive ethical climate, employees have a supportive work environment, which leads to higher commitment and job satisfaction of the employees.[10] Ethical leadership reinforces the beliefs of social learning theory that suggests that when the firm has role models for the employees, the employees will try to copy the behavior of the role models. Furthermore, recent evidence has shown that top manager ethical leadership has a direct impact on the subordinate supervisors, who, in turn, have a direct impact on the lower-level employees. As a result, the ethical leadership at the top of the organization does "trickle down" to the lower organizational levels of the firm.[11] In addition, ethical leadership has been shown to have a positive impact on the perception of top management effectiveness and has been shown to have a positive influence on the level of subordinates' optimism about their own contributions to the firm as well as the firm itself.[12]

Ethical leadership is demonstrated in the leader's various actions. The ethical commitment of the leader affects the leader's character, which influences the leader's motives and influences strategies.[13]

Characteristics of an Ethical Leader

Ethical leaders are those who are effective, are credible, and are legitimate role models to their subordinates. In addition, ethical leaders present a powerful and salient ethical message to their subordinates through effective communication and reinforcement.[14] Leaders can influence the attitudes, beliefs, and behaviors of the employees through either the transactional or the transformational leadership style.[15]

Transformational Leadership

A transformational leader is focused on developing a long-term vision for the company. This vision is the starting point for the development of the firm's values, beliefs, policies, and strategic focus. Transformational leadership is based on inspirational motivation, idealized influence, individualized consideration, and intellectual stimulation,[16] in which the leader uses a charismatic personality to communicate his or her vision to the employees. The ethical component of the transformational leader is part of the idealized influence component.[17] The transformational leadership style has a very strong positive ethical effect on the firm. Through this form of leadership, the employees are free to develop ideas and make decisions in an autonomous setting. In addition, this leadership style is altruistic in its focus and is, therefore, more effective to guide employees and more enduring by the employees. By its very characteristics, ethical leadership is transformational. The leader is the soul of the firm, and the leader's beliefs, attitudes, and values influence the ethical environment of the firm. The leader can develop ethical power from the transformational aspect. The principles of ethical power are purpose, perspective, patience, and persistence. The *purpose* of ethical power refers to the leader establishing a long-term vision and determining the means by which such attributes as personal sacrifice and building trust with the employees to implement the leader's ethical vision is formed. The leader must use *perspective* to make decisions based on prudence and justice. The leaders must also use *patience* and understand that there will always be roadblocks to implementing the leader's ethical vision. Leaders must also use *persistence* to remain strong to their commitments regardless of the setbacks that occur during the implementation of the leader's ethical vision.[18]

Transformational leadership is a much more effective style in which to implement an ethical vision to the employees. This is because transformational leaders are able to influence the employees by presenting their long-term ethical vision, inspire and foster commitment of the employees instead of trying to control them, set the ethical standards by being a role model, foster intellectual stimulation of the employees, develop clarity and provide meaning to the goals and expectations of the employees, demonstrate confidence in the ability of the employees to achieve higher and higher personal goals, give employees the ability to achieve their self-actualization goals, use intrinsic motivation to empower the employees, and develop and maintain collective identity among the employees.[19] These actions are those of an "authentic" transformational leader. Authentic transformational leaders integrate their own moral character in their everyday actions as leaders. However, "pseudo" transformational leaders use their power to manipulate others and focus on their own self-interests in their decision-making processes. As a result, this type of leader does not embrace or support an ethical climate within the firm.[20]

Transactional Leadership

Transactional leadership is based on the assumption that the interaction between the leader and the subordinate is based on the mutual benefit of a transaction between the two parties. Transactional leaders focus on operational and routine activities within the firm. These "maintenance" activities allow the leader to allocate resources, monitor the activities of the employees, and direct employees to achieve the firm's goals and objectives. Jay Alden Conger and Rabindra Nath Kanungo argued that this is not a true style of leadership but, rather, "managership" in which control is used to protect the status quo of the firm.[21]

Due to the compliance nature of transactional leadership, this type of leadership does not support an ethical commitment. This lack of commitment is due to the negative impact this leadership style has on followers' self-esteem by exercising options such as power brokering and quid pro quo behavior. Transactional leaders focus on control issues instead of influencing the values and ethical beliefs of the employees. Instead of being true leaders, transactional leaders use contingent rewards and management by exception to manage the employees. *Contingent rewards* are based on an agreement between the leader and the employee that if certain tasks are accomplished, certain rewards will be given to the employee. *Management by exception* refers to the concept that the leader will become involved in issues only if some extraordinary events have occurred that need the attention of the leader.[22]

Manuel Mendonca argues that the transactional leadership style is inherently unethical because of the leaders' perceptions that the employees are similar to programmed robots and because the control system forces strict compliance that could be counter to the dignified treatment of the employees.[23] However, transactional leaders can use standard setting, performance appraisal, and rewards and punishment to support ethical behaviors.[24]

A Reconciliation of Ethical Values of Both Leadership Styles

To evaluate the ethical commitment of transactional and transformational leaders, one must understand the philosophical foundation of the two leadership styles. The values, motives, and assumptions for the two styles are based on two different philosophical theories: teleological and deontological. Transformational leaders have an organic and interdependent view of external events, and these leaders' moral altruistic motives are supported by the deontological philosophical frameworks in which the means or process justifies the ends. Transactional leaders have a much more independent view of external events, and their altruistic motives are supported by teleological philosophical frameworks in which the ends or results justifies the means. In addition, transactional leaders focus on the individual obligations, whereas transformational leaders focus on social obligations. Furthermore, transactional leaders develop pragmatic goals, whereas transformational leaders are more likely to develop idealistic goals.[25]

A Manager's Ability to Develop Trust, Commitment, and Effort[26]

LaRue Tone Hosmer proposed that managers must understand the various needs of the firm's stakeholders. Through identification and empathy toward the stakeholder's needs and beliefs, managers can be rewarded by the establishment of trust, commitment, and effort from the firm's employees and all the firm's stakeholders. The ability of managers to effectively identify and answer the questions related to moral problems (What is duty?), moral reasoning (What is right?), and moral courage (What is integrity?)

FIGURE 5.1 ● Hosmer's Model of Trust, Commitment, and Effort

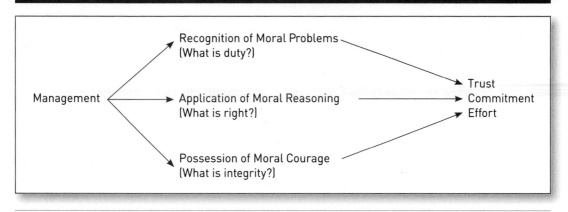

Source: LaRue Tone Hosmer, "Strategic Planning as If Ethics Mattered," *Strategic Management Journal* 15 (1994): 29.

guides the decision-making process. If managers understand their ethical responsibilities in addressing these three questions, the result will be the development of trust, commitment, and effort among the firm's stakeholders. The stakeholders will reward the firm with loyalty and commitment because the managers of the firm have been able to demonstrate their ethical commitment throughout their dealings with the various stakeholders. Hosmer's model with the proposed relationship is shown in Figure 5.1.

The Responsibility of Managers

The moral responsibility of managers was first presented by Chester Barnard in 1938 in his legendary book *The Functions of the Executive.* Barnard stated that managers or executives should view the decision-making process as based not solely on intellect but on moral responsibility as well. In addition, Barnard stated that executives should inspire faith in the common purpose of the organization.[27] Without an evaluation process for ethical values within the firm, employees may have difficulty accepting the strategic decisions developed by managers. Through this "ethical analysis," managers and employees can reconcile any differences in the value system that exist between the corporate and employee beliefs pertaining to ethical conduct.[28]

Through trust, strong ethical values can grow between the firm and stakeholders that will lead to strong organizational commitment. This strong commitment then leads to efforts that are cooperative, innovative, and could be integrated within the strategic decision-making process, leading to higher levels of profitability for the firm.[29]

In direct response to the needs of the stakeholders, a strong ethical commitment can be translated into a competitive advantage for the firm. A firm can use a strong ethical value system to help differentiate the firm's products and services in the marketplace. In a highly competitive environment, a strong ethical reputation may help convince potential customers to purchase goods and services from that firm rather than buying from a firm that has an ethically neutral or negative reputation.

Great leaders are stewards of the ethical commitment of the firm, and this commitment is transferred to the employees. Ethical stewardship is defined as "the honoring of duties owed to employees, stakeholders and society in the pursuit of long-term wealth creation."[30] When focusing on the long-term benefits to all stakeholders, leaders who are ethical stewards firmly believe that their roles are to provide the commitment needed for the employees and other stakeholders to also become ethical stewards. Leaders who are ethical stewards are motivated by virtues, values, and the needs of society. They also have high authentic moral principles that support the long-term growth and sustainability of the organization. Ethical stewards also believe that serving the needs of all the stakeholders enhances the growth and profit opportunities of the firm. Furthermore, the promise to be good ethical stewards allows the leader to build trust and honor in the relationship he or she has with the firm's employees. Transformational leaders focus on group goals and organizational needs that are enhanced through a commitment to ethical stewardship. A significant benefit of ethical stewardship is that it generates an ethically superior governance system within the firm that generates long-term wealth and sustainability by increasing the level of employee commitment to the firm.[31]

The Transformation From Moral Person to Ethical Leader

In their article "Moral Person and Moral Manager," Linda Trevino, Laura Hartman, and M. Brown highlight the duality of a manager's approach to ethical issues.[32] For one pillar, the manager must be a moral person based on his or her own values and beliefs. The other pillar is being able to transfer those values and beliefs to foster an ethical culture for the firm's employees. Trevino et al. argue that a decision maker must be both a moral person and a moral manager to establish an ethical leadership position within the firm. Through the complex code of morals first mentioned by Barnard, managers are able to create the traits necessary to be a moral person. In addition, the transfer of his or her moral codes to others makes a moral person a moral manager and gives the manager the ability to lead by example in the realm of ethical leadership. The two pillars of ethical leadership are presented in Figure 5.2.

Traits

Traits are fairly stable and predictable personal characteristics that remain consistent over time. Of the three traits of the moral person, integrity is the most important because it encompasses the other two traits of honesty and trustworthiness. The level of the manager's integrity drives the level of the other two traits. Furthermore, integrity in itself is not enough. Every stakeholder interacting with the manager has to trust the manager and has to assume that all transactions are done in an honest manner.

Behaviors

The behaviors of the managers must be consistent with what the managers say. A moral person is expected to always select the ethical option, with the result that the manager does the right thing. Furthermore, managers must show a genuine concern for people, which includes not just the manager's supporters, but also any stakeholder who has a vested interest in the firm. A moral manager must be open in that he or she is considered to be approachable for a discussion regardless of the topic and that the

FIGURE 5.2 ● The Two Pillars of Ethical Leadership

Moral Person	Moral Manager
Traits • Integrity • Honesty • Trustworthiness	**Role Modeling Through Visible Action**
Behaviors • Do the Right Thing • Concern for People • Being Open • Personal Morality	**Rewards and Discipline**
Decision Making • Hold on to Values • Objective/Fair • Concern for Society • Follow Ethical Decision Rules	**Communicating About Ethics and Values**

Source: Linda K. Trevino, Laura P. Hartman, and M. Brown, "Moral Person and Moral Manager: How Executives Develop a Reputation for Ethical Leadership," *California Management Review* 42, no. 4 (2000): 131.

manager is a good listener when it is necessary. Personal morality reflects ethical conduct outside the workplace. A moral manager makes no distinctions between doing the right thing at work and doing the right thing in private. Every action must be consistent with the moral and ethical beliefs of the manager.

Decision Making

Moral persons are expected to hold to a comprehensive and unwavering set of strong ethical values and principles. They are also objective and fair when they make decisions that can affect various stakeholders. Moral persons value all stakeholders when they measure goals and objectives by considering stakeholders who have a vested interest in the local community and the overall society. Furthermore, moral managers use a number of established ethical rules of thumb such as the Golden Rule and the newspaper test to aid them in the decision-making process.

Moral Manager

The transfer of the moral value of the moral manager to those he or she interacts with is based on how the moral manager is able to communicate the ethical values to others. A moral person should be a role model for ethical behavior. As a result, a moral manager is able to manage ethically by example. Subordinates to the managers will always look to the manager to interpret what is acceptable and ethical behavior. It is critical that a moral manager understand that every action taken by the manager becomes a model for the subordinates.

One of the most effective ways to relay to the subordinates the moral manager's commitment to high ethical standards is the establishment and implementation of the reward and discipline system. The use of both positive and negative reinforcement gives the moral manager an opportunity to help encourage the current course of behavior (rewards) or redirect the employee's behavior to get back on an ethical track (discipline).

Moral managers must also talk to subordinates about ethics and values without being condescending. Moral managers understand that communication of ethics and values is critical to establish for a subordinate what is and is not acceptable, and provides an opportunity for a two-way discussion about ethical issues.

Trevino et al. warn that not all supervisors are moral persons nor are they moral managers. In addition, a manager may be inconsistent from a moral person and moral manager perspective. The combinations of moral person and moral manager scenarios are shown in Figure 5.3.

Unethical Leader

A weak moral person and weak moral manager generates unethical leadership. Jeffrey Skilling of Enron, Bernie Ebbers of WorldCom, and Dennis Kozlowski of Tyco are three high-profile leaders who have acted unethically. Because of their drive to reward their self-interests, they did not seem to have the characteristics of moral people. In addition, trying, and quite often succeeding, in getting other employees within the firm to accept the unethical activities indicates these three former CEOs were weak moral managers.

Ethical Leader

The ethical leader is what Trevino et al. argue should be the ultimate ethical goal of any manager. It involves having the core ethical traits of behavior and decision making of a moral person but, more important, the ability to use those grounded ethical

---

FIGURE 5.3 ●   The Moral Person and Moral Manager Matrix

Strong	Hypocritical Leader	Ethical Leader
Moral Manager		
Weak	Unethical Leader	Inconsistent Leader
	Weak	**Strong**
	Moral Person	

Source: Linda K. Trevino, Laura P. Hartman, and M. Brown, "Moral Person and Moral Manager: How Executives Develop a Reputation for Ethical Leadership," *California Management Review* 42, no. 4 (2000): 137.

characteristics and transfer them to others within the organization through the characteristics of a moral manager.

Hypocritical Leader

A hypocritical leader is a dangerous position for a manager to establish with other employees within the firm. A hypocritical leader has destroyed all three of the critical traits of a moral person. When a leader says one thing about ethical values, then acts unethically, employees within the organization no longer view the manager as being a person of integrity, a person they can trust, or a person who is honest. Martha Stewart could be an example of a hypocritical leader in that her media empire was built on the correct way to entertain and interact with other people. However, Martha Stewart was found guilty of conspiracy, obstruction of justice, and making false statements. As a result, other employees within her empire may question whether any of her statements were true because she made false statements to government officials.

Inconsistent Leader

Although Trevino et al. did not name the fourth quadrant in the matrix, it could best be described as having the characteristics of an inconsistent leader. An inconsistent leader is a manager who has strong ethical traits, behaviors, and decision making of a moral person but is not able to transfer those values to other employees within the firm. As a result, the manager is inconsistent because of the contradictory strength of the individual moral values and the weak characteristics of a moral manager.

Ethics and Corporate Governance

Corporate governance can be defined as the system that is used by firms to control and direct their operations and the operations of their representatives, the employees. Through the corporate governance structure, firms can ensure that the needs of all their stakeholders are satisfied. The corporate governance system gives a method in which the ethical vision can be measured and validated. This system "governs" the behavior of the managers within the firm. The corporate governance system incorporates the objectives of the stakeholders and ensures that the behaviors of the employees within the firm are fair, just, and transparent.[33] From the corporate governance perspective, firms have the ability to interpret their ethical duty to their stakeholders.

Board of Directors

The board of directors was designed to represent the interests of the stockholders. This relationship, called *agency theory*, is based on the belief that managers are "agents" of the stockholders because managers should be making decisions to benefit the stockholders. As a result, the board of directors is a corporate governance mechanism to ensure that the agents do their job in maximizing the return for the investors.

Board members can be classified as either inside or outside board members. An inside board member is a person who has direct financial ties to the firm. Any person on the management team of the company is considered an inside board member. An outside board member is one who does not have any direct financial ties to the firm.

When discussing the composition of corporate boards, it is necessary to understand the areas of management power. As part of its fiduciary duty, the board of directors has a number of specific responsibilities that address the agency theory relationship the board has with its stockholders and all of its stakeholders. The responsibilities include establishing and maintaining internal financial controls, communicating financial situations internally and externally, establishing and revising when necessary the firm's code of ethics and ethical standards, selecting the external auditor, and establishing different board committees including the audit committee.[34]

Because the board members are stewards for the assets of the company and the interests of all stakeholders, six core ethical values are recommended to guide their behavior as board members:[35] honesty, integrity, loyalty, responsibility, fairness, and citizenship.

1. **Honesty:** Board members have an ethical responsibility to act in an honest manner. Board members are expected to be truthful and forthright with their decisions and board members should correct or dispute points or facts that they do not believe are valid.
2. **Integrity:** Board members are expected to act with honor, and their actions and decisions should always coincide with the ethical vision and standards of the firm.
3. **Loyalty:** Board members should avoid all deals that benefit their self-interests rather than the interests of the stakeholders. Board members are expected to be objective in their decision making and to hold classified any confidential or proprietary information.
4. **Responsibility:** Board members are expected to fulfill all their assigned responsibilities and their actions should be transparent. Board members should be willingly accountable for their actions.
5. **Fairness:** Board members are expected to make all decisions and treat others in a fair and respectful manner.
6. **Citizenship:** Board members are expected to act as good citizens for the communities in which the firm has operations. Board members are not expected to make decisions that could be considered harmful to the natural environment.

The responsibilities do not lie solely in the hands of the board of directors, however. If shareholders and other stakeholders want accountability from the board of directors, they must be proactive with their demands. As was shown in the example at the beginning of the chapter, integrity plays a role in any interactions between the board members and the CEO.

To have a smooth-running board of directors that accurately represents the views and demands of the firm's stakeholders, a number of recommended courses of action could help ensure harmony between the two groups. Clifton Wharton, Jay Lorsch, and Lord Hanson made five recommendations for an effective board of directors and five recommendations to ensure the shareholders and other stakeholders are well represented in the decisions of the board members:[36]

Board Members

1. The board of directors should make at least an annual evaluation of the CEO based on the established goals and strategies of the firm.
2. The evaluation of the CEO should be done solely by outside board members.

3. All the outside board members should meet at least once a year without the CEO present.

4. The members of the board should ensure that there are clear and appropriate listings of qualifications for proposed membership to the board, and those qualifications should be made available to the shareholders.

5. Outside board members should be the members who are responsible for the recruitment and selection of new board members based on the established qualifications.

Shareholders

1. Institutional shareholders should view themselves as active owners of the firm, not just investors.

2. The shareholders should not be involved in or question the day-to-day activities of the firm's operations.

3. Shareholders should use their rights to evaluate annually the performance of the members of the board.

4. Shareholders need to be informed when the firm does an evaluation of the board members.

5. Shareholders need to understand that a common goal of all shareholders is to support the firm so it continues to be an ongoing corporate concern.

Every board of directors is as unique as the firm it represents. However, there are some major issues that most boards of directors have in common, including the following:

- The annual business plan of the firm
- The hiring and compensation of the board members and other officials of the firm
- The issuance of stock options
- The investments in capital structure and level of firm indebtedness
- The issuance of dividends
- Discussions pertaining to risk management and insurance policies
- Acquisitions, divestitures, and capital expenditures beyond a certain dollar amount
- Litigation settlements greater than a certain amount
- Fines and penalties greater than a stated amount
- Restructuring of the firm that may exceed a particular amount
- Tax settlements that are greater than a certain amount
- Contingent liability issues greater than a particular amount
- Pension contributions that exceed a stated amount[37]

The Role of the Board of Directors

The role of the board of directors should be based on the belief that the actions of the board represent the objectives and needs of the stakeholders. As a result, the board needs to move beyond its traditional role, which was being passive to the decisions established by management, and take a more participatory role. David Nadler proposes a continuum of potential board involvement in the decision-making process within a firm: passive, certifying, engaged, intervening, and operating.[38] The continuum of board types is shown in Figure 5.4.

FIGURE 5.4 ● Types of Boards of Directors

Least Involved	⟵ ⟶	Most Involved
Passive	Certifying Engaged Intervening	Operating

Source: David A. Nadler, "Building Better Boards," *Harvard Business Review* 82 (2004): 4.

Passive Board

The passive, or "rubber stamp," board is one in which the board approves the recommendations from management with little or no opposition. It is also called a rubber stamp board because it automatically approves what is presented to the board for review.

Certifying Board

The certifying board provides the function of certifying to shareholders that the CEO is doing what is expected of him or her and that management will make corrective adjustments when necessary. This type of board emphasizes that outside board members need to meet without the CEO present. In addition, the board will design an orderly succession process and is willing to make adjustments to the management team when the shareholders demand change.

Engaged Board

The engaged board has a proactive role within the decision-making process. An engaged board provides advice and support to the CEO and the top management team. An engaged board judges the performance of the CEO and helps guide his or her actions. In addition, an engaged board will seek information from outside the company to aid in its understanding and making recommendations for the top management of the firm.

Intervening Board

The intervening board becomes actively involved in all the major decisions of the firm. The intervening board meets frequently and focuses intensely on all issues on the agenda at the board meetings.

Operating Board

The operating board actually makes the key decisions for the firm, and the top-level management is responsible for implementing the board's decisions. Management draws on the expertise and skills of the board members to help craft the overall strategic focus of the firm.

The critical role in the board of directors is the chair of the board. The chair sets the agenda for each board meeting, selects the members of each board subcommittee, and decides what type of information is available to the board for its meetings. When the CEO is also the chair of the board, this is called *CEO duality.* This can be a dangerous challenge to the corporate governance system. By being both CEO and chair, one person has significant control over the decision-making process for the firm. As a result, CEO duality could potentially lead to ineffective boards that may not have the power to veto the controlling power of the CEO. In fact, firms that had a separate chair of the board and CEO consistently outperformed firms that had a dual CEO and chair.[39]

A Contingent Perspective on Corporate Governance[40]

Paul Strebel argues that there are ebbs and flows to how a board of directors addresses governance issues. He argues that there are four major roles: auditing, supervising, coaching, and steering.

Auditing Role

The board views its role from an auditing perspective when there is an effective top management within the firm and the externalities facing the firm are insignificant. Because top management is formulating and implementing an effective strategy to compete in the marketplace and the competitive markets and efficient government regulations limit the impact of externalities, the board can focus on the financial aspects of the firm's operations. The role of the board usually occurs in a stable business environment that does not require large amounts of new investment.

Supervising Role

The board takes a supervising role when there are significant externalities impacting the firm and the top level managers are very effective in their strategic decisions. The supervising role includes ensuring that the needs of the critical stakeholders are addressed in the strategic decision-making process. As a result, the board focuses on strategic, societal, and risk-related issues to make sure the firm has strategic fit with these issues.

Coaching Role

The board takes a coaching roles when the management has not been effective with the development of its strategic focus. A coaching board seeks active participation in the decision-making process to help the top level manager make the most effective strategic decision. In this role, the board has the luxury of aiding in the development of the strategic decisions of the firm because the externalities facing the firm are not significant. As a result, the board has the time to give advice on how the firm should proceed strategically.

Steering Role

The board does not have the same luxury of time in a steering role. In a steering role, the management is ineffective in making strong strategic decisions and externalities have a significant impact on the firm. Therefore, a sense of urgency arises for firms with these characteristics. As a result, the board becomes extremely active in all aspects of the strategic focus of the firm. The board becomes actively involved in both the short-term and long-term strategic focus of the firm, in an attempt to ensure the firm survives. In this setting, an incompetent CEO will be replaced, usually in the interim, with a board member until a permanent replacement can be selected. In addition, the board takes an active role addressing the unmet needs of critical stakeholders.

Ethics and the Structure of the Board of Directors

There will be an inherent potential conflict of interest if the board is composed of a majority of inside board members. As shown in a number of the cases in this textbook, having an insider-based board allows for potential abuses of power by the top managers and the CEO. Inside directors might hesitate before reprimanding or punishing the performance of the managers within the firm because the inside board members, usually being employees of the firm, have a financial interest in the firm. This abuse of power could be enhanced if inside members make up a majority of the compensation committee. The compensation committee is responsible for the determination of the compensation for the CEO. If a member of the compensation committee is also an employee of the firm, it would be expected that the member may vote for a high compensation package in exchange for receiving higher compensation himself or herself. In addition, the compensation committee also determines the compensation package for the board members, leading to another potential conflict of interest.[41]

The Benefits of a Strong Board of Directors

In our study examining the relationship between strong boards of directors and financial performance, we found that having a strong board does have a positive impact on the performance of the firm.[42] By examining the financial performance of the best and worst boards of directors, which was published in *Businessweek*, we found that there were both short-term and long-term benefits of having a strong board. A strong board has a majority of its members be outside members, be large owners of stock in the firm, and be on only a small number of other boards of directors. Boards and board members with these characteristics yielded a higher level of financial performance than did boards that did not have those characteristics. Having good corporate governance supports the ethical requirements established by the stakeholders and the financial requirements established by the shareholders.

CEO Compensation and Ethical Reputation

In our study examining the relationship among CEO compensation, ethical reputation, and financial performance, we found a number of interesting results.[43] There was no direct relationship between CEO compensation and the financial performance of the firm. We had hypothesized that firms that had a high ethical supporting culture should have those high ethical standards represented in the interests of the CEO. Therefore, we expected that CEOs in highly ethical firms would not focus solely on their self-interests as they related to their level of total compensation. By examining the top 100 best corporate citizens as ranked by *Business Ethics* magazine, we found that firms with strong ethical reputations were not always able to transfer that reputation into superior financial performance. However, it appears that CEOs were financially rewarded through higher levels of compensation for those firms with high ethical reputations. Another interesting result of the study showed that firms that actually lost money had on average a higher level of CEO compensation than did firms that were profitable. The result contradicted the initial assumption, which was because these are the top 100 corporate citizens, all the CEOs of the companies would act in an ethical manner relating to the level of compensation.

This study was supported by a recent poll in the *Financial Times*, which reported that the British public views CEOs as people who mislead the public and are overpaid.[44] S. Finkelstein and others commented, Where is the personal shame of the CEOs who have performed poorly for their firms but demand higher and higher salaries?[45]

Ethical Viewpoints Explaining CEO Compensation

Some argue that CEOs' high level of compensation can be justified based on Kantian ethics.[46] Based on this ethical philosophy, CEOs will evaluate their decisions based on the answer to this question: "In this situation, would everyone else act this way, making it a universal law?" If the CEO's answer is yes, Kant would argue that the CEO is justified because everyone would act in the same manner given the same set of circumstances. In addition, a number of different ethical philosophies can be used to explain CEO compensation.[47] From an ethical egoism perspective, high levels of CEO compensation coincide with the agency theory model of maximizing the returns to the stockholders. If the CEO is able to maximize the returns, he or she should be rewarded with a maximum level of compensation. From a deontological perspective, it would be argued that CEO compensation is based on the rights of the individuals and the judgments made with a specific decision process instead of a focus on the decision choices. As a result, the compensation system for the CEO would be based on an analysis of performance from the compensation committee, which is made up of the CEO's peers. From a utilitarian viewpoint, compensation would focus on the consequences of the greatest good to the greatest number of people. Thus, if the CEO focuses on satisfying the needs of the shareholders and the other stakeholders, he or she would be rewarded generously for his or her commitment to the firm's stakeholders. From a relativist viewpoint, it is assumed that decision makers use themselves or their peers to develop ethical standards. Therefore, if the board of directors has a majority of inside members, it increases the probability that higher levels of CEO compensation could be rationalized within the board's decision-making process. From a virtue ethics perspective, prestige and image, as well as compensation, are also motivating factors for CEOs.

The Securities and Exchange Commission (SEC) proposed a more stringent reporting disclosure requirement for management compensation. The rules had not been changed since 1992, but the SEC began investigating possible changes in 2004 that were instituted in 2006. The new disclosures included a requirement to provide a table that shows the yearly compensation for the chair of the board, the chief financial officer, and the next three highest-paid executives. Included in these disclosures is information concerning stock options, total perks, and retirement benefits. Most important, the information included in the yearly filings must be written very clearly so the average investor can understand the information.

Corporate Governance and Stakeholders

This chapter has highlighted the complex relationship a firm has in the development and effective execution of its corporate governance system. Figure 5.5 highlights the relationship presented in this chapter.

Each of the stakeholders has established its own list of demands regarding what should be included in the firm's corporate governance system. The employees, suppliers,

FIGURE 5.5 ● The Relationship Between Stakeholders and Corporate Governance

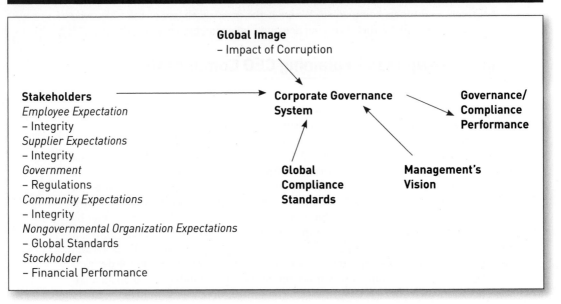

and community want and expect an honest and transparent relationship with the firm. Thus, they base their relationships on established mutual integrity in their business transactions with the firm. The stockholders expect the firm to perform at the maximum financial performance level. As a result, stockholders will support any actions in the corporate governance system that could enhance the ability of the firm to maintain or enhance its competitive advantage in the global marketplace. The governments in every country in which the firm has operations demand that the firm follow the legal requirements established by that country's norms. Nongovernmental organizations demand that firms respect the global human and worker rights of every individual who has a direct or indirect relationship with the firm in its global operations. Furthermore, the firm looks for guidance in establishing and revising its own corporate governance system by examining global compliance standards, how its actions could affect its global image, and how the ethical vision of top management may change over time. Based on the corporate governance system, an evaluation system should be in place to determine the overall effectiveness of the firm's corporate governance and compliance system.

Questions for Thought

1. In the opening vignette, a top level executive went into a rage over a bag of nuts. What do you think the underlying cause of this behavior is? Do you think a year in prison is the correct sentence for her behavior?

2. What are some ways in which a board of directors can increase its power? Under what circumstances can its power be decreased?

3. Do you perceive yourself as a transformational or transactional leader? Explain your answer.

Real-Life Ethical Dilemma Exercise

A True Global Ethical Leader: Tim Berners-Lee

The name *Tim Berners-Lee* may not be well known, but he is in our lives every day. Berners-Lee is the founder and creator of the software that became the basis of the World Wide Web.

A graduate of Oxford University in England, Berners-Lee addressed what was becoming an increasingly frustrating issue related to computer technology—the lack of ability to share data. Largely because of the operating systems developed by Microsoft and other traditional software developers, computers were designed to be stand-alone pieces of equipment without the ability to share information. That all changed in 1989 when Berners-Lee invented the software related to the establishment of the World Wide Web while working at CERN, which is the European Particle Physics Laboratory. A year later, he wrote the software for the first web client and server and was creator of the now common programs such as uniform resource identifiers (URIs), hypertext transfer protocol (HTTP), and HTML. In one of the more significant decisions related to not only business, but society, Berners-Lee made the software code "open source" so that anyone could use it, adopt it, and change it for free.[48] This one decision fundamentally changed how society operates and was in complete opposition to the stand-alone model that charges users for access to any type of "propriety" software. As a result, the actions of Berners-Lee should be studied by those would benefit society, even if it means that there will not be the same type of self-interest rewards for their action. One last point to consider: If Berners-Lee had used a "cost" model in which it would cost a user 5 cents to use the Internet, how would that affect your day-to-day behavior?

Questions for the Real-Life Ethical Dilemma Exercise

1. Why do you think Tim Berners-Lee "gave away" such valuable software?

2. If you had developed the software that established the Internet, would you make this software available for free to anyone in the world? Why or why not?

3. What do you think would have happened to the Internet during the past 20 to 25 years if a company had charged for Internet use?

Student Study Site

Visit the Student Study Site at **study.sagepub.com/stanwick3e** to access the following resources:

- Video Links
- SAGE Journal Articles
- Web Resources
- Web Quizzes

6

Strategic Planning, Corporate Culture, and Corporate Compliance

In fact, meaningful leadership—leadership that in the long run counts for something—cannot be accompanied by moral collapse. The leader who acts ethically will ultimately succeed. The leader who lacks in ethical foundation will ultimately fail.

—Willard C. Butcher, retired chairman of Chase Manhattan Corporation

Chapter Objectives

After reading and studying Chapter 6, students should be able to

1. Explain the concept of strategic planning with respect to ethics.
2. Explain the ethics life cycle.
3. Explain ethical strategic decision making from a global perspective.
4. Discuss ethical crisis and disaster recovery.
5. Define corporate culture.
6. Explain how ethical values can be changed.
7. Describe the process for embedding values and positive ethics in an organization.
8. Explain the difference between corruption, embezzlement, extortion, and bribery.
9. Describe the various forms of corruption.

When Ethics Drive a Change in Strategy[1]

In 2003, Charles Prince took over as CEO at the large financial services company Citigroup. He was handpicked by the previous CEO, Sanford Weill, to carry on the same strategic focus of aggressive growth, a large number of acquisitions, and high year-to-year earnings growth. Weill stayed on as chairman of the board to ensure his protégé was up to the task of steering Citigroup in the right direction for the future. After 2 years establishing his presence as CEO, Prince made dramatic changes at Citigroup. He stated that one of his primary goals was to improve the firm's corporate reputation and to focus on implementing stronger internal controls and a more comprehensive ethics program at the company. After the new initiatives were announced to the employees, two of the three highest-ranking employees at Citigroup left the company. The second-in-command, Robert Willumstad, and former global consumer banking head, Marjorie Magner, left the company. Weill also attempted to leave his position as chairman of the board. All were upset when their advice to Prince was ignored.

The obsession with implementing a supportive value system at Citigroup was based on a number of ethical issues that had taken place when Prince took over as CEO. Citigroup did not separate its financial analyst functions from its role as an investment bank. Citigroup also had to address government probes in England for its aggressive strategy related to bond trading. Citigroup lost its private banking license in Japan because of activities by some of its employees. Furthermore, the Federal Trade Commission accused Citigroup of purposely misleading customers in its consumer lending unit.

One of the driving forces to change the strategy at Citigroup was Prince's new interpretation of the role of Citigroup. Weill perceived Citigroup as primarily accountable to one stakeholder, the stockholders, through profitability, whereas Prince described Citigroup from a broader stakeholder perspective by styling the company as a "quasi-public institution." During the year before Prince made the strategic changes, he estimated that he spent half of his time focusing on culture and values issues. Prince stated that he needed to establish a new ethics model, which was not a priority for Weill.

Ethics and Strategic Planning

Strategic planning is the process by which future courses of action are developed to achieve the firm's short- and long-term goals. Part of the strategic planning process means that you are building trust with all of the stakeholders discussed in the earlier chapters.

It is critical that decision makers consider how the resolution of ethical issues affects others. Jeffrey Seglin recommends that everyone answer five questions before making a final decision:

1. Why is this bothering me?
2. Is it my responsibility?
3. What is the ethical concern?
4. What do others think?
5. Am I being true to myself?[2]

Peter Drucker calls this last question the mirror test. The *mirror test* involves the decision maker's ability to look in the mirror after the decision has been made and state that he or she has made the right choice.

The Ethical Cycle[3]

Since 1964, when the U.S. Civil Rights Act was passed, companies have been faced with an increasing array of ethical decisions related to their strategic development. These ethical decisions have created a new area for management—that of ethically managing the business. This may mean following prescribed laws and regulations or dealing with equal opportunity. It may mean dealing with a myriad of social responsibility issues, such as environmental issues and sustainability, or dealing with corruption. Whatever the issue, managers must take an active stance on the issues as they relate to strategic planning. In general, companies must take a look at the needs and demands of all stakeholders when making ethical decisions related to strategic planning. One method of understanding the underlying dynamics of strategic ethical decision making is based on the ethical cycle. The ethical cycle is presented in Figure 6.1.

Moral Problem Statement

The ethical cycle begins with the identification of the moral problem. The moral problem statement must be developed based on the responses to three conditions: a clear statement of what the moral problem is, an identification of who is affected by the resolution of the moral problem, and the moral issue of the problem.

Problem Analysis

To analyze the moral problem, three factors must be identified: (1) Which stakeholders are affected by the problem, and how does it affect their interests? (2) What are the moral values that need to be considered to analyze the problem? and (3) What are the relevant facts related to the moral problem?

FIGURE 6.1 ● The Ethical Cycle

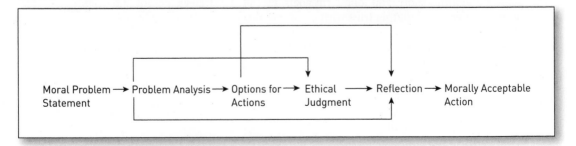

Source: I. van de Poel and L. Royakkers, "The Ethical Cycle," *Journal of Business Ethics* 71 (2007): 4–7.

Options for Action

Once the moral problem has been identified and the information related to the problem has been analyzed, the next step is to generate options to resolve the problem. By presenting these alternative solutions, the decision makers are able to understand how each alternative can affect the relevant stakeholders. During the identification of different viable options, the creativity of the decision makers should come to the forefront in the decision-making process. During this step, the decision makers should consider all ideas as initially viable until they are discussed in further detail.

Ethical Judgment

The evaluation of the different options takes place during the ethical judgment stage. For each of the options that were presented in the previous step, an evaluation takes place to see which of the options would be acceptable based on the moral values and beliefs of the decision makers and the organization as a whole.

Reflection

A reflection on the options that were considered viable in the previous step is needed to establish the final course of action. During the reflection stage, the outcomes from the ethical judgment stage are further evaluated so a definitive course of action can be determined. The different ethical judgment options that were the outcome of the previous step should be weighed against each other to identify what the decision makers would consider the optimal solution to the moral problem. The morally acceptable action is decided by the decision makers from the reflection stage and is implemented to resolve the moral problem.[4]

Using Strategic Ethical Decisions to Build Character[5]

The ethical cycle helps employees understand who they are and their strategic responsibilities from an ethical perspective. The cycle consists of the decisions resulting from resolving ethical dilemmas that could be considered defining ethical moments. These defining moments shape and mold the personal values and beliefs pertaining to each decision maker in the resolution of an ethical issue. Ethical decisions involve choosing between right and wrong. The classic example of a defining moment is when a decision maker has a choice between two plausible and acceptable strategic options. Based on the decision maker's ultimate decision, the individual has established a threshold of a defining point for what is considered acceptable and unacceptable. A defining moment could generate potentially conflicting feelings. This conflict is based on the tension that can arise when two valid perspectives are considered in the decision-making process. As a result, defining moments do not have a "correct" response, but, as John Dewey states, they help "form, reveal, and test"[6] the character of the decision maker. As a result, defining moments help decision makers form and define their personal character.

Who Am I?

Through these defining moments, individuals are able to identify themselves by answering three relevant questions: (1) What feelings and personal intuition are being conflicted as the individual decides on the course of action? (2) What are the individual values that are so deeply rooted in the core of the individual's being that they will not be compromised under any circumstances? and (3) What type of creative ideas and shrewdness can be developed by the individual to guide the individual to make the right decision?

Who Are We?

Defining moments can also occur for managers of various work groups. What is learned from the defining moments will be based on the answers to the following three questions: (1) What are different interpretations or points of view to the ethical dilemma that can make a convincing argument? (2) What focus or point of view would be considered the most persuasive to or supportive of the general beliefs of other employees within the organization? and (3) How can the manager of the work group create a process that will manifest the ethical values and beliefs that are important to the manager within the organization? In other words, what can the manager do to make his or her interpretation of the ethical issue be supported by the work group?

Who Is the Company?

Defining moments can also be used to clarify the ethical path company executives take within the organization. The questions that help identify defining moments for company executives are as follows: (1) As a company executive, have I done everything in my power to secure my own strength as well as the strength and stability of the organization to be able to make ethical decisions? (2) As a company executive, have I considered all the innovative ways in which my organization can help society, stockholders, and other stakeholders? and (3) What creative ideas can I develop as a company executive to help convert my ethical vision into a personal and organizational reality?

Is There a Link Between Strategic Planning and an Ethical Culture?

The decision-making process of all managers includes incorporating the goals and objectives of the firm into measurable evaluation points. Within the decision-making context, the decision maker also needs to integrate ethical issues into the process. By being able to demonstrate its ethical virtues to its various stakeholders, a firm that incorporates ethical planning as part of the strategic planning process will generate a positive reputation to its stakeholders.[7] In 2002, a survey of corporate and public sector organizations in Sweden was conducted. The survey was used to determine how well the information from each organization's code of ethics integrated with the firm's strategic planning. The researchers found that 55% of the corporations and 63% of the public sector organizations directly referred to their code of ethics during the strategic planning process.[8]

Constance Bagley proposed a decision tree process to help decision makers make the right decisions. Bagley proposed three major decision points to help guide the decision-making process. The first stage is asking if the action is legal. If no, then no action is taken. If yes, then the decision goes to the next stage, which asks whether the decision will maximize shareholder value. If no, then the follow-up question is whether it would be ethical not to take the considered action. That decision should

FIGURE 6.2 ● Ethical Decision Tree

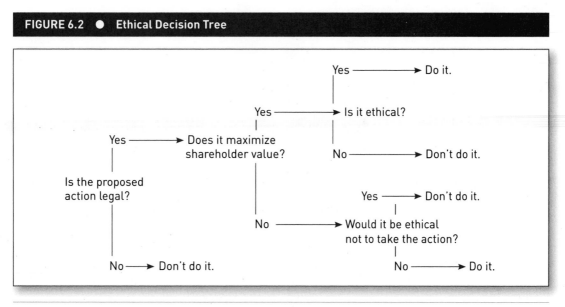

Source: Constance E. Bagley, "The Ethical Leader's Decision Tree," *Harvard Business Review* 81 (2003): 3.

be based on a cost-benefit analysis for the needs of the shareholders versus the cost benefit for the other stakeholders. If the answer is yes, it would be ethical not to take the action, then no action takes place. If the answer is no, then it would be ethical to take the action and the considered action should be implemented. If the action does maximize shareholder value, the follow-up question is, "Is it ethical?" which leads to the final determination of whether the action is implemented or not.[9] The ethical decision tree is shown in Figure 6.2.

How to Address Strategic Ethical Decision Making From a Global Perspective

Before managers can understand what constitutes appropriate and ethical behavior in countries other than their home country, they need to understand the unique differences of the companies and the countries in which they operate.[10] Although activities such as bribery and kickbacks are illegal in the United States, these actions may be considered ethical and a critical part of the negotiation process in other countries. As a result, it is essential to understand how certain factors may affect what is perceived to be ethical in other countries. Christopher Robertson and William Crittenden recommend that managers understand factors such as whether the country is capitalist or socialist, whether the culture aligns more with the traditional Western or Eastern culture, the dominant moral philosophy of the country, and the ethical and societal norms of the country. Once those factors have been identified, it is easier to understand the behavior of the citizens within the country. Robertson and Crittenden also proposed that ethical philosophy in a country is based on its culture and economic ideology. The positioning of the different ethical philosophies is shown in Figure 6.3.

FIGURE 6.3 ● A Mapping of Ethical Philosophies

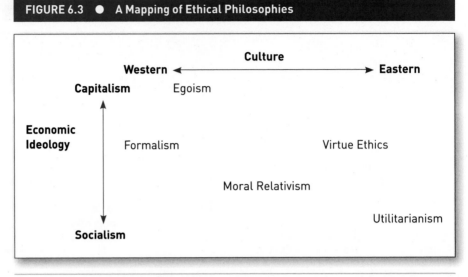

Source: Christopher Robertson and William Crittenden, "Mapping Moral Philosophies: Strategic Implications for Multinational Firms," *Strategic Management Journal* 24 (2003): 389.

How to Address Ethical Crisis and Disaster Recovery

An ethical crisis occurs when an event that was not part of the firm's normal course of action takes place and affects the firm. At present, many organizations are faced with recovering from disasters that were unexpected. The terrorist attacks of 2001, a variety of horrendous hurricanes hitting coastal cities, and mining disasters are just some of these unexpected disasters. Companies are finding they need a well-thought-out strategic plan to deal with these types of disasters, especially when they find their information technology (IT) systems have been compromised. Until the recent coverage of the disasters, many stakeholders had not even thought of companies having disaster plans in effect. For example, in the United Kingdom, power cuts have created a need for disaster planning in some organizations. Companies find that it is necessary to have continuity in their businesses during these disasters, or they will face drastic failures. When a firm faces an ethical crisis, top management can respond in a number of ways to address the issues. Peter Snyder and colleagues propose a framework to address these issues.[11] The crisis typology is whether the issue is internal or external in nature, called the Center of Gravity, and the second dimension is the frequency of the issues that are classified as normal or abnormal. The different components of the crisis typology are shown in Table 6.1.

Corporate Culture

Corporate culture comprises the shared values and beliefs of employees within any given organization. Corporate culture must have a strong ethical focus to ensure that various areas of unethical activities do not take place in the workplace. These include the following:[12]

TABLE 6.1 ● Typology of Crisis

Internal—Normal	**Internal—Abnormal**
Crisis occurs within the organization and is relatively predictable	Crisis occurs within the organization but is rare and unpredictable
Pre-crisis organization can occur	*Examples:*
Examples:	Corporate scandal
Product failure or recall	Information theft
Sexual harassment	Copyright infringement
Workplace violence	Records tampering
Vandalism	
Strike	
External—Normal	**External—Abnormal**
Crisis occurs outside the organization and is relatively predictable	All relevant organizations are affected by a crisis that occurs outside of the organization
Crisis could affect more than one organization	Crisis is relatively predictable for its timing and magnitude of the potential consequences, but the crisis is impossible to anticipate
Examples:	*Examples:*
Supplier failure	Terrorism
Industrial espionage	Industry deregulation
Product category failures	Reputation issues (e.g., rumors or slander)
Industry-wide technology attacks	Natural disasters

Source: Peter Snyder, Molly Hall, Joline Robertson, Tomasz Jasinski, and Janice Miller, "Ethical Rationality: A Strategic Approach to Organizational Crisis," *Journal of Business Ethics* 63 (2006): 371–383.

- Providing false or misleading promises to customers
- Violating workplace health and safety rules
- Engaging in employment discrimination
- Violating employee rights to privacy
- Allowing sexual harassment or a hostile work environment
- Being careless with confidential or proprietary information
- Engaging in activities posing a conflict of interest
- Providing false or misleading information to the public or media
- Allowing unfair competition or antitrust
- Allowing substance abuse
- Allowing environmental breaches
- Falsifying product quality and safety test results
- Offering improper gifts, favors, or entertainment to influence others
- Shipping a product that does not meet quality or safety standards

- Using dishonesty or unfair treatment of suppliers
- Falsifying or improper manipulating of financial data
- Embezzling funds or stealing from the organization
- Making false or misleading statements to government regulators
- Providing false or misleading information to investors or creditors
- Trading company shares based on insider information
- Providing improper political contribution to domestic officials
- Offering or paying bribes to foreign officials

Edgar Schein states that culture is based on norms and behavior patterns and can be represented by factors such as rituals and traditions.[13] Culture can be used by a firm to establish structural stability and integration of different components within the firm. Schein proposed that corporate culture exists simultaneously on three different levels within the firm. Figure 6.4 highlights the three levels.

Artifacts are factors such as what is seen and heard within a firm. Artifacts can also be the language used within the workplace as well as how people dress and the types of stories that are relayed to other workers within the firm.

Shared values are based on what groups within the firm learn about what is acceptable and not acceptable. A value can be shared, and it could become a shared assumption at a later time. The values of the firm are usually established by the founder of the firm or the CEO, and they are expressed to all the employees throughout the firm.

Basic assumptions are the agreed starting point for decision making within the firm. The basic assumptions are the linchpin for the establishment and maintenance of an ethical culture within the firm. Because the basic assumptions are the foundation for the decision-making process, during the assumption stage managers wanting high ethical standards within the firm are able to build ethical decision making from the ground up. From the basic assumptions, changes can take place within the value system of the firm. In addition, if manipulation of the value system is needed to support a

FIGURE 6.4 ● Schein's Three Levels of Culture

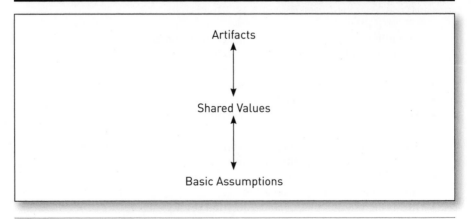

Source: Mary Jo Hatch, "The Dynamics of Organizational Culture," *Academy of Management Review* 18, no. 4 (1993): 659.

high order of ethical conduct, the value system could then drive the adjustment of the artifacts within the firm that would support a strong positive ethical climate.

How Managers Can Change a Corporate Culture

Schein proposed that managers can use two types of mechanisms to change cultures: primary embedding mechanisms and secondary articulation and reinforcement mechanisms.[14] Table 6.2 shows the various components of the two mechanisms.

As can be seen with the primary and secondary mechanisms, the top managers within a firm have many avenues available to have a strong ethical climate embedded within the firm. Top managers have the ability to use many mechanisms to lead by example, to communicate their ethical values to others, and to implement both positive and negative reinforcement to clearly establish what is acceptable and desirable behavior within the firm.

How to Change Ethical Values[15]

Kurt Lewin established a three-stage model in which change can be implemented throughout the organization. Schein built on the original model to develop what he called "cognitive redefinition" of individuals within the firm. Several stages are involved with cognitive redefinition. Stage 1 is the unfreezing of the individual's existing beliefs. The unfreezing of the existing beliefs allows the individual to be motivated to accept change. From an ethical value perspective, this unfreezing allows individuals to consider alternative facts and arguments that support a strong ethical culture.

TABLE 6.2 ● Culture-Changing Mechanisms

Primary Embedding Mechanisms

What leaders pay attention to, measure, and control

The reaction of a leader to a critical incident or crisis

What is observed to be the leader's criteria of allocating resources

The observation of the leader's behavior as a role model

What is observed to be the leader's criteria for the allocation of rewards and status decisions

What is observed to be the leader's criteria for the recruitment, selection, promotion, retirement, and excommunication of his or her subordinates

Secondary Articulation and Reinforcement Mechanisms

The design and structure of the organization

The systems and procedures of the organization

The rites and rituals of the organization

The design of the firm's buildings, facades, and the physical space within the buildings

The stories that are told to the employees about important events and people

The formal statements developed by the firm to represent the firm's philosophy, creeds, and charters

---

Source: http://www.tnellen.com/ted/tc/schein.html.

Stage 2 occurs when the beliefs have been unfrozen and the perceptions and attitudes of the individual are allowed to move to a new state. This is when the actual change occurs in the ethical beliefs of the individuals. During stage 2, top management needs to ensure that what is considered acceptable and unacceptable is clear to each individual within the firm.

Stage 3 is when the refreezing takes place and the new perceptions and ideals are "locked in." Also during stage 3, top managers must reinforce their commitment to support strong ethical behavior.

From a manager's perspective, two key responsibilities need to be implemented to ensure the firm's employees have a strong ethical value system to guide them. Management's first responsibility is to verify that ethical decisions are made by all levels of managers. The second responsibility is to develop an organizational culture that supports the ethical decision-making process.[16] Employee behavior is important in establishing a positive corporate culture because everyone within the company is ultimately responsible for the ethical behavior of the firm. Alan Graf believes that to formalize a culture of ethics, a company should focus on employee behavior.[17] He believes that this culture should include three basic components:

1. Define your philosophy and corporate values in a mission statement.
2. Develop guidelines for employees.
3. Establish a formal channel for employees to report violations.

From the top down, management must make sure that employees are operating in an organization filled with trust. There should be no hidden agendas for any of top management or for the employees. What is important is the employees' view of the ethical leadership of those at the top. It is critical in the process of establishing an ethical culture to create a culture where the leaders of the organization prove that they are committed to the process of changing the culture of the company. Executives must be held responsible for their actions, and employees must see this taking place.

Evaluation of Corporate Culture

Managers must be the individuals to model, communicate, and reinforce ethical behavior to their employees. In addition, top management must model to lower-level managers in these same ways to create an environment of ethical integrity. The top-level managers are responsible for ensuring that the corporate culture supports ethical behavior. A tool that can be used to evaluate how supportive the culture is to ethical behavior is to have management do a cultural assessment of the firm. Deloitte recommends that managers ask the following questions as part of their cultural assessment of their firms:

- Do rank-and-file employees understand the tone set by senior management?
- Do you know, without a doubt, that your organization's culture encourages ethical behavior at all levels?
- Can employees throughout your organization describe the company's code of ethics?

- Do employees in all areas of your organization ask questions and express concerns?
- Do your employees believe that the mechanisms are in place to allow them to voice opinions without fear of retribution?[18]

One professional stated, "As a young executive, at first I didn't understand what the president meant when he said that we weren't to reveal the real numbers. I later found out we actually had two sets of books."[19] It is critical that an organization create a climate of integrity. Employees need to feel that management is interested in ethics, that the discussion is not just another topic that they cover just because government regulations say they must, as in the case of publicly traded companies under the Sarbanes-Oxley Act. It may be that the real culprits are top management rather than the employees. (See, for example, the specifics of Enron, HealthSouth, WorldCom, and other cases in this textbook.) Some suggestions for creating a climate of integrity include the following:

- Set an example through strong leadership.
- Set realistic goals.
- Provide training.
- Distinguish between compliance and ethics.[20]

Compliance must be an accepted part of the company's corporate culture. It means that each employee, including those at the top, must understand what it means to have compliance entrenched as part of the organization's culture. A recent study has shown that there are still challenges facing firms as they develop and maintain a strong ethical culture. The 2011 National Business Ethics Survey[21] found some disturbing results. In this survey, 45% of the respondents had witnessed misconduct in the workplace. Types of misconduct included sexual harassment, substance abuse, insider trading, stealing, environmental violations, improper contracts, health or safety violations, and anticompetitive practices. In addition, 22% of the respondents who reported misconduct experienced some form of retaliation. The retaliation methods included verbal abuse, getting the cold shoulder from coworkers, hours and pay being reduced, demotion, physical harm, online harassment, and threats about losing their jobs. Furthermore, 13% of the employees felt pressure to compromise standards so they could perform the duties of their jobs. In addition, 34% of the respondents perceived that their supervisor does not display ethical behavior. A staggering 42% of the respondents stated that their company had a weak ethical culture.

Key attributes needed for an organization to be fully integrity based include the following:

- Employees feeling a sense of responsibility and accountability for their actions and for the actions of others
- Employees freely raising issues and concerns without fear of retaliation
- Managers modeling the behaviors they demand of others
- Managers communicating the importance of integrity when making difficult decisions
- Leadership understanding the pressure points that drive unethical behavior
- Leadership developing processes to identify and remedy these areas where the pressure points occur[22]

An example of an action that, although not reflected in its ethics code, reflects poor judgment by a top company official is that of Harry Stonecipher, the former chief executive officer of the Boeing Company. Stonecipher was asked to resign after he admitted to having a consensual affair with a female executive of Boeing.[23] This is a prime example of a company's board of directors examining the personal conduct of its top officials and taking action against conduct that appears to be inappropriate. The public exposure and ultimately the public's view is becoming more and more important because of the many corporate scandals.

Using Organizational Integrity to Link Corporate Culture to Corporate Compliance

Lynne Sharp Paine argues that the development of a strong corporate culture based on values and integrity can be used to ensure effective corporate compliance.[24] Paine argues that effective corporate compliance is not just providing a training program and a rule book, but it is the firm's responsibility to foster a corporate culture that supports integrity. These commitments to integrity are based on focusing on the firm's values, aspirations, and decision-making process. Management must be able to develop trust before managers can implement an effective corporate compliance system. With trust, the employees will challenge problems with the system especially if there are severe potential sanctions for noncompliance. In addition, employees who are not involved in the development of the compliance system will have less of a vested stake in the system and, therefore, a reduced level of commitment. In addition, Payne argues that a compliance system based solely on legal compliance does not inspire or motivate the employees to do their best ethically and professionally.

Furthermore, a legal compliance system is considered one based on moral mediocrity. As the former chairman of the SEC, Richard Breeden, stated, "It is not an adequate ethical standard to aspire to get through the day without being indicted"[25] By developing a corporate governance system based on integrity, the firm is held to a higher moral standard. Using organizational integrity as the basis of the governance system allows the employees to self-govern their actions based on a set of guiding principles established by the firm. The benefits of an integrity-based system includes bringing to life the guiding moral values of the firm, developing an ethical climate that supports ethical actions, and developing unified accountability of the actions among the employees.

A number of components need to occur before a firm can develop an effective integrity strategy: (1) The guiding moral values and commitments are communicated well and are easy to understand; (2) the top-level managers must be personally committed to the values and must be credible with their actions and be willing to take the necessary actions needed to support the values; (3) the moral guiding values must be integrated into the day-to-day decision making of the managers in the firm; (4) the company's information system and organizational structure must support the guiding moral values; and (5) the lower-level managers must have the autonomy, skills, knowledge, and competences to make ethical decisions based on the guiding moral values.

Ethics and Corporate Compliance

Deloitte argues that corporate compliance should not be considered a penalty of doing business, but an opportunity to incorporate a value-based approach to compliance issues.[26] Firms can use compliance programs to place positive ethical beliefs deep within the corporate culture of the firm. Incorporating values into the compliance programs decreases the exposure the firm has to legal liabilities and penalties in the future. Deloitte recommends a five-step process to embed positive ethics and values within the culture of the firm through its compliance program.

Step 1 is for the firm to do a risk and cultural assessment. During this step, management asks its employees via surveys and interviews what their assessment of the firm's culture is. In addition, management reviews any relevant documentation to see if there are any compliance gaps between the actual job performance of the employees and the ethical standards that have been established by the firm.

Step 2 is to review the current compliance program to determine if any revisions need to be made pertaining to the reporting structure, the methods of communication for employees, and any other components of the current compliance program.

Step 3 is to review the current ethical policies and procedures of the firm to ensure both the content and responsibilities coincide with the current ethical vision of the firm.

Step 4 is to review and revise, if necessary, the communication, training, and implementation phases of the compliance program. During this step, any gaps that were identified in the cultural assessment in step 1 can be resolved so there is no ambiguity about the ethical vision of the firm.

Step 5 is to develop an ongoing self-assessment of the compliance program. During this step, any revisions to the monitoring and reporting components of the compliance program can be adjusted if necessary.

Firms can approach designing a corporate governance system based on legal standards or one that is based on ethical standards. Surendra Arjoon compares the two approaches, which are shown in Table 6.3.[27]

The U.S. Federal Sentencing Guidelines for Organizations

No matter what changes are made in corporations, what changes are made in boards of directors, or what changes are mandated by regulations, there will always be some unethical activity. It is difficult to completely eliminate unethical behaviors in all people. However, many of the measures proposed recently are intended to help identify these unethical people and stop them before major scandals, such as those occurring recently in the business world, take place again. Top management will be forced to be more connected with what is happening in the organizations they direct. "If the Federal Sentencing Guidelines issued in November 1991 created the ethics profession, Sarbanes-Oxley created an entire industry. The new standards of doing business,

TABLE 6.3 ● A Comparison Between a Legal and Ethical Compliance Approach	
Ethics	
Legal View:	Ethics is viewed as a set of limits or a requirement
Ethical View:	Ethics is a set of agreed-upon principles that help guide choices
Objectives	
Legal View:	Objectives focus on preventing illegal acts
Ethical View:	Objectives focus on achieving responsible conduct
Method	
Legal View:	Focuses on rules and implements high level of monitoring and penalties when rules have been violated
Ethical View:	Views ethics as being integrated into all the actions of the firm (e.g., role of leadership, core business systems, strategic decision making)
Behavioral Assumptions	
Legal View:	Based on deterrence theory (identifying the negative consequences before the individual does the illegal action)
Ethical View:	Based on the development of individual and communal ethical values

Source: Surendra Arjoon, "Corporate Governance: An Ethical Perspective," *Journal of Business Ethics* 61, no. 4 (2005): 348.

introduced by legislators, regulators, and prosecutors over the past several years, have made the skills and experiences necessary to manage these risks by ethics and compliance officers much more important," said Keith Darcy, the executive director of the Ethics & Compliance Officer Association.[28]

The U.S. Federal Sentencing Guidelines for Organizations were passed in 1991 and were revised in 2004.[29] The guidelines state that organizations, like individuals, can be charged with and convicted of federal crimes. Although organizations cannot be sent to prison, they can be fined, sentenced to probation for as long as 5 years, and ordered to pay restitution to their victims. The most common criminal charges brought against organizations from the Federal Sentencing Guidelines, in order of frequency, are fraud, environmental waste discharge, violations of taxation, antitrust violations, and food and drug criminal violations. A major component of the sentencing guidelines is the requirement that organizations have an effective compliance program. Organizations can have their potential fines reduced by as much as 95% if they can prove to federal government officials that they had an effective compliance program in place when the criminal violation was committed by the organization. The seven criteria to be classified as an effective compliance program are (1) the firm must establish appropriate standards and formal procedures to detect and prevent criminal conduct; (2) oversight by a high-ranking employee within the organization; (3) implementing due care when assigning delegation responsibilities; (4) having an effective means of communicating the compliance system to everyone within the organization; (5) implementing "reasonable" steps to ensure compliance, including systems for monitoring, auditing, and reporting any illegal activity without any fear of reprisal; (6) having a consistent level of enforcement of the compliance standards including disciplinary procedures, when necessary; and (7) showing a good-faith effort to respond to and to prevent future illegal actions after the violations have been identified.

The Challenge of Compliance

PricewaterhouseCoopers conducted a global survey about the Sarbanes-Oxley Act. One of the interesting discoveries in this survey was about the benefits that businesspersons feel they will receive from the disclosures required in Section 404 of the Sarbanes-Oxley Act. These benefits include better information, better-informed management, greater reliance on audited accounts, greater transparency, reduction of overall risk, fewer frauds, more predictable earnings, and greater confidence.[30] It seems that Section 404 compliance is creating one of the biggest challenges for public companies. Deloitte has identified 10 possible threats to compliance with Section 404:

1. Lack of an enterprise-wide, executive-driven internal control management program
2. Lack of a formal enterprise risk management program
3. Inadequate controls associated with the recording of nonroutine, complex, and unusual transactions
4. Ineffectively controlled post-merger integration
5. Lack of effective controls over the IT environment
6. Ineffective financial reporting and disclosure preparation processes
7. Lack of formal controls over the financial closing process
8. Lack of current, consistent, complete, and documented accounting policies and procedures
9. Inability to evaluate and test controls over outsourced processes
10. Inadequate board and audit committee understanding of risk and control[31]

In addition, KPMG expanded the concept of management's documentation of internal control over the financial reporting aspect of the business. KPMG suggests that the documentation should include many kinds of supporting material, including company policy manuals, process models, accounting manuals, memoranda, flow charts, job descriptions, documents, forms, decision tables, procedural write-ups, and self-assessment reports.[32]

Corporate Compliance Systems and Global Corruption

Corruption is the conscious abuse of public roles and resources for the private benefit of a firm or the individuals of the firm. *Corruption* can be broadly defined as the use of bribery, extortion, or embezzlement for the benefit of one's own interests. *Bribery* is giving a financial benefit in return for influencing the decision of a person in a position of trust. *Extortion* is the use of intimidation or power in return for a financial benefit. *Embezzlement* is the taking of money illegally from a firm or other source.[33]

In general, corruption can be classified into three major types: petty corruption, grand corruption, and influence peddling.[34]

Petty corruption occurs when private individuals give illegal financial incentives to nonelected public officials in exchange for favorable dealings with certain government transactions. These transactions usually are related to taxes, low-level regulations, licensing, or some other low-level government issue.

Grand corruption occurs when illegal financial incentives are given to higher-ranked public officials. These high-level decisions usually include major infrastructure contracts, the purchasing of military equipment, or other major industry-based decisions.

Influence peddling occurs when illegal transactions take place along with legal transactions. An example of influence peddling would be illegal political campaign contributions.

Transparency International is a global civil society organization whose mission is to try to reduce corruption around the world. Transparency International developed an annual ranking of the level of corruption globally called the Corruption Perceptions Index (CPI). Table 6.4 shows the top and bottom countries with some notable others from the 2014 CPI ranking. The higher the CPI score, the lower the level of corruption within that country.

Transparency International also ranks global bribery in the Bribe Payers Index (BPI). The BPI identifies the propensity to pay bribes. A high BPI means there is a low likelihood that government officials will accept bribes. A listing of the 28 countries in the BPI index for 2011 is shown in Table 6.5.

TABLE 6.4 ● Corruption Perceptions Index for 2014

Rank	Country	CPI Score	Rank	Country	CPI Score
1	Denmark	92	14	United Kingdom	78
2	New Zealand	91	15	Belgium	76
3	Finland	89	15	Japan	76
4	Sweden	87	17	USA	74
5	Norway	86	100	China	36
5	Switzerland	86	103	Mexico	35
7	Singapore	84	136	Russia	27
8	Netherlands	83	171	South Sudan	15
9	Luxemburg	82	172	Afghanistan	12
10	Canada	81	173	Sudan	11
11	Australia	80	174	North Korea	8
12	Germany	79	174	Somalia	8
12	Iceland	79			

Source: http://www.transparency.org/cpi2014/results.

TABLE 6.5 ● BPI Scores by Country for 2011			
Country	BPI Score	Country	BPI Score
1. Netherlands	8.8	15. Hong Kong	7.6
1. Switzerland	8.8	15. Italy	7.6
3. Belgium	8.7	15. Malaysia	7.6
4. Germany	8.6	15. South Africa	7.6
4. Japan	8.6	19. Taiwan	7.5
6. Australia	8.5	19. India	7.5
6. Canada	8.5	19. Turkey	7.5
8. Singapore	8.3	22. Saudi Arabia	7.4
8. United Kingdom	8.3	23. Argentina	7.3
10. United States	8.1	23. United Arab Emirates	7.3
11. France	8.0	25. Indonesia	7.1
11. Spain	8.0	26. Mexico	7.0
13. South Korea	7.9	27. China	6.5
14. Brazil	7.7	28. Russia	6.1

Source: http://bpi.transparency.org/bpi2011/results/.

The ethical issues related to corruption are twofold for U.S.-based firms. Corruption is illegal under the U.S. Foreign Corrupt Practices Act (FCPA), and any act of corruption significantly negatively affects the image and perception of trust and honesty that the firm has with its various stakeholders.

The Cost of Corruption

Robert E. Kennedy and Rafael Di Tella argue that the costs of global corruption can be staggering. Its impact affects the country in which the corruption occurs and has a ripple effect in every country that has the same types of business transactions. Because corruption is used to gain a favorable advantage over others, corruption in one country can result in unfair trade practices relative to a country in which there is a low level of corruption. Kennedy and Di Tella present some estimated economic costs for different corruption activities. The comparison between economic cost and corruption activities is shown in Table 6.6.

The U.S. Foreign Corrupt Practices Act

The FCPA has evolved from the Corrupt Practices Act of 1907, which forbids firms from contributing to foreign political campaigns. FCPA was passed into law in 1977 and was amended in 1988. FCPA prohibits any U.S. firm and its foreign subsidiaries

TABLE 6.6   ● The Estimated Economic Cost of Certain Corrupt Activities

Corrupt Activity: Bureaucrat accepts money to speed up the issuing of licenses.

Economic Cost: 3% to 10% premium above licensing fee passed on to the consumers

Corrupt Activity: Organized crime operations control and set prices in the marketplace.

Economic Cost: Goods sold to the consumer at a premium of between 15% and 20%

Corrupt Activity: Tax collectors allow for the filing of underreported taxes in exchange for a bribe.

Economic Cost: Income tax revenue for the country can be reduced by up to 50%.

Corrupt Activity: Government official orders expensive capital good or purposely overpays for public works in exchange for a kickback.

Economic Cost: Goods and services in that country are priced 20% to 100% higher than necessary.

Source: Robert E. Kennedy and Rafael Di Tella, *Corruption in International Business (A)* (Boston: Harvard Business School, 2001), 4.

from giving foreign government officials any financial incentives in exchange for either obtaining or retaining any government business in that country. FCPA includes both U.S.-based firms and domestic concerns and individuals who are either citizens, nationals, or permanent residents of the United States. Criminal penalties for violation of FCPA can be as high as $2 million for a firm and $100,000 and 5 years in prison for an individual. Until the mid-1990s, FCPA was the only major government regulation in the world to make it illegal to pay bribes to get favorable actions from government officials. In comparison, other countries—including France, Germany, and Japan—tolerated having their nationals give bribes in other countries, and the bribes could be written off as business expenses on the firm's tax statements. After constant and intense lobbying by government officials in the United States, the 29 countries that are members of the Organisation for Economic Co-operation and Development (OECD) agreed to abide by an anticorruption agreement, called the Convention on Combating the Bribery of Foreign Public Officials, in November 1997.[35]

Questions for Thought

1. In the opening vignette, why do you think Sanford Weill believed it was important to stay on as chairman of the board after Charles Prince was picked as the new CEO? Why did three top-level employees at Citigroup want to leave after 2 years with Prince as CEO? Why do you think there were multiple ethical problems at Citigroup when Prince took over as CEO?

2. Explain why ethical decision making is so important in the strategic planning process.

3. Explain corporate culture in light of ethical conduct.

4. Examine the compliance program of a publicly held company. Does the company have a mission statement related to ethics? Comment on the program.

Real-Life Ethical Dilemma Exercise

IOC Investigates Selling Olympic Tickets[36]

The International Olympic Committee (IOC) started an investigation into allegations that Olympic officials from various countries offered to sell tickets for events at the London Olympic Games at highly inflated prices. The officials had legally obtained the tickets as part of their ticket allotment and had offered them for sale at very high prices. For example, tickets were being offered with an asking price of close to $10,000 for high-profile, high-demand events during the summer 2012 Olympics. The official rules of the IOC state that members of the official Olympic committee are not allowed to sell tickets outside their country, are not allowed to ask premium ticket prices, and are not allowed to sell tickets to unauthorized resellers. The *Sunday Times* newspaper in England presented evidence to the IOC about 27 officials who were willing to sell tickets at inflated prices to undercover reporters who posed as ticket dealers.

Questions for the Real-Life Ethical Dilemma Exercise

1. Should selling tickets at a higher price than the actual cost be illegal?

2. If the officials stated the money was going to government programs of their respective countries, would that make any difference in the decision from an ethical perspective?

3. Should the real solution be that the IOC charge a higher price for the tickets so that demand will equal supply?

Student Study Site

Visit the Student Study Site at **study.sagepub.com/stanwick3e** to access the following resources:

- Video Links
- SAGE Journal Articles
- Web Resources
- Web Quizzes

7

Decision Making and Human Resource Issues

If you don't have integrity, you have nothing. You can't buy it. You can have all the money in the world, but if you are not a moral and ethical person, you really have nothing.

—Henry Kravis

Chapter Objectives

After reading and studying Chapter 7, students should be able to

1. Describe the six stages of Kohlberg's moral development model.
2. Describe the two ethical studies done at Yale and Stanford Universities.
3. Describe the two components of organizational justice.
4. Explain the importance of workplace diversity from an ethical viewpoint.
5. Explain equity theory.
6. List the reasons employees steal from organizations and some of the red flags that could indicate employee theft.

The Triangle Shirtwaist Factory Fire: How Tragedy Can Create Change

During the early 1900s, the Lower East Side of Manhattan was a mecca for the garment industry. Thousands of people, mostly young women, worked in garment factories sewing the latest fashions. Many of the women were immigrants, and some were as young as 10 years old. One such business was the Triangle Shirtwaist Factory. The women worked 14 hours a day, 6 days a week for $2 a day or less. The owners would subtract from the paychecks the cost of needles, thread, and electricity used to make the shirts. The owners, Max Blanck and Isaac Harris, had a very profitable business, with sales of more than $1 million annually. The factory made only one type of women's blouse called the shirtwaist. They mass-produced the blouses because they faced ever-growing competition of 500 blouse makers just in Manhattan alone, and the shirtwaist was slowly becoming less fashionable after being stylish for 20 years. As part of their cost-efficient strategy, the owners charged the women for every mistake they made on the job, and the owners would not let the women stop for necessities such as a drink of water or to go to the bathroom.

On October 4, 1909, the workers at Triangle Shirtwaist went on strike for better working conditions, including shorter hours, more pay, and the ability to take breaks during the day. They also demanded the right to organize and form a union. The owners of Triangle hired people to threaten and beat up the strikers as they walked the picket line outside the factory. The workers finally went back to work after the owners agreed to concessions related to pay and work hours, but the owners refused to agree to let the workers form a union.

The Triangle Shirtwaist Factory was located in the Asch Building in Greenwich Village. The factory floor was on the 9th floor, and the owners had their offices on the 10th floor. On March 25, 1911, someone accidentally dropped a lit cigarette that caught fire on the 8th floor of the building. The owners of Triangle Shirtwaist were warned by a phone call that a fire had started in the building, and they were able to get on the roof and jump to a building next door. None of the 200 women on the factory floor on the 9th floor were told about the fire. The employees only realized there was a fire when they saw smoke moving into the ninth floor. The main exit was blocked by fire and the women's only option was going out the window onto the fire escape or crowding into a small elevator. Within minutes, the fire escape was pulled from the wall due to the weight of the women trying to escape. As a result, this was no longer a viable escape route. The elevator took two groups of women before it stopped working, leaving only one exit, the alternative stairway to the ground. When the women tried to escape through this exit, they quickly realized the door was locked and they could not get out. They were trapped inside. Some of the women jumped from the ninth floor. When the firefighters arrived, they realized that their ladders were not long enough to reach the ninth floor. In fact, the ladders could barely reach the sixth floor of the building. A total of 53 people had jumped from the window to their deaths, 19 more died when they fell in the elevator shaft, and another 20 died when they fell off the fire escape. At least another 50 burned to death on the ninth-floor factory level. A total of 23 of the dead were men, and nearly 50% of the women who died were teenagers. Altogether, 146 people died during the fire.[1]

The death of these workers was not in vain. This fire became the "final straw" in the belief that business owners can regulate themselves for the good of the workers. It created a fundamental shift in the government's role in protecting the rights and safety of the workers. In New York State, this fire led to the introduction of laws requiring fire sprinklers and fire drills in factories, requiring that doors must be unlocked and swing outward to allow employees a quicker exit, and limiting the work week to 54 hours without overtime. The federal government used this focus on worker reform to pass the National Labor Relations Act, also called the Wagner Act, in 1935, to protect the rights of workers and allow them to organize into unions. In addition, the federal government later passed legislation that related to maximum hours in the work week, set the minimum age of employment, set what would become the minimum wage, and led to the eventual introduction of the social security system. It was not a coincidence that the secretary of labor during Franklin D. Roosevelt's administration when these acts were passed was Frances Perkins, who 20 years earlier had watched the Triangle Shirtwaist fire from the street.[2]

Ethical Decision Making: Kohlberg's Six Stages of Moral Development

Throughout a manager's career, there are many opportunities to determine what ethical path the manager will take when making decisions. Although some decisions will be black and white, many others are shades of gray in which there are multiple "correct" solutions. Therefore, it is important for managers to understand how the "right thing to do" is determined when making decisions representing themselves and their organizations.

Lawrence Kohlberg[3] argues that there are six stages in the moral development of the individual. There are unique aspects to each stage and the type of ethical decisions made by the individual can vary from stage to stage.

Stage 1: Obedience and Punishment Orientation

In stage 1, individuals make moral decisions based on the consequences and repercussions of their actions. During this stage, individuals will make decisions that are accepted and obedient to others to ensure that they will not be punished for their actions.

Stage 2: Instrumental Purpose and Exchange

In stage 2, the individuals interpret the rules to determine whether they are beneficial to themselves. If the rules serve the self-interest of the individual, the rules will be followed. The individual will exchange his or her actions with another party if the perception is that the exchange is fair.

Stage 3: Interpersonal Accord, Conformity, Mutual Expectations

In stage 3, interpersonal relations and mutual respect affect the decision-making process of the individual. The individual acts based on what is expected of him or her by others. In addition, this "good" behavior is also based on the development of favorable interpersonal relations with others.

Stage 4: Social Accord and System Maintenance

In stage 4, decisions are made based on the obligations and duties that have been accepted by the individual. In this stage, the individual focuses on making a commitment to improving society and to upholding the laws of the land unless they directly conflict with the individual's perceptions of what is right for society.

Stage 5: Social Contract and Individual Rights

In stage 5, the belief becomes that because individuals may have a different set of values, it is important to view rules relative to the group, which must accept them. In this stage, the individual supports the rules that agree with society's social contract.

Stage 6: Universal Ethical Principles

In stage 6, the individual is governed by his or her own chosen ethical principles. As a result, the individual will support these principles even when they violate the law.

The result is that as the individual moves up the stages in moral development, the individual is driven more toward considering others and society. As individuals' moral development increases, so do their values. Their values become entrenched with the idea of refusing to implement immoral activities. Therefore, cheating decreases as the moral judgment level increases. The perception of how the manager reacts to an ethical dilemma varies significantly based on the moral development stage of the manager. In addition, obedience to immoral activities is also challenged as the level of moral judgment increases. As a result, individuals with higher moral development will refuse to obey orders that the individuals perceive as immoral or unethical.

The Role of Emotion in Moral Decision Making

Michael Wheeler and Juliana Pillemer argue that to understand how moral decisions are made, emotion must be included in the decision-making process.[4] Although the traditional belief is that moral decision making follows a linear pattern of problem, reason, and judgment, they argue that included in the reason component is an interaction between reason and emotion. Decision makers use heuristics or rules of thumb to help facilitate the decision-making process. Just as managers use intuition when they are making strategic and operational decisions, they also have moral intuition that guides their ethical decision-making processes.

Moral luck also has a role in moral decision making. Wheeler and Pillemer separate moral luck into three categories: resultant luck, circumstantial luck, and constitutive luck. An example of *resultant luck* occurs when two people fire guns at one another, and one shooter kills the other person but was not hit by the person killed. Even though both individuals performed the exact same actions, the results of the actions were vastly different. *Circumstantial luck* occurs when certain conditions or circumstances occur that allow the individual to demonstrate his or her moral values. An example is that one person could save the life of another person because he or she had the means and opportunity to save that life (i.e., pulling someone from the tracks of a subway), whereas another person may have the exact same moral beliefs but never have an opportunity to demonstrate it to others. The third type of luck is called constitutive luck. *Constitutive luck* is based on the background, family support system, and life experiences a person has before the moral decision is made. Influences from parents, teachers, friends, and members of the immediate family can help shape the moral value system of the decision maker.[5]

In 1963, Stanley Milgram's study of obedience was published in the *Journal of Abnormal and Social Psychology*. The Yale psychologist wanted to determine whether individuals in particular settings would be willing to obey orders even if they knew the consequences could be fatal. The origin of the study was based on the actions of soldiers in Nazi Germany who systematically killed millions of people based on direct orders from their commanders. The volunteers were picked at random for Milgram's study. An advertisement was published in a New Haven newspaper, and a mail solicitation was sent to people in the surrounding New Haven, Connecticut, area. Forty males between the ages of 20 and 50 were selected from those who responded to the advertisements, which described the study as one in which the volunteers would be testing the memory and learning of subjects at Yale University. The occupations of the volunteers who were selected included salesmen, engineers, manual laborers, postal workers, and high school teachers. In actuality, the study was to determine whether these volunteers would obey orders even if it could result in the death of the subject. No one was actually in danger—because all of the subjects were working with Milgram on the study. Milgram had developed a simulated or fake electric shock generator that was used by the volunteers. Whenever the subject failed to say the correct answer, the volunteer was to "shock" the subject. For each wrong answer, the volunteer was ordered to increase the power of the shock. The fake electric shock generator had levels marked with a range from 15 to 450 volts. At the highest levels, the description with the volts was "Danger: Severe Shock." As the volunteer became more hesitant about administering the shock, the experimenter would prod the volunteer by saying that the volunteer must continue. The second time the volunteer hesitated, the experimenter reminded the volunteer that the experiment must be completed and that the volunteer must continue. The third time the experimenter stated that it is absolutely essential that the volunteer continue, and by the fourth time, the volunteer is told he does not have any other choice but to continue with the experiment. As the volt level increased, the subject would yell and beg the volunteer to stop the process of shocking him. Before the experiment started, the researchers expected that only a very few people, if any, would obey the order to administer the most extreme shock of 450 volts. The researchers expected that the level of Very Strong Shock (195 to 240 volts) would be the point where most, if not all, the subjects would refuse to go any farther.[6]

The results showed that *all* 40 volunteers went past the 240-volt stage. The first stopping point came at the top of the Intense Shock range at 300 volts. Five volunteers refused to go any further. In the Extreme Intensity Shock range, four volunteers left at 315, two left at 330, and one left at each 345 and 360. In the Danger: Severe Shock range, one volunteer refused at 375 volts. All of the remaining 26 volunteers went to the extreme "XXX" voltage of 450 volts, which would have likely caused death if it were actually administered. Thus, 65% of the participants would have obeyed the order to "kill" the subject.[7] Milgram proved that ordinary people can do horrendous things when they are ordered to. People are willing to inflict extreme and potentially fatal punishment on others without having the self-control to stop themselves from performing the "torture." Individuals will seek to rationalize their behavior if they believe there are ethical issues related to that behavior.

Rationalizing Unethical Behaviors

Ethics is about doing the right thing and making the right choices, not just presenting the right idea. Corporations are not responsible for making ethical decisions; the people working at those corporations have the ultimate responsibility for decisions made, ethical or unethical. Managers will begin to cut corners and play accounting games when trying to raise share prices, ultimately trying to satisfy the shareholders and increase their own bonuses. The Institute of Business Ethics has identified three simple ethical tests to use for a business decision: transparency, effect, and fairness.

Transparency

Transparency refers to deciding if one accepts having others know what one has decided. The more open and transparent a person is in discussing his or her actions with others, the more comfortable the person is that he or she has made the right decision.

Effect

Effect refers to determining whom the decision affects. Decision makers must always be aware who will be directly or indirectly influenced by their actions. The decision maker must not assume that the effect will be only minimal to others.

Fairness

Fairness refers to determining if the decision would be considered fair by those affected by it. A decision maker must understand the perspective of each person who is affected by the decision to ensure that the decision is just to all.

In defining the boundaries of business ethics, one could view the binary considerations: discretionary actions and nondiscretionary actions. *Discretionary actions* are those actions that one can compromise within established boundaries. *Nondiscretionary actions* are those that one cannot change; that is, there is only one acceptable way of acting. Nondiscretionary actions include laws and regulations, public and employee safety, and truthfulness of records and statements.[8]

Without appropriate support from upper management or from an enforceable code of ethics, many employees may struggle with what should be done. Employees must understand what is expected of them when facing ethical dilemmas. For example, Texas Instruments first addressed the issue of ethics more than 60 years ago when managers developed ethical principles for the company, but the first written code of ethics appeared for the company in 1961. Then, in 1987, the company opened the Texas Instruments Ethics Office and appointed an ethics director. All current Texas Instruments employees are issued a small booklet with a short test that encourages the company's employees to make the right ethical decisions. The test consists of seven steps, which include the following:

- Is the action legal?
- Does it comply with our values?
- If you do it, will you feel bad?
- How will it look in the newspaper?
- If you know it's wrong, don't do it!
- If you're not sure, ask.
- Keep asking until you get an answer.[9]

No matter what the decision, each person will ultimately be responsible for his or her ethical choices. But knowing what an ethical dilemma is may be difficult for some people.

Interactionist Model of Ethical Decision Making in Organizations

Linda Trevino developed an interactionist ethics model in which both individual and situational variables were considered.[10] Trevino believes that ethical decision making can be explained by the interaction of the individual and situational components. The cognitive moral development stage of the individuals determines how individuals approach resolving an ethical dilemma. Trevino identifies the critical individual variables as ego strength, field dependence, and locus of control.

Ego strength is the strength of conviction or self-regulation by the individual. Individuals with high ego strength will follow their convictions and resist impulse decisions. *Field dependence* refers to the ability of using external information to help resolve an ambiguous situation. *Locus of control* refers to the individual's perception of how much control he or she has over an activity or event. If an individual has an internal locus of control, the individual believes he or she can have control over the activity. If the individual has an external locus of control, he or she believes that the outcome of the event is beyond his or her control.

The situational variables Trevino included were immediate job context, organizational culture, and the characteristics of the work. *Immediate job context* refers to the rewards or punishment that will be assigned to individuals based on their behavior related to the ethical issue. *Organizational culture* can allow individuals in the firm to be given autonomous decision-making authority that gives them the freedom to make their own decisions. By giving the individuals the authority and accountability for their decisions, companies can enhance the individual's moral stage development. *Characteristics of work* refers to the ability of the individual to develop expanded job responsibilities and roles within the firm and, therefore, "mature" as an employee. This resulting process can encourage the maturing of the moral development as the employee moves to a higher moral development stage.[11]

Ethical Decision Making and Moral Intensity

Thomas Jones argues that the level of moral intensity affects the ethical decision-making process.[12] *Moral intensity* refers to the extent in which the severity of the moral issues affect the decision maker. Moral intensity has a number of components: magnitude of consequences, social consensus, probability of effect, temporal immediacy, proximity, and concentration of effect.

Magnitude of Consequences

The magnitude of consequences relates to the aggregate of the harm or benefit done to the victims or beneficiaries based on the moral decision made by the manager. This utilitarian approach views whether this decision will benefit many or none in relation to the impact on others.

Social Consensus

Social consensus refers to the degree to which society would agree that the act is either good or evil. For example, it could be argued that the evil of bribing a customs official in Texas would be higher than the evil of bribing a customs official in Mexico. In other words, local society values determine the level of morality of the action.

Probability of Effect

Probability of effect refers to the decision maker's perception of the probability that the act will take place and the probability, if the act does take place, that harm or benefit will affect the stakeholders of the firm. For example, if a gun is sold to a criminal, the probability is that harm would come to various members of the community.

Temporal Immediacy

Temporal immediacy refers to the amount of time that will take place between when the decision is being made and the consequences of the action. The shorter the length of time is, the greater the level of immediacy will be. For example, the reduction of retirement benefits will have a greater level of immediacy to current retirees than to those workers in their forties.

Proximity

Proximity is the feeling of closeness or nearness the decision maker has with the individuals affected by the moral dilemma. For example, a manager would have a greater feeling of proximity in making a decision to lay off workers in a plant in his or her hometown than in a plant in another country.

Concentration of Effect

Concentration of effect occurs when a relatively small number of people with a large stake in the action of the firm are affected by the decision. For example, a concentration of effect would occur when a firm changes its warranty policy under which 10 people would lose a claim of $10,000 compared with a change in policy in which 10,000 people would lose their claims of $10 each.

The Role of Power and Influence in Ethical Decisions[13]

Power tends to corrupt, and absolute power corrupts absolutely.

—Lord Acton

With great power comes great responsibility.

—Uncle Ben Parker reminding Peter Parker (Spider-Man) of his duties

As is highlighted in most of the cases in this textbook, managers have to make sure that they do not cross the legal and ethical boundaries when they use their formal and informal power within the organization. Abuse of power can lead to rampant unethical behavior, resulting in the ultimate demise of the organization (e.g., WorldCom and Enron).

A disturbing validation of Lord Acton's warning was highlighted in the Stanford prison experiment. A Stanford University researcher wanted to research how ordinary, normal people would respond when some people were arbitrarily given power over other people. A sample of mentally stable, middle-class, intelligent male subjects was divided into two groups: prisoners and guards. Both groups were clearly told that this was just an experimental simulation to observe their behavior. The 2-week study was shut down after 6 days because the behavior of the subjects got out of control. The "guards" inflicted continuous punishment on the prisoners for minor "violations" or for no reason at all, and the "prisoners" emotionally broke down because they were helpless to defend themselves against the "guards." This experiment returned to the forefront when the treatment of the prisoners in the Abu Ghraib prison in Iraq became public in 2004.[14]

Managing Power

The Stanford experiment highlighted that anyone can potentially use power to abuse others and enhance his or her own self-interests. To use power in an ethical manner, a person must meet two standards. The first concerns the power being exercised to benefit others who have granted the decision maker the power with the expectation that the decision maker will serve others. In other words, the decision maker uses his or her power to support the best interests of the firm. The second standard is that the power conforms to both the legal and accepted cultural standards of what is considered ethical behavior. Therefore, it would be unethical or illegal to use the decision maker's power to enhance the interests of the firm while not abiding by the ethical standards established by society. For most new managers, a transformation takes place as a shifting takes place in job responsibility.[15] What was once an employee who has specific skills and job responsibilities becomes a manager who is now a generalist seeking to address agenda items. In their previous capacities, employees were considered individual workers, but as managers, they need to establish networks to get compromises and agreements. As such, managers must be political to accomplish their agendas. Managers must develop their own informal power to manage key relationships. Formal power is the type of power that is associated with the job title. Informal power is the type of power that managers can develop by having strong positive relationships with others. The benefit of informal power is the ability of others to act for the benefit of the manager when the manager's formal power cannot be used to "order" that action to take place.

Influence

Influence can be defined as the ability to change the viewpoint of another person based on verbal and nonverbal actions. Power is something an individual has, but influence is something that an individual can do. As a result, people use power to influence the actions of others. Influence can be an effective tool because it is not a direct use of power. As a result, the manager can "save" the direct use of power for when it is the only option available to change the actions of another employee.[16]

Influence can be used ethically if the adjustment of the viewpoint of another person results in both parties achieving a beneficial result. An unethical use of influence can occur when manipulation is used to alter the viewpoint of another person. Manipulation occurs when the true intentions of the person are hidden and may only become evident after the decision has been implemented. Manipulation tactics can include exaggerating your demands when negotiating with another party; strongly recommending an employee for another job not because of his or her merits, but because the manager does not want that employee to be working for the manager any longer; and spreading misleading or false information to force another party to respond in a manner that will support the self-interests of the manager.[17]

A Machiavellian Approach to Decision Making

Niccolò Machiavelli was born in Florence, Italy, in 1469. In 1532, his book *The Prince* was published. He began writing this book in 1513. Drawing from his previous experience in Italian politics, Machiavelli described how a prince was able to obtain and maintain his power. His "ultimate" prince was one who was calculating and amoral and did whatever was necessary to stay in power. The value of the leader is based on the ultimate success of the leader. This includes using force when necessary against internal and external enemies to ensure the most favorable result. The leader must crush any people who oppose or challenge him or her to send the message to all potential future challengers not to attempt to oppose him or her. Machiavelli described the perfect leader as one who was able to manipulate, was bold in his actions, and was stealthy when he needed to be. The prince, or leader, must be able to execute his actions based on not what ought to be done but on what actions served the leader's self-interests. The prince reminds the reader, "It is better to be feared than to be loved."

After *The Prince* was published, Machiavelli was forever linked with his amoral prince. In fact, the noun *Machiavellian* means one who uses whatever means possible to obtain and maintain power within an organization. Furthermore, two researchers, Richard Christie and Florence L. Geis developed a survey called Mach-IV to evaluate an individual's level of Machiavellianism.[18] Questions on the Mach-IV include "Do you never tell anyone the true reason you do something unless there is some benefit?" and "Is it true that everyone has a vicious streak in them and it will emerge when given an opportunity?"[19]

How to Control Power and Influence

A number of avenues are available to ensure that power and influence are exercised in an ethical manner. Firms must make sure that the policies and standards of the firm are based on the highest ethical standards possible. Furthermore, these policies and procedures must be enforced at all times. It is also imperative that each individual's performance evaluation is based, in part, on his or her ethical performance. An evaluation must occur to ensure that managers are not misusing their power and influence. Top executives must interact with lower-level employees so they can be role models for ethical behavior.[20]

Human Resource Issues

By providing an ethical climate in which ethical actions are expected, supported, and rewarded, the firm can strengthen employees' commitment to the firm and increase the level of job satisfaction, which will result in lower employee turnover rates. Having job satisfaction means the employee is pleased with the achievement and appraisal of his or her job performance. A strong ethical climate positively reinforces the positive aspects of the employee's job as well as reduces the level of ambiguity by having established policies and procedures pertaining to the ethical conduct of the employee. Employee commitment is based on the ability of employees to be committed to the goals and values of the firm, which results in their remaining loyal to the firm and providing high levels of effort as part of their job performance. Thus, employee commitment can be perceived as a psychological bond that connects the employee to the firm. Low levels of employee commitment can lead to dysfunctions in the firm, whereas high levels lead to increased motivation and productivity of the employees. Furthermore, low levels of employee commitment increase the probability of employee turnover. If the employee is not committed and loyal to the firm, the employee is more willing to seek a job with another firm. By developing organizational practices and procedures that support ethical conduct, the firm shows that its organizational ethical commitment will support the employees' ethical commitment. In addition, a strong positive ethical climate relies on the use of rewards and punishment to ensure the behavior of the employees coincides with the ethical vision of the firm.[21]

In other words, there must be an ethical fit between the employee and the firm.[22] The ethical matching between the employee and the firm starts before the employee is hired. During the selection process, it is one of the duties of the human resources department to evaluate whether the potential employee is a correct match for the job. The correct matching includes technical and interpersonal skills as well as ethical values and commitment. The ethical match starts at the very beginning of the employee's career. However, it does not stop at this point. This employee–firm ethical matching continues throughout the employee's career.

Although many firms and employees remain constant in their ethical values and commitment, variances can take place. For example, over time either the firm or the employee can shift ethical values "toward the dark side." Therefore, just as Darth Vader and Luke Skywalker battle good versus evil, the firm and the employee battle between a disconnect of their ethical fit. If the employee feels that the ethical climate of the firm has shifted away from a positive ethical value system, the employee is more likely to become less productive and eventually leave the organization.[23]

Enlightened firms realize a strong positive ethical climate improves the commitment of the employees and can help employees be more successful in reaching their career objectives.[24] A positive ethical climate results in increased productivity and the reduction of stress, which allows the employee to establish and achieve aggressive career goals knowing that the firm's ethical commitment supports the employee's career progress. Therefore, fostering an ethical climate that supports organizational justice also allows the employees to focus their time on achieving their individual performance objectives instead of "wasting" time on political battles and building up their stress related to how they are being unfairly treated by biased or subjective decisions made by the supervisors.

The establishment of a transparent organizational justice system within the firm eliminates employees' mistrust and anxiety about unfair treatment. Organizational justice has two components: distributive justice and procedural justice. *Distributive justice* relates to the fairness of management decisions on performance issues such as salary and promotions. *Procedural justice* refers to how managerial decisions are made based on formal rules, regulations, and due process, which directly or indirectly affects the employee.[25]

The Role of Workplace Diversity

As the economy becomes increasingly unified globally, the necessity of diversity within firms will only increase in importance. Although in the past, one argument was that it was easier to have decision makers from the same background and viewpoint make decisions, a more enlightened viewpoint is that alternative perspectives will no longer be a luxury but will be a requirement for a business to be sustainable in the long term. Because alternative viewpoints are presented that may match the alternative consumer preferences globally, diversity is the ethical thing to do, and it is a good business decision. The ability to adapt, to understand differences in consumer tastes, and to address country and culture specific issues results in higher financial performance for the firm.

There are different types of diversity: task-related diversity, traits and values diversity, and demographic diversity. *Task-related diversity* is based on having employees with different educational and or professional backgrounds. *Traits and values diversity* relates to diversity in personalities, values, or vision of the firm's future course. Demographic diversity relates to having employees of both genders with different ages, different ethnic backgrounds, and different belief systems.[26] With diversity comes an ethical climate that fosters psychological safety. Psychological safety refers to the employees' perceptions that they will be accepted in the workplace and that their ideas will be heard and considered by management. In addition, this may foster a creative and innovative environment because the employees are not "afraid" to present their ideas. The diversity of the workplace can build and revise the strategic vision of the firm. Managers must facilitate this type of supporting climate by encouraging input and feedback and developing a trusting relationship with their subordinates.[27]

Although diversity will enhance a firm's competitive position, some firms will challenge the benefits of demographic diversity by downplaying their effectiveness. These negative attitudes of diversity are based on prejudice, racism, ignorance, discrimination, and stereotyping. Furthermore, some individuals can feel "uncomfortable" around people who are not similar to themselves.[28]

Ethical Climate and Organizational Misbehavior

Organizational misbehavior or misconduct is any behavior by an employee or group of employees that defies or violates the organizational norms, values, or standards of proper conduct. Organizational misbehavior can be classified into three different types: Type S is misbehavior that benefits oneself, Type O is misbehavior that is intended to benefit the organization, and Type D is misbehavior that is intended to inflict damage to the organization. For example, the personal use of company equipment is Type S misbehavior, whereas giving false information to try to sell the firm's product would be Type O misbehavior. If the employee destroyed or otherwise damaged company property, that would be considered Type D misbehavior. Yoav Vardi and Ely Weitz found that employees who exhibit Type S and Type D organizational misbehavior are more likely to evaluate the positive and negative consequences of their actions before they act compared with employees exhibiting Type O misbehavior.[29]

The employee's imagination is usually the only limit to the type of destructive behavior that he or she can implement in the workplace. Mild examples of destructive behavior include calling in sick to miss work or using the work computer for personal business. More drastic measures can include sexually harassing other employees, sabotaging production, stealing material goods and money, behaving violently, misusing alcohol, and using illegal drugs. Furthermore, these dangerous behaviors can "catch on" with other employees who will copy the same type of behavior. Wendi Everton and colleagues argue that deviance or misbehavior can be classified into four categories: production deviance, political deviance, property deviance, and personal aggression.[30] Production deviance and political deviance are considered less severe behavior than are property deviance and personal aggression. In addition, production deviance and property deviance are more harmful to the firm, whereas political deviance and personal aggression are more harmful to individuals within the firm.

Production Deviance

Production deviance includes such actions as pretending to be sick to miss work, using firm equipment for personal use, not being as efficient as possible with the use of resources, working at a slower pace than is possible, and taking numerous breaks from work.

Political Deviance

Political deviance includes actions such as acting in an uncivilized manner, accusing and blaming the wrong people when mistakes are made, starting false rumors and gossip that can be harmful to employees, and supervisors requiring employees work beyond their job description and responsibilities.

Property Deviance

Property deviance includes actions such as stealing money or material items from the firm, misusing discount privileges given to the employees, claiming more money than was actually spent on an expense account, accepting bribes and/or kickbacks, and sabotaging or destroying firm property.

Personal Aggression

Personal aggression includes actions such as physical and verbal aggression, sexual harassment, and a boss refusing to provide resources, including compensation that was promised.[31] Misbehavior of the employees can be "taught" through the example of the managers. Similar to a parent–child relationship, employees will observe the behavior of the managers and assume that this behavior is acceptable. By "talking the talk" and not "walking the walk," managers allow their subordinates to develop organizational misbehavior if the manager is also misbehaving from an organizational perspective. By setting the example and communicating the firm's values and expectations, managers can support positive employee behavior, but when they set negative behavior as the example, the employees might follow the same type of actions as the managers.

Another avenue where the manager sets the ethical tone for the employees is the reward system. If employees perceive that they are unfairly rewarded for their efforts, they will potentially reduce their efforts or execute deviant behavior such as stealing. An employee rationalizes this behavior as "equalizing" the inputs to outputs. This is the basis of equity theory, which states that every employee will compare his or her inputs (effort, productivity, loyalty) with his or her outcomes (raises, promotions, recognition). If the employee perceives that his or her inputs to outcomes ratio is not equal to that of other employees, the employee will either reduce the inputs (exerting less effort) for the same outcomes or provide the same inputs for higher outcomes (stealing resources) because he or she feels entitled to these additional resources because of the inequality that is supported by the organizational climate. Therefore, an ethical climate would ensure that there is an equitable distribution of rewards and other outcomes based on the same level of inputs by the employees.[32]

Just as the manager plays a critical role in determining whether an employee implements organizational misbehavior, so does the work group of which the employee is a member. If the group presents a positive ethical climate, it will facilitate the employee supporting the group and the firm. Factors that could affect the positive nature of the work group include group cohesiveness, helping others, and peer leadership support and facilitation. As a result, if the employee is a member of a group that supports his or her effort and the group supports each member's actions, all members know that they will be treated fairly and will support this type of ethical climate as part of their everyday operations and will not engage in organizational misbehavior.[33]

By acknowledging the powerful impact equity theory can have on an employee's decision whether to misbehave, managers need to ensure that there is effective justice in the workplace. Managers need to consider three types of justice: distributive justice, procedural justice, and interactional justice.

Distributive justice is the distribution of rewards on an equitable, and not a political, basis. This type of justice is effective if provided in a fair ethical climate where the conditions and criteria of the awards are announced to the employees before the employees are evaluated. A firm's most valuable resource is its people, and the value added by the employees is through ideas.

Procedural justice focuses on the development, implementation, and maintenance of fair and unbiased procedures in which unintentional mistakes are viewed as part of the learning process where corrections can be made. Procedural justice is a bottom-up approach in which managers ask *and* listen to what the subordinates are telling them.

Interactional justice is to ensure the manager has the proper interaction with the subordinates. The manager must communicate that only civil behavior is acceptable in the firm. In addition, if it is necessary, the manager needs to explain the rationale of why a decision has been made.[34]

Employee Theft

Of all the types of deviance or misbehavior, it appears that employee theft is the most common. A number of factors could explain this, including equity issues and an employee's desperate need of money or material items. Equity theory has been studied and linked as a direct cause of employee theft. One study examined what would happen if, in one group, employee pay decreased temporarily by 15% while another group did not have any reduction in pay. Researchers found that employee theft increased drastically in the group that suffered the pay cut. In addition, when the pay cuts were explained thoroughly and with sensitivity, the level of employee theft decreased in the pay cut group.[35]

It could also be argued, however, that theft may be the most common type of misbehavior because every day anyone within the firm has an opportunity to steal. Whether it is money from the petty cash or three pencils for home use, the work environment is always enticing for theft due to opportunity as well as low probability of being caught. Employees steal from their employers for four general reasons. The first reason is economic pressure the employees must address, and they believe that stealing can help "solve" their financial problems. The second reason is the opportunity to steal. Employees must be given the time and access to steal from their employers. The third reason is the employee's attitude. Whether it is equity theory or some other rationale, employees believe that they are not being treated fairly and they are "entitled" to these assets from the firm. The fourth reason that employees steal results from their social norms. They may believe that stealing is not wrong if they perceive that there is a good explanation or justification to steal based on their social beliefs.[36] The average organization will lose the equivalent of 5% of its revenue to employee theft annually. Based on this estimate, approximately the equivalent of $3 trillion is stolen by employees globally and approximately $40 billion in the United States. The U.S. Department of Justice estimates that approximately one in three employees have, or will have in the future, committed some form of employee theft. To understand the full impact of employee theft, it is estimated that one third of all business bankruptcies that have occurred in the United States are the direct result of employee theft. The bottom-line impact of employee theft can be staggering. For example, if an employee steals $150,000 from the firm and the firm has a bottom-line profit margin of 5%, the company would have to generate an additional $3 million in sales just to recover the cost of the theft.[37]

A number of red flags can lead to suspicion that an employee is stealing from the employer: always rewriting records for minor reasons such as making the notes look neater; refusing to take vacation or sick days that would mean someone else would be doing the employee's job; working extended hours; being very resistant to give other employees certain files or data; having the appearance of a standard of living that does not match the employee's level of compensation; liking to gamble given any opportunity; refusing to be transferred or being promoted; responding to questions in a vague and opaque manner; getting angry and hostile when asked certain legitimate work-related questions; very quickly correcting any mistakes or errors; trying to accuse others of wrongdoing to switch the focus of the investigation; having a close relationship with fellow employees that does not seem normal; and excessive drinking or dependence on legal or illegal drugs.[38]

Firms can take different approaches to reduce employee theft, including a three-stage approach presented by Arthur Gross-Schaefer et al.[39] Stage 1 is a prevention tactic for keeping the potential "thieves" away from the company by not hiring them. The firm should ensure that it has an effective screening system to block potential thieves from being hired by the company. This screening system should include using personal interviews, reference and credit checks of the applicant, and other types of verbal and written tests to attempt to identify potential misbehavior. Of course, these screening techniques are not guaranteed to always work to eliminate thieves from the organization, so once the individuals have been hired, the firm needs to focus on stage 2, which is the prevention and detection of a criminal behavior. During this stage, the firm's monitoring and control systems are tested. Tools such as surveillance cameras, monitoring software, employee tracking systems, security control systems, check and balances for financial transactions, control and auditing systems, training programs, and establishing an anonymous whistle-blowing system to allow employees to notify the firm about theft. Stage 3 involves addressing the actions that should be taken once an employee has been caught stealing from the firm. The type of disciplinary procedures that are adopted by the firm should have the flexibility to assign different types of punishment based on the severity of the theft. However, if a theft has been committed, it is the firm's responsibility to prosecute the employee to the full extent of the law. If firms are not aggressive in pursuing prosecutions, the message will filter back to the other employees that theft is not a serious offense in the firm.[40]

Sexual Harassment and Sexual Discrimination

One of the most serious types of deviance or misbehavior is sexual harassment. In 2011, the Equal Employment Opportunity Commission (EEOC) received 11,364 claims of sexual harassment. Of those claims, 16.3% of the claims were filed by males. The EEOC also recorded payments of $52.3 million in 2011 to resolve previous claims.[41] A typical example of sexual harassment is one in which the initial communication is not harassing but evolves over time to become more explicit and sexual. Communication could start with innocent comments, such as "I am glad you are my employee" or "You are a funny person." Using this as an invitation to pursue the relationship further, the harasser will become more explicit and harassing when communicating his or her desires. When the harassed employee refuses the sexual advances, the negative repercussions of the refusal are stated to the employee. With the advent of e-mail and electronic texting, what was usually done through verbal discussion now can be presented as valuable evidence.

Furthermore, sexual harassment can be very costly, financially. The best-case scenario for a firm might be to settle without a trial by agreeing on a summary judgment. The legal cost of this easy solution can be a legal bill of as much as $100,000.[42]

Sexual harassment cases now and in the future will less likely be based solely on a "he said, she said" debate.[43] However, there is still a subjective nature to the claim of sexual harassment and sexual discrimination. For example, one federal appeals court ruled that a manager asking an employee for dates, describing her as a "dumb blonde," and attempting to kiss the employee three times was not sexual harassment. However, in another case, a woman was exposed to pornography on computers, on televisions at work, and in office mail; another court ruled that the actions were sufficient for a sexual harassment claim. In addition, if the employee is charging his or her coworkers with sexual harassment, the employee must prove the employer knew about it and did not properly responded when notified about the harassment.[44]

Sexual harassment will make an ethical climate toxic and unworkable. Regardless of whether the harassment is verbal or physical, this type of behavior must be stopped immediately with a zero-tolerance level. If this type of behavior is allowed to continue, significant negative issues will occur including reduction of productivity, motivation, loyalty, and significant legal liability. Specifically, a victim can struggle with a number of very serious negative consequences from being sexually harassed. These consequences include having a much lower level of job satisfaction, lower levels of commitment toward the firm, the physical and mental withdrawing from his or her job and the workplace, physical and mental disorders, and significant levels of stress including symptoms of posttraumatic stress disorder. As a result, sexual harassment can significantly affect the career of the victim.[45] The principal law that makes sexual harassment a criminal activity is Title VII of the Civil Rights Act of 1964. Title VII outlaws any type of discrimination regardless of race, color, religion, sex, and national origin. Although not specifically presented in that listing, victims have used Title VII to explain that sexual harassment was a form of sexual discrimination. The EEOC defines two types of sexual harassment: "quid pro quo" and "hostile work environment."[46]

Quid Pro Quo

Quid pro quo refers to an arrangement between the harasser and the victim where the victim will provide a sexual favor in return for a job favor such as a promotion or bonus. Alternatively, the arrangement could be a sexual favor in return for the boss not firing or demoting the victim. Regardless of the arrangement, the boss is using his or her level of authority and power to coerce the victim into providing sexual favors.

Hostile Work Environment

In a hostile work environment, one act does not necessarily create a hostile environment, but a series of events or activities can create a hostile atmosphere where the victim's fear results in loss of productivity and commitment to the firm. Within a hostile work environment, the victim will either report the environment or attempt to move to a different firm that does not have a hostile environment.[47] Six major categories of sexual harassment can occur within a hostile work environment: making sexual comments, sexual looks or gestures, nonsexual touching, sexual touching, expected socializing by the victim with the harasser, and expected sexual activity by the victim.[48]

The organizational climate plays a key role in the development and elimination of sexual harassment. First, a positive ethical climate will support the rights of the victim and should stop sexual harassment before it actually occurs. To succeed with this goal, management must first make sure the organizational climate does not make it "risky" to report harassment. The victim must be able to report any action without any fear of retaliation by the harasser. Second, the organizational climate must support appropriate punishment for sexual harassment. If there is a lack of sanctions against the harasser, it will invite the harasser to do it again, and it will encourage others to harass as well. Third, when a victim does report an incident, it must be followed through in a serious and professional manner. The victim must feel comfortable that judgment will be served at the end of the investigation. Another factor that can affect the level of sexual harassment within a firm is the gender context of the job. Job gender context refers to the ratio of men to women in the work group, the sex of the supervisor, and the perception of whether the job has been traditionally dominated by one gender.[49] Sexual discrimination is also covered under the Civil Rights Act and is related to the unfair treatment of employees because of their gender. As with sexual harassment, sexual discrimination is used when someone in power has the ability to unfairly manipulate the work environment for the employee.

A Silicon Valley Example of Sexual Discrimination[50]

Ellen Pao, a junior partner with the venture capital firm Kleiner Perkins Caufield & Byers, filed a sexual discrimination lawsuit against the company and selected employees. Kleiner et al. had helped fund start-ups such as Netscape, Amazon, and Google. Pao received a degree in electrical engineering from Princeton University and a law degree from Harvard University.

Although one might assume that venture capital companies investing in future-oriented Silicon Valley enterprises would be gender blind in their operations, this lawsuit claims that this is not the case. One colleague told Pao that women would never succeed at the company because they are too quiet, and another colleague explained that women are not invited to a big deal dinner because they will distract from the business atmosphere and "kill the buzz." The lawsuit claims that Kleiner had discriminated against Pao and other women in the company "by failing to promote them comparably to men, by compensating them less than men through lower salary, bonus and carried interest, by restricting the number of investments that women are allowed to make as compared to men." Pao also claimed that women are excluded from meetings and discussions and were not given the opportunity to be visible and successful. The bias toward women may be spread across the industry. Women are on only 9.1% of the boards of directors of Silicon Valley–based companies, whereas the Standard & Poor's 500 average is 16%. In 2009, only 11% of women who were either the CEO or founder of the company received venture capital funding.

Office Bullying

Office bullying is related but subtly different from sexual harassment. Office bullying often includes both verbal and physical harassment, but the actions are not based on the gender of the employee. Indeed, it could be argued that office bullying could be renamed *office harassment* without losing any of the negative impacts of office bullying that is inflicted on others. However, one critical difference between discrimination and bullying is that claims against discrimination are protected by the Civil Rights Act. Although it is illegal to discriminate based on gender, age, and race, this protected legal status does not apply to office bullying. Most office bullying is based on a dislike for another person, and it is not illegal to not like a colleague or subordinate. As with sexual harassment, there are a significant number of gray areas in which it could be argued that the actions should be punished.[51]

Supervisors use their power to bully their subordinates, and even the famous are not immune to bullying charges. As CEO of eBay, current CEO of Hewlett-Packard Meg Whitman was accused of pushing an eBay employee into a conference room when she got angry with the employee. The employee subsequently hired a lawyer, and the case was settled out of court for an estimated $200,000.[52] Office bullying is a very common experience felt by millions of American workers. In a study of U.S. workers, a staggering 41.4% of the respondents, which represent 47 million workers, have experienced psychological aggression at least once during the previous year. In addition, 13% of the respondents representing 15 million workers experience psychological aggression on a weekly basis. Examples of bullying include unwarranted or invalid criticism of the worker, blame given to a worker without proper justification, an employee being treated differently than the rest of the group for no valid reason, the employee having to listen to offensive language, the employee being isolated during meetings and discussion, the employee being shouted at, the employee being humiliated, excessive monitoring of employees or micro-managing the actions of the employee, and the employee being given unrealistic objectives or deadlines.[53] The consequences to the employee are real and can be severe. Employees who have been bullied have reported that they developed stress disorders such as posttraumatic stress disorder, their financial security is reduced because of absenteeism, their self-esteem was reduced, they have sleep and digestive problems, and they have increased occurrences of depression.[54]

Bullying is not just a superior–subordinate dynamic, however. Peers can also bully each other. The American Psychological Association (APA) recommends four steps that a supervisor can take to stop office bullying: foster improved communication skills so that every employee understands each other's role and dependence to maintain an effective organization; teach employees to understand each other so that misunderstandings can be avoided; identify the root causes of the bullying, which could be perceived as favoritism; establish a policy of respect that defines *bullying* and explains the consequences available for the firms if office bullying takes place.[55]

Employee Monitoring

As with any control or monitoring strategy, firms must balance the fine line of protecting their assets and their employees versus infringing on the privacy rights of the employees. Firms can argue that they must take an aggressive and comprehensive step in monitoring the employees because it is management's fiduciary duty to make sure the employees are productive and law abiding in the workplace. Furthermore, managers also have a duty to the stockholders to protect all resources controlled by the firm, whether human, physical, or financial. In addition, without an effective monitoring system, the firm is exposed to potential legal liability resulting from the misbehavior of the employees, whether accepting bribes or e-mailing inappropriate material such as pornography from company computers.

Although employees have the right to privacy, firms have the right to monitor e-mail and other electronic communications if the firm can prove these communications are a necessary part of the "ordinary course of business" as an exception to the rights of the employees that were stated in the Electronic Communications Privacy Act of 1986. This threshold can easily be achieved by firms because they can claim monitoring electronic communications is necessary to protect themselves from legal liability and to protect the proprietary information the firm needs to stay competitive.[56]

Firms can use a number of methods to monitor their employees.[57]

Undercover

One method is for managers to physically go undercover to see how the employees perform during the day. In fact, going undercover is the idea behind the show *Undercover Boss* in which the CEO of the company pretends to be someone else and works with the employees in the day-to-day operations of the firm.

Viewing Social Media

A relatively new and easy way to monitor the activities of the workers is to view their social media accounts. Whether from Facebook, MySpace, or Twitter, employers can obtain a lot of "unfiltered" information pertaining to the employee.

E-Mails and Instant Messaging

With the widespread use of personal digital assistants (PDAs) in the corporate setting, firms now have an opportunity to monitor employees by viewing the content on their computers and the content on their firm-issued phones. As long as the equipment "belongs" to the firm and is "loaned" to the employee for use, the employer has the right to monitor all information that flows from those sources. In addition, the global positioning system (GPS) capability of PDAs can track the physical location of each employee. To support why e-mail monitoring is so important, a 2007 study of employees found that 14% of the employees e-mail confidential information pertaining to the firm to outside parties; 89% of the employees in the survey send jokes, rumors, and gossip or critical comments about the firm to outsiders; and 9% admitted they sent sexual, romantic, or pornographic material to outside parties via the workplace server.[58]

Tapping Landline Phones

Even though more and more companies are shifting exclusively to smartphones, most firms still have landline phones. As a result, those phones can be tapped so that the employers can monitor the conversations that take place with that phone.

Monitoring Personal Web Postings

Personal blogs are a gold mine of information for current and potential employers. As with the social media, the individuals are less likely to "filter" out their true beliefs on these online formats. In addition, if employees have posted their résumés on a job-hiring website, their current employers know that they are ready to move to another company when they get the chance.[59]

The Ethical Issues Related to Extreme Jobs

Extreme job employees are individuals who dedicate a disproportionate amount of time to their job. It is estimated that there are employees in certain industries, such as financial services, who spend between 90 and 120 hours a week at their job. An employee is considered to have an extreme job if the employee works 60 or more hours a week and is a high wage earner. In addition, to be considered to be working at an extreme job, the employee must hold a position that meets at least 5 of the following 10 criteria: the flow of work is constantly unpredictable; the work is fast paced and under extremely tight deadlines; the position involves a broad range of job responsibilities that can be considered to be more than one job's worth of effort; there is a requirement to be at work-related events that occur after regular working hours; the position provides around-the-clock availability to the firm's clients; the position is responsible for profit and loss of at least one area of the firm; the position is responsible for the recruiting and subsequent mentoring of new employees; there is a significant portion of time spent traveling; the position is responsible for a significant number of direct reports; and the employee must be physically in the workplace at least 10 hours daily. The results of one study showed that 62% of the respondents worked more than 50 hours a week, 35% of the respondents worked more than 60 hours a week, and 10% of the respondents worked more than 80 hours a week. Furthermore, among those with an extreme workload, 48% stated they were working, on average, 16.6 more hours a week than they did five years ago. Traditional vacations are also becoming a distant memory to extreme job employees. Forty-two percent of the respondents took 10 or fewer vacation days annually, and 55% stated that they had to cancel vacation plans on a regular basis.

When asked why they were working at an extreme job, respondents gave multiple reasons. The top five reasons are stimulation and challenge, high-quality colleagues, high compensation, receive recognition at work, and power and status. As Table 7.1 highlights, there are some significant differences in the responses based on gender.

Of course, there is a downside with the complete commitment of an extreme job. In response to the question, "What are life factors that interfere with the dedication of an extreme job?" the top four factors given were being able to maintain my house, having a strong relationship with my children, having a strong relationship with my spouse/partner, and having a satisfying sex life. Table 7.2 also highlights the gender differences in the life factors that interfere with working at an extreme job.[60]

In order to create some balance between employees' work and their family, some companies are giving financial incentives for employees to take vacation. It can be a significant challenge for employees to take vacation time because a recent survey done by the career website Glassdoor showed that 15% of the respondents had not used any of their vacation time in the previous year. Furthermore, the corporate culture can encourage the employees not to take vacation. A survey done by Oxford Economics showed that 13% of the managers in the survey were less likely to promote employees who take all of their vacation time. Furthermore, the survey published in 2012 by DIW Economic Bulletin found that employees who took less than their full allotment of vacation time earned, on average, 2.8% more the following year than their colleagues

TABLE 7.1 ● Comparison of Men's and Women's Reasons Why They Work at an Extreme Job		
Stimulating/Challenging		**Difference**
Men 90 %	Women 82%	8% Men Higher
High-Quality Colleagues		
Men 52%	Women 43%	9% Men Higher
High Compensation		
Men 43%	Women 28%	15% Men Higher
Receive Recognition at Work		
Men 37%	Women 42%	5% Women Higher
Power/Status		
Men 23%	Women 30%	7% Women Higher

Source: Adapted from Sylvia Ann Hewlett and Carolyn Buck Luce, "Extreme Jobs: The Dangerous Allure of the 70-Hour Workweek," *Harvard Business Review* (December 2006): 6.

TABLE 7.2 ● Comparison of Men's and Women's Life Repercussions		
Being Able to Maintain My Home		**Difference**
Men 66 %	Women 77%	11% Women Higher
Having a Strong Relationship With My Children		
Men 65%	Women 33%	29% Men Higher
Having a Strong Relationship With My Spouse/Partner		
Men 46%	Women 46%	0%
Having a Satisfying Sex Life		
Men 49%	Women 53%	4% Women Higher

Source: Adapted from Sylvia Ann Hewlett and Carolyn Buck Luce, "Extreme Jobs: The Dangerous Allure of the 70-Hour Workweek," *Harvard Business Review* (December 2006): 8.

who did take all of their vacation time. In addition, the peer pressure within the workplace can make it difficult for an employee to take a vacation when other employees in the same department are not using their vacation time. Therefore, the firm's corporate culture is critical to how employees respond to the demands of an extreme job.[61]

Questions for Thought

1. Describe the similarities and differences between the studies conducted at Yale University and Stanford University.

2. Sexual harassment is a critical area for misbehavior in companies. Can a company eliminate sexual harassment? Why or why not?

3. Diversity is an important issue in all organizations. What is the importance of addressing diversity, and how can diversity be achieved?

Real-Life Ethical Dilemma Exercise

When the Stork Delivers a Pink Slip

In December 2011, Sarah Fielder's company was preparing to lay off some its employees. Sarah, who was 7 months pregnant at the time, wasn't worried because her friends told her they wouldn't lay off a pregnant employee because it was against the law. Sarah received her layoff notice five days later. Sarah's stunned response was "It was awful—I was planning to work until I went into labor, and to

(Continued)

(Continued)

return after taking my allotted maternity leave . . . Instead of being given an office baby shower, I was given a pink slip." The company stated that the layoff was not related to Fielder's pregnancy because that would be against the law. It is a violation of the Civil Rights Act to fire an employee specifically because she is pregnant, which is why firms never mention pregnancy when firing an employee. However, it is not a violation of the act to lay off an employee while she is on maternity leave, so long as the pregnancy was not the reason for the decision. Some experts claim that the downturn in the economy gives a ready excuse for a company just to lay off one employee, which could be a pregnant employee that it no longer wants on the payroll. Of course, a company would have the "bonus" of not having an obligation to pay for maternity leave if the pregnant employee was fired. To compound the problem, if the pregnant woman works for a small company with fewer than 20 employees, she may not be able to obtain affordable health coverage to pay for the delivery. In 2011, 6,285 cases of pregnancy-based discrimination were filed with the Equal Employment Opportunity Commission. Furthermore, in 2008, a federal judge in Brooklyn, New York, ruled that an employer does not have to make special accommodation for pregnant women. For example, an employee does not have to allow a pregnant employee to take more bathroom breaks, nor does the employer have to suspend the job duties that require heavy lifting if the employee is pregnant. The reason these accommodations are not required is that pregnancy is not considered a disability, so the employers do not have to provide the same reasonable accommodations that are required under the Americans with Disabilities Act.[62]

Questions for the Real-Life Ethical Dilemma Exercise

1. Do you think employers need to give pregnant women special accommodations?

2. How often do you think pregnancy is part of the decision process when layoffs occur within a firm?

3. Do you think there are certain industries that would be more likely to fire pregnant women? Do you think there are certain industries that would be less likely to fire pregnant women?

Student Study Site

Visit the Student Study Site at **study.sagepub.com/stanwick3e** to access the following resources:

- Video Links
- SAGE Journal Articles
- Web Resources
- Web Quizzes

EXTERNAL FOCUS ON ETHICAL ISSUES

8

Ethics and the Environment

Earth provides enough to satisfy every man's need, but not every man's greed.

—Mahatma Gandhi

Chapter Objectives

After reading and studying Chapter 8, students should be able to

1. Explain the concept of the tragedy of the commons.
2. Comment on the natural environment as a stakeholder and as a competitive advantage.
3. Identify areas in which firms can be environmentally proactive.
4. Describe the various environmental stakeholders.
5. List some of the major environmental regulations in the United States.
6. Describe some of the benefits of establishing a voluntary partnership with the U.S. Environmental Protection Agency.
7. Explain environmental justice.
8. Describe the importance of a firm's carbon footprint.

The Intersection of Billboards and Environmental Sustainability: A Peruvian Example[1]

In early 2013, in Lima, Peru, the University of Engineering and Technology developed an advertising billboard that can capture drinking water from the air. Despite being located in desertlike conditions, Lima's air has a high level of humidity, which usually approaches approximately 98%. In addition, Lima has to rely on water draining from the Andes Mountains and from glacier melts, which are both in decline due to climate change. The billboard uses electricity as its energy source, which powers five condensers linked to the billboard's inverse osmosis filtration system. It is estimated that the water captured through the filtration system can satisfy the water needs of hundreds of families weekly.[2] The billboard can produce 96 liters of water daily, and the water is stored in tanks at the top of the billboard with the water being dispersed at the base of the billboard through a tap.[3]

In May 2014, the University of Engineering and Technology introduced a new type of billboard, one which converts polluted air into purified air. The billboard purifies 100,000 cubic meters of air daily and is equivalent to 1,200 mature trees capturing the pollutants. The billboard works on thermodynamic principles of combining incoming air with water into a device that balances its internal heat. The net result is that the pollutants stay in the water and the purified air leaves the device.[4]

The Tragedy of the Commons

Although Garrett Hardin usually receives credit for the concept of the tragedy of the commons, the roots of the concept go back to Aristotle, who stated that what is common to the most people will receive the least amount of care.[5] The underlying belief of the tragedy of the commons is that free access to with unrestricted use of any resource that is finite will ultimately ruin the resource through overexploitation. In the context of the natural environment, the tragedy of the commons predicts the eventual use of all the natural resources on Earth because of the lack of control over their use. Hardin argues that only a finite amount of energy is available on Earth, and as the population grows, the human race needs to reduce its level of energy consumption instead of increasing it. Hardin gives an example of herders who have cows grazing on the open land. For each additional cow that the herder adds to his group, the herder would receive the financial benefit of one more animal. However, all the other herders would receive a negative benefit because there is now less grazing land than there was before the new cow was added to the herder's group. Therefore, one herder received all the financial gains, and all the other herders shared all of the financial losses. Hardin refutes the benefits of Adam Smith's invisible hand by arguing that the self-interests of each individual do not always translate into the promotion of the public good for everyone. Hardin continues by identifying other commons that face the same tragedy as the grazing land. These other commons include air, water, soil, forests, and energy resources. Hardin recommends that the "management" solution to the tragedy of the commons is to privatize resources, have polluters pay for their damage, and have government regulations to control the use of natural resources.[6]

Natural Environment as a Stakeholder

The natural environment could be considered a stakeholder without a voice. The resources used in the manufacturing of a product, the energy used to run a plant, and the disposal of waste products are just some of the links the natural environment has with firms. Although Greenpeace and Friends of the Earth play a role in representing the natural environment as a stakeholder, they represent only one component for the firm to consider when it develops strategic decisions based on the needs of the environment. On the surface, this argument goes against the view that a stakeholder has to be a human being. As Mark Starik argues, the classification of a stakeholder has been artificially limited to human beings.[7] According to Starik, a stakeholder is any entity that has an impact on the operations of the firm. As a result, the natural environment is a vital component of the external environment in which the firms compete and, therefore, needs to be incorporated in the decision-making process with every other party that has a vested interest in the firm's operations. An explanation of why the natural environment was not considered a stakeholder in the past is that the philosophical justifications for ethical actions by humans relate to decisions made by humans that affect humans. Therefore, nonhuman entities were not considered in the consequences of an individual's actions because they never had a voice to air their concerns. In addition, decision makers would consider the natural environment as a stakeholder only if the consequences that affect the natural environment also have an impact on the performance evaluation of the firm or the individual decision maker. Both the utilitarian and the Kantian viewpoints of ethical philosophy do not allow nonhuman entities to be factored in the decision-making process. However, a true utilitarian view would focus on the greatest good to the greatest number of living things, not just the greatest number of humans. Furthermore, Kant's ethical view of focusing on a human's duty should be expanded to consider that it is the decision maker's duty to other humans, and to all living things.[8]

Natural Environment as a Competitive Advantage

In their landmark article examining the relationship between the natural environment and competitive advantage, Michael E. Porter and Claas van der Linde argue that the natural environment should not be considered a cost of production, but should be viewed as a potential area to develop or maintain a competitive advantage.[9] By focusing on environmentally friendly strategies, firms are able to market their goods as eco-friendly, which helps differentiate their products from others on the market. In addition, by focusing on the efficiency issues in the production process, firms can reduce the amount of waste generated by the firm and the costs. Renato J. Orsato extends the argument presented by Porter and van der Linde by presenting a typology that represents the type of competitive business strategies a firm uses to convert the natural environment as a stakeholder into a competitive advantage.[10] The typology is shown in Table 8.1.

Firms can reconcile the potentially different interests the firm's stakeholders have related to the natural environment by focusing on the natural environment to create a competitive advantage. The local community and society achieve their objective of having the firm reduce its negative impact on the environment. For the shareholders, incorporating the natural environment in the strategic decision-making process to yield potential competitive gains addresses their demand of maximizing the rate of return for their investments. For the employees, the proactive approach to the natural environment enhances their level of satisfaction within the firm because it generates a positive corporate image, which potentially increases the loyalty of the employees. Therefore, utilitarianism could be used to explain the use of competitive advantages

TABLE 8.1 ● Generic Competitive Environmental Strategies

		Competitive Focus	
		Organizational Processes	**Products and Services**
Competitive Advantage	**Lower Costs**	**Strategy 1:** Eco-efficiency	**Strategy 4:** Environmental Cost Leadership
	Differentiation	**Strategy 2**: Beyond Compliance Leadership	**Strategy 3:** Eco-branding

Source: Renato J. Orsato, "Competitive Environmental Strategies: When Does It Pay to Be Green?," *California Management Review* (Winter 2006): 131.

because incorporating the natural environment in the firm's overall vision can bring the greatest good to the greatest number of people.

Strategy 1: Eco-Efficiency

In the eco-efficiency strategic focus, productivity is the key element that allows companies to gain an environmentally competitive advantage. If the firm is able to enhance its resource productivity, it could see the benefits in material savings, increases in its manufacturing process, and better use of the by-products in the manufacturing process. Under an eco-efficiency strategy, waste products are considered an inefficient use of resources. Therefore, firms will focus on eco-design and eco-efficiency measures that will lead to new business practices. As a result, stakeholder pressures from the government by means of regulations and from the market due to the demands of the customers, investors, and nongovernmental organizations (NGOs) justify the firm's commitment to improve its operations by internalizing environmental costs.

Strategy 2: Beyond Compliance Leadership

In the beyond compliance leadership strategic focus, the firm makes a conscious effort to acknowledge the demands of its stakeholders. In this strategic focus, firms are able to provide "proof" to their stakeholders pertaining to their commitment to the natural environment. This proof can be in many forms. Ways in which firms can show their stakeholders their environmental commitment include having Environmental Management Systems (EMS) certification, which shows that the firms have followed the guidelines of a certification organization such as having an ISO 14000 certification, having a formal environmental code of conduct, and investing in environmental improvements that do not increase the level of profitability of the firm in the short run. Firms that have EMS certification from an international agency such as the International Standards Organization (ISO) can also enhance their competitive position because some manufacturing customers require ISO certification from their suppliers. For example, global automobile manufacturers such as Ford, GM, and Toyota demand that all of their suppliers have ISO 14000 certification before they will buy parts from the suppliers. A core component of the beyond compliance leadership strategy is that the firm's proactive environmental commitment must be promoted so that the firm's customers are acutely aware of the firm's environmental policies. As a result, it is expected that customers would migrate toward firms that have an environmental commitment beyond mere environmental compliance. However, a risk associated with a beyond compliance leadership strategy is ensuring that the firm's environmental commitment is consistent over time. Shell Oil had a large negative backlash from its stakeholders when it planned to dump the Brent Spar oil rig in the North Sea. Although it was common practice to sink old oil rigs to develop artificial barrier reefs in the ocean, the stakeholders were angry because of the presence of residue oil and oil by-products that were still part of the oil rig if it sank. As a result, Shell immediately lost environmental goodwill it had built with its stakeholders. It was able to recover that goodwill when Shell officials reversed their decision to dump the platform in the Atlantic Ocean.[11]

Strategy 3: Eco-Branding

In the eco-branding strategic focus, firms use their proactive environmental commitments in an attempt to differentiate their products and services for their customers. Eco-branding allows potential customers to consider the natural environment when they are purchasing products and services. Before a firm can generate an effective eco-branding strategy, it must meet the following three prerequisites:

1. Customers must be willing to pay a premium for products that are eco-friendly.
2. Reliable and current information about the product's overall environmental performance must be made available to the customers.
3. The environmental product differentiation must be difficult for competitors to copy.

As a result, the consumers need to see a clear environmental benefit with the purchase of the firm's product or service for this strategy to succeed. If the firm is able to differentiate its products in an eco-friendly perspective, it will be rewarded with good stakeholder relationships, and it may be able to generate a higher profit margin for its products and services.

An example of a company that has embraced eco-branding to its fullest is Timberland.[12] Since 2006, Timberland has put a "nutrition label" on the boxes that contain its shoes. On this label is a description of how much energy has been used to make the shoes (e.g., 3.1 kilowatt hours of energy), how much of that energy was renewable (e.g., 5%), and the labor record of the factory (e.g., no child labor) that produced the shoes. Jeffrey B. Swartz, president and CEO of Timberland, stated that the company wanted to give its customers the ability to make their own judgments on Timberland's commitment to the environment. In tracing the amount of energy used to make the shoes, Swartz stated that you have to go back to the cow that supplied the leather. Timberland found that more than half of the energy used to make the shoes comes from the processing and the production of the raw materials. The next major contributor to energy use was the retailer that sold the shoes in the brightly lit stores. The third major contributor was the factory operations and the transportation of the shoes. Swartz observed the majority of energy is used after Timberland actually receives the raw materials from the suppliers.

Strategy 4: Environmental Cost Leadership

In an environmental cost leadership strategy, firms that compete on low price can offset their environmental investments. Firms that use this strategy embrace proactive environmental ideals as long as they can help reduce the overall costs of production. Firms using this strategic focus concentrate on radical product innovations such as material substitution or using fewer materials to yield cost savings.

Voluntary Environmental Compliance

Firms that recognize that the natural environment is a concern to all stakeholders, whether human or not, realize that they must establish an environmental compliance system based on an agreed-upon set of policies and procedures. Those policies and procedures are usually in the form of environmental codes of conduct. Catherine A. Ramus recommends 13 areas in which environmentally proactive firms should address environmental issues:[13]

1. Release an environmental policy that is available for all stakeholders to review.
2. Establish specific targets to be measured for annual environmental performance benchmarks.
3. Publish an annual environmental report.
4. Implement an environmental management system.
5. Use environmental criteria when making purchasing decisions.
6. Provide employees with environmental training.
7. Make the employees accountable and responsible for the overall environmental performance of the company.
8. Use life cycle analysis that evaluates the environmental impact of a product from its creation until it is no longer in use.
9. Have top-level managers who understand and attempt to address the issues of sustainable development.
10. Implement a system to try to reduce the level of fossil fuel use.
11. Implement a system to reduce toxic chemical use.
12. Implement a system to reduce the use of unsustainable products.
13. Ensure that the same environmental standards are consistent globally.

What Does It Mean to Be Green?

To be a "green" company, the company must make many adjustments in its strategic choices. Some may be relatively simple, but others may be more complicated and require a significant capital outlay. Table 8.2 shows several types of strategic adjustments that could be made in a corporation to make it a more "green" company.

How to Adopt Sustainable Strategies Using Firm Transformation[14]

The transformation of a firm to integrate sustainable strategies is a six-stage process. The stages are (1) develop the strategy—envisioning a new future, (2) translate the

TABLE 8.2 ● Examples of Strategic Adjustments That Could Be Made in the Greening of a Corporation	
Marketing	• Incremental change to existing products and new product development • Consumer awareness, press releases, advertising, sponsorships • Product labeling and packaging • More sensitive pricing strategy
Manufacturing	• Adjustments to the current manufacturing process • Introduction of new production processes • Incorporate waste reduction and recycling in the manufacturing process
Research and Development	• Develop new products that are more environmentally friendly • Consider redesigning the product and the production process • Select raw materials that are more environmentally friendly • Reduce the generation of by-products and develop waste recovery technologies

Source: Adapted from "Customers Drive Corporations Green," *Long Range Planning* 23, no. 6 (1990): 10–16.

strategy—the need for new analytic frameworks, (3) align the organization—developing and deploying the sustainability strategy, (4) plan operations—implementing the sustainability plan, (5) monitor and learn—evaluating sustainability performance, and (6) test and adapt—reenvisioning sustainability.

Stage 1: Develop the Strategy—Envisioning a New Future The first stage is to evaluate the firm's vision of sustainability. If sustainability is only considered a cost of production, the firm will not support the transformation to a sustainability focused firm. It is in first stage that the top-level managers need to consider sustainability as a potential new source for its competitive advantage as well as increasing the opportunity to enhance their financial performance.

Stage 2: Translate the Strategy—The Need for New Analytic Frameworks As part of the transformation process, firms must conduct life-cycle analysis on all activities within the firm to access their sustainability impact. These life-cycle analyses would be used to evaluate the potential long-term growth opportunities, including the value of new revenue streams and the new positioning of the firm's products. In addition, market segmentation sustainability evaluations need to be done to match future consumer needs with the products and services offered by the firm.

Stage 3: Align the Organization—Developing and Deploying the Sustainable Strategy At this stage, the sustainability strategy moves from simpler incremental improvements to more holistic change, focusing on establishing and maintaining a firm-wide commitment to sustainability. The comprehensive sustainability objectives must flow from the top-level managers and be incorporated into the performance objectives of each individual unit within the firm. In addition, the development and implementation of comprehensive responsibility and accountability assignments are made throughout the firm.

Stage 4: Plan Operations—Implementing the Sustainability Plan In Stage 4, the firm needs to establish sustainability objectives at each step in the value chain. The establishment of policy and stewardship objectives moves the focus away from new product development through research and development to value chain issues such as sourcing, logistics, and supply chain.

Stage 5: Monitor and Learn—Evaluating Sustainability Performance It is at this stage that the development and implementation of monitoring policy and procedures should take place using a sustainability management system. This monitoring process is critical to ensure that the proper sustainable actions have taken place; as well, it is an effective tool to evaluate how well the firm is progressing in its sustainability strategy.

Stage 6: Test and Adapt—Reenvisioning Sustainability Stage 6 demonstrates that the development of a sustainability strategy is never a completed task. As a firm moves through these six stages, the firm's sustainability performance is measured. It is at Stage 6 that the firm reenvisions its vision of sustainability based on its past performance. It is at this stage that the firm can recalibrate its vision and its sustainability strategy based on how easy or difficult it was to achieve its sustainability goals.

Employees as Environmental Stakeholders

Catherine Ramus argues that firms must use employees to implement the environmental commitment of the firm and to be actively involved in the formulation of the firm's environmental commitment.[15] Ramus states that one reason environmental initiatives may fail within the firm is because there is not a high level of commitment by the employees. Management must allow and foster the employees' development of original discussions that could lead to inventive solutions to the firm's environmental issues. As a result, employees, individually or in groups, could develop environmental innovations that could enhance the firm's environmental commitment. Some examples of employee-led eco-innovations are alternative methods to reduce pollution, the replacement of toxic or hazardous materials with benign materials, and the dematerialization of products. Ramus argues that the lack of support by the line managers within the firm blocks employees from presenting eco-innovative ideas. She states that three types of environmental initiatives can be generated from an employee at any level within the firm:

1. Initiatives that decrease the environmental impact of the company using the policies of reuse and recycling
2. Initiatives that solve an environmental problem such as hazardous substance use reduction
3. Initiatives that develop a more eco-efficient product or service that uses fewer resources or less energy

For example, employees at GE Plastics in the Netherlands took responsibility for developing environmental programs that focus on waste reduction and recycling, and those programs became part of a company-wide program to reduce the environmental impact of GE Plastics on the environment. At Lucent Technologies, the employees developed a cleaning process for microchips that uses water instead of hazardous and volatile cleaning compounds. At Neste Oil in Finland, employees developed a cleaner diesel fuel that resulted in cleaner air and increased the level of profitability of the firm.

Firms that view employees as proactive stakeholders regarding the environment realize that there are opportunities for both intrinsic and extrinsic rewards for the employees. The extrinsic rewards include giving the employees a financial reward for developing an innovative environmental idea, giving the employees resources and time during the workday to experiment with their ideas, and giving formal recognition to employees for advancements made. However, enlightened firms also realize that employees receive intrinsic rewards for their environmental ideas. Employees who put a high value on their quality of life with regard to a clean environment are internally motivated to develop ideas that help the firm help the environment.

NGOs as Environmental Stakeholders

Over the years, NGOs supporting environmental causes have grown significantly. Initially, the pressure from these stakeholders forced some firms to reevaluate their strategic focus as it related to the environment. The modern environmental movement started in 1962 with the publication of Rachel Carson's book about the extensive use of pesticides and other chemical toxins, *Silent Spring*. After *Silent Spring* was published, the next major environmental milestones were Garret Hardin's *The Tragedy of the Commons* in 1968 and the first Earth Day celebration in 1970. These were followed by the formation of the first global environmental interest group, Greenpeace. Beginning with Greenpeace, brief summaries of some of the major global environmental groups are presented here.

Greenpeace

Greenpeace is a nonprofit organization that has offices in 40 countries around the world. Greenpeace does not accept donations from either governments or corporations, but does rely on donations from foundations and individual supporters. Greenpeace's major focuses are climate change, protecting the old-growth forests, stopping whale hunting, protecting the oceans, and eliminating toxic chemicals. Greenpeace has 2.8 million supporters globally. One of its many slogans is "When the last tree is cut, the last river poisoned, and the last fish dead, we will discover that we can't eat money."[16]

Sierra Club

With a membership of 1.3 million people, the Sierra Club is the oldest and largest environmental group in the United States. Its mission is to explore, enjoy, and protect the earth; to practice and promote responsible use of the earth's resources; and to help educate people to protect the environment.[17]

Environmental Defense Fund

In 1967, a small group of scientists came together to address the issue of the pesticide DDT, the focus of Rachel Carson's *Silent Spring*. They presented evidence to the court to stop the use of DDT because of the negative impact it had on bird eggshells. The scientists won the decision, and the group was incorporated as the

Environmental Defense Fund. It currently has 500,000 members consisting of economists, engineers, computer analysts, and various PhDs.[18]

Friends of the Earth

Founded in 1969 in San Francisco, the Friends of the Earth is an activist group with chapters in 70 countries. It has identified some of the environmental accounting tricks that companies may play.[19] These tricks include methods of overstating earnings and understating losses related to environmental issues and include the following:

1. **Lowballing superfund liabilities:** Companies may delay remediation expenses by drawing out litigation related to the Superfund sites. Superfund sites are contaminated with hazardous substances. After the passage of the Comprehensive Environmental Response, Compensation and Liability Act (CERCLA) in 1980, the EPA was authorized to identify parties responsible for the contamination and ordered the parties to clean up the sites.
2. **Hiding asbestos liability:** Some companies try to manage earnings by minimizing the impact of asbestos claim liabilities on their balance sheets.
3. **Painting a rosy picture:** Some companies neglect to identify their environmental problems in their corporate disclosures, even though the Securities and Exchange Commission (SEC) requires these types of disclosures.
4. **Underreporting environmental legal proceedings:** Even though required by the SEC, many companies are failing to report environmental legal proceedings that are initiated or contemplated by an environmental agency that would result in monetary sanctions of more than $100,000.

Communicating the Firm's Environmental Commitment to Its Stakeholders

Although information pertaining to the firm's commitment to the natural environment can be transferred through many mediums, environmental disclosures are usually the first information source used by stakeholders. This is because they are convenient and easy to obtain from a firm's website, and they are usually comprehensive in describing the different methods used to address environmental issues.

There is a relationship between a firm's environmental disclosures and its financial performance.[20] Firms that had both a formal environmental policy and a detailed description of their environmental commitment had higher financial performance levels than did firms that were low financial performers. Firms that had a medium level of financial performance had the highest incidences of environmental policies. We concluded that firms in the "middle of the pack" financially were usually environmentally committed as a potential course of action to enhance their competitive advantage within their industries. As a result, the communication of the firm's environmental commitment satisfies the needs of both the shareholders of the firm as well as the other stakeholders in the company. Furthermore, a comprehensive environmental commitment by means of environmental disclosures allows both the firm and the stakeholders to establish benchmarks for the firm's future performance.

United States Government Regulations

The U.S. Environmental Protection Agency has the major responsibility for setting laws and regulations to protect the environment. The following major laws have been passed, some of which have been amended, to help protect the public from environmental problems:

- Federal Food, Drug, and Cosmetic Act (1938)
- Federal Water Pollution Control Act (also known as the Clean Water Act) (1948)
- Air Pollution Control Act of 1955
- Clean Air Act (1963)
- Solid Waste Disposal Act (1965)
- National Environmental Policy Act (1970)
- Ocean Dumping Act (1972)
- Endangered Species Act (1973)
- Safe Drinking Water Act (1974)
- Resource Conservation and Recovery Act (1976)
- Toxic Substances Control Act (1976)
- Comprehensive Environmental Response, Compensation, and Liability Act (1980)
- Nuclear Waste Policy Act (1982)
- Emergency Planning and Community Right-to-Know Act (1986)
- Ocean Dumping Ban Act (1988)
- Food Quality Protection Act (1996)
- Chemical Safety Information, Site Security, and Fuels Regulatory Relief Act (1999)[21]

Environmental Accounting Issues

Many companies are not as forthcoming about issues related to environmental liabilities. Although the reporting of environmental liabilities centers around two accounting rules, "FAS 5—Accounting for Contingencies" and "FIN 14—Reasonable Estimation of Loss," many companies fail to provide appropriate disclosures about their environmental liabilities. These two rules provide guidance for companies, but they don't provide precise guidance about what should be reported. Pressure from stakeholders will encourage more companies to be more forthright in disclosures of these liabilities, especially in the Form 10-K reported to the SEC. Discussion of these items should be included in the management's discussion and analysis section.

The EPA has advocated environmental auditing for companies. *Environmental auditing*, as defined by the EPA, is a periodic, objective, and documented assessment of an organization's operations compared with audit criteria.[22] An environmental audit will allow managers one measure of ensuring that they comply with environmental regulations. It will also allow them to consider ways in which to better their organization from an environmental standpoint by helping them identify ways that environmental issues can be integrated into their current operating strategy.

Environmental Justice

Environmental justice can be defined as the systematic equal allocation of environmental benefits and burdens. Environmental justice evolved from the perception that lower-income areas or areas with minority ethnic groups within a community would receive a disproportionate amount of environmental burdens (e.g., toxic dump sites and heavy manufacturing facilities) and would receive a disproportionately low allocation of environmental benefits (e.g., parks, walking trails, and hiking areas). An offshoot of this movement was the NIMBY philosophy, which most communities wanted to adopt. NIMBY, or Not In My Back Yard, was based on the view that local communities, regardless of their economic standing, wanted to have fewer heavy polluting facilities within their communities.

Regardless of ethnicity, culture, or income, the EPA is committed to environmental justice. It is the agency's belief that all people should be treated fairly with respect to environmental laws and policies, including development, implementation, and enforcement. Thus, the EPA has identified that this goal requires four activities:

1. Conducting our programs, policies, and activities that substantially affect human health and the environment in a manner that ensures the fair treatment of all people, including minority populations and/or low-income populations
2. Ensuring equal enforcement of protective environmental laws for all people, including minority populations and/or low-income populations
3. Ensuring greater public participation in the agency's development and implementation of environmental regulations and policies
4. Improving research and data collection for agency programs relating to the health of and the environment of all people, including minority populations and/or low-income populations.[23]

A study of environmental justice issues in the San Francisco Bay Area in 2007 found that two thirds of the residents who lived within 1 mile of a pollution source facility that is regulated by the EPA were minorities. A report titled "Still Toxic After All These Years," produced by Greenaction, states that close proximity to these pollution sites will affect the citizens of the areas with higher cancer risks and higher rates of asthma and other breathing problems. The report also stated that new immigrants to the Bay Area were almost twice as likely to live within a 1-mile radius of a pollution source. Two and a half miles is considered a safe distance. The report also states that given the same income levels, minority residents were more likely to live closer to the pollution source than were white residents.[24]

Environmental Sustainability

Environmental sustainability is the ability of an organization or a country to protect the use of future resources by properly maintaining and protecting the resources that are currently being used. Anne Grafé-Buckens and Sebastian Beloe define *sustainability* as having three major components: a system to ensure the sustainable management of the earth's natural resources, the development of social and institutional structures that would support the sustainable management of the natural resources, and changes in the economic framework to support the sustainable management of the earth's natural resources.[25] Grafé-Buckens and Beloe argue that an effective way to approach environmental sustainability issues is to focus on some general governing principles that have to be accepted for environmental sustainability to take place. Once those principles are in place, the firm can then convert those principles into operational strategies.

Stuart L. Hart argues that to view sustainability from a global perspective, it must be understood that different countries address sustainability differently.[26] Hart classifies countries based on their stage of economic development. The three types of economies are survival, emerging, and developed. Survival economies are at the lowest level economically from a global perspective. The countries could still be considered underdeveloped. Emerging economies are countries such as China and India, which were considered underdeveloped in the past but are becoming developed countries. The third type of economy is the developed economy, which coincides with economically developed countries. Based on those classifications, Hart identified the major challenges facing each type of economy based on sustainability issues. The sustainability challenges Hart proposed are shown in Table 8.3.

Among the financial institutions adopting these principles are Barclays, Citigroup, Credit Suisse, and Unibanco.

Many environmentally friendly companies want to do business with other companies that embrace the environment. It may be necessary to ask questions such as, What are you doing for the environment or what do you do for the environment beyond simply complying with applicable government regulations when making a decision whether to buy supplies and products from other companies?

Ethics and Climate Change

What Is the Greenhouse Effect?

Greenhouse gases have been heating Earth for millions of year. Without greenhouse gases, Earth would be too cold to support human and nonhuman life. Earth receives

TABLE 8.3 ● Major Challenges to Sustainability

	Pollution	Depletion	Poverty
Developed Economies	Greenhouse gases Use of toxic materials	Scarcity of materials Insufficient reuse and recycling	Urban and minority unemployment
Emerging Economies	Industrial emissions Contaminated water Lack of sewage treatment	Overexploitation of renewable resources Overuse of water for irrigation	Migration to cities Lack of skilled workers Income equality
Survival Economies	Dung and wood burning Lack of sanitation Ecosystem destruction due to development	Deforestation Overgrazing Soil loss	Population growth Low status of women Dislocation

Source: Stuart L. Hart, "Beyond Greening: Strategies for a Sustainable World," *Harvard Business Review* 75 (1997): 70.

a large amount of energy from the Sun every day. It is estimated that a few days of sunshine on Earth is equivalent to all the energy stored in fossil fuels. Approximately 30% of the solar radiation that points toward Earth is reflected back toward the Sun. The remaining 70% is absorbed by Earth. The greenhouse gases trap the radiation so it stays within Earth's atmosphere. This creates a blanket, or greenhouse, effect whereby the heat remains on Earth and does not escape back into space. Before humans' use of fossil fuels, there were natural greenhouse gases that were used to help support life on Earth. The problem is that the amount of greenhouse gas has increased rapidly in the past hundred years. As a result, more and more of the Sun's radiation remains trapped in Earth's atmosphere, and Earth's temperature continues to increase.[27] As was shown in the Exxon example at the beginning of the chapter, some people do not believe that the greenhouse effect is having a dangerous impact on the planet.

Kyoto Treaty

The Kyoto Protocol to the UN Framework Convention on Climate Change was created in December 1997. The aim of the treaty is to have every industrialized nation in the world voluntarily reduce the level of greenhouse gas (GHG) emissions into the atmosphere by 5.2% compared with 1990 GHG emissions levels. There are six GHGs: carbon dioxide, methane, nitrous oxide, sulfur hexafluoride, hydrofluorocarbons (HFCs), and perfluorocarbons (PFCs). The majority of GHG emissions come from carbon dioxide. Without reductions in GHG emissions, the global temperature will rise between 2.5 and 10.4 degrees Fahrenheit from 1990 to 2100. The danger of even

TABLE 8.4 ● Estimated Cost If Atmospheric Carbon Dioxide Were to Double From 2002 to 2050 (in Billions of US Dollars)					
	United States	European Union	Former Soviet Union	China	World
Coastal Protection and Losses	8.1	5.3	2.4	0.7	49.7
Other Ecosystems	7.4	9.8	2.3	2.2	40.5
Agriculture and Forestry	8.4	9.9	6.8	7.8	42.5
Energy Industry	6.9	7.0	−0.7	0.7	0.7
Water Management	13.7	14.0	3.0	1.6	46.7
Human Casualties and Dislocations	17.1	22.9	4.1	5.5	86.3
Air Pollution	6.4	3.5	2.1	0.2	15.4
Total	*68.0*	*72.4*	*20.0*	*18.7*	*304.2*
Share of GDP	*1.4%*	*1.6%*	*0.8%*	6.1%	1.5%

Source: Andrew J. Hoffman, "Climate Change Strategy: The Business Logic Behind Voluntary Greenhouse Gas Reductions," *California Management Review* 47 (2005): 33.

a slight increase in the global temperature is that it can also affect climate change greatly. It can affect the level of rainfall, causing significant changes in vegetation in some areas and resulting in severe flooding in low-lying areas around bodies of water. Table 8.4 shows the estimated annual cost in billions of dollars if the level of carbon dioxide concentrations were to double from 2002 to 2050.

The treaty would be ratified if countries that in aggregate release at least 55% of the world's greenhouse gases would sign it. It was not initially ratified because President George W. Bush announced that the United States, the largest emitter of greenhouse gases with 36% of the world's total, would not sign the agreement. The treaty was finally ratified in February 2005 when Russia joined the treaty, which increased the aggregate level of GHG emissions to 55%. By December 2006, 169 countries had agreed to the treaty, representing more than 61% of GHG emissions from developed countries. The two notable exceptions from the treaty are the United States and Australia. China and India are exempt from the Kyoto requirements because they were not main contributors to the GHG emissions in the past. This is a dangerous exemption because China was predicted to take over the number one position of GHG emissions from the United States by 2011.

A number of different components within the treaty could have a significant impact on the level of greenhouse gas emissions. One stipulation of the treaty is that those countries agreeing to the treaty would help fund development of new technology to reduce GHG emissions for less-developed countries. There would be strict monitoring and control systems in place to ensure that each country in the treaty could verify and report its GHG emissions. Countries that have dense forest areas could use these forest areas to offset the GHG level. The heavily forested areas within a country are called "tree sinks" because the trees absorb the carbon dioxide during photosynthesis. If a country in the treaty fails to maintain its promised GHG emission levels, it could face legally binding consequences.[28] Additional meetings in Copenhagen in 2009 and Cancun 2010 attempted to facilitate a clearer understanding of the role countries would have in the future related to the reduction of GHG emissions but both conferences ended with limited success.

On February 25, 2007, Al Gore won an Academy Award for his documentary *An Inconvenient Truth*. It was unique because he was the first former vice president of the United States to win the award and because the movie focused on global warming. This film was considered by many as the turning point in which climate change and global warming started to become a major political and economic issue.

Climate Change as a Strategic Option

With the passing of the Kyoto Treaty, countries around the world are expected to implement government regulations that will greatly restrict the level of acceptable GHG emissions by firms. In addition, firms whose assets are directly affected by weather patterns must now plan for fundamental changes in the global climate. Firms that are involved in insurance, real estate, agriculture, and tourism will all be greatly affected by shifting climate patterns. A number of strategic options are available for companies that want to incorporate climate change in their strategic decision-making process. Ans Kolk and Jonathan Pinkse present a framework that highlights the strategic options,[29] shown in Table 8.5.

TABLE 8.5 ● Strategic Options for Climate Change			
		Main Aim	
		Innovation	**Compensation**
Organization	**Internal (Company)**	Process Improvement	Internal Transfer of Emission Reductions
	Vertical (Supply Chain)	Product Development	Supply-Chain Measures
	Horizontal (Beyond the Supply Chain)	New Product/Market Combinations	Acquisition of Emission Credits

Source: Ans Kolk and Jonathan Pinkse, "Business Responses to Climate Change: Identifying Emergent Strategies," *California Business Review* 47 (2005): 8.

Process improvement focuses on adjusting the manufacturing process so it has less impact on climate change. Adjustments in the manufacturing process could include using less energy or increasing the level of production efficiencies. Internal transfer of emission reductions is the ability of the firm to internally "transfer" emission credits from a facility that is not generating the maximum allowed GHG emissions to a facility that is generating more than the GHG emission limit. New product development could focus on product design and use of materials to reduce GHG emissions. An example of supply chain measures would be for a firm to acquire electricity from only renewable energy sources. New product/market combinations would focus with a partner to develop a new product category or market segment. An example would be an oil company and an automobile company forming a joint venture to develop automobiles that receive their power from fuel cells. Emission credits are purchased on the open market from firms that are selling their emission credits because they are not at their GHG emission limit.

The Effects of Climate Change on the Firm

Jonathan Lash and Fred Wellington[30] argue there are numerous risks to the firm because of the impact of climate change, including regulatory, supply chain, litigation, reputational, and physical.

Regulatory risk is based on the belief that as the climate change continues to affect the global environment, governments from around the world adopt stronger and more rigid regulations to control GHG emissions. Regions such as Western Europe are predicted to continue to adopt more comprehensive environmental regulations to combat GHG emissions.

Supply chain risk is based on the assumption that as climate change continues to affect the world, the vulnerability of suppliers and the raw materials needed for manufacturing will decrease. Furthermore, the suppliers are expected to pass on to the customers the increased cost of conforming to new regulations in their own industries. Furthermore, the location of the suppliers could also affect the ability of the suppliers to fulfill the order. If the suppliers have facilities near coastal areas, the increased chance of flooding due to the melting of glaciers and polar caps could have a significant impact.

Litigation risk is based on the premise that firms with high GHG emission levels will be threatened more frequently with lawsuits similar to those established in the tobacco, pharmaceutical, and asbestos industries.

Reputational risk is related to how the customer perceives the firm. If the reputation and image of the firm are negative because of its high level of GHG emissions, this could reduce or eliminate the firm's competitive advantage in the marketplace.

Physical risk relates to how changes in climate result in weather disasters such as droughts, floods, storms, and rising sea levels.

Firms can improve their climate competitiveness by implementing four steps. Step 1 is quantifying the firm's carbon footprint since firms can only manage something they are able to measure. The firm needs an accurate count of all sources and levels of GHG emissions in its facilities throughout the world. Step 2 is having the firm determine the carbon-related risks and opportunities. The firm must determine both the direct and indirect impact it has on the global climate. In addition, the integration of the risks and potential opportunities related to GHG must be incorporated in the decision-making process of the employees. Step 3 is adjusting the firm's operations based on its risk and opportunity assessment related to GHG emissions. This assessment is needed so firms can set future climate change goals as well as determining where the firm's resources should be allocated to address climate changes. The fourth and most critical step is ensuring actions are unique, rare, and hard to imitate, which will enhance the firm's competitive advantage in its actions related to the reduction of GHG emissions.[31]

A Firm's Carbon Footprint

A *carbon footprint* refers to the amount of carbon via GHG emissions that have been generated by a firm. It is called a carbon footprint because the GHG emissions have an impact on the earth but do not disappear as a footprint on the ground does. The firm's carbon footprint[32] is based on the total annual GHG emissions that are a direct result of the firm's operations. This includes the combustion of fossil fuels and different types of chemical reactions that can occur in some manufacturing industries as well as GHG emissions related to electricity that has been purchased by the firm. An analysis must be done at both the organizational and product levels. There are three levels of scope for both the organizational and product footprint.

Scope 1 refers to direct emissions that are generated by sources that are owned or controlled by the firm. Some examples of these sources are *stationary combustion*, such as the production of electricity, steam, heat, or power from equipment that has a fixed permanent location; *mobile combustion*, which refers to transportation and construction sources that use motors such as cars, trucks, tractors, and airplanes; *physical and chemical processes*, which are sources of GHG emissions due to the releases during the heavy manufacturing processes such as aluminum and cement manufacturing;

and *fugitive sources*, which refer to GHG emissions that were unintentional. These releases could result from accidental leaks and evaporation of GHG materials into the atmosphere.

Scope 2 refers to indirect emissions sources that are not owned or controlled by the firms. These emissions could include purchased electricity, heat, and steam from external sources.

Scope 3 includes all other indirect GHG emissions related to the firm that have not been captured in scopes 1 or 2. These GHG emissions could be based on employee travel, the extraction and processing of raw materials, the transportation of the firm's products to its distribution centers, retailers, customers, and product disposal.[33]

The Carbon Disclosure Project 2010 Global 500 Report[34] highlights a number of interesting facts related to carbon disclosure. The report is based on data collected from 410 firms of the Global 500 firms. Scope 1 emissions reported by the firms in the sample equaled 3.4 billon metric tons, 11% of total emissions. The data support the belief that firms are moving away from a strategy based solely on addressing future risks and are instead focusing on potential opportunities. Of the firms reporting data, 187, or 48% stated they now include climate change and carbon management into the decision-making process at the group business strategy level. The report concluded that four functions dominate those firms that have taken leadership roles in carbon performance: the firm's strategy, the corporate governance system, stakeholder communications, and goals and achievements.[35] The firm's strategy focuses on integration of climate change risks and opportunities into the overall strategic focus of the firm. The firms also established GHG reduction targets and are proactive in engaging with policy makers related to climate policy. The corporate governance of the firms is based on establishing formal accountability of GHG reduction strategies to individuals to ensure oversight and management. In addition, the firms also establish incentives for actions related to climate change events. Stakeholder communications can be in the form of mainstream reporting as well as government reporting. In addition, proactive firms also verify the GHG emissions data through a third party. The firm's achievements in GHG emissions reduction is based on the effective implementation of the firm's GHG reduction strategy. This achievement is based on the actual reduction of GHG emissions as well as the enhancement of the firm's competitive advantage by focusing on the opportunities available when addressing GHG emissions reduction.[36]

Questions for Thought

1. The opening vignette is an inspiring example of social entrepreneurship. Why do you think there are not more examples of intertwining social commitment and entrepreneurship?

2. What role should businesses take in climate change? What should government's role be in climate change?

3. Do you believe that a business's carbon footprint will be an important competitive issue in the future?

Real-Life Ethical Dilemma Exercise

The Bhopal Disaster

On December 3, 1984, 40 tons of toxic methyl isocyanate (MIC) gas, a chemical used in pesticides, leaked from a Union Carbide facility in Bhopal, India. The gas killed at least 3,000 people immediately and thousands later. The gas injured thousands more and created a toxic waste dump in the heart of the city where the 11-acre plant was. More than 500,000 people were declared affected by the gas leak and were given an average compensation of $550. The chairman of Union Carbide at the time, Warren Anderson, was arrested while he was in India but posted bail and fled India, never to return. He has retired and lives comfortably on Long Island, New York. India had demanded $3.3 billion in damages, but Union Carbon refused to pay that amount. In 1989, Union Carbide agreed to pay a $470 million settlement for damages that were caused to the local residents. Union Carbide abandoned the facility without cleaning up all the toxic material. Hundreds of tons of toxic waste still are located within the facility and seeping into the nearby soil and water table. Dow Chemical bought Union Carbide in 2001 and claims no responsibility because it did not cause the leak. A Dow Chemical spokesperson stated, "As there was never any ownership, there is no responsibility and no liability—for the Bhopal tragedy or its aftermath."[37] Dow argued that the property had been turned over to the Madhya Pradesh State government in June 1998. In 2010, eight former senior officials from Union Carbide India were finally convicted of negligence and were sentenced to two years in jail and fined $2,100. One of the defendants died before the sentencing took place. At present, the area around the facility has been settled by scores of poor people who are looking for cheap land on which to build a house. An open pit just beyond the factory walls was used as a storage area for chemical sludge that was a by-product of the manufacturing process. The pit is now used for swimming by the children and as an open toilet.[38]

Questions for the Real-Life Ethical Dilemma Exercise

1. Why has the U.S. government not extradited former Union Carbide Chairman Warren Anderson to face his charges in India?

2. How would Union Carbide's reaction to the gas leak be different if the plant was located in the United States?

3. Do you think a payment of $550 is fair for the victims of the disaster? What do you think the payment would be if the disaster occurred in the United States?

4. Compare the U.S. government's response to the BP Deepwater Horizon disaster with its response to the Union Carbide disaster.

Student Study Site

Visit the Student Study Site at **study.sagepub.com/stanwick3e** to access the following resources:

- Video Links
- SAGE Journal Articles
- Web Resources
- Web Quizzes

9

Ethics and Information Technology

Computers are like Old Testament gods; lots of rules and no mercy.

—Joseph Campbell

Chapter Objectives

After reading and studying Chapter 9, students should be able to

1. Explain the types of critical analysis that can be used to evaluate information technology.
2. Discuss the issues associated with the privacy of employees.
3. Describe the issues associated with the privacy of customers.
4. Identify ethical issues facing Internet usage.
5. Discuss areas for technology fraud, including those associated with the Internet.
6. Explain the USA PATRIOT Act.

The Interview: Two Big Thumbs Down From North Korea

On November 24, 2014, Sony Pictures Entertainment was hacked by a group calling themselves the Guardians of Peace (GOP). The hacking froze the computer monitors of the employees at Sony Pictures, and a red skeleton appeared on the screen with a warning that a comprehensive set of data files would be released to the public, including internal communications related to corporate correspondence, unreleased Sony motion pictures, and personal data. Personal data that were hacked included employee Social Security numbers, performance reviews, salaries, home addresses, and passwords.[1] Sony Pictures speculated that the government of North Korea may have been involved in the hacking because Sony was getting ready to release the movie *The Interview*. *The Interview* is about two American reporters who are hired by the CIA to kill the leader of North Korea, Kim Jong-un. Not only had the hackers stolen 100 terabytes of data, but they also had erased a large portion of the data from Sony's hard drives.[2]

On December 1, 2014, the FBI started investigating whether the government of North Korea was involved in the hacking at Sony Pictures. On December 7, 2014, the Korean Central News Agency described the hacking as a "righteous deed" but also stated that the involvement of the North Korean government was a "wild rumor." On December 8, 2014, Sony's speculation was confirmed when the GOP demanded they "stop immediately showing the movie of terrorism which can break the regional peace and cause the War!"[3]

On December 16, 2014, the GOP posted a message online that threatened that 9/11-type attacks would take place in theaters that showed *The Interview*. The result of these threats was that the major movie theater chains refused to show *The Interview*. On December 17, 2014, Sony Pictures announced that it would not release *The Interview* to theaters on Christmas Day. On the same day, a United States government official announced that North Korea was responsible for the hacking of Sony Pictures. This claim was confirmed by the FBI on December 19, 2014. On December 22, North Korea experienced an Internet outage that lasted almost 10 hours. On December 24, 2014, Sony Pictures released *The Interview* online through Google Play, YouTube Movies, Microsoft's Xbox Video, and through the website www.seetheinterview.com for $5.99. On Christmas Day, *The Interview* was shown in 330 independent theaters nationally.[4] On January 1, 2015, Sony announced that *The Interview* would be available to view on national cable and satellite systems.[5] On February 5, 2015, Sony announced that Amy Pascal, Sony's co-chairman and head of Sony's movie business, would step down. Ms. Pascal's personal e-mails were released as part of the data dumped online by the hackers. A number of those e-mails were considered damaging to her relationships with actors and other executives in the movie industry.[6]

Why Are Information Technology Ethical Issues Important?

The intersection of ethics and information technology can clearly be seen when the results of the American Management Association/ePolicy Institute survey on electronic monitoring and surveillance are reviewed. A staggering 30% of the respondents reported that they had fired workers for misusing the Internet. The causes for dismissal were for the following violations: violation of company policy, 64%; inappropriate or offensive language, 62%; excessive personal use, 26%; breach of confidentiality rules, 22%; other, 12%. In addition, 28% of the respondents reported that they had fired employees for misuse of their corporate e-mail accounts. The causes for dismissal were for the following violations: viewing, downloading, or uploading inappropriate/offensive content, 84%; violation of company policy, 48%; excessive personal use, 34%; and other, 9%. A total of 73% of the firms use technology tools to automatically monitor employee e-mails.[7]

In the same survey, 66% of the firms reported that they monitored employees' computers to determine which websites had been selected. Of the firms responding to the survey, 65% stated that they used software to block connections to inappropriate Web sites. In addition, 45% of the firms monitored the content, the keystrokes used, and the amount of time spent on the computer by their employees. Forty-three percent of the firms in the survey saved and reviewed computer files of their employees. Twelve percent of the firms track blogs to see what was written about the company, and 10% monitor social networking sites.[8]

Furthermore, the survey highlighted the legal ramifications of information technology issues: 24% of the firms in the survey have had e-mail subpoenaed for legal cases, and 15% of the respondents had to address workplace lawsuits that were the result of employee e-mail.[9]

Six percent of the employers fired employees for misusing company phones. Forty-five percent of the firms monitor the time spent and the numbers called on the phone, and 16% recorded phone conversations. Nine percent of the firms monitor employee voice mail messages. Of the firms that monitor office phones, 84% of the firms notify the employees they are monitoring the phone, and 73% of the firms notify the employees that they are monitoring the employee's voice mail.[10]

Forty-eight percent of the firms in the survey reported using video monitoring to deter theft, violence, and sabotage. In addition, 7% of the firms reported using video surveillance to monitor the actions of their employees.[11]

Monitoring can also occur on a global scale. Three percent of the firms in the survey used global positioning systems (GPS) to track cell phones; 8% of the firms used GPS to track company vehicles, and less than 1% used GPS to track employees via the employees' corporate identifications or Smartcards.[12]

Management Issues and Policy Areas for Information Technology

From a stakeholder perspective, a manager has to consider a number of factors when understanding the potential ethical issues that relate to information technology. As an agent for the stockholders, the manager must try to use information technology to enhance the level of competition of the firm. However, it is also the manager's responsibility to ensure that the rights and needs of other stakeholders are not sacrificed to maximize the firm's level of profitability. The critical underlying framework that is required to identify the actual and potential ethical issues that can be raised from information technology could be separated based on management issues and policy areas. Mary Gentile and John J. Sviokla present a matrix in which management issues and policy areas are integrated. In the matrix, they identify with an X an area where a company policy can address a specific management issue. The matrix is shown in Table 9.1.

Management Issues

Privacy Through information technology systems, managers are able to have unlimited access to information that could be considered private and personal. In addition, the ability to capture information at great speeds and permanently store it allows

TABLE 9.1   ●   Management Issues and Policy Areas for Information Technology Activities

Management Issues	Policy Areas			
	Data Policy	Intellectual Property Rights	Workers' Rights	Competitiveness
Privacy	X			
Ownership	X	X	X	X
Control		X	X	X
Accuracy	X			
Security	X		X	

Source: Mary Gentile and John J. Sviokla, Information *Technology in Organizations: Emerging Issues in Ethics and Policy* (Boston: Harvard Business School, 1990), 13.

managers permanent access to private information pertaining to various stakeholders including employees, customers, suppliers, and even special interest groups. Therefore, managers can have access to the information history of any person for which data have been collected by the firm. To protect the privacy of the individuals for which information has been collected, Gentile and Sviokla recommend that managers ask certain questions of themselves before they collect, store, and release potentially private information: What is the nature of the data? If the information were known to the public, what would be the net effect on the individual? Who should have access to this information? Who is responsible for screening potential users to ensure they have a valid reason to request access to the information?[13]

Ownership The collection of information raises the question of property rights. Ownership is based on the answer to the question, "Who has the legal ownership of the information?" As a result, identifying the legitimate owner resolves the ambiguity of who is the ultimate decision maker pertaining to the information. From a privacy perspective, the individual has ownership of his or her own personal information. From a property rights perspective, a firm has to verify whether the owner or some other party is the legal owner of information that has been created and captured during the operations of the firm.

Control Information technology has allowed managers to have the ability to implement many different types of control mechanisms through capturing, tracking, and monitoring information flows inside and outside the firm. Information control has moved beyond simple inventory and asset tracking to include the ability to track the movements, actions, and communications of each employee within the firm.

Accuracy As access and accumulation of information become easier within a firm, so does the probability that some of the information may be inaccurate. As a result, managers must be sure that the source of the information has generated accurate data and has interpreted the data in an accurate manner.

Security As availability and the dissemination of information become easier, so do the security issues that are related to data become more challenging. The manager must ensure that comprehensive steps have been implemented to guarantee that data collected by the firm are protected diligently so there are no negative impacts on stakeholders based on the content of the information.

Policy Areas That Can Address Information Technology Management Issues[14]

Data Policy The company must establish an explicit and inclusive data policy to ensure that every employee who has access to corporate data understands what is acceptable and what is unacceptable in releasing information. In addition, a data policy is also a declaration to the firm's stakeholders of its commitment to being a good steward of the data. An effective data policy needs to address issues of privacy, control, accuracy, and security.

Intellectual Rights Policy An intellectual rights policy should clearly spell out what intellectual property is owned by the employee and what intellectual property is owned by the firm. A standard intellectual rights policy will state that because the employee is using assets of the firm, any intellectual property developed in the workplace belongs to the firm unless the employee can verify that there were unique circumstances to prove otherwise or that it is part of the employee's contract to maintain all intellectual property rights as a condition of employment.

Workers' Rights Policy Managers of the firm must explain, through the firm's workers' rights policy, the conditions the employees may be subject to during their employment with the firm. Issues that need to be addressed in the workers' rights policy include the type of monitoring that can take place within the firm, the type of information that may be collected pertaining to the employee, and the identification of what information would be considered private versus public.

The Next Step: Critical Analysis[15]

As managers identify and address these management issues pertaining to information technology, they need to be aware of how their decisions affect various stakeholders. As a result, managers should do different types of critical analysis to assist in their decision-making processes. Those analyses should include stakeholder analysis, utilitarian goal-based analysis, rights-based analysis, and duty-based analysis.

Stakeholder Analysis

Managers need to identify all the relevant stakeholders who will be affected by an information technology–based decision. Some questions to ask would be the following: Which stakeholders will be affected by this decision? What is at risk for each stakeholder? How do my decision options affect the interests of the stakeholders? Should certain stakeholders be considered a high priority for this information technology decision?

Utilitarian Goal-Based Analysis

After the identification of the relevant stakeholders takes place, the manager must consider the net results of his or her decision. The utilitarian goal-based analysis is used to help the managers determine a decision that will produce the greatest good to the greatest number of stakeholders. Not to be confused with a cost-benefit analysis, the utilitarian goal-based analysis is based on both the financial and nonfinancial impacts the decision will have on others. This analysis also attempts to determine the maximum benefits to all of the firm's stakeholders instead of focusing solely on one stakeholder group, the stockholders.

Rights-Based Analysis

Rights-based analysis occurs when a manager reviews the potential decisions and considers how each option would affect the rights of each type of stakeholder. For example, would the information technology decision affect a stakeholder's human rights, privacy rights, individual freedoms, or institutional rights?

Duty-Based Analysis

Duty-based analysis focuses on an evaluation of whether the options available to the manager affect any of the fundamental ethical duties of the manager. Ethical duties of the manager would include being honest, fair, and truthful and not causing any harm to any people.

Privacy of Employees

E-Mail

Virtually all jobs in today's society require use of e-mail. This leads to the question of privacy of e-mail messages. In general, most employees can assume that e-mail messages are not private. The computer systems are owned by the company, and thus, employers are allowed to monitor the messages being sent through the computer systems. Under the 1986 Electronic Communications Privacy Act, employers can consider individuals' e-mail corporate property. Sometimes, employers back up e-mail messages with other important data at the end of the day. This means that e-mail messages that employees thought they had deleted may have actually been saved. If the company policies state that the e-mails are to be kept private and are confidential, employees may have some recourse against an employer who, unknown to the employee, monitors e-mail messages.

Is any e-mail actually private? And just how far can you go without being unethical when it comes to others' e-mail? Can e-mail be used against employees? The answer to this last question is yes. Some believe that once e-mail is deleted from your e-mail system, it just goes away. But technology exists that allow this e-mail to be recovered and used as evidence against the employee in legal situations. In addition, employees need to be reminded that their e-mail accounts and individual e-mail messages really aren't private. This may be accomplished through an e-mail policy that is distributed and signed by all employees who have e-mail accounts. At www.enronemail.com, approximately 515,000 e-mail messages from Enron employees have become public documents. They were publicly released by the Federal Energy Regulatory Commission in 2003. So should employees think that their e-mails are confidential? Absolutely not. In many cases, e-mail content is shared among employees and may eventually find itself outside the company. Many companies have turned to monitoring the e-mail of their employees. E-mail can be subpoenaed and made public through court proceedings. It is becoming increasingly common for companies to eliminate e-mail or Internet privileges and possibly fine employees for misuse, especially if the use is illegal or degrading to the company.

Misconceptions Pertaining to E-Mail Privacy

With the underlying assumption that all e-mail is not private if sent from the workplace, why are there so many misconceptions about the level of privacy of e-mail? The first could be the lack of experience and understanding by the e-mail user. The user may not understand or realize that e-mail can be retrieved even after it has been deleted from the hard drive. The second reason could be a vague or nonexistent policy pertaining to e-mail from the firm. If the firm does not have a formal data policy, as mentioned earlier, the employees might not realize that the firm can take over ownership of their e-mail correspondence.[16]

Utilitarian Goal-Based Analysis Pertaining to the Use of E-Mail

As discussed previously in the chapter, one way to approach the ethical issues pertaining to information technology is to focus on what is the greatest good for the greatest number. As a result, an employee–employer stakeholder cost-benefit analysis can be used to determine whether the benefits of using e-mail outweigh the financial and ethical costs. Table 9.2 summarizes some of the costs and benefits.

TABLE 9.2 ● Costs and Benefits of Using E-Mail

Benefits

Cost benefits—e-mail is cheaper than other mediums of communication (fax, telephone, posted mail)

Efficiency—e-mail allows communication to a large population quickly

Documentation—e-mail is a written document that can be stored and retrieved

Access to resources—e-mail allows for easy access to information and people

Monitoring—employers can monitor the activities of the employees

Costs

Offensive communications—e-mail may relay inappropriate and/or offensive behavior

Frivolous use—e-mail can take a disproportionate amount of time relative to its real value

Information overload—e-mail can become the dominant form of communication within an organization; the sheer volume of e-mail may, at times, overwhelm the user

Source: Suzanne P. Weisband and Bruce A. Reinig, "Managing User Perceptions of Email Privacy," *Communications of the ACM* 38, no. 12 (1995): 45.

When the courts must decide about employee-monitoring disputes, the courts often try to balance "an employee's reasonable expectation of privacy against the employer's business justification for the monitoring."[17] What constitutes ethical use of a company's computer? Thomas Hilton surveyed 191 Fortune 500 companies about information usage. Of the respondents, 97% felt that it is management's responsibility to define ethical computer use for employees. Hilton argues that this thought is contrary to the usual view that ethics are personal in nature, and the response indicates that employees want a computer ethics code to guide them in their daily work. For example, Northumberland National Park Authority, located in the United Kingdom, has established several policies dealing with information technology. The policies include guidance on such topics as data backup, data protection, electronic mail, Internet access, and storage of data and records. All the policies established are done to help employees function in an efficient manner and to use all resources to their maximum potential.[18]

Types of Computer Monitoring

The Privacy Rights Clearinghouse suggests that there are two main types of computer monitoring that take place in companies. The first is a type of software that allows the employer to see what is on the computer screen in an employee's office or that allows the employer to view information stored on the hard drives. This makes it extremely easy for employers to monitor Internet use and e-mail use. A second kind of computer monitoring allows the employer to determine how long a computer has been idle, suggesting that the employee is not actually doing his or her job.[19]

One company, Aladdin Knowledge Systems in Tel Aviv, has introduced a prototype security system, called Biometric Security Systems, which identifies users based on heartbeats, rather than on PINs or passwords. Another company, SanDisk, makes USB fingerprint readers for security measures. PC makers such as Lenovo and Fujitsu sell laptops that boast built-in fingerprint readers.[20]

One private video surveillance company located in Ohio was the first known company to tag workers to electronically identify them. The tagging is being used to control access to a security video room, which houses video footage for government agencies. Ethical issues abound from this implantation procedure, mostly from the possibility of being able to track the employees' activities without their knowledge.[21]

Six criteria have been set forth by W. A. Parent to help determine whether an invasion of privacy is justifiable by an employer:[22]

1. For what purpose is the undocumented personal knowledge sought?
2. Is this purpose a legitimate and important one?
3. Is the knowledge sought through invasion of privacy relevant to its justifying purpose?
4. Is invasion of privacy the only or the least offensive means of obtaining the knowledge?
5. What restrictions or procedural restraints have been placed on the privacy-invading techniques?
6. How will the personal knowledge be protected once it has been acquired?

TABLE 9.3 ● Unethical Practices in the Workplace		
	Percentage Finding Action Seriously Unethical	
Action	**Employees**	**Managers**
The right of a company to monitor employee e-mail	44% (11% higher)	33%
The right of a company to monitor employees using video cameras	39% (5% higher)	34%
The right of a company to monitor voice mail	50% (8% higher)	42%
The right of a company to examine an employee's locker or work areas	47% (6% higher)	41%
The right of an employee to send and to receive personal e-mail during working hours	45%	50% (5% higher)
The right of an employee to use the Internet for personal use during working hours	58% (2% higher)	56%

Source: Adapted from *USA Today*, March 27, 2000.

There is a constant debate about monitoring of employees by the employers. Table 9.3 shows the results of a survey of both managers and employees on workplace ethics conducted by the Society of Financial Service Professionals.

These results show two things. First, managers don't seem to view these actions as unethical as employees do. This could be because managers are interested in protecting productivity and potentially thwarting ethical dilemmas before they arise. It may even be that the results would change if the managers were to consider their feelings if the actions were done to them. Second, as the Society of Financial Service Professionals has pointed out, employees seem more concerned than managers about protecting their privacy of thought and speech.

Telephone Monitoring

The issue of telephone monitoring is also still being debated. The Electronic Communications Privacy Act of 1986 allows monitoring of business-related phone calls. However, if the phone call is personal in nature, the monitoring must cease. If employees are explicitly told that they cannot make personal calls from business phones, calls may be monitored. Employers may also have to legally register a list of phone numbers and length of calls as an effort to monitor phone usage.

Cell phones create even further complications. Three vulnerabilities exist related to cell phones.[23] First, your conversations could be monitored while you are on the phone. If a person has a radio signal receiver, conversations can be tapped to listen.

Second, it is possible to change a cell phone into a microphone. Finally, cellular phones can be subject to cloning; to clone, the electronic serial number and mobile identification number are stolen and entered into another phone. Although it seems farfetched for some to believe, employers may suspect employees of ethical wrongdoing and monitor telephone conversations.

Privacy of Customers

Because companies are able to gather, store, match, and make more inferences about information because of greater technological advances, the issue of privacy has risen to the forefront of ethical issues related to computer technology. The importance of protecting customer information is vital. Few want information about them becoming public, but many corporations now employ technology that allows them to make inferences about customers that many customers do not even know the company is making. Information is being stored and used for future reference. This means that companies are able to use information to develop products and alter advertising claims.

For customer telephone calls, many employers have begun to monitor calls for quality control. In California, the California Public Utilities Commission requires that companies inform parties in telephone communications that their calls may be monitored.[24] This means that the companies must give some kind of warning, in many cases a recorded message, that calls may be recorded. In addition, the Electronics Communications Privacy Act, a federal regulation, allows unannounced monitoring of business-related calls. The Privacy Rights Clearinghouse suggests that privacy of personal calls made at work may be increased through using cell phones, pay phones, or separate phones that employers have designated for personal calls.[25] This will help eliminate the risk that an employer listens in on a personal call. Employees, however, should follow company rules if employers do not allow personal phone calls on the job. In some cases, a company may use a pen register to record calls. This device allows the employer to record a list of phone calls made from an employee's extension. In some cases, this device can also be used to record the time spent on the phone calls.

Many consumers are unaware of the business intelligence systems that many companies employ. These systems allow companies to monitor the behaviors of consumers using their products. Firms can monitor what kind of products the customers are ordering, how much is being spent each time the customer purchases a product, and how often customers are ordering their products. These systems allow companies to adjust their marketing plans to target specific customers and their preferences.

The main question to be addressed is the issue of maintaining the integrity of customers' personal information. Although companies have an ethical responsibility to provide safeguards for the information they gather on customers, the customers must also employ safeguards to protect their own information. Table 9.4 identifies several consumer protection tactics identified by the Federal Trade Commission (FTC).

Another issue that has raised controversial concerns is that of electronic monitoring for marketing and advertising purposes. Many consumers feel that this is an invasion of privacy, something that should be avoided at all costs. One of the most common ways of monitoring customers and potential customers is by using cookies. Cookies allow a company's website to gather and store information about consumers.

TABLE 9.4 ● Consumer Protection Tactics

1. Watch for catchwords and phrases.
2. Protect your private information.
3. Don't download files sent electronically by strangers.
4. When you buy items online, pay with a credit card.
5. Never give your password to anyone.
6. Pay attention.
7. When in doubt, check it out.
8. Use your common sense.
9. Don't be afraid to file a complaint.

Source: http://www.ftc.gov.

It is possible to disable cookies on your computer or at least delete cookies when an Internet session is finished. This type of computer surveillance is becoming more common, although it was originally set up to save customer passwords as a convenience to customers. Most information collected by companies can be considered value added to the company. However, privacy issues abound about when and how this information is being collected.

The Ethical Issues Related to Big Data[26]

Big data refers to the collection of large sets of data to be analyzed to help firms customize their strategic focus to their customers. Business analytics is a very useful tool for firms to enhance their customers' experience. The ethical issues associated with analyzing big data relate to when helping the customer's experience stops and the invasion of the customer's privacy starts. There are a number of risks that can develop when firms collect and interpret big data: loss of anonymity, self-protection, data patterns versus reality, and discrimination-based customer segmentations.

Loss of Anonymity

The standard disclaimer on any data collection process is that the personal information given by the user will not be identified at the individual level. This promise of anonymity gives a sense of security to the user submitting the data to firms. However, reidentification—in which "anonymous" data can be linked to a specific individual—can take place with data sets. For example, it is estimated that 87% of United States citizens can be identified in publically available databases if their birthdate, gender, and postal code are identified in the data set. This reidentification can then be linked to highly sensitive data such as medical, financial, and personal information.

Self-Protection

Many users are not aware of how the data will be used by firms. This ignorance about the uses of data collection may result in users later objecting to how information they have provided to a firm is being used. Even if the users read the "terms and conditions," there may not be specific descriptions of the use of data by the firm. In addition, the users may not be aware of potentially how long the firm can continue to use the data.

Data Patterns Versus Reality

Data analysis can show statistical patterns but it cannot predict the future. Firms may assume that data patterns can be used to identify the future activities of the individuals the data were obtained from. As a result, unjustifiable generalizations can be developed by the firm based on the past data collection of others. Therefore, a general profile can be developed by the firm that is not necessarily applicable to the behavior of any particular individual.

Discrimination-Based Customer Segmentation

The profiling as a result of the data analysis can lead the firm to apply discriminatory assumptions on the data patterns of the individuals. Information such as age, gender, ethnic background, health condition, and social economic status can be used by the firm to make unfounded conclusions about the potential behavior of an individual. In addition, firms may use these discriminatory data patterns to "customize" the experiences of the individuals, which could further entrench their discriminatory beliefs.

The FTC has issued a Safeguards Rule, which requires safeguarding of customer records and information. This rule is part of the implementation of the Gramm-Leach-Bliley Act and applies to all sizes of businesses. Specifically, each financial institution must develop a security plan that does the following:

- Designates one or more employees to coordinate the safeguard efforts
- Identifies and assesses the risks to customer information and evaluates the effectiveness of safeguards to control these risks
- Designs and implements a safeguards program and regularly monitors and tests it
- Selects appropriate service providers and makes them implement safeguards[27]

In addition, companies must carefully consider employee management and training, information systems, and managing systems failures to help mitigate the effects of security system failures.

Firms can take five steps to ensure that customers are satisfied with how a firm uses customer information:

1. Establish a clear process by which privacy complaints by customers can be addressed.
2. Establish an easy-to-understand privacy policy for customer information.
3. Identify the constraints of transferring customer information.
4. Establish an opt-in and opt-out customer policy for information sharing.
5. Establish a branding competitive strategy that includes privacy commitments.[28]

The Challenge of Technology

E-commerce is a major business opportunity that cannot be missed. However, several ethical issues surround doing business via the Internet. Many websites are beginning to ask for customers' permission to send unsolicited marketing e-mails to them. This response has surfaced because customers noticed that they were receiving unsolicited ads from companies after they made a purchase. In some instances, users of Internet sites realized that they were receiving e-mails after just visiting some sites. This began to raise concerns in consumers' minds about privacy issues.

Victoria Bush, Beverly Venable, and Alan Bush identified, through a survey of marketers, ethical issues facing Internet usage:

- Security transactions
- Illegal activity (fraud, hacking, etc.)
- Privacy
- Honesty/truthfulness
- Judged by same standards as other mediums
- Pornography
- Product warranty
- Plagiarism
- Targeting children
- Unsolicited e-mail
- False advertising[29]

Before a company can evaluate the effects of the electronic commerce in a positive and productive way, top managers must be computer literate and embrace e-commerce. In some cases, top managers are considered "dinosaurs." From a technology perspective, these dinosaurs are web illiterate and really know very little about computers. Several danger signs exist for identifying top managers who operate like dinosaurs:

- A recurring vacancy in the chief information officer position
- A reliance of executives on staff to handle e-mail
- Rare discussion of technology issues by the board of directors
- Low accountability for senior managers handling high-tech projects and budgets[30]

Absolute privacy will never be guaranteed for online transactions. Issues related to privacy will continue to mount because of the constant change in technology. This ability to gather, store, and use information will continue to be refined.

Fake Payment

Many online retailers feel the effects of fake credit card purchases. Approximately 14¢ of every $100 of online credit card purchases are fraudulent. This is in an industry of Internet retailing, which accounts for 11% of all credit card transactions.[31] Most important, Internet retailers are usually responsible for these fraudulent transactions because they have no way of checking the customer's physical credit card to verify the information given to them. For example, when Neil Kugelman opened his online jewelry business, www.Goldspeed.com, he realized that his first order was fraudulent. He realized the shipping address didn't match the mailing address, the telephone number didn't work, and the e-mail address didn't go through. He cancelled the order. Today, his company fills more than 50,000 orders per year, and Kugelman estimates about

30% of the online orders are fraudulent. In addition, Kugelman suspected another customer of making fraudulent orders and called the credit card company to verify the card several times. The credit card company assured him that the credit card was valid, and Kugelman shipped the items. Subsequently, the card was found to be fraudulent, and Kugelman was responsible for the loss. Online business owners must work even harder to identify fraudulent activities.[32]

Intellectual Property

The issue of intellectual property rights has resurfaced as Internet usage has increased, particularly relating to digital piracy. Illegal downloading of music and movies has become a large problem as more and more Internet users develop attitudes that if the music is there, it is for entertainment purposes and it is free. Some companies have tried to make illegal downloading and copying more difficult by installing measures that make downloading extremely difficult or by encouraging legal retaliations. People illegally download and copy music for many reasons. These range from "it is on the Internet, so I can copy it for free" to "CDs and DVDs are too expensive to purchase, especially if I want only one song." These attitudes can be changed only through a comprehensive crackdown on those who violate intellectual property rights.

The Role of Government Regulations

From an ethical perspective, should there be a government agency charged with policing the Internet? When this issue is explored, many would agree that this would be a most arduous task because the Internet is used for so many different purposes. In addition, how or in what capacity would this policing effort be enforced? Who would be responsible for the enforcement of any regulations? This issue is being debated, with many new regulations being considered and debated by lawmakers. Should the Internet be regulated in only one country if other countries fail to provide adequate Internet regulation? Would regulation of the Internet be considered censorship in the United States, thus constituting a violation of our First Amendment rights? Many questions must be answered before the Internet can begin to be regulated.

The Sarbanes-Oxley Act, while posing new regulations concerning internal controls, affects companies regardless of size, geographical location, or customer base. Companies must, despite the specifics of their businesses, comply with the act's provisions. Part of this compliance means investing in the appropriate computer technology. The compliance section has given rise to many compliance-oriented software packages. These packages have been developed to help companies comply mainly with Section 404 of the Act, assessing the effectiveness of internal controls. (Section 404 applies only to companies that file reports with the Securities and Exchange Commission pursuant to the Securities Exchange Act of 1934.) Thomas Vartanian and Mark Fajfar offer several basic guidelines when one is dealing with the issue of information security compliance:

- Check information security controls each time the business changes.
- Design information systems to permit later auditing.

- Hold third-party service providers to high standards.
- Monitor personnel to prevent information misuse or loss.[33]

Other global government regulations that pertain to information technology issues include the following:

- The World Intellectual Property Organization—WIPO has two treaties that protect the copyrights of intellectual property worldwide on properties such as books, songs, films, and pirated CDs and DVDs. The Digital Millennium Copyright Act, passed in 1998 by the U.S. Congress, was based on one of the WIPO treaties.
- The European Union's Electronic Commerce Directive—This directive forced companies to abide by the information technology laws of their country of origin and of a total of 15 countries.[34]

The Volunteer Censoring of Internet Search Information

In February 2006, a U.S. congressional committee sought answers from Google, Microsoft, and Yahoo! regarding their relationship with the Chinese government. All three of the companies sold Internet search technology to the Chinese government, which allowed the government to monitor all activities on the Internet system and allowed the government to block user access to information on the Internet. This censoring of information was counter to the three companies' public beliefs that all information on the Internet should be available to anyone in the world who seeks to find it. Google allowed the Chinese government to block results from certain search terms such as *freedom*, whereas Microsoft agreed to censor the software before it was sold to the Chinese government, and Yahoo! agreed to give the Chinese government information that led to the arrest of government "dissidents."

Google had spent more than a year internally discussing the moral and financial considerations of operating in China. Google officials concluded that a censored version of Google was the best solution. They rationalized that if the censorship is transparent, the users will know why the search has been blocked, and their presence in China could be used to put pressure on the Chinese government's policy on human rights.[35] Elliot Schrage, who represented Google at the congressional hearing as the vice president of global communications and public affairs for the company, stated that Google had to decide whether to "compromise our mission by failing to serve our users in China or compromise our mission by entering China and complying with Chinese laws that require us to censor search results. . . . Based on what we know today and what we see in China, we believe our decision to launch the Google.cn service in addition to our Google.com service is a reasonable one, better for Chinese users and better for Google. . . . Self-censoring, like that which we are now required to perform in China, is something that conflicts deeply with our core principles. . . . This was not something we did enthusiastically or something that we're proud of at all."[36]

Microsoft also sold software that censored searches such as "democracy" and "freedom." When asked to explain Microsoft's justification for this action, Microsoft stated, "abides by the laws and regulations of each country in which it operates."[37] When

Yahoo! was asked why it gave the Chinese government information to lead to the arrest of dissidents, Yahoo!'s senior vice president and general counsel stated that they had no choice because "Yahoo! China was legally bound to comply with the requirements of Chinese law enforcement. . . . When we receive a demand from law enforcement authorized under the law of the country in which we operate, we must comply. . . . Failure to comply in China could have subjected Yahoo! China and its employees to criminal charges, including imprisonment. Ultimately, U.S. companies in China face a choice: comply with Chinese law or leave."[38] Richard De George argued that corporations doing business with China do not have to follow laws that are unethical.[39] De George cited the example of General Motors disobeying laws related to apartheid when the company did business in South Africa. De George concludes, "Disobeying unethical laws is ethically justifiable; otherwise, one is forced to conclude that one has an ethical obligation to act unethically because it is commanded by law."[40]

Technology-Based Fraud

Because information is collected, stored, and transmitted via the Internet, there are many opportunities for fraudulent activities to occur. These fraudulent activities will continue to occur as Internet technology continues to change. Table 9.5 identifies some of the types of Internet fraud affecting individuals and companies.

The e-mail and websites used in phishing schemes look like legitimate business e-mail and websites, but they are not. One way of abusing e-mail systems, phishing is the use of e-mail to try to mimic a legal, legitimate company to "fish" for personal or financial information from individuals. In many cases, the information obtained in this fraudulent manner is used for identity theft. In all cases, the fraud perpetrators are trying

TABLE 9.5   ●   Types of Internet Fraud

Type of Fraud	Description
Auction and Retail Schemes	Schemes offering high-value items that are likely to attract many consumers by inducing them to send money but then deliver nothing or a lower-value item than what was promised
Business Opportunity or "Work at Home" Schemes	Schemes advertising business opportunities that would allow individuals to earn thousands of dollars a month, but first requiring the individual to pay an upfront fee before failing to deliver the necessary information
Identity Theft and Fraud	Obtaining and using someone else's personal data in a fraudulent or deceptive way
Market Manipulation Schemes	Disseminating false and fraudulent information to cause increases in thinly traded stocks or stocks of shell companies then selling off the stocks before the price falls back to its usual low level, disseminating false or fraudulent information in an effort to cause a price decrease, or combining mass-marketing technology with telemarketing schemes
Credit Card Schemes	Using unlawfully obtained credit card numbers to order goods or services online

Source: http://www.usdoj.gov/criminal/fraud/internet.

to get individuals to reveal financial and personal data that can be used for identity theft, credit card theft, or outright fraudulent transactions. Some of the schemes used may even contain computer viruses that will infect other users if the original e-mail is forwarded. The participants in the phishing schemes may be committing the following:

- Identify theft
- Wire fraud
- Credit card fraud
- Bank fraud
- Computer fraud

Other fraudulent activities are listed in the CAN-SPAM Act.[41]

The ultimate goal of phishing or other types of technology fraud is to acquire personal information pertaining to an individual that could be used in the future for illegal activities. As a result, all computer users must ensure they are not victims of identity theft.

An interesting initiative by the Federal Bureau of Investigation (FBI), in conjunction with other government agencies, called Operation Web Snare, was developed to help target and convict cybercriminals. Operating between June 1, 2004, and August 26, 2004, officials sought to convict those operating criminal schemes online. These frauds included the following:

- Criminal spam
- Phishing
- Spoofed or hijacked accounts
- International reshipping schemes
- Cyber-extortion
- Auction fraud
- Credit card fraud
- Intellectual property rights fraud
- Computer intrusions or hacking
- Economic espionage or theft of trade secrets
- International money laundering
- Identity theft
- More "traditional" online crimes[42]

Through this program, there were more than 150 investigations. These investigations represented more than $210 million lost by more than 870,000 victims through these Internet crimes. When completed, there were more than one hundred arrests and convictions. Table 9.6 shows some recommendations from the Federal Deposit Insurance Corporation (FDIC) on how individuals can protect themselves from identity theft.[43]

Internet Attacks

Since September 11, 2001, many U.S. citizens are acutely aware of terrorism. Although no one can be 100% safe from terrorist attacks, it is possible to take precautions to better protect businesses from cyberterrorism. Cyberterrorism is the use of computer technology to commit terrorism crimes. Though no company, large or small, can shield

TABLE 9.6 ● FDIC Strategies for Fighting Identity Theft
1. Protect your Social Security number, credit card and debit card numbers, personal identification numbers, passwords, and other personal information.
2. Protect your incoming and outgoing mail.
3. Keep your financial trash "clean."
4. Keep a close watch on your bank account statements and credit card bills.
5. Avoid ID theft on the Internet.
6. Exercise your rights under the Fair and Accurate Credit Transactions Act to review your credit record and report fraudulent activity.

Source: http://www.fdic.gov/consumers/consumer/fighttheft.

itself from all terrorist attacks, some industries may be more vulnerable than others. These industries include defense contractors, medical and health care companies, pharmaceutical companies, and financial institutions.

Several types of cyberterrorism crimes can be committed. These include e-mail crimes, identity theft (breaking into company computers to steal customer information), viruses that can wipe out all or parts of a company's computer system, and installation of spyware on computers without the company's knowledge. Tommie Singleton and Aaron Singleton identify several measures that can be used to protect businesses:

- An effective risk assessment
- A comprehensive review of the company's policies and procedures related to security
- A sound business recovery plan described in the company's policies and procedures
- Development of an incident response plan
- Education for key managers and employees, including training and seminars
- Insurance to provide coverage if an attack occurs[44]

Spyware is fast becoming one way to gather information to send to users, mainly unknown to the owner of the computer technology. *Spyware* is software that can be loaded onto a computer so an outside party can monitor the computer operations without the consent of the computer user. Many computer users are not familiar with the underlying operations of the computers they use in their day-to-day employment. Many times, this spyware is downloaded in tandem with other free software that the users get from the Internet.

The European Union has enacted the European Data Protection Directive (EDPD), which also requires consent of the user before the manufacturer can collect data on the user. All told, the subject of spyware can be summarized as an issue of privacy. Mainly, is it ethical to install software and monitor users without their express consent? In trying to balance the issues related to computer technology, the ethical issue of using spyware will continue to be debated in the business community.[45]

Evidence has arisen about programs that use keylogging to copy keystrokes of computer users. Considered by many to be Trojan horses, these programs may be hidden in software with the intent of affecting the computer. In Brazil, a fraud ring of 55 people was arrested for using these keyloggers to steal $4.7 million from accounts at six different banks. Authorities in Brazil believe that keylogger schemes are overtaking phishing schemes.[46]

The USA PATRIOT Act

The terrorist attacks on September 11, 2001, have fundamentally changed the world. In direct response to the attacks, on October 26, 2001, President George W. Bush signed into law the Uniting and Strengthening America by Providing Appropriate Tools Required to Intercept and Obstruct Terrorism Act, which is also called the USA PATRIOT Act. Companies should be aware of several components of the USA PATRIOT Act because they can significantly affect a firm's operations.

The act provides expanded government authority over matters such as electronic communications and the use of computer and monetary transactions. Under the current conditions of the act, government officials are allowed to request and monitor electronic communications that they believe may have a terrorist link. They do not have to have evidence of terrorist activity to make this request. As a result, all electronic communications are now considered available for government inspection. Although it is not expected that legitimate firms would experience any negative impact from this provision, companies need to be aware that all electronic communications may be viewed by third parties. As a result, firms must ensure that highly sensitive and confidential information is not relayed through electronic communications. Fraud, theft, or extortion linked to computer use will be considered terrorist acts but are defined very broadly.[47]

The USA PATRIOT Act also has a broad definition of which types of companies are included within the act. The act is designed to monitor the activities of financial institutions; however, the act considers many types of businesses that are involved in financial transactions. Banks, savings and loan companies, and credit unions are included, as are other businesses such as mutual funds, securities brokers, credit card operators, and money transfer companies are included. In addition, companies that have high volumes of cash transactions could be considered as included within these guidelines.

The responsibilities of the businesses that are eligible to be included in the provisions of the USA PATRIOT Act consist of a comprehensive system to ensure accurate customer identification and account monitoring. In addition, each company included within the act must have developed a number of control mechanisms that involve establishing internal policies and procedures to ensure compliance. Furthermore, the firm must implement independent audits and training programs for employees so each employee is aware of his or her responsibilities. Each company must also have a compliance officer who is responsible for the overall monitoring system. A number of questions need to be asked to ensure compliance with the act:

1. Has the board of directors approved a written anti–money laundering program?
2. Are there written policies, procedures, and controls to prevent and detect money laundering?
3. Has a compliance officer been designated?
4. Is there an independent audit function to periodically test the program?
5. Is there an ongoing employee training program on the institution's anti–money laundering program, the money laundering laws, the various schemes, and how to prevent and detect them?[48]

Questions for Thought

1. In the opening vignette, was it the correct decision for Sony to stop the initial release of *The Interview?* What message did that action send to the hackers? The movie industry? The actors? How would you respond to the same situation that Sony had to address?

2. Analyze the costs and benefits of using e-mail presented in Table 9.3. Why are the employees' and managers' responses different?

3. How has control of the data collected by firms pertaining to customers changed over the years? What type of government regulations are in place to ensure the data do not go to unauthorized users?

Real-Life Ethical Dilemma Exercise

The Dark Side of Technology[49]

There was a unique buzz at the 2012 South by Southwest Technology Conference. It was not related to the latest video game system, nor was it related to the latest smart phone. No, the unique buzz was concerned with having homeless people wear wireless transmitters. Homeless people were hired by a marketing agency, BBH Labs, to walk around the conference with mobile Wi-Fi devices so that the attendees of the conference could receive Internet access. The homeless people were paid $20 a day and allowed to keep any tips given to them. Thirteen homeless people walked around the conference carrying the device, passing out business cards for BBH Labs, and wearing T-shirts advertising BBH. The T-shirts had their names and function, such as "I'm Clarence, a 4G Hotspot." The homeless people were told to go to the most crowded parts of the conference area so they could advertise BBH Labs "Homeless Hotspots" projects, which the marketing firm classified as a "charitable experiment." One attendee, Tim Carmody, who is a blogger for *Wired* magazine, seemed to capture the consensus of the conference attendees. Carmody stated that the whole idea and project was "completely problematic," and he compared the idea of using human beings as Wi-Fi transmitters as "something out of a darkly satirical science-fiction dystopia." A spokesperson for BBH Labs, Saneel Radia, director of innovation, claimed that the company was not taking advantage of the homeless people and compared the Wi-Fi project to traditional projects such as homeless people selling newspapers on the street. Radia stated, "We saw it as a means to raise awareness by giving homeless people a way to engage with mainstream society and talk to people . . . The hot spot is a way for them to tell their story." Although all their homeless participants volunteered for the project and appeared to appreciate the opportunity to make money, the image the project represents to the high technology industry may be difficult to reconcile. As Adam Hanft, CEO of the marketing advisory firm Hanft Projects, states, "There is already a sense that the Internet community has become so absurdly self-involved that they don't think there's any world outside of theirs."[50]

Questions for the Real-Life Ethical Dilemma Exercise

1. Your boss has presented the idea of using homeless people in a project similar to what BBH Labs has done. What would you tell him? If your boss was determined to move forward with the project, what would you do?

2. BBH Labs compared its project to homeless people selling newspapers on the street. Do you agree with this analogy?

3. Do you agree with the perception that the Internet industry and Silicon Valley are self-absorbed and do not care about anyone other than themselves?

4. Is there any difference between paying a homeless man to work in the United States for $20 a day and paying an 11-year-old girl to work for $2 a day in India? Explain your position.

Student Study Site

Visit the Student Study Site at **study.sagepub.com/stanwick3e** to access the following resources:

- Video Links
- SAGE Journal Articles
- Web Resources
- Web Quizzes

10

Marketing and Advertising

It is true that you may fool all the people some of the time; you can even fool some of the people all the time; but you can't fool all the people all the time.

—Abraham Lincoln

Chapter Objectives

After reading and studying Chapter 10, students should be able to

1. Describe the green marketing movement.
2. Explain the ethical issues that arise from relationship marketing.
3. Explain the effect of boycotts on business and the origin of boycotts.
4. Describe the activities of Johnson & Johnson around the Tylenol scare.
5. List the reasons why product recalls occur.
6. Describe the costs of conducting a product recall.
7. Explain the ethical considerations of purchasing and sales transactions.
8. Describe the marketing campaigns of tobacco companies.

There Is Now an App for Chauvinism[1]

On October 9, 2009, an energy drink by Pepsi called AMP began to amp up the controversy and buzz in the advertising industry. To establish a "cutting edge" marketing focus, Pepsi decided to develop an app called "amp up before you score." This app was designed to help men pick up women based on certain stereotypes. Pepsi described the app as "a roadmap to success with your favorite kinds of women."

Pepsi identified 24 stereotypes: artist, aspiring actress, athlete, bookworm, businesswoman, celebrity, cougar, dancer, foreign exchange student, Goth girl, indie rock girl, married, military girl, nerd, out-of-your-league girl, political girl, princess, punk rock girl, rebound girl, sorority girl, tree hugger, trouble, twins, and women studies major. Suggested pick-up lines for the foreign exchange student included "Let's try a little cultural exchange." A pick-up line for the artist included "You know the Mona Lisa has no eyebrows. I wonder what else she shaves." Users of the app click on the stereotype that most closely resembles the women they are trying to pick up, and the app coaches the user on "useful" facts and potential pick-up lines. For example, a tree hugger would be impressed if you talked about carbon footprints. For the Indie girl, there was a built-in thrift store locator. The app also allows the users who "scored" to post the woman's name, date, and comments for his pals on Facebook and Twitter. Pepsi's response was that the app was intended for users older than 17 and was designed to appeal and to entertain AMP's target demographic. On October 22, 2009, Pepsi announced that the app was removed because of the criticism that the app supported stereotyping women. Pepsi officials thought that it was the most appropriate action to take after listening to feedback from various audiences.

Alternative Views of the Foundation of Marketing and Advertising

In 1960, Jerome McCarthy presented the idea of the marketing mix that he represented with the four Ps: product, price, promotion, and place.[2] Although subsequent researchers have fine-tuned and broadened these classifications, these four areas are still considered the foundation for the success of a good marketing campaign. Firms must address each of these four areas from an ethical standpoint. A cynic and skeptic about the "value" marketing has for society would argue that the negative impacts far outweigh the positive aspects of marketing. Whether by misleading customers, presenting false demand and scarcity, or charging a price that is not equitable when considering the overall cost of the product, marketing has received its share of controversy. For example, there are hundreds of brands of cigarettes around the world yet all the brands have basically the same commodity ingredients, tobacco, cigarette paper, and an optional filter. Therefore, because the products are basically the same globally, there is only one way to differentiate products—marketing. A more effective way to describe the marketing mix is to focus on the emotions of the consumers. Whether through fear, jealousy, or pride, marketing enhances product messages by attempting to strike a chord with the inner emotions of the consumer. Thus, an effective alternative method to describe a firm's marketing strategy is to apply the seven deadly sins: lust, gluttony, greed, sloth, wrath, envy, and pride.

Lust

It is well known in the advertising industry that "sex sells." Sex has been a common theme of advertising campaigns for more than a century. Lust is generated not just by the spokesperson of the advertising but, on occasion, by the product itself.

Gluttony

Examples of gluttony are numerous in fast food industry advertising. With the 24-ounce drink and the supersize French fries, fast food has increased the opportunities for consumers to become gluttonous. In addition, gluttony can be manipulated when advertising focuses on collections and limited edition products. The advertising focuses on the consumer not being happy with one product but being completely satisfied when the consumer has acquired *all* the products in the set.

Greed

Greed is the cornerstone of any marketing campaign. A core component of greed is the accumulation of material goods that are of enhanced value when they are only available to a certain segment of the marketplace. For example, the acquisition of a rare, expensive Rolex watch demonstrates the consumer's wealth, status, and power in society.

Sloth

From military recruitment to weight-loss marketing campaigns, marketing is used to motivate and inspire so the consumer can "be all he or she can be." Sloth needs to be more subtle than the other sins in marketing because the campaign must show that people can do better if they try harder, while not insulting the consumer by accusing the consumer of being lazy.

Wrath

Advertising for political campaigns or controversial issues uses wrath or anger as an effective tool to present its message. Although politicians claim that they do not like to run "negative" campaign advertising, most eventually do it because of its effectiveness in linking the anger of the voter with that of the candidate he or she will support.

Envy

Like greed, envy is a universal theme of marketing campaigns. The purpose of the marketing campaign and the advertisement is for the consumer to become envious of the person in the advertisement. Consumers want to be exactly like the person in the campaign because of that person's connection with the product. Therefore, envy will motivate the consumer to consider and (the firm hopes) eventually buy the product.

Pride

Pride is the consumer's result from an effective marketing campaign. Consumers are proud of their purchases and cannot wait to show friends and family what they have obtained. Therefore, through the motivating forces of greed and envy, the consumer will finally be able to realize the emotion of pride regarding the purchase.

Green Marketing

Consumers' increasing awareness of the natural environment in the 1990s encouraged the development of environmental or green marketing. Firms assumed that because consumers are focusing on green issues, promoting the firm's proactive commitment to environmental ideals would be a way to enhance their competitive advantage in the marketplace. This resulted in the initial "green selling" approach that was a post hoc evaluation and promotion of environmental features of existing products. This was a short-term focus, and consumers became suspicious of the motives of the firms because it appeared that no proactive action was taken to incorporate the natural environment in the decision-making process, yet the firm had jumped on the green bandwagon. The promotional campaigns to highlight these "green" products were perceived as opportunistic by consumers and the creditability of the campaigns quickly weakened. Firms also presented meaningless or unproven environmental claims on their existing products, which heightened consumer cynicism and resulted in significant negative public backlash. Many of the claims could not be determined as either true or false because there was no independent authentication pertaining to the claims made by the firm.

In addition, another marketing flaw is the pricing of green products. Although some products are the result of more expensive manufacturing processes, many products were actually produced at a lower cost due to cost savings on energy for packaging and materials. Instead of passing these cost savings on to the consumers, firms charged a premium price to differentiate themselves in potential niche markets. As a result, consumers equated green products with higher prices and, therefore, were hesitant to buy the products. By following the process of "green harvesting" firms were able to pick the "low hanging fruit" related to green products, but did not have the commitment to make fundamental changes in product design or processes that could facilitate a long-term focus on green products. Green harvesting firms focused on the short-term cost savings that increased profitability and shareholder value. With the tepid success of green products, firms rationalized their lack of financial commitment to long-term environmental solutions as not worth the value from a cost-benefit perspective.[3]

One reason why green marketing campaigns have failed in the past is based on the firm's ineffective targeting to the correct consumers. It can be argued that consumers have very different perceptions about the natural environment. Consumers can be classified into five different categories: true blue greens, greenback greens, sprouts, grousers, and basic browns. *True blue greens* have a strong environmental commitment and believe that their actions can have a positive environmental impact. Approximately 9% of U.S. consumers fall into this category. *Greenback greens*, which are represented by 6% of consumers, are not as politically active in environmental causes, but they are more willing than the public is to purchase green products. Sprouts (31% of the consumers) understand the issues related to the natural environment but are not willing to pay more for proactive environmental products. However, they are also open-minded to the extent that if they can be convinced of the benefits of a green product, they may purchase it. Grousers (19% of consumers) are not well informed about environmental issues and are cynical about their ability to have a positive environmental impact on society. Grousers are convinced that green products are not a good choice because of their high price and lower performance when compared with competing products. Basic browns (33% of consumers) do not think about environmental issues at all in their purchasing patterns.[4]

An alternative viewpoint is to focus on the concept of green purchases rather than green consumers.[5] Many purchases made of green products will result in either a compromise or trade-off between the green and non-green product. The trade-off or compromise can be in the form of paying a higher price for the green product, accepting a product that may not have state-of-the-art technology, or accepting the nontraditional distribution systems for the products. In addition, consumers must be confident that the green product actually addresses what it claims to address. Therefore, the consumer must believe that the product does address a real environmental issue, that the product has a better environmental performance compared with its competitors, and that purchasing the product does affect society from a material perspective. Compromise and confidence are two critical factors in determining the level of effectiveness in green products.

Win-Win Purchases

Products in the win-win category have a clear and transparent environmental benefit with little compromise needed by the consumer. The products do not necessarily have a green premium pricing strategy, yet they have good technical performance and, therefore, market acceptability is easy. An example of a win-win product is recycled non-chlorine-bleached paper products.

Feel-Good Purchases

Feel-good purchases are those for which the consumer makes a significant level of compromise in purchasing the product. This compromise requires a high degree of confidence that the product will have a positive material impact on the environment. The Body Shop is an example of a company that sells products that provide a feel-good purchase. Body Shop products are usually higher in price than traditional cosmetics but the creditability of the company's environmental commitment fosters customer loyalty, which continues to support the Body Shop's strategy.

Why Bother? Purchases

Why bother? purchases are those products for which consumers must accept a high level of compromise but have little confidence that their purchases will have a material environmental impact. Unless the companies can provide a convincing case why the product should be bought from a proactive environmental perspective, the products are not likely to survive in the marketplace. An example of a why bother? product would be nondisposable diapers.

Why Not? Purchases

Why not? purchases have a low level of compromise and confidence. The result is that these purchases have little environmental impact but there is also little compromise needed by the consumer. As a result, there is no risk or trade-off with this purchase, so . . . why not? These purchases are based on the assumption that the consumers can state that some effort is being made to acknowledge the natural environment, but it does not have any negative impact on the consumer. Examples of why not? products include using unleaded gasoline and reusing detergent bottles by buying detergent refills.[6]

Enviro-Preneurial Marketing Strategies

For a firm to be successful in implementing an effective green marketing strategy, the firm must identify which levels within the firm are committed to proactive environmental strategies. The different levels of commitment have been described as "enviro-preneurial" marketing strategies that include functional or tactical level strategies, quasi-strategic or business level strategies, and the firm's strategic level.[7]

Tactical Level The tactical level of commitment focuses on the marketing and production managers for its strategic focus related to environmental issues. Specific objectives for the functional areas are developed, and metrics are used to measure the success of the environmental programs.

Quasi-Strategic The quasi-strategic level focuses on how addressing environmental issues can enhance the competitive advantage of the firm. Within this level, firms evaluate the effectiveness of their green marketing compared with their competitors in the marketplace. As a result, the natural environment is viewed as an opportunity in which a firm is able to differentiate itself in the marketplace through its green marketing program.

Strategic Level The strategic level refers to commitment by the top-level executives of the firm to develop and implement a proactive environmental marketing strategy. The result is an overall commitment of the firm from both a micro-organizational and macro-organizational perspective.

Jaime Rivera-Camino argues that green marketing strategies can be integrated within the green marketing concept (GMC), which focuses on all stakeholders rather than just the consumers. By focusing on all stakeholders, GMC has a holistic approach to green marketing. It gives the firm the ability to address the needs and demands of the consumers as well as the special interest groups, the government agencies, and the communities in which the firm operates. In addition, the GMC approach acknowledges that stakeholders have the ability to influence the type of green marketing strategies that will be developed and executed by the firm. GMC focuses on the firm's green products or services, the communication of the firm's environmental commitment through green publicity and green sponsoring, the pricing of the green products, and the distribution system for the green products. The firms implementing a GMC program would develop an analysis of the potential green markets, the type of actions needed to satisfy the demands of the green market, and an analysis of the competitor's green strategy.[8]

Ethical Issues and Social Media[9]

With the explosion of social media as a medium for firms and consumers to communicate with each other, consumers rely on the information provided by social media sites. Therefore, firms must ensure that the information provided by social media sites is accurate and trustworthy. There are four ethical issues firms need to be aware of when using social media sites: unreported endorsements, improper anonymity, compromising consumer privacy, and overly enthusiastic employees.

Unreported Endorsements

Pursuant to regulations imposed by the Federal Trade Commission (FTC), firms must disclose if they give any financial compensation to any individual using social media who endorses the firm's products. If financial compensation, including free products, is given to the individual, it is considered to be a compensated endorsement, and this fact must be disclosed to the public.

Improper Anonymity

Improper anonymity occurs when an individual submits a review without identifying himself or herself. This becomes an ethical issue when there is an apparent conflict of interest in the review. For example, if an employee submits a negative review pertaining to a competitor without identifying himself or herself, the review may not be an accurate representation of the experience the individual had with the competitor's products. In addition, a conflict of interest occurs if the individual gives a favorable review of his or her own company's products.

Compromising Consumer Privacy

Firms that share individual information pertaining to their customers from social media sources without the consent of the individual user have compromised the consumer's right of privacy. The collection and distribution of data from social media sources should follow the same terms and agreements as the firm's other data collection.

Overly Enthusiastic Employees

Firms must be aware of the activities of their employees on social media sites. The employees represent the firm in any communication that is available to the public. Therefore, inappropriate comments and viewpoints expressed on social media sites could have a significant backlash on the reputation of the firm. In addition, the employee may inadvertently release sensitive and proprietary information that would be available to the competitors.

Ethical Consumer Behavior

Consumer behavior can be defined as an examination of how and why consumers behave when purchasing goods and services. To understand ethical consumer behavior, one can argue that consumers "share" the responsibility for their ethical conduct with the conduct of the firms with which they do business. Thus, if a consumer knowingly buys products from firms that outsource their product manufacturing to companies that use child labor, then the consumer is indirectly supporting this action by buying the company's products. As a result, if the firm offers the consumer ethical trade and ethical shopping initiatives, it gives the consumer the opportunity to demonstrate his or her ethical commitment by his or her purchasing pattern. Furthermore, if consumers do not believe a firm is acting ethically they can withhold their support by not purchasing products from the firm and they can go further and establish or join a boycott to publicize to the public the unethical activities of the firm.[10]

Relationship marketing focuses on the relationship between the customers and the firm from a commitment perspective. The establishment of a strong customer relationship facilitates the firm's ability to develop an effective marketing strategy. In addition, this relationship develops a commitment between the customer and the firm so that the ethical behavior of both parties becomes more critical in satisfying the needs of both the customers and the firm. The beneficial outcome of an effective relationship marketing strategy is one of the higher levels of relationship satisfaction, trust, commitment, and loyalty.[11] By applying relationship marketing to the ethical scenario of giving too much change at the checkout in a store, Sarah Steenhaut and Patrick Van Kenhove found that the customers' ethical actions varied based on the type of relationship they had with the firm. When the customer had a weak relationship with the firm, the customer who received too much change was less likely to report the mistake. Customers who had a strong commitment to the firm, however, were more likely to report the mistake than were those with a weaker commitment. In addition, weakly committed customers were driven by opportunism in keeping the excess money, but those with a high commitment had strong guilt-related feelings that encouraged them to report the mistake.[12]

Relationship Marketing and Privacy

At the bottom, the elimination of spyware and the preservation of privacy for the consumer are critical goals if the Internet is to remain safe and reliable and credible.

—U.S. congressman Cliff Stearns[13]

The use of relationship or direct marketing also leads to a number of ethical issues. Foremost from a consumer perspective is how relationship marketing affects the level of privacy of information pertaining to the consumer. Firms continue to acquire increasingly specific information pertaining to their customers to customize their relationships with the consumers. Of the 17 market sectors in the United States, companies who have more than 1,000 employees in 15 of the sectors collect an average of 235 terabytes (terabytes equals more than a thousand billion bytes) of data, which is more data than is held in the U.S. Library of Congress. As a result, data resources have become as valuable an asset for firms as are financial and human resources. In addition, the benefit that enhancing data collection can have on a firm's competitive advantage further encourages firms to collect more and more data.[14]

Through market research and market analytics, firms are able to develop a comprehensive profile on each individual consumer. This allows the firms to direct specific marketing and advertising programs to address the specific needs of each consumer. However, this accumulation of information results in consumers having less control over their private decisions and information. Therefore, the protective shield that ensured that private information would not be available to third parties, including criminals, has been eroded. As a result, there is a fine balance between using consumer information to acquire and/or maintain existing consumers and the infringement this information has on the privacy rights of the consumer. The relationship between the consumer and the firm shifts through relationship marketing. Instead of just being a passive recipient of the marketing strategy of the firm, whether willing or not, the consumer is now actively producing data that will be used in the development and revision of the firm's marketing strategy. The privacy issues related to consumer information relates to three stages: how the information is collected, how the information is used by the firm and how the firm controls the information so that other parties have access to it.[15]

An underlying issue related to consumer privacy is the significant variance in how consumers view the privacy of their information. As Frank Cespedes and Jeff Smith state, "information privacy is an ambiguous term, and consumers have different privacy thresholds depending on the information collected, how it is collected, and who collects it."[16] For example, consumers are more willing to provide information pertaining to their opinions and attitudes than pertaining to demographic or financial data. Furthermore, consumers are more willing to provide information if they are "rewarded" with some type of financial incentive but are hesitant to provide any personal information if they know that the firm will provide this information to third parties.[17]

Therefore, relationship marketing needs to be a two-way relationship to assure consumers that their privacy rights have been protected. Without this two-way relationship, what is perceived by the firm as using data to become more familiar with the needs of the consumer can be perceived as a direct intrusion of the privacy by the consumer. Building this two-way relationship is based on the belief that the firm has certain attributes to support the relationship, including developing a high level of trust between the consumer and the firm, identifying and explaining the mutual interests related to the collection and maintenance of the personal data, the firm's explicit commitment to the interests of the consumer; the firm's explicit demonstration of its respect for the customer's personal information and privacy in the form of actions, and the firm's policies.[18] The two-way relationship can facilitate the development and execution of the customer relationship management model.[19] This model incorporates the use of consumer data to drive the relationship marketing focus of the firm. The first step in the process is developing a database that is the foundation of the model. The database contains data related to the current customers that the firm is serving. Some examples of data collection are the type of transactions made by the consumers, the contact information of the consumers, descriptive information related to the consumers, and the type of response, if any, to previous marketing efforts targeted toward the consumers. The second step is analyzing the consumer data. The analysis would be used to develop groups or clusters of consumers with similar buying patterns. This clustering allows the firm to categorize the consumers based on the market segment their buying patterns represent. In addition, the analysis of the data can be used to calculate the existing and future profitability of each consumer. By determining the "lifetime customer value," the firm can be more effective in allocating its resources to target the specific clusters and individual consumers.

The third step in the process is selecting the customers. Customer selection is based on targeting the current and future most profitable customers. The customer selection can also be used to "fire" customers whose costs outweigh the potential future benefits of maintaining the customer. The fourth step is targeting the customers. The ultimate goal of relationship marketing is to develop a one-to-one relationship between the individual customer and the firm. Through data analysis, firms can target the specific needs of each individual customer. The fifth step is developing relationship marketing, which can include many different avenues available to the firm including establishing loyalty or reward programs, customizing advertising and benefits, and customizing customer service.

The sixth step is addressing the privacy issues related to the customer relationship management model. Customers' privacy concerns run the continuum from a simple irritation to feelings of being "violated" to the fear of being harmed by identity theft.

Firms must be proactive in being transparent in their privacy policies so they can react quickly to any violations to ensure these relationships continue with the customers. The seventh and final step is metrics. Metrics are used to measure the success of the customer relationship management program. The metrics should include financial performance measurements such as profitability, market share, and revenue growth and should focus on customer-based performance measurements.[20]

The Role of Consumer Boycotts

A small body of determined spirits fired by an unquenchable faith in their mission can alter the course of history.[21]

—Mahatma Gandhi

In 1880, Irish tenant farmers faced a very poor harvest. Charles C. Boycott was an English estate manager for wealthy landowners in Ireland. Even though the crop did not produce significant enough yield to support the farmers, Boycott refused to reduce the land rent for the farmers. As a result, the local workers refused to farm the land that Boycott was managing for the English owners. The Irish people led peaceful protests to highlight the unfair treatment they were receiving from Boycott. As a result, Boycott was isolated and ostracized by the local community, and the term *boycott* became part of the English language.[22]

More than 130 years later, boycotts are still effective tools used by individuals to present their viewpoints to the public. A *consumer boycott* can be defined as "an attempt by one or more parties to achieve certain objectives by urging individual consumers to refrain from making selected purchases in the marketplace."[23] Boycotts are usually started by special interests groups or nongovernmental organizations (NGOs), so the action to boycott a business is an example where the stakeholders directly affect the firm's financial performance. In addition, a boycott is an effective tool for incorporating social and ethical factors into the decision-making process of the firm's top managers. Boycotts can be such a powerful tool that they can make fundamental changes in society—for example, the 1955 Montgomery bus boycott that started the civil rights movement in the United States, the boycott of British sales of cloth in India led by Mahatma Gandhi, and the boycott by businesses, sporting events, and entertainers in South Africa during the apartheid regime. Effective boycotts on businesses include the boycott of Shell Oil when it was planning to sink the Brent Spar oil platform in the Atlantic Ocean and the boycott of Nike after information had been released about alleged sweatshop conditions of the factories that were producing Nike's products.

Boycotts usually occur following an event that "triggers" the consumers' motivation. This trigger event is considered to be the "egregious" action that fosters a negative attitude toward the company. In response to this negative perception, consumers evaluate participating in the boycott from a cost-benefit perspective. In an evaluation of the costs versus the benefits, each consumer determines how the egregious action can result in negative and potentially dangerous consequences to various stakeholders as well as to society as a whole. This evaluation can be subjective and based on each consumer's individual perceptions.[24] Jill Klein, N. Craig Smith, and Andrew John[25] found four factors that predict whether a consumer will participate in a boycott: the desire to make a difference, the scope of self-enhancement, counterarguments that inhibit boycotting, and the cost to the boycotter of constrained consumption.

The Desire to Make a Difference

The desire to make a difference is based on the belief that participation in the boycott can lead to adjustment in the firm's behavior. The result is that the boycott will result in ensuring the message to stop this behavior will be sent to the target firm and to other firms in the same industry. This belief is referred to as *perceived efficacy* in which the individual consumer, joined with others, has the power to achieve the collective goal of changing the behavior of the firm.

The Scope of Self-Enhancement

The *scope of self-enhancement* refers to the intrinsic benefits that boycotting can create for the individual consumer. By boycotting, consumers feel better about themselves because they are "doing something" to change the status quo. In addition, consumers who boycott believe that their actions will have a direct impact on helping other individuals. The individuals are able to increase their level of social and personal self-esteem by associating themselves with a moral cause or viewing themselves as moral persons by participating in the boycott.

Counterarguments That Inhibit Boycotting

A potential boycotting consumer will evaluate what the potential negative outcomes of participating in the boycott would be. For example, a negative consequence of boycotting products made in sweatshop conditions is that the factory workers may be fired and subsequently have no income to support their families. Another factor that could persuade consumers not to join a boycott is the perception of having no power and influence. If consumers perceive their individual contributions as having no value, they may not make the effort. In addition, they may also perceive the "free rider" benefits of supporting the boycott in voice but not in deed. In other words, they support the boycott, but they will let other individuals actually participate in the boycott activities.

Cost to the Boycotter of Constrained Consumption

The direct cost related to boycotting varies greatly on the amount of use the consumer has for the firm's products. A heavy user of the firm's products will suffer significantly by not having access to the product. As a result, heavy users have the most individual negative affect of constrained consumption of the firm's goods. As a result, the egregious action must be significant so the consumer can voluntarily constrain his or her consumption of the firm's products through boycotting.[26]

The Ethical Challenges of Product Recalls

In 1982, after seven people died in the Chicago area after taking Extra-Strength Tylenol capsules that were contaminated with the deadly poison cyanide, Johnson & Johnson withdrew all Tylenol capsules across the United States. The capsules were not contaminated in the manufacturing process, but one or more persons went into various retail outlets in Chicago and injected cyanide into the capsules. Even though Johnson & Johnson was not responsible for the contamination, it spent a week pulling the Tylenol capsules off the market at a cost of $100 million.[27] The Tylenol recall is considered the gold standard against which other recalls are compared. Johnson & Johnson reacted quickly to take responsibility for the illegal actions of others. Though Johnson & Johnson certainly had a financial incentive to rebuild Tylenol, it also relied on its credo that focuses on protecting the safety of its customers. In 1986, a federal judge ruled that Tylenol, and not Johnson & Johnson's insurance company, was responsible for the $100 million cost. Because of its prohibitive cost, Johnson & Johnson did not have product recall coverage in its insurance policy,[28] yet company officials ordered the recall knowing that it would be unlikely that the company would receive any insurance money to cover the recall cost.

The Reasons for Recalls

There are numerous reasons why a product needs to be recalled from the marketplace.[29] The first reason is a design flaw in the product. A weakness in the design of the products threatens the integrity of the product when it is used. The second reason is a production defect. A production defect occurs when a problem develops during the manufacturing process but goes unnoticed by the firm until the consumer starts using the product. The third reason for a recall occurs when new scientific information is released to the public that links dangers in the product or materials that were not previously known to the firm or the public. The fourth reason is accidental contamination of the product occurring during the manufacturing process. The fifth reason is product tampering. The Tylenol example highlights how a third party can directly cause a recall. The sixth reason occurs when there is an unforeseen misuse of the product by consumers. Firms attempt to identify potentially harmful scenarios for which they will present warnings on the product package, but they cannot anticipate all potential uses and misuses of their products. The seventh reason is the product's failure to meet the safety standards established by a governmental regulatory agency. This is the fault of the firm by not ensuring that its product met the minimum safety standards that have been established for the product.[30]

The Steps of a Recall

An effective product recall should be based on a sequential set of decisions that are made by managers within the firm that include policy and planning, product development, communications, and logistics and information systems.[31]

Policy and Planning Management sets the tone for the recall in the policy and planning stage. Before the recall takes place, managers need to stress the importance of being ready if a recall is needed, including developing instructional manuals and assigning responsibilities to specific employees during the recall process. Once a recall has occurred, managers need to establish a response team to determine the scale and scope of the recall. After the recall has been implemented, a strategy is needed for the reintroduction of the product, if viable.

Product Development Before a recall takes place, the firm should have in place safeguards to ensure that a recall is not needed. This includes using total quality management techniques and evaluating current products to verify they meet the quality and safety standards established by the firm. In addition, the design and manufacture of new products should include methods with which to trace the cause of the problem if a recall is needed. During the recall stage, it is critical to act as quickly as possible to determine the cause of the defect in the product. It is also necessary to calculate what type of adjustment is needed to satisfy the consumers. During the recall stage, recording the defect issues is imperative to ensure future products do not have the same flaw. After the recall has occurred, the firm must revisit the design and manufacturing process to determine all the elements that led to the defect. In addition, the firm must monitor the customer's level of satisfaction as it relates to the firm's handling of the recall.

Communications Before the recall starts, the firm must identify which critical stakeholders would be affected by a recall. In addition, managers are responsible for incorporating recalls into the corporate crisis communications plan. During the recall, the firm must quickly communicate what the problems are and what the firm is doing to correct them. It is important that the firm send a clear, honest, and transparent message to the critical stakeholders. The firm must also provide a timeline for the recall from problem identification to resolution of the problem.

Logistics and Information Systems Before the recall takes place, the firm must establish a traceability system for the product as well as provide quick notification of product defects. During the recall, the firm must trace the product and develop a recall-management information and logistics system. After the recall has taken place, management must continue to maintain recall logistics after the recall deadline and record the recall notification procedures. In addition, suggestions for possible revisions and improvement to the information and logistics systems should be encouraged.[32]

Financial Costs of a Recall[33]

Numerous costs are involved in recalling a product. Investigation costs include visiting plants, interviewing employees, reviewing written documents pertaining to the product, and product and equipment testing. Communication costs are involved in transferring the firm's plan of action to the media and the public. Financial incentives are given to the consumers to encourage them to try the product again in the future. Physical distribution costs are related to collecting and returning the related products back to the firm that produced the recalled products. There are the potential engineering costs to redesign the product. Labor costs are involved throughout all parts of the recall process. There are costs to legally dispose of the recalled products. Legal costs are involved in defending the likely lawsuits related to the product recall. There is also the cost of lost sales and profitability because of the decrease in demand for the recalled product. There are also potential costs to pay the government and fines and penalties related to the recalled product.[34] These costs can be a significant burden on the firm.

The Ethics of Fair Pricing

In a free market system, transactions between buyers and sellers are based on relative supply and demand. If there is a larger supply of the product than demand for it, the price of the product will likely decrease because the seller wants to sell its products within a predetermined deadline. Alternatively, if the demand is higher than the supply, the price of the product will likely increase because consumers would be willing to pay a higher price because of the scarcity of the product. However, is the increase of price ethical when it is due to a short-term disaster such as a hurricane? For example, before a hurricane in 2002, a store in Baton Rouge, Louisiana, was selling flashlights for $4.97 each. After it sold out, the next 1,000 flashlights were initially sold at $4.97, but then the supervisor in one store ordered the clerks to start charging $11.98 for the flashlights with the justification that this was the list price of the flashlights. After consumers complained, the price was brought back down to $4.97. Research has shown that consumers will campaign about "opportunistic" price increases but will not campaign if the company has to raise prices for its products because of increased costs of their raw materials. However, firms argue that if they are not allowed to increase their prices due to the supply and demand disequilibrium, then there would have to be rationing of the products. Furthermore, what is to stop a person from buying the $4.97 flashlight and then walking out the door and selling it to a consumer for $11.98?[35]

Ethics of Purchasing and Sales

The ethics of purchasing is based on the relationship between two parties in which transactions take place. The ethical focus of the purchasing is based on the trade practices and rules of both parties as well as the country in which the transactions take place. A common ethical gray area is offering or accepting gifts as part of the relationship between the two parties. The offering of a paid business lunch also can raise concerns from some parties, but other parties perceive this as just a normal cost of doing business with a customer. The gray area related to these gifts is whether there is a quid pro quo arrangement. If the salesperson offers a gift, will this salesperson and firm receive preferential treatment in exchange for the gift? This potential reciprocity agreement implies an unfair and unethical treatment given to one supplier versus the competition.[36] This is a gray area because it is not illegal to try to establish being a preferred supplier or vendor. It is part of the active strategy of each supplier to be ranked above the competitors in its relationships with its customers. A preferred vendor status can ensure the long-term relationship with the customer. As a result, some argue that purchasing agents "expect" some type of gift in return for guaranteeing the long-term standing of the vendor because they have the power to determine who should be considered to receive preferred status. As a result, a strong code of ethics is needed from both the purchasing and vendor firms to explicitly state what is acceptable and not acceptable pertaining to the transfer of a financial gift from one party to another.[37]

Wal-Mart has a zero tolerance for accepting gifts. In fact, a Wal-Mart employee may not even accept a cup of coffee from a vendor. Wal-Mart policy states,

Accepting gifts and entertainment can cause a conflict of interest, or the appearance of a conflict between personal interests and professional responsibility. The Wal-Mart culture is to never accept gifts or entertainment from any supplier, potential supplier, government, or any person the associate has reason to believe may be seeking to influence business decisions or transactions. Associates also may not accept a gift or gratuity from a customer for work performed by the associate in a store or club, except as required by local or national policy. We may not accept items donated to Wal-Mart by suppliers for the purpose of raising funds for charities or non-profit organizations. Also, we should not accept or approve of them making donations on behalf of Wal-Mart. Our policy of declining all gifts and entertainment stems from our value of maintaining Every Day Low Costs. Since such gifts and entertainment increase the cost of doing business, we help our suppliers to give us low costs on products by not expecting the gifts and entertainment they may have to spend on other customers. We recognize, as a global company, we may encounter situations where local practices will come into play. The Global Ethics Office will review these situations on a case-by-case basis.[38]

Amit Saini argues that unethical activities between purchasers and suppliers are based on three concepts: interorganizational power, interorganizational relationships, and interpersonal relationships.[39]

Interorganizational Power

Interorganizational power is based on who has the greater bargaining power, the purchaser or the supplier. If the purchasing agent has the edge in the balance of power, he or she will potentially use that power for his or her self-interests. The result is that the party with the greater power would be more likely to use that power for unethical results. In addition, if one party becomes more dependent on the other party, the less-dependent party can potentially use this type of power for its own goals. For example, if a supplier builds a warehouse or manufacturing plant on land owned by the buyer, the supplier has become significantly dependent on the buyer for its success. This can be called idiosyncratic investments because these investments are unique to the relationship between the purchaser and the seller. The idiosyncratic investments enhance the power of the purchaser and, therefore, create a sense of entitlement in the purchaser and a sense of obligation in the supplier.

Interorganizational Relationships

Interorganizational relationships concern the long-term focus of the purchasing firms and the level of satisfaction between the purchaser and supplier. Similar to a preferred status supplier, purchasers view the relationship with suppliers from a long-term perspective. The result is that the long-term perspective allows the purchasers to develop comprehensive dependent bonds with the supplier. This higher level of dependency also can encourage unethical purchasing behavior. The dependence of the supplier allows the purchaser to exercise opportunism by serving the self-interests of the individual or the firm. In addition, this dependence guarantees future continuity, which justifies the purchaser's rationalization to implement unethical practices.

A purchaser's level of satisfaction affects the long-term orientation, the morale of the purchaser, and the willingness to cooperate with the supplier. Satisfaction can be separated into economic and noneconomic satisfaction. *Economic satisfaction* refers to the financial rewards of the partnership, whereas *noneconomic satisfaction* refers to the comfort and quality of the interaction between the purchaser and the supplier.

Interpersonal Relational Issues

Interpersonal relational issues refer to the personal dynamics between the purchasing individual and the supplier salesperson. These personal dynamics can include social ties, personal friendships, and trust. Interpersonal social ties can facilitate the development of a long-term relationship by having common interests between the purchaser and supplier. In addition, these ties can enhance the level of trust within the relationship and create process efficiencies within the two parties. However, prolonged interpersonal ties can foster the conditions of unethical behavior by making decisions that help a "friend" instead of helping the firm. The level of trust in the relationship can be determined by five different processes: calculative process, which is the ability to calculate the costs and benefits of cheating with the partner; prediction process, which is the ability to forecast the actions and behavior of the partner; capability process, which is the ability to determine the partner's ability to meet the agreed-upon obligations; intentionality process, which is the ability to interpret the partner's words and actions to understand the partner's intentions; and transference process, which is using an external third party to evaluate the level of trustworthiness of the partner.[40]

False and Misleading Advertising

In 1938, the Federal Trade Commission (FTC) prohibited the use of any false advertising. The FTC defined *false advertising* as advertisements that were misleading to the public from a material perspective. Firms can use false or misleading advertising in numerous ways to try to sell a product to a consumer.[41]

Going Out of Business Sale

For example, when a retailer is having a "going out of business" sale, the retailer will raise the prices of the remaining inventory and then "discount" them so it appears the consumer is able to buy the products at a reduced rate. Alternatively, the firm may have continuous "going out of business" sales with no intention of actually going out of business.[42]

Manipulation of Product Size or Weight

Firms will attempt to misled consumers by presenting their products in different sizes or weights than expected by consumers. For example, in the United States, consumers expect products to be described in the traditional English measurement system. A manipulation can take place when the product is only described in metric terms and the opposite occurs in other parts of the world. Firms can also reduce the amount of the product without identifying the change to the consumers. When the change does occur, the weight of the product could be presented in small type. For example, a "pound" of coffee or bacon is now sold in 12-ounce packages instead of

16-ounce packages. Another example is a product that displays "bad" ingredients as "only" having 120 calories per serving. The customer usually does not realize that the firm has calculated that amount based on a serving size, which is less than the full amount in the package or container.[43]

Use of Fillers

In food products, fillers can be used to increase the weight of the product. For example, liquids are added to food products to increase the weight at a very low cost. Another example is restaurants that offer free refills but then fill the glasses with ice. The ice costs less than the drink so the consumer is receiving less actual drink for the price.[44]

Use of Vague or Undefinable Terms

Firms will use terms that are too vague or impossible to define to describe their products. Whether it is *healthy, organic,* or *natural,* each firm could have its own interpretation of the meaning of the term. If there is no legal definition for the term, the firm is allowed to make its own interpretation about how to describe its product. As a result, consumers do not have a realistic method to compare these adjectives from one product to another if different companies have different definitions of the term.[45]

Misleading Pictures or Illustrations

A common way to mislead consumers is to have a picture on the product that does not represent the product being sold. These misleading pictures can be on advertisements, websites, catalogs, or the packaging of the product.[46]

Bait and Switch

Another common misleading advertising practice is the technique called *bait and switch*. The consumers are "baited" into coming into the store because of a "fantastic" offer that is usually a high-demand scarce product priced below retail cost. The retailer does not have any intention of selling the product that has been advertised. After the consumer has come into the store, the practice moves from the bait to the switch. The consumer asks for the baited product and is told that they are sold out but there is another product that would better suit the needs of the customer. The customer is now offered the new more expensive product and the switch has taken place.[47]

Fortunately, consumers have become much more sophisticated in interpreting the messages presented in advertising. For example, one study found that 46% of the consumers in the sample believed that most or all television advertising was misleading, and another study found that more than half of the sample disagreed with the statement that advertising of a product presents a true representation of the product.[48]

The Eventual Truth in Advertising

On November 21, 2011, the Australian parliament passed the Tobacco Plain Packaging Act 2011 and the Trade Marks Amendment Act 2011, which were significant pieces of legislation pertaining to the tobacco industry. The legislation required that all tobacco products sold in Australia be in plain packaging by December 2012. The packaging will not contain any company logos but will contain warnings such as smoking causes mouth and throat cancer and smoking causes blindness. In addition to the warning, there will be graphic pictures showing how smoking can negatively affect the human body.[49] This is a significant setback for an industry that prided itself on its advertising prowess. For example, to encourage more women to smoke in the United States in 1920s, smoking was linked to losing weight in campaigns such as reaching for a Lucky Strike cigarette instead of a sweet. During World War II, all American soldiers were given cigarettes in their c-rations, which were the food rations, regardless of whether they smoked or not. Cigarettes were a valuable commodity during wartime, and nonsmokers would trade them for other items such as chocolate or coffee. The cigarette companies hoped that the boredom between battles would "encourage" nonsmoking soldiers to try cigarettes so they would become addicted and loyal customers once the war was over.

By the 1960s, specific tobacco brands were targeted for women by attempting to link glamour and femininity with smoking. In continuing their targeting toward women, cigarette companies offered "low tar" and "light" cigarettes, which actually were no safer than other types of cigarettes. Both men and women were "reassured" about the health benefits of smoking because advertising for products such as Camel cigarettes made the claim that more doctors smoked Camel cigarettes than any other brand. The Flintstones cartoon had Barney and Fred taking a Winston cigarette break. Winston cigarettes was one of the sponsors of the Flintstones cartoon.[50]

Cigarette companies also targeted their potential to the next generation of consumers—children. A classic example is the development of the Joe Camel marketing campaign. Joe Camel was a cartoon character introduced in 1987 as the advertising "mascot" of Camel cigarettes. In 1997, the FTC issued a report stating that RJ Reynolds (maker of Camel cigarettes) had done a survey that showed 86% of the children knew who Joe Camel was, and almost all of the children who knew Joe Camel were able to link the character with Camel cigarettes. Cigarette companies targeted children as young as 14 to start smoking because the sooner the individual becomes addicted to cigarettes, the longer the potential sales of cigarettes to the person. In 1996, RJ Reynolds spent $48.3 million on advertising on Joe Camel.[51] Because of pressure from the FTC, Joe Camel "died" in 1997.

The legacy of promoting tobacco use continues to harm people around the world. Four hundred thousand people die each year in the United States as a result of cigarette smoking, and 50,000 adult nonsmokers die each year from exposure to secondhand smoke. In 2011, an estimated 8.6 million people in the United States were suffering from smoking-caused illnesses. In totality, smoking is the cause of the death of an estimated 100 million people globally in the 20th century, and the number is estimated to be 1 billion for the 21st century if current trends continue. An estimated 8 million people die globally from tobacco products. Almost 1 billion men and an estimated 250 million women smoke globally. In addition, an estimated 80,000 to 100,000 young people become addicted to tobacco daily.[52]

Advertising to Children

Since the early 1970s, government agencies such as the FTC have focused on the negative impact advertising has on children. Children are usually quick to accept the message that is presented in advertising and are less suspicious of the message than adult viewers are.

Sugary Cereals

For decades, food producers of high-sugar, low-nutritional breakfast cereals have targeted children as their main demographic. In 2007, the average child in the United States watched 757 ads related to cereal of which 98% were for cereals with high-sugar and low-nutritional value. This cereal advertising accounted for 17% of all food advertising viewed by children in 2007. In addition, 92.3% of the cereal advertising was on cable networks that are targeted exclusively toward children. The advertising for healthy cereals was targeted toward adults rather than children.[53] The "empty calories" of high-sugar, low-nutritional cereals add to the obesity problem in the United States and other countries in the world. Obese children will have lifetime health problems, including developing high cholesterol, high blood pressure, and type 2 diabetes and having shorter life spans than will non-obese children. Since the 1970s, the obesity rate for children 2 to 5 years old and 12 to 19 years old has more than doubled, and the rate has tripled for children 6 to 10 years old.[54]

Children's Educational Television Rules

The exposure children have to advertising has exploded since the number of TV channels and time slots have grown tremendously in the last two decades. Until the introduction of cable television, children's products were targeted for Saturday morning when children would be watching their weekly cartoons. With the choice of hundreds of channels and numerous channels dedicated to children (i.e., Disney Channel, Nickelodeon Channel, Cartoon Network), marketers have the opportunity to advertise their products 24 hours a day, 7 days a week. In 1996, the Federal Communications Commission (FCC) demanded increased accountability from the television stations regarding the type of programming they present that is targeted toward children. Broadcasters have to report how they fulfill their obligation to present programming when it is specifically designed to serve the educational and informational needs of children. In addition, this requirement is mandatory for broadcasters to have their licenses to broadcast renewed by the FCC.[55]

Fast-Food Strategies

Morgan Spurlock filmed a documentary titled *Super-Size Me* in which he eats McDonalds' food three meals a day for 30 days. It is fascinating to watch how his body deteriorates so quickly from eating a diet containing high-fat and high-sugar foods. In one scene in the movie, Spurlock showed children portraits of George Washington, Jesus Christ, and Ronald McDonald. Ronald McDonald was the only picture that every child was able to identify. Similar to the strategy of the cigarette companies, fast-food restaurants target children because they will be potential future consumers for many decades. To enhance the incentive for children to demand fast food, "toys" are included in the children's meals. In actuality, the "toys" are marketing tools in themselves. They are usually designed around a new movie or television show that is targeted to children.[56]

These toys are a tie-in between the movie or television show and the purchasing decision taking place at the fast-food restaurant. The result is that the fast-food restaurant brings in the families because the children want the toys, so the promoters of the movie are advertising by partnering with the restaurant to "give away" the toy. In November 2011, San Francisco's board of supervisors voted to ban McDonald's from providing free toys with its happy meals. The California city joined the California county of Santa Clara forbidding the use of toys to be marketed to children when they eat McDonalds' food. The only exception to the ban is if the children's meal, including the food and drink, had a combined calorie amount of less than 600. San Francisco's board of supervisors argued that this was a starting point in addressing the issue of childhood obesity.[57]

The Sydney Principles

The International Obesity Taskforce has established the Sydney Principles to attempt to protect children against the negative impact of food and beverage advertising. The first principle is to support the rights of children. Children have the right to eat safe and nutritious food. The second principle is that protection of the children should be the responsibility of various stakeholders including parents, government, society, and the private sector. The third principle is to be statutory in protecting children. Governments must establish and enforce regulations that protect children from targeted advertising and the negative impact the products have on the children's long-term health. The fourth principle is to establish regulations that cover a broad array of commercial targeting including all media types. The fifth principle is to ensure that no product advertising is allowed in certain venues, including schools and day care facilities. The sixth principle is establishing international agreements to ensure that negative commercial advertising does not "link" from one neighboring country to another country. The seventh principle is that all government regulations need to be evaluated, monitored, and enforced. Metrics need to be set to ensure that compliance is always met by the firms.[58]

The Magic of Disney[59]

In June 2012, the Walt Disney Company announced that all products that will be advertised on the children-based television channels, radio stations, and websites owned by the company must comply with strict nutritional standards. The new set of requirements will also be implemented for Saturday morning cartoons on ABC stations that are owned by Disney. A number of standard products will no longer be allowed to advertise on Disney including Capri Sun drinks, Kraft Lunchables, a wide range of candy, sugared cereals with 10 grams or more of sugar per serving, and fast-food restaurants. Disney also announced that the 12 million children's meals sold in its theme parks annually would have 25% less sodium. The new requirements will not go into effect until 2015 because of long-term contract commitments.

Questions for Thought

1. Why do you think Pepsi decided to release the AMP app in the opening vignette? Do you think Pepsi officials were surprised by the response of the public?

2. Why is there such concern about protecting children from marketing and advertising?

3. What should consumers demand when companies recall products? What are the ethical considerations for recalls?

4. Is green marketing just a fad? Explain your view.

Real-Life Ethical Dilemma Exercise

Calculating the Financial Cost of a Life

In his January 1971 review of the Ford Pinto, *New York Times* car reviewer John Radosta stated that Ford had finally developed a car to compete with the compact cars coming from Europe and Japan. Listed at just over $2,000, the Pinto was going to help Ford recapture its lost consumers who had moved to higher-quality, more fuel-efficient foreign competitors. Price was a driving force because of the stiff competition from overseas. In an incredible prophesy worthy of Shakespeare, Radosta complained about the braking of the Pinto as being very abrupt and forcing the car to shift to the left or right, which requires "alert countersteering by the driver."[60] This foreboding statement came back to haunt Ford because the Ford Pinto was designed with its fuel tank in the center of the back of the car. In this position, a low-speed rear-end accident could result in the leaking and explosion of the Pinto gas tank. The Pinto was rushed into production because Ford was falling farther and farther behind its European and Japanese competitors. In 1977, *Mother Jones* magazine printed an article titled "Pinto Madness" in which the first national exposure took place identifying the design flaw in the Pinto. The *Mother Jones* article described an accident in which the driver of the Pinto stalled in a merge lane and another car rear-ended hers at an impact speed of 28 miles per hour. The impact of the collusion ruptured the gas tank of the Pinto, and gas vapors quickly filled the car. A spark from the car ignited the gas, and the car exploded into flames. The driver died hours later. The details were told because a passenger in the car had survived despite horrendous burns all over his body. The article in *Mother Jones* magazine stated that Ford engineers knew there was a design flaw with the gas tank because its own preproduction crash tests showed the gas tank rupturing after a rear-end collision. The article also explained that because the assembly-line machinery had already been tooled for the flawed gas tank, Ford planned to continue manufacturing the Pinto with the flawed gas tank even though Ford also owned the patent for a much safer gas tank. The Pinto was intended to be a special car to reverse the declining market share for Ford, and it was "Lee's car." Lee Iacocca, president of Ford, wanted the car to be in the showrooms in 1971, so Ford sped up the whole production process. The traditional time span at that time for a new car to be introduced was 43 months from conception to production. The Pinto accomplished that goal in less than 25 months.[61]

The Pinto Memo

The article in *Mother Jones* magazine identified a chilling document that is still difficult to comprehend: an internal Ford memo that contained a cost-benefit analysis of replacing the Pinto's gas tank with a safer one. In 1972, the National Highway Traffic Safety Administration (NHTSA) calculated the worth of the life of a person who has died in a traffic accident. Considering future salary losses, medical costs, legal costs, pain and suffering, property damage, funeral costs, and other associated costs, the NHTSA concluded that the value was $200,725 per victim. Ford then used that figure to compare the "benefits" of not correcting the flaw with the "costs" of correcting the flaw. The cost of correcting the flaw was $11 per unit. Yes, to correct the problem, Ford would need to spend $11 to retrofit the existing cars with a safer gas tank. There were 11 million cars and 1.5 million light trucks, so the total cost would have been $137 million. The "benefits" were based on an estimated 180 burn deaths at a payout of $200,000 per death; 180 serious burn injuries with a payout of $67,000 per injury; and 2,100 burned vehicles with a payout of $700 per vehicle. The total cost of the "benefits" was $49.5 million, so Ford would "save" $87.5 million by letting its customers burn to death.[62] On June 9, 1978, as a result of investigations by the NHTSA and the negative publicity generated by the *Mother Jones* article, Ford recalled 1.5 million Pintos for "modifications" to their fuel systems to reduce the risk of leaking gas tanks. All Pintos from 1971 through 1976 were recalled except station wagons. In addition, Ford had to recall 1975 and 1976 Mercury Bobcats, which had the same gas tank. The estimated cost of the recall was between $12 and $20 million.[63]

Questions for the Real-Life Ethical Dilemma Exercise

1. What issues do you think the managers and engineers faced while developing a cost-benefit analysis of replacing the Pinto gas tank?

2. How could this cost-benefit analysis be implemented in the United States at the end of the 20th century?

3. If you were working at Ford when the Pinto gas tank issue was discovered, what would you say to your boss if he or she told you this is what Ford was going to do to "correct" the problem?

Student Study Site

Visit the Student Study Site at **study.sagepub.com/stanwick3e** to access the following resources:

- Video Links
- SAGE Journal Articles
- Web Resources
- Web Quizzes

11

Ethical Issues in the Developing World

America did not invent human rights. In a very real sense . . . human rights invented America.

—Jimmy Carter

Chapter Objectives

After reading and studying Chapter 11, students should be able to

1. Describe the ethical issues that multinationals must focus on when dealing with Bottom of the Pyramid markets.
2. Describe the seven key principles for being profitable for BOP markets.
3. Define social entrepreneurship.
4. List and discuss the types of social entrepreneurs.
5. Describe the Grameen Bank's purpose.
6. Discuss the concept of fair trade and explain its significance for third-world countries.
7. Explain why human rights are important.
8. Explain why hunger and poverty must be addressed by businesses.
9. List the causes of hunger.
10. Explain the food versus fuel debate.
11. List the Millennium Development Goals.

Samsung Electronics and the Cycle of Child Labor[1]

On August 7, 2012, New York–based nonprofit labor group China Labor Watch released an investigative report on the use of child labor by one of Samsung's suppliers, HEG Electronics. Investigators from China Labor Watch worked in the factory in June and July 2012 and observed seven children under the age of 16 working in the same department as the investigators. The investigators estimated that between 50 and 100 children worked at the factory. The children worked under the same conditions as the adults but only received 70% of the adult pay rate. In addition, they were often required to perform dangerous tasks that resulted, in some cases, in injury.[2]

On July 10, 2014, China Labor Watch issued another investigative report stating that another Samsung supplier was using child labor, Shinyang Electronics in Dogguan, China. The investigators found that the factory hired children and underage students during its peak demand periods when there is an urgent need for labor in the factory. The underage workers would be employed from three to six months and would work 11-hour days and only be paid for 10-hour days. The underage workers were 15 years old and used IDs from other people. Samsung commented on the report by stating, "We are urgently looking into the latest allegations and will take appropriate measures in accordance with our policies to prevent any cases of child labor in our suppliers."[3] The underage workers were paid approximately $1.20 an hour because they were considered temporary workers and had actually been hired by a labor dispatch company. The typical worker wage is $1.45 an hour. The underage workers claimed that the factory borrowed real identification cards from other factories to register the underage workers.[4] On July 14, 2014, Samsung announced that it was "temporarily" suspending using Shinyang Electronics as a supplier due to its use of child labor. Samsung's own investigation into the plant confirmed that the factory was employing underage workers. This occurred two weeks after Samsung had released its annual global sustainability report on June 30. In the report, Samsung stated that for the second year in a row, no child labor was identified in the audits of Samsung's 130 suppliers in China.[5] On August 5, 2014, Samsung lifted the ban on using Shinyang Electronics as a supplier. Samsung did state that it would be reducing its orders to Shinyang by 30%. Samsung's rationale for lifting the suspension was that the underage workers were not directly hired by Shinyang but were contracted to Shinyang by the labor dispatch company. Samsung stated that it had "decided to still take measures against Dongguan Shinyang to hold the supplier responsible for failing to monitor its subcontractors, in accordance with Samsung's zero tolerance policy on child labor."[6]

The Bottom of the Pyramid

The base or bottom of the pyramid (BOP) refers to the 4 billion poor people who are virtually ignored by most corporations because they are perceived as "high risk" and "low resource" customers. C. K. Prahalad[7] argues that ignoring 65% of the world's population is not a good strategic move because this group represents $5 trillion in purchasing power.[8]

As multinationals continue to try to find avenues for global expansion, whole continents such as Africa are not even considered on the list of potential growth opportunities.

As a result, billions of people are either unserved or underserved by multinational corporations. Prahalad argues that investment in these underdeveloped markets will lead to significant positive effects for both the country and the firm doing business in the country and argues that the correct way to view the BOP is to consider the viable and profitable growth opportunities for firms. The resulting investment in BOP strategies can result in poverty reduction by developing established markets and financial institutions. Indeed, BOP strategies could foster explosive growth for the firm and local individuals and businesses that seize the opportunity to develop highly motivated emerging entrepreneurs. In addition, customers need to be perceived as viable customers instead of being dependent on aid for survival. Prahalad advises those firms that are interested in addressing these markets to remember that success is based on focusing on small unit packages, low profit margins on a per unit basis, and high volume to maximize the return on the capital investment for the project.[9] In addition, Prahalad and Hammond state that even though these customers are "poor," it does not mean they do not have any money.[10] Each individual may have little money, but as an aggregate, there is buying power available in the villages. For example, a single entrepreneur funded by Grameen Telecom will buy one phone that the entire village will use. The entrepreneur can make, on average, $90 monthly by charging the villagers for every minute they use the phone. In addition, the BOP customers do not just buy basic necessities. The poor also buy "luxury" items such as televisions, pressure cookers, and gas stoves. Furthermore, BOP customers do not always buy the lowest-priced products. These customers also balance the cost and benefit of price versus quality.[11]

V. Kasturi Rangan, Michael Chu, and Dijordjija Petkoski argue that strategies to be used to address the needs of the customers at the BOP depend on the income level of the customers.[12] Income can be categorized as extreme poverty, which is earning less than $1 per day; subsistence, which is earning between $1 and $3 per day; and low-income, which includes earnings between $3 and $5 per day. For those markets of extreme poverty, Rangan et al. recommend that firms form commercial partnerships with governments and nongovernmental organizations (NGOs). The people living in extreme poverty lack basic essentials such as sufficient food, clean water, acceptable shelter, and infrastructure, and most business transactions are done informally and irregularly. As a result, there is not a true "marketplace" to serve the customers so help is needed through government or NGOs to support market transactions. For those markets where the customers are at subsistence income levels, Rangan et al. recommend either enlisting individuals or small local businesses to help develop the markets or encouraging the local community to help support the firm by developing coproducing value by improving the infrastructure and/or supply chain for the firm. If the market is based on low-income earners, the firm can provide appropriate and affordable products that are sold directly to the consumers without direct support from a partner.[13]

Firms that focus on BOP customers may need to review their traditional strategic focus.[14] The firm and stockholders must accept a large-volume, low-profit-margin competitive focus. In addition, the firm must accept that transactions will take place in an informal market where "proper" business procedures may not be executed. The managers of the firm must have a long-term view of the project because BOP projects usually take an extended period before they become profitable. The firm must also make sure that its culture supports and encourages BOP innovation because its products must be tailored to the unique aspects of the markets.[15]

Certain ethical issues can be raised by multinational corporations focusing on BOP markets. For example, consider the appropriateness of the products. Is it appropriate for companies to sell products such as tobacco products or alcohol that could significantly negatively affect the individuals and communities in the marketplace? A second factor is the price points established by the firms. Even though the customer does not have to buy the product, there are potential monopolistic type profits available for firms in which there is no viable competition in the local marketplace and the firm holds the bargaining power over the customer. The third factor is the potential misuse of advertising and promotion. As occurs globally, firms use advertising and promotion to generate awareness and demand for their products. However, if firms mislead the consumers or have implemented questionable sales promotion tactics, there is a potential to "exploit" the customers. Furthermore, the multinationals are not required to maintain the profits from their BOP in the local communities. Often, the profits from this strategy are transferred back to the home country, which results in a lack of potential investments in the local communities.[16]

New Generation Business Strategies for the Bottom of the Pyramid

Ted London and Stuart Hart present a discussion based on the next generation of business strategies available to firms that focus on the BOP.[17] They argue that the first generation of business strategies targeted to the poorest customers focused on "fortune finding," which is the attempt to sell existing products to the poorest four billion people. The second generation of business strategies focuses on "fortune creating" by forming partnerships with local businesses within the poorest countries. Seven key principles help a company be profitable while addressing the needs of the customers at the BOP: (1) create market opportunities, (2) craft solutions with the BOP, (3) orchestrate effective experiments, (4) manage failures, (5) establish or comingle competitive advantage, (6) leverage and transfer social embeddedness, and (7) enhance mutual value. *Creating market opportunities* includes exploring partnerships with other businesses and determining the potential demand for the new products. *Crafting solutions with the BOP* entails following the advice of London and Hart, who state that firms need to "be patient," "stay longer," and "come back." Thus, it means that the firm must listen to the local customers and must not come into the negotiations with certain preconceived notions about the partners or their needs. *Orchestrating effective experiments* is the ability of the firm to do one or more pilot studies before the strategy is fully implemented. The firm must be willing to experiment, learn, and be innovative based on the feedback. *Managing failures* relates to understanding that the pilot studies can and will fail by their very nature. They are considered "pilot" studies because the firm does not have enough information to effectively implement the strategies. The information obtained from these pilot studies is, therefore, building the skill and knowledge base of the managers who will do business with the partners. *Establishing the competitive advantage* is based on identifying, leveraging, and enhancing the currently available platforms. Current platforms could include the current infrastructure, the existing distribution channels, and the role of the existing informal leaders in the marketplace. *Leveraging and transferring social embeddedness* is to understand the social impact of the firm's project. *Social embeddedness* refers to the ability to understand the social context of the firm's project along with the ability to understand the intrinsic economic rationale of the local economy related to the firm's project. The firm can use these social contacts to scale deep and wide. *Scaling deep* refers to providing new products to established customers of the firm. *Scaling wide* is the offering of similar products that have been accepted by the existing customers to potential new customers. The seventh principle of *enhancing mutual value* relates to the ability of the firm to understand its impact in the local community. The firm first must view its contribution based on a holistic approach and consider both the short-term and long-term impacts of the project.[18]

Social Entrepreneurship

Social entrepreneurship can be defined as organizations that have created business models that cater to basic human needs that are not currently being served. Social entrepreneurs can be described as individuals who use their drive and motivation as traditional entrepreneurs and focus on a mission that can positively affect society.[19] In other words, social entrepreneurship entails reconfiguring resources so the organization can achieve specific social objectives, which creates a social transformation.[20]

As with traditional entrepreneurs, a social entrepreneur must have three critical attributes to be successful. The first is a specific vision of the purpose and goals and objectives of the organization. The second attribute is the ability to use his or her leadership skills to champion the implementation of his or her vision. The third attribute is the will and motivation to be committed to developing the business so that it will be sustainable in the long term.[21] Social entrepreneurs need to focus on four types of capital to succeed in their vision: financial capital, social capital, environmental capital, and aesthetic capital. *Financial capital* is the creation and growth of wealth for the firm, which is also the mission of any entrepreneurial firm. *Social capital* is the "wealth" that is generated to the community and society through the operations of the social entrepreneur's organization. *Environmental capital* is the "wealth" created by having the organization focus on environmental sustainability issues. *Aesthetic capital* is the intangible "wealth" that is created by developing a "feel good factor" by making the world a better place to live in.[22]

Ten Characteristics of Successful Social Entrepreneurs

John Elkington and Pamela Hartigan present 10 characteristics of successful social entrepreneurs.[23] The first characteristic is to try to disregard the constraints of ideology or discipline. The second characteristic is using innovation, resourcefulness, and opportunity to determine what practical solutions are viable to solve the social problem. The third characteristic is using innovation to focus on the development of new products or services. The fourth characteristic is to focus on how the organization's mission will be used to create social value and be able to share its knowledge with other social entrepreneurs. The fifth characteristic is to not wait until all resources are available to capitalize on the opportunity. The sixth characteristic is to recognize everyone has the ability to contribute to the economic and social development of the organization. The seventh characteristic is that every entrepreneur is willing to take risks to succeed. The eighth characteristic is to make sure to balance the passion for the project with the ability to measure and monitor the social impact of the project. The ninth characteristic is that successful social entrepreneurs are also good teachers so others can learn how to achieve their social goals. The tenth characteristic is that sometimes entrepreneurs have to be patient when they do not see the type of progress that is needed for a successful competition of the project. Another aspect of successful social entrepreneurs is that they are considered by many to be unreasonable. They are considered to be unreasonable because they want to change the system, are insanely ambitious, are motivated by emotion, believe they are predicting the future, try to create profit in unprofitable markets, will disregard the evidence that does not support their vision, attempt to measure goals and objectives that are unmeasurable, are not qualified to run their organization, refuse to accept the actions are those of superheroes, and are, finally, unreasonable.[24]

Typology of Social Entrepreneurs

Shaker Zahra and colleagues propose a typology of different types of social entrepreneurs. The first type is the *social bricoleur*, who usually focuses on addressing the social needs of local communities. *Bricoleur* can be defined as the ability to use existing resources to address the strategic issue. Therefore, a social bricoleur is one who uses his or her existing resource base to address the social mission of the organization. An example of a social bricoleur is an individual who sets up a relief organization to help individuals who have been affected by a natural disaster. For example, Paige Ellison-Smith developed a program called Project K.I.D. after Hurricane Katrina hit the United States Gulf Coast. Project K.I.D. provided day care for children who were playing unattended in the water and debris after the hurricane hit the coast. Within 4 months, she was able to find 220 volunteers, many of whom were teenagers who also needed safety and shelter.[25]

The second type is called the *social constructionist*, who focuses on exploiting the market gaps that do not serve certain customers. By identifying and serving these previously "missed" opportunities, social constructionists know how to increase awareness that will lead to social reform. A social constructionist may not necessarily see opportunities to capture his or her social mission from the local community but does scan for opportunities that he or she could capitalize on through the development of new goods and services. Social constructionists focus on the identification of current customer needs that have not been addressed effectively by other firms. Social constructionists focus on financial and social wealth in the development and growth of their organizations. An example of a social constructionist entrepreneur is Jacqueline Novogratz. In 2001, Novogratz established the Acumen Fund, whose mission is to use entrepreneurial approaches to solve global poverty problems. The fund allocates its philanthropic funding to entrepreneurs and organizations whose mission is to deliver affordable basic necessities such as water, food, health care, and housing.[26]

The third type is the *social engineer*, who identifies systemic broad problems within the existing social structures and addresses these problems with frame-breaking revolutionary change. Muhammad Yunus is one of the most famous social engineers. Yunus established the Grameen Bank to set up microloans for poor villagers in Bangladesh because he realized that the villagers had to rely on high-interest moneylenders for any type of loan. The high interest rates resulted in the villagers becoming further and further in debt. Yunus went to the traditional banks, and none would lend money to the villagers, so he loaned 42 people a total of $27 to be split among themselves in a village in Jobra, Bangladesh, which broke the cycle of increasing levels of debt for the villagers.

Building Social Businesses

To me poor people are like bonsai trees. When you plant the best seed of the tallest tree in a flower-pot, you get a replica of the tallest tree, only inches tall. There is nothing wrong with the seed you planted, only the soil-base that is too inadequate. Poor people are bonsai people. There is nothing wrong in their seeds. Simply, society never gave them the base to grow on. All it needs to get the poor people out of poverty for us to create an enabling environment for them. Once the poor can unleash their energy and creativity, poverty will disappear very quickly.[27]

—Muhammad Yunus,
Nobel Peace Prize Lecture, Oslo, Norway, December 10, 2006

As an economics professor, Yunus realized something was wrong. He would talk about supply and demand curves in the classroom, then he would walk outside and see poverty and despair. How can he teach about a strong market-based economic system when his own country, Bangladesh, is not receiving the benefits of a strong formal economic system? As a guarantor of those 42 loans, Yunus proved that the poor can be as responsible, if not more so, to ensure the payment of debt as those in developed countries. Yunus defines *social business* as a new form of capitalism that is based on the selflessness of people.[28] Yunus argues that the existing theory of capitalism is flawed because it is based on the assumption that people are motivated solely by self-interests. Yunus proposes that human beings have the capacity to be multifaceted with their motivation and can be driven to succeed based on their selfish and unselfish interests.

Yunus took that first small step that eventually led to the creation of the Grameen Bank, which currently has more than 8.3 million borrowers and $10 billion in loans. Ninety-seven percent of the borrowers are women. This high percentage of women entrepreneurs is due to their motivation to use the profits from the businesses to help their children and their families improve their standard of living.

Yunus proposes seven principles for social business: (1) The business objective of the organization is to address a social problem and not to maximize profitability; (2) the firm will need to obtain both financial and economic sustainability; (3) investors of the organization will only receive back their full investment amount; (4) when the investment amount is paid in full to all the investors, the subsequent profits will be invested into the firm for expansion and improvement opportunities; (5) the firm is mandated to be environmentally conscious and sustainable; (6) the employees of the organization will receive market wages with superior working conditions; and (7) the running of the organization needs to be done with joy!

The success of Grameen Bank allowed Yunus to expand his operations into multiple areas, including Grameen Telecom (providing phone service to rural areas), Grameen Shakti (solar home power systems for villages), Grameen Kalyan (providing health care), Grameen Fisheries and Livestock Foundation (maintain fish ponds and provide veterinary service), Grameen Shikkha (provide education), Grameen Veolia (provide clean drinking water), and Grameen Uddog/Grameen Shamogree (textile and traditional handloom products). However, in a set of circumstances reminiscent of a Greek tragedy, Yunus was forced to step down as managing director of Grameen Bank in May 2011. Yunus was accused of mishandling donors' money, which he denied, stating that the issue was raised because of misinformation. Grameen Bank's official statement was that Yunus, 71, had to leave his position because he was past the mandatory retirement age of 60 years.[29]

Microfinance

Microfinance is the process by which small loans are given to entrepreneurial individuals in developing countries to generate income that will benefit the individual as well as the local village through poverty reduction. In addition, many microfinance programs include an educational component to help develop a comprehensive skill base for the individuals. Yunus believed that if financial resources were made available to the poorest people, the aggregate of these resources would result in a large impact on poverty reduction for the country. One of the unique aspects of microfinance loans is that no collateral is needed, and the loans are usually repaid between six months and a year after the loan was given. When the loan has been repaid, the money is then "recycled" as loans to other entrepreneurs in the village to create additional business opportunities. An example would be a woman purchasing chickens in order to sell the eggs. The woman would borrow $50 from the microfinance institution (MFI) to buy the chickens. As the number of chickens increases via reproduction, the woman can sell the eggs and the chicks to others in the village. She is a customer of the MFI, so the MFI would give her business advice about how to grow her business. In return, this increases the probability that the loan would be paid off. In addition, the MFI could provide other services, such as basic health care for the borrower and her family. As her business becomes larger, she will have enough money to improve the standard of living for herself and her family. The additional money will be spent in the village and will improve the standard of living of the other entrepreneurs who are providing goods and services she needs. The payback rate for the loans is between 95% and 98%, which is a higher rate of payback than the payback rate for student loans and credit card debt in the United States.[30]

Fair Trade

Fair Trade [is] all about creating a win-win business proposition for third-world farmers and for U.S. industry. Many people think of corporate social responsibility as a zero-sum game. They think it's a fixed pie that you're just re-slicing so that some other stakeholder gets more and the company gets less. So here's my premise: Fair Trade is innovative precisely because it explodes that perception about corporate social responsibility. Creating a platform in which interests are aligned and all stake-holders profit together.[31]

—Paul Rice, president and CEO of Transfair USA

The underlying foundation of the concept of fair trade is that a free market–based trade system does not always produce sustainable livelihoods for the farmers and other members of the global food chain. As a result, farmers and other workers are not able to generate enough income to create a sustainable standard of living. However, if the farmers and workers are provided "fair" wages and payments, the farmers and workers can develop a sustainable standard of living,

The Fairtrade Labeling Organizations International (FLO) is the global certifier of Fair Trade activities around the world. FLO defines Fair Trade in the following manner: "Fair Trade is a trading partnership, based on dialogue, transparency and respect that seeks greater equity in international trade. It contributes to sustainable development by offering better trading conditions to, and securing the rights of, marginalized producers and workers—especially in the Southern Hemisphere. Fair Trade organizations, backed by consumers, are engaged actively in supporting producers, raising awareness, and campaigning for changes in the rules and practice of conventional international trade."[32]

In 2010, 905 producer organizations globally were Fair Trade certified. These organizations represented 980,000 farmers and 173,000 workers for a total impact on 1.15 million people. In the fiscal year 2009–2010, total reported Fair Trade sales were 550 million euros, and the total Fair Trade premium was 51.5 million euros.[33]

Core Principles of Fair Trade

The core principles of Fair Trade developed by the FLO are providing market access for marginalized producers, developing sustainable and equitable trading relationships, developing knowledge and skills of the producers to increase their empowerment, increasing consumer awareness and advocacy, and developing a "social contract" with the buyers to do more than the minimum expected of them in the marketplace.[34] Fair Trade–certified producers also must agree to adhere to labor standards such as those provided by the UN-based International Labour Organization (ILO). ILO standards include allowing workers the freedom of association and collective bargaining, providing safe and clean working conditions, placing limits on the number of working hours daily, not tolerating harsh or inhumane treatment of workers, promoting nondiscrimination policies against any type, and respecting the rights of children. In addition, certified producers must agree to continuous improvement of environmental conditions on their land and agree to be monitored and evaluated to ensure compliance.[35]

Ethical Issues Related to Fair Trade[36]

Fair Trade has become a brand upon itself in which the FLO gives companies a license to be allowed to use the Fair Trade logo on their goods. In the United Kingdom, 85% of the revenues for the British organization Fair Trade Foundation are earned by licensing fees, with the remaining amount coming from donations and government grants. At least 70% of the revenue from licensing in the United Kingdom is spent on promoting the brand name and logo. The remaining 30% is to be spent on administrative costs and monitoring systems for the licensee. The licensees receive three benefits of being Fair Trade certified: they can charge higher prices, they can expect higher revenues, and they can improve their images and reputations.

The money that is intended to help the third-world farmers and workers does not pass through the Fair Trade organization. In the coffee industry, a number of levels are involved in the Fair Trade supply chain: The farmers, the primary cooperatives that assemble and process the coffee, and the secondary cooperatives, which export the coffee that has been processed by the primary cooperatives. The secondary exporting cooperative receives a premium of 10¢ per pound higher than the market price if the coffee is certified and sold with the Fair Trade brand logo. The exporting cooperatives have the power to determine how this social premium should be used. It could be used to pay the farmers a premium, it could be used to pay off the costs of being a Fair Trade cooperative, or it could be spent on other social projects in the local community. The result is that the Fair Trade premium may never get back to the farmer. Therefore, if the exporting cooperative is not ethical and does not pass the premium back along the value chain, it could be considered "unfair trading." Under unfair trading, it is unethical to misrepresent the program to the customers, and it is unethical not to give customers relevant information that could affect their purchasing decisions. In addition, it is unethical to misrepresent the program to donors and government agencies that have given money to support the Fair Trade program. In fact, in the United Kingdom, lying about the Fair Trade program could be considered a criminal act and in violation of Unfair Commercial Practices.

Another ethical issue is that retailers are allowed to charge whatever price they want for Fair Trade coffee. FLO does not monitor nor has any justification pertaining to the premium retailers put on the price of a cup or pound of coffee. Another ethical issue is that Fair Trade inspectors make pre-announced trips to the farmers and cooperatives every 5 to 6 years. The result is that cooperatives have ample opportunity to buy uncertified coffee and label it as certified. Furthermore, FLO only monitors the price paid to exporters, so it does not have any information on or control over how much, if any, money reaches the farmers. Therefore, consumers must have faith that the Fair Trade system works ethically.[37]

Human Rights

One of the first actions of this General Assembly was to adopt a Universal Declaration of Human Rights in 1948. That Declaration begins by stating that, "recognition of the inherent dignity and of the equal and inalienable rights of all members of the human family is the foundation of freedom, justice, and peace in the world." The idea is a simple one—that freedom, justice, and peace for the world must begin with freedom, justice, and peace in the lives of individual human beings. And for the United States, this is a matter of moral and pragmatic necessity.[38]

—President Barack Obama,
Address to the United Nations General Assembly, September 23, 2010

Human Rights can be defined as the "rights held by all individuals solely by virtue of their status as human beings . . . human rights belong to everyone, regardless of creed or nationality."[39] The ethical focus is how human rights affect the day-to-day operations of firms. Human rights such as civil rights, property rights, and labor rights can directly affect the strategic focus of a firm.

A number of steps need to be implemented to ensure the firm's human rights responsibilities are integrated throughout the organization. The first step is the development of a clear and comprehensive human rights policy that is championed by the top management leaders. The second step is to transform the vision and intent of the human rights policy into actionable policies and guidelines that every employee must observe. The third step is to ensure that the human rights beliefs are integrated into the decision making and strategic focus of the top management team. The fourth step is the development of a training program that links human rights with the actions of the employees throughout the firm. The fifth step is establishing and maintaining a monitoring function, including an auditing and tracking system that ensures employee compliance with the human rights policy. Managers must also be aware of country-specific risks. Countries with an unpredictable political system can quickly change from a country that supports human rights to one that does not. As a result, any firm that does business in that country must decide what course of action should be taken if, for example, a repressive regime takes over the government and withdraws the citizens' protection of their human rights.[40]

Why should organizations promote human rights? John Kamm identifies four positive reasons for promoting human rights:

1. Respecting human rights enhances worker productivity and management creativity. In short, it raises enterprise profitability.
2. Promoting rights opens markets.
3. Promoting respect for human rights goes hand in hand with development of rule law.
4. Promoting respect for human rights is good for a company's image, both at home and in the host country.[41]

In 2003, seven companies (ABB Ltd., Barclays PLC, MTV Networks Europe, National Grid PLC, Novartis Foundation for Sustainable Development, Novo Nordisk, and The Body Shop International) joined forces to help lead a corporate response to human rights issues. In developing the Business Leaders Initiative on Human Rights, these organizations made a commitment for three years to develop tools and methodologies to help corporations apply human rights principles. Five additional corporations have joined the original group (Hewlett-Packard, Statoil ASA, Gap Inc., Alcan Inc., and AREVA). In 2006, all of the organizations involved believed that there was still much to accomplish, and they extended their initiative.

In addition, companies could achieve Social Accountability 8000 certification. The certification is based on the agreement of the participating firms to abide by human rights standards established by the Social Accountability International (SAI). These standards are audited by SAI to verify compliance. This certification standard provides a way for companies to ensure that they are offering a humane workplace. The standards cover nine areas: (1) child labor, (2) forced labor, (3) health and safety, (4) freedom of association and right to collective bargaining, (5) discrimination, (6) discipline, (7) working hours, (8) compensation, and (9) management systems.[42]

Poverty and Hunger

In vast stretches of the earth, men awoke today in hunger. They will spend the day in unceasing toil. And as the sun goes down they will still know hunger. They will see suffering in the eyes of their children. Many despair that their labor will ever decently shelter their families or protect them against disease. So long as this is so, peace and freedom will be in danger throughout our world. For wherever free men lose hope of progress, liberty will be weakened and the seeds of conflict will be sown. But in working together to create that hope of progress, we raise barriers against tyranny and the war which tyranny breeds.[43]

—Dwight D. Eisenhower, November 10, 1958

Although the United States has had many presidents during the past six decades, there has, unfortunately, been no change in the message that there are millions of people every day who are food insecure globally. Religious scholars comment that discussing poverty is as old as human civilization. With the world's population more than 7 billion people, poverty will continue to be a dominant discussion point for countries and government leaders to ponder. Poverty and hunger go hand in hand because they have such a strong reciprocal relationship. Poverty will lead to hunger, and without food it is difficult to financially support oneself (and other family members), which reinforces the cycle of poverty.

The poor can only guess at what wealth is; the rich don't know what poverty means.

—Chinese Proverb

A Global Challenge

One of the many ironies pertaining to the discussion of hunger is that it is preventable. The technology is available today to supply food for all 7 billion people. Through technology breakthroughs, companies are able to develop new strains of seeds that are pest resistant and increase the yields of food production significantly. In 2007, 457 million people in sub-Sahara Africa were undernourished with a death rate of 25,000 daily. The number of deaths is equivalent to 60 jumbo jetliners crashing every day.[44] The facts related to global hunger are staggering. A total of 925 million people globally do not have enough food to eat, and of those, 98% are in developing countries. The Asian and Pacific regions of the world have one half of the world's population and have nearly two thirds of the world's hungry citizens. Women make up one half of the world's population yet account for more than 60% of the hungry in the world. Of the world's hungry, 65% live in just seven countries: Bangladesh, China, the Democratic Republic of Congo, Ethiopia, India, Indonesia, and Pakistan. There is an annual death rate of 5 million children under the age of 5 in developing countries. In developing countries, 25% of all children, approximately 146 million children, are underweight. Annually, 10.9 million children under the age of 5 die in developing countries. Of those deaths, malnutrition- and hunger-related diseases are the cause of 60% of the deaths.[45]

What Causes Hunger?[46]

There are a number of root causes of hunger. Some causes are discussed here.

The Natural Environment Natural disasters such as floods and drought can severely damage the crops in developing countries. In addition, these disasters can also wash away or destroy seeds that would be planted in the following year. Drought is considered the most common cause of food shortages in the world because it affects crops and livestock. The additional impact on climate change has made factors such as drought even more intense. Warmer temperatures and drier air due to changing climate conditions has had a further devastating impact in developing countries.

War Civil and external wars drain valuable and precious resources that could be used for food production. Wars destroy lives and land and force people to be displaced from their homes. Subsequently, a potentially large and migrating population that has no source of income needs to be fed. For example, the Darfur region in Sudan has been at war since 2004, and the result is that more than 1 million people have left their homes, which has generated a severe food crisis. Furthermore, food can be used as a weapon during a war. Soldiers can destroy crops and livestock to force the villagers to obey their commands. In addition, fields and water wells have been destroyed by explosives to force the farmers off their land. When wars started throughout Central Africa during the 1990s, the proportion of people who went hungry grew from 53% to 58%.

The Poverty Gap Farmers in developing countries cannot afford to buy the seeds and tools needed to develop a good harvest. Craftspeople can't develop their crafts because they cannot afford the tools. As was mentioned previously, the poor cannot afford to buy food so that they have energy to be able to concentrate to perform well at a job.

Poor Infrastructure In developing countries, poor infrastructure greatly restricts the availability of food across large distances. Poor roads limit the availability of the food, and poor or nonexistent warehouses limit the amount of supply that can be stored for future sales. In addition, poor irrigation systems force farmers to rely on the weather for water for their crops.

Overexploitation of the Environment Poor farming techniques such as overcropping, overgrazing, and deforestation greatly limit the sustainability of the farms over time. The soil is also being attacked by erosion, salination, and desertification, which reduce the fertility of the land over time.[47]

Food Versus Fuel

Biofuels are liquid transportation fuels that are developed from the organic material biomass. Biomass can come from plants or animals. Some sources of biomass are agricultural and forestry waste, industrial and solid waste, cornstalks, switchgrass, and wood, but the most common origins are corn, sugar cane, and soybeans. The energy generated from biograss is the conversion of the starch and cellulose in the organic material through a biochemical or thermochemical process into the energy. To be classified as a biofuel, the product must be made of at least 80% renewable materials and be produced from living organisms or from organic or food waste products. The results include methanol, biocrude, methane, ethanol, and biodiesel.[48]

Ethanol Ethanol is also known as ethyl alcohol or grain alcohol. This clear and colorless liquid is the result of converting starch to sugar. Regardless of the source—corn, sugar cane, grain sorghum, or wheat—the resulting ethanol is exactly the same.

Consumers are most familiar with E10, which is composed of 10% ethanol and 90% gasoline. The U.S. Congress passed the Energy Policy Act in 2005, which required an increased use of renewable fuel in gasoline. To create an incentive to produce ethanol, the United States subsidized some of the manufacturing costs for the production of ethanol and included tax credits. The net result was a rapid increase in corn prices even as farmers shifted more and more of their land for corn production. Although the actual ethanol releases fewer greenhouse gasses (GHG) than fossil fuels do, large amounts of carbon dioxide are released during the manufacturing process of ethanol. The manufacturing plant that produces the ethanol using fossil fuel or coal for energy releases GHG emissions. Furthermore, fossil fuels are used by the farming equipment in the planting and harvesting of the corn. In addition, nitrogen fertilizers are commonly used in corn production that are made with natural gas and could contaminate the ground and seep into the water table.[49]

A number of concerns relate to the use of corn as a biofuel. It appears the GHG advantage of biofuels is optimistic and that the sustainability of the market and industry are questionable since government subsidies are giving incentives to farmers that traditional food markets do not. In addition, the most significant drawback to using corn as a biofuel is the argument that the larger increase in demand for corn has led to a "competition" between food and fuel for the production on farmland. The result is a reduction of the supply of a food staple, corn, and increasing worldwide prices for the same staple, corn.[50] The U.S. Council of Economic Advisors estimated that in 2007 retail food prices had increased by approximately 2% because corn was being used as biofuel.[51]

An example of how biofuels have shifted supply decisions has occurred in Thailand. Thailand is the world's largest supplier of cassava chips, which are made from cassava roots. In 2010, 98% of all cassava chips exported in Thailand went to China to make biofuel. However, cassava chips are also used as an ingredient for tapioca pudding, ice cream, paper production, and animal feed. The result is an increase in the price of the chips because the supply is no longer going to the traditional customers for traditional needs. As a result, crops such as cassava, corn, sugar, and palm oil are now shifting customer focus from food-based products to biofuel, resulting in higher global prices. In 2011, the UN Food and Agriculture Organization announced that its index for global food prices had reached the highest level in more than 20 years of tracking world food prices. From October 2010 to January 2011, the global food price index had increased by 15%, which resulted in pushing 44 million people globally into poverty. The shortage of food staples can also lead to increased political instability. For example, palm oil, which is a major ingredient in cooking in Algeria, Egypt, and Bangladesh, has risen in price due to shortages of supply, which has caused riots and political turmoil in these countries. In the United States, corn prices rose 73% from June 2010 to December 2010, which resulted in increased global prices for this commodity. The demand for corn to be used as biofuel will only increase in the future because the U.S. Congress has demanded that biofuel use must reach 36 billion gallons by 2022, and the European Union (EU) is demanding that all EU countries must have 10% of their transportation fuel come from renewable sources such as biofuel or wind power by 2020.[52] In the marketing year 2010–2011, 4.9 billion bushels of corn grown in the United States would be converted into ethanol. The ethanol industry's response to the fuel versus food debate is that misinformation is misrepresenting the impact ethanol has on world food markets. The ethanol industry states that the corn used is "No. 2 corn," which is fed to animals and not humans. In addition, as many as 2 billion of the 4.9 billion bushels can remain after the distillation process and can then be used as animal feed. The ethanol industry also argues that increasing population and severe weather events also affect the price of food globally and that ethanol reduces the dependence of the United States on foreign oil.[53] In a surprise to many, on December 31, 2011, the U.S. Congress let the federal tax credit on ethanol expire. This tax credit was created more than 30 years earlier. The U.S. government has given the industry more than $20 billion in subsidies to encourage the support and sustainability of the industry. This included almost $6 billion in subsidies in 2011. Almost 40% of the corn crop in the United States goes to ethanol and its by-products, including animal feed.[54]

Food and Jobs[55]

In 2008, the government of Madagascar announced that Daewoo Logistics of South Korea was going to receive a 99-year lease of 1.3 million hectares of land for free. The land, which is equivalent to half the size of Belgium, will be used to plant maize and palm oil. Madagascar is offering the land for free in return for job opportunities to cultivate the land. Madagascar has a total of 2.5 million hectares of arable land, so the agreement will take more than half of the total available farming land in this small African island. The World Food Programme estimates that more than 70% of Madagascar's population lives below the poverty line, and 50% of the children younger than 3 years of age suffer from retarded growth resulting from malnutrition. This deal could be seen as a way for Madagascar to move itself out of poverty, or it could be perceived as another example of multinational corporations exploiting the resource base of a developing country.

How Domestic Hunger and Poverty Can Be Used in the Decision-Making Process of Managers

The issue of hunger is global in its realm. Firms in the United States and other parts of the world do not have to focus on developing countries to try to resolve hunger and poverty issues; they just need to look in their own backyards. In 2013, 45.3 million people lived in poverty in the United States. In addition, the official poverty rate was 14.5 percent of the total population in the United States. The poverty rate for children under 18 was 19.9 percent in 2013.[56] In 2014, the poverty line for a single adult was $11,670, and it was $23,850 for a family of four.[57]

In 2014, 46.5 million Americans were served food from Feeding America, including 12 million children and 7 million seniors. Each week, 5.4 million people receive emergency food assistance. Thirty-nine percent of the families served by Feeding America have at least one child under the age of 18. In addition, one third of the household have at least one senior who is 60 years or older. The average monthly income for family that use Feeding America is $927.[58]

It seems apparent from these staggering statistics that firms in the United States have multiple opportunities to focus on a universally underrepresented market segment, the poor. This is the link firms need to understand how they can have a positive role both domestically and internationally to address hunger and poverty issues. Whether in the Sudan or in Baltimore, individuals and families who are food insecure and do not have the financial resources to establish an ongoing standard of living need products and services. Therefore, a portable flashlight that does not need batteries is a potentially explosive product for both domestic and international segments. Strategies to develop higher crop yields can benefit both domestic and foreign farmers. As Yunus demonstrated, the poor are a viable market opportunity regardless of the location. Therefore, multinationals can synchronize their research and development to address hunger and poverty issues globally. This will enhance their financial objectives as well as their reputations and social images. The synergies created by focusing on this underutilized market segment both domestically and internationally will enhance the long-term sustainability of the firm.

The United Nations Millennium Development Goals

In September 2000 at the UN Millennium Summit, the UN Millennium Declaration was signed by 189 countries. The purpose of the summit was to establish global goals that address human development challenges. The results of the summit produced the eight Millennium Development Goals (MDGs). The MDGs have been identified as eight critical objectives that the United Nations proposed should be addressed by nations around the world by 2015: (1) eradicate extreme poverty and hunger; (2) achieve universal primary education; (3) promote gender equality and empower women; (4) reduce child mortality; (5) improve maternal health; (6) combat HIV/AIDS, malaria, and other diseases; (7) ensure environmental sustainability; and (8) develop a global partnership for development. See Table 11.1 for a description of the MDGs and targeted objectives.

TABLE 11.1 ● Millennium Development Goals and Targets

1. Eradicate Extreme Poverty and Hunger—Halve, between 1990 and 2015, the proportion of people whose income is less than $1 a day.
2. Achieve Universal Primary Education—Ensure that, by 2015, children everywhere, boys and girls alike, will be able to complete a full course of primary schooling.
3. Promote Gender Equality and Empower Women—Eliminate gender disparity in primary and secondary education, preferably by 2005, and in all levels of education no later than 2015.
4. Reduce Child Mortality—Reduce by two thirds, between 1990 and 2015, the under-five mortality rate.
5. Improve Maternal Health—Reduce by three quarters, between 1990 and 2015, the maternal mortality ratio.
6. Combat HIV/AIDS, Malaria, and Other Diseases—Have halted by 2015 and begun to reverse the spread of HIV/AIDS.
7. Ensure Environmental Sustainability—Integrate the principles of sustainable development into country policies and programmes and reverse the loss of environmental resources.
8. Develop a Global Partnership for Development.

Source: The Millennium Development Goals Report 2011 (New York: United Nations, 2011).

Progress Toward Reaching
the Millennium Development Goals by 2015

The UN 2011 Millennium Development Goals report presented some promising successes in reaching the eight Millennium Development Goals. Despite significant setbacks due to the slowing down of the global economy in 2008 to 2009, the goal to reduce the level of poverty by half from 1990 to 2015 is still considered feasible on a global scale. Some of the poorest countries have made the largest improvements in education for their children. Sub-Saharan Africa is the region with the greatest level of improvement. In addition, mortality numbers for children younger than age 5 have declined from 12.4 million in 1990 to 8.1 million in 2009.[59] The result is that 12,000 fewer children are dying daily. One quarter of the reduction in child mortality resulted from a 78% drop in measles deaths due to improved immunization coverage.

There has been a 20% reduction in deaths from malaria because of the efforts of governments and different partners to increase the distribution of mosquito nets. Due to improvements in sub-Saharan Africa, the number of new HIV infections is declining in Africa but are increasing in other parts of the world. Every region of the world has made significant progress in the availability of clean drinking water. From 1990 to 2008, an additional 1.1 billion people in urban areas and 723 million people in rural areas now have access to clean drinking water. A number of goals have not moved forward, however. The poorest children in the world have been slow to receive improved nutrition. In 2009, approximately 25% of the children in developing countries were underweight. In addition, women still have only limited opportunities to obtain and maintain paid employment. In developing countries, women were affected much harder by the global recession of 2008 to 2009. From a maternal health perspective, there has been some improvement in that more pregnant women have access to at least minimal health care. However, pregnancy remains a major health risk to women in most of the regions in the world.[60]

Furthermore, the probability has increased that a child will not be at school if the child is poor, female, or is living in a war conflict zone. In addition, more than 2.6 billion people lack access to proper sanitation including flush toilets.[61]

From an environmental sustainability perspective, forests are disappearing at a rapid rate in South America and Africa, but regions in Asia, especially China, have seen a net gain in the number of trees planted versus chopped down. Through a global partnership for development, foreign aid that was given to developing countries is at its highest level ever but is still woefully inadequate to fully service the needs of the countries.[62]

J. D. Sachs and J. W. McArthur presented four broad categories of factors that could explain why some regions have moved forward, but other regions have failed to move forward on the MDGs.[63] The first factor is poor governance. Governments that abuse the human rights of their citizens and are corrupt in their dealings with others will make it difficult to achieve MDGs because their actions are counterproductive to achieving the MDGs. However, the poor level of governance in the country could also be based on lack of knowledge, expertise, and infrastructure. As a result, the leaders of the country may not have the proper skills set to address these complex problems. The second factor is the poverty trap. A poverty trap occurs when a country does not have the financial resources necessary to implement the investments needed to improve infrastructure and reduce the levels of hunger and disease, which leads to stagnant economic development. Developing countries are caught in a vicious poverty circle that is very difficult to break. When the citizens of the country are extremely poor, they don't save money because they spend all their money just to survive. The result of having no disposable income reduces or eliminates any additional expenditures, which ultimately results in very low tax revenues for the country. The low level of tax revenues directly affects the ability of the country to help its citizens improve economically and limits the country's ability to make investments for improving the infrastructure within the country. An inadequate infrastructure then leads to lower levels of foreign investment, which further reduces the resources available to the government and could eventually lead to conflict and civil war within the country.

Once a conflict has taken place, the country now has the additional threat of having the most productive, wealthy, and educated citizens fleeing the country to reside in a safe haven. Therefore, the cycle of poverty becomes fully entrenched within the country with limited opportunity to stop it. The third factor is that many countries have persistent pockets of poverty. Countries such as Brazil, China, and Mexico have large middle classes that demand resources from the government. The result is that additional resources are not allocated to reduce these pockets of poverty. The fourth factor of some countries failing to move forward in achieving the MDGs relates to policy neglect. The concept of *policy neglect* refers to the inability of top-level governmental decision makers to understand the challenges and subsequent consequences of their decisions. Policy neglect traditionally causes biases, stereotypes, or ignorance. For example, the unequal treatment toward girls and women is not perceived as unfair by some government leaders. In addition, the destruction of environmental resources is not viewed from a long-term sustainability perspective.[64]

Private Sector Investment and MDGs

From a business perspective, the ability to reduce poverty can come from the private sector investment through economic growth and job creation, which results in higher income levels. An additional benefit of a traditional market economy is that people in developing countries are able to receive the benefits of products and services at lower prices due to increased levels of efficiencies resulting from economies of scale and economies of scope.[65] The combination of a number of factors—including strong infrastructures, a strong and objective legal system, and a government that supports economic growth—will encourage private sector investment. The result is enhancement of the economic standard of living of the citizens of that country. Firms are driven by market-based incentives, so a pro-investment strategy by the government will increase the firm's level of profitability and provide aid to further support country development goals.[66]

Jane Nelson and Dave Prescott propose that corporations can develop both core business operations and value chains that can be used to encourage higher levels of innovations by the firms, which are necessary for the country to enhance its market and economic opportunities.[67] Nelson and Prescott present three critical reasons why firms should contribute toward achievement of the MDGs: The first reason is that corporations make investments in developing countries that enhance the country's ability to establish a stable and secure business environment for both domestic and foreign firms. The result is standard-of-living improvements for the workers in the country, which means workers will be more productive and more motivated, ultimately resulting in higher levels of profitability for the firms. This will also enhance the long-term sustainability of the economy, which would be beneficial to both the country and the firms who have invested in the country.

The second reason it is beneficial for firms to contribute toward achieving the MDGs is that the firms have the opportunity to manage direct costs and risks. If the economic market is unpredictable due to the challenges presented in the MDGs, firms that do business in that country will be forced to address increases in operating, raw material, human resource, security, and insurance costs as well as the cost of capital. Therefore, an unpredictable economic environment could increase the level of both the short-term and long-term financial risks, market risks, litigation risks, and reputation risks. By addressing the challenges of the MDGs, firms can reduce the risk in business operations.

The third reason is the ability of firms to harness new business opportunities. As was discussed in the BOP section of this chapter, focusing on consumers in developing countries can lead to the successful development of new markets, services, and technologies and can eventually result in the overall evolution of the firm's strategic business model. Therefore, firms that are proactive in addressing the challenges established by MDGs will reduce business risk and enhance innovation, value creation, and competitiveness.[68]

Questions for Thought

1. Why are poverty and hunger seen as business issues?

2. Do corporations have a responsibility to help solve hunger and poverty around the world? Explain.

3. Why don't U.S. firms focus on the poor as a potential target market?

Real-Life Ethical Dilemma Exercise

The True Cost of Cotton

In India, the cotton gins are continuously working, with girls—some as young as 10 years old—employed to spin the raw cotton into commercial cotton for a global textile industry that generates trillions of dollars annually. The working conditions are dangerous, and the workers are not paid the minimum wage. A constant white cloud of cotton dust fills the factories, which can eventually cause lung disease for the children as they age. In addition, it is not uncommon for the exhausted children to fall asleep on the job and die from suffocation in the piles of raw cotton. The little hands of the girls pry open the cotton buds to get to the material to feed into the machines. In many cases, the children are sent by their parents to work the mills. The children do not see any of the money for their work because it all goes to the parents. The workers are paid just over $2 a day instead of the $7 for each 12-hour shift that is required by the labor laws in India. Indian law also does not allow children younger than 16 years old to work in the factories. Almost 500,000 children actually work in the cotton plants in India.[69] Therefore, consumers in developed countries who purchase these goods made from cotton do not realize the human cost in the development of cotton fibers.

Questions for the Real-Life Ethical Dilemma Exercise

1. Why doesn't the Indian government enforce its own labor laws?

2. Why would parents send their children to work in such horrible work conditions?

3. Is it better for the girls to be working in the factory or providing no income at home? Explain your position.

Student Study Site

Visit the Student Study Site at **study.sagepub.com/stanwick3e** to access the following resources:

- Video Links
- SAGE Journal Articles
- Web Resources
- Web Quizzes

DEVELOPING AND EVALUATING A STRONG ETHICAL FOCUS

12

Establishing a Code of Ethics and Ethical Guidelines

I have found that the greatest help in meeting any problem with decency and self-respect and whatever courage is demanded, is to know where you yourself stand. That is, to have in words what you believe and are acting from.

—William Faulkner

Chapter Objectives

After reading and studying Chapter 12, students should be able to

1. Describe the role of a code of ethics in organizations.

2. List the four types of statements that a corporation may use to communicate its ethical viewpoint.

3. Explain the benefits of having a living code of ethics.

4. Describe the three major stages of TRM systems used when setting up a code of ethics.

5. List the recommended items for a code of ethics.

6. Explain the necessary ingredients for ethics programs to add value to organizations.

7. Identify the major global codes of ethics.

How We're Fixing Up Tyco[1]

The new senior vice president of corporate governance at Tyco, Eric Pillmore, had a big problem. How was he going to try to repair the tarnished image of the diversified conglomerate Tyco? A major difference between the Tyco scandal and the WorldCom and Enron scandals was that Tyco had strong financial performance from its divisions. Although the other scandals falsified financial statements to give the appearance of financial strength, Tyco was still profitable during the scandal.

Realizing that to re-create its image, Tyco needed to start with a clean slate, Tyco changed all the board members who were part of the Kozlowski era to try to separate the company from $6,000 shower curtains. Tyco went through a two-stage process in which the board evaluated all the activities of the former top executives as well as reviewed all the financial statements for each business unit within the company. The board established Pillmore's job of vice president of corporate governance, which reported directly to the board of directors.

Tyco officials also realized that they would have to start from scratch to develop a new code of ethics. To reestablish credibility with its stakeholders, Tyco had to incorporate its new value system in a formal document. Tyco officials examined the code of ethics and corporate governance practices at General Electric, Johnson & Johnson, and Coca-Cola as a starting point for rewriting Tyco's code of ethics. From that foundation, Tyco established the Guide to Ethical Conduct, which applied to all employees at Tyco. The guide covered such ethical areas as sexual harassment, potential conflicts of interest, compliance rules, and what is considered to be fraudulent behavior of the employees. As a complement to the guide, Tyco also developed ethical vignette videos to highlight potentially unethical behavior in different situations. In the summer of 2003, the guide and access to the vignettes were given to every employee at Tyco. (The complete Tyco case is presented later in the textbook.)

Business ethics is based on determining where to "draw the line in the sand" in which the individual rights of a person infringe on the collective rights of society. Individuals need guidance, direction, and advice about what to do to make sure he or she goes down the right ethical path in his or her career. Corporations rely on government regulations to help ensure that employees do not break the law. However, ethics is much more than just the legal standards. Business ethics relates to the vision of the top-level managers and the culture that develops to foster this positive work climate. Every company should have a strong code of ethics that explicitly explains what is ethically expected from each employee in his or her day-to-day activities.

Role of a Code of Ethics

A *code of ethics* can be defined as a written document that explicitly states what acceptable and unacceptable behaviors are for all of the employees in the organization. The code of ethics of a firm represents the identification and interpretation of what the firm considers acceptable behavior. Jang Singh proposes that a number of components affect the development of the ethical standards of the firm:[2] social value, institutional factors, personal factors, and organizational factors. Together these result in the establishment

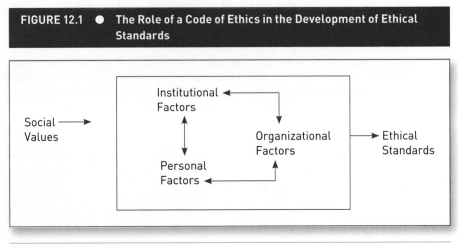

FIGURE 12.1   ●   The Role of a Code of Ethics in the Development of Ethical Standards

Source: Jang B. Singh, "A Comparison of the Contents of the Code of Ethics of Canada's Largest Corporations in 1992 and 2003," *Journal of Business Ethics* 64 (2006): 18.

of ethical standards. A model presenting the relationships proposed by Singh is shown in Figure 12.1.

The values of society drive the development of a code of ethics by affecting the relationship between institutional, personal, and organizational factors. Institutional factors are voluntary industry guidelines and government regulations. Personal factors are the values and ethical morals of the decision makers creating the code of ethics. Organizational factors are those factors that influence the development of a code of ethics within the firm. The result is establishing a strong positive ethical climate within the firm.

A corporation may adopt four types of statements to communicate the corporation's view of the subject of ethics:[3]

1. Values statement: A succinct document that is intended to set out the guiding principles of a company
2. Corporate credo: A statement that sets forth the company's beliefs and responsibilities to stakeholders
3. Code of ethics: A detailed statement of a firm's ethical policies
4. Internet privacy policy: A statement discussing the company's privacy policy for Internet transactions, usually written in legal terms relating to the firm's ethical values.

No matter what term is used, they all really represent the same thing—the company's commitment to doing the right thing. They represent a statement of values to give employees and managers guidelines about what to do in those gray areas that they may be faced with when working for the company to help guide them away from ethical misconduct. What is covered in each company's code may differ, being tailored to the specific industry or to the specific instances that the employees may face working for a particular company.

Code of Ethics and Stakeholders

The code of ethics gives a firm an opportunity to declare to all of its stakeholders its ethical vision. Firms can address the ethical needs of various stakeholders from information provided in the code of ethics. Cecily Raiborn and Dinah Payne suggest that firms consider four ethical values when developing or modifying a code of ethics:[4] integrity, justice, competence, and utility. Raiborn and Payne define *integrity* as presenting ideals in the code of ethics that highlight the attributes of honesty, sincerity, and transparency. They define *justice* as presenting the firm's commitment to unbiased and good-faith interactions with its stakeholders. *Competence* is identified as the duties and capabilities of the firm to execute its ethical vision. *Utility* is incorporating within the code of ethics values and actions that will do the greatest good for the greatest number.

One of the first corporate codes of ethics was developed by J. C. Penney, whose stores were originally called the Golden Rule Stores. In 1913, when the J. C. Penney stores were formed, the Penney Idea was adopted. The company introduced seven ideas, which formed one of the first ethical codes for corporations:

1. To serve the public, as nearly as we can, to its complete satisfaction
2. To expect for the service we render a fair remuneration and not all the profit the traffic will bear
3. To do all in our power to pack the customer's dollar full of value, quality, and satisfaction
4. To continue to train ourselves and our associates so that the service we give will be more and more intelligently performed
5. To improve constantly the human factor in our business
6. To reward men and women in our organization through participation in what the business produces
7. To test our every policy, method, and act in this wise: "Does it square with what is right and just?"[5]

It is important to put a code of ethics into writing regardless of the size of the business because it helps stakeholders know which behaviors are acceptable and which are not. Many codes of ethics leave out sanctions sections; however, it is important that employees and management understand the implications if they violate the code. Having a sanctions section shows the employees that this is a living document. If the sanctions section is overlooked or used on only select employees, however, then the code of ethics is nothing more than a piece of paper.

The Enron code of ethics began with a letter from the chairman and chief executive officer. Ken Lay stated, "We want to be proud of Enron and to know that it enjoys a reputation for fairness and honesty and that it is respected. Gaining such respect is one aim of our advertising and public relations activities, but no matter how effective they may be, Enron's reputation finally depends on its people, on you and me. Let's keep that reputation high."[6] The 65-page code of ethics at Enron highlighted the conditional value of a code of ethics. A code of ethics is valuable to a firm only if the employees believe in the code and the code has a direct impact on their actions within the firm. Sometimes companies require their employees to sign a statement that they have read the code of ethics and accept it. This signature may be used as part of employees' performance evaluations or as part of the requirements to advance in the organization.

Benefits of a Code of Ethics

Ethical issues are faced by business professionals on a daily basis. When companies have a code of ethics in place and enforce that code, the following happens:

- Employee loyalty increases.
- Questionable behavior decreases.
- Competitive positions improve.
- Managers become more confident.
- Employee relations improve.
- Customer relationships become more solid.[7]

W. Edwards Deming is well known for his 14 points, which define quality from a business perspective. When examining these points, which deal with employee skill, empowerment, and the absence of fear, one can see that approximately half of them can be related to ethical concepts:

- Adopt a philosophy that encourages high-quality and effective training and ensures effective supervision.
- Institute training.
- Institute leadership.
- Drive out fear.
- Break down barriers among staff.
- Eliminate quotas.
- Remove barriers to pride of workmanship.[8]

Content of a Code of Ethics

William A. Stimson believes that benefits from a code of ethics came from a Deming-inspired code of ethics and provide benefits to producers and consumers, which ultimately provides benefits to the marketplace. Beginning with a statement that says that profit is the company's goal and integrity is the means by which it will achieve that goal, the company achieves these benefits:

- Meeting customer expectations
- Honesty
- Nondelegable quality
- Traceability, which reduces occasions for waste and fraud
- Respect for privacy and avoidance of conflicts of interest
- Antidiscrimination, which is required by law but inserted to complete the code
- Empowerment through organizational freedom, responsibility, and authority
- True reports
- Integrity (encouragement of whistle-blowing reduces animosity and punitive action)[9]

For example, General Electric published its 2010 Citizenship Report, called "Sustainable Growth." In this 57-page document, the company sets forth its policy on several different areas and discusses each in detail. These areas address the stakeholders' expectations pertaining to the ethical commitment of GE.

Code of ethics content areas could include the following:

- Fiduciary responsibilities
- Compliance
- Accounting
- Governance
- Member communications and confidentiality
- Commitment to learning and skill enhancement
- Absence of prejudice and harassment
- Conflict of interest
- Human resources
- Cooperation with other credit unions
- Social responsibility

A Living Code of Ethics[10]

One of the many challenges facing organizations as they design a code of ethics is to ensure that the content of the code is integrated into the day-to-day decisions of the employees. A living code of ethics is based on a positive harmonious interaction among (1) the authentic leadership of the management, (2) five components of the organizational process of the firm, and (3) the firm's organization culture.

Authentic Leadership

Authentic leadership is based on a strong belief in the leader's value, character, and moral capacity. Authentic leaders focus on the needs of others and help in their development. Authentic leaders also support strong ethics through their actions and traits, which includes being a good role model and listener. Furthermore, authentic leaders set the ethical standards and accountability within the firm and ethically address the needs of the firm's stakeholders.

Organizational Components

Attraction-Selection-Attrition A firm can strengthen and enhance its integration of the living code of ethics if it is able to design an effective evaluation process in which ethical people are attracted to work for the firm, are selected to work for the firm, and stay employed by the firm.

The Socialization Process The socialization process allows the values, beliefs, attitudes, norms, and traits of the living code of ethics to be transferred to the new employees. The socialization process is embedded in the orientation and training programs designed by the firm. In addition, the socialization process should also foster the ability of new employees to identify and ask for guidance from a mentor.

Reward Systems Firms that have a positive ethical focus use reward systems to acknowledge the ethical behavior of the employees. The firm must ensure that the reward systems coincide with the living code of ethics. If there is a conflict in the rewards and the implied actions in the reward system, there can be confusion by the employees as to the best course of action to take to fulfil their obligations.

The Decision-Making Process The decision-making process by the employees must integrate with the living code of ethics in the day-to-day operations of the firm. Because the decision making process is driving the development and implementation of the living code of ethics, it is the most critical element ensuring the effective assimilation of the values and beliefs of the living code by the employees.

Organizational Learning Organizational learning is the process by which the firm generates and captures information relevant to its operations and transfers it to its employees. The ability to learn from this information allows the living code of ethics to be adjusted when required in order to be current with the external demands on the firm.

Organizational Culture

Organizational culture is a pattern of shared values and beliefs that are incorporated by the employees throughout the firm. A strong positive organizational culture can increase the employees' level of ethical awareness and can create a positive climate of ethical values and beliefs.

The Role of Total Responsibility Management and a Code of Ethics

An extension to Deming's total quality management (TQM) approach to firms is Sandra Waddock and Charles Bodwell's total responsibility management (TRM).[11] TRM starts with the premise that the vision of the firm drives the development of the code of ethics. Waddock and Bodwell argue that the creator's vision of the code of ethics must include the responsibilities that the firm has to its stakeholders and to the natural environment. By identifying the firm's responsibilities to its stakeholders, the firm can explicitly state what it considers acceptable conduct to support the needs and demands of the stakeholders. The firm's vision also establishes the benchmark goals in which the firm is now accountable to its stakeholders.

The firm's ethical vision was highlighted in the Tyco example at the beginning of the chapter. As Tyco tried to start its ethical commitment from scratch, it needed to start its ethical vision from scratch as well. Tyco used a method very similar to TRM to reestablish the ethical commitment to its stakeholders. The three major stages of the TRM system are inspiration process, integration process, and innovation and improvement process.

Inspiration Process

Vision Setting and Leadership Commitment During the inspiration process, the firm establishes its ethical leadership commitment and the vision-setting process. Vision setting is based on identifying the unique relationship each firm has with its competitive advantage, its stakeholders, and its historical development. Each of these three factors affects what will be appropriate for the firm's overall vision as it relates to its responsibilities to its stakeholders.

Responsibility Vision and Leadership Commitments During this stage, the formalization of the responsibilities and commitments to the ethical vision take place. The responsibility vision and leadership commitments need to be consistent and repeated often over time to all stakeholders. The two questions to be addressed during this step are, "What business are we in?" and "What do we stand for?" The second question is critical in developing a strong ethical vision because the answer to the question identifies the firm's core ethical values.

Stakeholder Engagement Processes The inspiration stage also incorporates the process to engage with the firm's stakeholders. During the engagement step of the process, the firm interacts with the stakeholders to ensure that the ethical vision the firm is developing coincides with the needs and expectations of all the stakeholders.

Foundation Values During the inspiration stage, a firm identifies its foundation values along with the international standards that apply to its operations. The foundation values are the minimally acceptable standards for any transactions with any stakeholder. Because these are considered minimally acceptable standards, firms are expected to move well beyond the minimal standards when they are developing their ethical visions to drive the TRM system.

Integration: Changes in Strategies and Management Practices

The integration process involves top management integrating the ethical vision, values, and leadership into the strategic decision-making process. The integration process involves integration into the corporate- and business-level strategies of the firm as well as identifying strategic implementation responsibilities, which include human resource and management systems issues.

Strategy From a TRM perspective, the ethical vision developed in the inspiration process is incorporated in all aspects of the firm's corporate- and business-level strategies. This integration process allows the firm to be proactive if a crisis arises. Furthermore, integration of the ethical vision in the strategic formulation stage of the decision-making process can eliminate the potential conditions for a crisis before it can occur. The question to ask from a strategic integration perspective is, "How do we do business here?"

Building Human Resource Capacity Integrating the ethical vision requires that human resource issues be identified so the ethical vision can be effectively executed. The ethical vision incorporates the beliefs about the most effective ways to treat employees and the most effective ways to develop the employees' skills. Furthermore, because the employees are the individuals responsible for executing the ethical vision, the employees must be trained on and informed of their specific role in executing the ethical vision. During this stage, decisions are also made and implemented pertaining to allocating resources to execute the ethical vision. Firms are able to set the tone for their visions and acceptable codes of conduct by establishing training and rewards programs that are linked to ethical behavior. As a result, the human resource element is usually a key and comprehensive component of any firm's code of ethics. The explicit explanation of what responsibilities the employees have within the firm and the expectations of how they will be treated by the firm become the cornerstones of the tone set in the code of ethics.

Integration Into Management Systems Another component of the integration process is to establish the link between the responsibilities of executing the ethical vision and the management systems within the firm. The integration affects the direct relationship the firm has with its external stakeholders. An example of integration into the management systems is for the firm to coordinate its ethical practices with its suppliers. Firms can and will demand complete compliance with their ethical visions from suppliers, or the firms will shift to other suppliers who will agree to their ethical commitments. As a result, the code of ethics will highlight the relationship that management systems play in the overall integration of the ethical vision of the firm.

Innovation: Focusing on Assessment, Improvement, and Learning Systems

Using the TRM system, firms are able to present their ethical vision to their stakeholders via their codes of ethics and will be able to generate new ideas about how to improve their TRM systems.

The Responsibility Measurement System Firms that use a TRM system have the ability to measure goals related to operating practices and to their stakeholder relationships. Therefore, by focusing on multiple stakeholders, TRM allows for the measurement of multiple bottom lines. Each stakeholder's interests can be evaluated based on how well the firm is able to execute its strategic ethical vision.

Transparency and Accountability Firms that implement a TRM system are able to generate relevant information of interest for both internal and external stakeholders. As a result, an effective ethical vision will allow, and even encourage, the release of all relevant information that could affect the stakeholders. Therefore, firms that use TRM are transparent in their information and are accountable. The firms have nothing to hide from their stakeholders.

Innovation, Improvement, and Learning Systems Firms that adopt a TRM system are able to learn from implementing the system. Similar to its cousin TQM, TRM is a continuous cycle in which the feedback from one year's execution becomes part of the input for the next year's cycle. From a code of ethics perspective, the innovative aspect of TRM allows the code of ethics to be a living document. By constantly measuring and reevaluating the ethical vision of the firm, the firm can adjust how the ethical vision is presented in the code of ethics.

Steps for an Effective Code of Ethics

Many companies begin their codes of ethics with mission statements. This statement sets forth a brief explanation about what the company stands for and why it exists. The mission statement also identifies many of the stakeholders of the company and explains the interactions within the company. The code should not be written by one person or one group. A task force should be developed with representatives from every employee level. Companies attempt to establish effective ethics programs, which include both the code of ethics and the implementation of the code, to allow their employees to actively think about ethics programs and to provide them with ways to address ethical issues on the job. By having an ethics program, employee concerns about ethical issues are validated, and they should no longer be wary of identifying and bringing these issues to light. Many use training programs to discuss the drafting of the code. This gives employees a chance to participate in the actual writing of the code. The employees may feel empowered to see the code change based on their input.

When developing a code of ethics, companies should follow several standard recommendations of what to include in the code. Deloitte recommends the following:

- An introductory letter from the senior leadership team or CEO that sets the tone at the top and defines the importance of ethics and compliance for each employee and the company
- The company's mission statement, vision, values, and guiding principles that reflect the company's commitment to ethics, integrity, and quality
- An ethical decision framework to assist employees in making choices. For example, a code might ask employees to answer some questions to guide them in making ethical decisions about possible courses of action. The goal is for employees to think before acting and to seek guidance when unsure. They should be encouraged to think about this type of question in the context of an ethical dilemma: "Would you be unwilling or embarrassed to tell your family, friends, or coworkers?"
- A listing of available resources for obtaining guidance and for good-faith reporting of suspected misconduct; for example, consider the following:

  o A means to report issues anonymously, such as a helpline or postal address
  o How to contact the ethics and compliance officer or office
  o A definition of the reporting chain of command (e.g., supervisor, department head)
  o A listing of any internal ethics and compliance websites

- A listing of any additional ethics and compliance resources and the identification of supplementary policies and procedures and their location
- Enforcement and implementation mechanisms that address the notion of accountability and discipline for unethical behavior; for example, unethical behavior will be subject to disciplinary action up to and including termination
- Generic examples of what constitutes acceptable and unacceptable behavior could be included to further explain risk areas; examples could be based on relevant company or industry experiences[12]

A good ethics program can be a value-added service to a company if it consists of the right elements.[13] These elements should include the following:

- A well-designed code of ethics
- The assignment of functional responsibility
- The proper employee training
- An ethics hotline

Rather than feeling the code is something that is imposed on them, employees should feel included in the process if they are involved in the writing of the code. The code of ethics should be seen as a document that can help strengthen the ethical working environment as well as protect the company legally. View the code as being a work in progress. The code is never actually finished. It is important to stress that ownership of the code of ethics is important. The company's code should be made public and should be readily available for public scrutiny to help increase transparency. Corporations need to be more sensitive about the public's expectations of their behaviors. Is it necessary to have the firm's legal team look over or even write the code of ethics? It probably is necessary for the legal team to look over the document to make sure that what the firm has expressed in the code is legal. However, it is probably unnecessary for management to have the firm's legal team write the code for the company. The code should realistically be written by those who use it.

Value of a Code of Ethics

In all cases actions will speak louder than words. Having good statements, or any statements at all, will never ensure that employees will comply with the code. If no one follows it, the ethical code is a useless piece of information in the company. Consider, for example, Enron. Enron had a code of ethics in place at the time of its collapse, as mentioned at the beginning of this chapter. However, few actually believe that given the collapse of this organization that Enron officials ever enforced this code of ethics. When the code of ethics was distributed to Enron employees on July 1, 2000, Lay stated in his letter to employees, "The Code of Ethics contains common-sense rules of conduct with which the great majority of Enron employees routinely conform. However, I ask that you read them carefully and completely and that, as you do, you reflect on your past actions to make certain that you have complied with the policies. It is absolutely essential that you fully comply with these policies in the future. If you have any questions, talk them over with your supervisor, manager, or Enron legal counsel" (Interoffice Memorandum, Enron, July 1, 2000).[14] In fact, the board of directors suspended Enron's code of ethics twice to approve the off–balance sheet transactions that were later shown to be illegal.[15]

Krista Bondy, Dirk Matten, and Jeremy Moon offer several reasons codes of ethics could be adopted:[16]

- As part of an internal control system
- To provide product differentiation in the marketplace
- As a signal to stakeholders about a firm's quality and would result in the stakeholders buying goods and services from the firm

- To reduce insurance premiums (because of less potential for risk) and to provide evidence of due diligence
- Because of peer pressure within the same industry
- In case of government failure
- To ensure applicability of codes of conduct across boundaries and borders beyond the borders of one nation-state
- To improve customer relationships
- To maintain standards along the supply chain

How to Make a Code of Ethics More Effective

The Institute of Business Ethics offers guidance to companies desiring to develop a code of ethics. One area that the institute focuses on is making codes of ethics effective. Table 12.1 presents the institute's comparison of good and poor practices in making codes of ethics effective.

TABLE 12.1 ● Directives for Making Codes of Conduct More Effective	
Good Practice	**Poor Practice**
Integrate the code in core ethical values	Post the code to the notice board without any action
Distribute to everyone in the company	Do not get the commitment of the board of directors
Allow a hotline or other method to report ethical breaches	Assign one unit within the company to be responsible for the effectiveness of the firm's ethical commitment
Include ethical training programs	Do not ask for employee feedback pertaining to their ethical concerns
Set up an ethics committee within the board of directors	Do not feature the code of ethics in training and management development
Include a report on the code's use in the annual report	Do not review the code of ethics for revisions
Make ethical commitment part of a contract for employment	Make exceptions to the code's application in certain circumstances
Make the code available in all the languages in which the firm does business	Failing to follow up when there is a breach of the code's standards
Distribute the code to business partners, including suppliers	Failure by top managers to set a good ethical example
Review and make adjustments to the code when necessary	View the code as a confidential and/or internal document
Make sure senior staff set the correct example by "walking the talk"	Make it difficult for staff to have continuous access to the code

Examples of Codes of Ethics

MetLife has a comprehensive employee code of business conduct and ethics.[17] All employees are responsible for "reading, understanding, and adhering" to the code. The code covers many different areas, including these:

1. In the workplace

   a. Respect
   b. Equal employment opportunity
   c. Sexual harassment and other discriminatory harassment

2. Business conduct certification program
3. Conflicts of interest

   a. Corporate opportunities
   b. Outside opportunities

      i. Office or director of another business
      ii. Second job

   c. Vendors, suppliers, and consultants
   d. Gifts and entertainment
   e. Communication of conflicts

4. Compliance with laws, rules, and regulations

   a. Insider trading
   b. Antitrust
   c. Money laundering
   d. Foreign Corrupt Practices Act
   e. Boycotts

5. Financial management and disclosure

   a. Accounting standards
   b. Audits and outside examinations

6. Protection and proper use of company assets
   a. Confidentiality
   b. Technology

7. Administration

   a. Reporting of any illegal or unethical behavior; points of contact
   b. Responding to improper conduct

Enron represents a company that stated its corporate values but didn't practice them at the senior management level.[18] Consider the values stated in the Enron code of ethics:[19]

- Respect: We treat others as we would like to be treated ourselves. We do not tolerate abusive or disrespectful treatment. Ruthlessness, callousness, and arrogance don't belong here.

- Integrity: We work with customers and prospects openly, honestly, and sincerely. When we say we will do something, we will do it; when we say we cannot or will not do something, then we won't do it.
- Communication: We have an obligation to communicate. Here, we take the time to talk with one another . . . and to listen. We believe that information is meant to move and that information moves people.
- Excellence: We are satisfied with nothing less than the very best in everything we do. We will continue to raise the bar for everyone. The great fun here will be for all of us to discover just how good we can really be.

Role of Government Regulations

In an effort to educate financial institutions about establishing an appropriate code of ethics, the FDIC issued guidance in 2005. The publication *Corporate Codes of Conduct: Guidance on Implementing an Effective Ethics Program* provides suggestions for the components of a code of conduct for financial institutions: (1) safeguarding confidential information; (2) ensuring the integrity of records; (3) providing strong internal controls over assets; (4) providing candor in dealing with auditors, examiners, and legal counsel; (5) avoiding self-dealings and acceptance of gifts or favors; (6) observing applicable laws; (7) implementing appropriate background checks; (8) involving internal auditors in monitoring corporate codes of conduct or ethics policies; (9) providing a mechanism to report questionable activity; (10) outlining penalties for a breach of the corporate code of conduct or ethics policy; (11) providing periodic training and acknowledgment of the policy; and (12) periodically updating policies to reflect new business activities.[20] As in practically all corporate codes of ethics, the FDIC recommends that financial institutions include specific information of applicable laws and regulations.

Section 406 of the Sarbanes-Oxley Act of 2002 (SOX) requires that companies that are publicly traded disclose whether or not they have a code of ethics. If they do not have a code of ethics, they must explain why. In addition, firms must report any amendments or any waivers from the code of ethics. However, based on the SOX requirement, only top-level managers are required to be held accountable to the firm's code of ethics. In a survey done in August and September 2002, which was shortly after the passage of SOX, 44% of the 291 executive respondents stated that their companies did not have a formal code of ethics.[21] To comply with the act, a company's code of ethics must be composed of standards that are reasonably necessary to promote the following:

- Honest and ethical conduct, including the ethical handling of actual or apparent conflicts of interest between personal and professional relationships.
- Full, fair, accurate, timely, and understandable disclosure in the periodic reports required to be filed by the issuer.
- Compliance with applicable governmental rules and regulations.[22]

The U.S. Sentencing Guidelines were revised in 2004.[23] These new guidelines strengthened the need for companies to have an ethics program and an associated compliance program related to ethics. By implementing an ethics program and compliance program, a company may be able to reduce the sentence if the company is convicted of a federal crime.

Global Code of Ethics

A number of organizations have shown the foresight to develop a global code of ethics that both for-profit and nonprofit organizations can use as a starting point to develop or revise their codes of ethics. Three of the major global codes of ethics are the Caux Round Table principles, the Organisation of Economic Co-operation and Development guidelines for multinational enterprises, and the United Nations Global Compact.

Caux Round Table Principles

The Caux Round Table (CRT) is an international network of business leaders who are committed to promoting the concept of moral capitalism. Using the CRT principles, businesses will be more socially responsible and promote sustainability of these ideals. The principles are based on the ethical ideals of kyosei and human dignity. *Kyosei* is defined as the ability to live and work together for the common good that allows mutual prosperity through cooperation. CRT defines *human dignity* as the sacred value of each human life, which should not be used solely for the betterment of others.[24]

Organisation for Economic Co-operation and Development Guidelines for Multinational Enterprises

Organisation for Economic Co-operation and Development (OECD) guidelines are recommendations made by governments for multinational enterprises to adopt into their own codes of ethics. The guidelines are voluntary principles and standards that support responsible and accountable business conduct. The goal of the guidelines is to encourage multinational enterprises to make positive contributions to the economic, environmental, and social progress of countries around the world.[25]

United Nations Global Impact

Established in January 1999, the United Nations Global Impact was based on a challenge by former Secretary-General of the United Nations Kofi Annan for businesses to adopt universal environmental and social principles. The principles are categorized into four major areas: human rights, labor, the natural environment, and anticorruption.[26]

A comparison of the principles presented by these three organizations is shown in Table 12.2. Table 12.3 presents some advice for companies that want to develop or revise their codes of ethics to ensure that they have captured all the global issues that directly or indirectly affect the firm.

TABLE 12.2   ●   A Comparison of Global Ethical Principles

CRT Principles[27]

Principle 1: The responsibilities of business are beyond shareholders and are to all stakeholders.

Principle 2: The economic and social impact of business should be toward innovation, justice, and world community.

Principle 3: Business behavior should be beyond the letter of the law toward a spirit of trust.

Principle 4: Businesses need to respect the global rules.

Principle 5: Businesses need to support multilateral trade.

Principle 6: Businesses must respect the environment.

Principle 7: Businesses must avoid illicit operations.

Stakeholder Principles: Businesses must treat all stakeholders with respect and dignity including customers, employees, owners/investors, suppliers, competitors, and communities.

OECD Guidelines for Multinational Enterprises[28]

Principle 1: Organizations must focus on sustainable development when contributing to economic, social, and environmental progress.

Principle 2: Organizations must respect human rights of all those individuals impacted by the organization.

Principle 3: Organizations must encourage local economic development through cooperation with the local community.

Principle 4: Organizations must encourage employment opportunities and employee training opportunities.

Principles 5: Organizations must not ask local or regional government for legal exemptions from legal requirements based on environmental, health/safety, labor, taxation, financial incentives, or any other legal issue.

Principle 6: Organizations must support and uphold good corporate governance principles and apply good corporate governance practices.

Principle 7: Organizations must develop and apply effective self-regulatory practices and management systems.

Principle 8: Organizations must make all of their employees aware of all compliance and company policies that affect the behavior of the employees.

Principle 9: Organizations must not be involved in any discriminatory behavior toward employees nor should they be unjust in the treatment of their employees.

Principle 10: Organizations must whenever possible do business with partners and suppliers who also agree to the OECD principles.

Principle 11: Organizations must avoid any improper conduct involving local political activities.

United Nations Global Impact Principles[29]

Human Rights

Principle 1: Businesses should support and respect global human rights.

Principle 2: Businesses should make sure they are not associated with any human rights abuses.

Labor Standards

Principle 3: Businesses should allow the freedom of association and recognize collective bargaining of their employees.

Principle 4: Businesses should eliminate all forms of forced or compulsory labor.

Principle 5: Businesses should abolish all child labor.

Principle 6: Businesses should eliminate all forms of discrimination in the workplace.

Environment

Principle 7: Businesses should support a precautionary approach to global environmental challenges.

Principle 8: Businesses should undertake all initiatives that promote a higher level of environmental responsibility.

Principle 9: Businesses should encourage the development and dissemination of environmental-friendly technologies.

Anticorruption

Principle 10: Businesses should stop all forms of corruption including extortion and bribery.

TABLE 12.3 ● Common Mistakes That Companies Make When Developing Global Ethics Programs
Not having consensus on objectives for globalization of ethics commitment
Not incorporating international-based employees in the development of the company's ethics policies
Not focusing on the potential competitive advantages of have a strong positive ethical program
Making the ethical policy in other countries match the country's legal requirements
Not committing resources and/or employees who focus on ethics issues in other countries
Not selecting only home country employees to fill any ethics-based positions
Not offering ethics training in languages other than English
Not making sure that all countries interpret the meaning of the ethics policy consistently
Failing to acknowledge the many cultural differences related to business ethics

Source: Adapted from International Business Ethics Institute.

Questions for Thought

1. Do you think codes of ethics really make a difference in an organization? Explain.

2. Find the Code of Ethics for United Health on the Internet. Comment on the topics addressed in United Health's Code of Ethics. Do you feel the code adequately achieves its purpose?

3. Many companies ignore or overlook differences in translating codes of ethics into other languages. Why is it important to have codes of ethics translated into the native languages of the countries in which the company may operate?

Real-Life Ethical Dilemma Exercise

A Preventable Disaster

On January 28, 1986, at 11:38 a.m., the space shuttle *Challenger* was launched. The evening before the launch, the temperature at the launch site had dropped to 18 degrees. It was also estimated to be near or below freezing when the *Challenger* actually launched. Seventy-three seconds after the launch, the *Challenger* exploded, killing all seven astronauts. If that were not tragic enough, it is more tragic to realize that those astronauts did not need to die. The cause of the explosion was a small rubber sealant called an O-ring. The O-rings are used to aid in the attachment of the different sections of the rockets to the shuttle. The O-rings were manufactured by Morton Thiokol (MTI). Both MTI and the National Aeronautics and Space Administration (NASA) knew there were problems with the O-rings at low temperatures. The rubber becomes stiff and brittle as the temperature decreases and, therefore, cannot flex back into place as the thrust from the rockets moves through the different components of the rockets. As a result, there was a real concern that the O-rings would fail for the *Challenger* launch because of the freezing temperature. However, there was immense pressure on NASA to launch because the launch had already been postponed, and Congress was threatening to reduce NASA's funding unless it started getting shuttles in the air. In addition, the day of the launch, President Ronald Reagan was going to read his State of the Union address on prime-time television and wanted to mention the success of the shuttle program. The first teacher in space, Christa McAuliffe, had scheduled to have a lesson in space, and without the launch, the schedule would not work for the lesson. There was also pressure from MTI officials to launch because it wanted to support NASA because NASA was a very important customer for MTI's financial stability. When the engineers from NASA and MTI met the evening before the launch to make the final decision, MTI engineers wanted to vote for a "no launch" because they had a difficult time quantifying the decision because no data had been collected from a launch at this low temperature. NASA engineers wanted to launch, but told MTI that NASA would not override MTI's decision for "no launch." MTI engineers believed this meant that NASA did want to launch. The MTI division head then told the MTI engineers to put on their "management hat" instead of their "engineering hat." This meant they needed to look at this decision not on safety issues but on how much revenue this would cost MTI if NASA no longer used them as a supplier. MTI and NASA finally agreed to the launch the following morning. Table 12.4 shows a portion of the American Society of Civil Engineers Code of Ethics (ASCE). The ASCE Code of Ethics was first adopted on September 2, 1914.[30]

TABLE 12.4 ● Portions of the ASCE's Code of Ethics

Fundamental Principles

Engineers uphold and advance the integrity, honor, and dignity of the engineering professions by:

1. Using their knowledge and skill for the enhancement of human welfare and the environment.

2. Being honest and impartial and serving with fidelity the public, their employees and clients.

Fundamental Canons

1. Engineers shall hold paramount the safety, health, and welfare of the public and shall strive to comply with the principles of sustainable development in the performance of their professional duties.

2. Engineers shall perform services only in areas of their competence.

3. Engineers shall issue public statements only in an objective and truthful manner.

Source: http://www.asce.org/uploadedFiles/Ethics_-_New/ethics_guidelines010308v2.pdf.

Questions for the Real-Life Ethical Dilemma Exercise

1. Which stakeholders' interests were included in the decision about whether to launch the *Challenger* or not? Which critical stakeholder's voice was missing from the discussion?

2. How could the engineers separate their decision from the very real possibility that the decision would kill seven people?

3. If you were at the meeting the night before the launch, what would you do? How would you try to convince others in the room to accept or agree with your decision?

Student Study Site

Visit the Student Study Site at **study.sagepub.com/stanwick3e** to access the following resources:

- Video Links
- SAGE Journal Articles
- Web Resources
- Web Quizzes

13

Evaluating Corporate Ethics

The man who goes up in a balloon
does not feel as if he were ascending;
he only sees the earth sinking
deeper below him.

—**Arthur Schopenhauer**

Chapter Objectives

After reading and studying Chapter 13, students should be able to

1. Describe the components of organizational fraud.
2. List some of the specific goals of ethics training programs.
3. Describe how firms can increase the ethical awareness of employees.
4. Explain the key elements in a global ethics training program.
5. Explain how companies can enforce their ethics policies.
6. Describe the concept of ethical auditing.
7. List items that whistle-blowers should consider.
8. Describe the steps for establishing an ethics hotline.

The Hillsborough Disaster: The Tragic Story of 96 Lost Lives

On April 15, 1989, a Football Association Challenge Cup (FA Cup) semi-final soccer game was held in Hillsborough Stadium in Sheffield, England. The match was between Liverpool and Nottingham Forest. The Liverpool and Nottingham Forest fans were allowed to enter the stadium at designated gates. The Liverpool fans entered at Leppings Lane, which had a small number of turnstiles. The match started at 3 p.m., but at noon the fans had already started to gather outside the stadium and the turnstiles were opened. By 2 p.m., the stadium started to fill up although there were more Nottingham Forest fans in the stadium than Liverpool fans. By 2:15 p.m., 12,000 fans had entered the Leppings Lane terrace and the central pens, pen 3 and pen 4, were filling up while the outside pens still had a lot of space for the fans. They were called pens because the fans stand there during the match and there are fences that stop fans from moving from one section to another. By 2:40 p.m., an estimated 5,000 fans were crowded around the Leppings Lane turnstiles. The enormous crowd made it impossible for all the fans to go through the turnstiles and get into the standing area by 3 p.m. At 2:47, the police superintendent in charge of the Leppings Lane entrance ordered the exit gates to be opened to relieve the pressure from the crowds. One of the exit gates was opened at 2:52, and an estimated 2,000 fans passed through the gate in 5 minutes. A majority of the fans coming through the exit gate headed to pens 3 and 4. The massive influx of fans created severe crushing in the pens. The central pens "safe" capacity was 1,600, but more than 3,000 fans moved into pens 3 and 4 before the match started at 3 p.m.

No one had instructed them to go to the side pens where there was still room to stand. At 2:54, the police ordered two other exit gates to be opened, increasing the flood of fans going toward the central pens. At 2:57, the first exit gate that was opened was closed and then was reopened 3 minutes later. At 3:05 and 30 seconds, the referee stopped the match as the policeman in charge of stadium ground control ran onto the field and asked for a stoppage in play after seeing the distress and panic in the stands, and the crush barrier in pen 3 collapsed, which resulted in fans falling on top of each other. The crush barrier is an additional fencing in the pens that separates the fans in rows within the pens. In addition, there were perimeter fences that separated the fans from the football pitch (field). The collapse of the crush barrier increased the panic and urgency to help the fans because they could be crushed to death. Some fans were able to climb the perimeter fences while other fans were able to get to safety by being pulled up by their arms to the second-tier level of the stadium. Because the police were unprepared for the disaster, fans started using the wooden advertising signs as makeshift stretchers to move out the injured fans. Firefighters who cut the fencing had difficulty getting to the pitch. In addition, dozens of ambulances were dispatched, but they could not get through the crowds to get onto the field until much later. The first ambulance did not reach the pitch until 3:13 p.m. Of the 96 fans who died in the disaster, only 14 were admitted to a hospital. The police superintendent in charge of the whole operation, Chief Superintendent David Dunckenfield, told Graham Kelly, the chief executive of the FA, that an exit gate had been forced open and the Liverpool fans had rushed in the open gate. At 4:10 p.m., the match was officially canceled.[1,2] A number of allegations were made against the Liverpool fans, including breaking the exit gate open, being intoxicated, arriving late to create a chaotic atmosphere, and stealing from those who were injured. These allegations were finally acknowledged as false when Prime Minister David Cameron apologized for how the Hillsborough disaster was handled. In September 2012, Prime Minister Cameron stated that "the Liverpool fans were not the cause of the disaster. The [investigative] panel has quite simply found no evidence in support of allegations of exceptional levels of drunkenness, ticketless-ness, or violence among Liverpool fans, no evidence that fans had conspired to arrive late at the stadium, and no evidence that they stole from the dead and dying."[3] Prime Minister Cameron was commenting on the investigative inquiry, which determined that many of the victims could have survived if they had received proper medical attention. Forty-one of the 96 victims could have lived if they had been transferred quickly to a hospital. In addition, the inquiry found that 115 witness reports submitted by the police had been altered to eliminate any unfavorable comments directed toward the police officers. The police also conducted computer checks and administered blood-alcohol level tests in order "to impugn the reputations of the deceased."[4]

Why Firms Need Ethics Training Programs

PricewaterhouseCoopers interviewed 3,877 senior executives from 78 countries to collect data for its 2011 Global Economic Crime Survey.[5] The results of the survey highlighted some staggering statistics: Thirty-four percent of the companies in the survey had been victims of economic crime in 2010. The results showed that almost 10% of the respondents had suffered losses of more than $5 million because of economic crime. Furthermore, 40% of the respondents feared that their reputations would be damaged because of cybercrime. Yet, 40% of the respondents didn't have the ability to detect or prevent cybercrime. A staggering 56% of the respondents reported that the most serious fraud committed was by the companies' own employees. Sixty percent of the respondents did not track their company on social network sites. In addition, the larger the company in the survey, the higher the probability that the company experienced at least one act of fraud.

The Size of the Firm

For firms with up to 200 employees, the percentage of firms that experienced fraud was 17%. For firms with 201 to 1,000 employees, the percentage rose to 29%. For firms that had more than 1,000 employees, the fraud percentage was 54%.[6]

PricewaterhouseCoopers provided a number of explanations why larger firms had higher incidences of fraud. One factor is that individuals have more opportunities to commit fraud in larger companies because of the level of complexity of the operations. In addition, there is greater ability to be anonymous within large firms. Employees may rationalize fraud as a victimless crime because they are only one individual in a giant corporation. Large firms often deal with a large number of complex transactions, which allow an individual to manipulate information without it being readily detected. To give credit to the firms, larger firms are more likely to have comprehensive fraud detection systems, which increases the probability of "catching" the fraud. As large firms expand internationally, the probability of fraud will increase as they expand into new markets.

Where in the World Does Fraud Occur?

Respondents in every region of the world reported cases of fraud. The range was from 21% of the respondents in the Middle East to 50% in Africa in 2014. Table 13.1 shows the summary of fraud by region in 2011 and 2014.

Every Industry Is Represented

Table 13.2 shows the percentage of fraud that was reported in various industries. The percentage ranges from 20% for professional services firms to 49% in financial services firms.

TABLE 13.1 ● Economic Crime By Region 2011 and 2014

Region	2011	2014	Difference
Africa	59%	50%	−9%
North America	42%	41%	−1%
Eastern Europe	30%	39%	9%
Latin America	37%	35%	−2%
Western Europe	30%	35%	5%
Asia Pacific	31%	32%	1%
Middle East	28%	21%	−7%
Emerging Eight: Brazil, China, India, Indonesia, Mexico, Russia, Turkey, South Africa	35%	40%	5%
Global	34%	37%	3%

Source: PricewaterhouseCoopers, "Global Economic Crime Survey 2014," p. 7, http://www.pwc.com/gx/en/economic-crime-survey/downloads.jhtml.

TABLE 13.2 ● Economic Crime by Industry Sector in 2011/2014

Industry Sector	Percentage of Fraud Reported 2011/2014	Industry Sector	Percentage of Fraud Reported 2011/2014
Communications	48%/48%	Engineering and Construction	31%/33%
Insurance	48%/35%	Energy, Utilities, and Mining	29%/31%
Gov't/State Owned	46%/41%	Aerospace and Defense	29%/28%

Industry Sector	Percentage of Fraud Reported 2011/2014	Industry Sector	Percentage of Fraud Reported 2011/2014
Hospitality and Leisure	45%/41%	Automotive	25%/28%
Financial Services	44%/49%	Manufacturing	23%/36%
Retail and Consumer	42%/49%	Pharmaceuticals and life sciences	23%/27%
Entertainment and Media	34%/31%	Chemicals	22%/27%
Transport and Logistics	32%/34%	Other Industries	23%/34%
Technology	N/A/27%	Professional Services	N/A/20%

Source: PricewaterhouseCoopers, "Global Economic Crime Survey 2011," p. 18, www.pwc.com/crimesurvey/; PricewaterhouseCoopers, "Global Economic Crime Survey 2014," p. 8, http://www.pwc.com/gx/en/economic -crime-survey/downloads.jhtml.

The Types of Fraud

PricewaterhouseCoopers identified 14 major categories of fraud. Table 13.3 shows the percentage of each kind of fraud for 2011 and 2014. As can be seen from Table 13.3, asset misappropriation had the highest percentage for both 2011 and 2014. Asset misappropriation is the misuse or stealing of the company's assets.

Who Commits the Fraud?

The common modus operandi of the typical fraud case was that a lack of adequate internal controls gave the individual the *opportunity* to commit the crime. The individual had a personal need to maintain a high standard of living, so there was an *incentive* to commit the crime. In many instances, the individual was not aware that his or her actions were wrong, which allowed for *rationalization.*

In 2014, when the fraud was committed by someone external to the company, 32% were customers, 18% were agents or intermediaries, 10% were vendors, 24% were other third parties, and 15% were not identified. Most of the individuals who committed the fraud were dismissed by their companies: 79% of the respondents dismissed the employee. In 49% of the cases, law enforcement was informed of the fraud, 44% of the respondents sought civil action, 23% notified relevant regulatory authorities, 17% gave a warning and/or reprimand, 5% did nothing, 3% transferred the employee, and 6% did other actions or didn't know the final action taken by the firm.[7]

How Are They Caught?

Three categories determine how the fraud was detected: corporate control, corporate culture, and beyond the influence of management.

TABLE 13.3 ● Types of Fraud Identified by the Respondents

Type of Fraud	2011	2014	Difference
Asset Misappropriation	72%	69%	−3%
Accounting Fraud	24%	22%	−2%
Bribery and Corruption	24%	27%	3%
Cybercrime	23%	24%	1%
IP Infringement	7%	8%	1%
Money Laundering	9%	11%	2%
Tax Fraud	4%	6%	2%
Illegal Insider Trading	6%	4%	−2%
Competition law/antitrust law	7%	5%	−2%
Espionage	2%	3%	1%
Other	4%	14%	10%
Mortgage Fraud	N/A	7%	N/A
Human Resources	N/A	15%	N/A
Procurement Fraud	N/A	29%	N/A

Source: PricewaterhouseCoopers, "Global Economic Crime Survey 2014," p. 6, www.pwc.com/crimesurvey; http://www.pwc.com/gx/en/economic-crime-survey/downloads.jhtml.

Corporate Control Fourteen percent of the respondents stated that the fraud was caught through internal audits, and 10% stated fraud risk managers caught the fraud. Other components were suspicious transaction monitoring, 18%; corporate security, 6%; and rotation of personnel, 2%.[8]

Corporate Culture The use of other employees and stakeholders is a valuable resource in detecting fraud. The survey showed that 11% of the respondents received internal tips about fraud, and 7% received external tips. The whistle-blowing system was used by 5% of the respondents.[9]

Beyond the Influence of Management Eight percent of the respondents found fraud by accident, and 4% used law enforcement or investigative media to find the fraud. Five percent of the respondents used other type of detection methods.[10]

Establishing an Ethics Training Program

Gary Weaver, Linda Trevino, and Philip Cochran argue that ethics training programs vary from firm to firm partly because of the differences in external pressures and the vision of the top managers within the firm.[11] They continue by stating the ethics programs, including the training programs developed by the firm, allow the firm to establish a control system. Through the training programs, firms are partly able to standardize the behavior of their employees. Compliance-oriented training programs should focus on ensuring that the employees follow the rules and explain what type of punishment will be implemented if there is employee misconduct. Alternatively, values-oriented training programs focus on the ethical aspirations of the employees as well as foster a forum to develop shared ethical values. Weaver et al. continue by stating that the training programs are influenced partly by external stakeholders such as government regulations, the pressure from the media, and business standard setters.

Debbie LeClair and Linda Ferrell argue that the culture of the firm can be influenced through the firm's ethics training programs.[12] Furthermore, an effective training program allows the firm to take advantage of any self-regulatory incentives by establishing and communicating the firm's ethical values. The goals of ethics training programs are to enhance the employees' knowledge of ethical issues, develop skills to support a strong ethical climate, and ensure proper ethical decision making by the employees. Some specific goals recommended by LeClair and Ferrell include the following:

- Provide the necessary tools needed by the employees to understand the ethical decision-making process. This could include an explanation of specific terms and the rationale behind the ethical focus.
- Give the employees an opportunity to assess ethical priorities.
- Explain the procedure used when employees violate the ethical standards established by the firm.
- Give the opportunity for employees to be able to identify ethical programs based on the firm's ethical standards.
- Increase the level of sensitivity of the employees' view pertaining to specific ethical issues.
- Enhance the ability of the employees to increase their level of individual reflection as it relates to ethical issues.
- Create a strong, positive ethical work climate in which ethical support systems and codes are in place within the firm.[13]

Corporations have found that it looks very good to stakeholders if they provide an ethics policy. However, it looks great if they actually follow the policy and enforce it. Enforcing the ethics policy is probably one of the greatest challenges in the ethics arena. A recent study conducted by the International Association of Business Communicators suggests that formal training programs for ethics are missing in most companies. Of the 1,800 respondents, 65% indicated that they had not received any formal ethics training. Respondents indicated that, at most, ethics was usually mentioned on their first day then largely ignored from then on within the organization.[14]

When setting up training programs, managers must first conduct an "inventory" of ethical feelings. Firms must ask employees where they stand on ethical issues. Managers must then ask employees to evaluate ethical issues. This will give managers a foundation from which to operate. Managers will be able to see the ethical tone of the employees, and the manager can move from that point into the training programs. It may also be informative to ask what ethical dilemmas employees are concerned about. This will provide information about what to cover in the training program, as well as provide feedback about topics covered in the code of ethics. Employees must know firsthand from management what the ethical expectations are for working at the company. This is something that must be communicated clearly to employees. Pat Croce offers advice for admitting mistakes. We all make mistakes, but his advice is to follow the Three Rs: assume responsibility, demonstrate regret, and offer a remedy to fix the problem.[15]

Some companies include a discussion of the code in the new employee orientation sessions. One of the goals of an effective ethics program in companies is to increase the ethical awareness of employees at all levels. This can be accomplished in many ways, including the following:

- Encourage a commitment by senior managers, and particularly the CEO, that an ethical organization is an essential part of the organizational vision.
- Write codes of conduct in simple terms.
- Ensure ethical policies are not one sided.
- Clarify what the ethics training program objectives are.
- In large organizations, use direct-line employees rather than staff personnel or outside consultants.
- Avoid having the senior management briefing sessions, the "train the trainer" workshops, or the actual training sessions turn into general organizational gripe sessions.
- In the ethics training sessions, define what *ethics* is.
- Ensure relevancy, genuineness, and reality.
- Ethical violations of subordinates should be recognized and consequences established.
- Ethical dimensions should be incorporated in new employee orientation programs.
- Be willing to identify and discipline employees guilty of ethical violations, as well as rewarding ethical employees.
- All employees should be cognizant of their roles in developing an ethical climate.[16]

Establishing a Global Ethics Training Program

As multinational corporations approach the issue of ethics training programs, the level of complexity increases greatly because of the intricacies of doing business in a global environment. The more countries in which a firm does business, the more potentially different cultural beliefs need to be addressed in the firm's global ethics training programs. The increased level of business complexity is based on the variation of ethical, cultural, and legal diversity the firm must address in its ethical vision. This can be especially challenging when there are different interpretations of how "doing the right thing" is related to ethical behavior.[17] Kevin Jackson recommends a number of key elements in any global ethics training program.

Ensure Morally Sensitive Cultural Education

The firm must understand that employees in other parts of the world will interpret ethical information through their own cultural lenses. As a result, firms must be aware of the cultural differences in the countries in which they do business. Furthermore, the firms must ensure that the information presented to their employees in different countries will not be misinterpreted based on the cultural grounding of the employees.

Provide Education on International Human Rights, Not Only on Foreign Law Compliance

As a global-focused firm, the responsibility of the firm is to embrace global ethical issues to guarantee that the ethical vision is consistent around the world. By adopting a blanket stance on international human rights, which is relayed in the ethics training program, the firm ensures employees will not have to address any ambiguity in the firm's message.

Try to Get Beyond "Rule Formalism"

Firms need to focus on presenting strong, rational, principled judgments in their ethics training programs instead of a checklist-based compliance focus. By fixating on rules, firms give up the opportunity of presenting the global ethical picture to all their employees. In addition, rules-based approaches work only when the rules are still valid. The firm does not want to depend on rule makers to dictate the ethical vision of the company.

Present a Rational Dialogue for Important International Issues When There Is Dissent

Firms must present a rational, moral dialogue to impart their viewpoints pertaining to global ethical issues in their global training program. If the firm cannot justify its position, it may be time to revisit that position. Furthermore, firms must tolerate, and even encourage, debate within the training program on important global ethical issues. As a learning organization, global firms must learn to adapt to changing global viewpoints.[18]

Consider Global Cultural Dimensions and Ethics Training Programs

Before a firm can implement an effective global ethics training program, it needs to understand how different cultural dimensions can affect both the message of the programs and how the message is presented to its employees around the world. Extending the work of Geert Hofstede, Weaver recommends that ethics training programs should be adjusted to consider these culture differences.[19] Table 13.4 shows the dichotomies related to global cultural dimensions.

TABLE 13.4 ● Global Cultural Dimensions
Individualism vs. Collectivism
High-Context Communication vs. Low-Context Communication
High Uncertainty Avoidance vs. Low Uncertainty Avoidance
Masculinity vs. Femininity
High Power Distance vs. Low Power Distance

Source: Gary Weaver, "Ethics Programs in Global Businesses: Culture's Role in Managing Ethics," *Journal of Business Ethics* 30 (2001): 6–9.

Individualism Versus Collectivism *Individualism* focuses on achieving individual goals, whereas *collectivism* focuses on attaining group-based goals. Individualists will abide by ethical standards to satisfy or protect their self-interests. Collectivists would comply with ethical standards if they are based on the ethical norms of the group. As a result, individual-based rewards and punishments for ethical behavior would have a minimal impact in a country with a collectivism-based culture. In addition, adversarial and legalistic ethical tools such as grievance committees, investigations officers, and external ethics auditors would conflict with the desire for collectivism-based cultures to maintain group harmony because these tools would identify single individuals to blame for the unethical behavior. In addition, internal communication ethical tools such as an ethics hotline would be considered too impersonal and not appropriate for a collectivism-based culture.

High-Context Versus Low-Context Communication *Low-context communication* culture focuses primarily on the actual words spoken or written to interpret the meaning the other person is trying to communicate. A *high-context communication* culture interprets the words that have been spoken or written and uses nonverbal cues such as body language and tone of voice to aid in the interpretation of the meaning of the words.

    As a result, an ethics training program that just focuses on the language and written documents to relay its ethical vision will be effective in a low-context culture but will be ineffective in a high-context culture. In a high-context culture, the presentation of ethics codes and formal procedures will be perceived as irrelevant and, therefore, most likely ignored by the audience. As a result, the ethics training program must use nonverbal cues to help a high-context culture audience interpret what the true ethical vision of the firm is.

High Uncertainty Versus Low Uncertainty Avoidance *High uncertainty avoidance* culture is based on the view that the individuals do not want any ambiguity in their jobs. By embracing the status quo, high uncertainty avoidance cultures will not accept any part of an ethics training program in which there is potential unpredictability in their actions because they will not accept that level of uncertainty. A *low uncertainty avoidance* culture accepts risk and ambiguity and even embraces them. High uncertainty avoidance individuals prefer specific rules and guidelines to help them understand what is considered acceptable ethical behavior, and high uncertainty avoidance cultures would refuse to embrace any tools that would result in anonymous reporting, such as an ethics hotline.

Masculinity Versus Femininity *Masculine* cultures focus on material goods, status, accomplishment, and reward for ambition. *Feminine* cultures focus on caring for human needs and supporting others within the group. As a result, high-masculine cultures require more comprehensive ethics training and more ethics monitoring and control mechanisms for the employees. In addition, individual punishment is needed to identify to others the individual consequences of unethical behavior. For feminine cultures, nonpunitive ethics programs would be more effective.

High Versus Low Power Distance *High power distance* cultures embrace the hierarchical relationship that occurs between the manager and the subordinate. High power distance culture individuals are less likely to change or provide input to their supervisors. Employees in a low power distance culture would not be too shy to speak their minds to their supervisors and present new ideas. In high power distance cultures, firms need to focus on accountability and blame for the upper levels of management because this is "where the ideas come from." For low power distance cultures, the accountability and blame should be distributed based on the actual job responsibilities of the employees.[20]

Benefits of an Ethics Training Program

Effective ethics training can yield a number of critical benefits for a firm. The first benefit is that it ensures that the employees are aware of the ethical standards of the firm. In addition, the employees are given guidance regarding the procedure set up within the company to report unethical behavior. Furthermore, effective ethics training aids in integrating the value systems of the top managers with the other employees within the firm. A detailed list of benefits is shown in Table 13.5.

Enforcement and the Ethics Training Program

It may be that some employees are taking the ethical internal control process too personally and reporting every action seen as a violation of the code of ethics. How should an employer deal with this? First, it may be necessary to ask if the employee is reacting in a retaliating way. Maybe the employee is mad at management for a certain decision that was made, maybe the employee is mad at other employees, or maybe the employee feels that he or she has been given an unfair share of the workload. If the answer to any of these questions is yes, then it will be necessary to deal with the employee through human resources, rather than through the ethics department. However, if an employer finds that the complaints are valid and are actual violations of the ethical code, then the employer will have to take steps to enforce the code. Otherwise, employees will begin to ignore the code of ethics. Although a certain amount of resources are

TABLE 13.5 ● Benefits of Managing Ethics in the Workplace
Company focus on business ethics has improved society.
Ethics programs allow companies to maintain a moral course regardless of the economic conditions.
Ethics programs develop strong employee teamwork and productivity.
Ethics programs develop strong employee growth and vision.
Ethics programs help ensure that the company is doing legal activities.
Ethics programs help integrate ethical values in the day-to-day decisions of management.
Ethics programs establish a positive public image.
Having a formal ethical commitment is the right thing to do.

Source: Adapted from http://mapnp.nonprofitoffice.com.

expended with each investigation of the complaints, it could be necessary to investigate all of the valid complaints because of the effort expended when establishing the code of ethics. It may mean that a code change is necessary because the code might not have been written to cover day-to-day occurrences.

For a compliance program to work effectively, the code of ethics must be enforced properly. Employees may begin to ignore the code if they realize that the code will be enforced only sporadically, not at all, or just for certain people. And the policy must be enforced at all levels in the organization. The "tone from the top" is important when enforcing the code of ethics in an organization. Part of the compliance aspect is to provide training programs for employees to know what is expected of them and how the code of ethics will be enforced. Companies such as Lockheed Martin have developed programs that help train individuals on gray areas that they may face in their jobs. These training programs must be given to all levels on the employment ladder. Employees need to see top management and their supervisors participating in the same programs they do to learn about ethics programs. In determining whether ethics training programs will be successful, two measures can be viewed: the level of support from the participant's direct supervisor and the support of peers in accepting the new behaviors covered in the training programs.[21] To enforce a code of ethics within an organization, corporate leaders must say that the code of ethics is a living document, not just something that is shared with employees then forgotten.

Sending the Right Message to the Employees

It is critical that management does not just pay lip service to ethics training programs. The purpose of the program is not a public relations tool to be used to promote the image of the firm. The true purpose of the training program is to be able to give the firm's employees a viable outlet in which ethical behavior can be maintained. As a result, the employees must view their disclosures of information as being taken seriously.

Corporate Ethics Officers

In the United States, the role of corporate ethics officer moved to the forefront in the decision-making process of firms when the Federal Sentencing Guidelines for Organizations Act was passed in 1991. A component of the act was the government's encouraging firms to implement internal controls to help prevent, detect, and report criminal activities. In addition, the government gave firms incentives to hire corporate ethics officers. Muel Kaptein proposes that the role of the ethics officer or ethics coordinator is to be the liaison between the employees and the firm in matters of company security, be an ethics counselor for the employees, and be responsible for ethics compliance.[22] The relationships presented by Kaptein are shown in Figure 13.1. As Kaptein demonstrated in his research, a corporate ethics officer has to wear many hats. Similar to playing the roles of both "good cop" and "bad cop," an ethics officer is the first line of defense for the firm as it relates to company security. The ethics officer is responsible for making sure that appropriate actions are taken if unethical activity leads to a breach of company security. In addition, the corporate ethics officer is responsible for all ethical compliance issues. This would entail attention at both the individual and at

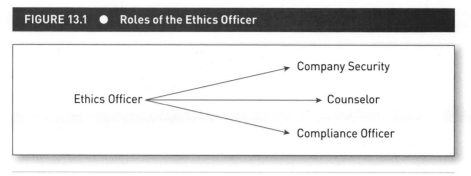

FIGURE 13.1 ● Roles of the Ethics Officer

- Company Security
- Ethics Officer
- Counselor
- Compliance Officer

Source: Muel Kaptein, "Guidelines for the Development of an Ethics Safety Net," *Journal of Business Ethics* 41 (2002): 227.

the corporate level. Finally, the corporate ethics officer is also an ethical ombudsman in helping employees with any ethical issues that must be addressed. In the role of counselor, the corporate ethics officer can be the emotional link between the ethical vision of the firm and the individual ethical dilemmas of the employees.

Henry Adobor takes Kaptein's model one step further by identifying what critical factors affect the level of effectiveness of the corporate ethics officer.[23] Figure 13.2 shows Adobor's framework for understanding the ethics officer's performance. Adobor's model highlights the complex relationships that affect the overall effectiveness of the ethics officer. The officer must have the skills and competencies in both technical and business issues to make informed, effective decisions. In addition, the ethics officer must be able to tolerate ambiguity, believe that he or she has control over ensuring that ethical behavior takes place within the firm, be of good moral character, and have strong leadership skills. The challenges for the ethics officer include having many roles, or hats, that he or she is responsible for, as was shown in the Kaptein model. The many roles can potentially lead to role conflict and ambiguity. In addition, a number of the technical functions of the corporate ethics officer can be highly complex, yet other members in the firm may not realize the level of complexity. Furthermore, organizational factors such as the ethical culture, the reporting structure within the firm, the level of authority to make decisions, and the recruitment of the employees also can affect the ethics officer's overall level of performance.

When developing ethics programs, managers must evaluate the program by considering different parts of the organization and the people involved with the program. Table 13.6 provides eight tests that can be used to evaluate ethics programs and describes each.

Many corporations are finding themselves appointing ethics officers. These new corporate officials help in many ways. This officer will help with the evaluation of the ethical decision-making process that may be already established in the company. Or the ethics officer may be charged with creating an ethics program for the company. Large or small, public or private, all corporations need to consider ethics in their day-to-day operations. These officers may be charged with communicating the ethics programs to employees, setting up effective reporting mechanisms, and maintaining oversight of the program established. Most important, the ethics officer will

FIGURE 13.2 ● A Framework for Understanding the Ethics Officer's Performance

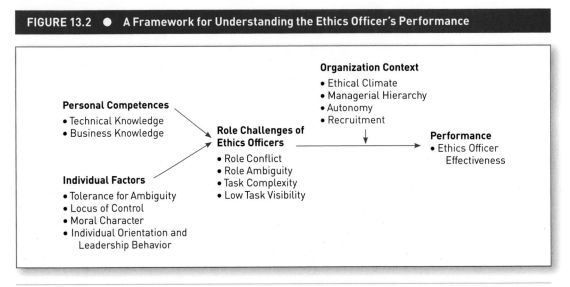

Source: Henry Adobor, "Exploring the Role Performance of Corporate Ethics Officers," *Journal of Business Ethics* 69 (2006): 58.

be charged with evaluating and investigating ethical charges. It is most important to establish the reporting scheme for these officers. This reporting may be done to an ethics committee that has final say in all ethics matters in the organization.

TABLE 13.6 ● Ethics Programs Decision-Making Tests

Name of Decision-Making Test	Description/Question to Ask
Relevant Information	How much information is needed to make an informed decision?
Involvement	How many people are involved, and are the correct people involved in the decision-making process?
Consequentialist	Who will be significantly affected by this decision?
Ethical Principles	Does this decision coincide with the company's ethical principles?
Fairness	Are all the stakeholders treated fairly with this decision?
Universality	Would this decision be acceptable as a "universal law" that applies to all?
Preventative	Does this decision prevent or limit the possibility of this issue arising again?
Light of Day	Could we defend this decision if our actions became public knowledge?

Source: Adapted from http://www.managementhelp.org/ethics/long.htm.

Ethical Auditing

Ethical auditing can be defined as the regular comprehensive evaluation of the compliance with the firm's ethical policies and procedures. Ethical auditing attempts to look at an organization's faithfulness to its ethics program. This includes examining the mission in conjunction with the ethics code. Most important, an ethics audit will help an organization recognize risks related to questionable practices in the organization.

The ethical auditing process is an evaluation tool used by management to ensure that the ethical conduct described in the code of ethics is enforced throughout the organization. The auditing process involves asking employees if they have seen or have any information pertaining to unethical activities within the company. This information is collected through questionnaires and interviews. In addition, internal "ethical" auditors make visual inspections of the different operations of the firm to ensure that each unit is complying with the ethical standards established by the firm. A summary of the information collected by the employer and the audit team are brought together into a final report. The report should be distributed throughout the organization. Based on the results of the report, adjustments are made to specific procedures with the firm's ethics training program. The five-part auditing process is shown in Table 13.7.[24]

Components of the Ethical Audit

John Rosthorn identifies 12 areas for which investors want information pertaining to the firm's ethical vision: (1) environmental record, (2) human rights, (3) operations in countries with oppressive political regimes, (4) business transactions dealing with military contracts, (5) stance on nuclear power, (6) production of tobacco and habit-forming drugs, (7) production of alcoholic beverages, (8) gambling, (9) pornography and prostitution, (10) animal rights and animal testing, (11) marketing codes, and (12) holders of developing countries' debt.[25]

Whistle-Blowing

Whistle-blowing is the process by which an employee informs another responsible party in the company about potentially unethical behavior. Janet Near and Marcia Miceli present a four-step process to address potentially unethical behavior.[26] The first

---

TABLE 13.7 ● Five Parts of an Ethics Audit

1. Questionnaires are filled out by the employees.
2. Employee interviews are conducted.
3. Ethics auditors make a firsthand inspection.
4. Ethics auditors develop a final report.
5. Ethics auditors follow up on the recommendations in the final report.

Source: Adapted from Michael Allen, "The Ethics Audit: A Tool Whose Time Has Come," *Nonprofit World* (November/December 1995): 51–55.

two steps are decisions made by the potential whistle-blower, and Questions 3 and 4 relate to decisions that would be made by the firm.

Question 1: Did the individual observe behavior that was illegal, immoral, or illegitimate? If yes, move to Question 2.

Question 2: Should the activity be reported? If yes, move to Question 3.

Question 3: Should the questioned activity be halted by the firm? If yes, move to Question 4.

Question 4: What should be done concerning the whistle-blower?

There is a high risk involved in becoming a whistle-blower. It takes courage to risk an unjust punishment to report the unethical actions of others within the firm.

The Government Accountability Project has existed for more than 25 years with a goal of offering support to whistle-blowers. Recognizing that the Sarbanes-Oxley Act was a breakthrough legislative attempt to offer protection to corporate whistle-blowers, the Government Accountability Project offers the following elements to consider when advising people about whether to pursue internal or external disclosure of wrongful acts in an organization. Whistle-blowers and those advising them should consider the following:

- Establish credibility.
- Provide visible personal leadership.
- Put in place a broad prohibition against retaliation.
- Identify problems early.
- Protect confidentiality.
- Extend broad coverage.
- Create an independent, neutral forum.
- Train managers and employees.
- Provide comprehensive relief.
- Hold wrongdoers accountable.[27]

Hotlines

Human nature suggests that not everyone is comfortable with reporting misconduct through channels suggested in the code of ethics. Many people would rather remain anonymous when reporting misconduct, often out of fear of retaliation, either through job loss or discrimination. The Sarbanes-Oxley Act offers protection to whistle-blowers. One way of allowing people to remain anonymous while still reporting ethical violations is through a confidential hotline. These ethics hotlines provide assurance to the person reporting the incident, but they also allow the company to become aware of internal and external problems that may need to be investigated. There are several steps in establishing an ethics hotline.

How to Set Up the Hotline

To set up an effective hotline, the firm must be willing to operate and staff the hotline for 24 hours per day. Some employees might not be comfortable reporting the suspect activities during the workday. By offering the service around the clock, the firm is effectively cutting across any geographical borders that may exist for the company, especially those operating in a global context. Employees must be assured that their confidentiality is protected if the hotline is to be successful. In addition, you should ensure that the call is toll free. This may mean setting up several different hotline numbers so employees in different countries can call to report incidents. Success may also mean that the hotline is operated by a reliable third party. One such service is offered by the Association of Certified Fraud Examiners, EthicsLine. This service offers a 24-hour, toll-free service that is provided in 150 languages. Callers to this service talk with a trained specialist. The hotlines can help uncover activities such as violations of governmental regulations, fraud, falsification or destruction of company records, workplace violence, substance abuse, discrimination, sexual harassment, conflicts of interest, and release of proprietary information.[28] Most important, the company must provide a feeling of trust through the hotline. Table 13.8 provides information about three models of hotlines available.

How to Get the Word Out to Employees About the Hotline

The success of the hotline will depend on management's commitment to the program. Management should make the program known to employees to help express support for the program. If top management does not truly support the hotline, the success of the program and the related benefits will not be realized. It is impossible to assure employees and other stakeholders that their comments will remain anonymous. But communication of the manner in which the hotline is handled will help alleviate some of the fears. For example, many state agencies and companies print the hotline number on payroll checks or on invoices. Some companies, such as Texas

TABLE 13.8 ● Types of Ethics Hotlines

Type of Hotline	Who Receives the Information	Benefits of This Type of Hotline
In-house	Staffed internally by employees of the company	*Quicker response time to resolve ethical issues *Maximum level of control over system operation by the company *Helps guarantee confidentiality of the reporter because no third parties are involved in the process
Outsourced	Expert, independent third party represents the company by receiving the information	*Employees may perceive that they may have a high level of anonymity *Could be cheaper than having an internal company hotline
Hybrid	A combination of both internal and external parties	*Allows flexibility for the company if it desires a 24/7 operation Allows for the outsourcing of foreign calls if company staff can handle domestic calls

Source: Adapted from "Installing an Effective Hotline," *International Business Ethics Review* (Fall 2004): 10.

Instruments, even provide wallet-sized copies of their codes of ethics with the hotline number printed on them for all employees. The hotline information should also be discussed at all ethics training programs. In these ethics training programs, management should stress that unethical conduct is not acceptable. The hotline may also provide answers about the company's code of ethics.

How to Handle Tips Resulting From the Hotline

In handling tips from the hotline, the company must establish designated company representatives who will be responsible for receiving the tips. More than one person should receive the tips. In the case of items that need immediate attention, company representatives' contact information should always be available. In many instances, it takes a lot of courage for an employee to report an incident. A certain amount of trust must be established between the employees and the company before employees will use the hotline. Therefore, the company must take seriously all of the tips received and properly investigate each one. If handled improperly, the company may be forgoing important future information about abuses and wrongdoings within the corporation. By using a third party to receive tips, such as EthicsLine described earlier, companies are relying on trained professionals to ask the right questions about the tips they are hearing, and they are trained to record the information in a usable manner. If the caller asks for a follow-up, it may be that the caller can be given an identifiable code to find out how the problem is being addressed. Many people do not want to just report an incident; they want to be privy to the actions and the consequences that the firm has levied against the party who committed the inappropriate activity.

Another example of a hotline is the Integrity Helpline offered by Deloitte LLP. The hotline is administered by a third party 24 hours a day, 365 days a year. The company offers two options for contacting the hotline: web access or telephone access. In addition, the company offers toll-free numbers for callers outside the United States. Most important, Deloitte specifies circumstances under which the hotline should be contacted:

- If you believe that ethics and compliance issues are not being resolved
- If you don't feel comfortable reporting through normal channels
- If you'd like confidential assistance on ethics and compliance issues
- If you wish to remain anonymous when filing a report[29]

Government Regulations and Whistle-Blowing

One of the provisions of the 2002 Sarbanes-Oxley Act protects whistle-blowers. According to the act, employees may not be discharged, demoted, suspended, threatened, harassed, or discriminated against because the employee provided information showing evidence of fraudulent activities in an organization. Without this protection, many people may feel that reporting the problem is just not worth the risk of potentially losing their jobs or being treated unfairly on the job.

As the first whistle-blower to receive his former job back under the Sarbanes-Oxley Act, David Windhauser, a former controller for Trane, has said that the financial and emotional tolls of the act of whistle-blowing are extremely high. Windhauser complained that many managers were recording fraudulent expenses on financial statements at Trane and was then fired.[30] One of the key provisions of the Sarbanes-Oxley Act is that whistle-blowers can be reinstated in their old jobs. However, many whistle-blowers do not file under the Sarbanes-Oxley Act because they really don't want to go back to their old jobs with the new title of "whistle-blower" attached to them. They may feel that animosity against them may make it impossible to perform satisfactorily in their old jobs.

It may be difficult to get employees outside the United States to report ethical violations because of cultural differences. A number of reasons may discourage reporting to the organization, including the following:[31]

- Divided loyalties can arise because in many countries many members of the same family work at or own the company. In many foreign countries, employees are discouraged from questioning any policies or decisions.
- The historical context of the country may preclude whistle-blowing. In some countries, such as China, Germany, and South Africa, creating approaches to secretly report corporate misdoings may remind people of the historical happenings that caused people to mistrust government and others who want secret disclosures of wrongdoing.
- Geographical logistics may prevent whistle-blowing unless the company creates phone lines and ethics offices in the countries of operations.
- Most important, the fear of retaliation by their colleagues may override any employees' thoughts of reporting misdoings.

Several strategies may help overcome the cultural differences associated with whistle-blowing. Table 13.9 provides a list of several strategies that companies can adopt that will encourage ethical behavior in companies and that will help encourage employees across the globe to report fraudulent activities.

Although many businesses are approaching their daily operations in a global context, they may approach the new boundaries without considering the cultural boundaries that exist. Managers must actively consider these cultural boundaries to establish a comprehensive ethical program for the company.

TABLE 13.9 ● Strategies for Encouraging Whistle-Blowing Across the Globe

1. Make sure that international managers are involved in the process.
2. Have clear definitions and guidelines pertaining to acceptable and unacceptable behavior by the employees.
3. Ensure that employees have the opportunity to blow the whistle on unethical activities via company policies and procedures.
4. Make sure the message given to the employees is tailored to the culture of the country.
5. Encourage the use of the reporting process.
6. Have financial commitments for ethics for both local and regional issues.
7. Review and revise when necessary the ethical policies and establish performance measures.

Source: Adapted from http://www.business-ethics.org.

TABLE 13.10 ● Notable Whistle-Blowers		
Name	**Organization**	**Description of Act**
Ed Bricker	Hanford Nuclear Reservation (taken over by Westinghouse Electric Corporation)	Bricker disclosed the safety deficiencies at the facility.
Cynthia Cooper	WorldCom	Cooper told WorldCom's auditing committee that the company had been using suspect accounting practices to inflate its financial results.
Coleen Rowley	Federal Bureau of Investigation	Rowley informed FBI director Robert Mueller about the bureau's failure to investigate intelligence reports about possible terrorist attacks on the United States before the attacks took place on September 11, 2001.
Sherron Watkins	Enron	Watkins notified CEO Ken Lay through an anonymous letter that she had many concerns about the off–balance sheet transactions that were taking place at Enron. She later revealed that she was the author of the letter and met with Lay to talk about her concerns.
Jeffrey Wigand	Brown and Williamson Tobacco Corporation	Working for Brown and Williamson, Wigand discovered that tobacco companies had misled consumers about the addictive nature of nicotine.

Source: Adapted from http://www.corporatenarc.com.

Interestingly, the Occupational Safety and Health Administration (OSHA) has authority to enforce the whistle-blower section of the Sarbanes-Oxley Act. Corporate fraud is not something that most people associate with OSHA because the Occupational Safety and Health Act provides protection for workers involved in health and safety matters. The act was established in 1970, and its whistle-blower protection authority is covered in a variety of federal regulations. Most of the investigators at OSHA agree that there is a learning curve associated with the Sarbanes-Oxley Act, which involves developing a general knowledge of the new industries OSHA may be investigating and the technology that may be used in those industries.[32] In addition, investigators must be intimately familiar with securities laws. Notable whistle-blowers are presented in Table 13.10.

A similar piece of whistle-blower legislation, the False Claims Act, originally enacted during the Civil War, was amended in 1986. This statute allows persons with knowledge of or who discover fraudulent actions against the federal government to file a lawsuit against the party committing the fraud, on behalf of the government. These whistle-blowers are considered *qui tam* (which means to sue on behalf of oneself as well as for the state) plaintiffs who will be entitled to a portion of the proceeds if the lawsuit is successful, which is usually between 15% and 25% of the amount recovered if the government intervenes in the lawsuit. The following states have even enacted their own false acts legislation, which means that plaintiffs in state and local lawsuits can share in the proceeds: Arkansas, California, Delaware, the District of Columbia, Florida, Hawaii, Illinois, Louisiana, Massachusetts, Nevada, Tennessee, Texas, Utah, and Virginia.

Evaluation of Ethics and Stakeholders

The evaluation of the ethical commitment of a firm addresses both the teleological and deontological philosophies as they pertain to stakeholders. By ensuring that the employees are properly trained and that an ethical safety net is in place to support and protect them, the individual ethical egoism needs of the employees are served. In addition, by incorporating global issues such as human rights, environment sustainability, and economic development, ethics training programs serve the utilitarian need of doing the greatest good for the greatest number. Of course, included in the greatest number are the needs of various stakeholders including suppliers, customers, government, local communities, and society as a whole.

Furthermore, ethics training programs and other evaluation tools also serve the deontological philosophies of the stakeholders. By realizing their duty to perform in an ethical manner to all stakeholders, firms use the ethical audit to validate their commitment and duty. This duty to the stakeholder is the starting point for the model that links the relationships discussed in this chapter. The framework that relates stakeholders to the other components in this chapter is shown in Figure 13.3.

As can be seen in Figure 13.3, the needs and goals of the stakeholders drive the evaluation process. Recognizing the stakeholders' demands allows the firms to craft their codes of ethics and other formalized documents that present their ethical vision during the strategic ethical formulation process. Once these standards have been agreed on, the firm must implement its strategic ethical vision in the implementation stage. During this stage, the internal stakeholders, the employees, are the focus of the firm because they are actively involved in the implementation stage of the ethical vision of the firm. After the implementation stage takes place, the ethical monitoring mechanisms are used to ensure that the ethical formulation and implementation has resulted in an effective transfer of the ethical vision from the

FIGURE 13.3 ● Framework of the Evaluation of Corporate Ethics and Stakeholders

Stakeholders → Strategic Ethical Formulation → Strategic Ethical Implementation → Ethical Monitoring Mechanisms → Ethical Performance

- customers
- suppliers
- NGOs
- community
- government
- society

- code of ethics
- formal policies and procedures

- ethics training programs

- ethics officers
- ethical audit
- whistle-blowing

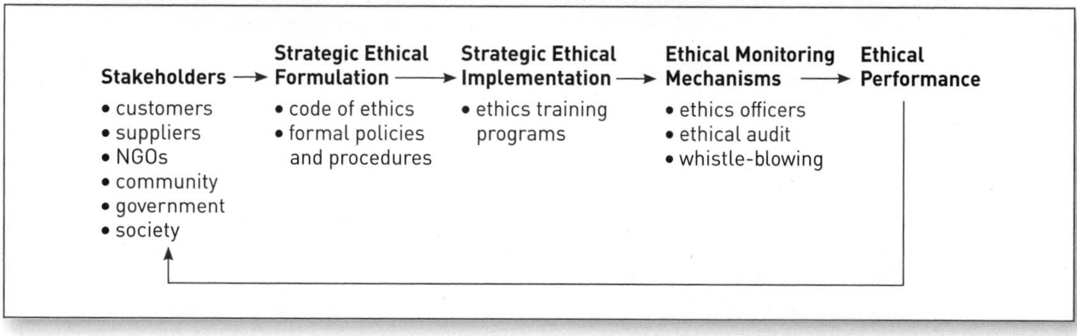

firm to each employee within the firm. During this stage, ethical officers, ethical audits, and whistle-blowing can be used to notify the firm if there are any actual or potential issues with the ethical vision as it is being interpreted by the employees. The final step in the process is an evaluation of how well the firm has performed from an ethical vision perspective. During this stage, the firm's ethical goals and objectives will be compared with the actual ethical performance of the firm and its employees. The information on the ethical performance is then relayed back to the stakeholders for their review. At this point, the process starts again and creates a perpetual circle of ethical evaluation.

Questions for Thought

1. Why do you think that many firms establish ethics policies but do not enforce them?

2. Can a company be ethical without having a formal ethics policy? Explain.

3. Do you believe that CPAs would be the best group to perform ethics audits? Why or why not?

4. Do you think hotlines for reporting ethical violations work? Explain your answer.

Real-Life Ethical Dilemma Exercise

How About Some Free Popcorn?

Released on December 3, 2010, the movie *Black Swan,* about a ballerina slowly becoming mentally unstable, received great reviews. The star, Natalie Portman, received an Academy Award for Best Actress and was paid $2 million to perform in the movie. Including her fee, the production cost of the movie was $13 million. A year and a half after the opening, *Black Swan* has grossed more than $100 million in the United Sates and more than $222 million outside the United States to make its worldwide gross revenues almost $330 million. However, behind the scenes when the movie was made, there were scores of unpaid interns who were promised the chance to get their foot in the door of the entertainment business in exchange for their labor. In September 2011, two of those unpaid interns sued Fox Searchlight, the production company that made *Black Swan.* Their lawsuit states that "Fox Searchlight's unpaid interns are a crucial labor force on its productions, functioning as production assistants and bookkeepers and performing secretarial and janitorial work . . . In misclassifying many of its workers as unpaid interns, Fox Searchlight has denied them the benefits that the law affords to employees." More than 100 unpaid interns had worked on various projects for Fox Searchlight. The movie industry defended the use of unpaid interns by stating that the internships are educational, valuable, and a unique opportunity to enter the industry.[33] On June 11, 2013, a Federal District Court judge ruled that Fox Searchlight had violated federal and New York minimum wage laws by not compensating its interns. The judge ruled that the interns were essentially performing the same functions as regular employees.[34] Table 13.11 lists the conditions that must be met by a firm if it is going to use unpaid interns. These conditions are set out in the Fair Labor Standards Act (FLSA) that was passed in 1938.

TABLE 13.11   ●   Conditions That Must Be Met to Exclude an Unpaid Intern From the Fair Labor Standards Act of 1938

1. The internship, even though it includes actual operation of the facilities of the employer, is similar to training which would be given in an educational environment;
2. The internship experience is for the benefit of the intern;
3. The intern does not displace regular employees, but works under close supervision of existing staff;
4. The employer that provides the training derives no immediate advantage from the activities of the intern, and on occasion its operations may actually be impeded;
5. The intern is not necessarily entitled to a job at the conclusion of the internship; and
6. The employer and the intern understand that the intern is not entitled to wages for the time spent in the internship.

Source: http://www.dol.gov/whd/regs/compliance/whdfs71.htm.

Questions for the Real-Life Ethical Dilemma Exercise

1. Do you think the responsibilities of the intern programs at Fox Searchlight meet the conditions required by the Fair Labor Standards Act?

2. Are the criteria established in the FLSA related to unpaid interns obsolete?

3. Why do companies decide not to pay interns?

4. How committed is Fox Searchlight in its promise of a "foot in the door" to get a permanent position in the industry?

5. If 100 unpaid interns had received a salary and benefits of $20,000 a year, it would have added $2 million in expenses to the production of *Black Swan*. Would this amount be a financial burden for Fox Searchlight, based on the worldwide gross revenue of the film?

Student Study Site

Visit the Student Study Site at **study.sagepub.com/stanwick3e** to access the following resources:

- Video Links
- SAGE Journal Articles
- Web Resources
- Web Quizzes

CASES

1

Bernard Madoff: How "One Big Lie" Can Destroy Thousands of Lives

I n the 1920s, Charles Ponzi introduced the "Ponzi" scheme to the American public. The scheme's simplicity is one of its best traits. By promising above-average returns for their investment, individuals appear willing to stand in line to give you their money. The only problem is that the Ponzi scheme makes no "real" investments other than paying back previous investors. The cycle of paying one investor (and pocketing a lot for himself) by collecting from another investor should only work for a short period before the "pyramid" of investors collapses under the weight of money owed.

Almost 100 years after Charles Ponzi showed the world how the scheme worked, people are still convinced that the administrator of the investments can guarantee above market returns. The underlying reason why Ponzi schemes will continue to be tried in the future is greed. As long as some people believe they can get more money from an investment than the average investor, they will continue to line up to give their money away in return for this empty promise.

Bernard Madoff went to prison for pulling off the largest Ponzi scheme in history, a fraudulent investment scheme that lasted an estimated 20 years.[1] The eventual downfall of Madoff's Ponzi scheme was not caused by regulators, investors, or even his employees but, rather, was the result of a global financial recession. When the financial crisis hit, Madoff had many billions of dollars of outstanding debt. Typical of a Ponzi scheme, when Madoff's investors made a "run on the bank" to take out the money that they invested with his firm, he did not have enough money to pay the above-average returns that he had promised. He did not even have enough to cover his clients' initial investment money.

Furthermore, there is no evidence that Madoff even made any trades to invest the money that his clients gave him. For example, Madoff had listed transactions in Fidelity Investments' Spartan Fund, yet Fidelity had no record of any account or transactions by Madoff's company.[2]

On the morning of December 11, 2008, the pyramid collapsed on Madoff when he was arrested in his apartment for criminal securities fraud. As a well-respected investor and part of New York's social elite, Madoff pulled off the largest Ponzi scheme in the history of commerce. Estimates are that Madoff stole more than $50 billion from investors over three decades. It is also estimated that Madoff, the former chairman of the NASDAQ Stock Exchange, had defrauded thousands of people including individuals, corporations, endowments, universities, foundations, and other investment funds. Before he was arrested, he told his sons Andrew and Mark, who worked for him, that his financial operations were "all just one big lie . . . basically a giant Ponzi scheme."[3] The day before his arrest, his wife Ruth withdrew $10 million from a brokerage firm that was partly owned by Bernard. This followed a withdrawal made November 25, 2008, for $5.5 million.[4]

As early as 2001, one of *Barron's* staff writers interviewed financial experts who questioned how only Madoff was able to achieve these types of above-average returns regardless of the market movement.[5] Madoff's standard response as to how he was the only person who could create these "miracle" returns was that his business strategy was too complicated for anyone outside the company to understand how he did it.[6]

In his response to the charges after being caught in 2008, Madoff stated, "'there is no innocent explanation' . . . and he 'paid investors with money that wasn't there.'"[7] After his confession to his sons, the sons turned him in to federal authorities.

Madoff ran his investment department of the company on a separate floor from the other parts of the company. He would not disclose his financial reports to anyone and would not tell his employees how he was able to provide guaranteed returns for the investors. He told one of the sons that investors had asked for approximately $7 billion in redemptions of their investments, and Madoff did not have enough money to cover those demands.

The day after Madoff's arrest, the first of many class-action lawsuits were filed against him. The lawsuit claimed that Bernard L. Madoff Investment Securities represented itself as a legitimate broker and dealer when in actuality it was a fraudulent Ponzi scheme.[8] His impact is staggering. A total of 13,567 customer accounts were listed with Madoff Securities. Young and old, famous and rich, the listing demonstrated that the fraud Madoff committed was global and piercing in its reach.[9]

Bernard Waving the Red Flags

The first fundamental red flag is a major one that occurs in all Ponzi schemes. The underlying premise of the Ponzi scheme is to guarantee a certain level of financial returns over an extended period. This guarantee cannot be proved. Wild fluctuations in markets both up and down ensure that no one can predict what the return will be next month or even next year. Therefore, both regulators and investors should have identified this guarantee as the basis of a Ponzi scheme. Harry Markopoulos, who was trying to identify how Madoff could make those guaranteed returns, wrote a letter to the Securities and Exchange Commission (SEC) in 2000 stating, "Madoff Securities is the world's largest Ponzi scheme."[10] For 8 years, Markopoulos tried to convince the SEC that Madoff was a fraud. After Madoff's arrest, the SEC stated that it would reopen the case.

Another red flag was the closed trading system developed by Madoff that ensured that no one else was able to verify the true asset value of the investment Madoff was making. In addition, a manager of funds should not use a related firm as a broker/dealer to make the trades because it creates an inherent conflict of interest. There were incentives for Madoff to encourage high trading volume because he would receive the benefit from his connection as asset manager and broker of the trades.[11]

A third red flag was that the volume that Madoff's reported trades for his clients does not correspond with the actual volume of trading on the Standard & Poor's (S&P) options market.[12]

When private investigators were hired by Aksia LLC, an independent hedge fund research and advisory firm, to examine Madoff's due diligence, they found the accounting firm he used to manage billions of dollars, Friehling & Horowitz, had three employees. One of the employees was 78 and lived in Florida, and a second employee, the secretary, operated the business in a 13-by-18-foot office.[13]

Where Was the SEC?

The SEC investigated Madoff numerous times during a 16-year period at Madoff's operations and found no evidence of any wrongdoing. In 1992, the SEC investigated Madoff in connection with two Florida accountants who were selling unregistered stock with very high return rates. The SEC traced the money under investigation to Madoff, and Madoff's response was that he did not know the accountants had collected the money illegally. In 1999 and 2000, the SEC investigated Madoff's trading practices with his firm. The SEC charged Madoff with not disclosing his order to other firms in the market, which is considered a trading violation. Madoff agreed to develop new procedures to remedy the problem. Markopoulos, who in 2000 claimed Madoff was running a Ponzi scheme, met with SEC officials in 2001 to explain in detail his concerns about Madoff's operations. The SEC found no wrongdoing. In 2004, the SEC again investigated the type of trading Madoff was doing and found no wrongdoing. In 2005, the SEC investigated whether Madoff was violating SEC rules related to the number of clients it was advising and the obligation to have Madoff's firm registered with the SEC. In November 2005, Markopoulos met again with the SEC investigators and provided them with a 21-page report highlighting his concerns.[14] Madoff used the investigation to his advantage by boasting to investors that the SEC had investigated his operation many times and still found nothing wrong with his company. The critical weakness of the SEC was that, despite repeated complaints about Madoff's operations, the SEC never verified the trades that Madoff claimed to be making over the decades.[15]

Madoff was described as a person who told the SEC "wonderful" stories during their interviews and bragged about his connections both in Wall Street and the SEC. He also became angry and refused to provide documents the SEC requested to review and told the SEC which documents investigators should request. When the investigators went back to their supervisor in the SEC Northeast regional office, the supervisor discouraged them from perusing the requested documents any further. In explaining why they did not follow up on the complaints from Markopoulos, the best rationalization the investigators came up with is that some of the SEC agents did not like Markopoulos personally. Another blatant lack of effort related to the idea of investigators requesting the National Association of Securities Dealers (NASD) to send the SEC independent trade data directly to verify Madoff's claims. The SEC decided not to make the request because it would become too time-consuming to actually review the data to verify the trades made by Madoff.[16] Furthermore, the SEC also should have realized that the steady profits obtained from Madoff could *never* work in the volatile financial markets. The chairwoman of the SEC, Mary Schapiro, summed up the SEC's lack of due diligence as "a failure that we continue to regret."[17] In November 2011, the SEC announced it had punished eight workers for their errors during previous investigations related to Madoff. The punishment varied from 3- to 30-day suspensions with and without pay reductions, and two people received "counseling memos," which is the lightest level of discipline the SEC allows.[18]

The Family Connections

Madoff boasted that his company was a close-knit family working for the investors. However, those family connections raised many ethical issues. Both of Madoff's sons, Andrew and Mark, worked for the company. Andrew was the director of trading, and Mark was director of proprietary trading. Madoff's brother, Peter, was the senior managing director and chief compliance officer, and Peter's daughter was Madoff Securities' compliance attorney. The closeness of these family members to the investment money should have raised multiple red flags. How could the company have an effective and objective evaluation of compliance when Madoff's brother and niece were in charge of compliance? How could Madoff state there was nothing to hide when both of his sons were top executives in the trading operations? Although not part of the "asset management" group where the fraud was committed, the sons may have had access to information that was being generated during the Ponzi scheme.[19]

The Impact on Charities

The impact of the Madoff fraud on charities was immense. Madoff was both a donor and, in many cases, the person responsible for investing money for the charities. Because of his religious faith, Madoff focused on many Jewish charities as being the "key" person for the financial sustainability. The promises of above-average returns convinced these charities that they were doing the right thing by having Madoff manage their money. From bone marrow transplants to human rights, Jewish charities have been desecrated by Madoff's fraud. For some charities such as the Justice, Equality, Human dignity, and Tolerance (JEHT) Foundation, which focused on criminal justice issues, the shutting down of its operations due to lack of funding was the only option. In addition, the Robert I. Lappin Charitable Foundation, which focused on Jewish youth, had to temporarily close its doors because of Madoff's actions. Yeshiva University lost $110 million from its Madoff investments. Madoff had served on the university's board of trustees since 1996. The $110 million was equal to approximately 8% of the university's total endowment.[20] Nobel Peace Prize winner, Elie Wiesel, was also a victim of Madoff, losing almost all of his $15.2 million in assets for his foundation. A concentration camp survivor, Wiesel has written more than 50 books and his Foundation for Humanity fights to resolve issues of indifference, intolerance, and injustice.[21]

The Social Network of Bernard Madoff

From Boca Raton to Park Avenue, London to Geneva, Bernard Madoff was a master of convincing ultra-wealthy people to invest in his company. Madoff used his image and status as the former chairman of the NASDAQ Stock Exchange to encourage people to beg him to accept their money. He refused some investors, heightening the intrigue and demand for his services. The elite group that was allowed to invest with him made Madoff in demand around the world. Madoff's clients usually referred potential new clients informally by word of mouth. The clients who invested usually did not understand if they were invested directly with Madoff or with feeder funds that would take clients' money, charge a fee, and then give it to Madoff. The largest hit feeder fund was the Fairfield Greenwich Group, which lost an estimated $7.5 billion from Madoff investments. With connections to the social elite around the world, Fairfield received a fee and then handed the investment over to Madoff. This arrangement lasted for 19 years.[22]

The Legal Issues Commence

On December 19, 2008, Bernard Madoff was placed under 24-hour home detention with electronic monitoring. In addition, Madoff's wife was ordered to pay for round-the-clock monitoring of the building where they lived, including supplying communication devices that transmitted a direct signal from Madoff's monitor to the FBI. Madoff also paid a $10 million personal recognizance bond for his release until his trial started.[23]

In what can only be considered one more bizarre twist in this story, Madoff and his wife Ruth were accused of mailing expensive jewelry and valuables to their sons and Madoff's brother in violation of the bail agreement. As part of the agreement, Madoff was not allowed to dispose of any of his assets because they could be sold with the proceeds going to the victims of the fraud. A total of three packages were sent containing expensive watches, a diamond necklace and emerald ring, other types of diamond jewelry including a Cartier diamond and Tiffany watch. Madoff's lawyers described the items as "a few sentimental personal items" that are valued at more than $1 million.[24] This information was revealed at the same time it was disclosed that Madoff had signed 100 checks worth $173 million that were found in his desk drawer on the day he was arrested. It is hypothesized that the 100 checks were for selected family members, close friends, and employees.[25]

The Consequences for Their Actions

On March 12, 2009, the 70-year-old Madoff pleaded guilty to all 11 felony counts brought against him and faced a sentence of as many as 150 years in prison. The charges included securities fraud, money laundering, and perjury. Government prosecutors announced that the amount of the estimated fraud had increased from $50 billion to $65 billion. The U.S. Department of Justice (DOJ) alleged that Madoff had maintained an ill-trained and inexperienced clerical staff so the fraud could work for so long. The staff generated "false and fraudulent documents" and provided false records and misinformation to regulators while moving money back and forth between numerous accounts to make it appear that actual trades were taking place.[26] Immediately after his plea, Madoff was handcuffed and led off to jail. His $10 million bail was revoked because he was considered a risk to flee the charges against him.[27] Six days later, Madoff's accountant was arrested. David Friehling was not charged with knowing about the Ponzi scheme but was charged with not doing the proper due diligence in his audits of Madoff's accounts. The "sham" audits allowed Madoff to commit the fraud for a much longer period than if the proper audits had been done on Madoff's books. The Federal Bureau of Investigation (FBI) stated that Friehling did not verify the existence of assets claimed by Madoff, nor did he examine the main bank account through which billions of dollars flowed with the clients' money.[28]

On June 30, 2009, Madoff was sentenced to 150 years in prison, the maximum allowed. There were no members of Madoff's family in the courtroom when the sentence was read. Ruth Madoff released a statement in which she says that she was expressing her grief for the victims of the fraud and that her reaction was of shock and betrayal when she "learned" about the fraud committed by her husband.[29] Prisoner number 61727–054 was sent to the Butner Federal Correctional Complex in Butner, North Carolina, to serve out his sentence. Madoff was sentenced to the medium security prison within the complex.[30] Madoff now rises at 6 a.m. and reports for mandatory work duty by 7:30 a.m. Inmates at the Butner facility are paid between 12 cents and $1.15 per hour based on the job they are performing. The end of the day occurs at 11 p.m. when the lights are turned off. Inmates tried to get Madoff to sign items for them in the hopes of trying to sell the items on eBay when they get out of prison because they are not allowed Internet access.[31]

On November 3, 2009, Madoff's accountant, Friehling, pleaded guilty to nine criminal charges including one charge of securities fraud, one charge of investment advisor fraud, four counts of making false filings with the SEC, and three counts of obstruction of the administration of federal tax.[32] Ten days later, two computer programmers who worked for Madoff were arrested for their role in the Ponzi scheme. Jerome O'Hara and George Perez were alleged to have created the software needed to generate a detailed paper trail of Madoff's "transactions." Both men had closed their accounts with Madoff in April 2006 because they had become uneasy about the fraud. In September 2006, Madoff confronted the men, who had remained quiet, but had demanded pay raises and bonuses—"hush money" in return for staying with Madoff and for not saying anything about the fraud to any outsiders. The software included programs that generated fake customer account statements as well as fake trading confirmations from the London Stock Exchange.[33]

The Impact of the Fraud on Family and Friends

In August 2009, Frank DiPascali Jr. pleaded guilty to 10 criminal charges for his role in the Madoff fraud. DiPascali admitted in court that the scheme was fake and fictitious, and he knew it was a fraud. He faces 125 years for his convictions. The SEC alleged that DiPascali and other Madoff associates used a "random number generator program" to give fictitious trading orders the appearance that trades were occurring at different periods. In addition, Madoff ordered that all old stationary and letterhead could not be destroyed in case they had to "backdate" a fictitious order to show to a client or regulators.[34]

On February 25, 2010, Daniel Bonventre, a senior executive who had worked with Madoff for more than 30 years, was arrested on federal fraud and conspiracy charges. Bonventre is accused of manipulating financial records to conceal the fraud. These fake records misled investors concerning the poor financial position of Madoff Securities. Bonventre was also accused of profiting from the fraud by collecting almost $2 million by using fake transactions in his own accounts at Madoff Securities.[35]

Cases

On November 18, 2010, two longtime Madoff employees were indicted for their roles in the fraud. Both Annette Bongiorno and JoAnn Crupi were considered "back room" employees but contributed valuable roles in maintaining the fraud throughout the years. Bongiorno had worked for Madoff for more than 40 years, and Crupi had worked for Madoff for 25 years. Bongiorno used a computer program to create blank account statements and to revise information on existing account statements. On occasion, she asked clients to return account statements that had been issued to them so she could adjust them to facilitate the fraud. Crupi was in charge of giving Madoff handwritten notes containing the daily balance from the primary bank account used to transfer funds in the fraud. She also produced a handwritten daily summary of the listing of clients and amounts that had been redeemed and those that had been requested but not yet fulfilled by Madoff. Crupi and other employees were in charge of creating the "special" financial books that were shown to the SEC during its investigations. Crupi also generated the listing of all the false transactions claimed to have taken place by Madoff. From 1975 to 2008, Bongiorno received more than $14 million from the fraud, and Crupi received more than $2.7 million in just 2008 from the fraud. During the final days before Madoff's arrest, Bongiorno convinced Madoff to use the last remaining money in the company to redeem the balances owed to employees, family, and friends instead of Madoff's other clients. More than $350 million in checks, which included the $173 million found in Bernard's desk, were seized by authorities before they could be sent. Bongiorno faces as many as 75 years in prison, and Crupi may have to serve as many as 65 years in prison. Authorities sought the forfeiture of approximately $5 million in assets owned by the two women, including a 2005 Bentley Continental and a 2007 Mercedes-Benz owned by Bongiorno and a New Jersey beach house owned by Crupi.[36,37]

In a tragic twist of fate, Mark Madoff, the eldest of Madoff's two sons, hung himself in his Manhattan apartment on the second anniversary of his father's arrest. Mark's 2-year-old son was asleep in another room in the apartment at the time of his death, while his wife, Stephanie, was vacationing at Walt Disney World with their daughter. Mark had become bitter and angry toward his father and had become increasingly anxious about the flood of lawsuits filed against him related to his father's fraud. Mark was also upset that a trustee had named his children as defendants in a lawsuit filed in the previous month. He was bothered by the rumors about his family, the news reports that stated that criminal charges against himself and his brother would likely take place in the near future, and his inability to find a job.[38] Bernard Madoff announced that he would not attend his son's funeral "out of consideration for the family's privacy." Madoff had his own private service for his son inside the federal prison where he is incarcerated. The Bureau of Prisons stated that inmates can request permission to attend a funeral of an immediate family member and the approval of the request is on a case-by-case determination.[39]

In January 2011, the estate of longtime Madoff friend Jeffry Picower agreed to return $7.2 billion to give to investors who were victims of the Ponzi scheme. Picower's widow, Barbara Picower, agreed to give what is the largest amount of money ever returned through a civil forfeiture proceeding. By agreeing to give up this money, the Picower estate is no longer liable for any future lawsuits related to Madoff. Jeffry died of a drowning resulting from a heart attack in October 2009. At the time, he was estimated to be worth $10 billion. Barbara stated she would continue her philanthropic contributions with the remaining money in the estate.[40,41]

In June 2011, another close friend of Madoff's, Eric Lipkin, pleaded guilty to conspiracy, bank fraud, and creating false financial records. Lipkin created false documents to mislead SEC investigators and created false payroll records. By using the false payroll records, Madoff paid friends retirement and other benefits even though they were not employees at Madoff Securities.[42]

In November 2011, yet another close friend of Bernard pleaded guilty for his action during the fraud. David Kugel pleaded guilty to conspiracy, securities fraud, bank fraud, falsifying business records, and falsifying the books of an investment advisor. Kugel could serve as many as 85 years in prison. Kugel admitted in court that Madoff had been using a Ponzi scheme since the 1970s, and he agreed to forfeit $3.5 million he received while working for Madoff.[43]

In December 2011, Madoff's former controller pleaded guilty to falsifying company records and filing false information to government officials. Enrica Cotellessa-Pitz starting working with Madoff in 1978 and was responsible for closing the company's financial statements monthly.[44]

In a haunting reminder of Mark Madoff's death, the U.S. bankruptcy judge ruled in April 2012 that the trustee could make financial claims against current and former spouses of Madoff's sons to collect money for Madoff's victims.[45] On June 29, 2012, Bernard's brother, Peter Madoff, pleaded guilty to fraud charges. Peter Madoff admitted that he falsified documents, lied to government regulators, and participated in other illegal activities to help Bernard Madoff cover up his Ponzi scheme. It was estimated that Peter Madoff received approximately $40 million from the Madoff firm between 1998 and 2008.[46] On December 20, 2012, Peter Madoff was sentenced to 10 years in prison and received a forfeiture order of $143 billion. That amount was selected to ensure that all of Peter Madoff's assets would be handed over to the government so the proceeds could be distributed to the victims. In the courtroom, Peter stated that he was "deeply ashamed. . . (and) tried to atone by pleading guilty. . . I am profoundly sorry that my failures have let so many people down, including my own loved ones and family."[47] On January 7, 2014, J. P. Morgan agreed to pay $2.6 billion to resolve the allegations that it had failed to notify government regulators about Madoff's Ponzi scheme. The United States Attorney and the FBI had alleged that J. P. Morgan had failed to put in place the proper controls that would have identified the fraudulent activities occurring in Madoff's firm. A number of internal documents demonstrated that various J. P. Morgan employees were raising red flags about Madoff's operations, but J. P. Morgan failed to act on this information.[48] On March 25, 2014, five former members of Madoff's staff were found guilty of fraud. Jerome O'Hara and George Perez, both computer programmers, were found guilty of creating false customer accounts. Annette Bongiorno and JoAnn Crupi, both former Madoff portfolio managers, were found guilty of creating fake trading records including backdating nonexistent trades. In addition, former operations director Daniel Bonventre was found guilty of generating false financial records.[49] On September 3, 2014, the only living son of Bernard Madoff died from mantle cell lymphoma cancer. He was 48 years old.[50] On June 24, 2014, Madoff's former accountant, Paul Konigsberg, pleaded guilty to falsifying records and conspiracy, which included illegally backdating trades.[51] On

December 8, 2014, Daniel Bonventre was sentenced to 10 years in prison and was also ordered to forfeit $155 billion. In court, Mr. Bonventre stated, "I was used by the ultimate con man. . . Bernard Madoff lied to me every day and I believed and trusted him."[52] On December 9, 2014, Annette Bongiorno was sentenced to six years in prison. In addition, Jerome O'Hara was sentenced to 30 months in prison and received a forfeiture order of $19.7 billion for his role in the Madoff fraud.[53] On February 9, 2015, Irving Picard, the trustee in charge of distributing the assets collected to the victims, announced that the payout to the victims had totaled more than $7.2 billion.[54]

Questions for Thought

1. Trust is extremely important in business transactions. Greed also plays a role in some business transactions. Discuss how these two concepts were intertwined in this case.

2. Describe a Ponzi scheme. Find several examples of other Ponzi schemes that have occurred in recent years.

3. In this case, it appears that Madoff had many friends and family members who were involved in the fraud. Speculate about how likely it is that Madoff's own sons, who were employees of the firm, knew nothing of the fraud, as they stated.

4. Explain the ethical issues associated with running a family-owned business. Were these issues present at Madoff's firm?

2

Siemens: How the Greased Wheels Slid off the Ethical Track

Cases

Headquartered in Munich, Germany, Siemens focuses on developing products for electronic and electronic engineering based industries. As with many large global manufacturing conglomerates, Siemens's customers are other companies and governments around the world. Within these industries, it is common to have long-term contracts with the clients that can be worth millions or billions of dollars. It is critical that Siemens and their competitors convince a relatively small group of people that their products provide the best overall value to the client. Therefore, Siemens and its competitors may always have the temptation to use "whatever means possible" to persuade decision makers to sign contracts with their firms. With this persuasion comes the temptation to give illegal financial incentives to close the contracts.

The Allegations Start

Siemens's illegal method of obtaining orders from clients was exposed when it was announced that six Siemens executives had been arrested for their actions related to giving bribes to German and other clients in the telecommunications industry. In addition, the executives were also accused of embezzling funds from Siemens to pay for the bribes. One of the executives arrested was Thomas Ganswindt, who was head of the telecommunications equipment unit. At this point, the estimated amount of the bribes was 200 million euros and allegedly included using bribes to obtain the security systems contract at the 2004 Olympic Games in Greece.[1]

The concerns started for Siemens when a senior executive, Michael Kutschenreuter, claimed he got a very worrisome phone call from Beit Al Etisalat in early 2004. Al Etisalat worked at a Saudi consulting firm that was a business partner with Siemens. Al Etisalat demanded that he be paid $910 million in "commission payments" by Siemens for his role in winning telecommunication contracts with Saudi Arabia. Al Etisalat continued by stating that he threatened to go to the SEC with evidence of bribes offered by Siemens related to the contracts if the company did not pay the commission payments. Kutschenreuter notified his superiors, including future Siemens CEO Klaus Kleinfeld and the then current CEO Heinrich von Pierer, that the company was being blackmailed by Al Etisalat. Kutschenreuter claimed he got approval from the Siemens management board to pay Al Etisalat $50 million in January 2005. Of that $50 million, $17 million was for past obligations and $33 million was for "hush" money to make sure that the information was not sent to the SEC. Kutschenreuter was one of six executives arrested in November 2006. It was alleged that Siemens used fake consulting contracts to transfer money as a bribe to clients. If Siemens were found guilty of fraud, the company would no longer be allowed to bid on public sector contracts by governments globally. Prosecutors alleged that the bribes were not isolated to one group of employees or to one business unit, but were widespread throughout Siemens and were very well organized. The allegations came at a time when Siemens was ready to merge its telecommunications equipment business with Nokia. Siemens announced that the proposed merger was put on hold until the results of the investigation were known.[2]

A Culture Built on "Don't Ask, Don't Tell"

The use of bribes in Germany has been very common in the past. In fact, only after stricter corruption laws were passed in 1999 were companies forbidden to offer bribes. Before 1999, German companies were allowed to write off as business expenses any bribes with foreign clients. Both Kleinfeld and von Pierer denied any knowledge of the bribes and claimed they did not offer any payments as hush money to stop Al Etisalat's disclosures. Kutschenreuter claimed that bribes were so wide spread that they even had a coding system for them using the phrase "Make Profit." Each letter in "Make Profit" corresponded to a number based on the sequence 1–2–3–4–5–6–7–8–9–0: M equals 1, A equals 2, K equals 3, and so on. Siemens executives used this code to tell their subordinates what the amount should be. For example, if they said "file this in the APP file," it would mean they were authorized to give a bribe equal to 2.55% of sales. Kutschenreuter stated he witnessed bribes being paid for power project contracts in Russia and Slovakia in the mid-1990s. In addition, he knew that bribes were being paid to the Argentine government for a contract to develop electronically scannable passports in 1999. He stated that the bribes stopped in 2001 only because there was a change in the Argentine government. Kutschenreuter also stated that the bribes were widespread partly because they were seen as a small sin (a peccadillo) in exchange for the large benefit to the company by obtaining these contracts.[3]

Another Siemens executive who had worked for the company for 40 years, Reinhardt Siekaczek, stated that he was ordered to set up bank accounts to establish slush funds to be used for bribes in either 1999 or 2000. One bank account in Salzburg, Austria, was used to transfer more than 75 million euros for bribes each year. The bribes were used to secure contracts in countries such as Cameroon, Egypt, Greece, Indonesia, Kazakhstan, Kuwait, Nigeria, Saudi Arabia, and Vietnam. The transferring of money for bribes became much more difficult after money laundering laws were tightened after the September 11, 2001, terrorist attacks. At the annual shareholders' meeting in January 2007, Siemens CEO Kleinfeld said he was "shocked" by the allegations and that Siemens was doing whatever was possible to clear up the allegations. At the same meeting, former CEO von Pierer stated that during his tenure as CEO he had taken major steps to control bribery and corruption. He also stated that he was "deeply distressed that these efforts were not successful enough."[4]

In fact, Siemens's decentralized organizational structure allowed bribes to take place without any real checks and balances. The vastness of Siemens's operations required that unit business managers be given a lot of autonomy to make their own decisions. Although this is an effective tool for decision making, it also weakens the potential accountability of the actions of the managers if there is not a control or monitoring system in place to ensure the decisions comply with German and foreign laws. Siemens had business unit managers and regional managers for their operations in 190 countries. Both unit and regional managers had the authority to create and implement contracts with consultants who aided Siemens in getting new client contracts. There was no standardized template that Siemens's managers were required to use to draw up these contracts. As a result, the responsibilities and compensation to be given to the consultants to obtain more business for Siemens were left to the discretion of each manager. After the bribery allegations started, Siemens established a requirement that any type of consulting agreement must now have approval of senior managers and the chief compliance officer.[5]

The Consequences Begin

In March 2007, former top Siemens executives stood trial for paying approximately 6 million euros in bribes so Siemens could secure a power generation equipment contract with the Italian utility Enel. Both Siemens's managers, Horst Vigener and Andreas Kley, a former finance chief at the power generation unit, admitted the bribes but argued they were not guilty. Their reasoning was that Siemens had benefited greatly by the bribes, and they were charged with bribing public officials whereas Enel is a hybrid public/private owned company. The Italian government controlled 68% of Enel's stock during the time of the alleged bribes, but the defense argued that Enel is partially privatized and is traded on Italian stock exchanges. In 2002, Germany passed an additional law stating bribery was illegal regardless of whether the official was with a public or private entity. The Siemens managers also stated that the Enel managers who were going to make the final decision on the contract asked for bribes during the bidding process. The charges against the Siemens managers were a breach of trust because they were accused of inappropriate stewardship of Siemens's money.[6] In May 2007, both former managers were convicted of giving bribes. Siemens was ordered to pay a fine of $51.4 million, and the former managers received suspended prison sentences. Kley received a 2-year suspended sentence, and Vigener received a 9-month suspended sentence. The $51.4 million is equivalent to the profit Siemens made on the power generator deal with Enel. Siemens's response was that the ruling was illegal because the court's decision was not based on law or fact.[7]

A New Beginning

In April 2007, von Pierer announced he would resign as chairman of the supervisory board of Siemens. Von Pierer stated he was leaving because of his duty to Siemens and not because of the ongoing bribery investigation.[8] Six days later, Kleinfeld announced that he would step down as CEO when his contract expired in September 2007. Siemens supervisory board voted not to renew Kleinfeld's contract. Kleinfeld had been CEO for only 2 years and was handpicked by von Pierer to take over the top position at Siemens.[9]

In July 2007, Siemens chief compliance officer, Daniel Noa stepped down from the job after 6 months. It was speculated that Noa's departure resulted from his lack of support from Siemens to be able to do his job. An anonymous source commented that Noa was not given enough power and responsibility to do his job properly in investigating illegal activities at Siemens.[10]

In July 2007, Peter Löscher, formerly of Merck, was named the new CEO of Siemens, and he promised to streamline operations to ensure bribery would not continue at Siemens. Löscher was the first CEO that was hired for the top position from outside of Siemens. Löscher's vision is based on Siemens having clear lines of responsibility, a high level of transparency, and the ability to make changes at maximum speed. He also stated that Siemens's strategic focus would be based on "performance with ethics—this is not a contradiction, it is a must . . . compliance becomes part of management culture internationally, from top to bottom and back again."[11]

The Fines Continue

In October 2007, Siemens was ordered to pay $284 million for its role in the telecommunication equipment bribes. Siemens was convicted of funneling money through consulting contracts that were actually bribes to ensure Siemens got the client contracts.[12] Siemens paid millions of euros in bribes to government officials in Nigeria, Russia, and Libya to win those countries' telecommunication contracts. It was estimated that a total of 77 bribes equaling approximately 12 million euros was paid by Siemens from 2001 to 2004. The bribes ranged from 2,000 euros to 2.25 million euros.[13]

An Amnesty Plan

Corruption had infiltrated to such a level within Siemens that it was difficult to determine the full impact of the effects of the bribes. As a result, in November 2007, Siemens declared an amnesty for all of its employees except the top 300 executives to disclose what type of illegal actions were taking place at various Siemens businesses around the world. The result of the amnesty was that 110 employees came forward and offered information about illegal activities occurring at Siemens. Through the information from the lower-level employees, Siemens officials could finally piece together which top-level managers were involved and knew about the bribes occurring globally. The newly appointed general counsel, Peter Solmssen, commented that in the past, Siemens's level of corruption was systemic and that there was "a cultural acceptance that this was the way to do business around the world, and we have to change that . . . [and that] . . . allowing crimes to persist is a form of aiding and abetting."[14]

The Investigation Continues

In April 2008, Erich Reinhardt, who was the head of the medical equipment division and was a Siemens board member, resigned after "new findings" were discovered about misconduct occurring in his division. The investigation had expanded to include 270 current and former employees.[15] In May 2008, German prosecutors started civil proceeding against Siemens's former CEO von Pierer, charging that von Pierer failed in his fiduciary duty to implement the proper oversight of the company when widespread bribery was committed by Siemens's employees.[16]

In May 2008, Siekaczek went on trial for 58 counts of breach of trust related to his role in the bribery scandal. Siekaczek testified that bribes were an open secret at Siemens and that managers would sign sticky notes that were affixed to the bribe contracts so that they could be peeled away if there were ever an investigation on the payments. As a result, the managers could not be identified as the source of the authorization of the bribe payment. Siekaczek argued that one problem was that it was difficult to shut down the bribes when the German government banned bribes in 1999 because many of the payments were over multiple years. As prosecutors developed a case for various employees under suspicion, they were processing confiscated material equal to 5 terabytes of data, which is equivalent to approximately 5 million pages.[17] In July 2008, Siekaczek was convicted, ordered to pay a fine of $170,000, and received a suspended prison sentence of 2 years.[18]

In a different type of "bribery," former Siemens board member Johannes Feldmayer went to trial on charges that he used Siemens money to support an employer-friendly union to counterbalance Siemens's workers most powerful union. Feldmayer gave $43.9 million to the Association of Independent Employees (AUB) to counteract the efforts IG Metall, which is Germany's largest union and represents workers at Siemens. He testified that he did not believe that any laws were broken because he believed the money did not directly influence the election of works council representatives at Siemens. The works councils in Germany are responsible for ensuring employees' rights are protected. Despite this protest, the AUB was known to be much more supportive and conciliatory toward Siemens than were other German unions that negotiated with the company. In addition, AUB helped propose and support labor concessions on pay and working hours that were agreed on in later union contracts even though IG Metall opposed these concessions.[19] In November 2008, Feldmayer was convicted of breach of trust and tax evasion, was ordered to pay a fine of $289,300, and was given a 2-year suspended prison sentence. In addition, the former head of AUB, Wilhelm Schelsky, was convicted and sentenced to 4½ years for breach of trust, embezzlement, and tax evasion.[20]

The Cost of Corruption

In December 2008, Siemens agreed to pay a fine of $800 million to settle charges from the DOJ under the Foreign Corrupt Practices Act. Of the $800 million, $450 million was given to the DOJ, and $350 million was given to the SEC.[21]

This penalty is approximately 20 times higher than the previous largest fine issued by the DOJ. The corruption at Siemens had spread to the point that former Argentine President Carlos Menem was accused of being part of the bribery machine. The DOJ was considering demanding a fine as high as $2.7 billion. The SEC estimated that Siemens had made at least 4,283 bribe payments that totaled $1.4 billion between March 2001 and September 2007. Some of the bribes that were given by Siemens include $55 million to Russian officials for medical devices, $40 million to Argentine officials for an identity cards project, $25 million for high voltage transmission lines and $20 million for metro trains to Chinese officials, and $20 million to Israel officials for power plant projects.[22] Therefore, with the $800 million fine and the previous settlements of $540 million and $290 million, Siemens has paid $1.63 billion in fines for its corruption.[23]

In July 2009, Siemens agreed to pay the World Bank $100 million for its role in bribing Russian officials in the urban transport project in Moscow. The World Bank helped finance that project and tried to ensure that fraud and corruption were not part of the business dealings in any project it financed. The $100 million will be used during the next 15 years to combat corruption through training and education and aid governments in recovering money stolen by corrupt leaders. Siemens also agreed not to bid on any World Bank–financed projects for 2 years.[24] In December 2009, Siemens reached a settlement with former CEOs von Pierer and Kleinfeld for their roles in the corruption scandal at Siemens. Von Pierer agreed to pay Siemens $7.5 million, and Kleinfeld agreed to pay $3 million. Von Pierer's lawyers stated that the settlement does not mean their client did anything wrong because von Pierer rejects all the accusations against him.[25] On December 13, 2011, eight former Siemens executives and contractors were charged by the DOJ with criminal bribery. Siemens managing board member Uriel Sharef was included in the individuals charged. An estimated $60 million in bribes were given in order to obtain the Argentinian national identity card contract. Assistant attorney general Lanny A. Brewer stated, "Business should be won or lost on the merits of a company's products and services, not the amount of bribes paid to government officials."[26] On February 6, 2015, former Siemens CFO Heinz-Joachim Neubuerger committed suicide. Neubuerger had, two months earlier, reached a settlement of $2.9 million with Siemens on his involvement in the bribery scandal. Neubuerger was the CFO of Siemens industrial group, which was the division responsible for paying more than $1 billion in bribes globally in order to win contracts.[27]

Cases

Questions for Thought

1. Should bribery be considered an unethical act or just another cost of doing business? Explain your position.

2. How do you change a culture that is built on bribery to make sales?

3. Due to the employee amnesty, 110 employees came forward with reports of wrongdoing. Does an amnesty program really work? Explain your position.

4. In 2009, two former CEOs reached settlements concerning their roles in the Siemens corruption scandal. However, one of the CEOs says that he did nothing wrong. Do you agree or disagree with this position? Does perception play any part in this settlement?

3

TOMS Shoes: Helping Soles All Over the World

I n 2002, Blake Mycoskie and his sister Paige competed in the CBS reality program *The Amazing Race.* During their travels in that competition, Blake and Paige travelled through Argentina. Although they lost the $1 million prize in the contest by 4 minutes, the experience had a significant impact on Blake. In 2006, Blake returned to Argentina for a vacation from his fourth entrepreneurial start-up, which was an online driver's education program for teenagers. While in Argentina, Blake noticed that a very popular shoe worn by the Argentinian people was a casual canvas shoe called the alpargata. The versatile shoe was worn in diverse areas of the country, on farms and in the cities, including in nightclubs. Blake thought this style of shoe would have a market in the United States. At the end of his vacation, Blake met an American women in a café who was volunteering for a local shoe drive for children. The shoe drive was needed because many of the children could not afford shoes, needed not only for school but also to help prevent diseases and problems related to the feet such as blisters, sores, and infections.[1] As a result, Mycoskie established TOMS Shoes in 2006. TOMS Shoes has a very simple premise it calls its One for One program. For every pair of TOMS shoes that are sold, one new pair of shoes will be given to a child in need. Mycoskie states that giving is the driving force behind the company, and it is the foundation for growing TOMS in the future.[2]

Mycoskie argues that shoes can have multiple benefits for children in developing countries. He cites that many schools require that shoes must be worn to attend school. In addition, the children usually must walk for miles to get to essential services such as education, clean water, and medical help. Furthermore, a number of soil-based diseases can enter the body through a child's foot. These diseases can also affect the cognitive development of the children, negatively affecting the long-term cognitive growth potential of the children. Potential trauma to the feet can be caused by factors such as hookworm, podoconiosis, jiggers, and tetanus.[3]

Why TOMS?

TOMS produces its shoes in 3 countries and provides shoes to children in 23 countries. TOMS makes shoes in factories in Argentina, Ethiopia, and China and is audited by a third party to ensure that the shoes are produced by workers who receive a fair wage and do not employ child labor.

By September 2010, TOMS, via its customers, had given one million pairs of new shoes to children around the world. TOMS will return to the same villages over time to replace any outgrown for newer, larger shoes.[4] By 2015, TOMS had given more than 35 million pairs of shoes to children in 70 countries. The underlying philosophy of TOMS is (1) identify communities that need shoes, (2) give shoes that fit, (3) use Giving Partners to help TOMS Shoes have a bigger impact, (4) give children shoes as they grow, and (5) ask Giving Partners to provide feedback to help TOMS Shoes improve.[5]

Hookworms

Hookworms are a global problem and affect an estimated 576 to 740 million people worldwide. Hookworms are parasites that enter the body and live in the small intestine. Hookworms lay eggs in the small intestine that are passed in the feces of the infected person. In areas with poor personal hygiene, the feces can come in contact with another person, and when the eggs are hatched, they then penetrate the skin of the next person. Hookworms can cause anemia through blood loss. In children, they can also cause protein loss. Hookworms were a major problem in the southeastern part of the United States until the early 20th century.[6]

Podoconiosis

Originating from the Greek words *podos* (foot) and *konia* (dust), podoconiosis is considered a tropical disease occurring in parts of Africa, especially higher altitude areas in the eastern and central part of the continent. Individuals develop podoconiosis from being barefoot in areas of red clay near active or inactive volcanoes. The silica found in the soil blocks lymph nodes in the lower limbs, especially the feet. This causes great swelling and pain in the individual and is commonly referred to as *big foot disease*. Podoconiosis usually starts with children in their early teens. The symptoms start with leg and foot pain at night and progresses to severe itching, swelling, and burning on the soles of the child's foot. Podoconiosis only occurs in individuals who walk barefoot.[7]

Jiggers

The jiggers, or female sand fleas, embed themselves in the feet of animals and humans. Jiggers feed on the human's blood to survive. The blood allows the jiggers the opportunity to develop eggs. Jiggers can cause severe inflammation and ulcers in the foot. In addition, permanent damage can include loss of toenails, amputation of toes, and ultimately death. Jiggers are able to survive and thrive in areas of dirt roads where animals and people walk freely without shoes. Children are especially vulnerable because they are less likely than adults are to have shoes.[8]

Tetanus

Tetanus is an infection of the nervous system caused by the bacteria *Clostridium tetani*. The bacteria lives in soil and can remain inactive for more than 40 years before becoming active. The infection occurs when the bacteria enters the body through an injury or open wound. As the bacteria spreads, it can affect the nerve signals from the spinal cord to the muscles. As a result, muscle spasms occur, usually first in the jaw, which is why tetanus is also known as *lockjaw*. A common form of contracting tetanus is stepping on a dirty and rusty object, usually a nail, which punctures the skin and introduces the bacteria into the body.[9]

How One for One Works

The first step in the One for One program is establishing partnerships with global humanitarian organizations that have a long-standing history with the communities in which they serve. With their partners, TOMS identifies communities in step 2 that would benefit the most from TOMS shoes. The criterion includes economic, health, and educational conditions and needs of the community. In addition, TOMS ensures that its involvement will not have a negative impact on local businesses in the area. In step 3, TOMS ensures that the children who receive TOMS shoes also receive additional support addressing the health and educational needs of the children.[10]

What Shoes Do They Give?

There is not a uniform type of shoes given to the children. The shoes are made to order to ensure the sizes match the needed sizes of the children. Based on the feedback received, TOMS has learned that there are cultural differences in the style of the shoes that the children want. Black is the most common color, most likely because it is the mandatory color of school shoes in many countries. In Argentina, TOMS found that the children liked very colorful shoes. In Ethiopia, the shoes are provided by local producers based on the needs of the local partners.[11]

TOMS Eyewear Products

In March 2012, TOMS expanded its product line to include eyewear. Working with its sight-giving partner, Seva Foundation, TOMS is using the same model as its shoes program. Initially, the eyewear will be sold at Selfridges in England, and every pair of eyeglasses sold will result in one child receiving a pair of glasses. This program includes the glasses, eye examinations, medical treatments, and sight-saving eye surgeries in Nepal, Cambodia, and Tibet.[12]

TOMS Coffee

In March 2014, TOMS announced that they had developed a line of coffees whose sales will be used to provide clean water for cooking and drinking in communities that do not have easy access to clean water. It is estimated that 2 billion people globally do not have access to clean water. Each bag of coffee sold will fund a week's worth of clean water for one person. Each cup of coffee would provide enough water for one day for one person when TOMS establishes its proposed cafes. Working with Water for People, TOMS Coffee will help in the development of sustainable water systems around the world, which could include building water tanks and piping systems to help bring clean water to people in need. The coffee for TOMS is grown in small farms located in Guatemala, Malawi, Peru, Rwanda, and Honduras.[13]

An Opposing Viewpoint

Although TOMS does an excellent job presenting its story, there have been critics of the overall philosophy and transparency. One issue is whether the donation of TOMS shoes will hurt local businesses that make shoes. Although providing shoes is a great cause, it reminds one of the old Chinese proverb that states that if you give a person a fish, that person will be fed for the day, but if you teach a person how to fish, he or she will be fed for a lifetime. The idea of a donation serves an immediate (and critical) need, but would it be better for TOMS to invest money to teach local businesses how to make shoes so that the children would receive access to inexpensive shoes and the local businesses would generate revenue to help improve the community? By establishing shoe manufacturing in these local communities, the people in the village would also be encouraged to consider additional entrepreneurial activities.

The second issue is the lack of financial statements. As a privately held company, TOMS is not required to release its financial statements. However, for improved transparency, it would be beneficial to the customers and other stakeholders to have access to TOMS' financial information. How much does it cost TOMS to make a pair of shoes? How much does it cost TOMS to give away one pair of shoes? These fundamental questions need to be addressed by TOMS. In TOMS' 16-page *2010 Giving Report*, there is no reference to any financial information related to TOMS' operations. This Giving Report would be the perfect opportunity for TOMS to show its stakeholders its past and current financial performance. Without transparency and accountability, TOMS' One for One campaign could be considered, by its critics, as more of a marketing ploy than a corporate social responsibility campaign.

A Shift in Strategic Focus for TOMS?

On August 20, 2014, Blake Mycoskie announced that the private equity firm Bain Capital was going to buy 50% of TOMS for an estimated $625 million. Blake Mycoskie explained that TOMS brought in Bain Capital as a partner so the company could take over the day-to-day operations and help TOMS expand globally and move into new product categories to fulfill his dream, which "is for TOMS to be the most influential and inspirational company in the world."[14] Bain Capital, cofounded by former presidential candidate Mitt Romney, pledged to continue the One for One program and match TOMS' level of charitable giving.[15] With the acquisition of half of the company by Bain, investors started to scrutinize more closely the operations of TOMS. Some investors are concerned about TOMS' heavy dependence on TOMS Shoes for revenue. In October 2014, it was estimated that 72% of TOMS' gross sales were from shoes. As a result, investors are looking at new markets TOMS will move into. TOMS announced that it would start selling handbags in 2016.[16] In response to the criticism that TOMS was not providing employment opportunities in areas that have the One for One program, TOMS partnered with shoe manufacturer LXJ Golden Pacific to start manufacturing shoes in Port-au-Prince, Haiti.[17]

Questions for Thought

1. If TOMS' model is so successful, why don't other companies try to be socially active in a similar way?

2. Is this concept just a self-serving model so Blake Mycoskie can say he is helping people when it is really the customers who are providing the mechanism for him to take credit for doing good?

3. Compare the philanthropic activities of Soles 4 Souls and TOMS Shoes.

   Describe the differences and similarities of the two organizations. Which group appears to help more people, from a philanthropic view? Explain your reasoning.

4. Is giving really the driving force behind TOMS shoes, in your opinion? Explain.

5. How do you think TOMS' model may change now that Bain Capital is its partner?

Cases

4

Disney Citizenship: Lending a Mouse Ear to Hear How to Help Society[1]

We believe that our efforts to be a good corporate citizen have a direct impact on our financial strength, as well as our reputation as one of the most trusted and admired companies in the world.[2]

—Jay Rasulo, Senior Executive Vice President and Chief Financial Officer, The Walt Disney Company

In 2014, The Reputation Institute ranked the Walt Disney Corporation third behind Google and Microsoft for their Global CSR Reputation. Disney scored a total ranking of 72, while Google had a ranking of 72.7 and Microsoft had a ranking of 72.1. It was the fourth year in a row that Disney was ranked as a company with one of the highest Global CSR Reputations.[3]

Citizenship Commitment

Disney has established a citizenship framework that focuses on two major components: acting responsibly by conducting its business in an ethical manner and inspiring others by promoting the happiness and well-being of families and children.

"Acting responsibly" is broken down into six areas: ethical conduct, responsible content, environmental stewardship, civic engagement, respectful workplaces, and responsible supply chain. "Inspiring others" is broken down into four areas: live healthier, think creatively, conserve nature, and strengthen communities.[4]

Acting Responsibly

One of the underlying values of Disney is to act responsibly. Disney states that being ethically responsible for its actions not only strengthens its bond with its consumers, but it is an effective recruiting tool to attract and retain exceptional employees. Disney has identified six components related to acting responsibly: ethical conduct, responsible content, environmental stewardship, civic engagement, respectful workplaces, and responsible supply chain.[5]

Ethical Conduct Disney believes that ethical conduct is critical to establishing and maintaining a positive relationship with its customers. If it does not conduct itself in an ethical manner, Disney will lose the authenticity of its communication and interactions with children, families, and society. Disney has established five goals related to ethical conduct: comply with governance policies and practices, disclose relevant citizenship information in a timely manner, encourage employees to be consistent with Disney's Standards of Business Conduct, integrate corporate citizenship in all daily decisions made by Disney managers, and integrate corporate citizenship into the daily conduct of Disney employees. Disney has established a corporate citizenship group that includes the following areas: community engagement, strategic philanthropy, healthy living, and the natural environment. Disney's Integrated Supply Chain Management group's responsibilities include labor standards, product safety, quality, environmental performance, and regulatory compliance.[6]

Responsible Content Disney's goals for developing responsible content include creating age-appropriate entertainment experiences for children; crafting marketing campaigns that consider the positive aspects of the entertainment experience while respecting the needs of the consumers; continuing the ban on cigarette smoking in Disney films; focusing on promoting safety for children, families, and guests; presenting diversity in cultures and backgrounds in Disney's entertainment experiences; giving parents and guardians relevant information on the content of the Disney entertainment experiences; using feedback from parents and guardians to improve the entertainment experience; and recognizing children for their positive contributions to society.[7]

Environmental Stewardship Disney's long-term environmental stewardship goals include zero-net greenhouse gas emissions, zero waste, and the conservation of water resources. In 2014, Disney had reduced its net greenhouse gas emissions by 31% from the levels established in 2012. Disney has established a goal of reducing the 2012 level by 50% by 2020.[8] Disney has also installed a 1-megawatt fuel cell in its Pixar Animation Studios to supplement its electricity use and is also planning to install a fuel cell in its Burbank Studio Lot campus.[9] Disney has a 2020 goal of diverting 60% of its generated waste from landfills and incineration. In 2014, Disney diverted 48% of its waste from landfills and incineration.[10] Disney also has a goal of maintaining the 2013 potable water consumption levels by 2018 and to develop water conservation plans for any new Disney sites.[11]

Civic Engagement Disney's civic engagement goals are to promote the idea of giving through entertainment and to engage with Disney's stakeholders on a regular basis. Disney identifies critical stakeholders as not only investors but also nongovernmental organizations, local communities, families, children, and Disney fans.[12]

Respectful Workplaces Disney's goals related to its workplaces include maintaining safe places to work, developing a workforce that is diverse and is engaging in the global marketplace, supporting the career development of all Disney employees, and encouraging the participation in health and wellness programs by Disney employees and families.[13] Disney has also established a United States Veterans Initiative and a Women's Initiative. Through its Heroes Work Here program, Disney hired 3,800 veterans as of October 31, 2014. Disney also has established programs to provide growth and support to female Disney employees.[14]

Responsible Supply Chain Disney's goals related to having a responsible supply chain include supporting the positive treatment of the labor force producing Disney products. This treatment includes the promotion of a safe, inclusive, and respectful workplace for workers producing Disney products; compliance with policies that support safety and chemicals management in the production of Disney products; and minimization of the negative environmental impact of the production of Disney products.[15]

Inspiring Others

Disney believes that it has a unique opportunity to inspire families and children to take actions that improve their lives and the lives of others. In addition, because children and families trust the Disney brand and develop an emotional bond with Disney, Disney has an obligation to use this strong bond to help improve the world everyone lives in. Disney has separated inspiring others into four components: live healthier, think creatively, conserve nature, and strengthen communities.[16]

Live Healthier In 2006, Disney was the first major media company to create nutrition guidelines for any food products associated with the Disney brand and characters through their media platforms, which included television channels and radio stations. By the end of 2015, Disney's goal is to have 100% of its advertising on food products in compliance with the nutrition guidelines established by Disney. In 2014, 50% of the advertising was in compliance with the nutrition guidelines.[17] Disney is also moving forward with the enhancement of the nutrition level of its licensed food sales. Disney has established a goal that 85% of its globally licensed wholesale food sales must meet its global nutrition guidelines. In 2014, its global wholesale food sales were 71% compliant, while the North American sales had met the global goal of 85%. Disney states that it would not be able to reach 100% compliance because there are certain foods that they produce, such as candy and cakes, that would not comply with the nutrition guidelines. Since 2006, Disney has been able to provide more than 4 billion healthy servings of fruits and vegetables to families.[18]

Disney also established the "Mickey Check" program, an easy way to identify healthy nutritious choices in all of Disney's parks, resorts, and cruise lines. Furthermore, Disney uses storytelling and endorsements from its characters to encourage children and families to try nutritious foods through its TRYit program. The TRYit campaign was able to reach 100 million households weekly in 2014, with 75% of the surveyed children expressing a willingness to make changes in their habits related to their health. Disney also is active in sponsoring programs that helped build more than 50 playgrounds, developed creative ways for children to spend their recess time outside, and helped food banks provide fresh fruit and vegetables.[19]

Think Creatively Disney has partnered with the Boys & Girls Clubs of America to establish a six-week creativity learning program that is targeted at middle school children, to help reduce the level of learning loss during the summer months. This program has been executed by 260 Boys & Girls Clubs and has had 8,500 participants. In addition, Disney has financially supported the Playworks program, which encourages innovative play among children in low-income schools. This program has been established in 44 schools and has had more than 24,000 participants.

Star Wars: Force for Change

> *The Force is an energy field created by all living things. It surrounds us. It penetrates us. It binds the galaxy together.*[20]
>
> —Obi-Wan Kenobi

Taking the words of the Jedi Master to heart, Disney and Lucasfilm sponsored a charitable program to create new and innovative solutions to some of the most difficult global challenges. The first challenge the program addressed was the needs of children in developing countries through UNICEF's Innovation Labs. Disney committed $1 million to support UNICEF programs related to clean water, nutrition, health, and education. As part of the campaign, Disney created a contest during the summer of 2014 for *Star Wars* fans to donate to UNICEF and be eligible to win the chance to be in the *Star Wars: Episode VII* movie. The campaign raised more than $4.2 million for UNICEF. Disney has had a relationship with UNICEF for more than 50 years. In fact, at the 1964 World's Fair, Disney introduced the "It's a Small World" attraction, which was a tribute to UNICEF.[21]

Conserve Nature In 1995, Disney established the Disney Worldwide Conservation Fund (DWCF), which focuses on protecting wildlife and natural habitats and developing sustainable conservation commitments. DWCF focuses on issues such as protecting threatened species and ecosystems and the creation of community conservation and environmental education programs in more than 100 countries globally. In 2014, DWCF contributed more than $25 million to fund more than 150 projects, which supported its long-term environmental commitment to eco-sustainability. Disney also actively promotes the natural environment through its Disney nature films, allowing millions of people to view various species in their natural habitats. Through its theme parks, reports, and its financial support of environmental nonprofit organizations, Disney was able to expose 13.4 million families and children to experiences related to the natural environment in 2014.[22]

Strengthen Communities The VoluntEARS program allows Disney employees to volunteer within their local communities. In 2014, more than 500,000 hours of volunteer service were performed by Disney employees. Volunteer activities included volunteering at a local food bank, helping in the construction of new playgrounds, and working with various nonprofit organizations. Since 2012, a total of 1.7 million volunteer hours have been generated by Disney employees. Disney's goal is to have an accumulated total of 5 million hours by 2020. In 2014, Disney introduced Disney Movie Moments, a program that sends first-run Disney films to more than 45 children's hospitals in the United States. In addition, Disney provides Hospital Care Packages to more than 430 hospitals globally. The children in the hospital receive a care package that contains toys, DVDs, books, Club Penguin memberships, and a Marvel comic book specially designed for hospitalized children. As a result, Disney positively impacted 9.8 million families and children through these various programs in 2014 alone.[23] Disney is also very actively encouraging reading by children. Disney donated 7.1 million books to schools and other educational programs in 2014. From 2012 to 2014, Disney donated a total of 23.1 million books, which was 5.1 million more than its target of 18 million.[24]

The VoluntEARS program provides funding for the "EARS to You" grants. EARS to You grants allow cast members and other Disney employees the opportunity to convert their volunteer actions into a financial contribution to various schools and charities connected with the Disney employees. Disney also has developed a Summer of Service campaign, which presents messages on its television networks encouraging the viewers to become actively involved in supporting their communities. Disney has created Friends for Change, a global community involvement initiative that encourages children and families to develop creative ideas to help their local community. Disney has also established the Disney Heroes Work Here program, which focuses on hiring, training, and supporting United States Armed Forces veterans and provides support to their families. Through activities from pledging online to protect the planet to volunteering in local communities, Disney encouraged families and children to take 3.7 million actions in 2014. Disney's goal is to increase that level to 20 million actions by 2020.[25]

Strategic Philanthropy

In 2014, Disney contributed a total of $315.7 million in philanthropic giving, which included $86.6 million in cash donations, $137.8 million in product donations, and $91.3 million in other types of contributions, including in-kind donations and Public Service Announcements (PSAs).[26]

Questions for Thought

1. Walt Disney's vision and values established the underlying CSR philosophy at Disney. How is Disney able to continue to embrace these values long after his death?

2. Disney claims that having a strong CSR reputation allows it to recruit and retain top-level employees. Do you agree? What characteristics do you look for in a company you want to work for?

3. Disney claims an emotional bond between the consumer and the company, which enhances its interaction with society. Identify an emotional bond you have with Disney.

5

World Food Programme: A Quarter a Day Keeps the Hunger Away

E stablished in 1961 by the United Nations and headquartered in Rome, Italy, the World Food Programme (WFP) is the largest humanitarian organization dedicated to eliminating world hunger.[1] It costs 25 cents to feed one person for a day in the developing world. The WFP's mission is to be the United Nation's link to eliminating poverty with the ultimate goal being the elimination of the need for food aid globally. Furthermore, food aid will help support economic and social development as well as providing immediate needs when emergencies arise.

In 2009, the WFP direct aid brought 4.6 million metric tons of food to 101.8 million people in 75 different countries. More than 1 billion people in the world are food insecure and are hungry on any given day because of the scarcity or high cost of food sources. Of the 101.8 million people receiving aid by the WFP, 84 million were women and children. Women are critical for food aid because they are more likely than men are to use the aid to support the whole family including the children.[2]

The WFP has 30 ships, 70 aircraft, and 5,000 trucks that can be used to facilitate emergency relief needed following natural disasters. In 2009, the budget of the WFP was $4.2 billion. The WFP is slowly shifting away from presenting foreign food for assistance and moving toward giving cash and vouchers so the people in need can support the local farmers and stores with their purchases. In 2009, WFP provided meals in schools for 21 million children and focused on the motto of providing "the right food to the right people at the right time."[3]

In 2010, the WFP was able to obtain food valued at $1.25 billion from 96 countries and purchased 2.6 million metric tons from local suppliers in developing countries. The WFP partners with more than 3,500 nongovernmental organizations (NGOs) in facilitating the distribution of food to those in need.[4]

In 2011, the WFP provided cash and voucher programs in 25 countries and was also developing nontraditional methods such as using debit cards, using vouchers texted to mobile phones, and online systems to aid in the distribution of money needed to buy produce from the local farmers and stores.[5]

In 2013, the WFP gave food assistance to 80.9 million people in 75 countries, which resulted, in part, in the reduction or stabilization of the undernutrition of 7.2 million children under the age of 5. A total of 18.6 million school children received meals in school and/or were given take-home food rations in 2013.

The WFP provided 3.1 million metric tons of food to areas in need. WFP responded to four Level 3 emergencies in Syria, the Philippines, Central African Republic, and South Sudan. A Level 3 emergency is the highest category classified by WFP. A Level 3 emergency requires the mobilization of global and corporate resources because of the severity of the emergency. In 2013, the WFP received $4.38 billion in aid from numerous countries.[6]

WFP Initiatives

One of the WFP's newest initiatives, started in 2009, was a focus on chronic malnutrition. Instead of using the "one size fits all" strategy of providing food rations, the WFP developed customized individual programs to serve the specific nutritional needs in different parts of the world. This was also integrated with its program to enhance the nutritional value of food that is delivered to people in need. Another initiative that was started in 2008, Purchase for Progress (P4P), focused on using WFP's buying power to stimulate production and small farmers in local areas that WFP is serving. In 2009, WFP bought 30,000 metric tons of crops from 80 farming organizations located in 13 countries.[7]

Nutrition

The WFP has a number of initiatives that enrich the nutritional value of the food. By fortifying the food with additional nutrients, the WFP can provide those in need with food that provides high caloric and vitamin intake in a relatively small amount of food. The challenges of this task are enormous. Approximately 200 million children under the age of 5 are stunted or undernourished in developing countries. Furthermore, an additional 130 million are underweight, and an estimated 3.5 million children die each year primarily because they are undernourished. The WFP has developed micronutrient powders that can be added to cooked food to increase the amount of vitamins and minerals in the food. Other examples of nutritionally enhanced food include micronutrient-enriched high-energy biscuits and Supplementary Plumpy, which is similar to peanut butter fortified with minerals, vitamins, and fatty acids, which are all essential to quicken the ability of the child to recover from undernourishment. In Egypt, the WFP has set up a program that enriches all the flour used to make the country's basic bread with iron and folic acid. The result was that in 2009, more that 70% of the flour used for the bread has been enriched from the participation of more than 500 millers in 106 mills.[8]

The 1,000 Days Plus Program

The curse of hunger knows no boundaries. It can start in the womb of the mother. The first 1,000 days are critical in the development of every child. If the child is malnourished during this period, the undernourishment can cause permanent damage to the child's mind and body. A child who is undernourished is more likely to be sick and find it more difficult to concentrate at school. Furthermore, mothers who were undernourished as children are 40% more likely to have children who die before the age of 5. Mothers who do not have enough nutrition run a higher risk of death while delivering a child. This cycle of misery, the intergenerational undernutrition cycle, can be difficult to stop without external aid from organizations such as the WFP. As an incentive to the child and the family, school meals and take home rations help in the growth and development of the child and are incentives for the family to send the child to school. This is especially critical for girls who are usually assigned to do chores at home during school hours. The direct link between education and financial security is indisputable. The WFP estimates that every year of primary school results in an increase of a girl's pay by 10% to 20% and if the girl reaches secondary school, each year adds 15% to 25% to the wages of the girl.[9]

WFP, HIV/AIDS, and TB

One of the great challenges facing people in need in developing countries is if they have a terminal illness such as HIV/AIDS. The lack of food and nutrition can significantly negatively affect the lives of people with HIV/AIDS. By providing food security, the WFP allows these people the opportunity to regain their strength and be able to continue with their productive lives. In addition, it also saves the family members the additional health care costs of the individuals as they battle the disease. Poor people who are treated for HIV/AIDS are usually already at an advanced stage of malnutrition, which compounds the challenge of supporting a successful reentry into the workforce of the infected individual. If an HIV/AIDS patient is malnourished, the mortality rate of the patient during the first months of the antiretroviral treatment is two to six times higher than if the patient has the necessary nourishment. The same challenges take place with patients infected with TB. Furthermore, the effective treatment for these diseases helps these patients survive and continue to be financial providers for their families so that the families do not fall any further in the downward spiral of food insecurity. In 2010, the WFP supported 2.5 million people with HIV/AIDs and TB in 44 countries. WFP support includes programs such as cash or voucher transfers, food aid, and the support of income-generating programs such as gardening that can yield long-term financial benefits for the individual and his or her family.[10]

The Dangers of Providing Food

The WFP faces dangerous situations on a daily basis while distributing food assistance worldwide. In 2009, the WFP had to deal with more than 600 security incidents related to WFP staff or operations. The types of incidents the WFP addressed included intimidation, harassment, detention, theft, kidnapping, and murder. One of the most dramatic incidents occurred in October 2009 when a suicide bomber in Pakistan killed himself and 5 staff members of the WFP. In 2009, 15 staff members were killed, and an additional 35 staff members were injured. The WFP will continue to have to deal with these dangerous situations because WFP is usually one of only a few humanitarian organizations that will provide aid on the front line of military campaigns including civil wars, cross-border wars, and military coups. In addition, the WFP is bound by its commitment to stay as long as possible in any conflict area in which food security is not guaranteed.[11] Furthermore, in February 2015, the WFP

Cases

was alarmed to see photographs of food parcels from the WFP given out in Syria with Islamic State (ISIS) logos pasted over the WFP logo. The WFP relies on local agencies such as the Syrian Arab Red Crescent (SARC) to help distribute the food in Syria. SARC admitted that it had to negotiate with ISIS when it distributes food in areas in Syria controlled by ISIS, but SARC claims it distributes the food itself.[12]

Providing Relief During Natural Disasters

The WFP is one of the first responders to natural disasters such as floods, earthquakes, typhoons, tsunamis, and hurricanes.[13] An area that represented the intersection of civil unrest and natural disaster was the January 2010 earthquake in Haiti. The 7.0 magnitude earthquake nearly destroyed most of the capital city of Port-au-Prince as well as the surrounding infrastructure. The WFP was able to provide more than 2 million people with more than 9,000 metric tons of food within the first 2 weeks after the earthquake. The organization was able to provide immediate relief by distributing food and cash for work projects to help with the recovery of the country. In addition, WFP was able to quickly work with the Haitian government in developing long-term recovery programs, including the establishment of the cash voucher system and the food-enhancing nutritional development program. Because the WFP was already stationed in Haiti, WFP staff members were able to respond quickly, but they were also affected personally. One staff member was killed, and two children of two of the drivers perished in the quake. In total, almost 90% of the staff members living in Haiti had their homes either damaged or destroyed.[14]

Financial Transparency

As the largest humanitarian relief agency in the world, the WFP has many critical stakeholders. Whether it is the people they serve or the organizations that support them (governments, NGOs, corporations, individual donors), the stakeholders expect the WFP to be good stewards of the aid it is providing globally. In June 2009, the WFP successfully implemented the International Public Sector Accounting Standards (IPSAS). IPSAS are global financial reporting and accounting standards developed by the International Federation of Accountants. The 26 standards evaluate the organization's accountability, transparency, internal controls, and organizational governance. The 2008 financial statements have received a clean audit opinion from the external auditors reviewing WFP's financial statements. The financial statements that were reviewed by the auditors included the statement of financial position, the statement of financial performance, the statement of changes in net assets/equity, the statement of cash flows, and the statement that compares budgeted expenditures with actual expenditures.[15]

Project Laser Beam

An example of a program that is based on partnerships with the private sector is Project Laser Beam (PLB). PLB is a $50 million partnership that includes participation from companies, including Kraft Foods, Unilever, and DSM (a Dutch life sciences company), in addressing the issue of child malnutrition. Malnutrition is caused by the lack of nutrients in the food and by contaminated water, poor personal hygiene, poor income levels, and chronic illnesses. It is called Project Laser Beam because the campaign focuses on a specific geographic region to maximize the long-term impact of the program. The focus is on food enrichment and on providing skills to generate income from such activities as farming by providing microfinancing opportunities. In addition, Unilever focuses on how to get clean water in the villages and how to improve personal hygiene through the initiatives such as a hand washing campaign. Unilever also generates revenue by working with Spanish retailers in developing a promotion in which if a customer bought two Unilever products, Unilever would provide a free school meal for a child in Bangladesh or Indonesia. When the promotion was implemented in Germany, the increase in sales of Unilever products resulted in paying for 500,000 school meals.[16] Unilever is investing $10 million in the program and uses its expertise in nutritious foods, personal hygiene, and clean water supply to facilitate the goals of the programs. The goals of the program include improving the nutrition of as many as 500,000 children; being able to provide clean drinking water to many local communities, along with good hygiene conditions and acceptable health care teaching more than 1 million people the benefits of good hygiene in both school and community settings; and improving the standard of living of 3,000 women who are part of the ultra-poor. The effectiveness of the program is based on being able to address the needs of numerous critical stakeholders simultaneously, providing a holistic approach to solving the problem of poor nutrition and developing a new type of public–private partnership that has specific tangible metrics that can be replicated in other countries around the world.[17]

DSM is using its researchers to develop locally grown produce that is rich in nutrients. Kraft is also involved in new product development of inexpensive products that can be sold in food carts and in the development of nutrition programs.[18]

Lessons Learned by the WFP

By constantly being the first responder to emergencies as well as being the largest organization dedicated to reducing hunger, the WFP has learned many lessons from members' past experiences. The first lesson is that innovation is vital for the long-term effectiveness of food aid. Circumstances and conditions are constantly changing, and the WFP must constantly innovate in new ways to approach this ancient problem. The second lesson is that innovation must be designed for the specific needs of the country and citizens. Differences in culture, geography, economic development, infrastructure, governments, and private corporations all play a role in the design of an effective food aid program. The third lesson is that innovation needs champions and leaders and must have a long-term financial commitment. There must be leaders who continue to move forward in addressing the issue of food assistance and ensuring the initiatives will be financially supported in the future. The fourth lesson is that free market systems are a powerful ally in implementing food assistance programs, but they cannot be the only source of innovation. The fifth lesson is that innovation is not a solo commitment but needs strong and progressive partners. The WFP found that partnerships with NGOs and private corporations are very effective in moving WFP's food security initiatives forward. The sixth lesson is that globalization needs to be perceived as both a threat and an opportunity. Although the worldwide challenges addressing hunger issues can be significant, they also need to be perceived as ample opportunities to learn from past experiences as WFP moves to future challenges.[19]

Questions for Thought

1. What should the role of corporations be in helping the WFP's mission? Explain.

2. Identify as many possible stakeholders of the WFP as you can. Comment on each group's involvement with the WFP.

3. Does it take a village to solve problems like hunger? Explain. How effective can organizations such as the WFP be in solving world hunger without the support from other NGOs? Explain.

4. Should issues such as world hunger be on corporate agendas? Explain.

6

Rupert Murdoch and News Corporation: All the News That's Fit to Hack

In November 2005, employees of England's royal family realized that someone was eavesdropping on their voice mail conversations. The communication secretary and the aide to Prince Charles and the private secretary to Princes William and Harry discovered that new voice mail messages left on their phones had already been played and listened to by someone because they were classified as "old" messages. Hundreds of voice mail messages were being heard by unauthorized listeners. Employees of the royal family were able to quickly narrow down the source of the privacy violation when the *News of the World*, a highly sensational British tabloid newspaper owned by Rupert Murdoch, published a story about Prince William hurting his knee. Prince William had told only a very small group of friends this information, making the newspaper the probable source of revealing the information.[1]

The royal family asked the police to investigate the phone hacking. In January 2006, Scotland Yard verified that the *News of the World* was indeed the party involved in hacking into the royal family's phones. The two principal people identified as the hackers were reporter Clive Goodman and private investigator Glenn Mulcaire. The two men had obtained the personal identification numbers (PINs) required to access the voice mail accounts of the royal family. The *News of the World* published voice mail messages verbatim that were hacked from royals' phones. The Queen and Prince Charles are not frequent cell phone users, so the hacking threat was limited to other royal family members.[2] On August 6, 2006, the British police arrested three people involved in intercepting phone calls and messages to Clarence House, Prince Charles's residence. The arrests were the result of a 7-month investigation by the police that had determined "public figures beyond the royal household have had their telephones intercepted which may have potential security implications."[3] Goodman pleaded guilty to conspiracy to intercept telephone calls "without lawful authority" and was sentenced to 4 months in prison. Mulcaire was also convicted of hacking phone messages while working as a consultant to the *News of the World* and was sentenced to 6 months in prison.[4] The editor of the

News of the World, Andy Coulson, resigned from his position after accepting responsibility for the hacking that occurred during his tenure.[5]

A major concern over the episode was that Scotland Yard was zealous in getting a conviction on hacking related to the royals, yet officers did not seem interested in pursuing leads on hacking that took place on phones not owned by the royal family. In fact, Scotland Yard was accused of not following up on many leads that would have led to a more comprehensive investigation of the role the *News of the World* and other newspapers had in hacking phones to get information. In 2006, the police had taken files belonging to Mulcaire that had a listing of thousands of mobile phone numbers and 91 mobile phone PIN codes used to get access to the victims' voice mail accounts. Critics of Scotland Yard stated that the police have a very strong positive relationship with *News of the World* and did not want to put that relationship in jeopardy by investigating the *News of the World's* involvement in hacking mobile phones. The police were able to get information from *News of the World* reporters about potential leads for high-profile arrests, and the *News of the World* wrote highly favorable stories about the police based on their leads to the police. The response by Scotland Yard to these criticisms was that officers' duties do not include the monitoring of the activities of the media. In addition, Scotland Yard had more important investigations to work on instead of moving forward on the phone hacking investigation.[6] However, Scotland Yard did release the names of some non-royals whose phones had been hacked. This led to lawsuits by the victims, and Scotland Yard could no longer control the level of the investigation because the plaintiff lawyers were demanding evidence obtained by Scotland Yard. This created a financial windfall for those names that were identified by Scotland Yard. As one plaintiff lawyer stated, "Getting a letter from Scotland Yard that your phone has been hacked is rather like getting a Willy Wonka golden ticket . . . Time to queue up at Murdoch Towers to get paid."[7]

News of the World

Murdoch bought *News of the World* in 1969, and its circulation in 2012 was 2.9 million readers, which is down from a high 10 years ago of 4 million readers. The culture at *News of the World* was a "take no prisoner" and "do what you have to do" attitude toward getting information that would lead to a good story. Coulson, the editor of the *News of the World*, was allegedly aware that the reporters were actively hacking into phones to get good leads. The hacking was usually a very simple process. In fact, when reporters were asked the origin of the information at staff meetings that included Coulson, the answer would be "We've pulled the phone records . . . [and/or] . . . I've listened to the phone messages."[8]

Most mobile phone companies will assign a generic password as the default PIN number to a phone for voice mail such as 1111 or 4444. Many users never change the default pin number, and as a result, the reporters and private investigators only need the person's phone number to hack into the phone. A common method of obtaining the voice messages is to make two phone calls simultaneously to the targeted phone. The first phone will lock up the phone line, and the second phone will be automatically sent to voice mail. The reporter then presses the PIN number to retrieve the messages and sometimes even deletes them to block any competing newspapers from also having access to the same voice mail messages.

After Coulson resigned from the *News of the World*, he was hired by the Conservative Party as the head of its communication team. The position is known in the media as the "chief spin doctor," whose job is to put a positive light on any information pertaining to the Conservative Party. This was a critical appointment for the party because Coulson had strong ties to the Murdoch empire and the Conservative party was trying to regain Murdoch's support, which had shifted to the Labour Party for Prime Minister Tony Blair and subsequently Prime Minister Gordon Brown.[9]

The leader of the Conservative Party is David Cameron. When Cameron won the general election and became prime minister on May 11, 2011, he promoted Coulson to be the top communication advisor in the prime minister's office. One of the objectives Murdoch wanted from the British government if Cameron were elected was to reduce the financial support for the British Broadcasting Corporation (BBC). The BBC was a major competitor for Murdoch's media empire, and it was one of the strongest critics of Murdoch's operations. Within a week of the election, Murdoch was invited to the prime minister's residence at 10 Downing Street for a private meeting with the newly elected prime minister. Two months later, the British government announced that it was going to review the expenses and budgets at the BBC because the government was concerned about the extraordinary level of waste that was occurring using taxpayer's money.[10]

The Murdoch Empire

In addition to the *News of the World*, Murdoch also owns *The Sun, The Times of London, The Sunday Times, The Wall Street Journal, The New York Post*, 20th Century Fox, Fox News, and Fox Broadcasting. Murdoch uses his newspapers as a vehicle to promote his pro conservative, pro-business viewpoint. During the 1970s, Murdoch supported Margaret Thatcher and helped secure her election as prime minister. He did the same again for Tony Blair when Murdoch switched alliances and supported Blair's Labour Party.[11] Murdoch's power was demonstrated when the singer Charlotte Church testified in a British inquiry on the ethics of the media. During her testimony, Church stated that she waived her performance fee of more than $154,000 to sing at Rupert Murdoch's wedding in return for a guarantee that she would get favorable coverage in Murdoch's newspapers. She told the inquiry that Murdoch had specifically requested her and that her management thought that it would be a great career move to offer her services for free. Murdoch had asked her to sing a requiem, which Church had pointed out to Murdoch was a funeral song. Church also testified that she did not receive the promised favorable press, and she thought she was being attacked on purpose by Murdoch's newspapers.[12]

James Murdoch, an Heir Apparent No More

James Murdoch had been groomed from an early age to eventually take over the Murdoch empire. James, one of three children of Rupert, was not the original heir apparent. Lachlan, the oldest son was originally groomed to take over the empire, but he quit in 2005 when he disagreed with other News Corporation (News Corp) executives over the strategic direction of the company and his father supported the executives rather than his son. James's sister, Elizabeth, left News Corp in 2000 so she could start her own production company. Elizabeth rejoined News Corp in 2011 when Rupert bought her production company, Shine, and thought she would eventually run News Corp's television companies. That path was evidently not what Elizabeth wanted because she refused to become a board member at News Corp. Therefore, more by default than by first choice, James was the only child left Rupert could groom to take over News Corp. James dropped out of Harvard to start his hip-hop label, Rawkus Entertainment. News Corp bought Rawkus in 1996, effectively letting James become part of the company. From 1996 to 2000, James was the vice president of music and new media for News Corp, and from 2000 to 2003, he was the CEO of Star TV, which focused on Asian markets. From 2003 to 2007, he was the CEO of British Sky Broadcasting (BSkyB) and was promoted in 2007 to CEO of Europe and Asia for News Corp. In 2011, he became the deputy chief operating officer (COO) at News Corp and eventually became the CEO of News International.[13] In December 2011, a British parliamentary committee saw e-mail messages from 2008 that James read and responded to that refer to "a nightmare scenario" of legal issues over hacking at the *News of the World*. This was a direct contradiction to James's previous testimony in which he stated he was not aware of the hacking activities that were occurring in 2008. The e-mails proved that James knew there was more than one "rogue" reporter involved in the phone hacking at *News of the World*.[14] Furthermore, former *News of the World* editor Colin Myler testified that James knew that payouts to hacking victims were to buy their silence to make sure the hacking scandal did not go public.[15]

On February 1, 2012, it was disclosed that the e-mail proving James Murdoch knew about the hacking at *News of the World* was deleted from his computer on January 15, 2011. The official explanation was that the deletion was part of an "e-mail stabilization and modernization program." The police inquiry into the phone hacking activities at *News of the World* started on January 26, 2011.[16] On February 29, 2012, James Murdoch resigned as CEO of News International to focus on News Corp's international television properties. He retained his title as deputy COO.[17] On April 3, 2012, James Murdoch resigned as chairman of BSkyB Group, but maintained a seat on the board of directors.[18]

The Involvement of the Police

On July 11, 2011, it was reported that employees of two of Murdoch's newspapers bribed police officers to obtain information pertaining to Queen Elizabeth II and former prime minister Gordon Brown. In addition, police were bribed so that *News of the World* could obtain locations of interest by using the police's restricted cell phone–tracking technology. The allegations included employees from two additional newspapers, *The Sun* and the high-end *The Sunday Times*. Evidence was found through e-mails that *News of the World* paid $1,600 to a royal protection officer who is eligible to be assigned to a royal palace for information about members of the royal family. The information obtained by the officer included the "Green Book," which has detailed information pertaining to the royal family including phone numbers and the day-to-day activities of the members of the royal family.[19] On July 17, 2011, the head of Scotland Yard (also called the Metropolitan Police Service), Sir Paul Stephenson, resigned from his position. He decided to step down because of the ongoing accusations and speculation that was taking place between the police and Scotland Yard. It was reported that Sir Paul had met with News International executives 18 times for meals during the phone hacking investigation. In addition, two more arrests took place. The former deputy editor of the *News of the World*, Neil Wallis, was arrested for his part in the hacking scandal. Wallis was serving as a public relations consultant for the police. In addition, Rebekah Brooks was arrested on suspicion of illegally gaining access to phone calls and for allegedly bribing the police.[20]

The Horrible Consequences of Hacking for One Family

A 13-year-old British school girl, Milly Dowler, had gone missing in 2002, and her body was found 6 months later. In the period before her body was found, *News of the World* reporters had hacked into her cell phone and listened to voice messages. They then deleted voice messages because the memory was full on the phone, in hopes that if any new messages were sent they could hear them. The result was that the family falsely believed that she was still alive because her messages had been deleted from her voice mail. The enormity of the crime is matched only by the time of the crime. *News of the World* had claimed that only a rogue reporter, Goodman, was involved in hacking in late 2005, yet this hacking occurred in 2002. The editor of the *News of the World* in 2002 was Brooks, who by 2011 was the CEO of News International, the British newspaper division of News Corp. In her response to the allegation that she knew about the hacking, she stated that she knew nothing about it and would never support such actions.[21] In September 2011, News Corp announced it would pay approximately 3 million pounds or $4.8 million for the hacking of Milly Dowler's phone. Approximately $3.2 million would go to the Dowler family and $1.6 million would go to a charity of the Dowlers's choosing.[22]

The Tangled Web That Was Woven

In July 2009, Myler, editor of the *News of the World*, told a British parliamentary committee that Rupert Murdoch's son, James Murdoch, approved the payment of $1.1 million to settle allegations of phone hacking related to the head of the Professional Footballers' [Soccer] Association, Gordon Taylor. In a meeting consisting of Murdoch, Myler, and the company lawyer, Tom Crone, it was agreed that the payment was needed to shut down any leaks about *News of the* World's usage of hacking to get information for stories. Rupert Murdoch denied that he had any knowledge of the payment made to Taylor.[23]

The *News of the World* announced it would cease operations on July 10, 2011, after publishing for 168 years. The ramifications were felt everywhere. Advertisers for the *News of the World*—including Ford, Mitsubishi, Lloyds Bank, and Virgin Holidays— had started pulling out ads. Former editor Coulson was forced to resign as communication director for the prime minister in January 2011 for his role in the hacking scandal. Another former editor and now CEO of News International, Brooks, was under intense pressure to resign after the allegations of the Dowler phone hacking and the newest allegations that *News of the World* had hacked into phones of family members of dead soldiers. The biggest concern for Rupert Murdoch was the potential takeover of the satellite television network BSkyB. News Corp owns 39% and wanted to have a controlling interest. Based on the actions of Murdoch's employees, the deal might

Cases

not be completed.[24] On July 7, 2011, Coulson was arrested for conspiracy in the phone hacking of his employees and for corruption for payments *News of the World* made to police officers in exchange for confidential information. The British government also announced it was going to review the proposal by News Corp to acquire a controlling interest in BSkyB.[25]

On July 14, 2011, because of intense pressure from the media and the British government, News Corp withdrew its proposal to buy a controlling interest in BSkyB. The announcement came hours before Cameron's party was going to submit a motion in parliament to stop the acquisition.[26] The following day, Brooks resigned from her position as CEO of News International. Brooks was under constant pressure after it was disclosed that she was the editor of *News of the World* during the Milly Dowler phone hacking scandal. On that same day, Rupert Murdoch met with Dowler's family and apologized for the actions of his newspaper.[27] A few hours later, Les Hinton resigned as CEO of Dow Jones & Company, the publishers of the *Wall Street Journal.* He was the CEO of News International from 1997 to 2005. It could be expected that, like Brooks, Hinton knew the *News of the World* was using hacking techniques during his tenure as chief of the British publications. Hinton had worked with Murdoch for 52 years, and Murdoch defended Hinton, stating he was not part of the hacking scandal. Hinton had misled two British parliamentary committees in 2007 and 2009 when he stated that *News of the World* did an internal investigation and found only one rogue reporter implementing hacking techniques to get information.[28] On July 20, 2011, Murdoch told a British parliamentary committee that he was sorry for the victims of the hacking but that he was not aware that this activity was going on in his company. He testified that he had trusted the people below him to use their best judgment when making decisions about obtaining information for his newspapers. While calling it the most humble day in his life, he did not take personal responsibility for the immense suffering his newspapers have inflected on its victims. He also said he may have "lost sight" of the *News of the World* because it had become such a small part of his global media empire.[29]

In January 2012, News Corp agreed to pay damages of more than $1 million to 37 victims of phone hacking. Sarah Lyall and Ravi Somaiya estimated that—similar to the boy trying to plug the hole in the dike with his finger —more than 800 victims of phone hacking could file for damages.[30] On January 30, 2012, police arrested four current and former employees of *The Sun* for allegedly bribing police officers[31] and on February 11, 2012, an additional five senior journalists at *The Sun* were arrested for bribery.[32] By February 2012, estimated costs to News Corp for the phone hacking scandal were almost $200 million.[33] News Corp is headquartered in the United States, so the company must abide by the Foreign Corrupt Practices Act, and the Federal Bureau of Investigation (FBI), the Department of Justice (DOJ), and the Securities and Exchange Commission all started investigations of News Corp's using bribes to get information.[34] On February 24, 2012, it was revealed that the e-mail archives from *News of the World* had been deleted from September 2007 and earlier. This deletion occurred despite warnings from lawyers that were working to sue *News of the World* that the news group should not destroy potential evidence. Millions of e-mails were deleted. News International stated that this deletion process was consistent with its e-mail deletion policy that was established in November 2009.[35]

On May 15, 2012, Rebekah Brooks was charged with three counts of conspiring to obstruct justice. The charges state that Rebekah Brooks concealed information from police, removed seven boxes of material from the News International archive, and concealed documents, computers, and other electronic equipment from police.[36] On July 24, 2012, Rebekah Brooks and former editor Andy Coulson were charged with conspiring to hack the voice mail of more than 600 people. Andy Coulson was the former chief communications aide to Prime Minister David Cameron. Rebekah Brooks was charged with three counts of phone hacking, and Andy Coulson was charged with five counts of phone hacking related to Milly Dowler's phone. Also charged with phone hacking were former *News of the World* managing editor Stuart Kutter, former chief reporter Neville Thurlbeck, and former news editors Ian Edmonson, Greg Miskiw, and James Weatherup. They had also been charged with conspiring to obstruct justice along with Rebekah Brooks in May 2012.[37] On October 30, 2012, prosecutors announced that Neville Thurlbeck, Greg Miskiw, and James Weatherup had pleaded guilty to a conspiracy to hack phones.[38] On June 24, 2014, a British jury acquitted Rebekah Brooks of all charges but found Andy Coulson guilty of illegally intercepting voice mail messages. The prosecutors had presented e-mail from Andy Coulson, which discussed and approved phone hacking, but they did not provide the same evidence from Rebekah Brooks. News Corp had stated that it had already spent $454 million in expenses related to the phone hacking issues.[39] On July 4, 2014, Andy Coulson was sentenced to 18 months in jail for his role in the phone hacking scandal.[40] On October 3, 2014, former News Corp editor Ian Edmondson pleaded guilty to illegally hacking voice mail messages from 2000 to 2006.[41] On February 2, 2015, The DOJ decided not to prosecute News Corp for its phone hacking actions. The DOJ had reviewed thousands of e-mails searching, in part, for potential violations of the United States Foreign Corrupt Practices Act.[42]

Questions for Thought

1. Is it likely that Rupert Murdoch did lose sight of the operations at *News of the World* because his empire had gotten so large? Explain.

2. Is phone hacking ever acceptable? Explain.

3. Are practices such as phone hacking used frequently in the media industry? Do you agree that this is always an unethical practice in this industry? Explain.

7

Enron: Were They the Crookedest Guys in the Room?

The Rise of the Big "E"

In May 1985, InterNorth Incorporated and Houston Natural Gas announced that they would merge. Their combined value was an estimated $2.3 billion. These firms were two of the largest gas pipeline companies in the United States. As part of the negotiations, the chairman and CEO of InterNorth, Sam Segnar, would be the head of the new entity until January 1, 1987, when the chairman and CEO of Houston Natural Gas, Kenneth Lay, would take over. The new company was initially called HNG/InterNorth and later was renamed Enron.[1] Lay's first choice for the new name of the company was "Enteron," but that was scrapped just days before it was announced to the public when Lay learned that *enteron* was the name for the digestive tract.

In 1990, Lay created a division of Enron called Enron Finance Corporation and hired Jeffrey Skilling to run the company. Skilling had been an accounting consultant to Enron through the firm of McKinsey & Company. Lay was so impressed with the accounting systems that Skilling developed for Enron that he custom-tailored the lead position at Enron Finance Corporation for him.[2]

By 1995, Enron had become the largest independent natural gas company in the United States. In 1996, Andrew Fastow, Enron's chief financial officer and one of the key players in Enron's downfall, was almost fired from Enron when he did an unsatisfactory job of managing a retail unit of Enron that competed against local utilities in different parts of the United States. But Fastow used his connections within Enron to keep his job and return to the finance department.[3]

In 1997, Skilling became president and chief operating officer of Enron. Fastow was in charge of the complex transfer of debt from Enron's balance sheet to two LJM partnerships, which Skilling and Enron's board of directors encouraged Fastow to form in 1999 and operate under his own name, so Enron could conduct transactions off its books and avoid reporting losses.[4] Fastow appeared obsessed with the accumulation of wealth and considered it the only true measure of success in the business world. His obsession was ironic because Fastow's wife, Lea, was an heiress to a real estate fortune in Houston. However, that did not dampen his desire to accumulate the $30 million he made related to the off–balance sheet partnerships and the $23 million he received for selling Enron stock in 1999 and 2000. During a congressional inquiry, Congressman James Greenwood of Pennsylvania called Fastow the "Betty Crocker of cooked books."[5]

Enron's strategic focus was to convince customers and the federal government that deregulation of the energy industry would result in more choices by customers and a more competitive marketplace, and to generate the same brand recognition as AT&T. The company took a number of measures to ensure the success of this strategy, including purchasing advertising time during the Super Bowl XXXI telecast in 1997, and reinforcing Enron's already strong personal relationship with the then governor of Texas and future president of the United States George W. Bush, whose family was a big player in the oil business.[6]

In July 2000, Enron released its code of ethics policies to its employees. The 63-page document, with two additional blank pages for notes, highlighted Enron's ethical commitment by top management. The foreword from this document written by Lay is shown in Table 1.

In October 2000, Jordan Mintz, a lawyer, was transferred from his position as vice president for tax at Enron North America to the position of vice president and general counsel for Enron Global Finance, which was the division run by Fastow. As soon as he started reviewing the documents pertaining to the agreements between Fastow's partnerships and Enron, Mintz was immediately troubled. He discovered

---

TABLE 1 ● Foreword From Enron's Code of Ethics Manual

As officers and employees of Enron Corp., its subsidiaries, and its affiliated companies, we are responsible for conducting the business affairs of the companies in accordance with all applicable laws and in a moral and honest manner.

To be sure that we understand what is expected of us, Enron has adopted certain policies, with the approval of the Board of Directors, which are set forth in this booklet. I ask that you read them carefully and completely and that, as you do, you reflect on your past actions to make certain that you have complied with the policies. It is absolutely essential that you fully comply with these policies in the future. If you have any questions, talk them over with your supervisor, manager, or Enron legal counsel.

We want to be proud of Enron and to know that it enjoys a reputation for fairness and honesty and that it is respected. Gaining such respect is one aim of our advertising and public relations activities, but no matter how effective they may be, Enron's reputation finally depends on its people, on you and me. Let's keep that reputation high.

July 1, 2000

Kenneth L. Lay

Chairman and Chief

Executive Officer

Source: http://www.smokinggun.com.

that Fastow was representing his own partnership as a negotiator, and that his subordinates were representing Enron in the deals. He also noticed that the approval sheets for deal transactions had not been signed by Skilling, even though there was a space on the documents for Skilling's signature. When Mintz went to Richard Causey, Enron's chief accounting officer, Causey's advice to Mintz was not to stick his neck out to investigate the details of the transactions.[7] Fastow did not sever the potential conflict-of-interest ties with the partnerships until July 2001.[8]

From 1998 to 2000, the total compensation paid to the top 200 executives at Enron went from $193 million to $1.4 billion. The top three Enron executives went from tens of millions in 1998 to each of the three earning more than $100 million by 2000.[9]

The Rank and Yank Culture at Enron

There was a simple understanding at Enron. The company believed it could get the best and brightest employees and pay them the most in the industry, but if they did not perform they would be fired. Skilling established a performance review committee to evaluate Enron's employees. It quickly got a reputation for being the toughest employee ranking system of any company in the United States. Although the official components of an employee's evaluation were based on respect, integrity, communication, and excellence, the employees quickly learned that the only performance measure that mattered in the evaluation was their contribution to Enron's profitability. Each employee's performance was compared with others' to generate an overall ranking. The top 5% were given a ranking as superior, the next 30% were ranked as excellent, and the next 30% were ranked as strong. The bottom two categories were satisfactory (20%) and needs improvement (15%), respectively. These evaluations occurred every 6 months, and anyone who did not move from the needs improvement category to one of the higher categories was fired. As a result, the culture at Enron became fiercely competitive and secretive, with each employee looking out for his or her own performance without regard to helping colleagues improve their performance.[10,11]

The Beginning of the End

In March 2001, the first crack in Enron's armor occurred when Bethany McLean from *Fortune Magazine* wrote an article titled "Is Enron Overpriced?" In the article, McLean questioned how it was possible for Enron's stock to trade at 55 times its earnings, two and a half times greater than one of Enron's chief competitors, Duke Power. She also questioned how Enron's stock could have more than doubled to $126, as forecast by Enron's top management. The core of her questions was a simple one: How does Enron make its money? She was unable to develop a clear picture of the revenue and cash flow streams at work at Enron, and when she asked Enron for more detailed information than was released to the public, Enron declined for proprietary reasons. The confusion about revenue generation was based on Enron's shifting its strategic focus over time. In the beginning of the 1990s, approximately 80% of Enron's revenue came from the traditional gas pipeline business. During the 1990s, Enron sold its iron and steel assets that were related to the gas pipeline business, and by 2000, 95% of Enron's sales and 80% of its operating profits were generated from the business Enron labeled as "wholesale energy operations and services." This business sector was described by Enron as the "financialization of energy," which McLean restated as the trading through buying and selling of energy. The lack of details on Enron's operations frustrated Wall Street analysts who were evaluating Enron's bonds and stock, as well as Enron's competitors, who could not understand how Enron always did better than the competitors when it came to financial performance.[12]

A key component of the contracts between the off–balance sheet partnerships and Enron was that the deals were financed by Enron stock. As a result, top management's only goal was to keep the stock price at high levels. In addition, the contracts with the partnerships had provisions called *triggers*. A trigger refers to the price of the Enron stock. If the Enron stock fell below certain trigger points, the losses and debt from the partnerships would have to be transferred to Enron's balance sheet. The contracts had trigger prices such as $57.78, $47.00, and $28.00 per share, which were not a threat when Enron's stock was at a high of $90.00 a share. However, as the stock price fell, there was increased pressure on Enron management and its accountants to do whatever they could to keep the stock price higher than the trigger points. One set of deals, made with four Fastow partnerships called the Raptors, would result in a loss of more than $500 million if the deals were transferred to the Enron books when the trigger point was met. Enron was facing an end-of-March quarterly closing of its books, which would have to absorb a $504 million loss from the Raptor dealings. It was resolved when an Enron accountant used several complex transactions to be able to refinance the Raptor transactions on March 26, 2001. Two weeks later, Enron reported its quarterly financial results, which included $425 million in earnings.[13] In an analyst's conference call on April 17, 2001, Skilling was upbeat because of the announced level of quarterly profits. There were no comments by Enron pertaining to the Raptors, which was considered the most important transaction of the quarter. One of the analysts, Richard Grubman, from Highfields Capital Management asked why Enron released only its profit figures and not its balance sheet information. Skilling's response was that it was not Enron's policy to release that information. Grubman responded that Enron was the only company that he monitored that did not release its balance sheet or statement of cash flows. Skilling's response was to say thank you very much and that Enron appreciated it. Grubman said thank you, and Skilling responded under his breath, "Thank you, a**hole."[14]

On June 12, 2001, Skilling was a featured speaker at the Strategic Directions technology conference. There he claimed that the Internet allowed Enron to implement all its strategic focuses. In addition, a question from the audience asked Skilling what his views were about the California power crisis. He responded with a joke in which he said the only difference between California and the *Titanic* was that the *Titanic* went down with its lights on. Less than 2 weeks later, a protestor hit Skilling with a cream pie when he visited California.[15]

On August 14, 2001, Skilling resigned as Enron's CEO and president. Skilling had taken over from Lay as CEO in January 2001, and Lay regained his title of CEO, which he had held for 15 years in addition to being the chairman of the board. As CEO, Lay had increased Enron's market capitalization from $2 billion to $70 billion with revenues of more than $100 billion in 2000.[16]

Skilling stated personal reasons as the explanation for his quick departure, although Enron stock had dropped by almost half in the 8 months during Skilling's reign as CEO. In response to Skilling's resignation, Lay stated that no accounting, trading, or reserve issues were related to Skilling's decision and that Enron was in the strongest financial shape in its history.[17]

The Role of Mark-to-Market Accounting

During the mid-1990s, Enron had adopted another one of its many controversial strategies, mark-to-market accounting. Mark-to-market accounting is based on the accounting procedure of recognizing the fair market value of long-term, outstanding, energy-related contracts. The challenge to recognizing the fair market value in the energy industry is that there are usually no sources from which to obtain a quoted price so an accurate evaluation can be calculated. As a result, energy companies such as Enron were allowed to determine their own valuation method to be used to calculate the fair market price.[18] Enron booked the full amount of the revenue from a 10-year contract immediately because there was no restriction on how to calculate the fair market value. Therefore, Enron was able to "control" its income levels for any given year through the manipulation of revenue recognition of its long-term energy contracts. Enron did disclose in a footnote in its 2000 annual report that managerial judgment is needed to estimate the fair market value of the long-term contracts. The aggressive use of mark-to-market accounting was one of the concerns that Sherron Watkins raised in her infamous letter to Lay.[19]

The Letter

After Skilling resigned as CEO, Lay asked employees to write to him if they had any concerns. He got more than he bargained for when a seven-page anonymous letter started with the simple question of whether Enron had become too risky to work for. The author of the letter revealed herself to Lay later. Sherron Watkins was an accountant who had worked for Enron for 8 years until she was laid off in 2000, only to be rehired in June 2001 to work for Fastow. Watkins wrote that Skilling's quick departure as CEO would raise questions and concerns about Enron's accounting practices. In addition, she went into great detail about her concerns about the Fastow partnerships that were playing a significantly larger role in Enron's operations. Watkins pointed out the transactions were based on a strong Enron stock price, which increased the level of risk as the stock price started to decrease. She also stated that to the layperson, it appears that the sole purpose of these partnerships was to hide losses for Enron for which the partners would be rewarded with future Enron stock. She also revealed her fear that Enron would implode via a series of accounting scandals and that Enron workers, herself included, would have no credibility if they had to find jobs if Enron went bankrupt. She warned that the legacy of Enron would be nothing more than an elaborate accounting hoax if corrections were not made. She said that the real reason Skilling resigned was that he saw that these transactions would be unfixable in the future. She continued by asking Lay whether there was a way "our accounting gurus" could reverse those deals and finished the letter asking whether Lay and chief accounting officer Causey could review the partnerships for 2002 and 2003.[20]

Lay showed the letter to Enron's general counsel, James Derrick, who recommended that the concerns be investigated. After Watkins identified herself to Lay, the investigation of the issues was done by the law firm of Vinson & Elkins. Lay met with Watkins on August 22, 2001, to discuss the issues raised in her letter. On September 21, 2001, Vinson & Elkins reported its findings to Lay and Derrick. The law firm concluded that there was no reason to be concerned about the transactions and that it would provide a written report in the following weeks outlining its conclusions. On October 15, 2001, Vinson & Elkins presented its written report to Enron. The law firm's cursory investigation and findings "appear[ed] worthy of Inspector Clouseau," according to Dan Ackman in his *Forbes.com* article, "Enron's Lawyers: Eyes Wide Shut?"[21] The following day, Enron announced that the partnerships with Fastow had generated a $35 million loss for Enron, which needed to be recognized on Enron's books. By October 22, 2001, the price of Enron stock had fallen to $20 per share, and the employees were locked out of selling their stock because of a shift in the administration of Enron's retirement plans. As a result, many employees lost all of their retirement savings.[22]

On October 16, 2001, Enron announced a third-quarter loss of $618 million based, in part, on the write-down of different investments, which included the limited partnerships between Enron and Enron's CFO, Fastow. A charge of $35 million was applied against the third-quarter results based on the early termination of some specific finance arrangements between Enron and Fastow's partnerships, LJM Cayman L.P. and LJM2 Co-Investment L.P. Other write-downs included the retail power business, broadband telecommunications, and other technology investments.[23] On October 24, 2001, Fastow was forced to resign as CFO of Enron after the Securities and Exchange Commission (SEC) stated that it was going to investigate the financial reporting at Enron, including a $1.2 billion write-down on shareholders' equity based on the partnership deals between Fastow and Enron. The write-down occurred when Enron wrote off a promissory note that had been on the books, but the transaction related to the note was not visible in Enron's quarterly financial results.[24] Investors raised concerns about the write-off because of the transaction's lack of visibility in the financial statements and raised questions about whether Enron was hiding other off–balance sheet transactions that could negatively affect Enron's financial performance.

Fastow was replaced by Jeffrey McMahon in October 2001. He had been Enron's treasurer but stepped down from that position in 2000 when he raised concerns about Fastow's partnerships as they related to Enron's financial operations. After leaving the treasurer position, McMahon became the head of Enron's industrial-markets division. After Enron's fall, McMahon was not charged with any crimes but was ordered to pay $300,000 to settle civil allegations.[25]

By the end of October 2001, the questions continued to mount about Enron's operations. Some critics asked how the deregulation that Enron had touted as the American way could result in the state of California having to deal with soaring energy costs and frequent blackouts during 2001. Additional questions were raised about Enron's broadband operations and how Enron would be able to make a profit on the venture. Furthermore, investors were asking why Enron was releasing public statements that it did not have enough cash to survive when it had reported such high levels of profitability. The stock price had fallen 80% from January to October 2001, which resulted in a decrease of $50 million in market capitalization. Enron's stock price closed at $15.40 on October 26, 2001.[26]

By November 2001, Enron's off–balance sheet transactions may have hidden billions of dollars in debt and Enron's profit may have been misstated for many years. When Lay was asked about the details pertaining to the off–balance sheet transactions involving Fastow, his response was that he could not give the details and that the transactions were way over his head. In trying to salvage some value for the company, Lay tried to negotiate selling Enron to one of its competitors, Dynegy. Dynegy initially agreed to buy Enron on November 9, 2001, but less than 3 weeks later on November 28, 2001, Dynegy had enough concerns about Enron's operations and financial stability to stop all negotiations.[27] Dynegy had initially agreed to pay Enron $9 billion and assume $13 billion in debt to take over the company but walked away from the deal when Enron released more information that raised concerns about the long-term financial viability of the company. From a high of $90 per share in August 2000, Enron stock closed at 61¢ on November 28, 2001.[28]

To Chapter 11 and Beyond

On December 2, 2001, the seventh-largest company in the United States, Enron, filed for Chapter 11 bankruptcy. With assets of just less than $50 billion, it was the largest bankruptcy filing in U.S. history. The previous largest bankruptcy filing was Texaco in 1987 when the oil company had $36 billion in assets. The complexity of the filing was shown when Enron provided a combined list of creditors that was 54 pages long. At the time of the filing, Enron had $13.15 billion in debt on its balance sheets but also had an additional $27 billion in debt based on off–balance sheet transactions. On the same day, Enron filed a $10 billion lawsuit against Dynegy for breach of contract for not fulfilling the purchase of Enron.[29] More than 6,000 employees lost their jobs when Enron filed for bankruptcy. On December 12, Congress began its investigation into the reasons Enron collapsed. On January 10, 2002, the Department of Justice (DOJ) announced that it would start a criminal probe of Enron, and on January 22, 2002, the Federal Bureau of Investigation (FBI) searched Enron's headquarters in Houston for evidence. On January 23, 2002, Lay resigned as CEO of Enron but kept his position on Enron's board of directors.

On January 25, 2002, the first fatal tragedy occurred when former Enron vice chairman Clifford Baxter committed suicide in his car in a suburb of Houston. Baxter was found dead in his 2002 Mercedes-Benz with a gunshot wound to his head. Baxter had made an estimated $22 million from 1998 to 2001 when he was with Enron but became unhappy with the direction of the company's business dealings and resigned his position in May 2001. He stayed on as a consultant for Enron. Baxter had been informed that criminal investigators wanted to interview him about his knowledge pertaining to Enron's operations. Before he became vice chairman, Baxter was the CEO of Enron's North American division and later the chief strategy officer for Enron. In her infamous letter to Lay, Watkins stated that Baxter had complained to Skilling about how the limited partnerships were inappropriate.[30]

Lay resigned from his board position on February 4, 2002, one day before the U.S. Senate panel subpoenaed Lay to testify in the congressional investigation of Enron. On February 7, 2002, Fastow and Skilling both refused to answer questions related to Enron during congressional hearings. On February 12, 2002, Lay followed suit by citing his protection under the Fifth Amendment and refused to testify before Congress.

As a direct result of the accounting scandals that occurred at WorldCom, a global telecommunications company that declared bankruptcy in 2002, and Enron, President Bush signed into law the Sarbanes-Oxley Act on July 30, 2002. The act required publicly traded firms to abide by a number of new corporate governance requirements or face severe penalties and potential prison time for the executives involved in the firm's decisions.

The Role of the Board of Directors

In the October 2000 issue of *Chief Executive Magazine*, Enron was ranked as having one of the top five boards of directors in the United States. The criteria that the magazine used to determine the best board of directors were those boards that work in harmony with the CEO and that are respected in the community and industry for their activities. In addition, each of the five best boards makes an "extra effort" to accomplish good corporate governance, which allows them to be good role models for other companies.[31] But by November 2001, the luster was definitively off the best board reputation at Enron, because it was now known that the board members had consulting and other financial agreements with Enron.

The board of directors played an active role in the decisions that eventually led to the spiral decline of Enron. They suspended Enron's code of ethics to allow the creation of the partnerships between Fastow and Enron in June and October 1999. The waiver was needed to allow the Enron CFO to also serve as a general partner in the other entities.[32] At a February 12, 2001, meeting of the audit committee, none of the members of the committee, all outside directors, challenged a single transaction that was presented related to the dealings in 2000 between Fastow's partnerships and Enron. The result was that a large amount of debt was taken away from Enron's balance sheet, and Fastow pocketed more than $30 million. One of the potential criticisms of the audit committee was that half of its members did not live in the United States, which made 100% attendance of the committee difficult to achieve. For example, one audit member, Ronnie Chan, missed more than one quarter of the audit meetings in 1996, 1997, and 2000.[33]

One board member on the audit committee, Lord John Wakeham, was paid a consulting fee of $72,000 in 2000 for his advice on Enron's European operations. Another audit member, Wendy Gramm, who is the wife of Senator Phil Gramm, worked at the Mercatus Center at George Mason University, which received $50,000 in donations from Enron from 1996 to 2001. Another audit member, Dr. John Mendelsohn, worked at the University of Texas M. D. Anderson Cancer Center, which received more than $2 million from 1993 to 2001 from Enron. In 2001, Enron's board members were considered some of the highest paid in the United States with an annual compensation of cash and stock of $400,000 based on the price of the stock when the annual meeting was held.[34]

Although Congress admonished Enron's board members for their lack of oversight, they were never indicted as parties to the Enron scandal.[35]

Arthur Andersen

On February 5, 2001, accountants at Arthur Andersen's Houston office met to discuss the off–balance sheet partnerships that Enron had started in 1999. They were uncertain how to address the issue until they decided to recommend that a special board committee be formed to review the transactions. One week later, on February 12, 2001, the audit and compliance board met to review the transactions and did not raise any concerns.[36]

On January 3, 2002, Arthur Andersen's lawyers went to Houston to review and retrieve all the related documents for the Enron audit for the government investigation. They found that the electronic files had been deleted from all the computers in

Andersen's Houston office. In a panic, the lawyers called Andersen's general counsel, Andrew Pincus, and Andersen's CEO, Joseph Berardino, to notify them that the documents were not available to retrieve. In a conference call the following morning, the lawyers told Andersen that the deletion of the e-mails was both abnormal and suspicious, and there appeared to be significant shredding of documents. On January 10, 2002, Andersen announced in a press release that the Houston office had destroyed an undetermined but significant number of documents that were related to the Enron audit.[37]

On January 15, 2002, the lead partner for the Enron audit, David Duncan, was fired by Arthur Andersen. Arthur Andersen released information that stated that Duncan was the person primarily responsible for the order to destroy thousands of e-mails and other documents that were related to the Enron audit. The destruction of the documents occurred as the SEC was ready to request the documents at the start of its investigations of Enron's financial reporting. The destruction of the documents was an attempt by Duncan and other members of Andersen's Houston office to try to control the Enron investigation at the local office and not have the investigation affect the firm at a national level. Duncan's response to the charges was that he was just following the instructions that were sent to him by an Andersen lawyer, Nancy Temple, on October 12, 2001, stating that Andersen's corporate policy allows the disposal of many documents as a common course of action. Duncan called a meeting on October 23, 2001, to discuss how to dispose of the documents related to Enron in a quicker manner. The destruction of the documents occurred until November 9, 2001, when Duncan's assistant sent out an e-mail to "stop the shredding." That was the day after Andersen received a subpoena from the SEC. Berardino stated that he first learned of the destruction of documents on January 3, 2002, and notified the DOJ and the SEC the following day.[38]

It was also revealed by an unnamed person who was close to David Duncan that Andersen's corporate office in Chicago appeared to be aware of the off–balance sheet transactions that occurred between Fastow's partnerships and Enron. The conclusion of the corporate office being aware of the transactions was based on a report from Enron's law firm, Vinson & Elkins, dated October 15, 2001, which reported that all the material facts related to the partnerships were disclosed and reviewed by Arthur Andersen.[39]

On March 2, 2002, Andersen was informed that the DOJ was ready to ask that Andersen be indicted for obstruction of justice. On March 3, 2002, Andersen executives accompanied by the firm's legal team met with DOJ officials in Washington. The lawyers argued that there was "inappropriate behavior" made by some Andersen employees, but the firm as a whole should not be charged. If charges were made against Andersen, it would be a deathblow to the firm because clients would leave and foreign offices would split from the parent firm. The DOJ was not convinced and stated that this was not the first occurrence of this behavior by Andersen. DOJ officials cited Andersen's involvement in the fraud cases of Sunbeam, Waste Management, and Baptist Foundation of Arizona as examples of a pattern of inappropriate behavior by Andersen. The government also raised concerns about whether Andersen officers realized the severity of their actions. The next morning, the message was conveyed to Andersen that if it did not plead guilty, it would be charged with obstruction of justice. After Andersen's lawyers recommended that Andersen enter a guilty plea, Andersen fired their law firm and told the new law firm to fight the indictment.[40]

In a last attempt to salvage the firm, Arthur Andersen executives started negotiations with Deloitte Touche Tohmatsu on March 7, 2002. By March 9, 2002, the negotiations had turned for the worse for Andersen when the lawyers for Deloitte advised against acquiring all of Andersen because of the legal liability. Deloitte wanted to pick which offices it wanted to acquire but not take over responsibility of the U.S. office. The proposal was submitted to the Andersen board, which was split on the recommendation. Some board members believed that the issue was solely isolated to the U.S. operations and would not affect the foreign offices. As the negotiations were taking place, Andersen continued to lose more clients, which increased the threat of additional legal liability and reduced the firm's level of cash flow. On March 12, 2002, Andersen was informed by a class-action lawyer that any merger would have to include the agreement that the acquiring firm would have to set aside $1 billion to resolve all class-action lawsuits. On that same day, Andersen's Spanish office announced that it was moving its operations to Deloitte. Even with the writing on the wall, Andersen executives continued to fight what was in hindsight a lost cause. The DOJ filed an indictment against Andersen on March 14, 2002. Berardino stepped down as CEO, and on April 5, 2002, Andersen officials were drawing up a negotiated deal with the government to resolve the indictment in return for admitting wrongdoing. That deal fell apart the following day when Duncan pleaded guilty to document destruction in return for cooperating with the DOJ. On April 17, 2002, the government presented Andersen with its final offer, which included the cooperation of Andersen partners even after they had left the firm, to Andersen lawyers. Andersen executives needed to agree to this offer by 5 o'clock Pacific time that evening. Andersen lawyers argued that no one accounting firm would hire the employees under those conditions. The government withdrew that requirement but stated that Andersen had to agree to all the other terms in the proposal by 8:30 a.m. Pacific time the next day. Andersen's lawyers tried in vain to contact all the members of Andersen's management team that evening to discuss the offer. The lawyers could not contact all of the executives, and the government withdrew the offer the next morning at 8:30 a.m. Pacific time.[41]

On May 6, 2002, Andersen's trial for obstruction of justice began in federal court in Houston. After 6 weeks of trial and 10 days of jury deliberations, on June 15, 2002, Arthur Andersen was convicted of obstruction of justice for destroying Enron documents while the firm was under notice of a federal government investigation. The jurors commented that Andersen lawyer, Temple, was a "corrupt persuader" by sending the e-mail to remind Andersen employees that it was firm policy to destroy some documents. By the end of the trial, Andersen had laid off 7,000 employees and had lost 650 of its 2,300 clients.[42] In September 2002, Arthur Andersen closed down as a firm when all of its state licenses were suspended. On May 31, 2005, the Supreme Court overturned the conviction against Arthur Andersen on the grounds that the judge at the trial went beyond the court's legal guidelines by not having the jury be required to find Andersen guilty of acting "dishonestly" when it destroyed the documents. The prosecutors argued that Andersen could be found guilty of obstruction of justice by destroying documents that would interfere with a government investigation regardless of Andersen's intent. By the time the conviction had been overturned, Andersen had fallen from employing 28,000 employees at its peak to 200 employees who were primarily responsible for resolving the outstanding lawsuits against the firm.[43]

The Fall of Enron's Smartest Guys in the Room

Andrew and Lea Fastow   On October 2, 2002, Andrew Fastow was formally charged with committing fraud, money laundering, and conspiracy in his role in the Enron scandal. On May 1, 2003, Fastow's wife, Lea, who was a former assistant treasurer at Enron, was charged with conspiracy to commit wire fraud and money laundering. On January 14, 2004, Fastow pleaded guilty to two counts of conspiracy to commit securities fraud and wire fraud, and agreed to cooperate with the DOJ. Under the terms of the agreement, Fastow agreed to serve 10 years in prison and give the government more than $29 million. The 96 other charges against Fastow were to be dropped if the government determined Fastow acted in good faith when cooperating with DOJ officials.[44] A summary of some of the reasons for Enron's fall are shown in Table 2.

Lea Fastow negotiated to plead guilty to filing false tax forms for not declaring more than $200,000 in income from one of Fastow's special purpose entities. Her lawyers and the prosecutors had originally agreed for her to serve 5 months in prison to ensure that one parent would be with their two sons as the Fastows served their time in prison. The presiding judge rejected the plea bargain based on the 5 months, and on May 6, 2004, Lea Fastow was sentenced to 1 year in prison and was ineligible to receive any time off for good behavior.

Jeffrey Skilling   On February 19, 2004, Jeffrey Skilling was charged with fraud, lying to auditors, and providing false financial records to the SEC. The SEC claimed that Skilling was responsible for defrauding investors by manipulating Enron's publicly reported financial results. The specific complaints included the manufacture and manipulation of reported earnings through the improper use of reserves; deliberately concealing the massive losses of Enron's retail energy business, Enron Energy Services; fraudulently promoting false information pertaining to the performance of Enron's broadband unit, Enron Broadband Services, to investors; and using special purpose entities and limited partnerships to manipulate Enron's financial results.[45] The low

---

TABLE 2   ●   Factors That Led to Enron's Demise Identified by Former SEC Commissioner Harvey Pitt

1. The failure to have effective internal controls to monitor actions
2. Board of directors that did not know or refused to find out what its role should be in the company
3. Multiple areas of actual and potential conflict of interest between Enron executives and Enron stockholders
4. The use of off-balance sheet transactions to drastically reduce the level of liabilities of the company
5. Illegal and unethical fraudulent activities that were difficult to identify that related to the accounting methods used by Enron
6. A corporate culture that condones illegal and unethical behavior by its employees without the employees taking any responsibility

Source: Adapted from Harvey Pitt, "Trials and Tribulations of Enron and S-Ox," *Forbes,* January 23, 2006, http://www.forbes.com.

point for Skilling came 2 months later when, on April 8, 2004, Skilling, who had had too much to drink, started a fight with two men outside of a New York bar on Manhattan's Upper East Side, where he and his wife were having drinks with friends. Skilling had accused the men of being undercover FBI agents, which they were not. In addition, he was alleged to have attempted to lift the blouse of a woman who was with the men to look for wires to record his conversations. The New York police had Skilling sent to a New York hospital in an ambulance, reporting that he was emotionally disturbed. His blood alcohol content was equivalent to that of a 200-pound man who had had nine drinks within an hour.[46]

Kenneth Lay On July 8, 2004, the SEC charged Kenneth Lay with 11 counts of fraud and insider trading. The specific complaints included Lay's early participation in the continuous activities that supported the defrauding of investors by constantly providing false or misleading statements to the public about Enron's financial condition. In addition, he was charged with failing to tell the public about the huge losses occurring in the Enron Broadband Services and Enron Energy Services divisions. Lay also had more knowledge about the limited partnerships, which resulted in the releasing of inaccurate financial statements to investors.

Another charge was that Lay knew about additional problems that occurred at Enron after Skilling had resigned as CEO, including stating publicly that there were no financial or accounting problems. Yet, he informed his managers about the deteriorating financial position at Enron. Lay was also accused of continuing to mislead the public in August and September 2001 when he talked in public about the robust financial performance and future growth of Enron although he had intimate knowledge about the true failing financial nature of the company. He sold more than $20 million in stock during this period. In addition, Lay was charged with insider trading for selling Enron stock from January 25, 2001, to November 27, 2001, in the amount of more than $135 million. During that time, he stated the financial growth of Enron was positive for the future although he had information that reflected the failing financial performance of the company.[47] Lay's response was that Fastow was at fault for the collapse of Enron and that Lay was not to be blamed. This response came 2 hours after he had been handcuffed and taken to a Houston courthouse. Lay acknowledged that wrongdoing was committed at Enron but claimed he was not aware of it during his time as CEO and chairman.[48]

Richard Causey On December 28, 2005, Enron's former chief accounting officer, Richard Causey, pleaded guilty to one count of securities fraud for his role in Enron's accounting fraud. The government agreed to ask for 5 years of prison for Causey if he cooperated fully with the government. If the government had determined that Causey did not provide full cooperation, it would recommend prison for 7 years. Causey, known at Enron as the "Pillsbury Doughboy," admitted that he was involved in a conspiracy along with other members of Enron's top management to generate false and misleading financial statements. The decision to plead guilty caught Lay and Skilling off guard because they had been presenting a unified defense until 1 week before the announcement of the plea bargain.[49] On November 15, 2006, former Enron chief accounting officer Richard Causey was sentenced to 5½ years in prison. Causey was also ordered to pay $1.25 million to the government.[50]

Lay and Skilling's Unified Defense Falls Apart

Less than 2 weeks before their trial was scheduled to start, Lay and Skilling presented their unified defense to the public. Both top Enron executives stated that not only did they do nothing wrong, but all the company moves during their tenure were legal. In legal circles, the "idiot" or "ostrich" defense created additional challenges to the defense team because if there were no illegal activities at Enron, why did the 30 lower-level Enron employees plead guilty to crimes they did not commit?

Skilling commented that his trial would be a business case, not a criminal case.[51] On January 30, 2006, the trial of Lay and Skilling started in Houston with the first surprise—the jury was selected in one day. It was extremely rare for a trial of this magnitude to have the full jury in place after only one day in the selection process.

On February 9, 2006, Lay's lead lawyer argued in court that Enron collapsed not because of accounting fraud but because of a market run on Enron stock. The lawyer pointed to a 2001 *Wall Street Journal* article that raised questions about one of Fastow's limited partnerships as the starting point of the rapid decline of Enron.[52]

During the trial, the prosecution accused Enron of manipulating the financial statements even if it meant one penny difference in the results. The "tweaking" of profits, the defense argued, is a standard practice of companies, and those adjustments were just routine refinements in their initial estimates. The defense claimed that accountants often would "sharpen" their pencils and "scrub" their books to look for any calculation to slightly adjust the final financial results.[53]

During the testimony of Kenneth Rice, former head of Enron Broadband Services, the jury heard Rice state that Skilling knew of the heavy losses that were occurring at the unit but told the public of strong financial performance of the division. In addition, former Enron accountant Terry West testified that she was told that Enron needed to have a quarterly profit of 35¢ per share and it was her responsibility to work backward through the financial statements to provide the income figure needed to reach those earnings per share objectives.[54]

Paula Rieker, former corporate secretary and deputy investor-relations chief at Enron, testified in court that Lay presented misleadingly optimistic statements about Enron's financial performance while knowing the true financial picture. Rieker recorded all the minutes of the board meetings as corporate secretary. In addition, Lay continued to sell Enron stock while misleading the investing public. Rieker presented documentation that showed the belt tightening occurring at Enron toward the end, which included canceling a Christmas party, laying off employees, and other efforts to raise money for the company all occurring as Lay was trading more of his Enron stock for cash. Rieker also testified that Enron's outside board members were outraged by Lay's dumping of stock while he was presenting false information and quoted Enron director John Duncan as stating that Lay was using Enron like an ATM to withdraw money from the company.[55]

Wesley Colwell, formerly of Enron's wholesale energy unit, testified in court that Skilling was looking to beat the street estimate for the second quarter results for 2000. As a result, Colwell was ordered to transfer $14 million from a reserves account to create a 2 cents per share increase in Enron's quarterly results.[56]

The next day of the trial, February 28, 2006, David Delainey, the former head of Enron's Energy Services unit, testified that he was told by Skilling to transfer losses that occurred in his unit's trading contracts to the wholesale division to try to hide the losses. Delainey told the court that the transfer had no business purpose other than to hide the loss, and he knew that it was not proper accounting. The transfer resulted in the announced result for the Energy Services unit of $40 million when the retail unit actually had a loss of approximately $260 million.[57] The credit reserve was used as a "cookie jar" to allow Enron to manipulate its earnings when its actual operations would not make the forecasted earnings per share. The cookie jar fund was established by transferring part of the huge profits that Enron was able to acquire via the California energy crisis.[58]

On March 7, 2006, former CFO Fastow took the stand to testify against his two former bosses. Fastow told the jury that Skilling was fully aware of the purpose of the limited partnerships and knew they were being used to hide debt. When a second limited partnership (LJM2) was proposed by Fastow, Skilling's response was to try to get as much "juice" out of the partnership as possible. LJM2 was used to "warehouse" Enron assets, which meant that Enron would submit transactions as if to buy assets but it was only to pretend to make the acquisitions. Enron would promise to buy them back for a premium to its trading partner.[59]

The original partnership, LJM1, was formed so Enron could "solve a problem" of trying to cover up investment losses from its operations.[60] An example of a deal with LJM1 was when the partnership bought an interest in a power plant in Brazil in 1999. Based on the investment by LJM1, Enron recorded income from the transaction and was able to achieve its earnings per share target. Fastow did not want his partnership to buy it because he thought the power plant was a "piece of sh**," but LJM1 did buy an interest when Skilling guaranteed Fastow that LJM1 would not lose any money on the deal.[61] It was a win-win situation for Fastow because he had no risk for his partnerships and he would be considered a hero at Enron for helping the company reach its financial goals. In 2001, Enron bought back the interest in the power plant from LJM1 for a premium after Fastow had sold his shares in the LJM1 partnership to ensure that Enron did not have to report the repurchase as a "related-party transaction" under SEC requirements. That was the first of many agreements between Enron and Fastow's partnerships. For each transaction, Fastow was guaranteed not to lose any money, which Skilling called a "bear hug" guarantee. The number of guaranteed transactions continued to build at such a pace that Fastow listed them and called it the Global Galactic agreement, which was the responsibility of former chief accounting officer Causey.[62]

Fastow also testified that Lay was informed in a meeting on August 15, 2001, that there was a "hole in the earnings" and that Enron would not make Wall Street forecasts by a significant amount. Fastow had estimated that Enron had between $5 billion and $7 billion of problems in its financial statements. Within a few days of that meeting, on August 20, 2001, Lay told *Businessweek* that Enron was in the strongest shape in its history and that it did not have any accounting problems.[63]

In a highly risky decision, both Lay and Skilling testified in court to defend their actions. Some experts stated that this was a dicey strategy because instead of objectively explaining their actions, former CEOs could become evasive and arrogant when challenged by the prosecution. One former federal prosecutor, Stephen Meagher, warned that in many cases the testimonies at trial of top executives blow up in their faces based on the executives' responses to questions. In addition, experts warned that a jury could disregard all the previous evidence that was presented in a trial after they heard the testimony of the top decision makers of a firm. Furthermore, top executives must ensure that their testimonies are presented in such a way that they appear very knowledgeable about all parts of the operation because this would void the "I didn't see anything wrong" defense. In addition, top executives also run the risk of increased sentences for perjury if their testimonies are not consistent with past statements. Lay did not give any sworn testimony before the trial, but Skilling gave prosecutors approximately two thousand pages of testimony to review. Skilling gave testimony before Congress, whereas Lay used his Fifth Amendment rights. Skilling also testified before the SEC and gave television interviews, which were used to explain his actions.[64]

When Skilling took the stand in his defense on April 10, 2006, he immediately stated that he was innocent of all charges and that a vast majority of Enron employees who had testified at the trial were also not guilty of any crimes. He told Lay that he wanted to resign from Enron because he was bothered by Enron's falling stock price. Skilling defended his actions at Enron, claiming his work at Enron helped the world become a better place.[65] He also gave as an example of his commitment to Enron that he accepted only $21.5 million in stock in 1997 when he became Enron president instead of the $70 million that was due him. He explained that he gave up almost $50 million that year to set an example for the other employees and to make a statement to the board of directors about his commitment to Enron.[66]

At the trial, Skilling claimed that he sold 500,000 shares of Enron stock on September 17, 2001, as a direct result of the September 11 attacks. September 17 was the first day after the attacks that the stock market was opened. Skilling, however, could not explain why he wanted to sell 200,000 shares on September 6, 2001 because he testified that he thought Enron's financial condition was still very strong and less than 3 weeks earlier told his broker that Enron stock was a good buy at $37.18.[67] The September 6, 2001, trade was not executed because the broker needed a letter from Enron that stated that Skilling was no longer an officer of the company and, therefore, the restrictions to sell his stock would be removed.[68]

On April 24, 2006, Lay took the stand in his own defense for his role in the Enron collapse and repeated the constant theme throughout his defense that Fastow was the mastermind of the financial operations at Enron. Lay testified in court that the deceit of Fastow and at most two other people were responsible for all the financial problems that plagued Enron. In addition, he claimed that he would not have taken over as CEO if he thought that there were fraudulent activities occurring at Enron.[69] He concluded that the collapse of Enron was a classic run on the bank that was started when Fastow's partnerships were made public to investors.[70]

During his testimony, Lay admitted that he probably violated Enron's code of ethics by making a $120,000 investment along with a $160,000 investment from Skilling into an Internet company, PhotoFete, which did business with Enron. Neither Lay nor Skilling notified the board of directors of their investments in the company, which was started by Skilling's ex-girlfriend, Jennifer Binder.[71]

Lay became flustered on the stand when the prosecution informed him that his son, Mark Lay, had executed four short sales orders for Enron stock in March 2001. A short sales order is bought when an investor believes that the stock price will go down in the future. Kenneth Lay's lawyer had stated that short-sellers of Enron stock were considered vultures. The prosecution asked Lay whether he would consider his son to be a vulture. In addition, the prosecution pointed out that as late as September 2001,

Lay was telling his employees to buy stock and that he also was buying Enron stock. The prosecution also showed that as Lay was saying that, he was selling millions of shares of Enron stock back to the company, not on the open market. As a result, those millions of transactions that totaled $70 million were not released to the investors. Lay's response was that he tried to hold as many shares of Enron as he could, but he had to sell some stock to cover margin calls on his personal loans.[72] The prosecution pointed out that Lay had millions of dollars in assets at his disposal, which he could have sold to pay for the margin call, including $14 million in non-Enron securities and $11 million in an unused line of credit that was available to cover the relatively small margin call. For example, in July 2001, Lay sold Enron stock back to Enron after receiving a margin call of $483,000.[73]

After his 6 days of testimony, experts thought that Lay hurt his case more than helped it. It appeared that Lay was not able to shift from being in charge of a boardroom to being under examination by others. As stated previously, Lay appeared to fall into the trap of using his self-confidence, which was necessary as CEO and chairman, to alienate the members of the jury. Lay seemed unprepared for some of the questioning and was testy and hostile during certain exchanges with the prosecution at the testimony.

The prosecution gave Lay many opportunities to admit that he was as least partially responsible for the downward spiral at Enron. Lay continued to blame the media and vulture short-sellers (but not his son) for Enron's demise. When the prosecution commented that Lay was developing a longer list of people to blame without including himself, Lay did not admit to any blame but said that he did all the things that were humanly possible to do at the time and that his decisions were based on real-time speed with a limited amount of information. Lay, from the beginning, made it clear to his lawyers that he wanted to control his testimony. After a series of questions from his lawyer, he asked his lawyer where he was going with that line of questioning.[74]

In his instructions to the jury, Judge Simeon Lake dealt a blow to the defense by stating that the jury could find the two former CEOs guilty if they consciously avoided finding out about the fraud at Enron. This defense—which is commonly referred to in legal matters as "willful blindness," "deliberate ignorance," or the "ostrich defense"—would have given a legal reason for Lay and Skilling to be found not guilty. This defense was unsuccessfully used by Bernard Ebbers in his trial for the WorldCom fraud. By allowing the jury to find Lay and Skilling guilty by not asking what was going on at Enron and the CEO was responsible for discovering them.[75]

Lay's and Skilling's Verdicts   On May 25, 2006, the federal jury found Lay and Skilling guilty of conspiracy and fraud. Lay was found guilty of all 6 charges against him, and Skilling was found guilty on 18 counts of conspiracy and fraud and 1 count of insider trading. Skilling was acquitted on another 9 counts of insider trading.[76] Lay was convicted of 1 count of conspiracy, 2 counts of wire fraud, and 3 counts of securities fraud. Skilling was convicted of 1 count of conspiracy, 12 counts of securities fraud, 5 counts of falsifying business records, and 1 count of insider trading. On the 9 charges that Skilling was acquitted of, the jury foreman stated that not guilty meant only not proven; it did not mean he was innocent. Lay faced as many as 45 years in prison, and Skilling faced as many as 185 years. One of the jurors, Kathy Harrison, stated that the verdict demonstrated that executives in charge need to be responsible for the operations of their companies. The jury also stated that the creditability of Lay and Skilling was hindered based on their testimonies because they argued that no crimes were committed at Enron. After the verdicts were read, Lay and his family and friends moved to one corner of the courtroom and prayed in a circle.[77] On June 30, 2006, federal prosecutors requested that Lay and Skilling pay almost $183 million in fines and penalties. The government was seeking relief in the amount of $139.3 million from Skilling and $43.5 million from Lay.[78]

A month after the verdicts had been read, Skilling reflected on his performance at the trial. He admitted that he was the best source of information for the prosecution and that the testimony he had given to the SEC came back to hurt him. He told the *Wall Street Journal,* the same publication Lay blamed for the downward spiral of Enron, that he was stupid to provide the information but that it was the "ethical" thing to do. After the conviction on the 19 charges, the government was able to put a lien on all of Skilling's assets including his 9,000-square-foot Florida home, his multimillion-dollar mansion in Houston, and $50 million in a brokerage account. Having battled depression and after considering suicide, Skilling concluded that life was better than the alternative.[79] His partner did not have the same option. Lay died of a heart attack in Aspen, Colorado, on July 5, 2006. He was 64. The cause of the attack was coronary artery disease. Lay had previously had two heart attacks, and his autopsy showed that three of his arteries were 90% blocked.[80]

Lay was finally able to do in death what he was not able to do while he was living—clear all criminal charges against him. A rule of U.S. law commonly called *abatement ab initio* states that a defendant's conviction is wiped clean if the defendant dies before he or she is able to appeal the conviction. As a result, Lay's conspiracy and fraud convictions no longer exist in the legal system. From a prosecution perspective, the elimination of Lay's charges made the job more difficult but not impossible for the U.S. government to seize ill-gotten proceeds from Lay's estate. Although the seizure of assets from criminal charges is not considered viable, civil charges against Lay can continue after his death. However, the government has to again prove any facts from the criminal trial before they are admissible in any civil proceedings.[81]

In September 2006, Lay's estate agreed to pay $12 million to settle a lawsuit by employees of Enron's pension plan.[82] On September 18, 2006, Delainey, the former head of Enron's Energy Services unit who had pleaded guilty in October 2003 to manipulating earnings, was sentenced to 2½ years in prison for insider trading. Delainey could have faced as many as 10 years in prison.[83] On September 26, 2006, former Enron chief financial officer Fastow was sentenced to 6 years for his role in the Enron fraud. After his prison sentence has been served, Fastow will be sentenced to an additional 2 years of house arrest. To add to the many quirks of the Enron case, Fastow received 4 years fewer than the 10 years he agreed to with the U.S. government in 2004. The judge determined that Fastow needed to have a sentence that was both just and merciful because Fastow had been subject to anti-Semitic remarks and personal threats. Furthermore, the judge reviewed the high level of cooperation Fastow displayed in aiding the government's case against Lay and Skilling.[84] Fastow reported to the minimum-security federal detention center in Oakdale, Louisiana, to serve his 6 years.[85] He was released on December 16, 2011.

On October 6, 2006, Paula Rieker, former corporate secretary and deputy investor-relations chief at Enron, was sentenced to 2 years' probation for insider trading.

Rieker recorded all the minutes of the board meetings and was found guilty of selling Enron stock after hearing that Enron's broadband unit had lost millions of dollars, but that information was not released to the public. Rieker could have served as many as 10 years in prison for her crimes.[86]

On October 23, 2006, Skilling was sentenced to 24 years 4 months in prison for his role in the Enron fraud. The judge noted that Skilling had repeatedly lied to Enron employees and investors and had sentenced many people to a life of poverty based on his actions. In his response, Skilling stated that he was remorseful for the toll that Enron had on people and commented that he had friends at Enron who had died, but he did not admit that he had done anything illegal. Skilling also continued to plead his innocence and vowed to continue to pursue his rights to have himself acquitted of all charges. Under U.S. federal law, Skilling must serve at least 85% of his sentence if it is not adjusted under appeal. As a result, the 52-year-old Skilling will be older than 70 before he can be released from prison. The judge had stated that Skilling's sentencing guideline calculation yielded a range of between 292 months and 365 months in prison and he was sentenced to 292 months. Based on the length of his sentence, Skilling would be initially assigned to a medium-security prison. On December 13, 2006, Skilling reported to a low-security federal prison in Waseca, Minnesota. He is now known as federal inmate 29296-179.[87]

In addition, based on a settlement reached between the prosecutors and the defense, Skilling agreed to forfeit his remaining $60 million, of which $45 million will be used to establish a fund for Enron victims and $15 million will help pay his legal bills. His legal fees are estimated as greater than $50 million, of which $20 million still had not been paid as of this writing.[88]

In an interview that was released in June 2010, Skilling reflected on his legal strategy leading up to his convictions. He would have done three things differently based on hindsight. The first was to exercise his Fifth Amendment Rights. Skilling wanted to explain Enron's business decisions but realized that he talked too much and gave the prosecution information that they did not have to discover on their own. The second lesson is to go on a public relations offensive. By remaining silent in the media, he was not able to challenge what was being said about him and Enron in the public. The third lesson was to avoid sarcasm. In May 2001, Skilling said, "They're onto us" to a series of Enron executives, which was perceived at trial as an admission of guilt instead of being humorous and sarcastic.[89] In June 2011, the U.S. Supreme Court reviewed the appeal of Skilling who claimed that he was unfairly convicted because of the technical legal interpretation of the benefits received by committing fraud. In 2010, the Supreme Court ruled that the jury in the Skilling case was not given specific enough direction pertaining to the legal terms and ruled that the Skilling case should be reviewed. In 2011, the Supreme Court did agree that the jury did not have the correct specific instructions but the Supreme Court determined that it could be considered a "harmless error." As a result, Skilling's case went back to a lower court, which determined that it was a harmless error, so Skilling's conviction was not overturned.[90]

The Domino Effect On June 12, 2005, Citigroup settled a class-action lawsuit brought by Enron investors for $2 billion for the bank's role in the energy company's collapse. This settlement followed the settlement by Lehman Brothers and Bank of America for a combined payment of $491.5 million.[91] Two days later, JPMorgan Chase agreed to pay $2.2 billion for its role in the Enron scandal.[92] On July 16, 2005, Enron agreed to pay the state of California $1.52 billion for its role in facilitating rolling blackouts and escalating energy prices in the Golden State. Because Enron was under bankruptcy protection when the settlement was reached, Enron was responsible for only 20% of the total settlement amount because California was an unsecured claimant.[93] On August 1, 2005, the Canadian Imperial Bank of Commerce (CIBC) paid $2.4 billion to settle its class-action lawsuit for its role in financially supporting Enron's operations.[94]

In 2007, Credit Suisse paid $61.5 million, UBS agreed to pay $115 million, and Deutsche Bank agreed to pay $25 million to settle litigation pertaining to their role in the Enron fraud.[95, 96] In January 2008, former lead auditor at Arthur Andersen, David Duncan, agreed to settle allegations filed by the SEC that he had violated securities law by signing audit reports that were false and misleading. No fine was issued, but Duncan was barred from appearing before the SEC as an accountant.[97] In March 2008, Citigroup settled litigation claims for $1.66 billion against it for its actions during the Enron scandal.[98]

In April 2010, *Enron* the play opened on Broadway. Written by British playwright Lucy Pebbles, *Enron* has played to two sold out runs in Britain before moving on to Broadway. In an irony even too much for Enron, the play closed less than 2 weeks after the theater critic of the *New York Times* called it flashy but also a labored economic lesson for the audience.[99] This cemented the authors' belief that *Enron* has become one of truly cursed words in the English language. On April 6, 2011, the United States Court of Appeals denied Jeff Skilling his appeal of his conviction.[100] On June 21, 2013, Skilling's sentence was reduced to 14 years by a federal judge. The reduction in the sentence was part of an agreement in which Skilling would halt any future appeals concerning his conviction.[101]

Questions for Thought

1. What are "cookie jar" reserves? Explain Enron's use of this concept.

2. Identify as many stakeholders as you can in this case. Explain how each was affected by the events surrounding the demise of Enron.

3. Summarize the main points of this case in one succinct paragraph.

4. All the executives in this case believed they were not guilty of the charges levied against them. Why would they believe this, given the evidence presented in their trials?

8

Google:
Don't Be Evil Unless . . .

From its start in a garage in Silicon Valley in 1998, Google has become one of the most powerful technology-driven companies in the world. Started by two graduate students at Stanford University as an improvement on the existing Internet search engines, Google's philosophy is to offer everyone in the world free access to all of the information in the world. As a result, the two main objectives of Google as it evolves are to organize the information around the world and "Don't be evil."[1] In 2005, Harris Polling and the Reputation Institute of New York did their annual ranking of the companies with the highest corporate reputation. Google entered the ranking for the first time in 2005 at number three behind Johnson & Johnson and Coca-Cola.[2]

The Privacy of Gmail

On April 1, 2004, Google announced in a press release that it was offering a new free e-mail system called Gmail.[3] The press release also mentioned that this decision was inspired by a customer who complained to Google about her e-mail service's low storage capacity and inefficient filing and searching technology. Google responded by developing an e-mail service that offered 1 gigabyte of storage capacity (which is equivalent to 500,000 pages of e-mail per user) and an easy way to organize e-mail messages. However, what the e-mail did not announce was that Google would search the contents of its customers' e-mails and design "customized" ads based on the content. This just was the first of many issues in which Google appeared to be caught off guard with negative comments related to its Gmail strategy. Some people even thought the Gmail press release was an April Fool's Day trick pulled by Google's cofounders when Google also announced that day that it was hiring positions for its lunar office.[4]

Google responded to the criticism, which started on April 2, 2004, by stating that no human being would read the customer's e-mail, but a computer program would do an automatic search for key content words. Google also stated that the e-mail system would have enhanced search features for the user to help coordinate the user's e-mails. Customers using Gmail would be able to search their e-mail storage by the traditional sender and by topic or any other search word the user wanted to choose. In addition, Gmail would have more antispam filters to help reduce the number of unwanted e-mails sent to the user's account. However, the underlying issue was whether Google could present this "free" e-mail system to users in which they potentially have their privacy compromised to ensure content-related advertising. Google tried to reduce the privacy fears by stating that the advertising would be used for *only* incoming e-mails and would not be attached to outgoing e-mails. Chris Hoofnagle, who was the associate director of the Electronic Privacy Information Center, compared the Google advertising methods to having a telephone operator listening to your phone calls and interrupting you with commercial messages when you are talking to another party. When Wayne Rosing, Google vice president of engineering, was asked whether it would be possible for a person writing about pro-life to have abortion advertising inserted in the e-mail, his answer was no because Google does not take advertising revenue concerning sensitive issues. However, he did admit that if the e-mail was talking about politics, an advertisement for a political candidate could be included in the e-mail.[5]

There are also potential problems with matching the content of the e-mails and the associated placement ads. When a Gmail user wrote about a British singer named Lily Allen, an ad for lily and lotus pond plants was placed in the e-mail. Another Gmail user wrote about going to a party in New York and an ad for bachelor party strippers was placed with the e-mail. In summarizing the placement of the ads, the user writing about Lily Allen stated that the ads are creepy when they match up exactly with the discussion and are hilarious when they do not match up with the written content.[6]

Another concern is the legal use of keeping information that is sent through Gmail without the user being protected by the rights given by the Electronic Communications Privacy Act.[7] The act states that Internet service providers (ISPs) and any other organizations are not allowed to monitor the content of electronic communications unless they have specifically identified a reason to do so, such as filtering spam or preventing the release of confidential information.[8]

The Privacy of Individuals

In a stunning show of hypocrisy, Google punished an entire news agency after one of its reporters searched for and published background information about the company's CEO, Eric Schmidt. It took Elinor Mills from CNETNews.com just 30 minutes to obtain as much relevant information as was available on Schmidt. Using only Google's search capability, Mills discovered that Schmidt was 50 years old, was worth approximately $1.5 billion, had sold $90 million in Google stock in the early part of 2005, and had sold another $50 million in shares in the middle of 2005. She also discovered that Schmidt and his wife, Wendy, live in Atherton, California, and she was able to get his home address from the Federal Election Commission database. Schmidt attended a Democratic fundraiser that cost $10,000 a plate in 2000. In addition, Schmidt is an amateur pilot.[9] When Google became aware of the article, Google's director of public relations, David Krane, stated that Google would not talk to any reporter from CNET for a year. This reaction seemed to contradict Schmidt's statement in May 2005 that the goal of Google is to organize all the information in the world.[10]

Google in China

In 2000, Google began a Chinese language version, which Chinese users could buy. It was operated from the United States through Google.com. In September 2002, Google refused to alter the search results of Chinese users, and the Chinese government blocked Google for a brief period. When the block was lifted from Google 2 weeks later, Chinese users no longer had access to politically sensitive websites. It was discovered that Google had voluntarily excluded several sites from the search results that were not allowed by Chinese censors. These websites are not excluded when users outside of China searched using the same key words.[11] Within the Chinese website, Google filtered out search words such as *human rights* and *democracy* from the search results.[12] In addition, antigovernment groups such as Falun Gong will not show up on a Google search. Google has adjusted its search process so it complies with the strict censorship and security laws imposed by the Communist Party in China. In response to a question about whether Google should censor results in China, cofounder Sergey Brin commented that it is a difficult question and the "don't be evil" statement may be open to interpretation regarding what exactly is considered evil. In September 2004, Google introduced a Chinese version of its news search service. However, the search excludes articles from news sources that the Chinese government considers subversive. Google's response was that it was not worthwhile for the users to get search results that they would not have access to in China.[13]

Google opened offices in China during 2005 and considered it a country for great revenue growth. In January 2006, Google stated that its special version of its search engine for the Chinese customers, called Google.cn, would be available without having any e-mail or blog features.[14] One British blogger commented on Google's restrictions of search words in China by wondering whether the Internet search company also banned the words *spineless, hypocritical,* and *cowards.*[15] When a comparison was made searching the word *democracy* in Google's U.S. and Chinese websites, the results were quite different. At Google.com, *democracy* yielded 33,000,000 results, with a link to the Taiwanese Democratic Progressive Party's definition ranking second. When *democracy* was searched on Google.cn, less than 20% of the sites selected in the U.S. search were found. In addition, the Taiwanese definition had been omitted from the results, and in its place was the website of the Chinese Communist Party's newspaper.[16] When a search was made for a picture of the Dalai Lama, more than 2,000 pictures were found on Google.com and only one on Google.cn—when the Dalai Lama met members of the Communist Party before 1959. In 1959, the Chinese military invaded Tibet and the Dalai Lama had to escape Tibet and live in exile.[17] In defense to Google's "don't be evil" credo, cofounder Schmidt rationalized that it was better for Chinese users to get the benefit of a speedy, restricted Google search than no access at all. Therefore, Google's solution was the lesser of the two evils. While at a World Economic Forum, Microsoft founder Bill Gates observed that "don't be evil" was not a relative commandment.[18] In February 2006, the *Financial Times* ran an online poll to ask whether Google is now considered evil for censoring the results for Chinese users. Of the 1,400 respondents, 70% believed that Google was being evil for its stand on accommodating the demands of the Chinese government.[19] A representative of the Chinese government stated that the purpose of the restrictions was to ensure that harmful information was not available to Chinese users. The Chinese government's actions are similar to those of newspapers in the United States that stated they would edit or omit any content the editor deemed inappropriate if it was posted to the newspaper's discussion group. The spokesman also stated that only a tiny percentage of websites are blocked from searches by Chinese Internet users.[20]

On February 15, 2006, Google, Yahoo!, Microsoft, and Cisco Systems were called to participate in a congressional human rights hearing regarding their role in limiting information to Chinese Internet users. Representative Christopher Smith stated that all the companies were involved in a sickening collaboration with the communist government in China and that they had decapitated the voice of Chinese dissidents by limiting the expression of free speech for people in China. It was revealed in the hearing that Google had learned the most effective ways of filtering out content by examining how the competitors and the Chinese government used software to filter out information.[21] Google vice president of global communications Elliot Schrage stated that although Google was not ashamed of its actions, it was not proud of what it had done with the design of Google.cn.[22]

In June 2006, Jason Dean reported that Internet users in China were having difficulty obtaining access to the Google global site but were not having any problems getting on the Chinese-based site. There was no official response from the Chinese government about why users logging on to Google.com were not successful, yet users had no problems logging into the censored Google.cn.[23] In January 2007, Google—along with Yahoo!, Microsoft, and Vodafone—agreed to establish a set of human rights principles that would include addressing the issue of censorship. This agreement came after the technology companies were pressured by human rights groups, Internet freedom activists, and other interested parties who wanted to see these companies protect individuals' human rights pertaining to the Internet.[24]

On January 12, 2010, Google announced that it would stop cooperating with the Chinese government to censor web searches in China using Google.cn. Google threatened to close down its Chinese operations if Google was "forced" to continue to censor the web for its Chinese users. Google stated that it would try to negotiate a new deal with the Chinese government that would provide uncensored results. Along with Google's concern of being hypocritical with its former stance on China and its belief of "don't be evil," it is also important to note that Google was not the market leader in China but was behind Baidu, which is a Chinese company with close ties to the Chinese government. Google's annual revenue in China in 2009 was $300 million.[25] On March 22, 2010, Google shut down its Chinese website and directed its users to go to its uncensored website in Hong Kong. The Chinese government responded by stating that Google did not abide by its contract, which stated that Google must provide filtered results to Chinese users.[26] In July 2010, the Chinese government renewed Google's license. Google was allowed to continue to operate a website in mainland China, and it continues to allow users in China to be referred to its uncensored search engine in Hong Kong.[27] Google's share of the web search market in China dropped from 36% in the fourth quarter of 2009 to 17.2% in the third quarter of 2011, Google admitted that it is hard to miss out on the world's largest Internet market and announced in January 2012 that it was hiring skilled employees in China to introduce new services to the Chinese consumers. Amir Efrati and Loretta Chao believe that Google wants badly to become a major player in the smartphone market with its Android-based phones.[28]

Refusing the Justice Department

On January 19, 2006, Google announced that it would vigorously challenge a request by the Department of Justice (DOJ) for Google to supply to the government information pertaining to Internet searches done on Google. The DOJ subpoenaed Google in August 2005, requesting all website addresses that were located through Google from June 1 to July 31, 2005. The request was to aid the DOJ in defending the Child Online Protection Act of 1998, the purpose of which was to protect minors from being exposed to sexually explicit material available on the web.[29] The DOJ wanted to use the data from Google to determine the effectiveness of filtering software compared with the protections that are supported in the 1998 act. The DOJ wanted to take the data from Google and use the more current filtering software that is commercially available to see how successful the current filters would be in excluding explicit websites from the search results. The Child Online Protection Act has faced a number of legal challenges. In 2004, the Supreme Court did not overturn an injunction that had been filed to block the enforcement of the law.[30] In October 2005, Google told the government that the DOJ request would imply that Google would be willing to reveal information pertaining to its users, which was unacceptable to Google. Google described the request as too vague, burdensome, and a form of harassment. Google also stated that the request would take up too much of Google's time and resources and that it would threaten Google's competitive advantage by exposing its proprietary secrets. When the DOJ tried to get Google to provide a list of 1,000,000 website addresses that are available via a Google search for only 1 week without any identification of who the users were, Google did not accept this compromise. Google continued to be firm that its decision stating that the DOJ request overreached what is expected from Google for compliance. The DOJ responded by stating that Yahoo!, Microsoft, and America Online were also subpoenaed in August 2005, and all three of Google's competitors complied with the government's request.[31] In March 2006, Google refused the DOJ's revised request for Google to provide 50,000 web addresses and 5,000 searches, of which the government would use 10,000 websites and 1,000 searches in testing its filters.[32] On March 17, 2006, a federal judge ordered Google to give the DOJ some search data including 50,000 websites but not the 5,000 sample searches.[33]

As a number of critics have pointed out, it appeared ironic that Google was a committed defender of privacy and freedom to control its data in the United States yet appeared to agree with every limitation the Chinese government had requested for its Chinese website.

Scanning Copyrighted Material and Other Copyright Issues

In December 2004, Google announced that it would scan the pages of the books located in various libraries across the world, including those of Harvard University, Stanford University, the University of Michigan, and Oxford University. This Google Books Library Project would have given Google users access to online copies of out-of-copyright books for no charge, as well as copyright-protected works, which would have partial content available. Critics were quick to point out that the program was an attempt to violate copyright laws by having copyrighted material available online without consent of the author. Google's response was that publishers could decide whether to participate in the program or not.[34] On September 20, 2005, three authors sued Google for copyright infringement. All the authors claimed that they had copy-righted material in at least one of the libraries that Google was using. In addition, they stated that they did not give permission to Google to copy their material. The lawsuit stated that Google should have been aware of the Copyright Act and should not have started the process of copying material without consent from the authors. The lawsuit claimed that the Google Print for Libraries program is not covered under the "fair use" rule for reproducing copyrighted material.[35] On October 19, 2005, five publishing companies located in the United States—Pearson Education, McGraw-Hill, Penguin Group, Simon & Schuster, and John Wiley & Sons—filed a copyright infringement lawsuit against Google for the Google Print for Libraries program.[36]

In September 2006, a Belgian court ruled that Google must stop publishing content from Belgian newspapers without permission. If Google did not comply, it would face a fine of as much as 1 million euros, or $1.27 million, per day.[37] Google appealed the ruling but on May 5, 2011, the Court of Appeal in Brussels upheld the 2007 lower court ruling.[38]

In October 2006, Google acquired YouTube for $1.65 billion. With the free access video website, YouTube comes with additional copyright issues. As was the case with Google, YouTube had copyrighted material on its website in which the copyright holders neither gave permission nor received a fee.[39] In November 2006, Google announced that its own video site, Google Video, had been served a copyright law-suit by Viacom for having copyrighted material on the site without permission or compensation. As a result, five different Google services faced copyright challenges: Google Web Search, Google News, Google Images, Google Books, and Google Video.[40] Jason Fry estimated that Google had set up a reserve of $500 million to resolve copy-right issues that were related to the acquisition of YouTube.[41] Six years later Viacom's suit remained unresolved. Google won an appeal in 2012, but on April 5, 2012, the U.S. Court of Appeals in Manhattan reversed the lower court's decision to throw out the case before trial.[42]

The Association of American Publishers agreed on October 4, 2012, to an out-of-court settlement with Google. Basically, the settlement offered the same deal that Google had offered copyright owners with books in Google's Library Project from the start: copyright owners whose books were scanned by Google under its Library Project could request that their books be removed. What will remain unknown is if a monetary settlement was involved, and if so, how much, because the suit was private and the details, therefore, will be kept confidential.[43] While the agreement settled the lawsuit brought against Google by Pearson Education, McGraw-Hill, Penguin Group, Simon & Schuster, and John Wiley & Sons, it did not resolve disputes between the other parties involved in the lawsuit, including the Authors Guild.[44]

On April 5, 2012, the U.S. Court of Appeals in Manhattan reversed a lower court's decision to throw out Viacom's lawsuit against Google before trial. The lower-court judge had ruled in favor of Google's request to dismiss the case by reasoning that YouTube's practice of removing infringing videos upon the request of the copyright holder protected Google from liability.[45] In October 2014, Google agreed to stop post-ing information from numerous German newspapers so that they did not have to pay for the right to post them. Its action was in response to a new German law that requires firms to obtain permission from publishers when content from the publishers is posted online.[46]

The Role of Click Fraud

Ninety-nine percent of Google's revenue comes from advertisers who pay Google every time a user clicks on the ads that are displayed within the Google results. The question that arises is this: Was the clicking of the ad a valid attempt by the user to examine the advertising of the firm, or was the click used in a fraudulent manner? It would be potentially beneficial for an unethical competitor to use click fraud to increase the overall advertising costs that would be paid to Google based on the number of recorded clicks. Another source of click fraud could be from businesses that allow Google advertising and split the revenue with Google under Google's AdSense program.[47] In addition, what role should Google have in verifying the accuracy of this critical revenue stream? Some estimates calculate that 20% of all clicks are fraudulent. In addition, critics of Google stated that the company is not responsive to the concerns its advertisers have about click fraud.[48] On March 8, 2006, Google agreed to settle a lawsuit for $90 million, including cash and advertising credits, by companies that paid click fees for their advertising on Google. The suit was originally filed by Lane's Gifts & Collectibles in Texarkana, Arkansas, a retailer that claimed it was paying for fraudulent clicks to its advertisement on Google. The lawsuit alleged that Google improperly charged retailers for clicks that were fraudulent. The settlement allowed any Google advertiser in the United States from 2002 to 2006 to make a claim for being overcharged for its advertising by Google.[49] Online advertisers spent more than $800 million on advertising that was based on fraudulent clicks. If true, that represents 14.6% of the $5.5 billion spent on online advertising in the United States in 2005.[50]

In July 2006, Google announced that it was introducing a new software program that would analyze the level of fraudulent clicks for its customers. An existing software program by a monitoring consulting firm called Click Forensics developed a "Click Fraud Index," which summarized the monthly percentage of fraudulent clicks. 13.7% of clicks on search engine web pages were fraudulent in the first quarter of 2005, and that number had increased to 14.1% for the second quarter of 2005.[51]

The Privacy Issues Continue: The Sting of Buzz

On February 9, 2010, Google introduced Google Buzz, which is a combination of the features of Facebook and Twitter. When Buzz was linked to Gmail, the users of Buzz opened a new account; they were automatically given a network of "friends" that were selected by Google. Google determined the user's "friends" by identifying people with whom the user communicated on Gmail and chat services. Google managers thought this was an efficient shortcut for the user because the user did not have to manually add each new friend. The users were not impressed. They complained that this was a blatant invasion of privacy and that Google did not ask permission of the user to share a Buzz contact with another user. Google officials did not take into consideration that communication such as e-mail can contain private information that the user would not want to share with anyone, including contacts for obtaining illegal substances or names of illicit lovers. One woman who writes a blog complained that she now feels fearful because her abusive ex-husband or writers who e-mailed her hostile comments now have her contact information. In addition, governments could use Buzz to identify contacts from subversives within their country. Google responded by stating that many users liked the convenience of the feature, and users can hide the list of Buzz contacts with a single click.[52] In September 2010, Google agreed to settle private class-action lawsuit filed by seven users of Gmail who had their private information linked on Buzz. Google agreed to pay $8.5 million, with most of money being allocated to help fund organizations whose mission is related to Internet privacy. Google also agreed to make future announcements concerning the privacy aspects of Buzz but denied that the company violated any laws.[53] In March 2011, Google settled with the Federal Trade Commission by agreeing to establish stricter privacy rules related to its Buzz program. In addition, Google agreed to develop a "comprehensive privacy program" and must submit to an independent audit every 2 years for the next 20 years.[54] On October 14, 2011, Google announced that it would retire Buzz in a few weeks and replace it with a new social network, Google+.[55]

Global Privacy Issues

Content Issues In February 2010, three Google executives were convicted of violating Italian privacy laws. The Italian court interpreted the role of Google as not just a search engine but as a media company like newspapers or television that provide content that needs to be regulated. The Italian court determined that Google is ultimately responsible for text, photographs, or videos that are available by third parties and are released to the public through Google or YouTube. In the Italian case, Google was accused of not acting quickly enough to remove a video that was posted in 2006 and showed a group of teenagers harassing an autistic boy. The Google executives were sentenced to six-month suspended sentences for violation of privacy.[56]

Street View In April 2010, privacy officials from 10 countries sent Google a letter that demanded that the company develop more privacy protections for its users. Representatives from Canada, France, Germany, Ireland, Israel, Italy, the Netherlands, New Zealand, Spain, and the United Kingdom all raised concerns about Google's lack of commitment to user privacy.[57] In May 2010, European officials were furious when Google informed them in response to their letter that Google had systematically collected private data since 2006 when Google was developing its Street View photo archive. The German government stated that Google violated privacy laws by illegally tapping into private networks to obtain the information. The German government concluded that privacy was a foreign concept to Google. Google was collecting data about locations of wireless networks and collected private information related to those networks.[58] The German government, followed by the governments of six other European countries, demanded that Google preserve the data it had obtained without permission from unsecured wireless networks. Joining Germany were Belgium, the Czech Republic, France, Italy, Spain, and Switzerland in requesting the information from Google. In total, Google had collected information from unsecure wireless networks from 33 countries. Google downplayed the value of the data, stating that it consisted of fragments from webpages and e-mail messages and claimed the data were inadvertently collected through a programming error. Three other countries, Denmark, Austria, and Ireland, requested that Google destroy all the data that were collected.[59] In October 2010, Google announced that it was toughening privacy controls and improving employee training and compliance procedures to ensure this unauthorized collection of data does not happen in the future.[60] On the same day, Google admitted that it had captured entire e-mails, URLs, and passwords during the Street View program development.[61] In March 2011, French regulators fined Google $142,000 for not being forthcoming with information[62] pertaining to the collection of data during the Street View program development.

Android Smartphones In a continuing theme of privacy violations, Google has also demonstrated invasion of privacy with its Android smartphones, which transmit their locations back to Google. The benefit for Google is that it can use this information that pinpoints the user's location for location-based services. Every few seconds, the smartphone transmits data to Google including the name, location, and signal strength of any Wi-Fi networks within a certain distance of the phone. These data are transmitted regardless of whether the user is using a location app or not.[63] In June of 2012, the U.S. National Telecommunications and Information Administration announced that it would address the issue of developing mobile privacy standards by holding a series of meetings with mobile carriers, app developers, and other stakeholders.[64]

New Privacy Policy In January 2012, Google announced that starting on March 1, 2012, it would utilize user information from multiple Google platforms including Google, YouTube, Google+, Android phones, and Gmail to coordinate data about the user to help make the search process "easier." This integrated information will be used to "customize" the user's search results based on the user's own preferences. Julia Angwin assumes that one reason for this integration is to give Google the ability to sell data "packages" of individual user information just as Facebook does.[65]

Anyone who is a registered user of Gmail, Google+, YouTube, or other Google products cannot prevent Google from combining the personal data it collects from all its services. But users can minimize the data Google gathers by making sure they are not logged into one of Google's services when they are using Google's search engine, watching a YouTube video, or perusing pictures on Picasa. Google does offer the option to delete users' history of search activity. Google can still track users even when they are not logged in to one of its services but only through a numeric Internet address attached to the computer or an alphanumeric string attached to the web browser, not by the user's name.[66]

Privacy and Safari The research of a Stanford professor and the *Wall Street Journal*, has shown that in February 2012, Google had bypassed the privacy setting of millions of smartphones and computers and was tracking the browsing habits of users who had "blocked" this type of monitoring. Google had developed a special computer code that fools Apple's Safari web-searching software into allowing Google to monitor numerous users. The default mode for the Safari software for both the computer and the smartphone is to block this type of monitoring. Of the top 100 websites, 22 sites installed the Google tracking software on the test computer. Once the software is linked to the computer or smartphone, it will continue to track web searching after the initial website has planted the software on the machine.[67] On August 9, 2012, Google agreed to pay $22.5 million to settle Federal Trade Commission violations related to the iPhone privacy settings.[68]

Current Issues Related to Google and Privacy

On May 13, 2014, the European top court representing the interests of the European Union ruled that Google can be forced to erase links to content pertaining to individuals on the Internet. As a result, individuals in the EU can request that Google and other search engines remove links to news articles, court judgments, and other published documents that contain the individual's name. The decision by the court is based on 19th-century French and German law that protects individuals' "right to be forgotten."[69] Google started removing search results in June 2014 for those individuals who had requested their removal under the "right to be forgotten" ruling.[70]

Questions for Thought

1. Given its mission of providing information to the world, should Google censor searches in China?

2. Why do you think Google was adamant about not wanting to supply information requested by the government concerning the Child Online Protection Act? Explain your position.

3. What do you think Google's rationale was for starting its Google Books Library Project?

4. Of all the issues discussed in this case, which issue is the most disconcerting to you? Why?

Cases

9

HealthSouth: The Rise and Fall of the Scrushy Empire

On October 29, 2003, Richard Scrushy, the former CEO of HealthSouth, was indicted by the federal government on 85 counts of fraud. He was released on a $10 million bond and a proposed trial date was set for August 23, 2004. The allegations against Scrushy included securities fraud and false certification of corporate financial statements. This indictment put a temporary end to the roller-coaster ride that HealthSouth, Scrushy, and the stockholders had been on for the previous 6 months. How HealthSouth got to this extreme should make even the most veteran roller-coaster rider scream.

The Birth of an Empire

Scrushy was born in the town of Selma, Alabama. He received his certification in respiratory therapy at the University of Alabama at Birmingham in 1974. After working in respiratory therapy for a brief period, Scrushy realized that Medicare was paying a large amount of money to diagnose and treat elderly patients. He saw an opportunity to open privately held clinics that could provide the same treatments with lower overhead than traditional hospitals had. In addition, he realized that as Baby Boomers aged, a higher level of sports-related injuries would occur. He saw this as a future growth opportunity. Scrushy decided that he wanted to develop a health care franchise that would be dedicated to physical therapy. In 1984 with $50,000 from four friends, he started AmCare, which eventually became HealthSouth.[1]

Soon after HealthSouth went public in 1986, HealthSouth started manipulating its financial statements. Scrushy's primary goal was to ensure that HealthSouth always met or exceeded Wall Street's expectations.[2] By 1988 HealthSouth operated 21 outpatient facilities, 11 inpatient facilities, and seven rehabilitation equipment centers in 15 states, By the end of1998 the company encompassed nearly 1,900 centers in 50 states, the United Kingdom, and Australia.[3]

In 1995, HealthSouth hired sport celebrities such as Tom Glavine and Bo Jackson to boost its corporate image.[4] By 2001, HealthSouth had hired former *Wonder Years* actor Jason Hervey to head HealthSouth's entertainment and marketing operations.[5] Hervey was in charge of the communications department at HealthSouth that, at its peak, employed 60 employees. Scrushy's fascination with the entertainment industry started in the late 1990s when he developed a "Go For It" road show that was supposed to present positive, healthful messages to children. An offshoot initiative of the road show was HealthSouth's involvement in developing a girls' group called 3rd Faze.[6]

In Birmingham, Scrushy was given almost royal status. A parkway, a community college campus, a building, a library, and a ball field are named after him. Scrushy's corporate helicopter was nicknamed "Bonus One" by the HealthSouth employees because it was purchased the same year that HealthSouth did not give out bonuses to the rank-and-file employees. It was estimated that the helicopter served three primary purposes: (1) take Scrushy from the corporate headquarters to the Birmingham airport, (2) take Scrushy and his family to their mansion on Lake Martin in Alabama, and (3) allow Scrushy's wife, Leslie, to make spontaneous shopping trips to Atlanta.[7]

According to the Security and Exchange Commission (SEC), Scrushy met with HealthSouth's senior officers each quarter to go over the firm's actual earnings. Scrushy then compared the actual earnings with what the market was expecting for the quarterly earnings. If the actual earnings were not as high as the expected earnings, Scrushy ordered the senior managers to "fix it." Scrushy denied this allegation to Mike Wallace during a *60 Minutes* interview.[8] HealthSouth's top accountants held "family meetings" in which they decided how to manipulate the financial statements. The accountants "fixed it" by "filling the gap."

The most common method was to make adjustments in the contractual adjustment account, which is used to estimate the variance between the amount billed to a patient and the amount insurance will pay. This account was used because it could be easily manipulated without scrutiny because it was impossible to verify the amount in the account. The accountants then had to manipulate the asset accounts to rebalance the balance sheet. They did this by adjusting the fixed asset account of plant and equipment to increase the asset levels. The accountants used a series of small adjustments so they wouldn't raise any red flags to the external auditors. In addition, the accountants had to generate false invoices to support the manipulations.[9]

The Red Flags Fly

In 1998, HealthSouth's auditor, Ernst & Young, received an anonymous letter identifying accounting irregularities. During a congressional House Energy and Commerce Committee hearing in 2000, James Lamphron, former engagement partner at Ernst & Young, admitted that the firm received the letter in 1998 but concluded that the issues raised in the letter did not affect HealthSouth's financial statements.[10] In the summer of 2002, Ernst & Young was notified again of accounting irregularities by a former bookkeeper, Michael Vines, at HealthSouth. Vines claimed that HealthSouth did not record certain expenses between $500 and $4,999 in order to lower the overall expense amount and, therefore, artificially increase the level of profits at HealthSouth. Vines explained that the number had to be less than $5,000 because that was the amount beyond which Ernst & Young started examining expenses.[11]

During an audit in 2001, the Ernst & Young auditor asked about the paper trail of a specific asset that was purchased. The problem was that the asset was never purchased. As a result, Vine's supervisor, Cathy Edwards, ordered Vines to alter an invoice from a different asset purchase. Edwards then scanned the alternative invoice and changed the information on the invoice so it matched the information on the phantom purchase. On April 3, 2003, Edwards pleaded guilty to committing securities and wire fraud. In accepting the plea bargain, Edwards admitted to the government that she altered accounting-related documents.[12]

In 1998, a HealthSouth patient in Texas filed a complaint with Medicare that HealthSouth used "unqualified personnel" for physical therapy by using aides and trainees instead of licensed therapists. In addition, the patient claimed that HealthSouth asked for financial reimbursements for services that it did not perform. In February 2003, after an investigation of the allegations, HealthSouth offered to pay the Department of Justice (DOJ) $150 million to settle the alleged Medicare fraud charges. The government refused, seeking more than $200 million, and would not agree to HealthSouth's condition that it would admit no wrongdoing.[13]

The Beginning of the Downfall

HealthSouth's rejected offer to pay $150 million to settle the Medicare fraud allegations came shortly before the SEC and the DOJ accused HealthSouth of falsifying its financial statements to increase net income by approximately $3 billion in order to keep the stock price from falling. An estimate of the amount of the overstatements is shown in Table 1. When Mike Wallace asked Scrushy in a *60 Minutes* interview in October 2003 if he had inflated earnings and betrayed his stockholders and employees, Scrushy's response was that there was no evidence of that happening at HealthSouth.[14] Scrushy put the full blame on his subordinates and pleaded no knowledge of the financial statement manipulations. The CEO must rely on his or her subordinates, and the CEO must delegate responsibility to the lower-level employees, he said. All the CEO can do is hire them and give them a good salary, and they are expected to do the correct thing every time. Scrushy stated that he just signed off what was given to him with the assumption that the information was accurate.[15] Both Scrushy and Ernst & Young were fired by HealthSouth Corporation's board in March 2003, less than two weeks after regulators charged Scrushy and HealthSouth with accounting fraud.[16]

After Scrushy was fired, he lost his celebrity status and all of the trappings that came with it. The Richard M. Scrushy Conference Center became just the "Conference Center." An entire room on the executive fifth floor was stripped of all the awards and pictures of Scrushy with various celebrities. Before he was fired, to ensure his security,

Income (Loss) Before Income Taxes and Minority Interests (in $ millions)	1999 Form 10-K	2000 Form 10-K	2001 Form 10-K	For 6 Months Ended June 30, 2002
Actual	$(191)	$194	$9	$157
Reported	230	559	434	340
Misstated Amount	421	365	425	183
Misstated Percentage	220%	188%	4,722%	119%

TABLE 1 ● SEC Calculations of HealthSouth's Overstatements

Source: http://www.sec.gov/litigation/complaints/comphealths.htm.

Scrushy had used a closed, private road to get to the corporate headquarters. On the inside of the building, he had access to an express elevator that did not stop for employees getting on and off at other floors. To get access to the executive floor, one needed a special elevator pass.

By October 2003, all five of HealthSouth's previous chief financial officers (CFOs) had pleaded guilty to fraud. Former CFO Michael Martin testified that he and Scrushy discussed the issue that the financial information in the SEC filing was false and that Scrushy told him to inflate the numbers to meet Wall Street's expectations.[17]

Another former CFO, Tad McVay, also claimed that Scrushy was aware of the financial statement manipulations. Scrushy responded by denying the allegation.[18] McVay claimed that Scrushy tried to rationalize the action by claiming that all companies manipulate their numbers.[19] Scrushy again denied the allegation. Scrushy was also quick to identify why the CFOs would have a motive to commit fraud and he would not: The CFOs had a personal financial incentive via bonuses, stock options, and the chance of promotion, which motivated them to manipulate the financial statements.[20] Yet Scrushy received more than $265 million in compensation between 1996 and 2002, which is the period when the alleged fraud took place. During this time, Scrushy was able to sell stock worth $99 million when the stock price was between $10 and $14. After the scandal became public, the stock quickly dropped to $3. Scrushy also sold five million shares of stock at $15 a share after announcing on CNBC that he was expecting the stock to go up into the twenties.

Some HealthSouth employees claimed that they were afraid of being fired if they said anything about the alleged fraud at the company.[21] Scrushy's directive ordered surveillance cameras and other equipment to monitor the actions of the employees. The federal government had initially claimed that HealthSouth inflated almost $3 billion in profits from 1996 to 2002. HealthSouth's new auditor, PricewaterhouseCoopers, stated that it may have uncovered closer to $5 billion in fraud from the company. Some of the new accounting irregularities included HealthSouth counting uncollected payments as revenue. In addition, HealthSouth understated the value of assets of certain acquisitions when the deal took place. HealthSouth would later increase, or "bleed," the true value in the financial statements to increase the net income estimates.[22]

Former HealthSouth CEO Speaks Out

In May 2004, HealthSouth appointed a new CEO, Jay Grinney. Grinney, a former top executive at HCA Healthcare, had the daunting task of taking over a company in crisis and helping to rebuild the image and trust for current and potential HealthSouth customers and investors. In January 2005, HealthSouth finally settled its Medicare lawsuit for $325 million. A component of the Medicare fraud by HealthSouth was having entertainment fees at management meetings in Orlando charged as Medicare expenses. Performers such as Faith Hill, Alabama, Brooks and Dunn, Amy Grant, Reba McEntire, and KC and the Sunshine Band performed at HealthSouth's annual management meetings. HealthSouth booked the cost of the annual meetings as "home office cost statements," which are allowed, in part, in Medicare claims as standard overhead costs.[23] By February 2005, HealthSouth had closed more than 300 rehabilitation and diagnostic centers that were not profitable, which was approximately 20% of the existing HealthSouth facilities.[24]

The Criminal Trial Starts

On January 25, 2005, the criminal trial of Richard Scrushy began in Birmingham, Alabama. HealthSouth was one of the first companies to be charged under the provisions of the Sarbanes-Oxley Act, which was passed by Congress in 2002. In fact, former chief financial officer Weston Smith resigned from HealthSouth on August 5, 2002, so he would not be forced to sign inaccurate financial statements, which is one of the provisions of the Sarbanes-Oxley Act.[25]

When the trial started, Scrushy and his lawyers already claimed a significant victory in their legal battle because the government dropped 30 criminal counts and stated that it would prosecute Scrushy on only 55 criminal counts instead of on the original 85 counts. Those 55 counts included conspiracy to commit fraud; filing inaccurate financial statements; and securities, mail, and wire frauds. The charges were later reduced to 36 after the trial had started.[26]

Scrushy and his lawyers failed to mention that even with the reduced number of counts, Scrushy faced as many as 450 years in prison, fines of more than $36 million, and the forfeiture of all assets that were acquired through "ill-gotten gains" including boats, houses, and cars. Foreshadowing the government's strategy, lead prosecutor Alice Martin stated that Scrushy was a very demanding and cunning CEO.[27] The defense showed its strategy in the opening arguments by stating that Scrushy was a successful CEO who did not know what lower-level managers were doing. Scrushy's lead attorney, Jim Parkman, stated that there was not a single piece of evidence that linked Scrushy to the fraud.[28]

The Consequences of the Fraud

On February 3, 2005, James Bennett, who was a former president and chief operating officer at HealthSouth, was indicted on 39 criminal counts including fraud, insider trading, money laundering, and telling false statements to the Federal Bureau of Investigation (FBI). Bennett was the 18th former HealthSouth manager charged since 2003. Also in February 2005, former HealthSouth controller and CFO Bill Owens stated in court that Scrushy was aware of the fraud and needed to continue to implement it for his own personal gain. Owens stated that Scrushy was fearful that a shareholder lawsuit would reduce his ability to sell his $100 million in HealthSouth stock.[29]

On April 6, 2005, HealthSouth accused its former auditor, Ernst & Young, of negligence for failing to discover the fraudulent operations of Scrushy and the other top executives at HealthSouth. This was in response to a lawsuit filed by Ernst & Young in March 2005 that stated that Ernst & Young wanted compensation for any potential class-action lawsuits against it from the HealthSouth account. Ernst & Young claimed that its reputation has been damaged by being connected with HealthSouth. In claiming its innocence, Ernst & Young stated that the fraudulent actions at HealthSouth were the direct result of HealthSouth's executives' and employees' calculated plan to deceive the external auditor by providing false information.[30]

The Phoenix Rises On June 28, 2005, after 21 days of deliberations, the 12-person jury found Richard Scrushy not guilty of all 36 criminal charges. The jury stated that the

Cases

government did not do a good job of presenting evidence that was beyond a reasonable doubt that Scrushy was guilty. In addition, the government had credibility issues with some of its star witnesses, according to jury members. One juror, Christopher Cooper, did not believe CFO Owens's statements about Scrushy's involvement in the fraud after it was disclosed that Owens was late filing his tax returns and lied about a HealthSouth loan of more than $1 million. Another juror asked why physical evidence was not taken to prove Scrushy's guilt. The juror, Debra Williams, stated that the prosecution should have tested the documents for fingerprints.[31] Another juror, Lutheran Harris, stated that there was fraud committed but that the prosecution did not provide enough evidence to prove that Scrushy committed the fraud.[32]

After Scrushy was released and walked out of the courthouse, he summed up his victory in religious terms, reminding his followers that Jesus had taught us how to love each other, and Scrushy questioned what had happened to all the compassion in the world.[33]

The Consequences Continue

In March 2006, HealthSouth announced that its losses for 2005 had more than doubled from the loss of the previous year. HealthSouth's loss of $446 million resulted largely from the settlements of lawsuits related to the accounting fraud. The loss was $271.5 million higher than the $174.5 million loss in 2004. The loss for 2005 included a reserve of $215 million to be paid for federal and state lawsuits. This payment was in addition to the $230 million that HealthSouth insurers agreed to pay to settle $445 million in lawsuits in February 2006.[34] In May 2006, HealthSouth agreed to pay the $3 million in fines to avoid criminal prosecution for its actions that occurred during the accounting fraud. The money went to the U.S. Postal Inspection Service's consumer fraud division. In explaining its decision to not prosecute, the DOJ predicted that criminal charges may have forced HealthSouth into bankruptcy with the loss of thousands of jobs. Furthermore, this would give HealthSouth the opportunity to increase the stock value for its investors. HealthSouth also agreed to implement more stringent internal controls for the company and would be on "probation" until 2009.[35]

Almost exactly 1 year after his acquittal, the compassion that Scrushy had wanted the world to have did not come to him in another courtroom. On June 29, 2006, Scrushy was convicted of giving a $500,000 bribe to the then governor of Alabama, Don Siegelman, in return for a position on a state regulatory board. Scrushy was found guilty of six charges, which included bribery, conspiracy, and mail fraud. The verdict came after the jury was deadlocked twice about the decision relating to the charges. The trial lasted 6 weeks, and there were 11 days of deliberations before the jury finally decided on a verdict. He faced a prison sentence of as long as 20 years for the mail fraud convictions[36,37] but served only 6 years; his prison sentence ended on July 25, 2012.[38]

In July 2006, a federal appeals court overruled former HealthSouth CFO Michael Martin's prison sentence, claiming the length of the sentence was too lenient. Martin had been sentenced to 5 years' probation and 1 week in jail. The appellate court stated that Martin's sentence was unreasonable and did not match the seriousness of the crimes that the former CFO had committed during his tenure at HealthSouth.[39] In September 2006, Martin was sentenced by a federal judge to 36 months in prison. Martin had pleaded guilty to fraud and had previously paid a fine of $50,000. In addition, he had forfeited $2.4 million that had been obtained through ill-gotten gains.[40]

In August 2006, the Alabama Supreme Court ordered Scrushy to repay HealthSouth $47.8 million in bonuses that were paid to him during the accounting fraud. The court agreed with the shareholder who sued Scrushy, stating that the former CEO received the bonuses without justification because HealthSouth was losing money during the payment period of the bonuses.[41] In November 2006, Scrushy negotiated to settle with HealthSouth for $31 million because Scrushy had asked HealthSouth to pay $21 million in attorney's fees from the company.[42]

In October 2006, a federal court refused to overturn the criminal convictions against Scrushy and former Alabama governor Don Siegelman.[43] In October 2006, HealthSouth began trading again on the New York Stock Exchange. It had been delisted from the exchange for 3½ years after the company struggled through resolving the issues of the fraud.[44]

In April 2007, Scrushy settled with the SEC for $81 million, which was composed of $77.5 million in forfeiture and $3.5 million in fines. In addition, Scrushy agreed not to serve as an officer or a director of a publicly traded company for at least 5 years.[45] In June 2007, HealthSouth announced that it would sell its Birmingham headquarters for $60 million. The headquarters, which had a Scrushy room of memorabilia and a private elevator so that Scrushy did not have to interact with his employees on the way up to his penthouse office, was the last tangible asset representing the Scrushy era at HealthSouth.[46]

In October 2007, HealthSouth received a tax refund of $400 million for the period when it overpaid taxes due on its inflated profits during the years when the company created fraudulent financial statements.[47]

The Phoenix Falls

On June 28, 2007, ex-Alabama Governor Siegelman was sentenced to 7 years 4 months in prison for accepting a bribe from Scrushy.[48] On March 27, 2008, Siegelman was ordered released from prison while his appeal went through the court system.[49] He lost his appeal and returned to prison on August 3, 2012.[50] Scrushy was not released because he was considered a flight risk. In February 2007, prior to Scrushy sentencing, prosecutors had alleged that Scrushy tried to flee the country in his 92-foot yacht, *Chez Soiree*, but bad weather kept him from reaching open waters. Scrushy explained that he had permission to travel to South Florida because the court had approved a family visit to Disney World. But Scrushy had neglected to tell his probation officer that his mode of transportation was to be a yacht. So prior to Scrushy's sentencing, the judge ordered Scrushy to wear a GPS device for all future trips out of Alabama, forbade him from using private travel, and ordered him to submit in writing a detailed itinerary of all future trips.[51]

In March 2008, HealthSouth CEO Jay Grinney estimated that the fraud cost the company $1 billion. His estimate was based on legal settlements and associated expenses. It also included $164 million spent on lawyers and accountants to reconstruct the financial statements. By 2008, HealthSouth employed 22,000 employees, a drop from a high of 52,000 in 2002.[52]

In May 2009, Scrushy stated he did not have any knowledge of the fraud during his civil lawsuit trial filed by HealthSouth stakeholders. Scrushy stated he was not aware of what the former HealthSouth CFO was doing with the numbers. Scrushy informed the court that every employee was given a plastic card with a toll free number to report fraudulent activities. In addition, at every management meeting, Scrushy asked the managers to hold up their fraud hotline plastic cards. Scrushy gave "evidence" to prove he knew nothing of the fraud by stating that HealthSouth would not have started the building of an expensive "digital" hospital if the company were in financial trouble.[53]

On June 18, 2009, the judge ordered Scrushy to pay $2.88 billion to settle the civil lawsuit with HealthSouth shareholders. It was the largest financial penalty ever assessed against one executive. HealthSouth had hired private investigators to see where Scrushy was potentially hiding his assets.[54] In the 2003 inventory of Scrushy's assets, among the assets listed were seven boats, three airplanes, 45 pieces of art including 1 Salvador Dali, 4 pieces by Pablo Picasso, 4 pieces by Pierre-Auguste Renoir, and 7 pieces by Marc Chagall. In addition, some of the jewelry listed included a 48.17-carat diamond bracelet with 30 stones and a pair of 6.09-carat diamond stud earrings.[55] Scrushy's 17,000-square foot Birmingham mansion was seized and was valued at $5 million. Leslie Scrushy was "forced" to move to a small house in a Houston suburb and claimed, "I buy a whole lot more at Wal-Mart and Target than before." In addition, she had to find a job so that she and her children could be covered by her employer's health insurance plan.[56] In January 2012, a U.S. district court in Montgomery Alabama reduced Richard Scrushy's sentence from 82 months to 70 months. The reduction in the sentence occurred after the federal appeals court dropped two charges of bribery and fraud against Scrushy.[57] On April 12, 2012, Richard Scrushy was released from a federal prison in Beaumont, Texas, and was moved to a halfway house in Houston. On May 10, 2012 he moved from the halfway house to house confinement. On July 25, 2012, his prison sentence finished and the three years' probation started.[58] On November 14, 2014, Richard Scrushy was released from his final eight months of probation.[59]

Questions for Thought

1. Why do you think Scrushy was acquitted of all charges related to the HealthSouth fraud?

2. Identify the stakeholders in this case. Explain the impact of the fraud on each of the stakeholders.

3. Do you think it is feasible for Richard Scrushy not to have known about the fraud if all CFOs admitted to it? Explain. Is it really feasible for a CFO to commit fraud without the CEO being involved? Explain.

10

De Beers and the Conflict Diamonds: A Monopoly Doesn't Last Forever

S ince the 1950s, humans have been able to make synthetic diamonds. Yet, consumers demand "real" diamonds for their jewelry, but at what cost? The diamond industry has been marred with numerous ethical issues. From child labor to a company controlling the global market, diamonds have had a phenomenal economic, social, and political impact globally. The image of the diamond is critical because the diamond does not have any intrinsic value. For more than half a century, humans have been able to develop synthetic diamonds that are used in industrial settings. Diamonds are carbon based, so they are one of the strongest substances known to man. Before the invention of synthetic diamonds, manufacturers bought diamonds on the open market to be used as drill bits and cutting tools. However, when General Electric developed the world's first synthetic diamond, there was no longer a viable need for natural diamonds. Diamonds were then delegated purely for cosmetic reasons. Thousands and thousands of people have died, been maimed, or been displaced from their homes because of a mineral that sparkles as a piece of jewelry.

The Challenge of Conflict Diamonds

Conflict or "blood" diamonds are diamonds that have been mined in a country that is in a civil war. The United Nations defines *conflict diamonds* as "diamonds that originate from areas controlled by forces or factions opposed to legitimate and internationally recognized governments, and are used to fund military action in opposition to those governments or in contravention of the decisions of the Security Council."[1]

The release of the movie *Blood Diamond* starring Leonardo DiCaprio as a diamond smuggler brought the issue of conflict diamonds to the forefront. *Blood Diamond* was set in Sierra Leone during its civil war and showed brutal images of murder, kidnapping, and mutilation. Some scenes included having children selecting which of their limbs would be amputated by the rebels to ensure children obey the commands of the rebels. Furthermore, additional scenes showed men being forced from their villages and being required to mine for diamonds as "slaves" to the rebels.

One of the reasons why conflict diamonds can be potentially common in funding civil wars is the location of the diamonds. In Western African countries such as Sierra Leone, Liberia, and the Ivory Coast, diamonds are located in marshy areas and river-beds. The diamonds are very close to the surface of the ground, so it is very easy for anyone to "mine" the fields. In addition, it is very easy for a rebel group to seize control of the marshy area and force workers to mine the area. In other areas of the continent such as Botswana, the diamonds are found inside dormant volcano tubes. This type of mining and removal requires additional heavy machinery and may be closely protected by the government. In addition, if the country believes there is a threat that these mines will be seized by the rebels, the government can order that the opening of the mine be closed using explosives. As a result, countries with marshy, easy to obtain diamonds fields are more likely to have extended civil wars than are countries that do not have these marshy areas.[2] For example, in 1999, $200 million in conflict diamonds were smuggled out of Sierra Leone. During the height of the conflict diamonds trade in the 1980s and 1990s, 4% of all global diamond trade involved conflict diamonds. Furthermore, the smuggling of conflict diamonds is a very effective way for terrorists and other criminal organizations to launder money. Ill-gotten gains from illegal activities would be used to buy conflict diamonds illegally and then the conflict diamonds would be smuggled out of the country and sold legally as conflict-free diamonds. This is one method al Qaeda used to fund its operations. The true tragedy of this illegal trade is the needless loss of life. Approximately 3.7 million people have been killed in Africa so others could gain access to conflict diamonds, and another 6 million people have lost their homes because of the forced evaluation of rebels mining for conflict diamonds.[3]

Diamonds and the Resource Curse Syndrome

The *resource curse syndrome* can be described as an imbalance between the positive and negative impacts of a country based on having a bountiful supply of a valuable resource. It is traditionally assumed that a country with abundant valuable natural resources will be able to capitalize on the sale of these resources by increasing the standard of living of the citizens of the country; however, this is not always the case. It has been shown that valuable natural resources can actually result in more negative than positive impacts for the country. Valuable natural resources can lead to corruption, political instability, and potential violent conflict including civil wars. These results show the ironic impact of natural resources. Therefore, a country like Sierra Leone can be "cursed" in having a large supply of diamonds, which results in the country being among the poorest in the world. Furthermore, Sierra Leone and other resource-rich countries tend to become dependent on the diamond trade. By focusing all their economic activities toward one industry, even if the political and social climate stabilizes, these countries will have unpredictability in the economic climate because the gross domestic product (GDP) of the nation is dominated by one industry.[4] For example, in Botswana, 33% of the GDP is directly related to the diamond industry.[5]

The Kimberley Process

In response to diamonds being sold in conflict areas, the United Nations developed the Kimberley Process certification scheme. The process is based on having the governments of diamond-producing countries certify that the diamonds being traded did not come from a conflict zone. This certification process included having a certificate that demonstrates the country of origin of the diamonds. To be a member of the Kimberley certification process, the country must pass legislation that monitors and certifies the diamonds based on the criteria established by the Kimberley certification process. To ensure that conflict diamonds are not included in the trade, Kimberley members are required to only deal with other members in the buying and selling of diamonds.[6]

The origins of the Kimberley process started in 1998 when the United Nations adopted a resolution that banned the export of diamonds from Angola. Angola was in the midst of a bloody civil war. The resolution did not stop the flow of conflict diamonds into the marketplace. In 2000, the United Nations developed a preliminary version of a policy related to conflict diamonds that would become the foundation of the Kimberley Process.[7]

The Kimberley Process resulted partly from the pressure from the nongovernmental organization (NGO) Global Witness. Global Witness provided evidence to the public showing the direct link between conflict diamonds and arms dealing. The initial meeting of member countries occurred in Kimberley, South Africa, which happens to be the birthplace of De Beers, the world's largest diamond-producing company. After the completion of 3 years of negotiation, the final agreement was approved in 2003 and was endorsed by the UN General Assembly and the UN Security Council. Since 2003, the members have met annually to discuss any issues related to the certification process.[8] In the past, members have been forced to withdraw their membership from the Kimberley Process. In 2004, the Republic of Congo lost its Kimberley Process membership when it could not explain its sudden significant increase in diamond exports.[9] One way in which smugglers in conflict zones can bypass the trade ban is to smuggle the diamonds from a conflict zone to a conflict-free zone. As a result, conflict diamonds will be certified as "conflict free" from a Kimberley Process member even though the true origin of the diamonds is from a conflict zone. One way to monitor this type of smuggling is to evaluate whether there has been a sudden jump in exported diamonds without a corresponding jump in new diamond mine discoveries. In 2007, the Republic of Congo rejoined the Kimberley Process when the country demonstrated the improvement of monitoring and control system for diamonds being traded in their country.

In September 2009, the Zimbabwe government was allegedly guilty of murder and human rights violations by its army and police pertaining to diamond mining. Zimbabwe is a Kimberley Process member. A Kimberley Process representative visited Zimbabwe and found evidence of killings and forced labor in the diamond fields. The team recommendation was that Zimbabwe suspend itself from membership in the Kimberley Process.[10] As expected, smugglers in Zimbabwe searched for an outlet for their potential "conflict" diamonds. They found an outlet in Zimbabwe's neighbor Mozambique. Although Mozambique does not have any diamond fields or mines, a significant market for rough diamonds developed. The diamonds are sold in Mozambique and shipped to another country to be cut and polished and then sold as "conflict free." Although no one knows exactly how many diamonds are being smuggled out of Zimbabwe, in the previous year, 2008, 59% of Zimbabwe's diamond product was not exported through official commerce channels. On the black market, conflict diamonds can sell anywhere from $1 to $4,000 per carat depending on the quality of the stone. In addition, buyers of conflict diamonds in Mozambique can earn as much as $100,000 a month buying and selling diamonds.[11]

In November 2009, the Kimberley members decided not to suspend Zimbabwe despite the evidence their own team collected on alleged human rights violations and murder. The members concluded that the military in Zimbabwe did have organized smuggling organizations and did use extreme violence against illegal miners. However, Kimberley Process members decided that instead of sanctioning, they would send a monitor to determine whether future exports from the disputed areas in Zimbabwe could be certified as conflict free. Human rights organizations and other NGOs voiced their complaints pertaining to the decision made by the Kimberley members, stating that the lack of sanctions proved that the Kimberley Process does not have the power to stop countries from committing illegal acts and human rights violations on its citizens. Global Witness, the NGO that started the pressure on the industry to develop the Kimberley Process, stated that the decision by the Kimberley members sets a bad precedent in which violations of laws and the requirements of the Kimberley Process agreement will result in no real punishment.[12] In December 2011, Global Witness withdrew from the Kimberley Process because of its continual non-action related to the alleged human rights violations in Zimbabwe. Global Witness stated that the Kimberley Process had failed and that its members should now be considered accomplices to diamond laundering.[13]

In 2011, 75 countries were members of the Kimberley Process and the diamond production from these countries represented 99.8% of the global diamond trade.[14] Although not a member of the Kimberley Process, the United States passed the Clean Diamond Trade Act in April 2003. This act created the Office of the Special Advisor for Conflict Diamonds located within the U.S. Department of State. The Department of State requires all rough diamond importers and exporters who do business in the United States to file annual reports verifying they are not trafficking in conflict diamonds.[15]

A Monopoly Is Born: De Beers

Cecil Rhodes established De Beers in 1888. Rhodes would later be known as only one of a few people in the world to have a country named after him (Rhodesia, which is now called Zimbabwe). In addition, Rhodes is known today as the founder of the Rhodes Scholar program for academically gifted students. The origin of the name De Beers is based on the family name of the owners of the first discovered diamond mine in South Africa. Located in Kimberley, the land was the starting point for the aggressive growth strategy for De Beers. Rhodes realized that the only way to become more efficient and reduce costs for mining was to acquire large tracks of land that adjoined or was close in proximity to each other. As a result, De Beers quickly bought out numerous landowners in the surrounding areas where they predicted would have additional diamond deposits. One influential turning point in the early strategy of De Beers was when the company signed an exclusive agreement with the London Diamond Syndicate, which had agreed to purchase all of De Beers's diamonds. De Beers quickly learned that having a guaranteed buyer was critical for the long-term success of the company. De Beers used this same model when it sold diamonds to dealers through the Central Selling Organization.

The Central Selling Organization

When De Beers became big enough to control the supply of diamonds, it was rewarded handsomely by serving the demand side of the diamond trade. For a large part of the 20th century, De Beers controlled approximately 90% of the diamond supply. This monopoly power allowed De Beers to establish the "single channel marketing" system in which it controlled the supply of diamonds globally. The result is that De Beers also controlled the demand of the diamonds by deciding which customers would be allocated which assortment of diamonds. De Beers justified the single channel marketing system by stating that the system guaranteed stability in the marketplace related to the buying and selling of diamonds.[16]

The single channel marketing system allowed De Beers to control the supply and the demand for diamonds through its "sight holders" system. De Beers invited clients to come to view its diamonds in London 10 times during the year. During each meeting, 125 clients, or sight holders, were allowed to see the diamonds that had been allocated to them by De Beers. These sight holders were required to buy, as is, the lot assigned to them. There was no negotiation on price, quality, or quantity. The client paid for the diamonds through De Beers Central Selling sales unit. If the client refused to buy the diamonds, the client would not be invited back to a future sight holders meeting, and another client would take that place.[17]

Controlling the Supply of Diamonds

Of course, this system can only work if De Beers controlled the supply of diamonds. This objective was accomplished through two principal means: land acquisition and contract buyers. De Beers continued to buy more and more land where diamonds were located. As a result, it became the dominant player in the diamond industry. In addition, De Beers had standing contracts with independent buyers such that these buyers would purchase whatever diamonds De Beers had available to sell. Therefore, De Beers could establish an artificial "scarcity" by controlling the supply of diamonds. For diamonds that were found in dormant volcano tubes, controlling the supply meant buying the land where the diamond deposits are located. The more difficult task was controlling the supply in the countries in which the diamonds were located in marshy, river areas near the surface of the ground. For these diamond deposits, it was much more difficult to control the supply and mining of the diamonds. To attempt to control the supply during the early 20th century, De Beers allegedly sought and received aid from the British government in controlling the diamond mining operations of countries that were British colonies. The government of these countries used intimidation and brute force to enforce the interests of De Beers.

As African countries broke away from Britain and became independent countries, De Beers shifted its focus to establishing strong relationships with whoever was in power. Therefore, De Beers controlled vast amounts of diamond deposits and used its influence to help control supply of diamonds for those areas that De Beers did not own. However, there was still a supply of diamonds that was not connected directly or indirectly with De Beers influence. For these diamonds, De Beers relied on its contact with the 1,300 independent buyers by offering to purchase whatever diamonds they had to sell. The new result was that De Beers was able to effectively control almost the entire supply of diamonds globally.[18]

De Beers and Marketing

De Beers officials realized that promoting diamonds had to include a glamorous image so that everyone would want to buy a diamond. In 1947, De Beers started the

"A Diamond Is Forever" advertising campaign.[19] Frances Gerety of De Beers's ad agency, N. W. Ayer, created the phrase after she had developed a number of ads for De Beers, and the initial response from De Beers was not overwhelmingly positive. However, the phrase helped create a permanent demand for diamond engagement rings. In the 1940s, N. W. Ayer had conducted a number of consumer surveys and discovered that the general perception of the American public was that diamonds were a luxury item only bought by the very wealthy. Most people thought that buying a diamond was a waste of money because it did not have a useful purpose like buying a washing machine or a new car. As a result, N. W. Ayer proposed a marketing campaign for De Beers

> to create a situation where almost every person pledging marriage feels compelled to acquire a diamond engagement ring. . . . Sentiment is essential to your advertising, as it is to your product. . . for the emotional connotation of the diamond is the one competitive advantage which no other product can claim or dispute.[20]

Voted the top advertising slogan of the 20th century by *Advertising Age* in 1999, this campaign is still used and consolidated De Beers's power in the luxury jewelry marketplace. The long-term "value" of a diamond became the focal point for engagement rings, with De Beers convincing women that the only type of engagement ring that shows "true long-term commitment" is a diamond. Before this campaign, a number of precious gems were considered viable and acceptable to be used for engagement rings. This viewpoint changed forever after 1947,[21] as can be seen in the purchasing pattern for engagement rings in the United States. In 1939, 10% of engagement rings were diamonds. By 1990, 80% of a much larger market of engagement rings were diamonds.[22] De Beers also convinced movie studios to include scenes in which the stars of the pictures wore beautiful diamonds. For one movie, *Skylark*, De Beers's ad agency was able to convince the studio to include a scene of the famous actress Claudette Colbert buying a diamond bracelet. In the movie *That Uncertain Feeling*, an actress wore $40,000 worth of diamond jewelry. The crowning jewel for De Beers occurred when De Beers's ad agency convinced the movie studio to have Marilyn Monroe sing "Diamonds Are a Girl's Best Friend" in the movie *Gentlemen Prefer Blondes*.[23] N. W. Ayer also developed the idea of evaluating a diamond based on the 4 C's: color, clarity, cut, carat. The idea of the 4 C's came about when De Beers had a surplus of very small stones and, at that time, size was the major determining factor in purchasing a diamond. N. W. Ayer added a box on all print advertising titled "How to Buy a Diamond" that listed the instructions on how to select a diamond based on the 4 C's. The instructions were "Ask about color, clarity, and cutting—for these determine a diamond's quality, contribute to its beauty and value. Choose a fine stone, and you'll always be proud of it, no matter what its size (carat)."[24] In addition, N. W. Ayer was responsible for establishing how much a customer should pay for a diamond. It was arbitrary but authoritative sounding: The advice "Isn't two months' salary a small price to pay for something that lasts forever?" was introduced in De Beers marketing in the 1980s.[25]

De Beers and Ethical Issues

De Beers and Conflict Diamonds De Beers had to buy diamonds from every source to control the supply of diamonds, which meant the company also had to buy conflict diamonds. De Beers could not pick and choose its suppliers because the origin of the diamonds did not matter from De Beers's strategic focus. In a report issued in 1999, Global Witness alleged that De Beers had bought diamonds from Angola during its civil war from 1992 to 1997. De Beers officials admitted that they had purchased the conflict diamonds. De Beers had bought diamonds from the rebels, who used the proceeds to acquire arms to fight the Angolan government. De Beers stated that it was not supporting the rebels, per se, but just wanted to ensure the stability of the diamond market by acquiring the diamonds.[26]

Bowing to overwhelming external pressure, De Beers agreed to stop purchasing any more blood diamonds in 2000. De Beers officials realized that they needed to do this from a marketing perspective, and they realized that if the government agreed not to export conflict diamonds (for example, by the future Kimberley Process), De Beers would not have to worry about these "excess" diamonds reaching the open market. De Beers let the governments be involved in the control of the supply of diamonds, and De Beers set up a verification and control system in which De Beers "guarantees" that the diamonds it sells are conflict free.[27]

De Beers and Apartheid Apartheid became the official ruling system by the government in South Africa in 1948. *Apartheid* is Afrikaans for apartness and meant that the government had the authority to separate the black and white races, as well as segregate "Asian" and "mixed races." Nonwhite races were forced to move from their own land and lived in mostly poor segregated areas. The whites of South Africa controlled 86% of the land, which included locations of all the major mineral areas in the country. The blacks of South Africa had their movements strictly controlled and were not allowed to vote or to own land.[28]

Although De Beers was "officially" against apartheid, in reality, it was a perfect system for De Beers. By having complete control over the black citizens of the country, De Beers could use the South African government as an ally to ensure that there was no employee uprising for the working conditions in the De Beers mines. In fact, the complaint that the head of De Beers at the time, Harry Oppenheimer, had related to apartheid was not for his concerns about human rights and equality but that apartheid could reduce the profitability of the production at De Beers's mines because of the inefficiencies of the workers.[29]

De Beers and Price Fixing In 1955, General Electric discovered a process in which to create human-made diamonds. In a process similar to cultured pearls, the diamonds can be developed to any carat, color, clarity, and cut specifications. The net result is that manufacturers no longer had to depend on "natural" diamonds for commercial applications. Thus, General Electric became a critical "competitor" to De Beers with one significant advantage; General Electric can make its own diamonds and does not have to mine them, as is the case with De Beers's other competitors. From De Beers's perspective, the obvious solution was to collude with General Electric for the price of commercial diamonds. De Beers has been charged four times with price fixing by the Department of Justice (DOJ). In 1994, criminal charges were filed against De Beers with the warning that De Beers's executives would be detained if they entered the United States.[30] De Beers was banned from doing business in the United States until the company resolved the pending criminal charges. Therefore, if De Beers wanted to

Cases

do business in the United States with the expansion of retail stores, company officials needed to address the price fixing charges and did so in July 2004. De Beers officials finally agreed to plead guilty to criminal price fixing charges, so they could execute their strategy of expansion into in the United States.

With 50% of the global diamond market in the United States, De Beers could no longer ignore the growth potential of doing business in the United States. The formal charges were based on De Beers violating the Sherman Antitrust Act by colluding on prices in the industrial diamond market.[31] As part of the final settlement, De Beers agreed to pay a $10 million fine.[32] In December 2005, De Beers agreed to settle four class-action civil lawsuits by paying the plaintiffs $250 million.[33]

The Current Status of De Beers

Until the early 1980s, De Beers controlled 90% of the global diamond market. By the mid-1980s, this had dropped to 85%. By 2000, De Beers's market share dropped further to 65%, and by 2005, it had dropped to 60%. In 2007, it had fallen to 40%. A number of factors caused this decline, but the major factor is the discovery of major diamond deposits in Canada, Russia, and Australia.[34] The result is that De Beers does not have the power or the resources any more to control the supply of diamonds in the marketplace. Furthermore, De Beers's monopolistic attitude toward its customers made it very easy for suppliers to buy their diamonds from alternative sources. In 2011, De Beers's market share had dropped to 36%, and its diamond production dropped from 33 million carats in 2010 to 31.3 million carats in 2011. Its sales had increased 26% from 2010 to $7.4 billion, while its earnings increased by 21% to $1.7 billion.[35] In November 2011, the parent company of De Beers, Anglo American, announced that it would pay $5.1 billion to buy the Oppenheimer family's share of De Beers.[36] In 2013, De Beers's sales were $6.4 billion and its earnings were $532 million.[37]

Questions for Thought

1. How does the diamond industry compare with other industries that have created demand for their products?

2. What are your views on De Beers purchasing conflict diamonds?

3. Does the consumer really care whether diamonds are conflict free? Explain the significance of the term *conflict free* with respect to diamonds.

4. Synthetic diamonds are now produced. If they choose to sell these diamonds, how would De Beers's corporate strategy change?

11

Interface: More Than Just a Carpet Company

Interface's dedication to sustainability has evolved into the company's Mission Zero commitment— our promise to eliminate any negative impact Interface has on the environment by 2020.[1]

—Interface's Mission Statement

This credo drives Interface's strategic focus as it competes in the highly competitive floor-coverings industry. Interface was started in 1973 by Ray Anderson to fill the need to manufacture flexible floor coverings for commercial customers. Started as a joint venture between British-owned Carpets International and a group of American investors, Interface began its operations in LaGrange, Georgia. Today, Interface is the largest producer of soft-surfaced modular floor coverings in the world. But what makes Interface unique is its ability to ship custom-designed flooring around the world while having environmental sustainability interwoven into every decision of the company, much like the fibers in its carpets.

Dan Hendrix, president and chief executive officer, stated, "I believe that not only must we do our best, but we must be the best at everything we do."[2] This underlying commitment to excellence in whatever it does helps drive Interface as it climbs "Mount Sustainability." Interface considers the sustainability impact of every operational decision from the raw materials that are selected to the best method used to recycle the flooring after the customer has finished with the product.

The Road to Sustainability

When Anderson started Interface more than 30 years ago, sustainability was not part of the strategic decision-making process. Over time, however, he realized that his company could reduce its environmental footprint on the earth while setting an example for other companies. In 1994, Anderson read Paul Hawken's book *The Ecology of Commerce* (1993) and *Ishmael* (1992) by Daniel Quinn. After reading those books, Anderson created the "Eco Dream Team" made up of some of the best-known experts on sustainability. From this starting point, Interface became fully competent in becoming a completely sustainable company. The first challenge was to define *sustainability*. Anderson proposed that a viable definition for *sustainability* would be "a dynamic process which enables all people to realize their potential and to improve their quality of life in ways that simultaneously protect and enhance the Earth's life support systems."[3]

Furthermore, Anderson stated that sustainability is not just an option, but a responsibility of everyone to protect the environment for future generations:

"Humanity has the ability to make development sustainable—to ensure that it meets the needs of the present without compromising the ability of future generations to meet their own needs."[4]

To climb Mount Sustainability, Interface has proposed that there are seven faces (or fronts) of the mountain: (1) eliminate waste, (2) benign emissions, (3) renewable energy, (4) closing the loop, (5) resource-efficient transportation, (6) sensitizing stakeholders, and (7) redesigning commerce.

Elimination of Waste[5] The sustainability challenge of eliminating waste is to reverse the enormous amount of waste that is generated when manufacturing products. Because there is only a finite amount of resources available on the planet, Interface was determined to eliminate waste wherever it was possible. The process began by first identifying what the current sources of waste at Interface were, then initially reducing the waste, and eventually eliminating the waste. Interface defines *waste* as any cost that does not produce value to its customers.[6] Therefore, waste is not only a by-product of production but also any activity that is not done correctly the first time, such as a misdirected shipment, an incorrect invoice, or a defective product.

The reduction of waste has been accomplished at Interface by redesigning products and the processes used to manufacture the products. In addition, what was previously considered to be a waste product was remanufactured into additional resources that could be used in the next step in the production cycle.

To help use opportunities that could occur to reduce waste, Interface established the QUEST program. QUEST stands for "Quality Utilizing Employee Suggestions and Teamwork." Through the QUEST program, Interface was able to save $300 million in 2005. An example of the simple way cost savings were generated at Interface occurred when the Interface manufacturing facility in Maine installed a brass nozzle, which cost $8.50. This nozzle reduced the amount of water needed in the plant by 2 million gallons annually.

Benign Emissions[7] The sustainability issue on this mountain face is to identify areas within the company that could reduce, or even eliminate, emissions into the ecosphere. The ultimate goal of this challenge is to have only products, clean air, and clean water being released from the Interface plants.

Interface monitors and evaluates all of the 247 air emissions stacks and the 19 wastewater effluent pipes in its global manufacturing ring operations. Instead of just trying to control emissions, Interface reviews the plant facilities to see if the air emission stack and effluent pipes are needed. By December 2004, Interface had reduced the number of air emission stacks in its facilities by 35% and the number of effluent pipes by 53%.

To evaluate the impact Interface's emissions have on global pollution, Anderson requested that Interface compile a list of emission standards from around the world and determine which standards were the most stringent. After that determination had been made, the emission releases for each emission stack and effluent pipe at Interface were evaluated using those standards as the benchmark.

In the area of water management, Interface examined how wastewater can be naturally treated and reused. At its Fabrics Division, Interface was able to reduce the number of gallons used per production unit by 30% by reusing the water in the production process.

In the area of toxic chemicals, Interface has established an initiative to eliminate the use of materials that are ecologically damaging in the production process. In 1996, Interface established the Toxic Chemical Elimination Team, which was responsible for analyzing the manufacturing processes in each of Interface's plants with the goal of eliminating the use of all toxic chemicals. The chemicals were defined as *toxic* based on the definition given by the Environmental Protection Agency (EPA) as part of the Emergency Planning and Community Right-to-Know Act (ERCRA), which is also known as SARA 313, referring to Section 313 of the Superfund Amendment and Reauthorization Act. The steps used to eliminate toxic chemicals included the elimination of chlorofluorocarbons (CFCs), hydrochlorofluorocarbons (HCFCs), and other ozone-depleting substances in the manufacturing process and the elimination of all volatile chlorinated chemicals, which are used primarily in the cooling and refrigeration stage in the manufacturing process. Interface also reduced the number of suppliers that provided chemicals in the manufacturing process so the company was able to better track and control what types of chemicals were coming into the manufacturing facilities.

An example of how the levels of chemicals were reduced in the manufacturing process occurred at Interface's Guilford, Maine, Dyehouse facility. The Dyehouse manager believed that Interface was using too much of the antistatic chemicals in the dye process. The manager felt that the amount of the chemical could be reduced without affecting the quality of the product and would result in cost savings as well as the reduction of chemicals used. The plant managers discovered that the manufacturing process would be the same with only 17% of the amount of the antistatic chemicals used in the dyeing process. Because of this result, Interface now tests all process chemicals before they are used in the manufacturing process.

Interface has developed numerous methods to evaluate the indoor air quality challenge that affects the products manufactured by Interface. It has developed a nonprofit partnership with other companies called the EnviroSense Consortium that evaluates indoor air quality issues. In addition, Interface's research and development department focuses on design products that have a minimal impact on indoor air quality. Furthermore, Interface integrates its toxic chemical elimination commitment by manufacturing products that have benign chemical properties.

Renewable Energy[8] Interface is committed to using less energy and to incorporating more renewable energy in its manufacturing process. Four of Interface's facilities operate with 100% renewable energy. Two of the four plants are located in the United States (Georgia and California), and the other two plants are located in Europe (United Kingdom and Northern Ireland). Interface is in the process of converting two additional facilities into 100% renewable energy uses. A total of 13% of Interface's global energy consumption is based on renewable energy sources.

Closing the Loop[9] Interface refers to "closing the loop" as the process used by the company to be able to continuously reuse and recycle materials in a "closed" circle process. The challenge is to continue to use the same resources multiple times instead of constantly extracting new resources from the ecosystem. One method Interface uses to close the loop is to reduce the use of petro-based materials via renewable energy and the rematerialization and dematerialization of their materials. Furthermore, Interface is committed to developing a closed-loop recycling program. The first step in the recycling process is to use recycled materials in Interface products. The next step that Interface has taken is to develop different technologies in the manufacturing process so the plants can use recycled raw materials from existing carpets and other textiles. Interface highlights the benefits of closed-loop recycling, which includes a reduction of the material needed to make the products, the reduction of new resources needed from the earth, the reduction of waste that fills up landfills, the reduction of the costs needed to manufacture the products, and the reduction of the costs of the products, which is passed on to the customers.

Interface also includes the design processes as part of the closed-loop system. One of the innovations in the design process at Interface was to develop new carpeting products that were more durable but required fewer materials than the previous design. Interface calls this redesign process the Sustainable Design Stairway. The stairway was designed based on the four principles used to reduce a company's environmental footprint on the earth. The four principles are reduce-reuse-recycle-redesign. The bottom step, reduce, focuses on asking the employees at Interface to do something by using less material. The second step, reuse, focuses on what Interface calls "zippered products," which are products that are designed to be dismantled easily to make it easier to reuse the components within the product again. The third step, recycle, relates to focusing on single-polymer products, which facilitate additional opportunities to recycle the material and, therefore, have the material stay within the sustainable "loop." The top step, redesign, focuses on the development of new products that are incorporated within the sustainability "loop" so the sustainability gains from the previous three steps support the development of new sustainable products.

Resource Efficient Transportation[10] Interface's Resource Efficient Transportation initiative uses the most sustainable transportation means available to move people, products, information, and resources. Interface's activities include belonging to the Business for Social Responsibility's Green Freight Group and the EPA's SmartWay Transport voluntary partnership program. In addition, Interface established the Trees for Travel program, which involves Interface planting trees to offset the carbon dioxide emissions from air travel. To date, Interface has planted more than 62,000 trees with its partnership with American Forests. In addition, Interface sponsors the Cool CO_2mmute program. In this program, Interface employees buy trees to be planted by American Forests to offset the CO_2 emissions that are released as they commute to and from work.

Sensitizing Stakeholders[11] "Interface's mission is to become a restorative enterprise, striving to understand and achieve sustainability and influence others to see the opportunity of 'Doing Well by Doing Good.'"[12]

Using these beliefs as a base for how Interface interacts with its stakeholders, the company makes all vested stakeholders aware of Interface's commitment to sustainability. As part of the process, in January 2000, all the top managers at Interface met to discuss how sustainability could be integrated into the five *P*s: people, product, process, place, and profit.

Redesign Commerce[13] Anderson said, "At Interface we seek to become the first sustainable corporation in the world, and, following that, the first restorative company. It means creating the technologies of the future—kinder, gentler technologies that emulate nature's systems. I believe that's where we will find the right model."[14]

The premise of redesign commerce calculates the true cost to manufacture a product. Instead of viewing Interface as a company that provides flooring products, employees view Interface as a company providing service and value. One of the initiatives of the redesign commerce initiative is the Re:Entry program, which takes materials that would have been thrown into a landfill and uses them in the production process.

The Continued Benefits of Sustainability

In April 2006, Interface announced that it had increased its use of renewable electricity in 2005 in its global operations to 22%, which was a significant increase over the use of 5% of renewable electricity in its plants in 2000. Five of Interface's plants were operating with 100% green electricity, which is made renewable by purchasing certified renewable energy certificates from wind and biomass projects. Furthermore, Interface was able to reduce greenhouse gas emissions by 35% though production efficiency and renewable energy purchases. In the carpet reclamation program, Interface captured 18 million pounds of carpet that would have been discarded in landfills. Of those, 71% was recycled, 28% was used for energy capture and conversion, and 1% was donated to charitable organizations.[15]

In May 2006, Interface was ranked 24th in *Business Ethics* magazine's top 100 Best Corporate Citizens list.[16] In November 2006, Interface announced that its new Chinese facility in Shanghai had received the Leadership in Energy and Environmental Design (LEED) gold certification from the U.S. Green Building Council. The Interface facility was the first building in China to receive this certification. The design of the building helped in such sustainability issues as water conservation, energy efficiency, and the use of reclaimed and reused materials.[17] Interface also announced that the seating fabric used in the 2008 Ford Escape Hybrid would be made from soft drink bottle resin.[18]

Interface in 2011

As Interface moves quickly toward its 2020 goal of zero emissions, company staff members continue to make tremendous strides in their commitment to the environment. Since Interface started Mount Sustainability in 1995, the company's energy use per unit has decreased by 43%; Interface now uses 35% renewable energy; greenhouse gas emissions have been reduced by 44%; the waste that was sent to landfills has decreased by 77%; the water use per unit has decreased by 80%; and recycled and bio-based raw materials compose 36% of Interface products. In addition, eight of the nine manufacturing plants operate with 100% renewable electricity. Interface's waste elimination program has resulted in a reduction of waste cost by 42% since 1995. Interface has identified the three major challenges in reaching its zero emissions goal by 2020. The first challenge is to be more productive and efficient in converting recycled raw materials into sustainable closed-loop products. The second challenge is to continue to motivate the culture within Interface so that the employees continue to be fully motivated to achieve the 2020 goals. The third challenge is to become more aggressive in moving toward the zero impact footprint goals on industrial waste, Interface's use of energy, and the reduction of greenhouse gas emissions.[19] But the largest challenge of all for Interface occurred on August 9, 2011. Ray Anderson, founder and visionary of Interface, died of cancer at the age of 77. In one of his speeches, he commented, "We are all part of the continuum of humanity and life. We will have lived our brief span and either helped or hurt that continuum and the earth that sustains all life. It's that simple. Which will it be?"[20]

Interface in 2013

In 2013, Interface continued using 35% renewable energy in its operations, with five of the seven factories operating at 100% renewable energy. The GHG Emissions per unit of product had decreased from 1.7 pounds in 2011 to 0.8 pounds in 2013. The amount of waste sent to landfills from carpet production has decreased from 2.5 million to 1.2 million pounds from 2011 to 2013.[21] Financially, Interface's net sales increased from $953.45 million to $959.989 million from 2011 to 2013, while net income increased from $38.721 million in 2011 to $48.225 million in 2013.[22]

Questions for Thought

1. Identify the companies that are part of the EnviroSense Consortium. Do you believe that any of these companies are as committed to sustainability as Interface?

2. Interface makes its commitment to sustainability issues seem so simple. Why don't other companies follow its example?

3. Define *sustainability*. What's so important about sustainability from a business perspective?

4. Compare and contrast Interface's environmental actions with a Fortune 100 company.

Cases

12

Facebook and Privacy:
Big Brother "Likes" Us

From the time of Facebook's inception in a Harvard University dorm room, Mark Zuckerberg's goal was to develop software to share information. His first software allowed Harvard students to see who had signed up for classes because he understood how important the social aspects of interacting with friends in the classroom really were. He moved on to a rating system for women that his friends could share and revise, based on their experiences. The software moved beyond these narrow focuses to become a social network that could link friends with other friends on the Internet. Named after his student and faculty guide at his prep school, "The Facebook" was born. It quickly spread to other Ivy League schools, and officially became Facebook in 2004.[1]

So, 20 years after George Orwell's future world of constant electronic monitoring of individuals was predicted to occur in his book *1984*, Facebook allowed the constant electronic monitoring of "friends" of individuals anywhere in the world. As a result, from its inception, privacy has been an issue of concern pertaining to Facebook.

The Early Days of Facebook

Zuckerberg's casual attitude toward others' privacy was evident from the start when he "hacked" into Harvard's database to get dorm ID pictures of the women he was evaluating on his software system. His view about privacy appeared to be entrenched in his, and later his staff's, belief system, which made the sharing of information part of Facebook's identity and mission.

Different rationales may explain the low priority that Zuckerberg gave to privacy. First, privacy does not work well with sharing information. In addition, since the original Facebook was basically a "closed" social network system with college students interacting with other college students, everyone was a "friend." This allowed frank and open discussions and pictures/videos posted because the "outside" world did not have access to the individual's Facebook page.

Facebook, whose first members were required to have a college e-mail address with an .edu suffix, kept its original strategy of being designed for college students to socialize with each other for only a year. Zuckerberg realized that if Facebook were to grow, it could not continue to support a closed system. Therefore, his first step to opening the system was to allow high school students to join.[2] This step occurred on September 2, 2005. By this date, Facebook was in 882 colleges and approximately 85% of students in those colleges had Facebook pages. The level of market saturation encouraged Zuckerberg to open Facebook. High school students were the first logical extension because they are possible future college students who would continue to use Facebook. As a result, the system opened somewhat but was still "closed" to outsiders. The degree of openness was hard to determine because high school students were not issued e-mail addresses. It became increasingly more difficult to monitor who was creating a Facebook account. Again, privacy was a major issue because it appeared market growth was the focus of Facebook's strategic actions.[3]

Invasion of privacy concerns started in Facebook's infancy. In a January 2006 article in the *New York Times*, college students complained that campus police were checking on Facebook for parties or other "activities." Police waited until the party was in full swing and then paid a visit to check for any illegal activities that were taking place at the party. The official response from the campus police was that noise rather than Facebook was the reason why the police showed up at the party. Even at this stage, though, people were complaining about privacy, as well as free speech, and the online "addiction" of checking their Facebook pages 20 times a day. In 2006, nearly 75% of the students checked their Facebook accounts once a day, and the average user checked his or her account six times a day.

In 2006, privacy concerns related to stalking caused the University of New Mexico to ban access to Facebook from its computer servers. In addition, in 2006, parents and students were worried about potential employers getting access to campus e-mail accounts and checking their prospective employees on Facebook before hiring them. Campus police around the United States started to warn students that if there are pictures of illegal activities posted on their Facebook accounts, they could be arrested with the picture used as evidence.[4]

Six months later, another article in the *New York Times* also highlighted the danger of posting "inappropriate" information and pictures on Facebook. One consulting company was reviewing candidates for a summer internship and looked at their Facebook pages, which showed an applicant smoking marijuana and describing personal obsessions. The hiring manager stated that he questioned how he could hire someone who would willingly post such material online, knowing that it could be reviewed by strangers. In another example, a candidate was rejected because there was a picture of her passed out from drinking too much, and another firm rejected a candidate when it read on his Facebook page that he liked "to blow things up."[5]

September 26, 2006

On September 26, 2006, Facebook, which now had approximately 9 million users, allowed anyone 13 years of age or older to set up a Facebook account. Thus, the system became completely open to almost everyone in the world. In addition to allowing anyone access to Facebook, Facebook also started implementing its News Feed feature. However, Facebook was still slow in addressing the privacy issues related to an "open" global social network system.

News Feed Feature

The News Feed feature gave users instant update information on individuals' Facebook pages by constantly monitoring the activities on every Facebook account. As a result, all posted friends automatically were informed about any adjustment made on a Facebook page. This was the first "tangible" example of Facebook infringing on the privacy of the users. Because the system was tracking every single action by every account holder, users became flooded with updates from "friends" they had forgotten about months or years ago. In addition, every user now realized that Facebook was monitoring every single Facebook action globally. This was a change from the previous method in which individuals had to physically search each friend to see if any revisions had been made to his or her Facebook account. Some users quickly realized that they did not need to know every detail about every friend's life.

When users complained to Zuckerberg about the News Feed tracking system, his famous response was "Calm down. Breathe. We hear you."[6] Facebook then allowed users an option to opt out of the News Feed feature or to shield specific information on their pages.

News Feed set two precedents for Facebook. The first was that, whether consciously or not, it was Facebook's first attempt to collect data on everyone, who could in the future be analyzed and potentially targeted for specific marketing campaigns. The second precedent was that it was the first in a number of occurrences where Facebook pushed the limits of privacy and reacted only after the users gave feedback or complaints. Almost 3 years later, in May 2009, Facebook reached an agreement to implement new safety and privacy rules to protect children from predators and inappropriate content.[7]

Marketplace Feature

In May 2007, Facebook started to allow free classified advertising listings for its 22 million members. It was the first of many ways in which Facebook started to offer diversified products to encourage enrollment and longer viewing times on Facebook. Again, whether conscious or not, Facebook was now evolving into a revenue-generating company. Although the classified ads were free when introduced, it gave Facebook the opportunity to charge for this service in the future at minimal cost because Facebook had already created the infrastructure to support it. In addition, the information would become increasingly valuable to Facebook and to the advertisers that would pay Facebook to advertise on their websites. By developing a marketplace feature, Facebook continued to expand its access to data that represent the personal involvements and interests of their users. This access provides another level of data that Facebook can use to build a customized data-driven profile of each user by setting up classified categories such as housing, jobs, items, and other services.[8] Facebook continues to develop detailed information on such critical user data as type of employment, where users live or want to live, and what their specific interests are. These data may not appear on their Facebook accounts but can be linked by Facebook to each individual user.[9]

OMG, My Mother Has a Facebook Account

Employers were not the only people who realized the value of obtaining information about individuals on Facebook. By June 2007, more than 50% of the users were not college students.[10] Parents also started to join Facebook.

Cases

A serious concern that parents have about Facebook is the opportunity it allows sexual predators to attempt to contact their children. A July 2007 article in the *New York Times* points out that Facebook, back then, did not have any monitoring system to ensure that inappropriate images and content were blocked from being shown on a Facebook account. The danger, of course, is having a predator become a friend with an underage child and start connecting with the child. Facebook had restrictions such as not allowing a full profile of someone under 18 to be available to someone over 18, but predators can always pretend to be underage. In addition, Facebook allowed the formation of sexuality-focused groups even though Facebook's code of conduct forbids any "obscene, pornographic, or sexually explicit" material. Facebook's reactive response to the complaints was to consider developing a database of names and e-mail addresses of known convicted sexual offenders that would be matched against the membership rolls of Facebook. At this point, only 13 states required that convicted sex offenders register their e-mail addresses.[11] Therefore, Facebook would have to wait until the other states pass laws requiring e-mail registration before this strategy could work. Again, Facebook was reactive rather than proactive concerning privacy issues.

This slow reactive policy has certainly cost Facebook. In October 2007, New York attorney general Andrew Cuomo settled with Facebook concerning charges that the company was not doing enough to warn children about using the site and the lack of control of inappropriate sexual messages. New York prosecutors accused Facebook of false advertising by claiming it was presenting a safe online environment while allowing this material to be posted on Facebook. The false advertising charges were connected to the consumer protection laws of New York State. As a part of a settlement, Facebook agreed to hire an independent company that would track Facebook's response to complaints. In October 2007, Facebook was estimated to have been the target of thousands to tens of thousands complaints daily. The independent company would report responses to Facebook and the New York attorney general twice a year.[12]

Social Advertising Feature: Beacon

In November 2007, Facebook decided to use blatant advertising related to the information shared on Facebook. Facebook decided to have users see ads for products that the users had purchased. The ads describing the product would also be sent to the users' "friends." For example, if someone rented a movie on Blockbuster.com, the user would be asked if it is okay to have this movie selection sent to all his or her friends. The friends would not have a choice of accepting or refusing the ad, which would describe the movie and provide a link to Blockbuster.com. At this point, Facebook had 50 million users, so a "friend" could quickly be inundated by Beacon with unsolicited ads from people they barely knew.

The Federal Trade Commission (FTC) raised concerns about the level of information obtained about consumers online by existing and potential advertisers. This type of advertising system was beneficial to Blockbuster.com or any advertisers because they can increase their exposure on Facebook, and they now have a continuously growing listing of people on Facebook that they can target with customized advertising. Again, New York was the challenger of this potential privacy invasion. New York's privacy law, written more than 100 years ago, states that any person whose likeness is used in advertising must give written consent before the ad is released. Under the

Facebook system, no written consent was required, which could result in a criminal misdemeanor in New York. Zuckerberg's response to the social advertising feature was that it was his belief that it would be "less commercial" because the ad was linked to a friend. When he was asked about people on Facebook who did not like the feature, his response was that Facebook was a business supported by advertising.[13,14]

The Beacon feature changed the "opt in" rule for Facebook users. In the past, when an activity was related to an external website, users had to choose to participate in the program or "opt in." Beacon's default was to automatically have users "opt in." Therefore, users who did not want the Beacon feature had to take action to "opt out." In less than a month, 50,000 Facebook members signed a petition objecting to the Beacon program. Again, Facebook managers did not understand the ramifications for the privacy of their users and again became reactive after protests started coming from users. Facebook managers stated that they would now get explicit approval from users each time their purchases from external websites were posted. Facebook also claimed that the 50,000 people were part of a marginal minority that did not like the program.[15]

Facebook predicted that Beacon would be accepted because Facebook viewed it as an extension of a user recommending a movie or book to another user. In one of the many issues related to Beacon, if you are buying any items in secret—for example, a birthday, Christmas, or wedding gift—and both you and your friend are Facebook friends, Facebook has just ruined the surprise because your friend received a posting related to the gift.[16,17,18] In August 2008, a lawsuit was filed against the Beacon feature by 19 Facebook users claiming invasion of privacy by disclosing personal information for advertising without the consent of the users. On September 22, 2009, Facebook was forced to pay $9.5 million to settle the lawsuit. Six million dollars was to be used to set up a nonprofit foundation that would award grants and projects that supported online privacy issues.[19]

In addition, Facebook agreed to shut down the Beacon program, although Facebook management continued to maintain that Beacon was a good program for the users because it kept them better informed about areas that interested them by getting "trusted referrals" from their friends.[20]

Who Owns the Data?

The underlying principle related to privacy pertaining to Facebook users is the question of ownership. Who owns the data? In February 2009, this question came to the forefront when Facebook changed its terms of service on its now 175 million active users. When "updating" its terms of service, Facebook deleted the statement that users could remove their content at any time and deleted the statement that the license allowing Facebook to store users' data would expire. Instead, the revised terms of service included a statement that said that Facebook would retain the content of the user and the license to store the data after the user account has been terminated. Zuckerberg's defense of the new policy was that users ownership of their information and control over whom they share the information with has remained consistent in the terms of service. This change in the "fine print" of the terms of service was not publicized by Facebook but was uncovered by the blog called *Consumerist*. In an attempt to clarify the change, Facebook stated that the terms do not state that Facebook owns the data but that the revised terms did a better job reflecting current user behavior such as leaving in place any comments the user had posted on a Facebook page.[21] Three days after the change of terms were publicized on *Consumerist,* Facebook had to reverse its decision. Bowing to overwhelming pressure from users, the threat of another lawsuit by consumer advocacy groups, and the threat of a formal complaint with the FTC, Facebook restored the earlier version of the terms of service. Chris Kelly, who was Facebook's chief privacy officer, summarized the fiasco as a misunderstanding that was based on a "clumsy" attempt to simplify the terms of service.[22,23]

The Price to Opt Out

Privacy issues continue to be a dominant part of stakeholder discussion pertaining to Facebook. On April 27, 2010, four U.S. senators sent a letter to Zuckerberg raising concerns about the privacy policies at Facebook. As a result, Facebook changed the classification of publicly available data to include the user's current city, the hometown of the user, the type of education the user has, where the user works, and the user's likes, interests, and friends. In addition, Facebook changed its policy of third-party data storage. Where previously, Facebook allowed third parties to store user data for 24 hours, that policy was changed so that third parties could store the data indefinitely.[24] Facebook's response was that the users are allowed to opt out of this type of data disclosure. Nick Bilton of the *New York Times* estimated that users would have to click more than 50 privacy buttons to make their personal information private. Once that is completed, the user must then choose from more than 170 different options.[25]

Even with all that effort, certain information cannot be blocked. For example, Facebook's community pages link user's information such as hometown or university attended to topic information related to the user's data. The only way to shut down community pages is to delete that personal information from the Facebook account. In addition, Bilton concluded that Facebook's privacy policy at 5,830 words is longer than the U.S. Constitution, whose 4,543 words have guided this country for more than 225 years. The word count at Facebook's privacy-related Frequently Asked Questions (FAQ) section contains more than 45,000 words in Facebook's Help Center.[26] In stating that Facebook really does believe in privacy, Zuckerberg announced on May 27, 2010, that there would be changes to the privacy controls at Facebook. Facebook would install a master control that would allow users to choose what information from their accounts they want to share with their friends or other Facebook users. This is another example of Facebook implementing a change to benefit itself and its current and potential advertisers and then being forced to reverse the decision after receiving a flood of complaints by users.[27]

The App Privacy Issue

In October 2010, another privacy issue was raised with Facebook concerning the use of application "apps" to receive information. The *Wall Street Journal* revealed that many of the most popular apps on Facebook had been used to transmit identifying information to numerous advertising and Internet tracking companies. The now 500 million users were not aware that this transmission of data was taking place by Facebook. The practice violates Facebook's own privacy policy and raises the question again of Facebook's commitment to the user to keep personal information private. In addition, the transmission of information took place even if the user had set the privacy settings to the strictest levels. After the *Wall Street Journal* exposed the privacy violation, a spokesperson from Facebook stated that the company was taking steps to "dramatically limit" the exposure of users' private information to third parties. The *Wall Street Journal* investigation discovered that the 10 most popular apps—including FarmVille (59.4 million users), Phrases (43.4 million users), Texas Hold 'Em Poker (36.3 million users), and FrontierVille (30.6 million users)—were transmitting user information to outside parties. In addition, 3 of the top 10 apps were also transmitting information pertaining to the user's friends to outside third parties.[28]

Facebook and the Federal Trade Commission

In November 2011, Facebook settled charges by the FTC for using "unfair and deceptive" practices in relationship to privacy of Facebook users. The settlement requires Facebook to respect the privacy wishes of the Facebook users and to submit to regularly scheduled privacy audits every 2 years for the next two decades. The FTC had concluded that Facebook had made public information that its 800 million users had wanted to remain private. Facebook was accused of allowing advertisers to gather personal information that could be linked to individual users when the user clicked on the advertisement of the firm on the user's Facebook page. Despite the settlement, Facebook continued to deny that it shares personal user information with third parties. Furthermore, the FTC accused Facebook of allowing advertisers access to photos and videos even after the Facebook user had "deleted" his or her account. The FTC had listed eight complaints against Facebook but did not force Facebook to pay a fine nor did it accuse Facebook of intentionally violating privacy laws. Zuckerberg's response was that Facebook had made "a bunch of mistakes," but that Facebook was already correcting the issues presented by the FTC. In addition, Zuckerberg stated that Facebook has always been committed to its belief to be transparent with the information on the user's Facebook account and Facebook has "led the Internet" in creating software so the users can see and control the information they share with others.[29]

Privacy Versus IPO

In February 2012, Facebook filed for an initial public offering (IPO) to make the company publicly traded. Based on the prices of the sales, the value of the IPO was estimated to be between $75 and $100 billion. In addition, Facebook was expected to receive $10 billion from the initial stock sold to investors. At the time of the announcement, Facebook had 845 million users globally. In a letter to potential stockholders, Zuckerberg stated that the goal of the IPO was not to become wealthy. He stated that Facebook did not build services to make money but rather made money to offer better services to the users, noting, "These days I think more and more people want to use services from companies that believe in something beyond simply maximizing profits."[30] However, the underlying question is how Facebook can increase sales and profit growth without infringing on the privacy rights of the users. The reason for the huge premium on Facebook stock was the anticipation of companies being able to customize advertising based on the specific interests of each individual user. To obtain that information, however, Facebook must transfer personal data to the firms. Therefore, there will be a constant battle between privacy issues and revenue generation.

If Facebook's commitment to privacy in the past is any indication of future commitment, it appears that revenue generation will prevail over protecting the privacy rights of the users. As David Carr states in the *New York Times*, the only way Facebook can now survive is to commodify Facebook users' communications and relationships. In addition, transparency of information and privacy rights now become part of the day-to-day operations at Facebook. Because of the accountability of being a publicly traded company, Facebook can no longer "hide" behind the "oops, I did it again" philosophy of stepping over the line on privacy issues and then apologize and "correct" it after the company has been caught. Those mistakes will now come with a much higher financial price tag and increased scrutiny by government regulators. Furthermore, Facebook managers realize that it can quickly alienate its users by violating their privacy rights. In the IPO filing, they warned that the company could be damaged if user sentiment changes about its products, including privacy and safety issues.[31] On August 29, 2013, Facebook announced that it had updated its privacy policy. Included in the update was a new provision that no longer allowed users to limit how their names and profiles could be used by Facebook for marketing. Once a person signs up for Facebook, he or she agrees to "give" Facebook the right to use the individual personal information.[32] On October 15, 2013, Facebook announced that it would allow teenage users to post status updates, videos, and images that can be seen by everyone on Facebook, instead of the previous policy that restricted these postings to friends or people who know the user's friends. Nicky Jackson Colaco, manager of privacy and public policy at Facebook, stated that "across the Web, teens can have a very public voice on these services, and it would be a shame if they could not do that on Facebook."[33] On November 13, 2014, Facebook announced it was going to simplify the privacy policy by reducing its length from more than 9,000 words to 2,700 words. In addition, the sections would be color coded to help the user find major subject areas.[34]

The Facebook Experiment

Data from a large real-world social network, collected over a 20-year period, suggests that longer-lasting moods (e.g., depression, happiness) can be transferred through networks . . . although the results are controversial. In an experiment with people who use Facebook, we test whether emotional contagion (transferring from one person to another) occurs outside of in-person interaction between individuals by reducing the amount of emotional content in the News Feed.[35]

The above paragraph is from a study published in the *Proceedings of the National Academy of Sciences of the United States of America* for a study that manipulated information being sent to Facebook users. The lead author of the study, Adam D. I. Kramer, is employed at Facebook as a Facebook Data Scientist.[36] The second author of the report, Jamie Guillory, works for the Center for Tobacco Control Research & Education.[37] The third author of the study, Dr. Jeffrey T. Hancock, is a Professor in the Communication and Information Science departments at Cornell University.[38]

After the study was published, Facebook admitted that for one week in January 2012, 689,003 randomly selected users had their news feeds manipulated by changing the number of positive and negative posts they read on their Facebook page.

The researchers measured how the manipulated news feed affected the tone of the posts the users created after reading the news feed. The results of the study showed that if users received positive news, they were more likely to subsequently write positive posts, and if they read negative news, they were more likely to be more negative in their subsequent posts. Even though the users were not informed of this manipulation, Facebook defended its actions by stating that when users agree to Facebook's terms of service, they also agree to having the information they receive be potentially manipulated by Facebook. Furthermore, Facebook stated that "none of the data used was associated with a specific person's Facebook account . . . [and there is] no unnecessary collection of people's data . . . We carefully consider what research we do and have a strong internal review process."[39]

General academic protocol requires that all human subjects need to give explicit consent before an experiment is conducted using the subjects. Mr. Kramer stated,

> The reason we did this research is because we care about the emotional impact of Facebook and the people that use our product...We felt that it was important to investigate the common worry that seeing friends post positive content leads to people feeling negative or left out. At the same time, we were concerned that exposure to friends' negativity might lead people to avoid visiting Facebook.[40]

Once the results of the study were released to the public, Adam Kramer apologized for the actions of the researchers of the study. He said, "I can understand why some people have concerns about it, and my co-authors and I are very sorry for the way the paper described the research and any anxiety it caused."[41] On October 2, 2014, Facebook announced that it was changing the process of conducting experiments on users. Facebook said it would increase the oversight of its data scientists with the establishment of clearer guidelines and form an internal review panel of senior researchers.[42]

Cases

Questions for Thought

1. Why is Facebook so successful?

2. Can Facebook survive as a publicly traded company? Why or why not?

3. It appears that Facebook operates with an "oops, I did it again" philosophy. Will this philosophy continue to work once the company is publicly traded?

4. Comment on each of the ethical issues mentioned in this case. Rank them on a scale from 1 to 10, 1 being the least ethical and 10 being the most ethical actions. Defend your rankings.

13

Outsourcing at Mattel: Elmo Sad . . . Elmo Covered in Lead Paint

Mattel has a long-standing relationship with Chinese manufacturers. For decades, Mattel has depended on Chinese suppliers to manufacturer its licensed products. In fact, 65% of all of Mattel's products are made in China, representing 50% of Mattel's total revenue. Mattel owns and operates 11 manufacturing plants in China that produce many of its products. Mattel also outsources a large number of its products to between 30 and 50 external vendors. Mattel started taking ownership of the factories in China in the 1980s when Mattel officials became concerned with control of its trademarked products and became worried that the toy market would be flooded with imitation Barbie dolls. For example, Mattel outsources short-term licensed products from Disney, Nickelodeon, and Sesame Street to other facilities but ensures the manufacturing of Barbies and Hot Wheels are done within Mattel's own facilities. Mattel has faced challenges in the past with its outsourcing. In 1996, NBC's *Dateline* did an exposé highlighting the sweatshop conditions in Mattel's Indonesian factory that showed the employment of underage workers.[1]

The First Recall

On August 1, 2007, Mattel announced that it was recalling 967,000 toys that were part of its Fisher-Price division because they could contain dangerously high levels of lead in the paint. The recall was estimated to cost Mattel $30 million and included 83 types of toys with characters from Sesame Street and Nickelodeon that had levels of lead that would be toxic if ingested by a child. Mattel stated that despite the size of the recall, the impact on the public would not be as dramatic because almost two thirds of the products were still in the warehouse and were not yet available to the public. Mattel stated that the toys were produced by a third-party manufacturer and not made in one of its own facilities. Mattel would not identify the manufacturer but said that the vendor had been a supplier for Mattel for 15 years. Mattel admitted that it allowed long-term vendors such as this one to do their own inspections, and Mattel relied on the results. As a result, Mattel officials trusted the audit reports presented to Mattel by the vendor.

Mattel admitted that it did not discover the high levels of lead in its own products. Mattel was informed about the high levels after a French retailer notified Mattel of the problem in early July 2007. Mattel stopped production at the facility around July 7, 2007, and notified the Consumer Product Safety Commission (CPSC) verbally on July 20, 2007. Mattel submitted a written report to the CPSC on July 26, 2007.[2] This was a tough announcement for Mattel to make because it was known in the industry as being the most conscientious related to toy manufacturing in China. Mattel was proud of its state-of-the-art testing facilities and independent manufacturing audits. In addition, Mattel was known to have some of the toughest and more stringent requirements for any company that becomes a vendor of Mattel in China.[3]

Recalls are not a rare occurrence for Mattel. In fact, this was the 17th recall that Mattel had to make in the past 10 years. When Mattel outsources the manufacturing of a product, it requires the vendor to only use raw materials that are provided by certified suppliers.[4] On August 9, 2007, the Chinese General Administration of Quality Supervision, Inspection and Quarantine suspended the export license of Lee Der Industrial, which manufactured the tainted toys for Mattel. Lee Der claimed that it used a paint that was described as lead free and implied that the supplier was the responsible party in the recall.[5] Four days later, Zhang Shuhong, owner of Lee Der Industrial, committed suicide by hanging himself in a company warehouse. It was also reported that Zhang Shuhong had used lead paint in the manufacturing process and that the paint was made by a company that was controlled by a close personal friend of his.[6]

The Second Recall

On August 14, 2007, Mattel announced its second recall of toys that were made in China. The recall included 436,000 toys due to high levels of lead. The toys were a die cast version of the character Sarge from the Pixar/Disney movie *Cars*. These toys came from a different manufacturing facility than Lee Der Industrial. In addition, Mattel also recalled, on the same day, 18.2 million magnetic toys that were considered a safety hazard because the magnets could become loose and then be ingested by a child. All of these toys were manufactured in China. Along with the announcement of the Sarge toy recall, Mattel officials announced that they were implementing a three-point check system to ensure that lead paint was not in its products. The first check was allowing only certified suppliers to provide the paint; the second check was tightening controls during the manufacturing process, including taking random samples; and the third check was testing for lead paint in every production run of a finished product. Mattel said that the manufacturer of the Sarge toys was Early Light Industrial, which had subcontracted the painting to another company, Hong Li Da, a noncertified third-party supplier of the paint.[7]

The Third Recall

Just over a month after the first recall, Mattel had to announce a third recall of toys manufactured in China. On September 5, 2007, Mattel announced the recall of 775,000 toys that had dangerous levels of lead in the paint. A majority of the toys were accessories for Mattel's Barbie doll. The recall was the result of a systematic review by Mattel of all its manufacturing processes. The results of the review found the defective toys and resulted in the elimination of a number of subcontractors that Mattel had used for manufacturing the toys in China.[8]

Why Manufacturers Use Lead Paint

Lead is added to the paint to give the paint more "desirable" features. Lead paint is quicker to dry than lead-free paint is. Lead paint is opaque so a small amount can cover a large area without needing a second coat of paint. Lead is insoluble, so when it is added to paint, the paint will be highly water resistant and be able to be cleaned with water easily. Lead can add to the richness of the color of the paint. In addition, lead paint is also easier to apply on hard surfaces. But the main reason is cost. Lead paint can be bought at approximately one third of the price of non-lead paint because in most countries it is forbidden to be used on consumer products, which reduces the demand related to the supply. For example, many countries in the Middle East do not have any restrictions on lead content of paint.

In China, industrial paint does contain lead, and it is used for outdoor applications such as buildings, bridges, and sidewalks. Therefore, the problem is that the lead paint is available to be misused by unscrupulous suppliers because the lead paint can "accidentally" be poured into "lead-free" paint containers. Suppliers that want to increase their profit margins will use the lead paint to improve their bottom line.[9]

Dual Apologies

On September 12, 2007, Mattel's CEO Robert Eckert apologized to Congress for failing to stop the tainted toys from coming into the United States. While Eckert explained that Mattel understood the problem and had implemented the three-check solution to solve it, many senators were discussing the idea of significantly increasing the fines for companies that imported tainted products. Also discussed was the fining and bringing criminal charges against the top executives responsible for bringing in the tainted products.[10]

A week and a half later, Mattel apologized again, but, this time to government officials in China. Thomas Debrowski, who is Mattel's executive vice president for worldwide operations, apologized to the Chinese government for harming the reputation of Chinese manufacturers. The response in the United States was disbelief that a company would apologize for the illegal actions of another country. Critics of Mattel complained that Mattel was afraid it would lose China as its manufacturing base so Mattel officers are doing whatever they could to reestablish good relations with the Chinese government. Based on this response, Mattel attempted to clarify the apology by stating that the apology was meant for the Chinese consumers and not the Chinese manufacturers, even though almost all the recalled toys were sold in either Europe or the United States. In another attempt to clarify the message, Mattel released a press statement in which Mattel apologized to the Chinese manufacturers for the 17.4 million magnetic toys that were recalled. The apology was based on the flaw being the design of the toy and not the manufacturing of the toy and was, therefore, Mattel's fault.[11]

Trust but Verify

"Trust but verify" were the words used by the president of Toys "R" Us to explain how major clients and retailers would address the issue of lead paint. In September 2007, both Disney and Toys "R" Us announced that they would do their own testing of Mattel toys to ensure they were in compliance with government standards. This was a radical change from the traditional relationship clients and retailers had with toy manufacturers in the past. The traditional procedure was for Disney to sign a contract with a toy manufacturer to produce licensed products and Disney would collect the royalty checks. Because of the consumer backlash of the toy recalls, both Disney and Toys "R" Us officers realized that their primary stakeholder, the customer, was not satisfied with the level of quality control at Mattel. Therefore, they decided to put the burden on themselves to trust but also verify the products that Mattel was producing for them. Both Sesame Workshop and Nickelodeon officials also realized that they needed to take control of the issue by hiring independent testers to verify the lead content in their toy designs. In addition, both Disney and Sesame Workshop stated they would start making surprise visits to the manufacturing facilities to ensure the products and the working standards were acceptable.[12]

Other toy manufacturers do not have to rely on the "trust but verify" model. Both Playmobil and LEGO manufacture the vast majority of their toys in Europe. For these two companies, the competitive advantages of manufacturing in Europe outweigh the cost of manufacturing in China. One of the reasons was that Playmobil and LEGO were not large enough to employ people who would inspect the factories in China. Even though there were continued pressures to move their operations to China, officers of these companies believed that the overall cost advantage of manufacturing in China was not worth it. They agreed that the labor costs are substantially lower, $1.50 an hour in China versus $30 an hour in Germany. However, there are significant transportation costs in moving the toys from China to the major markets in Europe and in North America. Furthermore, toys can have very limited selling periods. LEGO and Playmobil compete in an industry where fads can quickly come and go. Having operations in Europe allowed LEGO and Playmobil to quickly change their production times because they do not need the same lead times as they would if the toys were produced in China. In addition, LEGO and Playmobil were still able to ensure that stringent quality and work standards are met in their factories located in Europe. A top executive at Playmobil states that the company cannot have blind faith that everything is running exactly correct every minute of every day; however, it is much easier to jump in your car and drive 20 minutes to visit a plant, rather than have your toys made thousands of miles away from your headquarters.[13]

Trust, Now Sue

The first of many legal issues that Mattel had to address was the filing of a shareholder lawsuit by a Michigan pension fund in October 2007. The pension fund claimed that Mattel neglected its duty by not following proper safety procedures for its toys manufactured in China. Furthermore, because Mattel knew of the potential problems for weeks before they were actually disclosed, the pension fund also claimed that Mattel's directors, including its CEO Eckert, breached their fiduciary duty to the shareholders by not disclosing the problems within 24 hours as is required by law. Mattel also received many individual lawsuits from consumers who had bought a tainted toy and demanded compensation for Mattel's negligence.[14]

Mattel settled the first major lawsuit in December 2008. Mattel agreed to settle with 39 states that claimed that Mattel did not follow safety standards of the states. Mattel paid a total of $12 million and agreed to follow tougher standards in evaluating lead in toys. The company also agreed to keep at least 4 years of records on all subcontractors that produce any parts of its toys.[15]

Along with the records of the subcontractors, Mattel must also keep lead test records for the same period.[16] In June 2009, Mattel agreed to pay a civil penalty of $2.3 million to the CPSC for selling lead-painted toys.[17] In October 2009, Mattel settled a class-action lawsuit related to the lead-tainted toys. Final costs to Mattel are estimated to be more than $50 million for the plaintiffs. The final amount paid is based on the total number of claims of payment by consumers. The settlement resolves 22 lawsuits filed against Mattel and major retailers by millions of families who bought lead-tainted toys made by Mattel. Mattel agreed to provide refunds or other types of reimbursement for those customers who made a claim. Mattel agreed to pay either 50% of the total toy price or a $10 voucher, whichever amount was more. In addition, consumers would be reimbursed for the testing if they could prove they paid for lead testing of their toys.[18]

In November 2011, Robert Exkert, who was Mattel's CEO during the outsourcing crisis, retired from his position at Mattel.[19] His retirement had lasted less than 3 years when he joining the private equity firm Friedman Fleischer & Lowe as an operating partner in September 2014.[20]

Questions for Thought

1. Identify the stakeholders in this case. Which, if any, are the most important? Why?

2. Is 50% of the total price or a $10 voucher enough compensation to customers for the recall? Why or why not?

3. How can a company like Mattel appear to have such a blatant disregard for one of its major stakeholders, children? Explain.

4. Explain the steps for reporting a product recall to the U.S. government. Is the process adequate to protect consumers? Why or why not?

14

GM and the Ignition Switch: It Is Deja Vu All Over Again

A car company builds a car knowing that there is a defect in the design and parts of the car, but after calculating the cost of fixing the problem, the company decides it is more cost efficient to have the defective cars on the road than to recall the cars to have the problem fixed. The year is 1971 and the car was the Ford Pinto. (A vignette describing the Ford Pinto case can be found at the end of Chapter 10.) Fast-forward 30 years: General Motors (GM) discovered a flaw in an ignition switch part when testing its cars, but it waited 13 years before it started recalling the cars.

The Recall Starts

On February 13, 2014, GM announced that it was recalling 778,000 model year 2007 Pontiac GT and model years 2005 to 2007 Chevrolet Cobalt cars for ignition switch problems. The flaw in the ignition switch was that either a heavy key ring or a "jarring event" could cause the ignition to switch from the "on" to the "accessory" position, which cut off power in the car and prevented the air bags from deploying. GM stated it knew of five crashes in which six people died due to this faulty ignition switch. GM released a statement saying, "All of these crashes occurred off-road and at high speeds, where the probability of serious or fatal injuries was high regardless of air bag deployment. In addition, failure to wear seat belts and alcohol use were factors in some of these cases."[1] Less than two weeks later, on February 25, 2014, GM expanded the recall to include 1.6 million cars after consumers had complained that the initial recall was not comprehensive enough. GM increased the recall to include Saturn Ions with model years from 2003 to 2007, Chevrolet HHRs for model years 2006 and 2007, and Pontiac Solstice and Saturn Sky vehicles for model years 2006 and 2007. GM North American president Alan Batey apologized by saying, "We are deeply sorry and we are working to address this issue as quickly as we can." GM advised consumers whose vehicle had been recalled to use a single key on their key chain when operating the vehicle. In a report filed by GM to the National Highway Traffic Safety Administration on February 24, 2014, GM admitted that GM employees knew about the flawed ignition switch in 2004. In 2003, a GM engineer had recommended a redesign of the key head from a slot to a hole, which would have potentially eliminated the problem of the ignition switching off. The proposal was initially accepted by GM but was later cancelled without any reason given. In December 2005, GM issued a notice to dealers informing them that the ignition could switch off if the key ring was too heavy. In April 2006, a GM engineer who was responsible for the ignition switch approved changes to the ignition switch part, and in 2007, the part was changed. In 2009, the recommendation was made again to change the ignition design from a slot to a hole, and it was implemented for the 2010 model year. GM North American president Alan Batey also stated,

> The chronology shows that the process employed to examine this phenomenon was not as robust as it should have been . . . Today's GM is committed to doing business differently and better. We will take an unflinching look at what happened and apply lessons learned here to improve going forward.[2]

The Story Starts to Unravel

As stated in a deposition by a GM employee, GM had "repurchased vehicles from owners who had complained about the vehicle stalling or losing power." One customer had her 2005 Chevy Cobalt repurchased with only 600 miles on the vehicle. A team of high level executives was created in 2011 to investigate the ignition switch issue.[3] In November 2004, GM engineers were investigating the ignition switch problem, but in March 2005, the Cobalt project manager ordered the investigation to be closed because the "lead time for all solutions is too long . . . the tooling cost and piece price are too high . . . (and none of the solutions) represents an acceptable business case."[4] A 2005 memo stated that redesigning the faulty ignition switch would cost 90 cents per car and would return only 10 to 15 cents in warranty cost savings.[5]

On March 12, 2014, GM revealed that it knew of the faulty ignition switches as far back as 2001. GM also announced that the replacement part would cost between $2 and $5 per car and take only a few minutes to install. By March 12, 2014, 12 fatalities has been linked to the faulty ignition switch. In response to the latest information on the recall, GM spokesman Greg Martin announced,

> In keeping with our commitment to help customers involved in this recall, a special $500 cash allowance is available to purchase or lease a new GM vehicle. . . . We have been very clear in our message to dealers that this allowance is not a sales tool and it is only to be used to help customers in need of assistance. Neither GM, nor its dealers will market or solicit owners using this allowance.[6]

The program engineering manager for the 2005 Cobalt, Gary Altman, stated that GM engineering knew about the ignition switch problem but that the vehicles could coast safely to the side of the road if the vehicle lost power. In a June 2013 deposition, Gary Altman stated, "We've sold vehicles for many, many years without power assist and the car was maneuverable and controllable. . . . We've been through that several times, in fact, during this investigation looking at the car to make sure it still could be controlled."[7] In addition, Ray DeGiorgio, who was the project engineer for the

Cobalt ignition switch, said that he was not aware of any problems with the ignition switch and was not informed when GM issued a service bulletin to the dealers identifying the ignition switch issue. He stated that "as long as the vehicle can still be controlled . . . the vehicle is still safe."[8] On March 28, 2014, GM announced it would be recalling an additional 971,000 vehicles to replace the ignition switch, which resulted in a total recall of almost 2.6 million vehicles globally. In addition, GM announced that approximately 95,000 faulty ignition switches were sold to dealers and parts stores, of which 5,000 were in vehicles on the road.[9]

The Consequences of GM's Inaction

On April 10, 2014, the two main GM engineers involved in the ignition switch decision, Ray DeGiorgio and Gary Altman, were put on paid leave.[10] On May 14, 2014, the GM board of directors announced that it had hired a law firm to review how information related to potentially dangerous defects is received and reviewed by the board. The board stated that it was not informed about the ignition switch problems by GM management. The directors were facing at least three lawsuits in which it was alleged that the directors had failed to perform their governance duties related to GM operations.[11] On May 16, 2014, GM agreed to pay a $35 million fine for not releasing information related to the ignition switch problem. GM had told its employees not to use words such as *defect* in their communications related to the safety issues. Instead of defect, employees were told to use the phrase "does not perform to design."[12] On June 5, 2014, a 315-page report was released by the NHTSA that described a number of internal issues at GM that led to the lack of quick correction of the ignition switch issue. Two of the issues are related to the physical actions of the GM executives. The "GM nod" refers to the nodding of one head in agreement in a meeting but taking no action after the meeting is over. The "GM salute" occurred when GM executives would cross their arms and point outwards indicating someone else was to blame for the issue and, therefore, it was not his or her problem to solve. The report also revealed that GM had bought an ignition switch that was "far below GM's own specifications." Furthermore, the report stated that GM failed to look for the "root cause" of crashes in which the air bags were not deployed, which could have occurred if the ignition had been switched to "accessory."[13] On June 5, 2014, GM announced that 15 people related to the ignition switch problem had been dismissed from GM, including Ray DeGiorgio and Gary Altman.[14] On June 12, 2014, GM announced that its board of directors had created a new risk committee responsible for GM policies and procedures related to vehicle safety, product quality, and cybersecurity.[15] On June 13, 2014, GM announced an additional recall of more than 500,000 Chevrolet Camaros due to an ignition switch problem.[16] By June 30, 2014, 2.6 million cars had been recalled by GM for faulty ignition switches. The estimated replacement cost for each ignition switch was 57 cents.[17] By January 31, 2015, 4,180 claims had been made to the GM ignition switch compensation fund. GM estimated the payout of the claims could be up to $600 million. At that time, 51 deaths and 77 seriously injured people had been linked to the ignition switch defect problem. The estimated amount of compensation given to each victim was from $20,000 to $1 million.[18] By February 16, 2015, the death toll had risen to 56,[19] and it increased to 57 on February 23, 2015.[20]

Questions for Thought

1. Comment on the dismissal of Ray DeGiorgio and Gary Altman. Were their dismissals justified? Explain.

2. What value should be place on human life? How did GM value the life of its customers?

3. A cost-benefit analysis was conducted for the switches. What was problematic with the analysis?

15

McWane:
A Dangerous Business

McWane Corporation has been a fixture in the Birmingham, Alabama, business community since 1921. Started by J. R. McWane and still controlled by the McWane family, McWane Corporation has become an international manufacturer of water and sewer pipes and other heavy manufacturing products. With approximately 5,000 employees and 12 plants in the United States and Canada, McWane is considered one of the largest privately held businesses in the heavy manufacturing industry. It has annual sales of approximately $2 billion.

For the past three decades, McWane's overall corporate strategy has been to acquire older, inefficient manufacturing plants and increase the level of efficiency and profitability through its philosophy of disciplined management practices in the treatment of its workers.[1] McWane's stringent management practices were responsible, in part, for the high number of accidents that have occurred at the McWane facilities. One plant manager summarized McWane's philosophy as manufacturing time equals making pipe and making pipe equals making money.[2] As a result, there seems to have been a disincentive to properly review procedures after an accident. Corrections such as improving the safety features of the equipment and offering more safety training would mean a reduction in productivity. A police report after an accident at one of McWane's facilities in Alabama showed that the foundry supervisors restarted the conveyor belt to continue production before the safety inspectors for the federal government were allowed to inspect the accident site.[3] The drive for production was implemented at the worker level. Each line worker was evaluated based on meeting daily quotas set by McWane. If a worker did not meet his daily quota, he would get a "D.A.," or disciplinary action, on his employment record. After a worker had accumulated a number of D.A.s, the worker was considered on "death row." For the foundry managers, bonuses and profit sharing were directly related to the production level of their foundries compared with the other McWane facilities.[4] At some of the McWane facilities, the annual turnover rate of employees was almost 100%.

From 1996 to 2003, McWane was cited for more than 400 safety violations. The combined total of safety violations of McWane's six largest competitors over the same period was 100. In that 7-year period, 9 McWane workers were killed on the job, and more than 4,600 workers were injured.[5] In 2004, the death total of McWane workers went up to 10 when a maintenance worker working alone in the Elmira, New York, plant was crushed to death when he became caught in a conveyor belt used to collect sand.[6] This was the second death to occur at the Elmira plant. In 1995, Frank Wagner died after an explosion at the plant. Wagner was responsible for disposing of a large amount of highly volatile toxic paint. He was told to put the paint in one of the industrial ovens at the plant. The paint ignited and created a huge explosion. In an investigation after the explosion, it was discovered that the oven was modified to be used as an incinerator. The oven was never designed to be used to destroy toxic fluids. McWane paid a total of $500,000 in fines and donations and admitted guilt for violating environmental laws. The plant manager at Elmira paid a fine of $85 and pleaded guilty to a misdemeanor charge.[7]

After McWane acquired the Texas company Tyler Pipe in 1995, McWane laid off almost two thirds of its workers while expecting increased levels of productivity from the plant.

A previous McWane plant manager, Robert Rester, who had worked for McWane for 24 years, stated that the working conditions at the plant were probably the worst possible. He stated that they were more dangerous than working in an underground coal mine. He said that the employees were just numbers who could be replaced quickly if they were not doing their jobs. If an employee complained about the working conditions or was injured during the job, management would try to find an excuse to fire him or her.[8]

The former assistant secretary of labor for Occupational Safety and Health Administration (OSHA), Charles Jeffress, highlighted the frustration in trying to change the behavior of companies that ignore OSHA requirements. He stated that the penalties available for OSHA to address these safety issues are not adequate. The penalties that OSHA can issue to a business were established in 1970 and have increased only once in more than 36 years. If a company is responsible for contributing to the death of a worker, the maximum penalty issued by OSHA is $7,000. If the violation is willful by the company, the maximum fine is only $70,000.[9] The OSHA Act states that a willful violation by a company that leads to death results in a criminal violation. If a willful violation does occur, OSHA transfers the relevant information to the U.S. Attorney who represents the area where the facility is located. It is then up to the U.S. Attorney to decide whether the company will have criminal charges brought against it. The criminal violation is classified as a misdemeanor charge.[10]

One former plant manager at McWane summarized the impact OSHA has on its operations. He stated if OSHA comes to the plant for an inspection, the company policy is to delay the entrance of OSHA inspectors for as long as possible.[11]

Ron Howell, a former design engineer for the McWane Tyler Pipe plant, and one of Tyler's former workers, Marcos Lopez, described the conditions at the plant. Lopez had to go on permanent disability after having a serious back injury while working at the Tyler Pipe plant. Lopez was working on a pipe-molding machine when he injured his back. His supervisors did not believe that the injury was serious and sent him to a private clinic that had a financial agreement with Tyler Pipe for evaluations. Its diagnosis was that Lopez had just a sprained back, and he was sent home with an ice pack and a prescription for pain relievers. Ten days later Lopez went back to the clinic in horrible pain and requested an X-ray. The results of the X-ray showed that Lopez had broken his back in the accident.[12]

Howell stated that a human being can push only so many buttons on a machine within a given period. As soon as the employee became quick enough on one machine, he was assigned to also operate an additional machine and was expected to be fully productive on both machines. Once full productivity was achieved, the employee became responsible for a third machine.[13] Howell also stated that the workers were not allowed to leave their machines to go to the bathroom. Lopez stated that he worked as many as 16 hours a day, and his supervisor would tell him that he could go to the bathroom only when the supervisor said so.[14] In supporting this statement, Howell stated that he saw workers who would raise their hands to go to the bathroom, but the supervisor would refuse to let them leave their work area. As a result, the workers would relieve themselves in their pants at their work area.[15]

On safety issues at the plant, Howell stated that management would tell the workers to be safe while asking the workers to do dangerous activities within the plant. If a worker told management that he needed additional employees to help him with the dangerous task, the response by managers was they did not care what the employees did as long as they met the production numbers for the week. It was the employee's fault if the numbers were not met.[16]

A former mechanic at Tyler, Ira Cofer, lost his arm at work when the sleeve of his shirt became caught on an unguarded conveyor belt. Cofer was working by himself due to employee layoffs and watched his left arm get crushed by the machinery. He remembered that the belt on the machinery had taken all the flesh off his arm and had rubbed his arm all the way down to the bone.[17] The report by McWane on Cofer's accident stated that Cofer could not be located for more than 2½ hours, even though he was yelling for help during that whole time. Cofer was finally found and was standing on the top of his hard hat to try to relieve the pain and pressure of his injured arm.[18] Since the accident to Cofer occurred, four additional workers have had limbs amputated due to machinery accidents at the Tyler plant.

McWane supervisors were encouraged to discipline workers who were injured on the job. The belief was that if the workers were punished, they would be hesitant to report an injury in the future. Corporate executives at McWane reviewed the disciplinary actions of the foundry managers for injured workers. Workers who cited government regulations protecting their safety or wanted a second opinion on their injuries were prime targets for dismissal.[19]

When McWane took over the Tyler plant, it eliminated "luxury" items such as soap, medicated skin cream, and hand towels.[20] In addition, workers were told to bring their own toilet paper to work. Managers were also known to limit the amount of ice that workers were allowed in their drinks. Portable heaters were taken away from the loading dock, even though the heaters were needed during the winter months. The works manager, Dick Stoker, explained that McWane does not provide heat for the comfort of its employees.[21] McWane also replaced the workers' $17 heat-resistant gloves with cloth gloves that cost $2. In addition, McWane stopped ordering protective aprons, face shields, and safety boots after the inventory in the stockroom had been used.[22] The results of the change in management style when McWane took over were evident in the plant's level of profitability. In 1996, the Tyler plant generated $50 million in annual profits, which was twice the profit level for the previous 5 years.

After a review of the Tyler plant, OSHA inspectors commented that Tyler Pipe had not implemented a system to hold plant supervisors accountable for the safety issues

Cases

of the plant. Tyler Pipe, however, had done an excellent job ensuring that the same supervisors were accountable for the total level of production at the plant. OSHA argued that safety issues were in direct contradiction with production because putting up and taking down safety guards or preparing the workers before they enter dangerous situations results in a drop in the production level of the plant; safety precautions take time.[23]

In its Atlantic States Cast Iron Pipe foundry, McWane faced allegations of a cover-up in an accident that killed a worker. The worker was killed by a forklift that had a number of problems with its brakes. McWane managers were involved in trying to hide the facts of the accident and told one of the employees to mislead the investigation by not presenting an accurate account of the accident.[24]

The working conditions at the Tyler plant became so notorious that it was difficult for McWane to hire people. Tyler Pipe had to go to a pool of ex-convicts to try to get enough people to work at the plant. Howell stated that the local community knew the reputation of the working conditions at Tyler Pipe, so it was difficult to get local workers.[25] When asked whether management was concerned about the hiring difficulties at the Tyler plant, Howell responded by saying management was not worried because they eventually could always find another warm body to put on the production line.[26]

When addressing the costs of the injuries to its workers, McWane wanted to get the costs of medical services under control. An e-mail from a senior plant manager to a nurse at Tyler Pipe, Michelle Sankowsky, stated Tyler Pipe was spending too much money to cover workers' compensation claims. Sankowsky stated that McWane had an unusual philosophy regarding how to resolve the medical cost issue. She said that the policy of the company was to assume that all the injuries were fake. It was up to the employee to prove that he or she had a legitimate injury because Tyler Pipe believed that employees who were on workers' compensation were getting a free ride.[27] The employees did not receive any support when they reported an accident. In fact, at the Tyler plant in 2000 and 2001, more than 350 were disciplined by the managers for reporting accidents. The employee handbook at Tyler stated that employees would be disciplined in any manner short of termination for reporting an accident to help teach the employee what the correct behavior should be.[28] As the employees recovered from their injuries, they were put on "modified duty." Modified duty would usually include menial jobs such as cleaning the toilets. One of the senior managers of the Tyler plant, John Combs, identified the benefits of having the workers on modified duty. He wrote that modified duty would accomplish one of two things: either the employees would rush back to regular work so they would not have to clean the toilets at a lower wage or the employees would quit.[29]

When commenting on the conditions of the facilities, McWane President G. Ruffner Page, Jr. stated that McWane was committed to protecting the safety of its employees and ensuring it followed environmental regulations. He did say that the standards established by McWane have not always been met but that McWane is taking appropriate action to improve its safety and environmental record.[30] In addition, Page stated that McWane's operations keep manufacturing jobs in the United States while competing in a global market. Page stated that manufacturers in China and Latin America do not have the same safety and environmental standards that are in place in the United States, giving those manufacturers an unfair cost advantage. The foreign pipe manufacturers are not concerned about safety issues for their workers, nor are they interested in addressing environmental issues as they relate to their plants' operations.[31]

In March 2005, OSHA sent letters to 14,000 businesses that incurred the highest rate of injury and illness based on data from 2003. OSHA calculated the level of danger in the workplace by the facilities' DART rate: days away from work, restricted work, or job transfer injury and illness. OSHA considered the workplace to be dangerous if the DART rate was an average of 6.5 or higher for every 100 full-time workers. The average across the U.S. facilities was 2.6. Six U.S. McWane foundries were on the OSHA's most dangerous list: Atlantic States Cast Iron, Empire Coke, M & H Value, McWane Cast Iron Pipe, Union Foundry, and Tyler Pipe. Jonathan Snare, acting assistant secretary of labor, stated that this ranking is used to highlight the high number of injuries and illnesses that are taking place in these facilities. The goal of the U.S. Department of Labor is to provide advice to the companies on this list so they can improve the working conditions.[32]

In August 2005, McWane pleaded guilty to federal safety and environmental violations in its Union Foundry facility, located in Anniston, Alabama. In 2000, Reginald Elston was killed while working on an unguarded conveyor belt. Elston died when he went headfirst into the machine and was not able to shut it off in time.[33] McWane admitted that it purposely violated federal safety rules, which was a direct cause of the death of Elston. McWane agreed with the evidence that showed that there was no safety guard on the conveyor belt, which is required by law. McWane was charged with causing death to an employee by knowingly violating federal safety rules, which is a misdemeanor. With the guilty plea, McWane paid a fine of $3.5 million and was required to spend an additional $750,000 on a community project.[34]

In February 2006, OSHA cited McWane for 38 safety violations at the McWane Cast Iron Pipe facility. OSHA found violations pertaining to unacceptable silica levels, machinery that did not have safety guards, and the failure to have safety latches on a ladle that transports molten metal. Of the 38 violations, OSHA had classified 28 as serious, which meant increased risk of serious injury or potential death to the employees. The 38 violations were based on an inspection that was done in August 2005.[35]

In March 2006, OSHA had proposed a $332,000 fine against McWane after 38 alleged health and safety violations were identified in its Birmingham foundry. During an August 2005 OSHA inspection, OSHA issued McWane 10 repeat violations with a proposed fine of $242,700 and 28 serious violations with proposed penalties of $90,000. The alleged violations included carrying molten metal in a ladle without safety latches, having pipes improperly stacked, and having employees work on damaged equipment that had potential electrical hazards. McWane's senior vice president of compliance and corporate affairs, Michael Keel, stated that McWane placed a strong emphasis on employee health and safety and that the company continued to work diligently to have health and safety standards that were unsurpassed in the industry.[36] In April 2006, a federal jury found that Atlantic States Cast Iron Pipe was found guilty of conspiring to evade workplace safety and environmental laws and had to pay a fine of $8 million. It was alleged that managers lied to government regulators, tampered with evidence, and forced its employees to remain silent pertaining to the violations. Atlantic States Cast Iron Pipe was found guilty on 32 charges, and four managers were found guilty of multiple felony charges. It was alleged that employees at the plant tampered with smokestack tests, they dumped wastewater that was polluted away from plant facilities, and they stalled government inspectors at the front gate while they tried to hide numerous violations.[37] In April 2009, one of the plant managers, John Prisque, was sentenced to 70 months in prison for making false statements to federal investigators related to three accidents at the plant.[38]

Canadian Operations

McWane started operations in Canada as the Canada Pipe Company in 1989. At the time of this writing, McWane has three plants in Quebec, two plants in Ontario, one plant in Alberta, one plant in British Columbia, and one plant in New Brunswick. The plants in Quebec employ approximately 500 employees, and the New Brunswick plant has approximately 45 workers. Of McWane's $2 billion in annual revenue, approximately $100 million comes from its Canadian operations. As with its U.S. operations, McWane has had to address a number of safety violations in its Canadian plants. One plant in Quebec set a McWane record for number of injuries for 2001. In 1989, McWane contacted one of its U.S. competitors, U.S. Pipe and Foundry, to try to negotiate who would sell certain products in Canada. McWane wanted U.S. Pipe to stop any further sales of its ductile iron pipe in Canada. If U.S. Pipe refused, McWane threatened to start a price war in the northeastern market of the United States. U.S. Pipe agreed to stop selling the products in Canada.[39] In 1995, McWane was fined $2.5 million by the Canadian government for its agreement with U.S. Pipe.[40]

Environmental Issues

Between 1996 and 2003, McWane facilities were charged more than 450 times for pollution and emissions violations. A Birmingham environmental lawyer, Bart Slawson, has had a longstanding battle with McWane, trying to get McWane to correct its environmental policies. He stated that the philosophy at McWane was that there will not be any changes in the current operations unless they have been caught by a legal authority.[41] In May 2004, McWane president Page stated that McWane was getting close to the point where the company could not continue to have multiple complaints against it and remain a successful company.[42]

In March 2005, McWane was charged and subsequently pleaded guilty to two felony charges relating to environmental violations at the Tyler Pipe plant. It was the first federal prosecution of criminal charges against a foundry for environmental violations. McWane paid a fine of $4.5 million and stated that it was aware its environmental control equipment for air emissions was not up to the standards required by the Clean Air Act. McWane also admitted that it did not disclose all relevant information to the Environmental Protection Agency (EPA) during its investigation.[43] McWane built a new cupola furnace from December 1998 to January 1999 without filing the proper request and documentation to the state environmental agency. In addition, McWane hooked up the new cupola with the existing pollution equipment that had been developed in the 1960s. McWane was required to attach current pollution equipment technology to the new cupola. Furthermore, McWane was required to apply for a new Clean Air Act Title V permit when the new cupola went online. McWane claimed in its Title V filing that the foundry had not been modified since 1971. The EPA's acting assistant administrator for enforcement and compliance assurance, Thomas Skinner, stated that Tyler Pipe willfully made the improvements to the facility without obtaining the required air permits and then attempted to hide its actions.[44]

In May 2005, McWane stated that it would invest $9.3 million in environmental upgrades at its Atlantic States Foundry to avoid fines by the New Jersey government for emissions violations that occurred in 2003.[45] The managers of the plant disposed of contaminated wastewater by releasing it into the Delaware River. In addition, McWane falsified pollution-monitoring reports and burned environmental waste in the furnace used to convert scrap metal into molten iron.[46]

In June 2005, McWane was convicted of environmental violations at its McWane Cast Iron Pipe facility in Birmingham, Alabama. McWane was charged with discharging polluted water from its facility into a Birmingham creek.

In August 2005, McWane was found guilty of violating safety and environmental laws in its Union Foundry facility in Anniston, Alabama. The company admitted that dust in the facility contained lead and cadmium and had been in contact with the employees in the plant. Dust that contains these chemicals is a potential cancer hazard to the employees. McWane paid a $3.5 million fine and spent an additional $750,000 on a community project.

In December 2005, a federal jury convicted McWane of dumping wastewater into a Birmingham creek. McWane was fined $5 million and was required to spend $2.7 million on pollution mitigation in a community improvement project in Birmingham. McWane was also given 5 years of probation. James Delk, McWane former vice president and general manager, was fined $90,000 and was given 6 months' home detention and 3 years' probation. Michael Devine, the former plant manager at McWane Cast Iron Pipe, was fined $35,000 and was given 3 months of home detention and 2 years' probation. Charles Robison, McWane's vice president of environmental affairs, was fined $2,500 and given 150 hours of community service and 2 years' probation.[47] The three McWane executives were convicted of polluting Avondale Creek in Birmingham and conspiring to violate the regulations in the Clean Water Act. The illegal actions occurred between 1998 and 2001, when McWane and the plant managers gave orders to the employees of the plant to release polluted water that was used in the pipe-making process into the creek. The chief of the DOJ's Environmental Crimes Section, David Uhlmann, stated that guilty verdicts in McWane's home town showed that McWane and its management are accountable for their years of wrongdoing.[48]

The chairman of McWane, Phillip McWane, stated in court that he did not plan nor design for McWane Corporation to perform in a manner that would take it into a courtroom. McWane stated that he was ashamed about the failure of McWane Corporation to follow the guidelines of the Clean Water Act and that the company accepts responsibility.[49] Yet McWane's attorney, Doug Jones, stated that the company would appeal the conviction and that McWane was part of the solution instead of being solely the problem.[50]

In February 2006, McWane paid $3 million in fines for environmental violations at its Pacific States Cast Iron Pipe foundry in Utah. The indictment stated that executives at the Provo, Utah, foundry were involved in tampering with pollution-control devices and also made incorrect statements about their operations to the EPA in 2001 and 2002.[51] The fine of $3 million was the largest ever set in Utah for environmental violations. McWane also was put on 3 years' probation, and the general manager of the Pacific States foundry entered in a plea of guilty for tampering with environmental monitoring equipment that was required under the Clean Air Act. DOJ official Sue Ellen Wooldridge stated, "Today's guilty pleas by McWane and the former general manager of its Pacific States facility prove that the company and its employees engaged in a concerted effort to rig state-required compliance tests, and then to misrepresent repeatedly the level of pollution from Pacific States."[52] In June 2006, a former vice president and general manager of Pacific States was sentenced to 1 year in prison and required to pay a fine of $20,000 for violating the Clean Air Act requirements. Charles Matlock pleaded guilty to filing false emissions testing information with the EPA. The EPA had accused Matlock of manipulating the emissions test of the smokestacks in September 2000. In addition, Pacific States then filed inaccurate emissions inventory information from 2001 through 2003 based on the inaccurate September 2000 emissions test.[53]

In April 2006, McWane was found guilty by a federal jury in New Jersey for violating of workplace safety and environmental laws. The McWane-owned Atlantic States Cast Iron Pipe Company and four of its managers were found guilty of conspiring to commit fraud by lying to government regulators and by tampering with evidence and intimidating employees into not reporting violations to the government. Atlantic States was found guilty of 32 criminal counts, and the four managers were found guilty of multiple felony charges with possible prison time. During the trial, witnesses testified that Atlantic States manipulated the results of smokestack testing and dumped polluted wastewater during the night. From 1996 to September 2002, Atlantic States released between 50 and 100 gallons of oil-contaminated wastewater into the Delaware River. Furthermore, Atlantic States used the plant's high-intensity furnace, which was designed to melt scrap iron and to burn paint and waste tires, which released high levels of air pollution.[54]

In addition, employees stopped OSHA inspectors at the front gate until other employees could hide the most obvious safety violations. The prosecutors stated that the McWane way was to always blame the employees, not the working conditions, for accidents. Uhlmann stated that the verdicts in the case proved that McWane was one of the worst violators of safety and environmental laws in the United States. Assistant U.S. Attorney Norv McAndrew described Atlantic States as a plant where production is the number one priority and every other goal is incidental.[55] In July 2010, McWane agreed to pay $4 million to settle more than 400 violations related to federal and state environmental laws. In addition, McWane must also fund seven environmental projects for $9.1 million.[56]

A Dangerous Business Revisited

In 2008, *Frontline* went back to the McWane story to see what, if anything, had changed in the previous 5 years. The DOJ representative stated the DOJ was going to be more aggressive in its pursuit of McWane violations. The justice representative also admitted that most of his knowledge of McWane to that point was based on the *Frontline* broadcast and the articles from the *New York Times*. By 2006, the DOJ investigation resulted in the company and eight executives being charged and convicted of 125 environmental and health and safety crimes. In a complete turnaround, *Frontline* was invited to visit McWane's corporate headquarters in Birmingham. In the original broadcast, McWane refused any participation in the broadcast. Representatives stated that 90% of the senior management at McWane was new and that McWane had hired more than 125 new environmental health and safety employees. In addition, the company had invested in state-of-the-art computer software that can be used to track environmental compliance and injuries. The employees interviewed by *Frontline* stated the work environment has changed completely and that there is now proper safety equipment in the plant to protect the workers.[57] In January 2012, McWane was accused of illegally conspiring to fix prices of pipe fittings with two other companies. The Federal Trade Commission alleged that McWane invited two other pipe companies, Star Pipe and Sigma Corp, to join to collude on pricing of their products. McWane denied that any price fixing had taken place.[58]

On September 19, 2012, the United States Third Circuit Court of Appeals upheld the sentences and fines levied against four former McWane managers at the Atlantic States plant for OSHA EPA violations and obstruction of justice. Former plant manager John Prisque was sentenced to 70 months, former manager Scott Faubert to 41 months, former maintenance supervisor Jeffrey Maury to 30 months, and former supervisor Craig Davidson to 6 months. Atlantic States was fined $8 million and was placed on a 4-year probation. In a response to the court decision, McWane released a statement that the violations occurred during a period of "significant growth and change for the company. . . . McWane is now the industry leader in all facets of environmental, health and safety performance. . . . Virtually all of these efforts began several years prior to the formal enforcement actions."[59] On January 26, 2015, Atlantic States Cast Iron Pipe changed its name to McWane Ductile. Jeff Otterstedt, a senior vice president at McWane Ductile, commented on the name change by stating, "While we have many valued and rich traditions that are unique to each of our divisions, we believe that we become stronger collectively as one distinct brand."[60]

Questions for Thought

1. Explain the concept of *disciplined management*. Has it worked at McWane?

2. Identify the ethical issues associated with the McWane Corporation.

3. Research the McWane Corporation. Identify some of the positive things the company has done.

4. It seems every time one turns around, McWane is paying another large fine. How can the company sustain paying these fines?

16

Merck's Vioxx: How Would You Interpret the Data?

The Introduction of a Blockbuster

In the mid-1990s, Merck & Co. was at a crossroads. A number of its best-selling drugs would no longer be protected by patents within a relatively short period, and Merck had not provided a new set of blockbuster drugs to take their place. The company focused on one growth area—drugs used as painkillers. It had developed Vioxx as the main drug in this category, but it needed to make sure doctors and patients would see the benefits of this Cox-2 drug versus traditional pain relievers. Cox-2 is part of the family of enzymes within the body called cyclooxygenase, or Cox. The body has two types of Cox enzymes: Cox-1 enzymes protect the stomach lining from acids. Cox-2 enzymes cause pain and inflammation. Over-the-counter (OTC) painkillers such as aspirin, ibuprofen (in products such as Motrin and Advil), and naproxen (in products such as Aleve) block both Cox-1 and Cox-2 enzymes. Vioxx and other Cox-2 inhibitors block only the Cox-2 enzyme. As a result, Cox-2 inhibitors should not have an adverse effect on the patient's stomach while relieving pain and inflammation. One theory about the dangers of Cox-2 drugs is that Cox-1 enzymes may help the body clot blood while Cox-2 enzymes help the body reduce blood clots.[1]

Merck wanted to ensure the Vioxx was proved to be gentler on the stomach than OTC medications. More than 16,000 Americans die each year from gastrointestinal bleeding from the cheaper OTC medicines, and Merck wanted to prove that Vioxx was better than the OTC medicines.[2]

Getting Ready to Launch

In a November 21, 1996, memo, Merck officials warned that if the patients didn't take aspirin to relieve potential blood clotting along with Vioxx, there would be a higher rate of cardiovascular problems. Dr. Alise Reicin, who worked in the clinical research department at Merck, stated that giving an aspirin with Vioxx would create a "no-win" situation because the aspirin would increase the potential stomach problems, which Merck was claiming would not occur if the patient had taken Vioxx.

Reicin advised that patients with a high risk of cardiovascular problems should not be included in the study so the difference in cardiovascular problems between the Vioxx and non-Vioxx patients would not be evident. In 1999, Merck started the Vioxx Gastrointestinal Outcomes Research study (VIGOR) clinical trial to collect data to prove that Vioxx was better for the patients' stomach than naproxen.

On May 29, 1999, Merck launched Vioxx after receiving approval from the Food and Drug Administration (FDA). Vioxx was introduced in 80 countries in 1999. In March 2000, the results of the VIGOR study were completed. The study demonstrated that Vioxx users had fewer stomach problems than did those patients who had used naproxen but that Vioxx users had significantly higher numbers of blood clot–related problems. Furthermore, Vioxx users had four to five times higher rates of heart attacks than the naproxen group did.

The Trouble Begins

On March 9, 2000, Merck's research head, Edward Scolnick, e-mailed his colleagues at Merck and warned them, based on the results of the VIGOR study, that Vioxx created a higher risk of a cardiovascular event. He called the side effects a shame but stated that there are always hazards with using drugs. Scolnick also asked that additional data be developed to show that this result occurred in all Cox-2 inhibitors, not just Vioxx.

Merck sent out a press release describing the results of the VIGOR study. In contrast to the concerns raised by Scolnick and others at Merck, the press release was titled "Merck Confirms Favorable Cardiovascular Safety Profile of Vioxx." In the press release, Merck did acknowledge the results of the study but also highlighted other clinical trials and other data collected that had shown "no difference" in the rates of cardiovascular events for patients using Vioxx and a placebo or OTC pain relievers. Merck explained that the antiplatelet properties of naproxen might have helped the patients who took it.[3]

In November 2000, the *New England Journal of Medicine* published the results of a VIGOR study. The article was written by academic researchers who had received research grants or consulting contracts from Merck. The paper touted the potential benefits of Vioxx for stomach problems and heart attacks. The authors did not provide any information about the higher risk of serious cardiovascular complications from using Vioxx, such as strokes and blood clots. Based on the data in the study, the authors had concluded that Vioxx did not show a significant rise in heart attacks among patients who were not at high risk for heart attacks before they started taking Vioxx.[4] This study demonstrated that Vioxx patients were four times more likely to have a heart attack or stroke (0.4% to 0.1%) than were those patients who took the OTC drug naproxen. However, the focus on the paper was Vioxx's benefits. Merck argued that the results of the study could have been based on the protective effects of naproxen, rather than on the dangers of Vioxx.[5]

In February 2001, Merck won a significant decision from the FDA when the FDA allowed Merck to claim that Vioxx is safer for patients' stomachs than previous painkillers, giving Vioxx a significant competitive advantage over its chief rival, Celebrex, made by Pfizer. The FDA wanted to have the dangers of cardiovascular problems displayed prominently on the Vioxx label, but Merck refused, arguing that it wanted to promote the positive aspects of the drug. They compromised, resulting in a label showing the positive impact on stomach problems first, then the information about the risks of heart attacks and strokes. The new labeling was released in April 2002.

External Red Flags Start to Fly

In August 2001, the results of a Vioxx study done by the Cleveland Clinic were published in the *Journal of the American Medical Association*. Researchers concluded that a cautionary flag needed to be raised concerning the increased risk of cardiovascular events occurring in patients who use Vioxx. The authors stated that all Cox-2 inhibitors may increase the risk, but Vioxx appeared to be riskier than the other drugs in the marketplace. Merck met with the authors to argue that Merck did not believe that there was a problem with the drug and asked the journal to allow Merck to present a rebuttal to their findings. The journal refused Merck's request.[6]

On September 17, 2001, the FDA sent a letter to Merck's CEO, Raymond Gilmartin, warning Merck that it should stop marketing Vioxx as a drug with a minimal threat of cardiovascular problems when comparing Vioxx with naproxen. The FDA stated explicitly that Merck's promotional campaign discounted the fact that patients who had used Vioxx were observed to have four to five times higher risk of a heart attack than those patients in the other sample, which it claimed was a critical fact. The FDA also criticized Merck for claiming that the reason Vioxx patients had more heart attacks was because of the protective properties that were found in naproxen. The FDA claimed that Merck had no proof that naproxen had any protective properties for the patients' hearts. In addition, the FDA claimed that Merck was misleading the public by titling the press release of the VIGOR study "Merck Confirms Favorable Cardiovascular Safety Profile of Vioxx."[7]

How to Address the Concerns

An internal Merck marketing document for sales representatives told the reps to "dodge" any potentially tough questions that were asked by doctors about the side effects of Vioxx. This advice was part of the "obstacle handling guide" given to help the sales reps continue to convince doctors to prescribe Vioxx. When a doctor asked specifically about concerns related to heart problems, the sales rep was instructed to tell the doctor that Vioxx would not reduce the level of cardiovascular problems and that Vioxx would not be considered a substitute for aspirin. The sales reps were given a 16-page "Dodge Ball Vioxx" document that went through a step-by-step process teaching reps how to respond to questions from doctors about Vioxx. The final four pages of the document had the single word *DODGE* on each page.[8]

In addition, Merck attempted to control academics who started to question the benefits of Vioxx. Stanford University's Dr. Gurkipal Singh was a leading expert in Cox-2 research and was presenting lectures that were funded by Merck and other companies. Singh asked Merck for additional information pertaining to cardiovascular issues, and Merck refused to provide any. Singh added a slide to his PowerPoint presentations—a picture of a man hiding underneath a blanket—to represent the missing data that Merck would not supply. Merck canceled Singh's subsequent lectures, and the company also complained to Stanford University Medical School that Singh was anti-Merck and anti-Vioxx and was acting irresponsibly. Merck warned Stanford that if Singh's actions continued, there would be consequences for the doctor and for Stanford. Stanford replied that Merck had crossed the line and that other top-tier medical schools had also complained about Merck's threatening behaviors toward researchers who had studied Vioxx. Merck CEO Gilmartin responded that Merck had a strong commitment to have strong ethical standards with its dealings with all doctors and health-care providers.[9]

The Wonder Drug for Everyone

In October 2003, a research study by Merck demonstrated that Vioxx could significantly help children with juvenile rheumatoid arthritis. The results showed that the children in the study were able to tolerate Vioxx, and Merck started moving toward positioning Vioxx as a pediatric medication.[10] However, during the same month, another study funded by Merck showed that patients who had taken Vioxx had a 39% higher risk of heart attack within the first 90 days of taking the medication compared with Celebrex. Despite the results of that study, Merck continued to broaden the scope of uses for Vioxx. On April 1, 2004, Merck announced that the FDA had approved Vioxx to help reduce the pain associated with migraines in adults. Vioxx was the only Cox-2-specific inhibitor the FDA allowed to be prescribed for migraine relief.[11]

The Data Continue

On April 14, 2004, the results of a clinical trial sponsored by Merck and Harvard Medical School that were to be published in the American Heart Association's publication concluded that Vioxx had higher risks of heart attacks in the first 90 days of use of than Celebrex did. Merck had requested that the authors alter the conclusions so they were not as negative about the side effects of Vioxx. The authors refused to change the conclusion. On May 4, 2004, just before the paper was to be published, Merck had one of the researchers, Carolyn Cannuscio, who was an employee at Merck, removed from the article.[12]

On August 25, 2004, the results of an FDA study on Vioxx showed increased risk of heart attacks and sudden cardiac deaths. In the study, patients who took doses of Vioxx that were more than 25 milligrams daily had 3.15 times more chance of having a heart problem than did patients in the control group. Although only 10 cases of heart problems were discovered in the study, the results were statistically significant. The conclusion of the study was that Celebrex "may be safer" than Vioxx for heart problems. The results of the study raised concerns at Kaiser Permanente for its customers, and the HMO was considering no longer allowing Vioxx to be included in its drug program. Kaiser helped fund the study with the FDA by giving technical, clinical, and programming support. The spokesperson at Merck, Mary Elizabeth Blake, stated that Merck did not agree with the results and those previous randomized studies, which included thousands of elderly patients, did not find any significant increase in heart problems with the patients. At the time of the results of the study, Vioxx's market share had fallen from 43% in 2001 to 32% in July 2004.[13] On September 8, 2004, the FDA announced that Vioxx was approved to be used to help children with juvenile rheumatoid arthritis with the only limitation being that the children must be at least 2 years old and weigh at least 22 pounds.[14]

Cases

On September 24, 2004, Merck CEO Gilmartin received a call from the head of Merck's research department, Peter Kim. Kim had been notified the day before that an external panel that was supervising a clinical trial on Vioxx had told Merck to stop the trial immediately because the patients taking Vioxx were twice as likely to have a heart attack or stroke than were those taking a placebo in the control group. The trial lasted for more than 18 months and involved 2,600 patients. There were 15 heart attacks or strokes for every 1,000 patients taking Vioxx versus 7.5 heart attacks or strokes per 1,000 for those patients taking a placebo. There was no difference in the two groups for the first 18 months; both samples had 3.75 heart attacks or strokes per 1,000 patients in the first 18 months.[15]

The Withdrawal of Vioxx

On September 30, 2004, Merck announced that it was withdrawing Vioxx from the market based on studies that linked it to increased occurrences of heart problems. Vioxx had global sales in 2003 of $2.5 billion and more than 100 million prescriptions for the drug had been written since 1999, when the drug was introduced into the marketplace. Vioxx had accounted for 11% of Merck's global sales in 2003 and was estimated to contribute 20% of Merck's overall level of profitability. Approximately 2 million people had been taking Vioxx when the withdrawal was announced.[16] Sales of Vioxx had dropped in the second quarter of 2004 to $653 million from $801 million in the second quarter of 2003. With the announcement of the withdrawal, critics started asking whether Gilmartin should resign so Merck could regain its creditability. The cost of the cancellation of Vioxx was estimated to be between $700 million and $750 million for patient reimbursement and the write-off of the Vioxx pills that had already been manufactured. The cost of cancellation did not include any reserves being set aside for the settlements of future lawsuits.[17]

Critics of the FDA raised concerns about why it took so long to pull the drug when questions about its impact on heart problems were first discovered in 2000. In addition, some critics were asking whether Vioxx was worth both the physical and financial cost. One Vioxx pill sold for as much as $2.50, providing almost the same pain relief as aspirin, though Vioxx users were less likely to develop ulcers and stomach problems versus aspirin users.[18] Within a week of the announcement by Merck, it was estimated that Vioxx-based litigation could cost Merck more than $10 billion with an estimated 60,000 potential lawsuits to be filed against the pharmaceutical company.[19]

The Steamrolling Legal Problems

On November 8, 2004, the Department of Justice (DOJ) started a criminal investigation pertaining to Merck's handling of the Vioxx issue. In addition, the SEC notified Merck that it would be starting an investigation. Merck responded by stating that it had acted responsibly and appropriately to both the development and marketing of Vioxx.[20]

In his speech on ethics at the University of Michigan in November 2004, Gilmartin explained that patients come first at Merck and that Merck's withdrawal of Vioxx was a clear representation of the values that Merck upholds. Gilmartin reminded the students that ethics is all about your behavior and not what people say about you. He also reminded them that all that matters at the end of the day is what you have done. Gilmartin commented that the *Wall Street Journal* had misrepresented the facts and policies of Merck when it printed that Merck knew in 2000 that there were problems with Vioxx.[21]

In February 2005, Merck announced that it would consider reintroducing Vioxx into the marketplace if the FDA advisory committee decided that the risks associated with Vioxx were also found in other Cox-2 drugs. Merck argued that if the benefits of Vioxx outweighed the risks for some patients, that Vioxx could be sold to patients with appropriate warnings. Of course, the reintroduction of Vioxx would help Merck's legal argument that despite the risks, Vioxx is a valid alternative treatment for some patients.[22] Also in February 2005, Merck announced that Gilmartin would receive a bonus of $1.4 million for his effort in 2004. Using its own judgment and discretion, the board of directors at Merck determined the amount of Gilmartin's bonus.[23] On May 5, 2005, Gilmartin stepped down as CEO of Merck and was replaced by Richard Clark, who had been in charge of manufacturing at Merck. It was speculated that Merck wanted a new CEO from outside the company, but reportedly, the potential candidates Merck was interested in did not want the position. Clark was not given the chairman of the board position, which instead was to be composed of a three-person executive board committee to advise Clark. Gilmartin was to retire from Merck in March 2006, and he remain at Merck after he stepped down as CEO as a special advisor to the board's executive committee. By the beginning of Clark's tenure, more than 2,400 lawsuits had been filed against Merck by the families of former Vioxx patients.[24]

The first Vioxx-related trial with a jury started on July 14, 2005, in Angleton, Texas. The plaintiff's lawyer called Merck's marketing campaign the ability to turn science into science fiction and referred to the company's "Merck-y ethics." The Vioxx patient had died from arrhythmia, or an irregular heartbeat, and Vioxx had never been associated with causing that heart problem. By the start of this trial, the number of lawsuits against Merck for Vioxx-related problems had risen to 4,000 with the potential of between 20,000 and 100,000 total cases.[25] On August 19, 2005, the jury found in favor of the plaintiff in the trial against Merck. The jury found Merck guilty of wrongful death and awarded total damages of $253 million to Carol Ernst, whose husband, Robert, died after taking Vioxx for 8 months. Of the $253 million, $229 million were punitive damages for Merck's liability, negligence, and malice. The state of Texas has a limit of $2 million for punitive damages in any trial located in that state, so if the award was paid out, it would automatically be reduced by $227 million. Merck said it would appeal the verdict. The stock price of Merck fell almost 8% to just above $28 per share.[26] The jurors said that they were troubled by seeing the internal documents that showed the company appeared to suppress the risk of Vioxx in its marketing campaigns. The jurors also stated that Merck needed to make the warning clearer on the packaging. They explained that the warnings needed to be in layperson's terms so patients can decide whether it is worth the risk of taking the drug.[27]

In addition, the jurors criticized Merck for presenting very technical, scientific data but not explaining in terms the jury could understand about why Vioxx may have not caused the death. One juror compared it to the "wah wah wah" that the adults make when talking to the children in the *Peanuts* cartoon programs. Furthermore, the jurors did not like that Merck's former CEO and other top officials gave only a video-tape testimony and did not appear in person. One juror said that his interpretation was that Merck was admitting its guilt by not having the top officials present during the trial. In addition, the plaintiff's lawyer, Mark Lanier, had hired a shadow jury to help with his arguments. Lanier picked 13 people with the same demographics as the real jury and paid them anonymously $125 a day to listen to the trial and give feedback to a consultant working for Lanier at the end of each day at a nearby McDonald's restaurant. Two days before the closing arguments, the shadow jury voted 9 to 4 for the plaintiff with $115 million in damages. That was not good enough because at least a 10-to-2 vote by the real 12-person jury must take place to reach a verdict. Lanier also hired a psychologist and litigator, Lisa Blue, to observe the reactions of the real trial. Blue told Lanier that he was still weak on presenting causation and that he needed to tell the jury members they needed only 51% confidence that Vioxx was one of the causes of Robert Ernst's death. Blue also reminded Lanier that one juror wrote in her questionnaire that she loved watching Oprah Winfrey and tapes the show. As a result, during the closing arguments, Lanier wrote *51%* on the board to remind the jurors of the threshold of certainty they needed for the impact of Vioxx on cardiovascular events and also stated that he couldn't promise Oprah but that a lot of people would be interested in hearing their story if they had the courage to find Merck guilty.[28]

After the verdict was reached, Merck stated that it would continue to fight each lawsuit separately but might consider settling a few of the lawsuits that met very specific and narrow criteria: The patient had taken Vioxx for more than 18 months, and there were no other risk factors that were associated with heart attacks or strokes. By that point, 4,951 lawsuits had been filed against Merck for Vioxx-related problems.[29]

On September 19, 2005, the second Vioxx trial started in Atlantic City, New Jersey. By this time, approximately 5,000 Vioxx-based lawsuits had been filed against Merck. A researcher from the University of Michigan, Dr. Benedict Lucchesi, testified that Vioxx may cause a heart attack after one dose.[30] The patient, Frederick "Mike" Humeston, had a heart attack and lived after taking Vioxx off and on for 2 months. Merck stated that Humeston's poor general health and on-the-job stress, not Vioxx, were the cause of his heart attack. Merck's major defense tactic was to present the fact that the FDA had concluded that Vioxx would not cause heart attacks in low doses over a short term. On November 3, 2005, the jury found Merck not guilty of fraud and failure to warn customers about its products. The jury determined that Merck had adequately disclosed the risks about Vioxx and, therefore, should not be held accountable for Humeston's heart attack. By the end of the trial, more than 6,500 lawsuits had been filed against Merck.[31]

On November 30, 2005, the third Vioxx trial, the first tried in federal court, started in Houston, Texas. The widow of Richard "Dicky" Irwin sued Merck, claiming that Vioxx was the cause of her husband's fatal heart attack in 2001. On December 8, 2005, while the third Vioxx trial was in progress, the *New England Journal of Medicine* published an article titled "Expression of Concern" about the results of the Vioxx study that was published in 2000. The article revealed the academics who had received grant or consulting money from Merck and had concluded that Vioxx was better for stomach problems but did not increase the risk of heart attacks. The *New England Journal of Medicine* had discovered that three Vioxx patients in the study who had suffered heart attacks were excluded from the study and were, therefore, not included in the final data results. The exclusion of the three patients made the results appear that Vioxx was much safer than it should have been. Merck responded by stating that the three heart attacks were not included in the study because they occurred after a predetermined cutoff date for data collection for the study. The executive editor of the journal discovered the omission of the three patients' data after being deposed by one of the plaintiffs who was suing Merck.[32] After the journal made its announcement, the plaintiffs in the third Merck trial asked for a mistrial because of the new information pertaining to the VIGOR study.[33] On December 12, 2005, the third Vioxx case was ruled a mistrial when the jury could not come to a unanimous agreement on the verdict. Of the nine jurors, eight had voted that Merck was not guilty with one juror holding firm on Merck's guilt. The eight jurors who voted for Merck stated that they felt that Merck had made stronger scientific arguments supporting its case than the patient had; Irwin was already in a high-risk category for a heart attack.[34] The retrial for Irwin started on February 6, 2006, in New Orleans. After 2 weeks, the jury found Merck not responsible for the death of Irwin, giving the company its second legal win. By this time, more than 9,650 lawsuits had been filed against Merck.[35]

Merck defended itself against another plaintiff in Rio Grande City, Texas, on January 25, 2006. The family of Leonel Garza Sr. sued Merck over his fatal heart attack in 2001. Garza had heart problems for more than 20 years and was a smoker. In addition, he also had a quadruple-bypass operation in the past.[36] On April 21, 2006, the Texas jury found Merck liable for the fatal heart attack of Garza. The jury awarded the Garza family $7 million in compensatory damages and $25 million in punitive damages.[37] On December 21, 2006, the $32 million award was reduced to $8.7 million by state law that caps punitive damages at $750,000.[38]

On March 6, 2006, the next Vioxx trial started in Atlantic City, with a patient who had a heart attack while using Vioxx but survived. The patient, Thomas Cona, had a heart attack in 2003 but was in a high-risk category to have a heart attack. Another patient, John McDarby, also had a heart attack and survived and was in a high-risk category for heart attacks. The lawyer for the plaintiff was Mark Lanier, who was the lawyer who won the first Vioxx case in Texas.[39] On April 5, the jury in the McDarby case found Merck guilty of not properly warning patients. The jury awarded McDarby $3 million in compensatory damages and his wife, Irma, $1.5 million. The jury also found Merck guilty of committing consumer fraud against both McDarby and Thomas. A decision on punitive damages was scheduled later by the court.[40] On April 10, 2006, the jury added $9 million in punitive damages to the decision pertaining to McDarby's case.[41]

In April 2006, suing Merck became easier because of a "trial in a box" system that had been developed by lawyers. The system set up a step-by-step process in which smaller law firms could help their clients sue Merck. The package—which included select portions of video disposition, a trial theme grid that laid out the basic arguments in the case, and courtroom slides—was free to any law office, but lawyers who used the package had to pay a contingency fee between 3% and 6% of any rewards or settlements that were received from Merck. Shortly after it was introduced, almost 200 law firms had signed a contract to obtain the package. By using the package, the estimated cost of the trial for the law firm could be reduced to $50,000.[42]

In May 2006, Merck released data that showed that the risks of cardiovascular problems could occur starting at 4 months after first taking Vioxx instead of the 18 months, which was the cornerstone of its defense in its lawsuits. In the study called Approve, the data showed that patients taking Vioxx started to have more cardiovascular events than did those taking the placebo by the fourth month of the study. By this time, approximately 11,500 lawsuits had been filed against Merck.[43] A study published by the Canadian Medical Association showed that senior patients who took Vioxx had the highest risk of a heart attack within the first 2 weeks of taking the drug, which countered Merck's defense that Vioxx had only long-term effects.[44] On May 11, 2006, Merck released additional data that showed that patients who took Vioxx were at risk of having a heart attack or stroke for as long as 1 year after they stopped taking Vioxx.[45]

The November 2000 *New England Journal of Medicine* article that highlighted the benefits and downplayed the risks of Vioxx might have had "lax" editing. The journal's executive editor, Gregory Curfman, admitted in a disposition that the authors might have been allowed to make misleading claims in the article because of a lax review of the article's results by the journal's editorial staff. Curfman also admitted that the Vioxx article generated between $697,000 and $836,000 in revenue from selling 929,400 reprints, which were mostly bought by Merck.[46]

Merck received its fourth victory in seven verdicts when a New Jersey jury found that the company was not responsible for Elaine Doherty's heart attack. The jury stated that Merck had acted responsibly and the 68-year-old Doherty's doctor knew about the potential risk of taking Vioxx.[47] Merck was victorious in the next trial as well. A California jury also found that Merck was not responsible for the heart attack of a 71-year-old patient, Stewart Grossberg. The jury again cited that Merck had made the patient aware of the potential risks of taking Vioxx.[48] By August 2006, Merck was facing 14,000 lawsuits, but the recent victories in court led to the withdrawal of 300 federal cases in which the patients either had weak cases or could not prove that they had taken the drug.[49]

In a double dose of reality, on August 17, 2006, Merck lost in two separate cases. A federal court ordered Merck to pay the plaintiff in one case, 62-year-old Gerald Barnett, $51 million in compensatory and punitive damages. The jury found that Merck was negligent by failing to warn doctors about the risks linked to the drug. In addition, the jury stated that Merck had knowingly misrepresented or failed to properly disclose relevant information about Vioxx.[50] Furthermore, Merck's first Vioxx victory was thrown out because of the new questions pertaining to the data that was generated in previous Merck studies.[51]

On August 30, 2006, a federal judge in New Orleans described the $51 million verdict for Barnett as "grossly excessive" and ordered a review of the assignment of damages in the case. The judge agreed with the jury that Merck should be liable for Barnett's heart attack but stated that issues such as lost wages should not be included in the damages because the plaintiff was able to go back to many of his regular daily activities.[52]

In August 2006, Merck announced that it had developed a replacement for Vioxx called Arcoxia. Merck stated that it already had been sold in 62 other countries but had not received final approval from the FDA. The FDA had deferred a decision on the approval because it appeared that Arcoxia could have similar risks to the heart attacks that occurred with Vioxx. One of the side effects of Arcoxia was high blood pressure. On September 6, 2006, an internal investigation found that Merck behaved in an appropriate manner as it related to Vioxx. At a cost of $21 million and having taken more than 20 months and 53,000 hours to complete, the report stated that Merck executives did not hide the potential risks to patients taking Vioxx. The report concluded that Merck officials took "reasonable steps" in researching the potential health risks of taking Vioxx.[53] With 14,200 lawsuits waiting to be tried, the report could have been a critical part of future litigation if it had found that Merck was guilty of negligence. Even with the clean bill of health from the report, Merck was facing an estimated legal liability of between $4 billion and $30 billion.[54]

On September 12, 2006, researchers from Harvard Medical School released the results of the summary of 114 clinical trials that examined the associated risks of using Vioxx. More than 116,000 people were part of the trials, and the results showed that Vioxx increased both kidney disease and arrhythmia risks. Furthermore, the arrhythmia risks were shown to have started soon after the treatment had started.[55]

On September 26, 2006, a federal jury found Merck not responsible for the heart attack of a Kentucky plaintiff. After 3 hours of deliberation, the jury found the plaintiff had not proved that Vioxx was the cause of his heart attack 3½ years earlier.[56] By the end of September 2006, Merck had 22,000 Vioxx-related lawsuits filed against it. Part of the surge in the number of lawsuits was because a number of states have a 2-year statute of limitations for plaintiffs to file lawsuits, which expired at the end of September, corresponding with the 2-year anniversary of Vioxx's withdrawal from the marketplace.[57] By September 30, 2006, Vioxx had 23,800 lawsuits that involved 41,750 plaintiffs. The company also faced 275 class-action lawsuits and stated that it would increase its reserves for Vioxx-related legal costs from $685 million to $958 million.[58] In the 11th trial related to Vioxx, Merck recorded another victory when a jury spent just 90 minutes in deliberation to decide that Merck was not responsible for Charles Mason's heart attack. Merck successfully argued that Mason's clogged arteries, rather than the use of Vioxx for 10 months, caused the heart attack. That made the tally seven victories and four losses for Merck; the 11th case was an initial victory for Merck, but the decision was overturned.[59] In another victory for Merck, a federal judge ruled that the thousands of federal lawsuits against Merck could not be grouped into one national class-action lawsuit. Merck wanted to have each of the cases tried independently to highlight the unique characteristics of each plaintiff's complaint.[60] In an apparent increased level of momentum, on December 13, 2006, Merck also won its 12th case in New Orleans when a jury decided in less than 2 hours that Merck had given adequate warning of the heart risks associated with the drug. By December 2006, the numbers of outstanding lawsuits against Merck had climbed to 27,000.[61] Two days later, Merck won another victory when a jury in Alabama deliberated for less than 2 hours to decide that Merck was not accountable for Gary Albright's heart attack.[62]

By August 2007, Merck had spent more than $1 billion in legal fees to defend itself in Vioxx cases. As part of its legal strategy, Merck automatically appealed any judgment against it, which gave Merck a potential additional opportunity to present its case while not being required to make any payments in judgments against the company until after the appeal. Thus, 2 years after Carol Ernst won the first Vioxx case against Merck for the death of her husband Robert, neither she nor any of the 45,000 other plaintiffs had received any money from Merck. In the 2 years after the initial legal judgment against Merck, its stock price increased by 80%, and the estimated legal liability for Merck had decreased from $25 billion to $5 billion. The legal counsel responsible for Merck strategy pertaining to the lawsuits, Kenneth Frazier, was promoted to president of global health division, which is in charge of Merck's marketing and sales forces and includes approximately 30,000 employees.[63]

Cases

One month later in September 2007, the Supreme Court of New Jersey rejected a class-action lawsuit against Merck for its Vioxx litigation. The court ruled that a nationwide class-action lawsuit was not appropriate. The ruling was a huge victory for Merck because the company was now allowed to continue to have each case tried separately instead of having the plaintiffs' resources be pooled in a class-action motion. The shares of Merck rose more than 2% to $50.47 after the ruling was announced.[64]

In what could be considered one of the greatest legal bargains in corporate history, on November 8, 2007, Merck agreed to settle 27,000 Vioxx lawsuits covering approximately 47,000 plaintiffs for $4.85 billion or approximately $100,000 per lawsuit. Therefore, each plaintiff would receive just over $100,000 before legal fees and expenses, which can be equivalent to between 30% and 50% of the payment. As a result, the average plaintiff will receive between $50,000 and $70,000.[65] By March 2008, 44,000 of the 47,000 plaintiffs had signed up to be part of the $4.85 billion settlement.[66]

In February 2008, Merck agreed to pay $671 million to settle civil legal claims by the government that Merck had overcharged Medicaid health programs for four of its drugs. In addition, Merck was accused of offering doctors fees and gifts in exchange for the doctors prescribing Merck drugs. Merck's response was that there was just "a disagreement" over the rules of the Medicaid rebate program.[67]

Merck had drafted numerous research studies pertaining to Vioxx. In other words, Merck representatives had written the research papers and then gave credit to other authors. In one research paper for which Merck wanted to have a well-known researcher as the lead author, the lead author's name is not on the paper, which has the comment "External author?" instead. Merck acknowledged that it occasionally hired external medical writers to help draft research papers that would be given to doctors whose names would eventually appear on the article. Merck also stated that the authors of the paper were actively involved in the research or analysis of the data in the paper. The *Journal of the American Medical Association* (*JAMA*) examined published articles pertaining to Vioxx in which *JAMA* concluded, "It is clear that at least some of the authors played little direct roles in the study or review, yet still allowed themselves to be named as authors."[68]

In May 2008, Merck paid $58 million to settle civil claims that it down played the health risks of Vioxx in its marketing campaigns. In addition, Merck also agreed to submit all future television commercials to review by the FDA before they are aired for the next 7 years.[69] Also in May 2008, Carol Ernst's $26 million verdict from the first plaintiff Vioxx victory in 2005 was overturned by a state appeals court in Texas. The appeals court found that the plaintiffs had not proven that Vioxx caused Carol's husband's death.[70] In May 2009, it was discovered that Merck subsidiary in Australia was paying the Australian officer of an academic publisher, Elsevier, from 2002 through 2005 to have eight positive compilations of scientific articles published about Vioxx. The articles were published in the *Australasian Journal of Bone and Joint Medicine*. Elsevier did not disclose that Merck had paid to have the articles published, and readers perceived that the articles were based on peer-review evaluations, but they were not.[71]

In April 2010, shareholders won a lawsuit against Merck that claimed that Merck executives and board members did not perform their fiduciary duties in marketing Vioxx. Merck agreed to pay as much as $12.15 million of the shareholders' legal fees to settle the case. In addition, Merck agreed to hire a chief medical officer to be responsible for monitoring product safety and marketing.[72] In November 2011, Merck agreed

to pay $950 million in fines and civil settlements and to plead guilty to one crim-
inal misdemeanor charge for its role in marketing and selling Vioxx. The criminal
charge was based on the notion that Merck illegally promoted Vioxx to its patients.
Merck had made inaccurate, unsupported, or misleading statements of patient safety
when they used Vioxx. Merck pleaded guilty to introducing a "misbranded" product,
Vioxx, into interstate commerce, which is a criminal violation of the Food, Drug, and
Cosmetic Act. Merck agreed to pay a fine of $321.6 million and $628.4 million in civil
lawsuit settlements. The civil settlement was allocated to pay $426 million to the fed-
eral government and $202 million to state Medicaid agencies that had sued Merck for
civil claims. As a result, Merck has paid nearly $6 billion to settle lawsuits for a drug
that generated total sales of $11 billion from 1999 to 2004.[73] In 2012, researchers at
the University of Pennsylvania determined why using Vioxx can lead to heart problems. In order to relieve pain, Vioxx suppresses the production of a single enzyme,
Cox-2, which is needed to help protect the heart. The blocking of the Cox-2 enzyme
suppresses the production of molecules that are used to break up potential blood clots
and increase the blood flow inside the body.[74]

Questions for Thought

1. What are the ethical implications of
    the "Dodge Ball Vioxx" document
    given to sales representatives?

2. Do you think this is a case of putting
    profits first? Explain.

3. It took Merck 5 years to remove Vioxx
    from the market. Why?

Cases

17

The Music Industry: Ethical Issues in a Digital Age

The Long and Winding Road of Recorded Music

With the invention of the phonograph by Thomas Edison in 1877, music became available in a unique, new, and different medium. Before the phonograph, music could be listened to only when played live to an audience. With the ability to record and permanently capture music, an industry was formed. Through its more than 130-year history, the industry has had many peaks and valleys and has faced a number of unique issues as the industry evolves in a digital age. A historical summary of the music industry in presented in Table 1.

The Rise of Napster

A critical step is needed to transfer recorded music legally or illegally from one computer user to another. That first step is creating a software program that will convert and compress the information into a transferable file. The advent of MP3 files allowed music to be sent and stored electronically through the Internet. Napster became the mother ship of music transfer. Users could download and trade the music files without any third party being involved in the process. The first MP3 player, MPMAN, was introduced in South Korea by Saehan in February 1998 and was released in the United States in the summer of 1998. The MPMAN was the first portable player that could play MP3 files. The Recording Industry Association of America (RIAA) sued the manufacturer of the MPMAN player on October 9, 1998, for facilitating copyright infringement. The music industry claimed that it was unethical and illegal because the artists who were involved in the recording of the song received no payment when the user obtained the song via an MP3 file on the Internet.[1]

The software program used to transform a personal computer into a server that could be used to transfer music files was developed by an 18-year-old freshman at Northeastern University in Boston, Massachusetts. Shawn Fanning just wanted a method with which he could trade music with his friends, but his software changed the music industry forever. At 19, Fanning dropped out of Northeastern so he could

TABLE 1 ● The Long and Winding Road of the Music Industry

1877: Thomas Edison invents the phonograph record, which gives birth to the music industry.

1915: Records that make 78 revolutions per minute (RPM) are introduced in the marketplace. The 78 allowed shorter pieces of music to be purchased by consumers and was the forerunner to the single.

1948: Vinyl records (33.3 RPM) are introduced for mass production. Vinyl records were more durable and easier to play than the previous wax cylinders and shellac versions of records.

1949: Records that make 45 revolutions per minute are introduced. These 45s allowed customers to purchase a "single" song at a lower price than a 78.

1965: Audiocassette tapes are introduced to the public. This allowed customers to record music for their own personal use as well as transfer music to their friends.

1966: Eight-track tape decks are introduced in cars. This allowed a full album of music to be heard in a car.

1983: Compact discs are introduced in the United States. These discs contained digitally recorded music and would evolve into a recording medium when recordable CDs are introduced.

1998: MP3 files are introduced.

1999: Napster is born.

2001: iPod is introduced. Can store up to 1,000 songs.

2009: iPod Classic 160 GB is introduced. Can store up to 40,000 songs.

Source: Jon Pareles, "What Albums Join Together, Everyone Tears Asunder," *New York Times*, July 20, 2003, www.nytimes.com.

build Napster into one of the most visited websites on the Internet. Fanning's uncle, John Fanning, financially supported Shawn's vision and became Napster's largest shareholder. Napster's software allowed users to search quickly and effectively to identify where MP3 files were available on other websites.[2]

In 1999, the RIAA filed a copyright-infringement suit against Napster and claimed that Napster was the facilitator for the illegal transfer of music from one peer user to another. Napster claimed that it was just a service where peers could trade music between websites and was not involved in the actual transfer of music, whether it was legally or illegally done by the computer users. In January 2000, the RIAA sued MP3.com for compiling a database of RIAA members' music without permission from the artists.[3]

In April 2000, the heavy metal group Metallica sued Napster for allowing users to illegally transfer Metallica songs without the band receiving any royalty compensation. In March 2000, Nullsoft, a division of America Online, introduced Gnutella as a file-sharing system that does not have the centralized index server Napster used.[4]

From 1999 to 2003, between $700 million and $2 billion in sales were lost to the music companies and the artists through illegal music file sharing. By the end of 2004, the RIAA and the International Federation of the Phonographic Industry (IFPI) had filed more than 7,700 legal actions against individuals and organizations that share music illegally through file transfers.[5] The downloading of music files is predominately done by younger listeners. A poll published in the *Wall Street Journal* in 2003 revealed that 53% of respondents age 12 to 17 and 44% of respondents age 18 to 24 had downloaded music from the Internet. The percentage dropped quickly to 23% for the age range 25 to 34, 12% for respondents 35 to 54, and 3% for those respondents who were 55 years of age or older.[6]

On April 3, 2001, musician Don Henley of the Eagles testified before the Senate Judiciary Committee in Washington, representing the Recording Artists Coalition (RAC), a large group of musicians. Henley stated that the file-transferring system used by Napster and other swapping services such as Gnutella, Kazaa, and OpenNap did not allow the artists to collect rightful compensation for their work.[7] On June 5, 2001, Napster announced that it would start offering a subscription-based system in which the user must pay for access to music files from three of the major record labels.[8] The decision was based on the fact that the RIAA won the legal battle to force Napster to filter out all copyrighted songs from its file-trading system that the user does not have to pay a fee for.[9]

The battle over copyrighted songs was not over. Just as with the boy who put his finger in the dike, another hole opened. Kazaa seized on the vacancy of free music trading left by Napster to establish its own file-swapping system that was easier to use. By February 2002, more than 33 million users logged on to Kazaa to transfer music to each other. In early 2002, 1 billion files were traded daily on Kazaa, including music, software, and movie files. The RIAA filed suit against Kazaa and claimed that the company had created the equivalent of a 21st-century piratical bazaar, allowing the illegal trading of copyrighted material. Claiming the same defense as Napster, Kazaa stated that it could neither control nor be responsible for the illegal actions of its users. The parent company of Kazaa, Sharman Networks, also owned Streamcast, which had given out more than 60 million copies of its file-sharing software. The CEO of Streamcast, Steve Griffin, compared file sharing with photocopying. He stated at a music summit in Los Angeles in February 2002 that employees used a copy machine to make copies of articles to pass around the office so everyone in the office does not need to buy the magazine. So why would it be any different to share music files?[10]

The music industry lost the initial lawsuit against the file-transferring service Grokster on April 25, 2003, when a federal court ruled that Grokster was able to continue to offer its software to transfer music files. The court ruled that Grokster was not responsible for the illegal transfers because it did not have centralized computer services that would allow it direct access to monitor which files were being transferred from one peer to another. This system was different from Napster's "central list" system, which did allow Napster the opportunity to review what files were being transferred.[11] As a result, the RIAA decided on June 25, 2003, that it was going to start suing individual users who had illegally transferred large numbers of music files. On September 8, 2003, the first lawsuits were filed against individual users. In the text of the letter sent with the summons was an explanation of the music industry's position. The RIAA stated that copyright is not a crime with one victim: Many people are involved in the recording, manufacturing, and distribution of music, and their salaries depend on the legal purchase of music. The initial settlement amounts ranged from $2,000 to $5,000.[12] The RIAA targeted users who had shared more than a thousand files. The copyright law in the United States allowed the RIAA to sue users for as much as $150,000 per song for copyright infringement.[13] In October 2007, Jammie Thomas-Rasset became the first individual to go to trial for illegally downloading music. The jury found Thomas-Rasset liable for copyright infringement, and she was ordered to pay $222,000 for illegally downloading 24 songs.[14] In November 2010, a retrial resulted in a different verdict for Thomas-Rasset. Instead of having to pay $222,000, she was now ordered to pay $1.5 million. Needless to say, Thomas-Rasset's attorney stated they were planning to appeal the verdict.[15]

On June 27, 2005, a victory occurred for the music industry against Grokster when the U.S. Supreme Court ruled that file-sharing websites could be sued for encouraging illegal copyright infringement by the users of their services. The court ruled that Grokster or any other file-sharing service is liable for the actions of its users who infringe on copyrighted material.[16] On September 5, 2005, the federal court in Australia ruled that Kazaa's file-sharing system breached copyright laws in that country, and Kazaa was given 2 months to alter its file-sharing software. Kazaa was controlled by Sharman Networks, located in Sydney, Australia. Kazaa had taken over from Napster as the most popular free file-sharing website. Kazaa made its money by selling advertising on the webpages as the users searched for music files.[17] In July 2006, Kazaa agreed to pay the music industry $115 million to settle global lawsuits pertaining to illegal downloading. Sharman Networks also promised to use all reasonable means possible to discourage online piracy by its users. Sharman Networks stated that it would begin negotiations with the record labels to obtain legal access to the copyrighted songs.[18]

On November 7, 2005, Grokster closed down its operations without warning. The only message left on its website stated that the Supreme Court unanimously decided that Grokster had illegally traded in copyrighted material and that there were other services that offered legal downloading of music and movies, but Grokster was not one of them. Shutting down the operations was part of the settlement Grokster had reached with the music industry. The settlement also stipulated that Grokster was not allowed to directly or indirectly infringe on the copyright of any of the companies that filed the lawsuit against Grokster.[19] The settlement also included Grokster paying the RIAA $50 million to compensate for its past illegal activities.

On May 16, 2006, the RIAA filed a lawsuit against XM Satellite Radio for its portable device called Inno that can save as many as 50 hours of music for one monthly fee. Similar to an iPod, the Inno allowed a listener to hit a record button on the device whenever a song that the user wanted to save was broadcast on XM Satellite Radio. The RIAA claimed that the listener did not pay the copyright to "own" the song, which can be permanently stored on the hard drive within the Inno. The RIAA filed for copyright infringement and for unauthorized digital delivery, reproduction infringement, and unfair competition. The RIAA asked for $150,000 for each song copied by customers of XM that had been downloaded onto one of the portable devices.[20] XM had responded to a product offered by its competitor, Sirius Satellite Radio, called the S50. It offered the same features, and Sirius settled with the music industry by agreeing to make a payment to each music company from the proceeds for each S50 that was sold. XM argued that it was already paying broadcasting rights for the songs and wanted to know why it should have to pay additional royalties for a device that is similar to using a tape recorder to record songs. The music industry responded by stating that XM was indirectly "selling" the songs by allowing the listeners to capture the songs permanently on the device.[21]

In December 2008, the music industry waved a partial white flag when it decided to stop suing thousands of people for downloading pirated songs. The legal proceedings that had started in 2003 and had grown to 35,000 people were not effective in deterring illegally downloaded music. The music industry stated it would focus on working with Internet service providers to stop the downloading. France and the United Kingdom used this philosophy to address music piracy. Both countries require the Internet service providers to warn users about illegal downloads and then potentially shut down their Internet service if the providers refused to stop downloading pirated songs. In France, a new agency was formed that polices the Internet and requires that offenders who have repeated offenses must appear in court, After two written warnings, the users in France can have their Internet disconnected for as long as a year and can be fined more than $400,000.[22]

In May 2011, the major record labels won a 5-year battle when they settled a lawsuit with LimeWire for $105 million for copyright infringement. LimeWire is a file-sharing network that allowed its users to upload and download music without permission.[23]

The Savior of the Music Industry: iTunes

In April 2003, what saved the music industry's attempt to control illegal file transfers took place when the Apple iTunes Music Store service was introduced. The predicted success of iTunes was seen after 2 days when 475,000 songs were *legally* downloaded through the iTunes service for 99¢ per song. The ironic point about Apple being the savior for the music industry was that Apple officials were not concerned with illegal music transfers per se but wanted more people to buy its computers. Apple officials believed that an easy legal way to transfer music from a computer to a portable device would give Apple a competitive advantage. Apple managers realized the power of iTunes and offered a Microsoft Windows version of the software in October 2003 and focused on selling iPods to be used with iTunes. Of course, iTunes and iPods exploded in demand. In its first year, iTunes sold 70 million songs, and by the end of 2004, 10 million iPods had been sold. By the end of 2005, 30 million iPods had been sold and 600 million songs had been downloaded.[24]

The Role of Royalties

In August 2001, the members of the musical group Dixie Chicks sued their record label, Sony Music Entertainment, for fraud. The Dixie Chicks alleged that Sony committed thievery by not paying the full royalties that were due the band.[25] This was just one example of the continuous battle artists have had with their record labels over proper royalty payments. Numerous artists over the years have complained that the record labels purposely withheld payment of royalties. Sam Moore, from the soul group Sam & Dave, realized when he was in his 50s that his retirement fund would pay him only $63.67 a month because his record label did not put any money into his retirement fund. The monthly payment should have been $8,000, but Moore's record label, Atlantic, did not make any contributions to his retirement fund from 1965 to 1992.[26]

Don Engel, a lawyer who specializes in music industry issues, estimated that the record labels would underpay artists anywhere from 10 to 40% of their royalties. *Rolling Stone* writer Dave March described it as a firmly entrenched part of the music business that makes the fraud at Enron look like the amateur hour in comparison.[27]

In addition, the burden of proof is on the artists to provide evidence that the record labels have not paid in full. The artists have to rely on the bookkeeping done by the record labels as the calculation for their royalties. If they believe that improper payment has occurred, the artists must hire an external auditor to review the royalty documents. The Dixie Chicks alleged that Sony failed to pay the band $4 million in royalties. The Dixie Chicks settled for an undisclosed amount with Sony in June 2002. Conditions of the settlement included giving the band a $20 million advance when it signed a new contract and an increase in the royalty rate to 20% of sales. The settlement was reached after the band failed to reach a new record deal with EMI or Bertelsmann Music Group.[28]

In January 2002, singer Peggy Lee led a lawsuit against Universal Music for unpaid royalties. Universal agreed to pay $4.75 million to 300 artists who had recorded songs for Universal before 1962. The artists had alleged that Universal had underpaid their royalties and overcharged them for production services such as album packaging. Other artists (or their estates) who were paid included Billie Holiday, Louis Armstrong, and Patsy Cline.[29]

In May 2004, New York Attorney General Eliot Spitzer negotiated an agreement with the record labels for artists to receive nearly $50 million in unpaid royalties. The settlement was the result of a 2-year investigation by the New York attorney's office into the operations of the major record labels. The response from the record labels was they were not really paying close enough attention to ensuring the artists received their royalty checks. Spitzer pointed out that for some of the artists who received money in the settlement, such as David Bowie, Dolly Parton, and Willie Nelson, the record labels just needed to go to one of their concerts and throw the check up on the stage. A listing of some of the artists and the amounts due are shown in Table 2. The largest amount paid was to the estate of Tommy Edwards, who had a hit called "It's All in the Game" in 1958. His estate received $230,000 from the settlement. Other large payments included $107,000 to the Fontane Sisters and $78,000 to jazz saxophonist Gerry Mulligan.[30] Spitzer used New York State's abandoned property law, which stated that after 5 years of holding someone else's property, the property must be turned over to the state.[31]

Another avenue in which the record labels can manipulate the royalty payments is in charging overhead to the artists when they make albums and go on tour. An example of how artists can owe money after producing a "successful" album is shown in Table 3 (shown by * in table—before other payments).

Eminem sued his record label Universal Music Group for not providing his fair share of royalties because of differences about whether an individual song sold online should be considered a license or a sale. Most artists including Eminem have significant differences in their contracts based on the definition. Eminem received 50% of the royalties if the song is considered a license but only 12% of the royalties if the song

TABLE 2 ● Artists Included in the $50 Million Settlement and Amounts Due

[Rounded to the Nearest Thousands of Dollars]

Three Dog Night	71	Elvis Presley	10
Doc Severinsen	42	Hall and Oates	9
Jefferson Airplane	20	Everly Brothers	4
John Mellencamp	19	John Belushi	3
Dolly Parton	18	Frank Sinatra	3
Tom Jones	16	Willie Nelson	2
Dave Matthews Band	14	Dizzy Gillespie	2
David Bowie	11		

Source: Adapted from Lola Ogunnaike and Leslie Eaton, "Record Labels Must Pay Shortchanged Performers," *New York Times,* May 5, 2004, www.nytimes.com.

TABLE 3 ● Estimated Royalty Payment for a New Band

Suggested price of the band's CD	$20.00
Subtract packaging cost (25% of retail price)	(5.00)
Base rate in which royalties are calculated	15.00
Royalty rate	9.35%
Royalty rate per CD sold ($15.00 × 9.35%)	1.40
If the band sells 500,000 CDs (gold record) 500,000 × 1.40	$700,000
Subtract 15% for free goods (giveaways, radio promotions)	(105,000)
Subtract recording cost of the album	(300,000)
Subtract shared* independent promotion (using outside agents to secure radio airplay)	(100,000)
Subtract shared* video costs	(75,000)
Subtract tour support	(50,000)
Net total before agent/manager payment	***$70,000***

Source: Adapted from Edna Gundersen, "Bye, Bye, A Piece of the Pie," *USA Today,* May 16, 2004, www.usatoday.com.

*Shared = Artist pays 50% and the label pays 50%.

is considered a sale. Eminem argued in the lawsuit that his record label's arrangement with digital retailers resembled the actions of a license because the record label gave the digital retailer a single master copy of the song, and the retailer then duplicated it thousands of times. Alternatively, a physical sale occurs when the manufacturers create a physical disc, which has incremental costs not associated with a digital transfer of information.[32]

What Package Are We Breaking?

In April 2006, the band Cheap Trick and the Allman Brothers Band sued Sony BMG Music Entertainment for not paying a high enough royalty rate on downloaded music. The disputed royalty rate is based on the interpretation of how a downloaded song is classified based on the artists' contract. Sony had calculated that royalty rate as 4.5¢ per song using the same formula that is used to calculate CD royalties. The core of the argument is based on the original contracts signed by artists before the advent of digital downloads. Royalties in older contacts were all based on the distribution of "physical phonorecords" and considered CD sales as new technology and, therefore, reduced the royalty rates for CDs so the record labels could recover the investment costs of the new technology. For a 99¢ download from iTunes, Apple keeps 30¢ and the other 69¢ goes to the record label. The artists are arguing that the band and the record label should split the remaining 69¢ so each party gets approximately 35¢ per song. Cheap Trick argued that all the production costs have been recouped and that the label had no manufacturing or distribution costs. Sony is currently paying Cheap Trick 4.5¢ per song. Sony pays Cheap Trick $1.20 in royalties for every album sold on CD. At a list price of $11.98, this royalty rate is 10%, but the download rate is less than 5%. Therefore, based on Cheap Trick's original contract, the band gets a reduced royalty because it is not a phonorecord. In addition, Sony reduced the royalty by 25% for "container deduction" and 15% for "breakage reduction." The suit is seeking $25 million in damages and is open to any Sony artist who signed a contract from 1962 to 2002.[33] Since 2002, the Allman Brothers Band has sold approximately 538,000 digital downloads of their songs, and Cheap Trick has sold 425,000 downloaded songs.[34]

Sony's Ghost in the Machine

At the National Association of Recording Merchandisers conference in August 2005, the CEO of the RIAA, Mitch Bainwol, stated to the audience that the number one threat for the industry is casual piracy. The music industry defined *casual piracy* as the copying of music to be shared among friends via one person buying the CD and the other friends burning the files onto a blank CD. Bainwol presented the results of a market research study that showed that in 2004, approximately 55% of consumers gained access to music through a legal channel. The breakdown showed that 51% of the respondents bought CDs and 4% downloaded from a paid online website. The remaining 45% of the respondents acquired their music from peer-to-peer networks (16%) and from casual piracy (29%). Bainwol concluded that using copy protection technology was a solution to reduce the 29% of illegal copying by sharing with friends.[35]

In response to casual piracy, Sony BMG decided to include copy-protection technology called XCP with the music on certain CDs, which would limit the number of

Cases

times the music could be copied from the CD to three. This was one attempt Sony used to enforce digital rights management, or DRM, to help facilitate the control of music in the digital age. When a user put the CD into a computer drive, the user needed to agree to the statement that "it will install a small proprietary software program (that will remain) until removed or deleted" and the software would be automatically installed into the user's computer. The critical limitation was that the users were not told that XCP is the equivalent to agreeing to have spyware integrated into the hard drive of the computer. Furthermore, the software used "rootkit" techniques, which meant that the software was very difficult to identify on the hard drive and extremely difficult to remove from the hard drive. To remove the software, the users had to fill out a request form from Sony's website, download additional software, wait for technical support to call the user, then download and subsequently upload additional software. XCP was discovered only when a computer developer and an expert in Microsoft Windows, Mark Russinovich, found that he had the XCP software buried deep in his hard drive when he ran a program to identify whether his computer had any file-cloaking software called *rootkits*. He finally traced the software back to a Sony XCP-protected CD by Van Zant. Russinovich wrote his findings on his blog, and within 2 days, the issue had become a major media event. He discovered that his CD drive became disabled when he manually tried to remove the XCP software.[36] A spokesman for Sony BMG, John McKay, stated that the technology had been available for 8 months and that Russinovich was the first person to complain about the attributes of the XCP system.[37]

Rootkit software is traditionally used by computer hackers so that once the software is embedded into the hard drive, the hacker can gain control of the computer. The rootkit system also allowed hackers to have easier access to the computer that had downloaded the Sony XCP software because it allowed gaps in the security system of the computer by circumventing most antivirus software. The XCP software allows the hacker to go in through the "back door" of the computer, which would not be protected from Trojan horse programs used by hackers to acquire personal user information, help launch attacks on other computer systems, and help send spam. The XCP software hides its files, which were coded sys. As a result, any hacker could transfer files with the same code name (e.g., $hidethisfile$) and the antivirus software on the computer would not be able to detect it. In an interview on National Public Radio, Sony BMG's head of global digital business, Thomas Hesse, commented that most users did not know what a rootkit was, so why should the customers be worried about it? The "patch," which was to be used to resolve the security problems, actually generated a larger security risk. As part of the patch software, a program called CodeSupport was included, which meant that any website could access the user's computer through the CodeSupport program.[38]

Russinovich posted his discovery on October 31, 2005, and on November 1, 2005, the first lawsuit was filed against Sony for fraud, false advertising, trespassing, and violating state and federal laws that ban malware and computer tampering.[39]

In addition, the Sony XCP software was not compatible with files for Apple's iPod. As a result, music tracks from a Sony XCP CD could not be transferred to an iPod. The initial negative reaction forced First4Internet, the British company that designed the software for Sony, to make a patch available on its website so the XCP files would no longer be hidden in the computer.[40] Some of the 20 artists whose CDs included the XCP technology were Celine Dion, Neil Diamond, Van Zant, Dion, Ricky Martin, Gerry Mulligan, and Dexter Gordon.

Less than 2 weeks after Russinovich posted his discovery on his blog, Sony agreed on November 11, 2005, to withdraw using the XCP software on its CDs while defending its right to prevent customers from illegally copying songs from its CDs. The previous day, computer experts had verified that hackers had been distributing software programs that would have exploited the vulnerable computers that had installed the XCP software. Russinovich responded to the Sony announcement by stating that Sony should have withdrawn the software immediately and admit it was wrong to include the software on the CDs without informing the customer. Russinovich also pointed out that Sony would not promise that it would not try a similar type of spyware in the future to control illegal downloading.[41] When Sony made the decision to withdraw the XCP-based CDs, approximately 2.1 million CDs had been sold and another 4.7 million had been shipped to various retailers. Sony's official response was that the consumer experience is the primary goal at Sony, and Sony is committed to bringing the music by its artists to as wide an audience as possible while continuing to protect the rights of the artists.[42]

On November 16, 2005, Sony announced that it would replace the estimated 2.1 million CDs that contained the XCP software and would pull from the shelves the estimated 2.6 million CDs that had not been sold. The recall and replacement of the CDs cost Sony an estimated $2 million to $4 million and Sony finally apologized by stating that it deeply regretted any inconvenience the XCP software may have caused the customers. The XCP software was on 52 CD titles rather than just the 20 that were earlier reported.[43] On November 21, 2005, a digital rights advocacy group, the Electronic Frontier Foundation, and the attorney general for the state of Texas filed lawsuits against Sony for violation of consumers' rights and for transferring malicious software to consumers.[44] The number of lawsuits continued to increase, and on December 29, 2005, Sony BMG settled at least 14 of the class-action lawsuits filed by consumers. The consumers were to receive a non-XCP CD and additional forms of compensation. The estimated cost of the settlement of the 14 lawsuits was as much as $50 million depending on the participation rate of the class-action consumers.[45] The remaining class-action lawsuits were settled on May 22, 2006, with the same terms of replacing the XCP CD with a regular CD and either accepting a cash payment of $7.50 and one free Sony album download or no cash payment and three free Sony album downloads.[46]

On December 19, 2006, Sony BMG reached a settlement with customers in California and Texas over the placement of antipiracy software on its CDs. Sony BMG agreed to pay $1.5 million and provide thousands of dollars in rebates for customers.[47] On December 27, 2006, Sony BMG reached a similar agreement for customers in Ohio and 39 other states and agreed to pay $4.25 million. Sony also agreed to provide refunds of as much as $175 to customers whose computers had been harmed by the installation of the software.[48]

How Much Is That Song on the Radio?

Defined as the payment of cash or other gifts in return for radio airplay of a song, *payola* has almost as long of a history as the music industry itself. The term *payola* comes from "pay" and "Victrola," which was the first brand of record player. Payola came to the forefront in the late 1950s when one of the most popular disc jockeys in the United States, Alan Freed, was charged with accepting payola. The U.S. Congress subsequently passed the federal anti-payola statute in 1960, which increased the penalties for the record labels that tried to influence what would be played on the air. In 1986, Senator Al Gore started a congressional investigation into the rampant use of payola in the music industry. He was quoted as saying that payola had returned to the music industry.[49] The record labels' employees were directly involved in the alleged payola in the 1950s, but by the 1980s, the music labels had hired someone else to do their dirty work. These new representatives were called independent promoters and potentially worked for multiple record labels by meeting with radio stations to aggressively promote new singles. Independent promoters became an established part of the music industry in the late 1970s, when the major record labels greatly reduced their internal promotion departments. The independent promoters defended their actions, stating that they were only providing up-to-date information on the music and the artists and would sometimes give the radio station prizes as part of their promotion giveaways. In the mid-1980s, the record labels paid independent promoters a combined $80 million to promote their music.[50] By 1989, a number of independent promoters had pleaded guilty to payola by supplying the disc jockeys and radio station managers cash but also cocaine.[51]

In 1998, payola allegations again rocked the music industry with a new twist. Instead of straight cash payments, the record labels paid radio stations to broadcast hour-long music "showcases" of the artists' music. EMI was alleged to consider paying radio station groups approximately $1 million for an hour of prime-time programming by one or more of their artists. By 1998, failure to disclose the identity of who paid to have songs played on air was punishable by a fine of as much as $10,000 and as long as 1 year in prison.[52]

By 2002, the record labels started to complain that it was too costly to get their songs promoted on the radio. Each song that was promoted cost the label between $200,000 and $300,000 with costs sometimes escalating up to $1 million. The compensation to the promoters from the music label was between $500 and $2,000 for each station that added one of the label's songs on the station's playlist. The largest radio network, Clear Channel Communications, required that record labels pay $40,000 to be sponsors at one of the radio network's lunch or evening cocktail parties. In return for the $40,000, the record label was allowed to present its music to Clear Channel, and the radio network would give feedback to the label on which music to focus on.[53]

In an apparent cycle that rises like a phoenix every decade, payola became a focus of New York Attorney General Spitzer in 2004. Spitzer investigated the age-old question of how the music labels promote their music to the radio stations. The investigation started in early September 2004 when Spitzer had requested documentation from all four of the major record labels: Warner Music, EMI, Universal Music Group, and Sony BMG.[54] In addition, major radio networks including Clear Channel Communications also received subpoenas to produce documentation for the investigation.

Within 11 months, Spitzer was able to get his first settlement from a music label, Sony BMG. Sony BMG agreed to pay a fine of $10 million for its actions and admitted its misconduct. In addition, Sony BMG agreed to no longer use independent promoters for its music. Furthermore, it agreed to stop the practice of "spin programs," which occurred when Sony paid stations to broadcast the same songs repeatedly in the hope of influencing the chart position of the songs.[55] Spitzer discovered that Sony was giving a number of illegal incentives, including outright bribes to radio programmers, contest giveaways to be given to station employees and not listeners, payments to radio stations to help cover the operational expenses of the station, hiring independent promoters who made illegal payments to radio programmers, and spin programs where money was paid for multiple plays of the music under the guise of advertising payments given to the radio station.[56] In 2002, a promotion by Epic Records in which the winner would get to go to Las Vegas to hear Celine Dion and meet her in person was given to Infinity Broadcasting in return for the radio network's agreeing to add Dion's latest single to the playlist of 13 radio stations.[57]

The $10 million fine paid by Sony BMG was given by the attorney general's office to the Rockefeller Philanthropy Advisors of New York State to help fund music education and music appreciation programs.[58] After the settlement was reached, Sony BMG fired Joel Klaiman, who was the executive vice president for promotion at Song BMG's Epic Records Label. One of the complaints against Klaiman was that he misled even Sony's accounting department in one episode where he gave a $3,300 plasma television to a radio executive in San Diego in return for more airplay. The television was listed as a contest giveaway when the receipt was submitted to the accounting department.[59]

On August 8, 2005, the Federal Communications Commission (FCC) announced that it would start an investigation into Sony BMG payola activities. The FCC planned to examine the payola scandal from the perspective of the radio station involved in accepting the gifts from Sony BMG. Clear Channel Communications stated that it had severed all ties with independent promoters, but the investigation by the attorney general's office found that Clear Channel instead just increased its relationship with the promoters from within Sony BMG. Clear Channel also stated that an internal investigation had been started to review the relationships the radio network giant had with the music labels.[60] On October 18, 2005, a small independent music label, TSR Records, sued Sony BMG for illegally blocking music from independent music labels by using payola to ensure its own songs were on radio playlists. The CEO of TSR, Tom Hayden, claimed that deserving TSR artists were not allowed the opportunity to be played because of Sony BMG's illicit activities.[61]

On November 22, 2005, Spitzer settled with the second major music label, Warner Music, for its activities related to payola. Warner Music agreed to pay a $5 million fine for offering trips, gifts, and cash to have Warner Music artists added to radio station playlists. At the same time, Spitzer had announced that the two largest radio networks in the United States, Clear Channel Communications and Infinity Broadcasting, had been served subpoenas for their alleged roles in the payola scandal.[62]

By February 2006, hundreds of radio stations were included in the review by the FCC for alleged payola activity. The commissioner of the FCC, Jonathan Adelstein, called it potentially the largest and most comprehensive violation of FCC rules in the history of broadcasting in the United States.[63]

Not waiting for the FCC to conclude its investigation, Spitzer filed a lawsuit against the fifth-largest radio network in the United States, Entercom Communications, for payola on March 7, 2006. Entercom owned and operated 105 radio stations including

7 stations in Buffalo, New York, and 4 in Rochester, New York. The New York attorney general accused Entercom of accepting secret payments from the music labels in return for promised airtime for its artists. As the lawsuit was announced, Spitzer pleaded with the FCC to move faster to resolve the corrupt relationship that had taken place between the music labels and the radio stations. The specific allegations against Entercom included accepting gifts, cash, promotional items, and personal trips in exchange for airtime. In addition, Entercom allegedly took cash in return for airtime for the music labels so they could manipulate the positioning of the songs on the music charts through the use of a "CD preview program." A CD preview program was a system where the music labels would buy "spins" on specific radio stations. The music labels would be allowed to batch up a number of spins over a week for between $1,000 and $3,500 with the program generating annual revenue of $2 million. The result was constant repetition of songs. One station played Avril Lavigne's "Don't Tell Me" 109 times within 1 week (an average of more than 15 times per day), with one third of those plays based on compensation received from her record label, Arista Records. When an e-mail sent by a disc jockey complained that the CD preview program would result in losing listeners, the response from Entercom was that the program was not optional and it generated millions of dollars in income for Entercom. An e-mail from an Entercom executive acquired by Spitzer stated that Entercom preferred to work with the music labels directly instead of going through independent promoters because the music label promoters were more generous with their cash payments.[64] Spitzer stated that what made the Entercom case unique was the use of payola at every level of management throughout the company.

Spitzer had wanted a settlement with Entercom for about $20 million, but Entercom did not agree with that figure or the changes that the New York attorney general put in the agreement that Entercom would have to implement in the future. Another e-mail cited by Spitzer showed a Buffalo radio station asking Columbia Records if it needed "help" on Jessica Simpson this week, with the number *1250* after the question. The e-mail continued, stating that if Columbia didn't need help, then the radio station didn't need to play it. Another request came from a Rochester radio station that needed a new laptop. The station told an executive from Universal Music that if it were able to help with the station's computer needs, then the station would add two Universal artists to its playlist. Spitzer alleged that the CEO of Entercom, David Field, had received e-mails outlining the incentive systems Entercom was receiving from the music labels. Another program Entercom had established, called Total Access, allowed the music labels to pitch the songs directly to Entercom programmers in exchange for a commitment to pay for 20 advertising spots per station for an average cost of $100 an ad. The programmers would "seriously consider" the songs pitched to them but would not be required to play them.[65] One document obtained by Spitzer showed that of the 120 songs that were added to the playlist of one of the Entercom radio stations, 118 songs were linked to receiving compensation for the songs to be played.[66]

On May 11, 2006, the New York attorney general's office reached a $12 million settlement with Universal Music for its role in the payola scandal. Spitzer's office was able to provide documented evidence of "pay for play" incentives at Universal Music that included cash, computers, travel, concert tickets, and other financial incentives in return for having its artists played on the air. The sizes of the settlements requested by Spitzer were in relation to the size of the music label.[67] On June 15, 2006, the fourth and final major music label settled with Spitzer's office when EMI agreed to pay $3.75 million for its role in the payola investigation. Though stopping short of admitting that its employees were involved in illegal activities, EMI admitted that its employees were involved in certain promotional activities that were inappropriate and wrong.[68]

On October 19, 2006, CBS Radio agreed to pay a $2 million fine to settle payola charges brought against it by the New York attorney's office. CBS is the third-largest radio corporation with approximately 180 radio stations. Spitzer had commented that CBS's action of selling its valuable airtime to the highest bidder violated state and federal laws and robbed CBS's customers of their right to know how the radio stations determined what songs were selected to be played on the air. In a memo obtained by Spitzer's office, CBS Radio's affiliate in Rochester showed a summary of the station's "returns" from the record labels. Airtime for songs such as "Shut Up" by Nick Lachey and "You Are My #1" by Smash Mouth were "sold" to the station in exchange for airplane trips that could be used in contests.[69]

The Continuing Challenges of Digital Music

In October 2014, Apple announced that its midyear music sales from its iTunes Store had fallen between 13% and 14% worldwide from six months earlier. These permanent downloads are losing favor with music fans. The fans are shifting toward free videos and inexpensive unlimited subscription streaming. Apple became involved in the subscription streaming distribution of music when it acquired Beats Music, which was part of the $3 billion acquisition of Beats Electronics.[70] In the mid-2014 RIAA report, CD sales had fallen from $73.7 million in mid-2013 to $56.3 million (–23.7%) in mid-2014. This resulted in a reduction of revenue from $884.1 million to $715.6 million (–19.1%). Permanent downloaded singles had decreased from 707.0 million units in mid-2013 to 643.6 million units (–9.0%) in mid-2014. The revenue for permanent downloads had decreased from $842.4 million in mid-2013 to $752.9 million in mid-2014. Total digital and physical units of all music, including albums and singles, had decreased from 878.7 million units in mid-2013 to 783.1 million units in mid-2014. The total revenue had decreased from $3.352 billion in mid-2013 to $3.189 billion in mid-2014.[71] In 1999, the total revenue of music sold in the United States was $14.6 billion and by 2009 had fallen to less than half at $6.3 billion.[72]

Taylor Swift Versus Spotify

On November 3, 2014, Taylor Swift announced that she was going to pull her entire song catalog from the online streaming service Spotify. Swift's action was taken after Spotify refused to only allow the streaming of her album *1989* to occur outside the United States. Swift is an established artist in the United States, but not so in other parts of the world. Spotify stated that its policy was to make the artist's music available in all 58 countries in which it has operations. Swift's label, Big Machine Label Group, had also requested that Ms. Swift's music only be available to paid subscribers in the United States, and this request was also refused by Spotify. Spotify pays between $0.006 and $0.0084 per stream to the record labels and publishers. The record labels and publishers then pay the artists a percentage of this amount.[73] Spotify has

50 million users globally, with 12.5 million paying a monthly fee; the rest of the users get the songs for free along with advertising.[74] The paid subscribers generate a higher royalty rate for the artists as compared with the free users' advertising model.[75] In her response to withdrawing from Spotify, Taylor Swift commented, "I'm not willing to contribute my life's work to an experiment that I don't feel fairly compensates the writers, producers, artists, and creators of this music."[76] Singer and songwriter Aloe Blacc, who was the vocalist for the 2013 Avicii's hit "Wake Me Up," stated that the song was played 168 million times on Internet radio service Pandora, which resulted in only $12,359 in publishing royalties, of which he was given less than $4,000.[77] On January 23, 2015, Billboard announced that Taylor Swift's *1989* had sold 4 million copies in the United States. The last album to sell at least 4 million copies was Swift's previous album, *Red*.[78]

Questions for Thought

1. Comment on how widespread illegal transferring of music is on college campuses.

2. Should payola be allowed? What is the real ethical problem with it?

3. Why do you think Eliot Spitzer became involved in the music industry's problems?

4. Is it fair that artists must shoulder the burden of proof with respect to their royalty payments? Defend your position.

18

Apple Outsourcing in China: iSweatshop?

I n the past, Apple marketed that its products were made in the United States. In today's global marketplace, that is no longer the case. Almost all the products sold by Apple are produced outside of the United States. When President Barack Obama met Apple CEO Steve Jobs at a dinner in February 2011, Obama asked Jobs what it would take for those jobs now outsourced to return to the United States. Mr. Jobs's response was "Those jobs aren't coming back." Apple employs 43,000 people in the United States and another 20,000 in other countries, and in 2011 yielded a profit that is equivalent to $400,000 per employee. An additional 700,000 people are outsourced to manufacturer Apple products around the world.[1]

An example of the dexterity of the outsourced workforce occurred when Apple had to redesign, at the last minute, its iPhone screen to be made of glass instead of plastic, which forced a significant readjustment in the assembly line. The new screens at the assembly plant started to arrive at midnight, and the supervisor woke up 8,000 workers, gave them a biscuit and a cup of tea, and then started a 12-hour shift with the redesigned screen. In response to the question why Apple does not employ more American workers, an executive stated that Apple sells iPhones to more than 100 countries and it is not Apple's responsibility to solve the U.S. economic problems. Apple's only obligation is to produce the best products available.[2] Furthermore, there seems to be no pressures from stakeholders for Apple to change its approach.

When the *New York Times* did a survey in November 2011 asking the public their perceptions of Apple, a staggering 56% said they could not think of a single negative issue about Apple. Fourteen percent of the respondents stated that the worse thing they can say about Apple is that their products are too expensive to buy. A minuscule 2% of the respondents addressed the issue of labor practices related to Apple's outsourcing overseas.[3]

Apple uses a number of foreign manufacturers to outsource the production of their products. One of the dominant manufacturers is Hon Hai Precision Industry Co., which commonly goes by the name of Foxconn. Foxconn is one of the largest manufacturers of electronic components in the world. Foxconn has two massive production facilities in Shenzhen, China, which are used to manufacture and assemble many of Apple's products, including the iPod and iPhone. Hanging on the wall of the plants, a banner states Foxconn's management philosophy: "Work hard on the job today or work hard to find a job tomorrow."[4]

The Working Conditions in the Chinese Plants in 2006

In August 2006, the *Daily Mail* published a story that described the horrendous working conditions at Chinese factories that manufacture iPods. In 2005, 22.5 million iPods were sold, which represents a daily production rate of 61,644. One Foxconn factory in Longhua, China, has a facility for 200,000 workers, both in work areas and in dorm rooms for sleeping. The dorm size is large because 20 people share a three-bedroom apartment. The accommodation is free but no one outside the plant is allowed to visit the workers in the dormitories. The typical workers receive less than $50 a month for their 15-hour days. The workers are required to stand still for hours and will be punished if they move. They are required to work overtime when ordered, and they are only allowed to go back to their dormitories when their boss gives them permission to do so. Labor costs for an iPod are less than $10 per unit, and the total manufacturing cost of an iPod Nano in 2006 was approximately $75, less than half of the retail price.[5]

Apple claimed the investigation was an anomaly of plants but did admit that the factories did violate Apple's conditions for suppliers, which included having the employees work no more than 60 hours a week 35% of the time or work more than 6 continuous days without a day off 25% of the time. In addition, Apple found that employees were housed in former factories or in open areas with little privacy or were sleeping on bunk beds that were three levels high.[6]

The Suicides Start

The working conditions in the Chinese plants became an issue again in July 2009. A Foxconn employee committed suicide by jumping off a 12-story building. It was alleged that the employee had been stopped and questioned by a security guard before his death for suspicion of stealing a prototype of the next-generation iPhone. It was also alleged that the employee was beaten during the questioning.[7] The allegations continued in March 2010 when Apple's audit of its suppliers found 17 core violations of its policies including three cases in which a supplier hired underage workers as young as 15 years old. Apple describes core violations as actions such as employee abuse, employment of underage workers, involuntary labor, audit material that has been falsified, workers' safety has been threatened, supervisor intimidation, supervisor retaliation, and significant environmental violations. The annual audit started in 2006 after the *Daily Mail* article highlighted the working conditions in the plant in 2006.[8]

Suicides of Foxconn employees continue to haunt Apple. From January to May 2010, six Foxconn employees committed suicide. An additional two employees were injured in their attempts to commit suicide. The company established a "Foxconn Employee Care Center" to help employees contemplating suicide. It addition, for the size of Foxconn, the number of suicides is not exceptional because the suicide rate in China in 1999 was approximately 14 per 100,000. However, exhausted employees who must work in oppressive and dangerous work environments may see suicide as a viable option.[9] A spokesperson for Foxconn stated that most of the suicide victims were either severely depressed or had significant personal problems and rejected the hypothesis that the deaths were related to the working conditions in the plant. Foxconn stated that it had recently built modern dormitories, had improved the food at the dorms, and had included recreational facilities such as swimming pools to improve the standard of living of the employees. Critics say that recreational facilities are of no value if the employees do not have time to use them. For example, one worker stated that they are extremely tired and under continuous pressure and are required to complete each step in 7 seconds, which is faster than the machines.[10] Less than a week later, another Foxconn employee committed suicide by jumping to his death. The response from Foxconn was that it was not a sweatshop and that the company was doing everything possible to prevent future suicides. In addition, Foxconn was starting to build safety nets at the dormitories to stop workers from killing themselves by jumping from the building.[11] One Foxconn executive observed that there is a fine line between productivity and inhumane and strictly regimented treatment of the employees, and they "hope" that a company with $60 billion in sales treats its 800,000 employees with dignity and respect.[12] In reaction to the negative image the suicides had brought to Foxconn, it announced on June 1, 2010, that worker pay would be raised 33% from $132 per month to $176. This translated to a total rate of $1.11. The decision was officially based on the rationale that the company had not increased wages in a while. Foxconn stated the benefit of the pay wage was that it would give the workers more leisure time and it would attract more qualified workers to join Foxconn. Steve Jobs responded by stating that the Foxconn plant is not a sweatshop; that "for a factory, it's a pretty nice factory";[13] and that Apple is doing everything possible to understand what is happening to the Chinese workers.[14]

A Worker at Foxconn

An interview of the sister of one of the employees who committed suicide, Ma Xiangqian, paints a bleak and depressing portrait of life as a Chinese factory worker. She said her brother hated his job. He had to work an 11-hour overnight shift 7 days a week. He hated the dust and fumes forging plastic and metal into different electronic parts. He hated that after he had a conflict with his supervisor, he was demoted to cleaning toilets. For an equivalent of approximately $1 an hour, her brother had worked 286 hours in a month, which included 112 hours of overtime. That level of overtime is more than three times the legal limit of 36 hours in China. But his story is not unique because tens of thousands of employees quit Foxconn shortly after they are hired. The workers complained about the military culture at the plant and being constantly abused verbally by the superiors. In addition, they were forced to read their "self-criticisms" aloud and can be asked to work 13 days in a row during which they slept on the factory floor.[15]

A week after the June 1, 2010, announcement of the 33% wage increase, Foxconn announced a major increase in wages. Foxconn stated that within 3 months, it would raise the wages of many of its 800,000 workers in China to almost $300 a month, which is almost double what the wage rate was going to be after the 33% increase announcement in the previous week.[16]

In June 2010, Foxconn announced it was going to let a professional property management company control the dormitories in Shenzhen, China. The agreement with the property management company was to ensure Foxconn met the current and future needs of its employees.[17] In February 2012, Foxconn announced that it would implement another pay increase for its employees. For many workers, the monthly wage will increase as much as 25% to produce a monthly wage rate of $400. Foxconn stated it would also reduce overtime hours at its facilities.[18]

The Dangers of Explosive Dust

In May 2011, an explosion in a Foxconn plant that made iPads in southwestern China killed 3 employees and injured 15. The cause of the explosion was an accumulation of combustible dust from the polishing workshop. Production was halted until a full investigation could take place.[19] Foxconn also announced that it had closed all workshops that were involved in polishing electronic parts until the investigation was completed. Students & Scholars Against Corporate Misbehavior (Sacom) had warned Foxconn in March and April 2011 that the excessive aluminum dust floating in the air was dangerous and could lead to an explosion. Although unfamiliar to the public, combustible dust is well known as a dangerous threat in manufacturing plants that pulverize plastics or aluminum. Some other industries that are susceptible to dust explosions include grain storage facilities and candy manufacturing plants. Combustible elements become even more dangerous when they are in minute particles because the burning area of combustion is spread out across the facility where the dust is released.[20] The plants were reopened in June 2011 with increased ventilation and changes in the dust disposal policies.[21]

The Apple Supplier Responsibility Report

Apple's first code of conduct was established in 2005. The code stated that suppliers must treat workers with respect and dignity and that all manufacturing facilities must act in an environmentally responsible manner.[22]

On January 13, 2012, Apple released its first supplier responsibility report, which listed Apple's suppliers by name. Under Jobs's regime, Apple refused to release any information pertaining to its suppliers. This philosophy changed when Tim Cook took over as CEO of Apple. Apple finally joined the ranks of global companies such as Hewlett-Packard, Intel, and Nike by identifying to stakeholders with whom Apple does business related to the manufacturer of its products. In addition, the audit revealed that 108 facilities did not pay workers the proper amount of overtime as was required by law in China. In the previous 2 years, 137 employees had been seriously injured after being in contact with a toxic chemical, n-hexane, which is used to clean iPad screens. Complications for contact with the chemical can include nerve damage and paralysis.[23] Listed in the supplier responsibility report is Apple's supplier code of conduct. For its employees, the code of conduct protects the workers' rights by not allowing discrimination, providing fair treatment of the workers, preventing involuntary labor, preventing underage labor, protecting juvenile workers, limiting working hours, paying proper wages and benefits, and allowing freedom of association.[24] In its 2014 supplier responsibility report, Apple reported that it had established an Environment,

Health, and Safety (EHS) Academy that created an 18-month curriculum in order to increase the level of EHS expertise in its suppliers. In 2013, more than 240 individuals representing Apple suppliers enrolled in the EHS program. Apple also announced the establishment of a Clean Water Program that was implemented at 13 supplier sites that use more than 41 million cubic meters of water annually.[25]

Workers' Rights For the 2011 audit, the overall compliance rate for workers' rights was 74% and 81% in 2013.[26] The breakdown of practices in compliance for the over-all audit was as follows (2011/2013): antidiscrimination (78%/87%), fair treatment (93%/96%), prevention of involuntary labor (78%/87%), prevention of underage labor (97%/97%), juvenile worker protections (87%/73%), working hours (38%/95%), wages and benefits (69%/75%), and freedom of association (95%/99%). In 2011, discrimination found at the facilities included screening job candidates for hepatitis or other medical conditions, and 24 of the factories conducted pregnancy tests on employees. More than 50% of the workers exceeded their weekly working-hour limit, and in 90 facilities, more than half of the workers had worked more than six consecutive days at least once a month. Wage and benefits issues included delaying workers' pay, providing no pay slips, not providing adequate benefits, not providing employees with paid leaves or vacations, using wage deduction as punishment, and not paying proper over-time wages.[27] In 2013, Apple reported that it trained 1.5 million workers about their rights in 2013.[28] The suppliers had an overall 95% compliance rate related to Apple's policy of a maximum 60-hour workweek.[29] In 2013, Apple conducted 451 audits of the suppliers with underage workers and found that 23 underage workers were employed by the suppliers out of a total supplier employment of 1.5 million people.[30]

Workers and Safety For worker health and safety, the overall compliance rate was 76% in the 2011 audit and 77% in the 2013 audit. The breakdown of the percentages of practices (2011/2013) in compliance was occupational injury prevention (65%/72%); prevention of chemical exposure (86%/82%); emergency prevention, preparedness, and response (75%/77%); occupational safety procedures and systems (77%/80%); ergonomics (66%/70%); dormitory and dining (78%/80%); and health and safety communication (84%/73%).[31] In its 2013 audit, Apple found that 14 facilities had excessive recruiting fees, which Apple considered to be bonded labor. Apple required the suppliers to pay back any excessive fees, resulting in a total reimbursement of $3.9 million. In addition, the 2013 audit uncovered that 106 facilities did not pay the workers for legal holidays and 71 facilities underpaid overtime due to incorrect calculations.[32]

Environmental Impact For environmental impact, Apple's code of conduct for the suppliers (2011/2013) includes hazardous substance management (68%/72% compliance), wastewater management (89%/78% compliance), air emissions management (68%/71% compliance), solid waste management (90%/70% compliance), environmental permits and reporting (75%/72% compliance), and pollution prevention and resource reduction (94%/91% compliance), for an overall compliance rate of 79%/77%. Environmental violations included mishandling chemicals, failing to label hazardous waste products and storage locations, improper disposal of hazardous waste, failure to monitor and control air emissions, and failure to provide environmental impact reports.[33] In its 2013 audit,

Apple found that 159 facilities did not have proper storage areas for hazardous waste and 96 facilities disposed of hazardous waste using unqualified vendors.[34]

Ethics From an ethics perspective, Apple's code of conduct includes business integrity (97% compliance), disclosures of information (95% compliance), whistle-blower protection (93% compliance), and protection of intellectual property (97% compliance) for an overall compliance rate of 95%. Ethical violations included falsifying audit materials, providing misleading answers to the audit team, and blocking the audit team from obtaining payroll records.[35]

Questions for Thought

1. Do the outsourcing issues facing Apple really concern consumers? Explain.

2. Comment on the results disclosed in Apple's supplier responsibility report. Should these be disconcerting to investors?

3. Since Steve Jobs's death, it appears that Apple has become much more transparent in what officials publish about the company. Why do you think this has happened?

4. Should Apple have any responsibility for the events at Foxconn? Explain your position.

19

Patagonia: Don't Buy Our Stuff

Build the best product, cause no unnecessary harm, use business to inspire and implement solutions to the environmental crisis.[1]

—Patagonia's Mission Statement

Patagonia's Mission Comes From Its Founder's Values

Based in Ventura, California, Patagonia was founded by Yvon Chouinard. As a 14-year-old boy, he started rock climbing in 1953 as a member of the Southern California Falconry Club. While searching for falcons, Yvon fell in love with the means to get to the falcons, climbing up and down mountains.[2]

Because Chouinard is a famed mountain climber and outdoorsman, his commitment to the environment and his company are completely intertwined. Inspired by his love of the outdoors and climbing, he started designing his own hardened steel pitons, which support the person during the climb up the mountain. His designs had significantly better holding power than the traditional soft iron pitons, and, just as importantly, they did not damage the rocks because soft pitons could not be removed from the rock while hard pitons can be removed and used again. He started selling the pitons from the back of his car and expanded to trying to improve every piece of climbing equipment to benefit both the user and the environment. Chouinard continued to work on new designs until he found an alternative to pitons. He designed aluminum chocks that could be wedged by hand instead of pitons, which have to be hammered in and out of cracks in the rock. This "clean" approach to rock climbing demonstrated that companies like Patagonia can develop products that fulfill the needs of the customers without harming the environment.[3]

From his focus on improving equipment, he ventured into clothing and started introducing bright and unique colors that starkly contrasted with the traditional black and gray sports clothing. The origin of the colorful shirts was based on a climbing necessity of comfort and practicality. Yvon was on a climbing trip in Scotland in 1970 when he bought a rugby shirt to be worn during a climb. The shirt was durable enough to withstand the strains of rock climbing and was blue with red and yellow stripes. He wore the shirt when he returned to California and his friends wanted to know where they could buy one. Yvon started importing rugby shirts from England, New Zealand, and Argentina. The shirts sold out so quickly that he realized that clothing could generate the type of sales and profits that were not feasible from his mountain climbing equipment gear. With his newfound commitment to clothing, Yvon decided he needed to change the name of the company from Chouinard Equipment. At the time that Yvon founded his company in 1973, Patagonia, a geographical region that covers the lower sections of Argentina and Chile, was perceived as an isolated paradise. This perception of "Shangri-La" and the practicality of being pronounced the same way in any language led to Patagonia becoming the name of his clothing company.[4]

The Culture at Patagonia: Let My People Surf

It is not unusual to find surfboards stacked up in the mailroom at Patagonia, unless, of course, it is high tide and the boards are to be used on the ocean a few blocks away. There is a volleyball court in the back of the corporate headquarters, and there are showers in the restrooms. The corporate "uniform" is shorts and sandals, and the cafeteria is not allowed to serve beef. Their company's mission statement is to "do no harm" in its business transactions. Decisions that affect the employees are usually made by consensus. For example, when Patagonia needed to lay off employees in 1991 (due to a recession in the United States that started in 1990), managers allowed the employees to review the financial books of Patagonia to demonstrate why the layoffs were needed. The employees responded to the information by recommending and implementing the cost cutting needed for the long-term sustainability of Patagonia. To encourage a family-friendly atmosphere, Patagonia set up a child care center so that children are always close to their parents. At lunchtime, many parents will eat with their children. In addition, both new mothers and fathers get paid leaves.[5]

After the 1991 layoffs, Patagonia realized that to keep its strong positive culture, it must allow the employees to enjoy all the different parts of their life. As a result, Patagonia allowed and encouraged employees to go surfing during lunch or high tide whenever they could. This flexible work schedule practice prompted the creation of the Patagonia phrase "Let My People Surf." Management's underlying assumption was that the employees would still complete their work responsibilities within their deadlines.[6] This and Patagonia's many other employee-friendly policies, such as a company café that serves organic food and drink, and an infant and toddler care room, keep turnover remarkably low, especially for the retail industry.[7]

Patagonia's Corporate and Social Responsibility

Patagonia is committed to ensuring that its workers, regardless of their location in the world, work in conditions that are safe, fair, legal, and humane. Patagonia conducts a due diligence evaluation of any facility that manufactures Patagonia products. For new factories, the due diligence evaluation includes the following practices: the director of the social/environmental responsibility (SER) department must be involved in the decision to include a new factory, the SER representative must work with the sourcing and quality departments on the decision whether to include the new factory, the director of SER has complete veto power to override the choice of the new factory, and the SER staff are also responsible for ensuring all new factories comply with Patagonia's social and environmental standards included in Patagonia's code of conduct and code of conduct benchmarks as well as with all laws and union contracts (if it is a union shop). If the standards vary, Patagonia will apply the standards that are most beneficial to the employees.

Patagonia will also review the factory's SER management systems and will train the facility's employees to ensure they comply with Patagonia's code of conduct. In addition, a prescreening takes place at the facility by either the SER staff or a third-party monitoring firm that does a full social audit on the facility. The social audit includes a payroll analysis and interviews with workers in their local language. Patagonia will not tolerate any facility that supports child or forced labor, worker abuse, worker harassment, or worker discrimination and will immediately reject the facility if they find any of these conditions. For those facilities that have minor violations, the factory owner must agree to correct all the violations before the facility can start manufacturing Patagonia products.

Patagonia uses four criteria in selecting a new facility to produce its clothing: quality, business factors (technologies used in the plant, skills of workers, location of the plant, price per unit of clothing), customer service, and dependability based on the ability to deliver the final goods in time. In 2012, Patagonia made products in factories in Jordan, Nicaragua, Sri Lanka, India and Bangladesh, China, Thailand, Vietnam, Turkey, Mexico, Costa Rica, Colombia, El Salvador, Israel, the Philippines and the United States. The company tries to manufacture as many products as possible in the United States. In 2012, Patagonia had eight domestic factories in this country, but a lack of skilled garment laborers and higher labor costs prevent Patagonia from producing more clothing here.[8]

Patagonia's SER staff visits all of its factory sites regularly to check current conditions and ensure that previously cited violations have been corrected. The SER staff will also consult and perform training for the employees if they have specific concerns that need to be addressed at the facility. Furthermore, Patagonia tracks the wage rates for the countries to which it outsources its manufacturing. Management will negotiate with the owners of the factories to work toward a higher fair or living wage rate for the workers who produce the Patagonia clothing. Many of Patagonia's plants pay workers more than the minimum wage rate for the country. In 2010, Patagonia audited 90% of its supply chain for both social and environmental issues.[9]

The Natural Environment and Patagonia

With the founder's sustainability beliefs firmly entrenched, Patagonia has always been an environmental pioneer. In 1985, Patagonia became committed to donating 10% of pretax profits annually to grassroots environmental groups and later amended it to donating either 10% of pretax profits or 1% of sales, whichever amount is greater. To differentiate itself in the marketplace, Patagonia focuses on environmentally friendly materials. In 1996, Patagonia announced that its entire sportswear line would be produced using organic cotton. Patagonia also uses naturally grown hemp and recycled polyester in its clothing. Patagonia gets the material for its recycled polyester from used soda bottles and other sources.[10]

Patagonia tracks the carbon footprint of its products throughout its supply chain. For each product being tracked, the company measures energy consumption, carbon dioxide emissions, waste generation, and water use. Patagonia defines the start of the supply chain as occurring at the origin of the primary material (cotton, wool, leather, polymer) and follows the process through the production of the garment from a fiber to a finished product. The supply chain is completed when the garment reaches Patagonia's distribution center in Reno, Nevada. The energy consumption that is measured through the supply chain includes the energy consumed during transportation and the energy consumption at each step in the manufacturing process. The measurement of carbon dioxide and other greenhouse gas emissions is based on the transportation and supply chain energy use of the products sold by Patagonia. The amount of waste generated is based on solid waste that has been developed at each step in the production process. This waste metric does not include waste that has been classified as liquid, hazardous, or packaging. The water use is based on the calculation of the total amount of water that has been consumed at each step in the production process. The water use does not include water that has been recycled or water that has been discharged during the manufacturing process.[11]

In July 2011 in the United States, Europe, and Japan, Patagonia started taking back every single product made by the company for potential recycling. Clothing that is made from polyester and nylon is melted down and converted into a new fiber. Organic cotton and wool clothing are chopped up and recycled into new materials. Used fishing waders are recycled by a company called Recycled Waders into fishing bags, and used wet suits can be converted to beer koozies. Patagonia will also take products such as used shoes, backpacks, and luggage. Returned shoes that cannot be recycled are donated to the Soles4Souls program. Patagonia does not yet have a plan for recycling the backpacks and luggage.[12]

In April 2012, Patagonia launched the Patagonia Provisions Salmon Project, which promotes the sustainability of wild Pacific salmon, whose numbers have been dwindling. Chouinard wrote in an essay posted on the Patagonia website, "Our goal is to create a new model that demonstrates how selectively harvesting salmon is not only possible, but good business, and can help protect the future of wild salmon."[13]

In October 2014, Patagonia announced the opening of the Patagonia Park. Patagonia, along with its partner Conservation Patagonia, created a new national park in Patagonia, Chile. The park has almost 100 miles of hiking trails, three campgrounds, a lodge with a restaurant, and a visitor's center.[14]

The Integration of Cause and Capitalism: "Don't Buy This Jacket"

The integration of Patagonia's social beliefs and its for-profit business came to fruition in an ad that was published in the *New York Times* on November 25, 2011. The title of the ad was "Don't Buy This Jacket." The ad copy reads that retailers shift their focus from red to black on Black Friday, but in a culture of consumption, the economies of the natural ecosystems are clearly in the red. The ad continues by stating that humans are using one-and-a-half planets' worth of resources on our only planet. Patagonia wants to be sustainable as a business and allow the world's children to have the same benefits of the natural environment that today's adults currently have. So Patagonia asked the readers of the ad to reflect on everything they buy and buy less and don't buy the jacket that is pictured in the ad unless the reader really needs it. Patagonia reminds the reader that environmental bankruptcy is similar to financial bankruptcy in that the warning signs slowly appear until it is too late, and then there is a sudden and fatal decline. The earth is running out of natural resources at a rapid rate, and these ecosystems support both businesses and lives. Patagonia continues by listing the environmental impact of the jacket, which included the use of 135 liters of water and 20 pounds of carbon dioxide that is 24 times heavier than the jacket itself.[15]

This ad was part of Patagonia's Common Threads Initiative. The initiative is based on five Rs: reduce, repair, reuse, recycle, and reimage. Consumers need to *reduce* by only buying what they need and buying products that last a long time. Patagonia will help *repair* its products if the consumers are committed to helping the environment. Patagonia will find a new home for any of its products through *reuse* if the consumers sell or pass the Patagonia products on to others. Patagonia will *recycle* its products if the consumers pledge to reduce the amount of their waste that goes into a landfill. Both Patagonia and consumers will work together to *reimagine* a world in which whatever is taken from the natural environment can be replaced.[16] In May 2014, Patagonia started selling Fair Trade Certified apparel. The initial apparel line is supporting 10 women's sportswear styles that are sewn in three factories in India.[17] In addition, Patagonia introduced the first 100% traceable down products, in which all the down feathers can be traced back to birds that have never been force fed nor have had their feathers plucked while the birds were alive.[18]

Questions for Thought

1. Comment on the Common Threads Initiative. Will it be successful, in your opinion?

2. Can organizations effectively manage environmental issues while making a profit? Explain your position.

3. Patagonia appears to be concerned with being an environmentally friendly company. Do you think this effort will be sustainable in the long run? Explain.

4. Do consumers really care about preserving the environment? Cite examples to support your position.

20

Tokyo Electric Power and the Fukushima Daiichi Nuclear Power Disaster: A Tsunami of Problems

March 11, 2011

On March 11, 2011, at 2:46 p.m., a 9.0 magnitude earthquake shook Japan and created a tsunami of epic proportions. The earthquake was so powerful that it moved the Japanese coastline and made Japan "wider." The impact was shown by global positioning stations that were close to the epicenter that had moved eastward toward the United States by as much as 13 feet after the earthquake hit off the coast of Japan. National Aeronautics and Space Administration (NASA) scientists calculated that the earthquake was so strong that it redistributed the mass of the earth so that the day had been shortened by a couple of millionths of a second and the tilt of the Earth's axis had changed slightly. Japan is on the Pacific plate, which moves about 3½ inches each year in a west-northwest direction. The earthquake on the east side of Japan released the tension being built up, and Japan shifted in an eastward position. With the release of energy, the land "unbuckled" and 250 miles of Japanese coastline dropped 2 feet in altitude. These 2 feet made the tsunami even more devastating because it allowed the waves to move even farther inland from the coast.[1]

While the first responders were trying to address cataclysmic disasters, a third disaster started forming on the northeastern shoreline of Japan at the Fukushima Daiichi Nuclear Power plant owned by the Tokyo Electric Power Company (TEPCO). The Japanese government issued a broad evacuation, but the warning was not dire because government officials stated that only a small amount of radioactive material was likely to leak from the power plant. The reactors were shut down during the quake, but officials noticed there were critical failures in the cooling systems of the reactors. A 6-mile radius was evaluated from the Daiichi plant, which included 45,000 people, because when the cooling systems fail in a nuclear reactor, pressure builds up within the reactor, and "small" amounts of radioactive vapor are released into the atmosphere. The officials stated that the evacuation was a precaution, and the radiation level should not be high enough outside the plant to affect the health of people in the surrounding areas.

The First Hours of the Disaster

Cooling System With Reactor 1 A number of unprecedented challenges faced TEPCO employees as they tried to ensure there would not be a total meltdown of the active reactors at Daiichi. The first challenge they faced was that the emergency cooling system for Reactor 1 was not working consistently, if at all. It appeared that someone had manually shut down the valves of the condenser after the earthquake, but before the tsunami, to try to control the pressure inside the reactor. The valves had to be reopened with battery power, which was not available after the tsunami hit. Because the valves were shut, the temperature inside Reactor 1 quickly climbed, causing significant damage, which made recovery for the reactor not a viable option. The fuel pellets started melting 5 hours after the earthquake, and by the morning of the next day, the fuel was a lavalike substance at the bottom of the reactor. This series of events would not have taken place, at least not as quickly, if TEPCO could have opened the valves to release the built-up pressure.

Emergency Command Center The emergency response by the Japanese government was designed to be coordinated at an off-site command center near the Daiichi plant. When Kazuma Yokota, the person in charge of coordinating the emergency response, went to the center, he realized that there were some communication problems. The phone lines were down, the cell phone towers were down, the satellite phone was not working, and there was no backup power because of a broken fuel line for the backup generator. TEPCO's main emergency communication systems were still online, so TEPCO personnel could communicate with third parties from the Fukushima Daiichi earthquake shelter and provide a video link and phone communications with Tokyo. However, because the off-site center was not available, government officials in Tokyo had to rely on information from TEPCO headquarters, which created confusion and inefficient transfer of information from TEPCO to the government officials in Tokyo. Communication became a critical problem when TEPCO had to vent radioactive gas to reduce the pressure inside the reactor vessel. The final approval of this release must come from the president of TEPCO, Masataka Shimizu. Shimizu was stuck in the city of Nagoya and was trying to get back to company headquarters in Tokyo. His initial attempts failed. He eventually asked for a military transport to fly him back to Tokyo but was denied permission by the Japanese minister of defense. The plane was to first to give relief supplies to tsunami victims and would come back to take the TEPCO president who eventually got back to Tokyo.

Filter Problems TEPCO officials never thought that a disaster of this magnitude would hit the Daiichi plant, so they did not bother to install a filter on its emergency vent pipe to catch radioactive particles that would be released through the steam. In fact, the vent installation was not mandated by the nuclear regulators because they could not envision a scenario in which the pressure would climb to such a level that an emergency vent system would be needed. Therefore, the complete vent pipe system was voluntary. As a result, the venting of the steam was delayed until a 6-mile evacuation zone was completed instead of the original 2-mile zone.[2]

Power Problems TEPCO officials were completely unprepared to address the issue of auxiliary power during the first hours of the disaster. As the daylight faded during the first day, TEPCO employees were forced to go door to door of local neighborhoods trying to find flashlights. TEPCO employees also disconnected car batteries from automobiles nearby that were not washed away by the tsunami. The batteries were used to try to get the reactor gauges operational again. The lack of power also resulted in the shutdown of the automatic relief vents that would have reduced pressure quickly inside the reactor during the first critical hours. In addition, TEPCO employees did not have any way to check the strength of the plant's emergency batteries. The result was that because there was partial power inside the plant, TEPCO employees miscalculated the amount of time they had to make their repairs. The batteries were barely functional and shut down before the workers had a chance to make critical repairs to stop the fuel from melting, which occurred many hours before it was forecast to occur.[3]

Lack of Emergency Plans It was evident early on in the crisis that TEPCO and its employees were unprepared for these events during this time. At the Daiichi plant, there was only one stretcher, one satellite phone, and 50 protective suits that employees could use to shield themselves against radiation. The emergency plan was designed to address only small emergencies and outlined how to address issues related to backing up key operational systems. The emergency plan did not have the vision or scope to address a crisis of the magnitude that hit the Daiichi plant. There were contingencies in the plan to deal with the issue of communications being knocked out by the disaster, but the primary communication media used to link the plant with the outside world in the emergency plan was a fax machine. There were no contingencies to request help from outside sources if TEPCO employees could not manage the disaster themselves. For example, Tokyo firefighters, Japanese military forces, or the use of U.S. equipment was not included in the emergency plan. TEPCO's response was that the emergency plan met, and in parts exceeded, the legal requirements set by the Japanese government. Some critics in Japan argue that the Japanese government and Japanese companies would rather not focus on or discuss emergency disaster plans because the Japanese people would become scared.[4]

A Partial Versus a Full Meltdown

The degree of damage between a partial and full meltdown is enormous. A partial meltdown means that the uranium fuel in the reactor rods has melted. The fuels rods are damaged because they have been left exposed to the air without surrounding water. The exposed portion of the rods will likely crack, releasing small amounts of radioactive material. During a full meltdown, the rods are completely exposed to the air without any cooling water. The fuel pellets of uranium oxide in the rods fall to the bottom of the reactor and become part of a molten, lavalike pool of radioactive materials that can reach temperatures of several thousand degrees Fahrenheit. The worst-case scenario for the full meltdown is that molten lavalike material burns through the reactor's pressure vessel and then melts through the reactor containment wall and is released into the air with enormous levels of radioactivity. Therefore, it is critical that a reactor never to get to a stage where the rods are fully exposed. The challenge for TEPCO was that by pumping seawater into the reactor, the seawater evaporates and more water is needed. It could take weeks of pumping water to finally "cool" the reactor. It could take several thousands of gallons daily for as long as a year to finally control the reactor.[5]

Nuclear Plant Design Problems

As far back as three decades ago, critics warned about the potential flaws in the nuclear reactor at Daiichi. In 1972, reports had identified that if the cooling systems failed on the "Mark 1" nuclear reactor, the primary containment vessel protecting the reactor would explode because of the intense heat of the exposed fuel rods. Thus the Daiichi plant's Mark 1 nuclear reactor had a known potential to create a complete meltdown, which would release dangerous levels of radiation into the environment.

Mark 1 nuclear reactors were developed by General Electric (GE) in the 1960s. In this old design, the containment vessel around the reactor is not as strong as in more modern models. In newer nuclear reactors, the reactors are sealed inside a very thick steel and cement "tomb." The Mark 1 design has less capability of stopping radioactive leaks if there is a meltdown of the uranium rods. GE had marketed the Mark 1 designs as cheaper and easier to build for utilities because the reactors are smaller and have a less expensive containment structure.[6] The Daiichi plant was also built by GE and was in operation since 1971. The plant had a battery backup generator system that could last for 4 hours if there were a loss of electricity.[7]

The U.S. Atomic Energy Commission representative, Stephen Hanauer, recommended in 1972 that the Mark 1 systems should be discontinued because of the safety risks. Hanauer identified that the problem with the containment structure was that it was more likely to explode due to a buildup of hydrogen gas, which is exactly what occurred at Daiichi. Also in 1972, this future chairman of the U.S. Nuclear Regulatory Commission (NRC) stated that the banning of the Mark 1 system was a good idea; however, it had already been adopted in many countries of the world, so a ban would not solve the problem and could result in the countries being reluctant to use nuclear power in the future. The safety issue was revisited in the mid-1980s when an official of the NRC predicted that Mark 1 reactors had a 90% chance of exploding if the fuel rods overheated and subsequently melted. Industry experts challenged that estimate by stating that the probability of this occurring was only approximately 10%. After the Daiichi explosions, a GE spokesperson stated that the Mark 1 was a "workhorse" in the nuclear power industry and that it had a proven track record of safety for more than 40 years.

As of March 2011, 32 Mark 1 reactors were in use around the world, despite the fact that numerous utilities in the late 1980s had threatened to sue GE because internal documents had been released that had identified GE concerns pertaining to the Mark 1. The internal documents stated that GE had failed to implement proper safety testing and that GE had identified certain flaws internally with the Mark 1 that could compromise the safety of the reactor. Mark 1 reactors that are used in the United States have been modified to increase their safety levels, including redesigning the containment vessel and retrofitting venting systems to reduce pressure within the reactor. GE's potential liability in the Daiichi disaster is minimal because the regulatory system in countries such as Japan identify the plant operator as the responsible party for any safety breaches.[8]

Silence Is Not Golden

Once an explosion hit the reactors, TEPCO officials described the explosion as "a big sound and white smoke"[9] and told the media that the incident was under investigation. The media accused TEPCO of producing conflicting reports of the nuclear disaster that are based on ambiguous language and a lack of TEPCO officials to confirm even the most basic information regarding the status of the recovery. When asked about the steam escaping from Reactor 3, TEPCO officials stated they could not confirm anything, it was impossible to say anything about the issue, and they were sorry to cause such a bother. Translating from one language to another is also a challenge. For example, in one press conference, when Yukio Edano, the chief cabinet secretary, stated that all the staff members would be moved temporarily to a safer location, some foreign reporters incorrectly interpreted, perhaps due to confusion caused by a translator, that his remark meant that TEPCO staff members were leaving the plant.[10]

Another challenge was the lack of media coverage in Japan for certain aspects of the crisis. For example, 4 days after the reactor shutdowns, a top American nuclear official, Gregory Jaczko, described the Daiichi reactors in very serious and grave terms. He stated there was little if any water left in the holding pools in Reactor 4 and that the subsequent high levels of radiation could make any type of repair impossible to complete. This dire warning was almost completely ignored by the Japanese media. The U.S. government assumed Mr. Jaczko was correct and started evacuating American citizens on chartered planes flying out of the two Tokyo airports. Japanese officials replied to Jaczko's comments by stating that because they had been unable to go to the pools at Reactor 4, they could not confirm if there was water in the spent fuel pool or not.[11] The following day Japan's nuclear safety agency changed the danger level ranking from 4 to 5 on a scale of 1 to 7. The ranking scale is logarithmic, which means the movement from one rank to the next is equal to an accident that is 10 times more serious than the lower-ranked accident. A level 5 nuclear accident, which was the ranking of the Three Mile Island accident in 1979, is extremely serious. The Chernobyl nuclear accident in 1986 has been the only event to be rated a 7 for danger.[12]

Japan's government officials also depended on TEPCO to provide information, but TEPCO was providing opaque and vague information to government leaders who needed to demonstrate to the people of Japan that there was a plan in place to solve the emergency. The prime minister of Japan, Naoto Kan, complained, in front of the media, to TEPCO officials that he was not being informed about the status of the nuclear disaster because he saw the explosion on television before TEPCO informed him. The International Atomic Energy Agency also became frustrated with TEPCO officials who refused to provide information to the agency in a timely manner.

In TEPCO's defense, Japanese companies traditionally do not like to release any unpleasant information. Culturally, it is not acceptable to "air dirty laundry" to people outside the company.[13] Furthermore, Japan previously had to address the issue of radiation during World War II from the nuclear bombing of Hiroshima and Nagasaki, so the Japanese people already have a heightened awareness and fear of radiation. The Japanese resistance to telling negative information even affects the medical treatment of patients. It is standard practice for doctors to avoid telling patients when they are diagnosed with cancer to protect the patient from stress.[14]

TEPCO's Role

After the tsunami knocked out the generators at the Daiichi plant, TEPCO could have immediately taken complete control of the situation by releasing seawater into the reactor. During the first hours of the crisis, the pressure was much lower in the reactors as the rods first responded to the lack of cooling water. However, TEPCO did not release seawater until the following evening when the prime minister ordered TEPCO to do so. Why the hesitation? The most common conclusion is that TEPCO was trying to protect its "asset." Introducing seawater into the reactor immediately makes the reactor nonfunctional for any future use. TEPCO officials naively thought that there was still a chance to recover from the accident and use the reactors in the future. The shortsightedness of the decision was explained succinctly by one government official who stated that the Daiichi disaster was 60% human-made. He observed that TEPCO "failed in their initial response. It's like TEPCO dropped and lost a 100 yen coin while trying to pick up a 10 yen coin."[15] Less than 2 weeks after the accident, Japanese banks provided the $25 billion in emergency funding that TEPCO requested, to help the company financially weather the nuclear storm. As of March 2011, TEPCO was still struggling financially, with an almost 60% drop in its stock price since the crisis started.[16]

The Government Regulators' Role

Prior to the disaster, in February 2011, Japanese government regulators had approved a 10-year extension for Reactor 1, the oldest reactor of the six in the Daiichi plant. Reactor 1 had been in operation since 1971 and had stress cracks in the backup generators, which made the generator vulnerable to becoming inoperative due to corrosion from seawater and rainwater. The regulators found that the maintenance of the Daiichi plant was inadequate and that the quality of the inspection by TEPCO was insufficient. TEPCO admitted that it did not inspect 33 pieces of equipment that were connected with the reactor cooling systems, which included the water pumps and the generators. When a whistle-blower from another company was contracted to inspect the reactors in 2000, he reported that there were cracks over the shield that covers the reactor cores. The regulatory agency told TEPCO that it needed to look into the issue. But TEPCO kept the reactors operating. The regulators did not notify any third parties about the cracks until 2 years later in 2002.

The Wall Street Journal reported that from 2005 to 2009, the Daiichi plant had 15 accidents, the highest accident rate of any large-scale nuclear plant in Japan and of one that has more than three reactors within its facility. As a result, the workers at the Daiichi plant were exposed to more radiation than were the employees at most of the other plants in Japan. TEPCO's response was that, overall, the reactors at Daiichi are safe and the high number of accidents, which are all minor in nature, are due to the age of the reactors.[17]

The regulatory agency in charge of monitoring compliance issues for nuclear power plants is under the domain of the Ministry of Economy, Trade and Industry, whose mission is to encourage growth and development in the nuclear industry. Therefore, there is an inherent conflict of interest between the regulators and the government ministry that controls the regulators. In addition, to have a government regulatory job actually results in "heavenly" benefits. A Japanese tradition is to have companies hire former ministry officials for lucrative jobs after they retire from government. The practice of hiring former government officials is called *amakudari*, which is translated to mean descent from heaven. Therefore, the minister in charge of monitoring TEPCO was lax with the inspections because he did not want to rock the boat and risk losing the lucrative payoff that people in his position can expect, or the potential to become a paid consultant for TEPCO.[18]

The connection between government officials and the nuclear industry is well known in Japan. The interests have colluded with little transparency in their actions and information given to outside parties. The relationship is commonly called the "nuclear power village," in which nuclear power is continued to be encouraged and supported by the government in return for overlooking critical safety problems such as building plants near earthquake fault lines and not building seawalls large enough to block tsunami-size waves. Like any village in Japan where everyone shares the same interests, the nuclear power village has a nuclear official, a government official, and scientists all benefiting by rewarding each other with financial support, favorable jobs, and favorable funding. Those who refuse to play by the rules of the village are considered outcasts and do not receive the benefits of those who support the village. The creed of the village is to support a nuclear industry that maximizes profits so everyone will receive the benefits. With the watchdog government agency under the control of the Ministry of Economy, Trade and Industry, it is not uncommon for government officials to be transferred from jobs that review the safety and oversight of the industry to jobs that support promoting nuclear energy growth and vice versa.[19]

The revolving door between government officials and TEPCO can been seen by the hiring record at TEPCO. From 1959 to 2010, four top government regulatory officials were hired to serve as vice presidents at TEPCO. In fact, the musical chairs are so dominant that the vice president's position is considered a "reserved seat"—after one former government official retires from TEPCO, his second in command from the ministry becomes the next person to fill the vice president's position.[20]

The Crisis Continues

Even though the radiation levels were 1,000 times the normal level in the reactor control room and some radioactive material has seeped outside, TEPCO officials were stating there was no immediate health hazard for people outside the plant and that the radioactive leaks were "minute." After the earthquake struck, the emergency diesel generators started to give power to the reactor cooling system, but the generators shut down an hour after the earthquake. Early speculation was that the tsunami was responsible for the generators shutting down. Auxiliary power was restored using a battery-controlled generation system. However, TEPCO officials believed that a "controlled containment venting" of radioactive gas would be needed to stop a rupture and further damage to the containment unit. TEPCO stated everything would be fine because of the evacuation of nearby residents and a wind that was blowing out into the ocean.

Reactor 1 was the first to have the radioactive gas vented from it. One of the many major challenges is that shutting down the reactor does not solve the problem of cooling the unit. Even in shutdown mode, the reactor must still be continuously cooled. If the cooling does not continue, the water in the cooling system will boil away, and the fuel rods will melt and release particles of uranium. The continuation of water flow can only occur if the water pumps connected to the cooling system are working. The following day, Reactor 1 exploded, increasing the fear and urgency to resolve the crisis. After the explosion took place, nuclear power officials in Japan feared that Reactor 1 and the other three reactors could eventually lead to a nuclear meltdown with a massive release of radioactive material. One day after the earthquake, it appeared that the reactor problems were caused by the tsunami rather than the earthquake itself. The tsunami waves damaged the power generators at the power plant as well as the backup power systems, which resulted in the cooling system failure.[21] The generators were located in a low-lying area because plant officials felt that no waves would ever be higher than the seawall. The generators were flooded with water from the tsunami when the first series of giant waves struck the area near the nuclear plant.[22]

The following day, TEPCO officials believed that two of the Daiichi reactors had a partial meltdown. The addition of the second reactor, Reactor 3, compounded the issues for nuclear officials. To contain the meltdown in Reactor 1, Japanese government officials flooded the reactor with seawater. Plant officials had to release radioactive vapor from both reactors to decrease the pressure. The venting of the radioactive vapor may have been the cause of the explosion in Reactor 1. The likely cause was the release of the radioactive steam or the release of hydrogen, which resulted in the outer wall and the roof of Reactor 1 being blown off.[23] The following day, there was an explosion in Reactor 3 that blew the roof off the containment building, confirming that it too had been affected by a partial meltdown. The second explosion demonstrated that TEPCO officials still did not have control of the situation related to the cooling systems of the reactors and that the reactors could move to a full and complete meltdown.[24] On March 14, 2011, TEPCO announced that the cooling systems with a third reactor had failed and that seawater was being pumped into the reactor to cool the reactor rods. The use of the corrosive seawater meant that TEPCO officials had abandoned all hope of using the reactor in the future because, as mentioned earlier, once saltwater gets inside a reactor, it can no longer function as a power source.[25]

On March 15, 2011, an explosion occurred at Reactor 2. The explosion damaged the steel container of water known as a *torus* that wraps around the base of the reactor vessel. The explosion did not appear to damage the containment vessel of the reactor.[26] Reactor 4 also had an explosion on March 15 where the used fuel rods were stored. Reactor 4 had been shut down but was still vulnerable to explosion if the cooling systems failed within the reactor building.[27]

One month after the disaster, the Japanese nuclear regulatory agency raised the alert level from 5 to 7 on the nuclear disaster scale and the Japanese government made an ominous announcement that the disaster was now on par with the 1986 Chernobyl explosion. This highest ranking meant that the disaster was likely to have substantial and long-term impacts on the health and environment of the local communities. A level 7 nuclear accident ranking also meant that there was an "external release of a significant fraction of the reactor core inventory."[28] Although the Japanese officials downplayed the information, several reports stated that large amounts of radiation had been released into the air during the crisis. The spokesperson for the Japanese nuclear regulator stated although the crisis was now ranked a 7, it was different from Chernobyl because the radioactive material from the four damaged nuclear reactors was contained within the reactors. However, a TEPCO official contradicted the regulator by stating the reactors that were leaking radioactive material had not stopped and that the amount of radioactive material released could eventually be higher than Chernobyl.

With the justification again being trying not to scare people, Japanese officials justified that waiting a month to raise the accident level from 5 to 7 was in the public's interest. The officials explained that many foreigners fled the country when there appeared to be only a minimal risk, and if the officials had quickly moved to level 7, there would have been a mass panic of people trying to leave Japan.[29] On April 15, 2011, TEPCO announced it was planning to compensate 50,000 people who were forced to evacuate because of the disaster. TEPCO had allocated $600 million, which would result in individuals receiving approximately $9,000 and larger households receiving approximately $12,000.[30]

Almost 5 months after the disaster, on August 1, 2011, TEPCO officials announced that the radiation levels near Reactors 1 and 2 exceeded the maximum reading on their instruments, which meant that with prolonged exposure, the levels are fatal if absorbed by a human.[31] However, according to the authors of a paper that discusses potential health risks from exposure to the radiation, no acute radiation injuries have been observed, even among plant operators and accident responders.[32]

On May 20, 2011, TEPCO president Shimizu resigned from his position. He told the media that he wanted to take managerial responsibility for the accident and bring the crisis to a symbolic close.[33] Two days later, the Japanese government offered to set up a fund of $26 billion to help TEPCO pay compensation for those people affected by the crisis.[34] On August 9, 2011, TEPCO announced that it had lost $7.4 billion for the fiscal quarter. Of that loss, $7.3 billion was booked as a onetime loss associated with the disaster.[35] On October 21, 2011, the prime minister of Japan, Yoshihiko Noda, predicted that the cost of the radiation cleanup would be at least $13 billion.[36] On December 3, 2011, TEPCO announced the results of its internal investigation related to the accident. TEPCO officials concluded there were "no errors" on their part related to the accident. The plant had complied with all earthquake safety standards. The report did cite that TEPCO did not have enough preparation ready for a large tsunami like the one that took place on March 11, 2011.[37] Two days later, TEPCO announced that a new leak of contaminated water had been discovered that was taking the radioactive material out to the ocean.[38] On December 16, 2011, 9 months after the crisis started, Prime Minister Noda declared that TEPCO had regained control of the reactors. He stated the reactors were stable and were ready for a cold shutdown, which occurs when there is no energy being emitted from the reactor.[39] The following week, on December 22, 2011, Japanese officials announced a 40-year plan to decommission and clean up the Daiichi plant and the radioactive contamination of the surrounding areas. Estimated milestones during the 40 years include finally plugging the leaks in the reactor buildings in 2018 and the complete removal of the fuel rods in 2036.[40]

On April 7, 2013, leaks of highly radioactive water from the Number 2 and Number 3 underground storage pools were reported. Three quarts of contaminated water had leaked from Number 2 storage pool, and 32,000 gallons of radioactive water had leaked from Number 3 storage pool.[41] On July 9, 2013, the former Fukushima nuclear power plant head, Masao Yoshida, died of esophageal cancer at the age of 58. A spokesperson representing TEPCO stated that although Yoshida was exposed to radiation, it would take 5 years for that level of radiation to develop into a cancer.[42] On August 22, 2013, Japan's Nuclear Regulation Authority announced that there was a serious spill of 79,000 gallons of radioactive water from a storage tank at the Fukushima facility. This storage tank was among numerous tanks that were built after the disaster to store the contaminated water pumped out of the buildings in the facility. An additional 400 tons of contaminated water are pumped into these storage tanks daily.[43]

On September 9, 2013, Japanese prosecutors announced that they had decided not to indict former executives of TEPCO who were involved at the Fukushima plant. The rationale for the lack of prosecution of the executives was that the magnitude of the earthquake and subsequent tsunami could not have been predicted.[44] By March 2014, it had become more difficult for TEPCO to find qualified people to help in the Fukushima facility cleanup. As a result, the company posted an online ad that stated, "Out of work? Nowhere to live? Nowhere to go? Nothing to eat? . . . Come to Fukushima."[45] On December 20, 2014, TEPCO announced that it had safely removed the radioactive fuel from the Number 4 reactor building. The 1,500 fuel rods that were removed were in a storage pool. It was the first of the four reactors in which all the fuel rods had been removed.[46]

Questions for Thought

1. Develop a time line of all of the activities at TEPCO during the disaster.

2. Can these events be placed on the shoulders of just one group? Why or why not?

3. Can those who were harmed by the TEPCO events ever truly be compensated for their loss? Explain.

4. What are the benefits of nuclear power if disasters like this can happen? Is it worth it, or are there too many ethical and environmental problems to deal with?

21

Tyco: I'm Sure That It's a Really Nice Shower Curtain

The Rise of Dennis Kozlowski

On May 18, 2002, Tyco CEO Dennis Kozlowski, who had received his degree in accounting and finance from Seton Hall University in 1968, gave the commencement address to St. Anselm's College in Manchester, New Hampshire. He talked about the difficult decisions that the graduates would face during their lifetimes. He stated that the graduates would have questions that would test their moral standards. He told the students that the questions would get tougher and the potential consequences would be more severe, so his advice was to not do the easy thing, but to do the right thing.[1] Less than 2 weeks later, on June 1, 2002, Dennis Kozlowski, who had worked at Tyco since 1975, announced to the board of directors for Tyco International that he was the subject of a criminal investigation in New York for evasion of sales taxes on a painting he had purchased in Manhattan. The board of directors demanded that he step down as CEO, which he did on June 3, 2002. Tyco told the media that Kozlowski had resigned for "personal reasons." By resigning rather than being fired, Kozlowski was no longer eligible for a severance package that was valued at approximately $120 million. Previous Tyco CEO John Fort took over as interim CEO. Fort, Tyco's CEO from 1982 to 1992, had stopped using the company jet and sold off the president's house and other corporate-held apartments during his first reign. In an ironic example of déjà vu, Fort, who was on the board of directors of Tyco, had to address the same issues of management's misuse of corporate funds in 2002 that he dealt with in 1982.[2]

The Financial Troubles Begin

It was not a pleasant time for Tyco because the company had lost $86 billion in market capitalization due to concerns investors had about the company's strategic focus. In addition, a number of critics were complaining about the compensation levels given to Kozlowski and other members of Tyco's management. During his tenure, Tyco's stock had fallen from $60 in December 2001 to $16.05 in June 2002. In addition, Tyco had accumulated $27 billion in debt through various acquisitions. Kozlowski was called

"Deal a Month Dennis" for his aggressive acquisition style. He said his goal was to create the new General Electric. Some of the major acquisitions are shown in Table 1. In his 10 years as CEO, through growth via acquisitions, Kozlowski grew the size of Tyco from $2 billion when he took over the CEO position in 1989 to a conglomerate with annual sales of $36 billion at the end of fiscal year 2001. Tyco had a quarter of a million employees worldwide and had a market capitalization of $120 billion. By the time of his resignation, Kozlowski had exercised $240 million in stock options and had been paid almost $100 million over the previous 3 years. In addition, Kozlowski owned residences in New York, New Hampshire, and Florida and on Nantucket Island. His New York apartment was reportedly bought for $18.5 million in 2000. His distaste for paying taxes led him to move the corporate headquarters to Bermuda from Exeter, New Hampshire, in 1997 to reduce Tyco's tax liability to 20%, which is approximately half the average corporate rate for U.S.-based firms.[3]

Paying for Empty Crates

Kozlowski's distaste for paying taxes extended to his personal life as well. When he purchased approximately $8 million to $12 million worth of paintings in New York, he had the art gallery ship them to New Hampshire to avoid paying the 8.25% New York State and Manhattan combined sales tax, even though they were to be hung in his Fifth Avenue apartment.[4] On June 4, 2002, Kozlowski was indicted by a grand jury for tax evasion for avoiding to pay between $650,000 to $1 million in taxes on the six paintings that he had purchased in the fall of 2001. In addition, he was also charged with tampering with evidence and willfully falsifying financial records. He was ordered to surrender his passport and was released on a $3 million bond.

TABLE 1 ● Some of the Major Tyco Acquisitions During the Kozlowski Era

Date	Company	Products	Cost
July 1994	Kendall International	Medical	$1.4 billion
March 1997	ADT	Home Security	$5.4 billion
April 1997	AT&T Cable	Underwater Cable	$850 million
May 1998	U.S. Surgical	Medical Supplies	$3.3 billion
November 1998	AMP	Electronic Components	$11.3 billion
June 2000	Mallinckrodt	Health Care Products	$4.2 billion
February 2001	Scott Technologies	Lifesaving Equipment	$400 million
March 2001	CIT Group	Financial	$9.2 billion
May 2001	C. R. Bard	Health Care Products	$3.2 billion

Source: Adapted from Alex Berenson, "Tyco Chief Out as Tax Inquiry Picks up Speed," *New York Times*, June 4, 2002, www.nytimes.com.

Cases

One piece of evidence that prosecutors were able to obtain was a fax that listed the paintings Kozlowski had purchased, which were supposed to be shipped to New Hampshire, with the words *wink, wink* in parentheses. From August to December 2001, Kozlowski had bought approximately 12 paintings, including a Renoir and a Monet. In total, the artwork was valued at more than $15 million. Karen Kozlowski, Dennis's wife, worked with art gallery director Christine Berry to help purchase the art for the Kozlowskis' Fifth Avenue apartment. Some of the paintings were sent to the apartment to see how they looked on the walls before they were purchased. In December 2001, the Kozlowskis purchased a Monet for almost $4 million from a private Manhattan dealer. The art dealer, Alexander Apsis, did not charge sales tax on the painting because Kozlowski gave him a written document that stated that the painting was going to be shipped to New Hampshire. However, the painting went to the Manhattan apartment, which is less than two blocks from the art dealer's office. On January 2, 2002, five empty boxes were shipped to New Hampshire and signed for by a Tyco employee.[5]

The Investigation Expands

On June 6, 2002, prosecutors announced that the investigation had been expanded to examine whether Kozlowski used Tyco funds to finance the maintenance of his Florida homes as well as paying for other personal expenses. The investigation started to focus on whose money was used to purchase the artwork that was hanging in the Kozlowskis' Fifth Avenue apartment. In addition, it appeared that Tyco money was used to purchase the $18.5 million apartment in Manhattan for the Kozlowskis. The investigation also examined whether Tyco money was used to purchase the Kozlowski home in Boca Raton, Florida.[6] The Boca Raton home had been owned by Lord Michael Ashcroft, who became a Tyco board member in 1997 when Tyco purchased ADT, which Ashcroft's company owned. In October 1997, Ashcroft sold his house to his wife for $100. She sold it the same day for $2.5 million to a Tyco vice president, Byron Kalogerou. The investigation was expanded to determine if Kalogerou's name was put on the title to avoid the appearance that Tyco bought the home for Kozlowski from a Tyco board member.[7] By June 9, 2002, Tyco's stock had fallen from a high of more than $60 in December 2001 to $10.10, resulting in a reduction of market capitalization of approximately $95 billion.[8]

On June 26, 2002, Kozlowski was indicted on two additional charges of tampering with evidence in the tax evasion case. The new indictment was based on the disclosure that Kozlowski had physically taken a bill of lading from the Tyco offices in Boca Raton that falsified the shipment of the paintings from New York to New Hampshire before the files were sent to the New York district attorney's office in May 2002. As with all the previous charges, Kozlowski pleaded not guilty to the new felony charges.[9] On July 23, 2002, Tyco reported a third-quarter loss of $2.32 billion, compared with a net profit of $1.18 billion for the third quarter of 2001.[10] On July 25, 2002, Tyco announced that it had hired Motorola's president, Edward Breen, as the new CEO and chairman of the board. Breen had also previously been the CEO of General Instrument Corporation, which was acquired by Motorola in 2000.[11]

On September 12, 2002, Kozlowski and chief financial officer (CFO) Mark Swartz were indicted for illegally obtaining hundreds of millions of dollars from Tyco for their own use. The indictment alleged that the two former Tyco executives were involved in racketeering by being involved in stock fraud, the disbursement of bonuses that were not authorized to employees, and the falsification of expense accounts. The indictment also alleged that Kozlowski and Swartz "paid off" a Tyco board member and other employees to keep their fraudulent activities quiet. The prosecutors accused Kozlowski and Swartz of running a "criminal enterprise," a term that is commonly used when indictments are applied to members of organized crime. The Manhattan district attorney's office claimed that the two former Tyco executives started the covert fraudulent operation in 1995. The district attorney's office alleged that the two men had spent millions of Tyco's dollars for their personal use. It was also alleged that the two Tyco executives controlled the focus of Tyco's internal audits and filed disclosure reports with the Security and Exchange Commission (SEC) without any input from the legal department to avoid the chance that their activities would be discovered. The prosecutors calculated that Kozlowski and Swartz had stolen $170 million directly from the company and had illegally gained another $430 million by selling Tyco stock while the price was artificially high because of financial statement manipulations. The prosecutors also alleged that Kozlowski had defrauded the company by giving himself and other Tyco employees unauthorized bonuses and loans that were not repaid to the company.[12]

Kozlowski used a Tyco program designed to help executives pay taxes on stock options to improperly borrow an estimated $242 million for his own use. Kozlowski used the money to purchase paintings, real estate, yachts, and jewelry for himself and his wife. Swartz allegedly used the same program to borrow $72 million for his personal investments. In addition, Kozlowski and Swartz used $78 million in loans from Tyco's real estate "relocation" program, which was designed to help pay the costs of employees who were being transferred to the Boca Raton office from the New Hampshire office. The two executives allegedly used the money to purchase real estate and other personal expenses.[13]

The Payment of Expenses

On September 18, 2002, the company released the results of an internal review headed by David Boies, who found that Tyco paid for additional personal expenses of Kozlowski, including an $80,000 payment to American Express, a traveling toilet box that cost $17,100, an umbrella stand designed to look like a dog for $15,000, a sewing basket that cost $6,300, a $6,000 shower curtain, two sets of bed sheets that together cost $5,960, a set of coat hangers that cost Tyco $2,900, a metal wastebasket that cost $2,200, a $1,650 notebook, and a pincushion that cost $445.[14]

Tyco filed a lawsuit against Kozlowski, requesting the former CEO to return to Tyco his compensation and benefits since 1997 and to forfeit all of the components of his severance package.[15]

Happy Birthday, Karen!

One allegation was that Tyco paid $1.5 million of the $2.1 million total cost of the 40th birthday party for Kozlowski's second wife, Karen, on the island of Sardinia in Italy. Kozlowski had met Karen when she was working as a waitress in a New Hampshire restaurant near Tyco's U.S. headquarters. A memo given to the *Wall Street Journal* described the details of the $2.1 million party, which was described as a Roman Empire theme with Kozlowski being the emperor. The party included gladiators, exotic animals, and an ice sculpture of Michelangelo's *David* that dispensed Vodka through its genitals. Not to be outdone, there was also a woman-shaped birthday cake that had a bosom that exploded when sparklers were inserted in the cake. The servers were dressed in togas, and there was an open bar for the 75 guests and more than 25 staff members. An Elvis impersonator appeared on a huge screen, apologizing for not being able to appear in person, and an extravagant light show ended the evening. Jimmy Buffett also performed for a fee of $250,000. The guests did not have to pay for anything, including flying to Italy. The birthday "week" was so elaborate that a logo was included on bags, hats, and other gifts given to the guests. Also part of the weeklong events were a scavenger hunt, horseback riding, water skiing, and trips on Kozlowski's yacht. After the party was over, Karen and some of the guests took a Tyco jet and flew to Florence to participate in a cooking class. The only guidance Kozlowski gave the planners was not to do anything that he would be embarrassed to see on the front page of the *Wall Street Journal*.[16] In Tyco's 2001 annual report, which was published after the birthday celebration, Kozlowski informed Tyco investors that the company had a continuous drive to reduce costs throughout the organization.[17] Kozlowski described the party as primarily a business function.[18] During the 2005 retrial of the two executives (the six-month first trial was called to a halt after a juror received a menacing letter and telephone call), Mark Foley, who was the former senior vice president of finance, testified that the party was going to be a "management meeting" and would include a meeting with the board of directors.[19]

Mark Swartz, CFO

CFO Swartz was more involved with the deal making for the acquisitions than with the financial statements of Tyco. He was considered Kozlowski's protégé. From 1999 to 2002, Swartz received more than $170 million, which included a salary of $48 million and $125 million in stock options. His compensation was one of the highest for a CFO during that period.[20] New Tyco CEO Breen asked Swartz to leave Tyco on August 1, 2002. In agreeing to step down as CFO, Swartz gave up his original severance package, which estimated to be worth $100 million, and settled for $9 million and other retirement benefits when Breen threatened to challenge the previous severance agreement in court.[21] On September 11, 2002, David FitzPatrick was hired by Tyco as the new CFO. He was previously a CFO and senior vice president for United Technologies Corporation.[22] On February 19, 2003, Swartz was indicted for tax evasion for not paying federal income taxes on a bonus, originally in the form of a $12.5 million loan, which was given to him in 1999. The loan became a "bonus" after Swartz told a Tyco finance department employee that the board had authorized bonuses in the form of forgiveness. The tax due for the bonus would have been almost $5 million.[23]

Swartz received this loan via the Key Employee Loan Program, established in 1983 by then CEO Fort as a way for top executives to borrow money from Tyco to pay for taxes on their stock options. The premise behind the program was that Tyco did not want the executives to be forced to sell shares in Tyco stock to pay taxes when they exercised their stock options. The purpose of the program was to pay taxes only on stock options, which was explicitly stated in Tyco's 1995 proxy statement.[24] Tyco's former treasurer, Barbara Miller, testified in the first trial that in 1997 the scope of the program moved beyond loans for tax payments. Former Tyco CFO Swartz told Miller that executives could now borrow money for any reason with the only restriction being that the total amount borrowed must not surpass a calculated percentage of the executive's restricted stock holding based on the executive's tax rate. As a result, Kozlowski and Swartz borrowed Tyco money through this program to buy real estate, jewelry, and other personal items.[25]

One of the criminal charges made was that Kozlowski and Swartz were "stealing" $37.5 million from the loan program because Kozlowski had loans worth $25 million wiped out, and Swartz did not have to repay his $12.5 million loan. A third person, Barbara Jacques, who joined Tyco as a secretary in 1986, also had $1 million "forgiven" from the loan program. The prosecutors in the first trial asked why a secretary also benefited from the select Tyco forgiveness program. The reason was that Jacques had an affair with Kozlowski starting in 1986 when he was still married to his first wife. The prosecution concluded that Kozlowski must have controlled the forgiveness program to allow only himself, Swartz, and Jacques to be able to participate in it.[26] Jacques eventually became the event planner for Tyco and was in charge of coordinating the infamous 40th birthday party in Sardinia, Italy, for Kozlowski's second wife.

Linda Auger, head of Tyco's accounting department, testified in court that Kozlowski used his loan account to buy an $8 million painting, $50,000 in flowers for a Christmas party, and restaurant tips that sometimes reached as high as 50% of the bill on Kozlowski's corporate credit card.[27] In 1998, Kozlowski used his account to pay for his $8.3 million investment in the New Jersey Nets and to buy a 1999 Porsche Carrera for his future wife. In September 1999, he used the account to buy his own sailboat, *Endeavour*, for $13.5 million.[28] In 2001, Kozlowski used his account to purchase a $5 million diamond ring for his wife.[29]

On April 1, 2003, Tyco filed a lawsuit against Swartz, asking for more than $400 million that Swartz had taken from Tyco. The lawsuit was filed after Swartz refused to resolve the issue through arbitration.[30] In September 2004, Swartz's Manhattan apartment near Central Park was sold by Tyco for $12 million. Swartz, using Tyco funds, bought the apartment in 2002 for $15.274 million.[31]

On May 11, 2005, during his retrial, Swartz stated that he did not remember checking his 1999 W-2 form to see whether he had reported the Tyco forgiveness loan of $12.5 million. The former accountant testified in court that he only remembered seeing the W-2 2 years later in the summer of 2002.[32]

Mark Belnick, Tyco Legal Counsel

On June 10, 2002, Tyco fired its general legal counsel, Mark Belnick. The circumstances behind his firing are disputed. Belnick, who had been at Tyco since 1998, stated that he was fired because he lost a power struggle with one of Tyco's board members, Joshua Berman, and the lawyer who was hired in April 2002 to be included in the Tyco corporate governance committee, David Boies. Conversely, Tyco stated that the reason Belnick was fired was because he was disrupting the internal investigation by having Tyco pay for executives' personal expenses as well as issuing previously undisclosed loans to Tyco executives.[33] Berman also became part of the investigation when it was discovered that Tyco was paying his law firm as much as $2 million annually and Berman's compensation until 2000 was tied, in part, to how much business he could bring to the law firm from Tyco. Belnick had complained that Tyco was depending too much on Berman's law firm of Kramer Levin Naftalis & Frankel for its legal needs.[34]

Boies stated that Belnick had been given $20 million in compensation without the payment being disclosed to the board. Belnick's lawyer confirmed the payment of $20 million but stated that the proper disclosures had been made. The SEC requires that the compensation for the five top-paid officers be disclosed. Belnick's compensation would have put him in the top five, yet Tyco did not disclose this information to the SEC in its filings.[35]

In addition, initial results of the internal investigation done by Boies's firm—Boies, Schiller & Flexner LLP—raised questions as to whether Tyco money was used to buy Belnick's residences in New York City and in Park City, Utah, without full approval by the board of directors.[36] On June 17, 2002, Tyco filed a lawsuit against Belnick alleging that Belnick had accepted total payments of $35 million from 1998 to 2001 without disclosing it to the compensation committee of the board of directors or to the SEC. In addition, the lawsuit also claimed that Belnick purposely deleted files relevant to the investigation on June 10, 2002, which was the day he was fired. On September 12, 2002, the Manhattan district attorney's office announced that Belnick was criminally charged with defrauding Tyco. The indictment alleged that Belnick hid the fact he received a "relocation loan" from Tyco that he used to buy a resort home in Utah. The district attorney's office claimed that Kozlowski "paid off" Belnick with the loan so Belnick would not say anything about the internal transactions that were occurring at Tyco.[37]

On February 3, 2003, Belnick was indicted for three more criminal charges, including obtaining a $12 million bonus that was not authorized. The three charges were grand larceny, fraud, and falsifying documents.[38] During his trial, prosecutors claimed that Belnick did not disclose $14.9 million in company relocation loans that were used to purchase an apartment in New York and a home in Utah. Belnick was listed as the only Tyco employee in Utah in Tyco's records.[39] Belnick was accused of taking as much as $32 million through loans and bonuses without proper authorization. After a 2-month trial, during which the jury deliberated for 5 days, Belnick was found not guilty on all charges.[40] On May 2, 2006, Belnick agreed to pay the SEC a $100,000 penalty as part of the settlement for civil fraud charges. In addition, Belnick agreed not to serve as a corporate officer of a publicly traded company for 5 years.[41]

Tyco's Board of Directors

On June 13, 2002, the board of directors at Tyco was investigating the actions of interim CEO and board member John Fort for conflict-of-interest violations. Fort was an investor and advisor for DLJ Merchant Banking Partners II, which bought Tyco's flow-control products division for $810 million in August 1999. Fort did not disclose this information to the board of directors at Tyco. In addition, Fort had sold a Rye, New Hampshire, house to Kozlowski in 1996, which was paid for with Tyco funds. Furthermore, another Tyco board member, Stephen Foss, had a business relationship with Tyco by leasing an airplane to Tyco.[42] The lack of control by Tyco's board of directors pertaining to the decision-making process by the top executives at Tyco is evident by examining the compensation levels given to Kozlowski and Swartz from 1998 to 2001, as shown in Table 2. Although their combined salaries and bonuses ranged from more than $1 million to more than $5 million per year, the issuing of stock bonuses and options ballooned the total compensation package for the two top Tyco executives combined to almost half a billion dollars for the 4 years.[43]

TABLE 2 ● Compensation for Kozlowski and Swartz, 1998 to 2001

Dennis Kozlowski's Total Compensation from 1998 to 2001 (Rounded to Millions of Dollars)

Year	Salary	Bonus	Subtotal	Restricted Stock Bonus	Stock Options (Present Value)	Grand Total
1998	1.250	2.500	3.750	20.140	25.430	49.320
1999	1.350	3.200	4.550	25.707	68.420	98.677
2000	1.350	2.800	4.150	21.208	80.610	105.968
2001	1.650	4.000	5.650	30.399	21.810	57.859
Total	*5.600*	*12.500*	*18.100*	*97.454*	*196.270*	*311.824*

Mark Swartz's Total Compensation from 1998 to 2001 (Rounded to Millions of Dollars)

Year	Salary	Bonus	Subtotal	Restricted Stock Bonus	Stock Options (Present Value)	Grand Total
1998	0.559	1.250	1.809	10.700	14.540	27.049
1999	0.750	1.600	2.350	12.030	31.480	45.860
2000	0.769	1.400	2.169	10.061	41.560	53.79
2001	0.969	2.000	2.969	15.199	12.000	30.168
Total	*3.047*	*6.250*	*9.297*	*47.990*	*99.58*	*156.866*

Source: Adapted from Dan Ackman, "The Millions Kozlowski Didn't Steal," *Forbes*, May 23, 2005, www.forbes.com.

Cases

On June 17, 2002, former independent board member Walsh created a conflict of interest by taking a secret $20 million from Kozlowski for helping Tyco buy CIT Group. The fee was not disclosed when it took place, but 6 months later Tyco disclosed the fee, which resulted in a decrease of $16.7 billion in market capitalization of Tyco stock.[44] The $20 million "finder's fee" was given to Walsh so Tyco could buy CIT Group, which was owned by Walsh's friend Albert Gamper Jr. On December 17, 2002, Walsh pleaded guilty to securities fraud. Walsh admitted that he had taken a payment of $20 million for helping Tyco acquire CIT Group, but he did not disclose that information to any other members of the board of directors. In exchange for not being sentenced to jail, Walsh agreed to pay back the $20 million with an additional $2.5 million as a fine for his actions. Tyco bought CIT for $9.2 billion and sold it in 2002 for a loss of $7 billion.[45] In the first criminal trial against Kozlowski, evidence was presented that showed Kozlowski had admitted to Fort in a January 2002 phone conversation that the $20 million payment was a mistake and that it was an action that should have been done only with board approval. Fort testified at the trial that board members usually arranged potential acquisitions without any additional compensation. Fort told Kozlowski that the payment would have been denied by the board if the board had been aware of the deal.

Kozlowski also forged a close financial relationship with board member Richard Bodman. Bodman had been a Tyco board member since 1992, and Kozlowski had invested $5 million into a private stock fund that was managed by Bodman. Bodman was a member of Tyco's oversight board committees—audit, corporate governance, and nominating.[46] Contrary to other board members' willingness to keep quiet about Tyco's illegal financial dealings, Bodman's close relationship with Kozlowski did not hinder him from stating his opinion that a $20 million payment made to another board member, Frank Walsh Jr., without board approval was corrupt and a complete violation of the responsibilities given to the board of directors by the investors.[47]

The Wonderful World of Tyco Accounting

On June 13, 2002, the SEC announced that it was starting an investigation of Tyco based on its accounting procedures. The SEC wanted to determine whether Tyco was using its reserve accounts to artificially increase its level of profitability after a number of acquisitions by the conglomerate. This reopened an investigation that the SEC had started in 1999 and finished in 2000, after Tyco had acquired more than 120 companies in 6 years during the 1990s. There were questions pertaining to the $3 billion in restructuring charges that Tyco realized during the 6-year period during which these acquisitions took place. The 1999 SEC investigation was initiated when Albert Meyer, from the firm David W. Tice & Associates, raised concerns about how Tyco was using aggressive accounting methods during its acquisition splurge.[48] The internal audit to examine the books for Tyco took 25 lawyers, 100 accountants, and 65,000 hours to review the financial transactions of more than 45 Tyco operating units.[49]

On December 30, 2002, Tyco admitted that it had artificially inflated profits for years and would have to eliminate the $382 million in profits that had previously been reported by the company. A 5-month internal investigation revealed that Tyco had a corporate culture that encouraged managers to bypass accounting rules to inflate the results of their departments' performances. One department memo stated that the employees of one Tyco division had to try to reduce costs through the process of "financial engineering." Another division stated that the employees had to "create stores" to validate the accounting changes that occurred, which increased the level of profitability of the division. The internal audit also discovered that Tyco would force companies that it was acquiring to report lower performance numbers so when Tyco took over the company, it could present a dramatic increase in financial performance. The investigation also found that there was poor documentation of transactions, the policies and procedures in place to control for fraud were not adequate, and there were inadequate procedures for authorizations of employees' actions. Some examples of improper authorizations included employees' having company cars and also receiving car allowances, and having a $150,000 charitable contribution given to an organization that was not a charity.[50] By April 2003, Tyco had estimated that it had an additional $1.2 billion in accounting problems that had to be restated. This announcement came after two announcements in March in which Tyco had estimated restatement of its financial statements of $265 million and $325 million.[51] From October 2002 to August 2003, Tyco revised or restated its financial statements on five separate occasions with the result being a reduction of $2 billion in pretax profits from Tyco's previous financial statements from 1998.[52]

Key Employee Relocation Program

The employee relocation program was designed to compensate employees when they moved to the New York office of Tyco. After the board approved the design and use of the program in 1995, Kozlowski and Swartz adjusted the scope of the program. The limited scope of the program was based on the legal opinion of a Boston law firm that concluded that if additional benefits were given to the executives as part of the relocation program, it would be considered additional compensation for the executives, which would require a disclosure of that information in Tyco's proxy statements. The two executives told Miller, who was Tyco's treasurer from 1993 to 1998, that the relocation program would now include additional expenses such as paying for second homes for executives and paying for private school tuition for children of the executives. At the time of this adjustment, Swartz had three school-aged children. Miller had testified that Swartz would give her handwritten alterations to the criteria of the program.

Tyco Relocation Loan Bonus Program

On September 18, 2002, Kozlowski approved, without authorization from the board of directors, the forgiveness of loans to 51 Tyco employees to the tune of $96 million in return for their silence. The purpose behind his decision was to forgive relocation loans for employees who had bought homes and moved to the Tyco offices in Boca Raton, Florida. As a result, Tyco paid for the homes of the employees who transferred to Florida as well as the related taxes when they purchased the houses. When Patricia Prue, who was head of Tyco's human resources department from 1998 to 2002, asked Swartz if this bonus plan had been approved by the board of directors, he and Kozlowski told her that the program had been approved. Kozlowski received a forgiveness loan of $33 million from the program, and Swartz received $16.6 million.[53,54]

PricewaterhouseCoopers, Tyco's External Auditor

On February 7, 2003, prosecutors accused PricewaterhouseCoopers (PwC) of knowing about the unauthorized bonuses and loans and not investigating them. PwC executives met with Kozlowski and Swartz about the unauthorized transactions, and PwC had determined that they were not material and did not need to be disclosed.[55] The SEC accused Richard Scalzo, who was a partner at PwC and the chief external auditor for Tyco, of ignoring the accounting practices that were occurring at Tyco. The SEC claimed that Scalzo did not press for information pertaining to the unauthorized loans and bonuses and other extravagant perquisites that were given to the top executives at the company. Based on his actions in the Tyco account, Scalzo agreed to an SEC settlement that stated he would no longer be allowed to practice as an accountant before the SEC, meaning that he would not be allowed to be an auditor. An example of Scalzo not performing due diligence was that he knew that Tyco had a general reserve that was being used to offset expenses that management had not anticipated. Setting up this type of reserve is not allowed under generally accepted accounting principles. In addition, Scalzo knew that Kozlowski and Swartz had borrowed $35.5 million and

$8 million, respectively, interest free. Scalzo agreed with Swartz's argument that the loans were not material.[56] Tyco's former senior vice president for finance testified in court that Scalzo knew of the $96 million in forgiveness loans that were implemented in "Bonus 2000" and did not stop it when it was classified as a direct cost associated with an initial public offering of the Tyco optical fiber subsidiary. Scalzo reportedly stated that was an unusual accounting treatment but he would not overturn the transaction.[57] In court, Scalzo testified that he did review how some of the bonuses and loans were accounted for on Tyco's books. When asked if he ever verified that the board of directors had approved the bonuses and loans, Scalzo said that he did not because it was not part of the auditing procedure.[58]

The Beginning of the End for Dennis Kozlowski

On September 29, 2003, Kozlowski's first trial started in Manhattan. The prosecutor in the courtroom accused Kozlowski and Swartz of shamelessly violating the trust that investors had in the management of Tyco. In addition, the prosecutor accused the two former executives of considering Tyco assets to be their own and that they were using them when the executives wanted Tyco to pay for their expenses.[59]

On November 4, 2003, Tyco announced a net loss of $297.1 million for the quarter and stated that it would close 219 operations and lay off 7,200 employees, which represented 3% of its workforce.[60] On November 11, 2003, Tyco announced that it had signed a 5-year contract with Legal Knowledge Company so every employee could take ethics classes. This was the first comprehensive ethics training program ever at Tyco.[61]

On February 26, 2004, Swartz's defense attorneys rested their case. Kozlowski's attorneys rested their case two weeks earlier. On March 18, the prosecution in the trials of Kozlowski and Swartz concluded its closing arguments and the jury was sent out to reach a verdict. The chance of a mistrial became larger and larger as notes from the jury commented that the atmosphere within the jury room became "poisonous" with one jury member holding out. The suspected juror was Ruth Jordan, also known as Juror No. 4, who was a former teacher with a law degree. On March 26, 2004, Jordan gave the "OK" sign to the defense table as she walked past it.[62,63] On April 2, 2004, Judge Michael Obus declared a mistrial after he had been informed that one of the jurors had complained about being pressured into convicting the two former Tyco executives. The other jurors stated that after 12 days of deliberations that the rest of the group was ready to convict both men on many of the most serious criminal charges presented by the prosecution. The Manhattan district attorney's office immediately stated that it would have a retrial for Kozlowski and Swartz.[64] In October 2004, Kozlowski's New York apartment, home of the $6,000 shower curtain, was sold for $21 million. The price included many furnishings but not the shower curtain because prosecutors had taken it for evidence in his trial.[65] On April 27, 2005, Kozlowski took the stand in defense of the charges against him in his retrial. He did not take the stand in the original trial. He denied that he had committed any crimes and that his goal was for Tyco to grow as a company. Kozlowski could not tell the court why the $25 million that was a forgiveness loan from Tyco was not reported as income on his 1999 W-2 form. He stated in court that he wasn't thinking that he had a forgiveness loan when he signed the tax form.[66]

On May 31, 2005, the jury deliberations started for the retrial of the two executives. On June 17, 2005, Kozlowski and Swartz were convicted of fraud for falsifying business documents, grand larceny, and conspiracy. After 10 days of deliberations, both men were convicted on 22 criminal counts and were acquitted on 1 count of falsifying business records. Jordan, the "OK" juror from the first trial, commented that she was a little shocked because she still believed they were both not guilty.[67] The jurors in the second trial stated that they felt that Kozlowski was not believable and that Swartz was a very good liar.[68]

After Kozlowski and Swartz were convicted, the government inventoried assets of both men to determine what could be seized for restitution with the proceeds going back to Tyco and its investors. The government claimed that combined the two executives looted Tyco of more than $600 million, which included illegal stock transactions. Some of the assets are listed in Table 3.

On September 19, 2005, Kozlowski and Swartz were both sentenced to the same prison terms. The judge sentenced them both to 8 years, 4 months to 25 years for their crimes. Both men would be eligible for parole after 6 years, 11 months, and 9 days. The maximum sentence they could have faced was 15 to 30 years, and the minimum was 1 to 3 years. But the judge was not convinced that the men deserved the maximum sentence, even after prosecutors read a letter that Kozlowski had written in 1995 to request that the Houston judge who was in charge of sentencing a Tyco employee who was convicted of stealing from the company be given the maximum sentence.[69] The prosecution weighed whether to include this letter when Kozlowski and Swartz were to be sentenced for their crimes.

TABLE 3 ● Some of the Assets Available for Seizure From Kozlowski and Swartz	
Kozlowski	
Yacht called *Endeavour*	$17 million
Fifth Avenue, New York, apartment	$17 million
Park Avenue, New York, apartment given to his ex-wife	$7 million
Boca Raton, Florida, home	$15.2 million
Colorado Rockies home	$9.4 million
Nantucket home	$12.7 million
BMW Roadster	$150,000
Swartz	
Boca Raton, Florida, home	$16.1 million
Virginia estate	$12.2 million
Total value of assets that were to be seized from both men was estimated at $600 million	

Source: Adapted from Charles Forelle, "Seeking Restitution, Government Targets Tyco Duo's Fortunes," *Wall Street Journal*, June 30, 2005, www.wallstreetjournal.com.

The court also ordered the two executives to pay $134 million in restitution to Tyco, and Kozlowski was fined $70 million and Swartz was fined $35 million. The prosecutors had asked for the maximum sentence and concluded that Tyco had become a global symbol of kleptocratic management. Because Kozlowski and Swartz were convicted in state court rather than in federal court, they were sentenced to a state prison, considered to be a much harder place to serve their time than at a federal prison, which houses white-collar criminals.[70] In New York State, if a convicted felon is sentenced to more than 6 years in jail, he or she is usually sent to a maximum-security state prison. The state prison houses mostly violent offenders, and the inmates are paid $1.05 per day for doing 6 hours of work.[71]

On the same day as the sentencing, the SEC recommended that an accounting fraud case be started against Tyco for allegedly inflating its profits by approximately $1 billion. On April 17, 2006, Tyco settled with the SEC by paying a fine of $50 million for artificially inflating, by $1 billion from 1996 to 2002, profits it reported to the SEC.[72]

In an ironic twist, on May 3, 2006, Tyco sold two of the paintings that were "shipped" in empty boxes in New Hampshire for $7.8 million. *Fleurs et Fruits* by Renoir sold for $2.8 million and *Pres Monte-Carlo* by Monet sold for $5 million. Nine days later, Kozlowski agreed to pay $21.2 million to settle tax evasion charges that had been filed against him in New York for the purchase of the artwork. Kozlowski also agreed to pay $3.2 million in sales taxes that were not paid and an additional $15 million for fines and penalties related to the tax evasion.[73]

In June 2006, Kozlowski requested that Tyco reimburse his legal costs under his "officer and director" liability policy at Tyco. Kozlowski had submitted a claim of almost $17.8 million to Corporate Officers & Directors Assurance Ltd., which had provided liability insurance for Tyco.[74]

In an apparent case of "what have you done for me lately," Karen Kozlowski filed for divorce on July 31, 2006. Karen, who enjoyed her $2 million 40th birthday party in Sardinia, declared that their marriage had been irretrievably broken. She had requested that a lien be put on their Boca Raton mansion to protect the asset from the government and potential lawsuits. The 15,000-square-foot waterfront estate was purchased for $19 million using interest-free Tyco loans. The divorce settlement requested that all of the assets of the couple be equally distributed with the additional stipulation that Dennis pay Karen financial support.[75] A prisoner in the New York state penal system averages a wage rate of $1 per day.[76]

In an ironic full circle, on December 15, 2006, New York state sales tax charges against Dennis Kozlowski were dismissed when prosecutors reached a deal with the former CEO. Kozlowski had agreed to pay approximately $21.2 million to pay off his tax liabilities related to New York income and sales taxes. Kozlowski had also agreed to pay $97.7 million in restitution. The dismissed charge came after Kozlowski had already liquidated $125 million in assets to pay for the penalties and fines.[77]

In May 2007, Tyco agreed to pay almost $3 billion to settle investor-based class-action lawsuits against the firm. This amount is considered the largest ever spent to settle a class-action shareholder lawsuit. After the announcement, the stock price went up 19¢ to $32.38. The stock price had reached a low of $6.98 during the scandal in July 2002.[78] In July 2007, PwC agreed to pay Tyco investors $225 million to settle their legal claims.

In April 2009, Kozlowski and Swartz submitted their appeal to the U.S. Supreme Court to overturn their fraud convictions. Both claimed that they were not privy to evidence that was used against them during their trial.[79] In June 2009, Kozlowski and Swartz's appeals were rejected by the U.S. Supreme Court.[80] In July 2009, Kozlowski and Swartz agreed they would not take positions of officer or board member on any publicly traded company.[81] In December 2010, Kozlowski was ordered by a federal judge to forfeit his compensation and benefits that he had earned from 1995 to 2002 to Tyco, which had been requesting that Kozlowski repay the company the $505.8 million that he had accumulated over that time frame.[82] On August 10, 2012, Dennis Kozlowski and Tyco agreed to settle the long-standing dispute over whether the former CEO had to return $505.8 million in compensation and benefits. The terms of the settlement were not initially disclosed. Tyco's claim was based on the decision by U.S. District Judge Thomas Griesa, who ordered that Kozlowski must return all of his compensation and benefits he received from September 1995 to 2002.[83] On January 17, 2014, Dennis Kozlowski was released from prison.[84] Now living in a modest two-bedroom rental with a shower curtain from Bed Bath & Beyond, Kozlowski, married to his third wife, Kimberly, admitted, "I was piggy. . . . I'd go to Harvard Business School and get a standing ovation when I was introduced as the highest-paid C.E.O. in the country. . . . But, I'm not that person anymore."[85]

Questions for Thought

1. What do you think Kozlowski's motivation was for trying to evade sales taxes on his art purchases? Explain.

2. Explain the concept of *commingling assets* with respect to the Tyco case.

3. Would it have been possible for the board of directors to see the adjustments taking place in the many different programs at Tyco? Explain.

4. Is it realistic, in your mind, that the auditors could have missed such blatantly fraudulent transactions? Explain.

22

Olympus: A Corporate Governance Picture That Was Out of Focus

O n October 14, 2011, British-born Michael Woodford, CEO of Olympus, was fired after the firm's board of directors unanimously voted for his dismissal. Olympus is a Japanese company that is well known for cameras, but the company also produces products such as medical imaging equipment. Woodford had worked at Olympus for 30 years, starting as a junior salesman selling surgical instruments. Woodford's tenure as CEO barely lasted half a year because he was only promoted to CEO in April 2011. Woodford's vision was to not keep the status quo at Olympus but to shake up the organization. Although Japanese firms tend to focus on harmony and consensus in making strategic decisions, Woodford wanted to challenge the current mind-set of the Olympus executives by playing devil's advocate, forcing the executives to justify their decisions. It appeared that Woodford's rebel-like nature was his ultimate downfall because he wanted to make quantum adjustments in the corporate culture at Olympus. At the same time, the organization as a whole was resisting any change. Therefore, the initial justification of the firing of Woodward was that there was a disagreement between Woodward's view on the corporate culture and his management style.[1] In response to the firing, Tsuyoshi Kikukawa, the chairman of Olympus, stated that Woodford was not able to understand the way business had been done at Olympus for 92 years. Kikukawa also claimed that Woodford did not follow the proper chain of control and gave orders to lower-level employees without going through their supervisors. Woodford was warned that he was ignoring Olympus's organizational structure and that he needed to stop doing it. Woodford was told that even though he would no longer be CEO, he would still be a board member at Olympus.[2]

From the beginning of the controversy, however, Woodford claimed that he was not fired because of a disagreement over his management style or because of his vision to change the firm's corporate culture.

The Acquisitions

Woodford stated that he was fired for challenging Olympus officials to explain a story that was published in a Japanese financial magazine, *Facta*, in July 2011 that claimed that Olympus paid exorbitant premiums on four acquisitions that occurred between 2006 and 2008. When asked by Woodford to explain the story, the Olympus executives told Woodford that he was too busy to worry about it and that the Olympus executives would address the issue. For one acquisition of a UK medical equipment company, Gyrus ACMI, Woodford discovered that Olympus paid $687 million in advisory fees to a Cayman Islands–based company, Axam Investments, that did not have any ties to Olympus. The amount of the fees was equivalent to approximately one third of the total acquisition price of $2.2 billion.[3] In the other three acquisitions, Olympus bought a plastic medical-waste disposal company called Altis; a company that makes microwave cookware called New Chef; and the third company, called Humalabo, that was in the mail-order cosmetics business. Acquisitions have long been considered a part of sound corporate strategy, though companies usually select acquisitions that are related to their core business. The Olympus acquisitions, however, were not related at all to Olympus's core of developing products that use lens and camera-like devices. When acquisitions are unrelated, there is no chance for the firm to develop synergistic links between the different divisions based on such factors as similar customers or products. Despite their unrelatedness, Olympus put a value of $912 million on the purchase of these small unfamiliar firms that were not listed on a stock exchange. The premium paid for the acquisitions was supported by Olympus writing down the values of the companies from 68 to 83% one year after the acquisition took place.[4] On October 18, 2011, Kikukawa admitted to paying a high advisory fee for the Gyrus acquisition but refuted Woodford's estimates. Kikukawa claimed that Olympus "only" paid about one half of the $687 million ($390 million) that Woodford had claimed went to Axam Investments for advisory fees. Other Olympus executives had stated that the initial agreement was to pay the advisor $5 million and 1% of the value of the acquisition. This amount was renegotiated upward after many rounds, yet there did not appear to be any additional benefit for Olympus to agree to pay such a high fee.[5] The following day, Olympus reversed its course and agreed with Woodford's figure of $687 million being paid to advisors for the Gyrus acquisition. Olympus's response to the fee controversy was that it had performed the proper due diligence on the acquisition.[6]

The Ramifications of the Firing

Less than a week after Woodford was fired, Nippon Life and Harris Associates demanded an explanation from Olympus for the advisory fees paid for the acquisition. As two of the largest shareholders of Olympus—Nippon owned 8.26% of the stock, and Harris Associates owned a 4% share—both companies demanded accountability from Olympus's executives and board members. Furthermore, the Tokyo Stock Exchange, which trades Olympus shares, ordered the company to explain the advisory fees because the average amount of advisory fees is 1% of the acquisition price.[7]

Questions were also raised about the level of corporate governance at Olympus. A very firm "friendly" board had 12 of the 15 members being Olympus executives who were loyal to Kikukawa. In addition, a large percentage, 60% of the total shares, was held by Japanese corporations that believe that tradition and stability are needed by the board members. Within a week, the Olympus stock share price had fallen by 41%.[8]

On October 20, 2001, Olympus agreed to set up a third-party committee to investigate the acquisition. The probe was to be responsible for understanding how these fees were created and accepted as part of the negotiation. Olympus finally agreed to the probe, bowing to the increased pressure by major stockholders demanding transparency and objective information on how decisions were made during the acquisition process.[9]

On October 24, 2011, Kikukawa lashed out at Woodford in a memo posted on the firm's internal website. Kikukawa called Woodford's questioning of the acquisitions aberrant and unforgivable, and Kikukawa accused Woodford of using the controversy to try to consolidate his power base with top executives so they could force Kikukawa to resign. In addition, Kikukawa concluded that Woodford did not like Japan because he was always flying in his private jet to different countries in Europe and to his home in the United Kingdom.[10] On the same day, the Federal Bureau of Investigation (FBI) announced it was starting an investigation of the transactions that took place at Olympus. The U.S. link with the investigation was that the company that owns Axam Investments is Axes Americas, a securities firm based in the United States.[11]

On October 26, 2011, Kikukawa announced his resignation as president and chairman of Olympus. Kikukawa was not at the news conference when his resignation was announced. He was replaced by Shuichi Takayama who had been at Olympus for 41 years. Takayama stated that Kikukawa had acted appropriately during the acquisition process.[12]

The Cultural Treatment of Due Diligence

The Japanese culture is steeped in traditions and customs. Along with harmony and consensus is the belief that trust is enough for due diligence. Although U.S. investors expect and demand objective due diligence in any action committed by management and the board, the Japanese philosophy is that the due diligence has been done before the decision has been made. By trusting the relationship the managers have with each other and fostering a trusting relationship with other stakeholders, Japanese managers believe that trust will "guarantee" that the correct actions are taken.

In addition, a quirk in the Japanese corporate governance system occurred during the 1990s when aggressive deal making took place by Japanese firms. Small Japanese shareholders, including some individuals with alleged ties to organized crime, basically extorted money from the companies at their annual shareholders meetings. The individuals threatened to challenge and dispute the meeting unless they were given money to keep quiet. The result was that a culture developed in which managers were never challenged, even by stockholders, at their annual meeting.[13]

The Truth Starts Coming Out

On November 8, 2011, Olympus finally admitted that the payments were not for advisory fees. Actually, Olympus had incurred decades of investment losses and used a number of acquisitions to "write off" the losses by writing down the acquisition's goodwill after the purchases had taken place. Takayama admitted that Olympus had carried out accounting practices that were not appropriate. Takayama accused former chairman Kikukawa, Vice President Hisashi Mori, and Corporate Auditor Hideo Yamada of committing the fraud and disclosed that he did not know of the scheme to cover up the losses until the previous day when Mori admitted the scheme to him. Olympus had used the scheme to cover up investment losses that had started in the 1990s. The amounts from the losses were calculated and then funneled through the funds that were used for the acquisitions. The money was written off when the value of the acquisitions was reduced once Olympus had acquired them.[14]

The Use of Tobashi

The use of the tobashi procedure to write down trading losses is not a new one. This was a common occurrence in the early 1990s in Japan. Japanese companies would hide bad loans or they would divest unwanted stock through the practice of "tobashi." *Tobashi*, which in Japanese means "fly away," was used to "clean up" the financial statements of Japanese corporations. Tobashi usually involves transferring assets that have lost significant value to shell companies. By transferring the money-losing assets, the losses "fly away." Olympus would transfer the trading losses by pretending they were paying a premium on these different acquisitions. Olympus paid substantially higher advisory fees and other payments in the four acquisitions to cover up the losses. Approximately $2.6 billion in losses were hidden by making money "transfers" between Olympus and various clients.[15]

How the Fraud Occurred

Olympus had numerous securities that had lost significant value. By the late 1990s, the loss on the securities was more than $1 billion, and there was going to be a change in the accounting procedure by the Japanese government that would require the disclosure and writing off the losses. Olympus transferred the devalued securities assets at original cost to shell companies that did not appear to be affiliated with Olympus but were actually controlled by Olympus. The goal was that the gradual transfer of these bad assets would allow Olympus time to try to recoup the losses from other avenues. The first tobashi transfer occurred in 1998 when Olympus set up the company called Central Forest Corp. in the Cayman Islands. Olympus had deposited 21 billion yen (approximately $210 million) in Japanese government bonds in a bank in Liechtenstein. Olympus then asked the bank to lend Central Forest Corp. 18 billion yen (approximately $180 million) with the government bonds being used as the collateral. Central Forest Corp. planned to use the money to buy the bad assets from Olympus so they would no longer be on the balance sheet at Olympus. Olympus officials misled the bank by claiming that this financial arrangement was set up in this particular manner because Olympus wanted to make some secret acquisitions in Europe and did not want its competitors to know its actions.[16]

Olympus officials decided to close down the transfer of funds through two major initiatives. The first was acquiring the three small Japanese companies: Altis, Humalabo, and New Chef. Olympus paid the premium price for the three and wrote most of the acquisition amount off the following year, then repaid the outstanding loans it had set up with the Liechtenstein bank. Olympus did not pay the full amount of these acquisitions. The additional amount above the real market value of the acquisitions was transferred to an off–balance sheet subsidiary controlled by Olympus. For example, if a company was worth $50 million, Olympus paid $100 million, of which $50 million went to the owners of the acquisition and $50 million was transferred to the off–balance sheet subsidiaries. Olympus then wrote down the value of the acquisition to its correct amount of $50 million, so the asset value was shown correctly on the Olympus balance sheet and the transaction recorded for the off–balance sheet subsidiaries was not disclosed in the financial statements.[17]

The other initiative was to write off the remaining losses by using the $687 million in fees that corresponded with the Gyrus acquisition. The firm Axes America, which received the advisory fees, was owned by Hajime Sagawa who was a "partner" with Olympus in setting up the fraud from the beginning.[18] Again, Olympus wrote off the advisory fees, which are considered an acquisition-related cost and are included in the value of the acquisition. Therefore, the fees could be written off the following year so that the true value of the acquisition could be presented on the balance sheet. The reason why these initiatives raised red flags in the *Facta* article was the sheer size of the payments. The reason why these payments were so large is because Olympus was running out of time. Japanese accounting standards had changed. In the past, shell and off the balance sheet subsidiaries were not required to be consolidated into Olympus's main financial statements. This policy changed because of Enron. As was the case at Olympus, Enron used off–balance sheet subsidiaries to "dump" liabilities and have more "attractive" yet less accurate financial statements. This practice was outlawed in the United States with the passage of the Sarbanes-Oxley Act in 2002. In Japan, reform of this activity took much longer. The off–balance sheet transfers were no longer going to be a viable outlet for Olympus to manage its losses because Japanese accounting standards changed starting in 2008. In 2008, Japanese firms were required to consolidate any shell and off–balance sheet subsidiaries into their corporate financial statements. As a result, Olympus had to "dump" the remaining losses as quickly as possible. Olympus had to have a clean slate financially by 2008 or else Olympus officials would have to disclose all of the previous transfers used to cover up the losses.[19]

Rotten to the Core

On December 6, 2011, the outside panel appointed by Olympus to understand the cause and scope of the scandal released its report, which summarized Olympus's top executives as "rotten to the core." The panel found that Olympus officials had gone to several banks and asked them to submit incomplete financial statements pertaining to Olympus to Olympus's auditors. The cover-up included at least $1.7 billion of trading losses that were hidden. The report states that Olympus had told the banks that they were to refuse KPMG's request to verify the collateral for the loans given to Olympus because the collateral was being used to secure loans used to cover up the losses.[20] In addition, the panel found the origin of the trading losses actually started in the 1980s when the Japanese yen started to rise sharply against world currencies. The Olympus president at the time started an aggressive speculative investment strategy that became the cornerstone of its strategy. Olympus traded in highly speculative currency transactions. When the yen started to fall in the early 1990s, Olympus was caught with significant losses in currency trading transactions. To "recover" the losses, Olympus started to invest in highly speculative and complex financial instruments that were considered extremely risky. By June 1993, the financial losses from the risky financial asset instruments were significant, and the new president at Olympus tried to shift to more traditional businesses, but the losses were too large. The losses continued to spiral, but to "save face," Olympus officials did not want to acknowledge the losses publicly.[21]

The panel described the corporate culture at Olympus as opaque and lacking any corporate governance. The panel's report described top-level managers as a one-man system in which no one could challenge or object to the president. Olympus had a history of presidents who did not believe in the virtues of transparency or good corporate governance; the employees' sense of duty was to the president and not the stockholders. Only this type of laissez-faire attitude toward checks and balances could have allowed this type of fraud to occur for decades. The panel concluded that it appeared that the top-level executives at Olympus did not care and were not concerned with the fraud that was taking place. The belief system of the executives was based on following through with any actions that would avoid trouble and mind their own business by focusing on their own jobs and responsibilities. The panel concluded the report by stating Olympus needed to remove its malignant tumor (its top-level executives) and reinvent itself as a new company.[22]

On February 28, 2008, the board discussed the acquisition of the three nonrelated businesses. One director stated that the medical-waste company (Altis) could be an interesting opportunity, but the other two firms did not fit Olympus's overall corporate strategy. Executive Vice President Mori argued that all three companies had to be bought together as a "set" because they were all owned by the same shareholder. When another board member asked about the price, Mori stated that Olympus would eventually list all the three firms to be sold at a later time. Mori also stated that the board needed to act quickly on the acquisitions because there could be possible rival bids for the three companies.[23]

In a fine twist of irony, the two masterminds of the fraud, Yamada and Mori, were also responsible for overseeing Olympus's whistle-blowing hotline. The hotline system was designed to receive calls, letters. and e-mails from employees about potential ethics violations. Although approximately two thirds of major Japanese companies had their whistle-blowing systems outsourced to third parties, Yamada, who was heading the division responsible for the whistle-blowing system, opposed the idea of moving the system outside of Olympus because he considered it unnecessary. To further reduce the effectiveness of the hotline, the whistle-blower system would not accept anonymous tips. Olympus would ask the employee to identify him or herself if the tip required an investigation. One example of the impact of this requirement was that an employee had used the whistle-blowing system to notify Olympus of potential ethical violations by employees using fake vouchers. When the employee was requested to identify himself, he withdrew his statement. Another example was an employee who had used the system to complain about the behavior of his boss. The boss was hiring away employees from a client, which the employee thought was inappropriate. When the employee notified the hotline, the employee was reassigned and harassed by managers.[24]

Where Were the Auditors?

KPMG Azsa signed off on the financial statements in March 2009 even though KPMG disagreed with Olympus about the treatment of the Gyrus acquisition. After being challenged by KPMG, Olympus hired Ernst & Young ShinNihon as its new external auditor. It is not known what information was transferred to Ernst & Young. However, under Japan's accountancy rules, when a new auditor is hired, the auditor must ask the previous auditor 13 clearly defined questions that include whether the auditor had a dispute with the firm over the handling of any transaction or account.[25]

KPMG had a long history with Olympus, having been Olympus's auditor for 35 years when KPMG was replaced by Ernst & Young. During its tenure, KPMG appeared to have battled with Olympus on many occasions about transactions related to the fraud. In May 2009, KPMG had objected to Olympus's accounting interpretation of how the suspected acquisition would be recorded on Olympus's financial statements. In fact, KPMG had recommended that the top-level managers at Olympus step down, and KPMG officials threatened to take their suspicions to Japanese authorities if something was not done by Olympus. KPMG eventually agreed to sign off on the financial statements when Olympus agreed to accept a write-down of 71 billion yen (approximately $710 million) on acquisitions that were questionable from KPMG's perspective.[26]

The Aftermath After the Report

On December 21, 2011, Japanese authorities raided the corporate headquarters of Olympus in Tokyo. Authorities also raided the house of former President Kikukawa as well as the offices of three of the acquisitions under investigation: Humalabo, Altis, and New Chef.[27] Former CEO Woodford attempted to gather support from executives within and external to Olympus so he could return as CEO with a new management team. Because of the lack of support from Japanese institutional investors, his attempt failed, but he did file a lawsuit against Olympus for unlawful dismissal. He sought damages equal to the remaining 3 years of his contract and additional damages.[28] On January 10, 2012, Olympus filed a lawsuit against 19 current and former Olympus executives and board members for approximately $47 million for their role in the fraud. President of Olympus Takayama was one of the 19 people being sued by Olympus, but none of the 19 have been fired by Olympus.[29]

On January 17, 2012, Olympus announced that the external auditors, KPMG and Ernst & Young, were not negligent in their review of Olympus's financial statements but that Olympus's internal auditor should have seen the cues to become suspicious of the fraudulent transactions. The internal or statutory auditors are nonvoting members of the Olympus board of directors who are responsible for the internal evaluation of the financial transactions executed by the firm. Statutory auditors are usually former executives of the firm and independent outsiders.[30]

Olympus estimated that five current and previous statutory auditors at Olympus are liable for $109 million in damages.[31]

In another ironic twist, the statutory auditors are the individuals within Olympus who have the authority to sue the 19 current and former executives. As a result, the statutory auditors are suing the executives, and Olympus is accusing the statuary auditors of negligence.[32] On February 16, 2012, seven people were arrested in connection with the Olympus fraud. Former chairman Kikukawa, former executive vice president Mori, and former internal auditor Yamada were arrested, along with four people outside of Olympus. The four people included two who ran one of the shell companies and two bankers with links to the shell company who worked with Olympus setting up the financing of the fraud.[33] On February 27, 2012, Olympus announced its new top managers by selecting Yasuyuki Kimoto as chairman and Hiroyuki Sasa as president. Kimoto was a former director of Olympus's main lender Sumitomo Mitsui Bank, and Sasa was the head of Olympus's medical equipment marketing division. There were concerns from investors that Olympus did not make the fundamental change in its top management team that many financial experts expected. Of the 15 new directors and one auditor on the board, 11 members will be external outside members.[34]

On March 7, 2012, Japanese prosecutors filed charges against Olympus and six people, including three former Olympus executives. The company and the individuals were charged with violating Japanese law by creating and submitting falsified financial statements from 2006 to 2008. The three former Olympus executives, former chairman Kikukawa, former executive vice president Mori, and former internal auditor Yamada, were also arrested for inflating the asset value of the company from 2008 to 2010. If found guilty, Olympus could be fined as much as $17.3 million, and the individuals could be sent to prison for as long as 15 years or be fined approximately $185 thousand.[35] On September 25, 2012, all three pleaded guilty to the charges. They could face as many as 10 years in jail each and a fine of as much as $128,000 each.[36]

On December 20, 2012, the FBI arrested Chan Ming Fon for conspiracy to commit wire fraud for his involvement in using shell corporations to hide hundreds of millions of dollars in assets. It was alleged that in exchange for hiding the assets, Chan was paid more than $10 million.[37] On July 3, 2013, a court in Tokyo convicted former Olympus chairman Tsuyoshi Kikukawa, former auditor Hideo Yamada, and executive vice president Hisashi Mori of falsifying financial statements and gave them a three-year suspended sentence. The Tokyo District Court also ordered Olympus to pay the equivalent of $7 million in fines.[38] On September 18, 2013, Chan Ming Fon pleaded guilty to conspiracy to commit wire fraud and told the court, "I acknowledge that my conduct was wrong."[39]

Questions for Thought

1. If Olympus is found guilty, will the fine of $17.3 million be enough? Why or why not?

2. Ethics hotlines can be an effective resource for identifying unethical actions in a company. Why, in your opinion, did Olympus allow the hotline to be run internally?

3. Japanese culture seems to play a large role in this case. Explain the concept of *due diligence* and how it differs in American culture.

4. What stakeholders are affected in this case, other than the shareholders?

23

Wal-Mart: But We Do Give Them a 10% Employee Discount

Wal-Mart began as a simple dream by its founder, Sam Walton, to provide low prices for customers every day. That philosophy has taken Wal-Mart from one pre-Wal-Mart 5-and-10-cent store in Bentonville, Arkansas, to the first Wal-Mart, which opened in Rogers, Arkansas, in 1962, to the largest retailer in the world with an annual revenue in 2011 of almost $447 billion.[1,2,3] In 2005, Wal-Mart was the largest company in any industry in the world based on revenue, but slipped to number two in 2006 and again in 2011, when Exxon/Mobil took over the number one position.[4] Wal-Mart, which employs more than 2 million associates worldwide, expects fiscal year 2012 sales to be approximately $444 billion, thanks to the more than 200 million customers and members who visit, every week, Wal-Mart's 10,300 stores under 69 banners in 27 countries and the company's e-commerce websites in 10 countries.[5] However, in 2011, Wal-Mart came in last in the American Customer Satisfaction Index (ACSI), an annual survey conducted by the researching firm ACSI, and in a 2011 Harris Poll, only 37% of Wal-Mart customers reported having a high degree of satisfaction (Extremely/Very Satisfied) with their experience.[6,7]

Walton's vision and beliefs remain the cornerstone of Wal-Mart's business philosophy. However, the Southern "good old boy" culture cultivated in rural Arkansas has created a number of 21st-century problems for the company.

Off-the-Clock Work

In 2000, Wal-Mart settled a class-action lawsuit in Colorado for $50 million when 69,000 current and former Wal-Mart employees claimed that they worked for Wal-Mart without receiving any compensation. The lawsuits continued in August 2001, when additional lawsuits were filed against Wal-Mart for refusing to pay overtime to workers and failing to compensate workers when they worked during their scheduled breaks. Eleven states had lawsuits pending pertaining to Wal-Mart employees not being paid for their work. The lawsuits alleged that Wal-Mart forced the workers to work "off the clock" by requiring them to punch out with their time cards, yet told them they had to continue to work.[8] By June 2002, the number of states that had off-the-clock lawsuits against Wal-Mart had risen to 28. One employee in Kansas City, Missouri, Verette Richardson, had clocked out and was walking to her car when her manager ordered her to go back into the store and straighten up some merchandise in the apparel department. Richardson spent the next hour, without pay, getting the inventory back in order. In other incidents, Richardson was ordered to corral the shopping carts in the parking lot after she had clocked out.[9]

One complaint that the Wal-Mart employees had was the lock-in procedure managers would use at night. The managers would lock the doors after the store had closed and force the workers to stay in the store until all the work had been completed. The managers justified the lock-in procedure as a method used to try to reduce inventory theft but claimed that all employees were paid during the lock-in. However, many of the employees had stated that they had already clocked out when the lock-in took place. An example of the potential problems of a lock-in occurred in a Sam's Club in Corpus Christi, Texas. An employee's ankle was injured by some heavy machinery, but the employee was not allowed to leave the store. The manager was not in the store with the keys, and the employees had been told not to use the fire exit unless there was a fire or else they would be dismissed. Other personal emergencies such as a woman going into labor or a natural disaster such as a hurricane could greatly hamper the potential for an employee to leave the store quickly.[10]

The common philosophy of the store managers was that employees could not leave their positions until the work was finished, and if the employees could not complete that work in an 8-hour shift, then the employees must use their own unpaid time to complete their work. If they did not complete their daily tasks, the employees feared that they would be disciplined the next day by the manager. Employees were told they had to clock out so overtime pay would not show up on the store reports. In addition, 12 Wal-Mart employees, including 4 employees who worked in Wal-Mart's payroll department, stated that managers would come in and delete overtime hours from the worker's time cards so Wal-Mart would not have to compensate them for the additional time worked.[11] A deposition given by a senior payroll executive at Wal-Mart revealed that corporate headquarters gives the store managers a target total payroll expense and each store must be below the target amount. If the store goes over the target payroll expense, the store manager is disciplined and could be demoted or eventually dismissed from Wal-Mart. In addition, the Wal-Mart handbook stated explicitly that overtime pay would not be given to employees except during the busy Christmas season.[12]

Another common practice that Wal-Mart managers used was the "one-minute clock-out." This practice occurred when Wal-Mart employees failed to clock back in after their lunch. Managers clocked out the employees 1 minute after their lunch breaks began. As a result, the employees did not receive any payment for the hours worked after lunch, which could result in nonpayment of 4 hours or more per day for each employee. Wal-Mart responded by stating that it had broadcast a video to managers in April 2003 explaining to them that one-minute clock-outs would not be allowed. If the employee failed to clock back in, it was up to the manager to determine the number of hours the employee would get paid for that day.[13]

Wal-Mart's corporate objective was to keep its labor cost at 8% of sales, which were lower than the industry average of 9% to 10% in 2004. In addition, corporate headquarters wanted the store managers to reduce labor costs by 0.2% to 0.3% annually. An additional way Wal-Mart reduced labor costs was to have the assistant managers take over the responsibilities of the regular employees once the employees reached their 40-hour limit. Because the assistant managers are not required to receive overtime and are required to work at least 48 hours a week, Wal-Mart can shift the burden of multiple tasks to the assistant managers without any additional costs. In 2010, an assistant manager might work as many as 75 hours a week.[14] Wal-Mart's official response was that it has a strong policy that does not allow off-the-clock work, which is explicitly stated in the Wal-Mart handbook. Wal-Mart officials described the off-the-clock problem as minimal and isolated, and quickly corrected whenever it was brought to the attention of Wal-Mart management. In addition, officials stated that managers who force off-the-clock work will be disciplined and possibly dismissed.[15] Wal-Mart officials stated that off-the-clock work is in direct violation of the company's official policy and is against the law. On December 20, 2002, a jury in Portland, Oregon, found Wal-Mart guilty of not paying its employees overtime when it was due.[16] In 2009, a federal jury found that Wal-Mart forced Oregon employees to work unpaid overtime between 1994 and 1999, after more than 400 employees from 24 of Wal-Mart's 27 Oregon stores sued the retailer for violating federal and state wage laws.[17]

On October 13, 2006, Wal-Mart was found guilty of violating Pennsylvania labor laws by requiring its employees to work through rest breaks and off the clock. The jury in Philadelphia stated that Wal-Mart must pay its employees $78.5 million to settle the class-action lawsuit. The lawyer for the plaintiffs also stated that the employees would seek an additional $62 million from Wal-Mart because the jury found that Wal-Mart was acting in bad faith. Each plaintiff from the lawsuit was expected to receive from $50 to a few thousand dollars in the settlement. During the closing arguments of the trial, Wal-Mart attorney Neal Manne stated that Wal-Mart thought a lot of its employees and that they had missed their breaks or had a shorter break because of their own personal choices.[18] Evidence during the trial included computer records that showed that Wal-Mart employees in Pennsylvania had missed 33,000,000 rest breaks from 1998 to 2001.[19]

On January 25, 2007, Wal-Mart agreed to pay $33.5 million in back wages and accumulated interest to settle a lawsuit that claimed that Wal-Mart had violated federal overtime laws for 86,680 of its workers. The claims in the lawsuit included Wal-Mart's failing to pay time and a half to nonmanagement employees who had worked more than 40 hours a week. The federal lawsuit also claimed that Wal-Mart had violated the Fair Labor Standards Act by not including bonuses and geographical differences when calculating the time-and-a-half rate for its workers. The average payout to the more than 86,000 employees was $375. Seventy-five employees received more than $10,000, and the highest amount given was $39,775.[20]

In December 2008, Wal-Mart agreed to pay a settlement of $54.25 million to approximately 100,000 current and former employees who worked in various Minnesota Wal-Mart and Sam's Club stores. The judge ruled that Wal-Mart had failed to follow state laws regarding rest breaks and other wage-related rules more than 2,000,000 times from September 1998 to November 2008. Wal-Mart also agreed to develop and maintain an electronic tracking system to ensure it complies with state labor laws.[21] At the end of December 2008, Wal-Mart settled 63 lawsuits in 42 states related to not paying employees for off-the-clock work. The total final payment was approximately \$640 million. Wal-Mart's response was that this was a settlement of Wal-Mart's actions long ago, and they do not represent Wal-Mart's current policies related to working off the clock.[22]

In December 2009, Wal-Mart agreed to pay 87,500 Massachusetts employees a total of \$40 million to settle claims that Wal-Mart had denied the employees legally required rest and meal breaks. Wal-Mart also allegedly manipulated the time cards of the employees and had refused to pay them overtime. The amount of the settlement per employee ranged from \$400 to \$2,500. This settlement came 3 months after Wal-Mart had settled with the state prosecutors in Massachusetts by paying \$3 million for not allowing employees proper meal breaks.[23]

Sexual Discrimination

In a lawsuit filed in 2001 in San Francisco, Wal-Mart was accused of sexual discrimination with regard to its promotion policies. The lawsuit was based on the fact that in 2001, female employees at Wal-Mart were 65% of the hourly workers, yet they comprised only 33% of the managers. The potential lawsuit included 700,000 female employees who had worked at Wal-Mart from 1996 to 2001. In addition, the lawsuit claimed that women employees were also discriminated against in their pay rates. The lawsuit alleged that female employees received \$1,150 per month, 6.2% less on average than their male counterparts for similar jobs. The lawsuit also claimed that female managers were paid less than males were. Female managers received an average yearly salary of \$89,280, \$16,400 lower than male managers. Another fact presented in the lawsuit was that 89.5% of the cashiers, 79% of the department heads, 37.6% of the assistant store managers, and 15.5% of the store managers at Wal-Mart were women. The official response from Wal-Mart was that it does not discriminate against anyone. Wal-Mart stated that women did not have a high percentage of management jobs because they did not have an interest in working in management-level jobs at Wal-Mart. The example Wal-Mart gave was that whenever there is a management training program, only 43% of the applicants are women. Wal-Mart officials did admit that the companywide posting of management positions started after plaintiffs' lawyers had complained that Wal-Mart did not give every employee the chance to apply for a management position, which the lawyers argued were usually given based on favoritism. On June 22, 2004, the sex discrimination lawsuit achieved class-action status and covered 1.6 million current and former Wal-Mart employees. It was the largest class-action sex discrimination lawsuit ever to be filed in the United States.[24]

Depositions given by Wal-Mart employees for the lawsuit showed that a manager told one woman that a man was promoted instead of a qualified woman because the man had to support his family. In another deposition, a manager in a South Carolina Wal-Mart told a woman that men are paid more because, according to the Bible, Adam was created before Eve.[25] One plaintiff in the lawsuit claimed that a store manager told her that men work at Wal-Mart for a career and women do not. In addition, the store manager told her that retail is just for housewives who want to make some additional money. Another plaintiff stated that when she asked to work in the hardware department, the male store manager said, "Why do you want to work in hardware? You are a girl. You are needed in toys." Other claims in the lawsuit included a stripper performing at a store meeting to celebrate the manager's birthday and management's calling the women employees "Janie Q" and "girl." Yet the executive vice president of human resources at Wal-Mart, Coleman Peterson, had warned members of the board of directors in 1999 that Wal-Mart was falling behind other companies in the number of women it promoted to managers. Peterson also told the board that Wal-Mart was behind the rest of the world when it came to the treatment of women.[26]

In April 2010, the federal appeals court allowed the sex discrimination lawsuit against Wal-Mart to proceed as a class-action lawsuit. Wal-Mart claims that the lawsuit is without merit because sexual discrimination is unique to the individuals and cannot be combined together as a homogenous group.[27] In December 2010, the U.S. Supreme Court agreed to hear Wal-Mart's appeal of the lower court ruling. The Supreme Court agreed not to examine the pattern of alleged discrimination at Wal-Mart but instead agreed to examine whether the claims of more than a million people can be combined into a single class-action lawsuit.[28] In June 2011, the Supreme Court ruled that there are too many plaintiffs for the class-action lawsuit. The Court ruled in favor of Wal-Mart by deciding that the unique experiences of these 1,500,000 women cannot be combined into a single class-action lawsuit. Justice Antonin Scalia stated that it was not feasible for the women to sue pertaining to "millions of employment decisions" all at once.[29] In October 2011, current and former Wal-Mart employees in California filed a class-action lawsuit against Wal-Mart alleging discrimination. After the Supreme Court decision, the plaintiffs scaled down their lawsuit in hopes of supporting the argument that the patterns of discrimination are similar enough in the California stores to establish a class-action lawsuit. In this lawsuit, 90,000 women are represented who are former or current Wal-Mart employees.[30]

Health Benefits

In 2003, Wal-Mart's policy of lower costs in every part of its operation was highlighted based on the type of health benefits that it offered its employees. Wal-Mart made new employees wait half a year before they could enroll in the health benefits plan. Wal-Mart employees who had retired were no longer eligible to be part of the health benefits program. In some cases, the deductibles the employees had to pay for their health services went up to $1,000, which was three times the normal amount of deductibles. Wal-Mart's response was that employees can select the type of coverage they want. If they paid $13 every 2 weeks, then the deductible was $1,000. Employees willing to pay higher premiums had much lower deductibles.[31]

In 2002, the 500,000 employees covered by the plan cost Wal-Mart on average $3,500 per employee, which was 40% lower than the $5,646 average for all companies in the United States and 30% lower than the $4,834 average in the retail industry. In addition, Wal-Mart sent out teams of advisors who examined which network of doctors and hospitals has the lowest fees in every state. That program was abandoned in 2003 when an analysis showed that by having a national contract with Blue Cross and Blue Shield, Wal-Mart was able to further reduce its costs. Wal-Mart's response was that it offers health benefits to part-time workers, which some other retailers do not offer. In addition, Wal-Mart, like any other company, has tried to keep health-care costs under control. Wal-Mart also does not have a lifetime maximum, so if an employee or family member under the program has a long-term illness, he or she would also be covered under Wal-Mart's program.[32] On December 12, 2003, Susan

Chambers, who was the senior vice president of benefits and insurance for Wal-Mart, wrote a letter to the *New York Times* in which she stated that more than 90% of Wal-Mart employees have health coverage from either Wal-Mart's plan or their spouses' plans. A Wal-Mart employee can have individual health coverage starting at $15.25 every 2 weeks, and family coverage, regardless of the number of members in the family, starting at $66.25 every 2 weeks.[33]

In 2004, a survey done by the state of Georgia found that 10,000 children whose parents worked for Wal-Mart were part of the state health program for children. The cost to the state of Georgia was $10 million annually. A survey done at a hospital in North Carolina discovered that 16% of the 1,900 patients who worked for Wal-Mart had no health insurance coverage, and 31% of the patients were on Medicaid.[34]

On October 24, 2005, Wal-Mart announced that it would be offering a cheaper health insurance plan for its employees. The monthly premiums for the new plan would start at $11. Wal-Mart also announced that it would start a health savings account program called Value Plan for its workers. Wal-Mart stated that the new programs were in response to the feedback it had received from its employees, not from media criticism. Wal-Mart estimated that the monthly premiums for the employees would be between 40% and 60% lower than the previous health benefits program.[35] The following day, an internal memo authored by M. Susan Chambers, Wal-Mart's executive vice president for benefits, and sent to the board of directors explained how Wal-Mart could lower its health and benefit costs. Among the recommendations in the memo was for Wal-Mart to hire more part-time employees to try to discourage unhealthy people from applying at Wal-Mart. The memo recommended that all jobs at Wal-Mart should include some type of physical activity to weed out unhealthy applicants. Chambers also recommended in the memo that Wal-Mart should reduce the level of contribution in the employee's 401(k) retirement programs from 4% of wages to 3%. The memo stated that 46% of the children of Wal-Mart employees do not have health coverage at all or are covered by Medicaid. The memo also stated that 5% of all of Wal-Mart's employees were on Medicaid, which was higher than the average of 4% of all employees at companies with a national presence. In an interview in which Chambers was asked about the memo, Chambers stated that its purpose of was not to reduce costs for Wal-Mart but to recommend better options that could be available to employees by redirecting costs from one benefit area to another. One of the cost-cutting proposals made by Chambers was to reduce the time for a part-time employee to be eligible for health insurance from Wal-Mart from 2 years to 1 year. Another recommendation was to put health clinics in some of its stores to reduce the costs of employees' visits to emergency rooms.[36]

On January 12, 2006, the state legislature in Maryland passed legislation that would require Wal-Mart to increase the level of spending on its employees' health benefits program. The legislature overrode the veto of Maryland's governor, Robert Ehrich, who received $4,000 in reelection contributions from Wal-Mart, to pass the law. The law stated that any employer who has 10,000 or more employees in Maryland must spend at least 8% of payroll costs on employee health insurance. If it does not pay at least 8%, then the difference between the percentage paid and 8% would be given to Maryland's Medicaid fund.[37] On February 23, 2006, Wal-Mart announced that it would revise its health care programs to allow more employees to be eligible. Furthermore, Wal-Mart stated that it would reduce the 2-year eligibility waiting period for part-time employees to 1 year, and it would allow children of full-time and part-time workers to be eligible for coverage.[38] The children could be added to an employee's insurance plan for $15 a month, and Wal-Mart would provide a 10% employee discount on healthy foods sold at Wal-Mart and Sam's Club.[39]

On July 19, 2006, a federal judge in Baltimore ruled that the Maryland law, which had become known as the "Wal-Mart Tax," requiring Wal-Mart to provide more health care coverage was not valid. The judge ruled that the Maryland law was in violation of the federal law known as the Employee Retirement Income Security Act, or ERISA, which states that large companies are allowed to have uniform health care plans across the country.[40]

On January 11, 2007, Wal-Mart announced that the number of workers who had enrolled in the company's health plan had increased by 8%, or about 82,000 employees, from the fall of 2006. Wal-Mart identified the cause of the increase as the introduction of cheaper insurance policies. However, Wal-Mart did admit that even with the increased level of enrollment, only 47.4% of employees were receiving health insurance from Wal-Mart. Of those employees who were not covered by Wal-Mart's plan, 22.2% were covered by a spouse's plan, 3.1% were covered by either Medicaid or a state-sponsored plan, and 2.3% were covered through a military health insurance plan. For all of Wal-Mart's employees, an estimated 130,000 employees, or 10%, had no health insurance coverage under any plan. The lowest-price Value Plan insurance program costs $11 per month and covers three generic prescriptions and three doctor's visits before a deductible needs to be paid. The deductible is usually $1,000 for an individual worker and $3,000 for an employee's family. The average yearly salary of a Wal-Mart employee is less than $20,000.[41]

In January 2008, Wal-Mart announced that more than half, 50.2%, of employees had signed up for Wal-Mart's health insurance, and this number increased to 52% in 2009. Wal-Mart introduced a more flexible and generous health plan in which deductibles started at $350, and 2,400 generic prescription drugs could be bought at $4 per prescription. In addition, Wal-Mart stated that 92.7% of its employees belonged to some type of health insurance program.[42] In October 2011, because of rising costs, Wal-Mart announced that it had to reduce health care coverage for part-time workers and significantly increase the insurance premiums of many of the full-time employees. Part-time employees who worked less than 24 hours per week were no longer eligible for health insurance from Wal-Mart. Furthermore, new employees who averaged between 24 and 33 hours weekly would no longer be able to add a spouse to the Wal-Mart health insurance. Wal-Mart also informed smokers that it would cost them more for health insurance. Smokers who worked for Wal-Mart paid an additional $260 to $2,340 a year in health insurance premiums.[43] On October 7, 2014, Wal-Mart announced that it was going to end health insurance for some of its part-time associates. Approximately 30,000 employees who were working fewer than 30 hours per week were no longer eligible for health insurance from Wal-Mart. Sally Welborn, senior vice president of global benefits at Wal-Mart, stated, "We can't take our eyes off costs."[44]

The Role of Unions

A cornerstone of Wal-Mart's philosophy of "Everyday Low Prices" is to keep labor costs at the lowest level possible. As a result, Wal-Mart has always battled the efforts of its employees to become unionized. In February 2000, the meat department at a Wal-Mart in Jacksonville, Texas, became the one and only unionized operation within Wal-Mart in the United States. Two weeks after the union was formed, Wal-Mart disbanded the meat department in the Jacksonville store and 179 other stores by using prepackaged meat instead of butchers. On June 19, 2003, the National Labor Relations Board ruled against Wal-Mart for its handling of the meat department union in Jacksonville. The ruling ordered Wal-Mart to negotiate with the meat employees and the union about Wal-Mart's decision to phase out the meat department. In addition, the judge ordered Wal-Mart to bring back the meat department in the store until the negotiations had been completed with the employees and the union.[45]

From 1998 to 2002, the National Labor Relations Board filed more than 40 complaints against Wal-Mart for such illegal actions as firing employees who were union supporters and telling the employees that they would not receive any bonuses if they formed a union. By 2002, 8 of the 40 cases had been settled by Wal-Mart.[46]

In September 2012, Illinois and California workers at warehouses owned by Wal-Mart's parent company, Walmart, went on strike. In October 2012, approximately 60 Wal-Mart employees went on strike and fellow employees in other states quickly followed suit. The striking workers demanded that Walmart end retaliatory practices against employees who attempted to organize union membership. These alleged practices included harassment, cut hours, and other disciplinary actions. If the NLRB sides with the workers, Walmart may eventually be forced to pay a huge settlement in back pay.[47]

An example of the global measures that Wal-Mart uses to ensure a nonunionized workforce occurred when Wal-Mart entered the Canadian market in 1994. Wal-Mart bought 120 stores from the struggling Woolco retail store, a subsidiary of Woolworth's. Wal-Mart bought all of Woolco's nonunionized stores but none of the 7 unionized Woolco stores. Two former managers of the Canadian stores informed the corporate headquarters that union literature was given to the Canadian workers. That same day, two Wal-Mart specialists in labor relations were flown to Canada in one of Wal-Mart's company jets. It was later revealed that the labor relation experts visited stores considering unionization and showed anti-union videos to the employees in an attempt to convince the employees that the unions would have no benefit to them and would only cost them money in the form of union dues. In addition, the labor relations specialists attempted to determine which employees were pro union to discredit their efforts and even recommended the termination of the pro-union employees.[48]

Ten years later, the Quebec Labor Board certified the formation of a union at Wal-Mart's Jonquière, Quebec, store. Wal-Mart stated that it was disappointed that the company did not have an opportunity to express its views of unionization to the employees. Quebec law states that a union can be formed without an actual vote of the employees as long as a majority of employees sign union membership cards. A spokesman for Wal-Mart Canada, Andrew Pelletier, said that the results of a secret democratic vote on union membership failed 4 months before the certification.[49] The certification by the United Food and Commercial Workers Canada Union was the first step in trying to unionize now 241 Canadian stores. The union argued that the gap between union pay and Wal-Mart pay could range from C$10 to $20 per hour. Furthermore, the union argued that it would be available as a means to settle any disagreements that took place between the employees and management. Wal-Mart responded by stating that the pay gap was not that large and that Wal-Mart employees have the option of profit sharing, which could significantly increase the amount of pay given to the employees. Wal-Mart Canada also stated that whenever it opened a new store, it received 10 times more applications than job openings. In addition, Wal-Mart was ranked 14th in the listing of Canada's 50 best employers, published in *The Globe and Mail* newspaper.[50] Wal-Mart closed the Quebec store on April 29, 2005, before it could reach a collective agreement with the union. Wal-Mart said that it had been losing money since it had opened in 2001 and the financial performance was getting worse. In November 2009, the Supreme Court of Canada ruled that Wal-Mart was entitled to close the Quebec store in 2005. The court argued that no legislation can force a company to remain in business.[51]

In November 2004, Wal-Mart announced that it would allow trade unions in its Chinese stores. Wal-Mart's change of heart may have resulted from the pressure that was put on the company by the All-China Federation of Trade Unions, controlled by the government of China. However, Wal-Mart management still felt that the unions were not needed because the direct link between management and the workers was the best structure for the company.[52] On November 18, 2013, the National Labor Relations Board (NLRB) accused Wal-Mart of illegally disciplining and firing its employees over their actions in strikes and protests. In addition, the NLRB ruled that a Wal-Mart spokesman, David Tovar, unlawfully threatened employees on national television if they were part of a protest on Black Friday after Thanksgiving. Mr. Tovar stated on *CBS News*, "If associates are scheduled to work on Black Friday, we expect them to show up and to do their job, and if they don't, depending on the circumstances, there could be consequences."[53] Nineteen employees were fired by Wal-Mart for taking part in strikes and demonstrations against Wal-Mart. Wal-Mart stated that the firings were due to the employees breaking Wal-Mart's attendance policy.[54] On December 10, 2014, the NLRB ruled that Wal-Mart managers in California had illegally disciplined employees for striking. In its decision, the NLRB cited evidence that included the quote, "If it were up to me, I'd shoot the union" from a Wal-Mart manager.[55]

The Great Union Wall of China

As Wal-Mart expands internationally, it must address the issues of unions in every country in which it starts operations. However, Wal-Mart admits that China is a unique case. Wal-Mart's CEO at the time, Lee Scott, had constantly stated that China is the only other country in the world where Wal-Mart could effectively duplicate its U.S. strategy based on its population and geography. Furthermore, Wal-Mart purchased $18 billion in inventory directly from Chinese manufacturers in 2005, and a large percentage of its entire inventory made in China had been outsourced from other companies. The Chinese government advocates unions in privately held foreign companies such as Wal-Mart. The Chinese trade unions are unified under an umbrella organization named the All-China Federation of Trade Unions (ACFTU). The ACFTU is supported by the Chinese government and has links to the chairman of the Communist Party. In addition, Chinese law forbids companies from blocking or stopping employees from starting a union. Wal-Mart's biggest rival in China, Carrefour SA, is 70% unionized in China.[56] The power of the Chinese market was shown on August 9, 2006, when Wal-Mart announced that it would allow unions to be formed in all of its stores in China. Wal-Mart stated that it had formed an alliance with ACFTU to create a harmonious relationship with the employees. At the time of the announce-ment, Wal-Mart had 60 stores in China and employed 30,000 Chinese workers.[57] With the apparent thumping of Sam Walton rolling in his grave, on December 18, 2006, Wal-Mart announced that its Chinese employees had established a branch of the Communist Party at its Chinese headquarters.[58] This was quite a concession for a com-pany that is actively involved in the Students in Free Enterprise (SIFE) program, which encourages free enterprise education. Furthermore, Wal-Mart established a fellowship of SIFE faculty advisors named the Sam M. Walton Free Enterprise Fellows program.[59]

Use of Illegal Aliens

On October 24, 2003, agents from the U.S. Immigration Service raided 60 Wal-Mart stores in 21 states for suspected use of illegal aliens as the janitorial staff at Wal-Mart. Acknowledging Wal-Mart's "roll back the prices" marketing campaign, the name of the raid was called Operation Rollback. The janitors were hired by a third party to which Wal-Mart had outsourced janitorial responsibilities. The federal agents also seized doc-uments from Wal-Mart corporate headquarters in Bentonville, Arkansas. Even though a third party hired the illegal aliens, Wal-Mart was aware that illegal aliens were used to clean its stores. Wal-Mart's response was that it had specific requirements for every contractor it uses to employ only legal workers. The immigration agents arrested more than 250 workers as a result of the raids. Raids arresting illegal aliens had also taken place at Wal-Mart stores in 1998 and 2001, when approximately 100 workers who had been hired by contractors were arrested.[60] The results of those three raids were 13 fel-ony indictments and $5 million in fines for the two third-party contractors who had hired the illegal aliens. On November 9, 2003, nine illegal immigrants sued Wal-Mart, accusing the company and the contractors of failing to compensate for overtime and forcing them to work every night of the week.[61] Two days later, the nine illegal immi-grants filed a new lawsuit against Wal-Mart, which alleged that Wal-Mart was in direct violation of federal racketeering laws by agreeing with the contractors to not allow the workers to receive any overtime pay.[62]

In December 2003, Wal-Mart responded to the attacks by stating that the man-agers were aware of the illegal workers being used to clean the stores, but they were told by the government to continue to employ the workers until the government had completed its investigation of the contractors. Wal-Mart stated that it had been coop-erating with the government regarding the use of illegal workers and was waiting for the government's raid to stop using the workers through the contractors.[63]

On March 18, 2005, Wal-Mart agreed to settle the charges brought against the company for having illegal aliens clean its stores by paying a fine of $11 million. Wal-Mart was not charged with any criminal violations because it had cooperated with the government in the investigation. The settlement of $11 million was four times larger than the previous highest settlement given to the government by a corporation. Wal-Mart referred to the $11 million payment as a voluntary payment by Wal-Mart to help the government monitor violations of immigration laws.[64]

Child and Other Labor Laws

In March 2000, the state of Maine fined Wal-Mart more than $205,000 for violat-ing child labor laws in each of the state's 20 Wal-Mart stores. On January 13, 2004, the results of an internal audit at Wal-Mart showed that Wal-Mart's top executives had known since 2001 that they had violated child labor laws as well as state laws pertaining to time off for breaks and meals. The result of the audit that was done in July 2000 showed that in one week's time cards of Wal-Mart employees, there were more than 1,300 violations in which employees younger than 18 years old were working past midnight, were working during school hours, and were working more than 8 hours during a day. Wal-Mart's response was that the results were misleading because schools may have been closed on those days.[65]

On February 11, 2005, Wal-Mart agreed to pay $135,540 to settle charges of violating child labor laws in three states. The settlement of violations filed in Connecticut, New Hampshire, and Arkansas were based on having employees who were younger than 18 operating machinery that was dangerous, including chain saws and cardboard balers. One of the employees had injured his thumb when he used a chain saw to cut Christmas trees. As part of the settlement, Wal-Mart denied that it was involved in any wrongdoing with the actions of the employees.[66]

The one-week audit also showed that there were more than 60,000 violations of workers not taking their required breaks and more than 15,000 violations for workers not having any time off to have a meal. Wal-Mart responded by stating the results of the audit were not meaningful because the violations could have resulted from employees failing to clock in and out for breaks and meals. On December 22, 2005, a California jury awarded the plaintiffs of a class-action lawsuit against Wal-Mart $172 million as compensation for not being allowed to take their lunch breaks. The award included $57.3 million in general damages and $115 million in punitive damages. The plaintiffs were the 116,000 Wal-Mart employees in California. The jury decided that Wal-Mart was in direct violation of California law that required mandatory lunch breaks for all employees.[67] The lawsuit claimed that Wal-Mart had violated the mandatory lunch break law that states that every employee is entitled to 30 minutes for lunch if he or she works at least 5 hours. It was found that the break was denied more than 8,000,000 times from the beginning of 2001 until May 2005.[68]

On September 13, 2005, a labor advocacy group, the International Labor Rights Fund, filed a lawsuit against Wal-Mart for not enforcing the company's code of conduct with Wal-Mart's suppliers. The lawsuit claimed that Wal-Mart did not verify whether suppliers from five countries—Bangladesh, China, Indonesia, Nicaragua, and Swaziland—were in compliance with fair labor practices. The lawsuit claimed that factory workers in these five countries had experienced labor violations that included forced labor and nonpayment of work and overtime. The lawsuit also claimed that the suppliers obstructed any attempt to have unions formed in those factories.[69] In addition, the workers claimed that they were physically abused by the managers of the factories and were not able to leave the factories because the doors were locked. Wal-Mart responded by stating that it has the largest monitoring system for suppliers in the world. Wal-Mart has 200 full-time inspectors who visit as many as 30 factories a day. The inspectors are responsible for monitoring the activities of more than 5,000 factories. In 2004, Wal-Mart stated that it did not buy any goods from 1,200 of those factories for at least 90 days when inspectors found violations in the factories. Furthermore, more than 100 factories were banned permanently in 2004 for direct violations of child labor laws.[70] In November 2013, a Wal-Mart in Canton, Ohio, organized a food drive for its employees.

Storage containers were on display at the Wal-Mart with a sign that read "Please Donate Food Items Here, so Associates in Need Can Enjoy Thanksgiving Dinner."[71]

Wal-Mart Responds

As the pressure from Wal-Mart's stakeholders for the company to improve employee relations continued to rise, the largest retailer (Wal-Mart has always been the largest retailer but may not have been the largest company) in the world announced a new program called "Associates Out in Front." The managers at Wal-Mart agreed to meet with 10 rank-and-file workers every week from each of its 4,000 stores, to get employee feedback. In addition, workers who had been with Wal-Mart for more than 20 years received a special polo shirt. Furthermore, some employees were given a "premium holiday": Wal-Mart paid a portion of their health insurance premiums. Finally, to show its holiday spirit during the Christmas season, Wal-Mart allowed the employees to purchase one item at a 20% discount, twice their standard 10% employee discount.[72] On February 19, 2015, Wal-Mart announced that it would pay some of its U.S. employees at least $10 an hour by 2016, well above the federal minimum wage of $7.25. This action was taken due to a tightening labor market and more competition in the hiring of lower-wage employees. The pay rate of approximately 500,000 Wal-Mart and Sam's Club employees increased to $9 an hour in April 2015 and will rise to $10 an hour by February 2016.[73]

Questions for Thought

1. Are the ethical issues Wal-Mart faces really any different from those of other large retailers?

2. Wal-Mart management has stated that they don't feel women are interested in management positions at the company. Do you agree or disagree?

3. Wal-Mart is continually criticized for its health care policy. Is this really an ethical issue? Why or why not?

4. Should Wal-Mart be concerned about unionization of stores since allowing unionization of workers in China?

Cases

24

WorldCom: Can You Hear the Lawsuits Now?

From Humble Beginnings

In a coffee shop in Hattiesburg, Mississippi, in 1983, four men, including Bernard Ebbers, decided to form a long-distance telephone company called Long Distance Discount Service (LDDS). Their strategy was simple: They would acquire small "mom and pop" phone companies that had been created after the deregulation of the telecommunications industry and provide the service for a cheaper cost per minute to the customer. Within 2 years, Canadian-born Ebbers became the CEO of a company that became the second-largest telecommunications company in the United States by 2002, garnering more than 60 acquisitions along the way. Ebbers's acquisition strategy was based, in part, on his previous experience in the motel industry. He bought his first motel in 1974 in Columbia, Mississippi, and by the early 1980s, had built a portfolio of eight motels including a Hampton Inn and a Courtyard by Marriott.

Although born in Edmonton, Alberta, Ebbers had lived in California and New Mexico before settling down in Mississippi in the 1960s. After receiving a basketball scholarship, Ebbers enrolled in Mississippi College and graduated in 1967. He moved to Brookhaven, Mississippi, and moved up the ranks as a manager for a local garment manufacturer, working in the warehouse, before starting his motel empire. (Inside the WorldCom Scam. American Greed. CNBC.com)

In 1989, LDDS became a public company via its acquisition of Advantage Companies. In 1995, LDDS changed its name to WorldCom, and in 1997, Ebbers earned the nickname "Telecom Cowboy" for his bid to acquire one of the largest players in the telecommunications industry, MCI. A listing of some of the acquisitions made by Ebbers is shown in Table 1. WorldCom acquired MCI on November 7, 1997, for $37 billion.

Ebbers's Financial Problems

By 2000, Ebbers started to depend on financial support from WorldCom in the form of personal loans. In 2000, he needed to borrow more than $84 million from WorldCom to pay for the margin calls on WorldCom stock that fell from a high of $64.50 in June 1999 to $14 by the end of 2000. (Inside the WorldCom scam. American Greed. CNBC.com)

TABLE 1 ● Major Acquisitions of WorldCom
1989: Advantage Companies Inc. (LDDS becomes a public company)
1992: Advanced Telecommunications
1993: Resurgens Communications Group
1993: Metromedia Communications Corp.
1994: IDB Communication Group
1995: Williams Telecommunications Group
1996: MFS Communications Company
1996: UUNET Technologies Inc.
1997: MCI Communications
1998: Brooks Fiber Properties
1998: CompuServe Corp.
1999: Agree to merger with Sprint Corp. but was blocked by U.S. and European regulators
2001: Intermedia Communications

Source: Adapted from WorldCom Company Time Line, *Washington Post*, March 15, 2005, www.washingtonpost.com.

On February 1, 2002, Ebbers had to repay more than $180 million in loans from Bank of America and WorldCom, based on a $10 or less per share trigger price that had been set when he borrowed the money in 2000. Ebbers had borrowed the money to help cover a previous demand to put up additional collateral for WorldCom stock that he purchased on margin. When WorldCom's stock price hit $9.85 per share, Ebbers owned 27 million shares. The loans were equal in value to 18.3 million shares.[1]

Investors were concerned about the slowdown in growth of the telecommunications industry; they were also concerned about WorldCom's $28 billion in debt due to its aggressive acquisition strategy. But in response to rumors that WorldCom had potential accounting and financial problems in February 2002, Ebbers commented that there was no question that WorldCom was a viable company, even though it was considering writing down at least $15 billion to $20 billion in goodwill on the books based on numerous acquisitions.[2] One week after the announcement of the $180 million in loans, it was reported that Ebbers owed almost $340 million from margin calls, which was significantly higher than WorldCom's profit for that quarter, $258 million. WorldCom paid the $339.7 million that was due for repayment. *The Wall Street Journal* claimed that multiple loans from WorldCom to Ebbers totaling $340.8 million by 2002 could have been the largest amount ever to a top executive and was the largest in recent memory.[3]

Ebbers commented that he would not sell his 27,000,000 shares of stock but would sell other assets to pay off the debt.[4] WorldCom stock had dropped to the $7 to $10 range during the margin calls. On February 14, 2002, WorldCom suspended three employees and froze the commissions of at least 12 salespeople based on suspicions of false order booking. The sales managers improperly altered the commissions of their sales teams, which were used to evaluate the manager's performance. The sales teams included sales that had already been recognized by other units of the company. The legal counsel of WorldCom, Michael Salsbury, stated that there were just a few bad apples who knew how to manipulate the system. Ebbers claimed that WorldCom would be able to stand by its accounting.[5]

Securities and Exchange Commission's Investigation Starts

On March 11, 2002, WorldCom was notified that the Security and Exchange Commission (SEC) wanted information pertaining to specific accounting transactions and loans given by WorldCom to officers of the company. The SEC had asked WorldCom to voluntarily provide documentation pertaining to its results for the third quarter of 2000. The SEC was interested in examining WorldCom documents related to its wholesale accounts, sales commissions, disputed charges from customers, organizational charts, and an explanation of how it recognized goodwill. The SEC also wanted information pertaining to the loans made by WorldCom to its executives, how WorldCom was integrating its technology systems with MCI, and any state or federal government investigations that were being conducted on WorldCom.[6] This request came shortly after information about WorldCom's internal investigation of inappropriate booking of sales commissions and WorldCom's large personal loans to Ebbers were released to the public. From a high of more than $64 in June 1999, WorldCom's stock was now selling for less than $6.

In his response to the request by the SEC, Ebbers stated that he would be the first to tell the SEC if there were any issues that would be of concern.[7] After the request had been made, the large loan to Ebbers might have given the SEC the push it needed to establish an inquiry. WorldCom stated that the loan was in the company's best interest because Ebbers would have had to sell millions of shares of WorldCom stock to cover the margin call, which would have had a negative impact on WorldCom's stock price. However, a former SEC enforcement official, Seth Taube, stated that a large loan to a top executive of a company automatically raises a red flag for the potential conflict of interest and breakdown of the executive's fiduciary duty to the company's shareholders.[8]

Although the prevailing personal loan rates were between 9.75% and 16.67% in Jackson, Mississippi, when Ebbers received his loans, Ebbers's loan rate was 2.14% on a $198.7 million loan and an average of 2.16% on a loan of $142.1 million. For each percentage point that the loan was below the market rate, Ebbers reduced his interest amount by $3.4 million.[9] By receiving loans from WorldCom, Ebbers did not have to sell his assets to pay for his margin calls. These assets included a 164,000-acre ranch in British Columbia; a soybean farm in Louisiana; a yacht manufacturer in Savannah, Georgia; an investment in a refrigerated trucking company; and his 960-acre estate in Brookhaven, Mississippi.[10]

The Board Becomes Involved

The WorldCom board blocked Ebbers from selling shares when the margin call came in and the stock price was in the mid-20s. Ebbers could have paid off the debt by selling an estimated 18.3 million of his 27,000,000 shares at that time. However, Ebbers did not want to sell the stock and stated that he was waiting until the stock price went up again. In March 2002, a major strategy session was called by WorldCom for all top executives around the world. However, instead of presenting a clear vision of how WorldCom should change to reverse its decline, Ebbers talked about, in part, someone stealing coffee in the break room. It seemed that the CEO of WorldCom had matched the coffee filters with the bags of coffee, and at the end of the month, the number of filters was higher than the number of bags of coffee. One of the outcomes of the meeting was "Bernie's seven points of light," which included having the coffee bags counted, having someone check to make sure all the lights were off before the last person left the office, and increasing the thermostat in the summer by 4 degrees to reduce energy costs. Ebbers also ordered the installation of an outdoor video camera above the smoking area so a record could be made of how long the employees spent on cigarette breaks. Ebbers also stated that all purchases greater than $5,000 must have his approval and Ebbers must personally agree to all press releases.[11]

On April 4, 2002, it was announced that WorldCom would lay off 4% of its workforce, amounting to 3,700 employees. WorldCom stated that the layoffs were due to the slow-growing economy and excess capacity in the telecommunications industry.[12] In April 2002, WorldCom announced that Ebbers would not receive a 2001 bonus and his salary would remain unchanged at $1 million. The stock of WorldCom dropped to just above $4 as WorldCom adjusted projected sales figures from $22 billion to $21 billion for 2002 for the WorldCom Group unit. WorldCom also said it was going to review its external auditor because of the Enron scandal. WorldCom's auditor at the time was Arthur Andersen.[13]

On April 29, 2002, Ebbers was forced to step down as the CEO, president, and board member of the company he cofounded after outside board members could no longer accept a declining stock price, the continued negative publicity over Ebbers's personal loans, and the expanding scope of the SEC investigation of WorldCom. The closing price of WorldCom stock on the day of Ebbers's resignation was $2.35.[14]

A New CEO

When John Sidgmore took over as the new CEO of WorldCom, he had to try to determine the underlying value of the 78 companies that WorldCom had bought during Ebbers's tenure.[15] In addition, WorldCom's bonds that accounted for the debt of almost $30 billion had lost half of their value in the marketplace. Sidgmore stated the first goal was to reestablish creditability of WorldCom to investors and the public.[16] Sidgmore had been WorldCom's vice chairman in charge of WorldCom's Internet division, UUNet.

In May 2002, WorldCom stock was trading at less than $2 per share, and WorldCom's bond rating was reduced to "junk" status, meaning there was a high risk of a future default on the debt. Ebbers's personal loans from WorldCom now amounted to $408.2 million, including the interested assessed at 2.3%. Ebbers was to receive $1.5 million in yearly pension payments as part of his package, but the pension payments would stop if Ebbers defaulted on his WorldCom loans and declared personal bankruptcy. In addition, Ebbers would be given the title of chairman emeritus and would be allowed to use a WorldCom private jet for as many as 30 hours annually.[17]

On June 24, 2002, a negative report by Salomon Smith Barney helped push WorldCom's stock price to below $1. If stock stays below $1 for 30 consecutive days on the NASDAQ Stock Exchange, the stock becomes delisted.[18] WorldCom's probe found that expenses were improperly recorded as capital expenditures. The result was that WorldCom's cash flow and profit were artificially inflated for at least the previous five financial quarters. WorldCom should have actually had a net loss for the four quarters of 2001 and the first quarter of 2002 instead of the reported profit of $1.4 billion for the year in 2001 and $130 million for the first quarter of 2002. After that information was presented to WorldCom, the company's board of directors fired Scott Sullivan, WorldCom's chief financial officer, and David Myers, who was the senior vice president and controller for WorldCom. Arthur Andersen, WorldCom's auditor until May 2002, commented that Sullivan was responsible if there was inaccurate information in WorldCom's financial statements. WorldCom stated that it could not rely on Andersen audit reports to verify the information needed to investigate the inappropriate expense bookings. Andersen concluded that its audits complied with generally accepted accounting standards and were conducted in accordance with generally accepted auditing standards. KPMG took over as WorldCom's external auditor in May 2002. In summary of the new revelations, Lehman Brothers analyst Blake Bath said that this was the final straw for investors' confidence. WorldCom had violated the trust it had with the financial institutions with which it had dealings.[19]

Cynthia Cooper's Role

The fraud at WorldCom was actually discovered when WorldCom's vice president of internal auditing, Cynthia Cooper, did a spot check on the bookings of capital expenditures. WorldCom's new CEO, Sidgmore, asked her to examine the books as he tried to turn WorldCom around from the recent series of events.[20] Cooper found that one of the biggest expenses for WorldCom, charges paid to local telephone systems to complete phone calls, was not recorded as an expense but was recorded as a capital expenditure. This action broke one of the fundamental rules of accounting, which is that capital costs have to be associated with long-term investments and not current financial activities. In addition, a cost of an asset cannot be capitalized unless it is able to generate a value for the company in future periods. Sullivan had started this revised booking pattern at the start of 2001, and the net result was a huge increase in the level of profitability for WorldCom. Cooper contacted the chair of WorldCom's auditing committee, Max Bobbitt. Bobbitt met with Sullivan, who was reluctant to do anything to correct the actions. But Bobbitt notified WorldCom's new auditor, KPMG, of the issue. Cooper also stated that WorldCom's official course of events was not accurate. Cooper said that Sidgmore did not ask for a review of the books, but she took the initiative to examine the specific transactions of the capital expenditures account in May 2002. With the help of one of her subordinates, Gene Morse, Cooper reviewed thousands of transactions, often at night to avoid any suspicion from their superiors. Morse discovered an accounting entry for $500 million for computer expenses for which there were no supporting documents pertaining to the purchase. Morse thought this seemed to be a very large sum to be booked without any invoices or other written documentation. When Cooper, Morse, and a third internal auditor, Glyn Smith, dug deeper into the fraudulent transactions, they quickly realized that they needed to report their results to senior management as soon as possible. Sullivan was not interested in discussing it, and when Cooper and her colleagues went to WorldCom's external auditor at the time the transactions took place, Arthur Andersen, its response was to refuse to answer some of the questions from the internal audit team and that Andersen had approved the accounting methods used in the transactions.[21]

Cooper first realized that something was wrong with WorldCom's accounting in March 2002 when the head of WorldCom's wireless division, John Stupka, complained to Cooper that the $400 million he had reserved in the third quarter of 2001 to be used to cover nonpayment of customers was taken away from his division. A reserve for bad debts is a common and acceptable accounting practice in the telecommunications industry. Sullivan had informed Stupka that the wireless division was going to lose that money and that the $400 million would be used to increase the level of corporate income for WorldCom. Stupka had previously complained to Arthur Andersen about the transfer of the $400 million, and Andersen supported Sullivan's actions. Cooper felt that this transaction was not correct and also contacted Arthur Andersen. The response from one of the auditing partners was that Andersen reports directly to Sullivan and that Andersen did not believe that the $400 million reserve for bad debts was necessary.[22] Based on that response, Cooper gave the go-ahead for Morse to examine any transactions that could be in violation of accounting standards. On March 6, 2002, Cooper and Sullivan attended a board of directors audit committee meeting at which Cooper presented her concerns to the committee. Sullivan backed down from his support of the $400 million transfer. The following day, Sullivan tracked down Cooper by contacting her husband, who gave Sullivan Cooper's cell phone number. Sullivan told her not to interfere with the wireless division manager's business again.[23] That same day, March 7, 2002, the SEC notified WorldCom that it had filed a Request for Information, which is the starting point on the road to a formal inquiry. WorldCom's competitors, including AT&T, had complained to the SEC that they could not understand how everyone in the telecommunications industry was losing money in 2001 except WorldCom. In addition, after reviewing the public filing by WorldCom, the SEC could not understand how WorldCom's financial performance could be so superior to every other company. This raised suspicions to the point where the SEC requested WorldCom provide information to explain how the company was able to generate such a high level of profitability. As a result of the SEC's action, Cooper ordered her 24 subordinates to start collecting financial information to fulfill the request. Another potential issue for Cooper and WorldCom was the trouble that Arthur Andersen was having with the Enron account. This increased Cooper's suspicion, and she started to review all components of the financial statements. Cooper took on this additional role of accounting investigator without any official assignment from senior management. Without permission from Sullivan, Cooper started to have her department do complete financial audits, which up to this point, were the primary responsibility of Arthur Andersen.[24]

Arthur Andersen's Role

The approval of Arthur Andersen's auditing of the WorldCom account occurred after a May 1999 presentation Andersen made to WorldCom's audit committee in which Andersen claimed that WorldCom's audit cost more than what was actually billed to WorldCom. The cost structure was revisited in 2001, when it was calculated that Andersen spent a total of 15,000 hours on the WorldCom account, yet billed WorldCom only $2 million. This would mean that Andersen was charging an hourly rate of approximately $133 instead of the standard $500 for a major accounting firm. Andersen adopted a "risk based" model when auditing WorldCom and other accounts. The underlying assumption of this model is that auditors do not have to be as thorough in all areas of the audit as long as they concentrate on areas where the client may have potential weaknesses in the control systems or a high potential for risky transactions. As a result, the rigor of the audit decreased in many areas at WorldCom as Andersen depended on analyzing unusual patterns of activities to indicate where the auditors should focus a majority of their time. The underlying weakness of this new approach to auditing was that management could manipulate the accounts in a "normal" pattern, which would not come under increased scrutiny of the auditors. The SEC had been concerned since 1999 that accounting firms were becoming too trusting of their clients by examining only the exceptions to the rule as they pertained to the clients' financial statements. Based on the resistance of clients to pay more for an audit, accounting firms embraced the risk-based approach as a way to perform audits that are more cost efficient. Based on the risk-based approach of auditing, Andersen failed to investigate the expense that transferred $798 million and $560 million to capital expenditures.[25]

On May 21, 2002, Smith received an e-mail from Mark Abide, who was in charge of WorldCom's property, plant, and equipment, located in Richardson, Texas. Abide had attached to his e-mail a copy of an article from the local newspaper that reported the firing of a WorldCom employee in the Texas office who had raised questions concerning the capital expenditures account. The e-mail was forwarded to Cooper, who started to investigate further the various expense and capital accounts. Cooper and Morse came across a $2 billion entry that appeared to be transferring operating expenses to capital accounts for the sole purpose of improving the reported level of profitability for WorldCom.[26] After discovering the adjusted entry, Cooper and Smith went to the director of financial planning at WorldCom, Sanjeev Sethi, and asked the justification of the entry. Sethi's response was that it was for "prepaid capacity." Neither Cooper nor Smith was familiar with that term. They discovered the term had a reference to capital expenditures, but when asked for a clear definition, Sethi told them to ask WorldCom's controller, Myers. When Cooper and Smith asked Myers what the origin of *prepaid capacity* was, he referred them to the director of general accounting at WorldCom, Buford Yates. On that same day, May 28, 2002, Morse discovered the $500 million in computer expenses that did not include any invoices or other forms of documentation. To understand the severity of the questionable transactions, Cooper sent an e-mail to Smith asking him to investigate further the validity of the prepaid capacity transfer. She also wanted to know how much further they should press Sethi to give a comprehensive response to their questions. Myers was copied on the e-mail and quickly responded that Sethi worked for him and did not have time to respond to Cooper's questions.[27]

Although they did not know it yet, Cooper and Smith had discovered the underlying basis of the fraud at WorldCom. Top management was keeping two sets of accounting books to cover up the fraudulent transactions. In 2001, WorldCom was struggling financially because of overcapacity and high levels of competition within the tele-com industry. Until 2001, Sullivan had been able to "fix" the results by transferring reserve money to artificially boost WorldCom's profits. However, by 2001, the reserve amounts were not enough to reverse the huge losses occurring from WorldCom's oper-ations. As a result for the five quarters leading up to the SEC investigation, Sullivan started asking Myers to transfer line item costs out of operating expenses and book them as capital expenditures without the knowledge of Cooper and the internal audit department. Morse became a valuable part of the internal audit investigation because he was an information technology expert. Sullivan controlled who had access to every component of WorldCom's computerized accounting system. The internal audit department had limited access to the accounting system, but Morse was able to convince a senior manager in WorldCom's information technology department, Jerry Lilly, to give him full access in return for helping Lilly try out the new software system that was being implemented by WorldCom for its accounting records. With full access to the accounting system, Morse was able to quickly follow the complete audit trail of any transaction electronically. Within 2 weeks, Morse was able to identify almost $2 billion in accounting transactions that could be considered questionable.[28]

Roadblocks in the Investigation

In an internal memo dated June 12, 2002, that related to a meeting among Sullivan, Cooper, and Smith, Sullivan asked the internal audit department to delay its review of the capital expenditures account until the third quarter of 2002. That would give time, Sullivan believed, to start correcting the account. Sullivan stated that a number of issues were related to capital expenditures that needed to be "cleared up" in the second quarter of 2002.[29] Cooper refused to stop the audit, and they left the meeting without resolving the issue. On June 13, Cooper and Smith met with the chairman of WorldCom's audit committee, Bobbitt, about their concerns because they thought that Sullivan would try to block them. After Cooper informed Bobbitt of her con-cerns, the audit committee for WorldCom planned to meet for a regular meeting 2 days later. Bobbitt felt it was too premature to discuss the matter at the meeting, so no mention of the capital expenditure issue was made.[30] Cooper met with WorldCom's controller, Myers, on June 17, 2002, to discuss the booking made in the capital expen-ditures account. Cooper asked Myers if he had a justification why WorldCom was recording normal line expenses as capital expenditures, which violated accounting standards. Myers's response was that he could not identify any specific accounting pronouncements that would validate WorldCom's actions and admitted to Cooper that WorldCom should probably not have recorded the transactions in that manner. When Cooper asked Myers how he would explain the bookings to the SEC, he stated that he hoped he would not have to explain the transactions. Myers claimed that he and WorldCom had no choice because if they did not record those expenses as assets, the company would probably go bankrupt.[31] It was later reported that during a WorldCom board of directors meeting on March 6, 2002, Ebbers had proposed that the internal audit department, of which Cooper was in charge, should have its fund-ing reduced to half its current budget. The board did not agree but did decide to reduce the funding to the internal audit department by 10%.[32] After the June 17, 2002, meeting with Myers, Cooper told her subordinates that top management had no support for the transactions. KPMG met with Sullivan and Myers to have them explain the justification for the accounting treatment of the expenses. Sullivan said that because WorldCom was not receiving any revenue for the payments, he could defer the costs of leasing the phone lines until they were able to generate revenue for WorldCom. KPMG responded by stating that the costs of operating leases could not be recognized in a future period.[33]

On Thursday, June 20, 2002, Cooper, Smith, and Farrell Malone from KPMG went to WorldCom's audit committee meeting in Washington, D.C. Malone told the committee about the transfer of expenses to the capital expenditure accounts and stated that he did not believe that those transfers were in accordance with generally accepted accounting principles (GAAP). Sullivan tried to explain the transfers to the audit committee without success and asked for more time. The committee told Sullivan that he had the weekend to produce a valid explanation for the transfers into the capital expenditures account. On Monday, June 24, 2002, Sullivan was not able to produce valid support for the transfers, and the audit committee told him and Myers that they would be fired if they did not resign before Tuesday morning. Myers did resign and Sullivan refused, so he was terminated on June 25, 2002. On June 26, 2002, WorldCom announced that it had artificially increased profits from the five previous quarters by almost $4 billion.[34]

The Fraud Becomes Public

The $3.8 billion was the largest accounting fraud in corporate history and put WorldCom in violation of the covenants on its outstanding debt of almost $30 billion.[35] On June 26, 2002, the SEC filed civil charges of fraud against WorldCom by stating that the company presented itself to investors as a profitable company but that was not the case.[36] The trading of WorldCom's stock was stopped, and WorldCom eventually became delisted on the NASDAQ Stock Exchange. After the news of the scandal broke, members of the internal audit department were told by various WorldCom employees that they wished the internal auditors had just left the fraudulent transaction alone.[37]

By July 2002, questions began to arise about the true value of WorldCom's assets. WorldCom had reported $104 billion in assets, but analysts were starting to guess that the true asset value should have been closer to $3 billion to $8 billion. The drastic reduction in asset value is partly due to the fact that WorldCom had almost $50 billion of goodwill listed in its assets from numerous acquisitions. The goodwill's value was almost zero for those acquisitions with the exception of the MCI brand name. An additional $40 billion in property, plant, and equipment would have to be discounted significantly if they were sold because of the excess capacity in the telecommunications market. In addition, the market capitalization for WorldCom had dropped from a high of $120 billion in 1999 to $335 million. It is ironic that the loans to Ebbers that started the downward spiral of WorldCom had a higher value, $408 million, than the total market capitalization of the company that he cofounded. WorldCom's debt, with a face value of $30 billion, was trading at a market value of approximately $4.5 billion.[38] On July 15, 2002, the Federal Communications Commission (FCC) announced that it had rejected WorldCom's bid for $3.5 million in next-generation telecommunications network equipment. A former Arthur Andersen auditor who joined KPMG when it took over the WorldCom account, Ken Avery, was fired.[39]

In July 2002, an internal memo dated March 2001 was released. In it, Myers reminded one of his subordinates, Tom Bosley, that Bosley had promised Sullivan and Ebbers to do whatever was necessary to help WorldCom's financial position through increased levels of profitability. Bosley would e-mail Sullivan and Myers and ask them what numbers Sullivan wanted, and Bosley would try to ensure the numbers were met.[39] Sullivan would faithfully adjust the financial statements by shifting operating costs to capital accounts every quarter to ensure WorldCom reported high levels of profits. Sullivan's rule of thumb was that the quarterly line expense would equal 42% of WorldCom's quarterly revenue, which was within the "normal" range of expenses for WorldCom. A red flag that was ignored by investors was that WorldCom was always able to exactly meet Wall Street's quarterly forecast for the company. In two consecutive quarters, WorldCom was able to meet Wall Street's forecast within one-hundredth of a cent. The odds of that happening two quarters in a row are very low.[41]

On June 28, 2002, WorldCom announced that it would lay off 17,000 employees to reduce costs. On July 1, 2002, WorldCom released the results of an internal investigation that showed that the fraudulent financial transactions might have started in 1999 instead of 2001. On July 8, 2002, Ebbers and Sullivan pleaded the Fifth Amendment when a congressional committee asked them about their roles in the WorldCom fraud.[42]

The Bottom of the Downward Spiral

On July 21, 2002, WorldCom declared bankruptcy and had the dubious distinction of being the largest corporate bankruptcy in the history of American commerce. The reported pre-bankruptcy assets of WorldCom were $107 billion and $41 billion in debt, which dwarfs at that time the largest bankruptcy in U.S. history, Enron. In addition to having only $450 million in available cash, WorldCom was forced into bankruptcy by suppliers who required that WorldCom pay all purchases with cash on delivery. Sidgmore estimated that WorldCom had enough cash to operate for 2 months before it could no longer pay its financial obligations. The inaccurate financial statements at WorldCom made it extremely difficult to determine what WorldCom's true financial position was when it filed for bankruptcy. However, cash flow problems are a common "final straw" for a company that had fraudulent financial statements. One of the common causes is the lack of credit that WorldCom had available to pay off debts. As soon as the fraudulent activities at WorldCom were made public, WorldCom's lending partners declared that WorldCom was in default on its loans.[43] On August 1, 2002, Sullivan and Myers were arrested for securities fraud and for filing inaccurate financial statements with the SEC. On August 9, 2002, internal auditors identified an additional $3.8 billion in questionable transactions, which doubled the level of the fraud from $3.8 billion to $7.6 billion.[44]

On September 11, 2002, Sidgmore stepped down as CEO of WorldCom based on increasing pressure by WorldCom's board of directors. On September 27, 2002, Myers pleaded guilty to three counts of securities fraud, wire fraud, and conspiracy. On October 7, 2002, WorldCom's former accounting director, Yates, pleaded guilty to securities fraud and conspiracy. "Buddy" Yates may have been best known during the investigation when it was discovered that his response to an employee about a large discrepancy in one of the accounts was that if the employee showed the disputed numbers to the auditors, Buddy would throw him "out the f***ing window."[45]

By November 2002, the SEC expanded the scope of the investigation to uncover fraudulent transactions from 1999 that totaled more than $9 billion, resulting in a loss of $180 billion in shareholder value. In November 2002, the former president of Hewlett-Packard, Michael Capellas, became the new CEO of WorldCom, and the court approved his employee contract, which included compensation of $20 million over 3 years. On December 18, 2002, six WorldCom board members resigned from their positions.[46]

In February 2003, WorldCom announced that it would lay off another 5,000 employees to reduce costs and help move the company out of Chapter 11. On March 14, 2003, WorldCom wrote off $79.8 billion in assets as it moved closer to leaving bankruptcy. On April 15, 2003, WorldCom no longer existed; the company officially changed its name to MCI and moved its corporate headquarters from Clinton, Mississippi, to Ashburn, Virginia. On May 19, 2003, MCI agreed to pay $500 million to investors to resolve civil fraud charges. By June 2003, the estimated amount of the fraud had increased to more than $11 billion.[47]

In June 2003, the results of two external investigations on the fraud at WorldCom presented the first piece of evidence that directly linked Ebbers with the fraud. In an internal memo dated July 10, 2001, Ebbers wrote WorldCom's chief operating officer, Ron Beaumont, and asked him about the progress of finding a onetime item that could be used to "close the gap" between their actual and expected revenue numbers. The onetime item would be used to artificially support WorldCom's level of performance without raising a lot of questions. A subsequent memo on July 13, 2001, from a vice president of finance, Michael Higgins, stated that Higgins had reviewed the numbers with Ebbers and the two sets of numbers that showed the monthly results should not be forwarded because of the concerns Ebbers had about listing two sets of numbers. WorldCom's financial results were released to the public on July 26, 2001.[48]

By July 2003, the estimated amount of the WorldCom fraud had increased to nearly $12 billion, and a federal judge agreed to have MCI pay $750 million to settle claims with federal regulators. On August 27, 2003, Oklahoma attorney general Drew Edmondson filed criminal charges against MCI and six executives, including Ebbers. On September 3, 2003, Ebbers pleaded not guilty to the fraud and securities charges filed in Oklahoma. On October 14, 2003, MCI announced that the position of chief ethics officer was created and that the position would report directly to the CEO.[49]

On January 7, 2004, the U.S. government removed the 5-month suspension of federal contracts that had been imposed on MCI. On March 15, 2004, MCI separated the positions of CEO and chairman of the board. In March 2004, Sullivan pleaded guilty to fraud charges for his role as chief financial officer at WorldCom. Sullivan stated in court that he and other WorldCom employees purposely conspired to present a false and inaccurate representation of WorldCom's true financial position. As part of his plea, Sullivan agreed to cooperate with federal authorities and sell his Florida home to give the proceeds to investors who lost money because they owned WorldCom stock. On the same day, it was announced that Ebbers was charged with securities fraud for making false statements and conspiracy. In March 2004, MCI announced that the company would restate its financial results for 2000 and 2001 and reduce pretax income by $74.4 billion.[50]

The Trials Start

On April 20, 2004, MCI officially emerged after 21 months in Chapter 11 bankruptcy. On May 10, 2004, MCI announced that it would eliminate 15% of its workforce, equal to 7,500 jobs. In November 2004, Citigroup agreed to pay WorldCom investors $2.58 billion in exchange for settlement of legal claims based on Citigroup's actions during the scandal. Citigroup was accused of having one of its investment banking divisions aid WorldCom in its presentation of fraudulent transactions. On January 25, 2005, Ebbers's trial started in New York after he failed to have the trial moved to Mississippi. During the trial, Myers testified that Ebbers stated in a 2001 meeting that all the finance managers must cut costs and be able to turn around the financial condition because Ebbers's personal wealth was in jeopardy. Ebbers reminded the managers that if the WorldCom stock price fell below a certain price level, Ebbers would lose everything from a company he had built from scratch. He stated that his stock and the board's stock were their lifeblood and if the stock price went below $12, he would be financially wiped out.[50] Ebbers told the managers that line-item costs were increasing at an unacceptable rate that needed to be corrected. He also told the managers that the company was dealing with an extraordinary time in its history and extraordinary things had to be done to make sure WorldCom survived. Myers stated that Ebbers knew about the fraud and understood the severity of it and the amount of dollars involved in the fraudulent transactions.[52] Myers also admitted in court that the improper accounting methods at WorldCom started in 1997 when he became controller, not in 2000, as it was first believed.[53] Sullivan also testified that Ebbers had a great ability to understand financial matters and compared his knowledge base to that of a chief financial officer. Sullivan also testified that he informed Ebbers in a March 2001 dinner meeting that the accounting department would need to classify item costs as assets to meet Wall Street expectations. When the prosecution asked whether Ebbers told Sullivan not to do it, Sullivan replied that Ebbers said that WorldCom needed to get its revenue stream moving forward again. When Sullivan showed Ebbers the revised financial statements for the first quarter of 2001, which included $700 million of expenses that were booked as assets, Ebbers mentioned that WorldCom needed to hit its numbers for that quarter.[54] Sullivan also stated in court that WorldCom was reluctant to have merger discussions with Verizon Communications in 2001 not because of the potential impact of the merger, but because Ebbers and Sullivan were afraid that Verizon would discover the fraud when it started examining the books during the negotiations. Ebbers was also concerned because WorldCom would not get a good deal from the merger due to the low price of WorldCom stock. Sullivan also testified that Ebbers had told him to stop talking to the board of directors about ways in which WorldCom could try to boost revenue to match the forecasts from Wall Street.[55]

When chief operating officer Beaumont presented information to the board about some of the proposed adjustments that could be made, one of the board members asked him after the meeting if he really was going to make the adjustments. In addition, Sullivan testified that Ebbers did not want the corporate treasurer, Susan Mayer, to see the monthly cost information because Mayer started to ask questions about the large variances in the balances of some accounts. When Ebbers asked Sullivan where Mayer was getting the information, Sullivan replied that she was the corporate treasurer. Ebbers told Sullivan that she needed to be removed from the distribution list for the monthly results.[56]

When Ebbers took the stand, he stated that he knew nothing pertaining to the fraudulent activities. Ebbers stated that Sullivan did not inform him of the unacceptable accounting transactions that were occurring and that Ebbers acted more as a coach than as an active participant in the financial operations of the company.[57]

During the jury deliberations, seven banks agreed to settle lawsuits based on the actions related to the WorldCom fraud, and they paid more than $750 million in settlement costs. On March 15, 2005, former CEO Ebbers was found guilty of all nine criminal charges against him: conspiracy, securities fraud, and seven counts of filing false financial statements with the SEC. In rejecting Ebbers "Aw, shucks" defense, one of the jurors stated that it was hard to believe that the man in charge of the company didn't know what was going on.[58]

On March 19, 2005, 11 board members agreed to pay $20.25 million from their own pockets to settle lawsuits by investors. This amount was in addition to the $35 million that was paid by insurance companies that held policies on the WorldCom board members. The $20.25 million was more than the cumulative compensation for the 11 board members during their tenures at WorldCom. On March 21, 2005, another former WorldCom board member and former chairman of the board, Bert Roberts, settled the investors' lawsuits against him by personally paying $4.5 million. He was the final WorldCom board member to settle the investors' lawsuits. On May 9, 2005, MCI announced it would pay the state of Mississippi $100 million that was owed, in part, in back taxes from the years 1998 to 2002. When MCI was WorldCom, it owed the state of Mississippi approximately $1 billion in total back taxes.[59]

The trial of Arthur Andersen's involvement with WorldCom started on March 29, 2005. The prosecution claimed that Andersen was so eager to please its client that in return for millions of dollars in auditing fees, the auditors saw, heard, and spoke no evil. Government prosecutors claimed that Andersen constantly took at face value whatever WorldCom told it or gave it as appropriate documentation.[60] On April 25, 2005, Arthur Andersen agreed to pay $65 million to settle a class-action lawsuit brought against the firm by WorldCom investors. Combined with the settlement amounts paid by investment banks, auditors, and former board members of WorldCom for their roles in the WorldCom fraud, Arthur Andersen's $65 million brought the total to more than $6.1 billion.[61]

On June 30, 2005, Ebbers agreed to pay $5 million and transfer almost all of his personal assets into a liquidation trust to settle civil charges against him. It was estimated that the total amount of the trust would be $40 million. Ebbers was allowed to keep only enough money to pay his legal bills and establish a modest living allowance for his wife.[62] On July 13, 2005, Ebbers, the 63-year-old former founder and CEO of the second-largest telecommunications company in the United States, was sentenced to 25 years in prison for his role in the WorldCom fraud. The judge commented at the sentencing that Ebbers was the instigator of the fraud and his statements purposely misled investors in their actions. The judge stated that if Ebbers had been truthful about WorldCom's performance, investors might have made different investment decisions. Under federal sentencing guidelines, Ebbers must serve at least 85% of his sentence, which would be 21 years 3 months. If he were to be released at that time, he would be 85 years old.[63]

On July 26, 2005, Sullivan agreed to forfeit his Boca Raton estate that was valued at $10.9 million. In addition, he agreed to hand over the $200,000 that he had in his 401(k) account.[64] The retirement account had been worth millions but had dropped substantially because a majority of the account was based on WorldCom stock. On August 11, 2005, Sullivan was sentenced to 5 years in prison for his role in the WorldCom fraud. Sullivan was facing as many as 165 years in prison but received a reduced sentence for his key role in providing information to the government to aid in its prosecution of Ebbers. Sullivan still could have received as many as 25 years in prison after cooperating with prosecutors. The judge commented during the sentencing that Sullivan would have received a much more substantial sentence if he had not cooperated with the government.[65]

On August 5, 2005, former director of corporate reporting, Betty Vinson, was sentenced to 5 months to a year after she had cooperated with the prosecution in Ebbers's trial. Troy Normand, the former accounting department manager, was the lowest-ranking WorldCom executive charged. He received no jail time and was given 3 years of probation. On August 9, 2005, the former director of general accounting, Yates, was sentence to 1 year 1 day for his role in the WorldCom fraud. Yates had cooperated with prosecutors by helping them in Ebbers's trial. On August 10, 2005, Myers was the final member of the six employees to be sentenced for his role in the WorldCom fraud. He was sentenced to 1 year 1 day. Table 2 shows a summary of the

TABLE 2 ● The Legal Results of the WorldCom Case

WorldCom

Name	Position	Charges/Legal Result	Jail Sentence
Bernard Ebbers	CEO and Chairman	Convicted of all nine charges: conspiracy, fraud, filing false financial statements	25 years
(reported to prison September 2006)			
Scott Sullivan	Chief Financial Officer	Pleaded guilty to securities fraud: three counts	5 years
(reported to prison November 2005)			
David Myers	Controller	Pleaded guilty to three counts: fraud, conspiracy, filing false financial statements	1 year 1 day
(reported to prison October 2005)			
Buford Yates	Director of General Accounting	Pleaded guilty to two counts: securities fraud, conspiracy	1 year 1 day
(reported to prison October 2005)			
Betty Vinson	Accounting Dept. Manager	Pleaded guilty to two counts: conspiracy and fraud	5 months and 5 months' house arrest
Troy Normand	Accounting Dept. Manager	Pleaded guilty to two counts: conspiracy and fraud	3 years' probation

Source: Adapted from Online WSJ Editors, "WorldCom: Keeping Track," *Wall Street Journal*, August 14, 2005, www.wallstreetjournal.com.

Cases

results of the six WorldCom executives who were criminally charged by the government. In October 2005, MCI settled 32 individual lawsuits from 60 organizations that had filed financial claims against WorldCom. MCI paid $651 million to settle the claims.[66] On July 27, 2006, Sullivan was not required to pay a fine to the SEC because he no longer had any money with which to pay them. Sullivan had previously agreed to pay $13.6 million in penalties.[67]

The saga of Ebbers ended as humbly as it began, but with a twist. On September 27, 2006, the former CEO of one of the largest telecommunications companies in the world arrived in the federal penitentiary in Oakdale, Louisiana. However, Ebbers arrived in style, driving his Mercedes-Benz through the prison gates. Ebbers left his mansion in Mississippi that morning at 9 and arrived at the prison at 2 in the afternoon. He pulled down the bill of his cap and hid his face from reporters and photographers who were waiting for him at the prison gates as he started his 25-year sentence.[68] In December 2008, Ebbers filed a petition asking President George W. Bush to revoke his 25-year prison term and pardon him for his role in one of the largest accounting frauds in corporate history.[69] President Bush did not sign the pardon.

The Aftermath of the Demise of WorldCom In November 2002, Richard Breeden, former chairman of the SEC, was appointed as a corporate monitor by the court as part of WorldCom's settlement. His position evolved into being in charge of making recommendations pertaining to WorldCom's corporate governance structure. As part of the settlement with the SEC, WorldCom agreed to implement the recommendations based on the Breeden report. The results of Breeden's work were released to MCI in August 2003. Under the title "Restoring Trust," Breeden recommended 78 specific changes along 12 distinct themes. The major themes are the following:

1. MCI must establish a governance constitution.
2. MCI must establish electronic town hall meetings so shareholders can communicate directly with MCI.
3. One new board member must be selected every year.
4. An active, independent board in which all the board members except the CEO are from outside MCI must be established. The full board of directors must meet at least eight times annually, and the board must visit the company facilities every year separate from the board meeting. In addition, the board must meet with the chief financial officer and general council independently. No compensation will be given to board members other than board retainers.
5. The chairman of the board can be neither the CEO nor any other member of management.
6. MCI must establish audit, corporate governance, compensation, and risk management board committees.
7. Board members and the external auditors may last only a term of 10 years.
8. Any compensation at MCI that is higher than $15 million must have approval of the shareholders.
9. There would be strict limits on the amount and frequency of stock options.
10. MCI would ensure complete transparency of its transactions as well as having strong internal controls.

11. MCI needed to develop a more comprehensive ethics program and a stronger legal department.
12. MCI would not have any poison pill or any other provisions in case of a hostile merger or acquisition.[70]

After Ebbers's trial was over, Steve Rosenbush from *Businessweek* wrote about the five lessons to be learned from WorldCom.[71] The first is to beware of companies that have corporate cultures that resemble a cult. WorldCom had a charismatic leader, and the employees behaved more like a tribe following Ebbers than like employees. As a result, they were more likely not to challenge unethical actions if the actions were for the "good" of the tribe.

The second lesson is to beware of companies that have to depend on government contracts for their long-term survival. If the government changes its policy, the company would have to quickly find alternative sources of revenue to satisfy Wall Street. As a result, WorldCom "manufactured" alternative revenue streams that were not always legitimate.

The third lesson is to beware of companies that rely on mergers and acquisitions for revenue growth. As was the case with WorldCom, mergers and acquisitions became the end rather than the means for growth. WorldCom paid huge premiums in goodwill for its acquisitions and was caught with inflated asset levels that could not be written down due to the continuous pressure on WorldCom's stock price.

The fourth lesson is to beware of companies in which the top managers have a close relationship with the board of directors. By offering Ebbers more than $400 million in loans, the board became an accomplice of WorldCom's actions. The board had a vested interest in Ebbers's personal financial position based on the loan. In addition, the board members also had huge personal investments in WorldCom stock and supported actions that would protect the price level of the stock.[72]

The fifth and biggest lesson is to beware of companies in which it would be difficult for the CEO or other top executives to defend their actions in court. This is similar to the ethics television rule, which states, "Could you defend your actions if there was a report on television explaining what you had done?" Investors need to ensure that if a top manager of a company is on trial, he or she can legally explain his or her actions before a judge and jury. Bernie Ebbers is currently incarcerated at the Oakdale Federal Correctional Institution and is expected to be released on July 4, 2028.[73]

Questions for Thought

1. Why do you suppose Bernard Ebbers was treated more like the leader of a cult than as a CEO? Explain.

2. Evaluate the recommendations in the Breeden Report. Will these accomplish the objectives they are supposed to achieve?

3. Do you view Cynthia Cooper as an ethics exemplar in this case? Explain.

4. Arthur Andersen auditors would not speak with Cynthia Cooper, saying they reported to Sullivan. Is it correct to say that a public company's auditors speak only with one person in the organization? Explain.

25

BP and the Deepwater Horizon Disaster: "I Would Like My Life Back"

We're sorry for the massive disruption it's caused their lives. There's no one who wants this over more than I do. I would like my life back.[1]

—Former **BP CEO Tony Hayward, May 30, 2010**

The Explosions on the Deepwater Horizon

This statement by Tony Hayward is just one of the many ironies in an environmental disaster of epic proportions. Not just Hayward, but the unfortunate many thousands of people who resided around the Gulf of Mexico would have liked to have had their lives restored to what they were like before that fateful day on April 20, 2010. That evening, at approximately 10 p.m., the first in a series of explosions that killed 11 people occurred on an oil drilling rig in the Gulf of Mexico. The explosion shot huge plumes of flames and smoke hundreds of feet into the air. The name of the rig was Deepwater Horizon, and it was owned by Transocean but had been under contract to BP since September 2007.[2] Another irony of the disastrous day was it had started on such a positive note. Four Transocean executives had landed, by helicopter, that morning on the Deepwater Horizon to recognize the employees for their outstanding safety record.[3]

A critical problem that occurs at any offshore oil rig is that goals and objectives of the different companies involved in the process can conflict. This was the case on the Deepwater Horizon. The crew members stated that there was a "natural conflict" of interest between Transocean and BP. BP focused on getting the job done as quickly as possible to reduce costs. The speed of work became even more imperative when the Deepwater Horizon operation was already running over budget. The Deepwater Horizon work was 43 days overdue, which had cost BP $21 million. Conversely, Transocean received a leasing fee of $500,000 for every day BP continued to use the rig. Thus, Transocean had a financial incentive for delaying the completion of the project because it would create more revenue for the company. In addition, Halliburton was hired to provide the cementing process needed to plug the final hole, and a subsidiary of Halliburton was responsible for checking the drilling fluids. Another company was responsible for providing the drilling fluid system, another provided the well casing, and still another company gave the worker remote-control vehicles used to check the bottom of the ocean. The result was that multiple companies were doing multiple specific jobs on the Deepwater Horizon, which resulted in a breakdown of leadership and a chaotic atmosphere where no one was in control. Halliburton had warned BP on April 1, 2010, that BP's use of cement was not in accordance with Halliburton's best practices. On April 18, 2010, Halliburton sent BP another warning, explaining that the method used by BP to cement the plug could result in a "severe" gas flow problem if the casing being cemented around the pipe was not centered.[4]

As the explosions hit the rig, panic ensued among the crew members. The safety guidelines required that they had to call two senior management members and be told what to do. The safety guidelines also required that multiple people had to jointly make a decision about how to respond to "dangerous" levels of gas, yet the procedures did not identify who would make a decision about whether to shut down the rig. Transocean responded after the disaster by stating its chain of command was in place and did not hinder the process to start an emergency shutdown of the rig. At the time of the blast, Captain Kuchta, the captain of the ship/rig, was entertaining two BP executives who were honoring the Deepwater Horizon for its 7 years without a serious accident.[5]

At 9:47 p.m., the workers heard a hissing of methane gas. This is a huge red flag because methane gas is usually in or near crude oil reservoirs. The pressure of the methane gas forced the gas to move up quickly through the pipe toward the top of the rig. As the methane gas moved upward, the captain of a supply ship docked at the Deepwater Horizon described the flow of drilling mud through the top of a pipe like lava from a volcano. Because no methane gas had reached the top of the derrick yet, the Deepwater Horizon was not at a safety level where there is a "dangerous" level of gas present, meaning the emergency protocol was not initially started. Therefore, the crew was not notified of the danger, and no order was issued to shut down the rig. Within minutes, the methane gas ignited, probably due to a spark from an engine. This fire destroyed critical parts of the platform that were needed to attempt to shut down the rig. In addition, large parts of the rig were on fire and the explosion allowed crude oil to leak into the ocean.

A series of explosions followed that destroyed the motor room and blew crew members across the rig. There were no fire pumps available that they could use to try to put out the fire so the crew members started moving toward abandoning the rig. The crew members did not know what to do until the public address system started blaring that there was a fire on the rig. The crew members found they could only get to two lifeboats, which could each hold as many as 75 crew members. At this point, flames were shooting 250 feet out of the well pipe, and one crane boom had collapsed and

Cases

melted due to the intense heat from the fire. Many crew members could not find their way because debris blocked their paths and destroyed staircases. Crew members who were injured littered the remaining part of the platform. No one took charge on the rig to try to produce an orderly evacuation. One Transocean executive was helping the injured workers onto the lifeboat and told the deck crew not to lower the lifeboat until it was full.

Simultaneously, the 50 people inside the boat were yelling at the deck crew to lower the lifeboat while it was still operational. The panic continued as crew members could not wait any longer and jumped into the dark cold ocean 75 feet below. Once word had reached the Transocean managers that people were jumping overboard, a "man overboard" call was given, and the supply ship that had moved away from the Deepwater Horizon returned to see a sea of shining objects near the crippled rig. The shiny objects were the reflective life vests of the crew members. The supply ship put a small boat into the ocean and started to retrieve the workers.

Although the abandon ship order should have been given by the captain and top executives at Transocean, one of the subordinates finally announced on the PA system to abandon ship after one lifeboat had already been released. By the time the 10 remaining people got to the boarding station for the lifeboats, they realized they were too late. The first boat was out of view and the second lifeboat was on the water moving away from the rig. The crew members found a 25-foot life raft that they inflated, and some of the people jumped in. The people still remaining had to jump into the ocean. After landing on the water, the 25-foot life raft floated but did not move away from the rig. Panic started again with the thought that the intensity of the fire from the rig was creating a fire draft that was pulling the raft back toward the rig. The supply ship with the rescue team realized that this was not the case. The crew had forgotten to release the rope that was attached to the rig on the life raft. A member of the rescue team yelled for them to cut the line, and the life raft was set free. The supply ship, the *Bankston*, which just happened to be at the Deepwater Horizon, is the epitome of being at the right place at the right time. The *Bankston* rescued 115 crew members, including 16 who were seriously injured. Untold lives would have been lost if the *Bankston* had not been there to rescue the crew.[6]

The Sinking of the Deepwater Horizon

Two days later, still burning and now out of control, the Deepwater Horizon sank into the Gulf of Mexico. This was the ultimate worst-case scenario because Transocean and BP had zero control over the crude oil dumping into the ocean. The official response from a vice president of Transocean was that their response team "was not able to stem the flow of hydrocarbons" into the ocean. On April 24, 2010, approximately 1,000 barrels of crude oil was leaking from an underwater pipeline that had linked the Deepwater Horizon to the seabed.[8] Two days later, the estimated release of oil had increased from 1,000 to 5,000 barrels a day.

The initial investigation found that the Deepwater Horizon did not have a remote control shutoff switch that is used in other countries as a final emergency safety measure to stop underwater oil spills. The switch, called an acoustic switch, is operated with a remote control that sends acoustic pulses through the water to trigger an underwater valve called the blowout preventer. The blowout preventer will shut down the flow of oil from the well, even if the oil rig is damaged and inoperative. The acoustic control is a "redundant" back to the two primary methods of shutting down the rig: the hard-wired controller, the primary safety measure, and the dead-man switch, which is the secondary safety measure. The hard-wired controller is handled manually, but the dead-man switch should work automatically to cut the flow of oil from the rig. The acoustic control is the third level of safety. Both Norway and Brazil require all offshore oil rigs in their territory to have one just in case of an extreme disaster such as the Deepwater Horizon. The U.S. regulators had previously considered in 2000 requiring an acoustic safety switch, but the oil companies had complained to the Department of the Interior about the potential cost and effectiveness.[9]

The Minerals Management Service ← 5 H

The Minerals Management Service (MMS) in the U.S. Department of the Interior is the government agency responsible for regulating offshore oil drilling. The MMS warned offshore rig operators on at least three separate occasions that they needed to have this additional backup system in place in case of an emergency. In 2000, 2004, and 2009, MMS gave warnings, but never made the backup system a mandatory part of the drilling operations. The oil industry continued to reassure MMS that there would never be a need for this additional safety system because the other two systems are sufficient. Yet, from 2001 to 2007, the oil industry was responsible for 1,443 drilling accidents to offshore operations that resulted in 41 deaths, 302 injuries, and 356 oil spills. The MMS rationalized that the industry was the best expert to determine what type of safety measures are needed in offshore drilling. Furthermore, in 2009, BP joined forces with other offshore operators to oppose more stringent safety and environmental standards for the rigs as well as more frequent regulatory inspections. BP told MMS that "extensive, prescriptive" government regulations were not needed in the offshore oil drilling industry and that the operators should be able to design the process needed to ensure a safe offshore operation. The deputy inspector of MMS stated a few weeks after the explosion, in response to criticisms about the minerals service, that MMS has inspectors going offshore every day when weather conditions make it feasible to check rig operations and that enforcement of the regulations is strict, with MMS shutting down offshore operations 117 times in 2009. However, based on requests from the operators, MMS inspections of blowout preventers became less frequent and occurred once every 2 weeks, although it previously had been once a week. The oil rig operators complained that the inspections disrupted the operations with their frequency.[10] One of the challenges is that MMS has two potentially conflicting duties. The MMS is responsible for the enforcement of safety and environmental regulations, yet it is also responsible for encouraging growth in the oil drilling industry. The incentive for continued growth is that MMS collects royalty payments from oil companies as well as levies fines against the same companies. Therefore, there is a potential conflict of interest in having the enforcer also be financially rewarded by letting the oil rig operators do whatever they want. The secretary of the interior, Ken Salazar, who controls MMS, admitted that the oil companies have had a history of "running the show" and getting the full cooperation from the MMS. However, MMS is only part of the regulatory enforcement that the oil rig companies must accommodate. The Environmental Protection Agency (EPA) examines oil rigs to ensure there are no environmental violations. The U.S.

Coast Guard inspects the vessels and crew to ensure the ships are seaworthy, and the National Oceanic and Atmospheric Administration (NOAA) is responsible for monitoring weather conditions.[11]

The MMS concluded in 2003 that the acoustic switch should not be required on offshore oil rigs because they are very costly and the rigs already had a backup system with the dead-man switch. The cost of the acoustic trigger is approximately $500,000. A week after the disaster, the estimated cost of the Deepwater Horizon disaster was $560 million for the oil rig and $6 million a day to try to battle the oil spill.[12] On May 27, 2010, the director of MMS, S. Elizabeth Birnbaum, resigned from her position. President Barack Obama had commented that Birnbaum had failed to provide enough urgency in turning around the MMS and that the president wanted people to fix problems instead of making excuses when things break down.[13]

BP's Problematic Safety Past

BP has faced a number of safety challenges in the past. In 2005, a BP refinery exploded in Texas City, Texas, and killed 15 workers. The refinery was built in 1934 and was acquired by BP when it bought Amoco oil. Workers in the Texas City plant filled a 170-foot tower with liquid hydrocarbons, including gasoline. The liquid mixture rose too high in the tower, yet the workers did not recognize it, probably because they had been on 12-hour shifts continuously for more than a month. The mixture overflowed the top of the tower and was released into the sky. At that same moment, a contractor started his stalled pickup truck, which produced enough spark to ignite an inferno. The U.S. Chemical Safety Board concluded that the explosion was "caused by organizational and safety deficiencies at all levels of BP."[14] The Occupational Safety and Health Administration (OSHA) found more than 700 violations related to the Texas City explosion and fined BP $87.4 million. Investigators had discovered that routine maintenance had been delayed at the refinery in an effort to reduce costs by BP. In 2007, this supported the view of the independent review panel that was appointed by BP to examine BP's safety track record and concluded that BP's culture supported the belief that the company focuses on profits before safety when managers make decisions.[15] In August 2010, BP agreed to pay a $50.6 million fine for safety violations related to the Texas City explosion. In addition, BP promised to invest $500 million to improve safety at the plant.[16]

In 2006, 200,000 gallons of crude oil spilled in Alaska North Slope after an oil pipeline ruptured. Investigators had found that several miles of the pipe were corroded and undermaintained. In addition, investigators found that the pipes were also poorly inspected. BP paid more than $20 million in criminal fines and restitution for the North Slope oil spill.[17] In May 2011, BP paid an additional $25 million in civil fines to settle charges related to its involvement in two oil spills from its network of Alaska pipelines in 2006. BP was charged with willfully failing to comply with a government order to maintain the pipeline and avoid corrosion on the pipes.[18]

Transocean's Problematic Safety Past

The safety track record for Transocean is really no better than BP's. From 2008 to 2010, 73% of all federal investigations into deepwater oil drilling in the Gulf of Mexico were on oil rigs that have been operated by Transocean. Yet, Transocean only operated 42% of all the oil rigs in the Gulf of Mexico during that same period. In November 2007, Transocean took over another offshore oil rig company, GlobalSantaFe, paying $18 billion for the company. Some of Transocean customers have stated that the decline in the safety performance at Transocean is partly because Transocean was merging its operations with GlobalSantaFe, resulting in a preoccupation with integrating the two companies while still trying to control costs. Transocean responded by stating that the merger went smoothly, and Transocean was committed to having a strong safety record.[19]

Cause

The Deepwater Horizon won a MMS award for safety in 2008. The cause of the Deepwater Horizon explosion has been hypothesized to be based on either a problem with the cement seal put on the well to prevent oil and gas from escaping from the well or a problem with the blowout preventer. Transocean has had safety problems in the past dealing with both of these issues. In addition, MMS had discovered that the source of a number of previous accidents that have occurred on Transocean rigs have resulted from workers not following the proper safety procedures during the rig operations.[20]

BP's Response to the Disaster

Less than a week after the explosion, BP officials publicly stated that the oil spill was BP's responsibility, and it is responsible for the cleanup. BP deployed 32 spill response ships and five aircraft into the area of the spill so they could spray as much as 100,000 gallons of chemical dispersant, which could then be used to skim the oil off the top of the water.[21] By the middle of May 2010, BP had set up a large command center in Houston, with 500 people representing 160 firms in the oil industry. BP had announced that it was well prepared for the emergency and was doing all it could to stop the oil spill.[22] On May 24, 2010, BP announced that it was giving a total of $500 million in grants to different universities to study the impact of the oil spill on the marine and coastal environment. The first university to receive funding from the grant was Louisiana State University. An independent panel was to determine which other universities would receive funding from the grant.[23] By the end of May 2010, BP had 30 aircraft flying around the Gulf of Mexico searching for any signs of oil.[24] By the middle of June 2010, BP had spent $1.6 billion on the cleanup, which included the help of 100 companies. In addition, local residents started complaining about some specific actions that took place during the cleanup. Cleanup workers had trampled pelican nests and tossed around pelican eggs, caution tape that was used to block access to the media was flying away and ending up in marshes where it could harm the ecosystem, and cleanup workers had left oil-soaked mops on the beaches that eventually were buried in the sand due to the tides. Many of the cleanup personnel were outsiders and were not aware of the fragile ecosystems when they were cleaning up the oil.[25]

Cost

Environmental impact of cleanup

The Wit and Wisdom of Tony Hayward

A former geologist, Tony Hayward, faced the largest challenge any CEO must face, a catastrophic disaster that becomes a global media event. Hayward seemed ill prepared to resolve the issue or even discuss it in logical terms. For example, he described that the spill was not going to have a large impact on the Gulf of Mexico because the gulf is located in a very big ocean and continued by stating, "The environmental impact of

Cases

this disaster is likely to have been very, very modest."[26] Furthermore, Hayward admitted that BP did not have the right "tools" in its toolkit to address resolving a deepwater oil rig disaster. Of course, the most striking quote is the one that is at the beginning of the case. Critics jumped on Hayward's decision to attend a yacht race with his son during the crisis by stating that apparently Hayward *did* get his life back. The official BP response was that Hayward was "having some rare private time with his son."[27]

On June 16, 2010, Hayward testified before Congress regarding his lack of involvement in the decision-making process at Deepwater Horizon. Hayward stated that he did not have any prior knowledge of the drilling of the well and could not recall reading any of the numerous warning reports describing the potential disasters that could take place on the Deepwater Horizon. When Congress accused him of "stonewalling," his response was that he was not stonewalling and that he was not involved in any part of the decision-making process. BP had just agreed to set up a $20 billion escrow fund account to pay for damages from the disaster.[28] Hayward finally got his life "back" when BP announced he would no longer be the CEO of BP as of October 1, 2010. Robert Dudley was then appointed lead executive on the spill response. Dudley had extensive experience with the Gulf of Mexico because he grew up in Mississippi and spent his summers fishing and swimming in the Gulf.[29]

The Investigation Starts

On May 12, 2010, a congressional investigation into the Deepwater Horizon disaster focused on problems the rig had related to its blowout preventer. This critical piece of equipment had a dead battery, was leaking hydraulic fluid, and was not strong enough to shut down the well in emergency conditions. The preventer had also been modified in 2005 on BP orders. The modification removed one set of valves, which made testing the preventer easier and cheaper but reduced the level of safety the preventer would provide in case of an emergency. Furthermore, a MMS supervisor testified that the MMS office does have regulatory standards for the operation of the blowout preventer, but he was not aware of anyone at MMS or another regulator that actually checks the blowout preventers to determine if the equipment is at regulatory standards. In addition, Transocean CEO Steven Newman testified that the blowout preventer might not actually shut off the oil flow in all situations. The preventer would not be able to shut down the oil flow if other debris such as pipes, cement, and rocks also are flowing through the same pipe. Hayward stated that the blowout preventer is a "failsafe piece of equipment that clearly has failed."[30]

Information was presented during the congressional investigations that BP continued to finish working on the well even though combustible natural gas had seeped into the well. Initially, this gas was not an immediate threat because there was still heavy drilling fluid "mud" in the pipe that blocked the gas from escaping from the well. However, BP started removing the drilling fluid before workers had finished capping the well with a cement plug. Once the mud was withdrawn, the gas was released from the well, and as it moved up the pipe, the gas began to get warmer and started expanding. As it expanded, the gas's force pushed the drilling mud and seawater that were in the pipe upward until the gas reached the surface. Once the natural gas reached the surface, the explosions started on the rig.[31] Donald Vidrine, the highest-ranking BP executive on the rig, made the decision to pull out the mud before sealing the cap.[32]

BP sped up the final procedures to reduce the number of days over budget that had been allocated for the job. BP shortened certain procedures during the final days of the Deepwater Horizon to speed up the completion of the project. Halliburton, the company responsible for putting the cement cap on the well, advised BP to install 21 devices during the sealing process to make sure that the drilling pipe was in the center of the well. The location of the pipe is critical because if it is not in the center, there is a danger natural gas will flow through the pipe. Instead of 21 devices, BP used just 6 devices to aid in centering the pipe. Furthermore, BP did not run a time-consuming, but critical from a safety standpoint, procedure that could determine whether natural gas was building up in the well. BP ran a condensed version of the procedure that took 30 minutes to complete instead of the industry standard 6 to 12 hours. Furthermore, BP did not run tests and did not check the final part of cement that was pumped into the well to seal it to determine if the seal was satisfactory. BP had hired Schlumberger to work on the rig, and Schlumberger workers could have included the test as part of the job. BP told the Schlumberger workers that they were no longer needed, so the test was not done. The Schlumberger workers left the rig the morning of the explosion. The Transocean workers disagreed with this action but were overruled by BP. The drilling mud was removed before two more tests could take place that would have determined whether natural gas was seeping into the well.[33]

In May 2010, internal documents from BP showed that there were severe safety concerns pertaining to the Deepwater Horizon months before the explosion. Problems involving the well casing and the blowout preventer were highlighted in documents that discussed the issue of losing control of the well at least a year before the explosion. The well casing BP managers in the Gulf wanted to use for the Deepwater Horizon required special approval from corporate headquarters of BP because it did not meet the company's safety and design standards. The casing also did not meet the safety regulations of MMS. The BP documents showed that the blowout preventer leaked fluid on at least three occasions, which the manufacturer, Cameron Manufacturing and Design, states would weaken the ability of the device to shut down the rig in an emergency.[34]

On July 22, 2010, it was disclosed that a critical alarm system that would have warned workers on board the Deepwater Horizon had been disabled. Transocean rig managers had ordered that the alarm be shut off so that workers would not wake up at 3 a.m. to a false alarm. Survivors stated they had no warning of the disaster until they felt the explosion and saw the flames shoot up out of the well pipe. The alarm system had to be activated manually and that was not done during the disaster.[35]

In June 2010, BP still had not controlled the oil spilling into the Gulf of Mexico. Various methods to plug the leak failed, and BP acknowledged to the U.S. government that it was abandoning any further attempts to plug the leak. This included a "top kill" procedure in which BP pumped drilling mud back into the well to try and reduce the pressure of the oil and gas being released from the well. This procedure failed because BP could not push the mud far enough down the well to reduce the pressure from the oil and gas. This failure occurred after a previous failure when BP tried to put a 98-ton containment dome over one of the leaks. The dome could not seal properly because particles of gas, which are transformed into crystals in the water, formed on the dome and blocked the top of dome so that oil could not escape via a pipe. In addition, the crystals are lighter than water so once they formed inside the dome, the dome starting floating above the ocean ground. At this point, the only viable option was to try to contain the oil and gas as it flowed from the leak, siphon it upward to the surface of the water, and put the collected oil on a barge. This process continued as BP started drilling relief wells that eventually cut off the flow of oil and gas.[36]

The Results of a Global Disaster

In June 2010, BP was finally able to fit a containment cap on the leak that allowed the capture of 11,000 barrels. Unfortunately, the leak was dumping between 15,000 and 25,000 barrels of oil daily into the Gulf at that point. Under the Oil Pollution Act, written after the *Exxon Valdez* disaster, BP must pay $1,000 for every barrel of oil that it spills and that amount would increase to $3,000 per barrel if BP were found to be guilty of gross negligence. By June 7, 2010, the well had been dumping oil for 40 days. If the average release is 25,000 barrels daily and BP had to pay $3,000 per barrel, BP would already owe $3 billion in fines to the U.S. government.[37]

On June 17, 2010, BP announced that Hayward would no longer be in charge of the Deepwater Horizon crisis. The chairman of the board, Carl-Henric Svanberg, stated that Hayward's comment has upset people and it has become "a reputational matter, a financial squeeze for BP and a political matter, and that is why you will now see more of me."[38] In addition, Svanberg stated that American Robert Dudley, who eventually became CEO of BP, would be the lead executive on the spill response and that BP had set up a specific unit that would focus on the issues related to the spill.[39]

On July 15, 2010, BP was finally able to cap the leak but not before it was the largest oil spill in history. An estimated 5 million barrels of oil were released into the Gulf, of which BP was able to capture only approximately 800,000 barrels. As a result, an estimated 4.2 million barrels of oil had contaminated the Gulf of Mexico. By the time BP was successful with the capping process, 53,000 barrels a day were being released into the ocean. The daily level had reached a high of 63,000 barrels, but it slowly decreased as the reservoir of oil slowly decreased in the well.[40]

In its internal investigation of the Deepwater Horizon disaster, BP not surprisingly pinned most of the blame on others and not BP. BP officials blamed Halliburton for doing a poor job on the cement seal because it allowed gas to enter the well. BP's report cited both BP and Transocean for misinterpreting a critical test whose results would have warned the supervisors that the cement was not properly sealed against the gas entering the well. In addition, BP blamed Transocean for not detecting and not responding when there were signs that gas entered the well. Once the gas was released, the workers pointed the gas toward the rig instead of safely away from the rig. In addition, safety devices on board the rig that would have prevented the gas from igniting failed to work. The last failure was the "last chance" blowout preventer device that failed to shut off the well. The report noted that the blowout preventer had temporarily shut off the well, but it was too late because the natural gas had already escaped and was moving up the pipe. Therefore, if the workers had acted more quickly, they could have prevented the disaster by being able to shut down the well before the gas had escaped. Transocean's response, not surprisingly, claimed that BP was in charge of making the critical decision and that BP was the company that decided to implement a number of cost-saving measures that threatened the integrity and safety of the rig, such as the design of the rig. Halliburton's response was that BP had omitted a few of the key points and that some of the facts were not accurate.[41]

On September 18, 2010, almost exactly 5 months after the disaster, the well that the Deepwater Horizon was drilling was permanently sealed. The cost to BP at this point was approximately $9.5 billion, which included costs for spill response, containment of the oil and other operational procedures, drilling relief wells, grants to Gulf States, individual claims paid, and payments to the federal government.[42]

The oil reservoir where the well was located could contain approximately 50 million barrels of oil, of which 5 million was released into the Gulf. BP had paid the federal government $34 million to lease the part of the ocean where the reservoir is located. An option for BP would be to continue to drill in the area at a later date or sell the lease to another oil operator. At the time of the spill, the oil reservoir was estimated to be valued at $3.5 billion.[43]

In April 2011, BP sued Transocean, Cameron, and Halliburton for their involvement in the Deepwater Horizon disaster. BP sued all three companies claiming that their negligence and misconduct directly lead to the disaster. Cameron is the company that makes the "fail safe" blowout preventer.[44] On December 15, 2010, the Department of Justice (DOJ) filed a civil lawsuit against BP, Transocean, and seven other companies that were involved in the Deepwater Horizon disaster. At the same time, the DOJ was also starting a criminal investigation into the wrongdoing at the disaster.[45]

The Payout to the Local Communities

After receiving increased pressure from the U.S. government, BP set up a $20 billion compensation fund and hired Kenneth Feinberg to administer the money. Feinberg would decide how much money each legitimate claim against BP should get. Feinberg was also in charge of distributing the payouts for the victims of September 11, 2001, attacks. Once the Deepwater Horizon victims agree to the payments given by Feinberg, they no longer have any legal claim for any future monies related to the disaster.[46] The payouts for the workers who died on the Deepwater Horizon are in the range of $8 to $9 million. Called "Deepwater premium" by plaintiffs' lawyers, these settlements are millions of dollars higher than a "normal" wrongful death claim. It is evident that BP did not want additional bad press by not paying enough money to the widows of the workers and their families.[47] Emergency claims from individuals were to be handled within 48 hours after the request had been made. Evidence of financial hardship because of the oil spill was sometimes difficult to provide. Many workers were paid in cash and did not have a pay receipt. Restaurants had to prove that if sales had declined after the spill, it was because of the spill and not for other nonrelevant reasons. The easiest claims to prove were those of fisherman, shrimpers, seafood producers, and beachfront property businesses.[48] Between May 2010 and December 2011, $9.3 billion had been paid to individuals and businesses who had been affected by the oil spill and filed a claim. In addition, BP focused on helping promote tourism and seafood as the Gulf of Mexico recovered from the disaster. In 2011, BP spent $63.5 million on tourism marketing, $7.1 million on seafood marketing, and an additional $9.3 million on seafood testing. All the commercial fishing waters had been reopened in the Gulf in April 2011. Furthermore, BP funded more than 150 studies to examine the impact of the oil spill on the Gulf Coast natural resources. In November 2011, the U.S. Coast Guard approved the shoreline cleanup process as completed by BP.[49] On March 3, 2012, BP agreed to a class-action lawsuit settlement involving thousands of individuals and businesses at a cost of $7.8 billion. The payment of claims would be based on two categories: economic-loss claims and medical claims. The $7.8 billion would come from the $20 billion settlement fund already set aside by BP.[50]

A Better, Safer BP

BP enhanced safety standards in oil drilling when the industry was allowed to drill again in the Gulf of Mexico. BP officials have also strengthened their risk management systems and have put in place new responses for oil spills and containment. In addition, BP has developed a new type of capping system that will be used in the event of another deepwater oil spill. BP has enhanced the requirements for the blow-out preventers to reduce the chance of failure at a future blowout. In addition, BP also enhanced the standards for cementing wells in case of a spill.[51]

In November 2012, BP pleaded guilty to 14 criminal charges for its involvement in the Deepwater Horizon disaster. It also agreed to pay $4.5 billion in fines and other payments to the DOJ. The 14 criminal charges included 11 felony counts of misconduct or negligence. In addition, two senior BP officials were charged with manslaughter and a third was charged with one count of obstruction of justice.[52] Transocean, owner of the Deepwater Horizon, agreed to settle civil and criminal charges with the United States government for $1.4 billion. In addition, Transocean pleaded guilty to one criminal misdemeanor charge related to violating the Clean Water Act and received a fine of $100 million. Transocean also agreed to pay the National Academy of Sciences and the National Fish and Wildlife Foundation each $150 million, which will be used for oil spill prevention and natural resource restoration projects.[53] On January 15, 2015, a U.S. federal court ruled that BP was liable for spilling 3.19 million barrels of crude oil into the Gulf of Mexico. The ruling resulted in BP being ordered to pay a fine of up to $13.7 billion. The fine was based on the maximum pollution penalty under the Clean Water Act of $4,300 per barrel.[54]

Questions for Thought

1. Identify the stakeholders in this case and comment on how they have been affected by the Deepwater Horizon disaster.

2. Blame is usually part of disasters. Comment on the actions of Tony Hayward.

3. How long does it take geographical areas to recover from disasters such as the one described in the case? Can the area ever have complete economic recovery? Explain.

4. Comment on the ironic event of the Deepwater Horizon's safety awards just hours before the disastrous event.

26

Greyston Bakery:
The Zen of Philanthropy

Based in Yonkers, New York, Greyston Bakery has been baking brownies since 1982. The company was founded by a Zen Buddhist priest, Bernard Glassman. Glassman was a former aerospace engineer with a PhD in applied mathematics from the University of California who borrowed $300,000 to open a small bakery in the Bronx. Greyston moved to Yonkers in 1985. The original mission of the bakery was to produce high-quality products locally made by Glassman's meditation group that would provide a sustainable living. The mission soon evolved to allow others the same opportunity to provide financial support for themselves. Greyston Bakery quickly became known as a producer of high-quality brownies sold in some of the top-rated restaurants in New York and in some of the top retailers, including Bloomingdale's, Saks, and Godiva.[1]

The mission continued to evolve until the hiring of the workers became as important, if not more so, than the brownies. Greyston Bakery's current mission statement includes Greyston's commitment for personal transformation and the ability to contribute to community renewal. This mission is achieved by producing high-quality baked goods with a commitment to customer satisfaction.[2] The current vision of Greyston is to be a leading model for other organizations on how to develop a social enterprise that creates a partnership with employees, the community, and Greyston's shareholders. Greyston hires men and women who have minimal or no work experience. In many cases, they have never had an opportunity to find a job because of homelessness, substance addiction, incarceration, domestic violence, or illiteracy. Greyston enrolls potential employees into a 6-month apprenticeship program where the employees learn technical skills and general business skills, such as appropriate behavior and attitude. The trainees are evaluated every 2 weeks, and one mistake such as being late for work can result in dismissal from the program.[3]

Greyston is a for-profit company with annual sales of $8 million and 50 employees. All the profits from the bakery go to the Greyston Foundation, which funds various self-sufficiency programs such as housing for the homeless, children's programs including child care, health and social services, housing for HIV/AIDS individuals, and community gardens.[4] In February 2012, Greyston Bakery enrolled as a benefit corporation (B Corp). A B Corp focuses on financial projections, as well as on social and economic goals and objectives.[5]

Greyston Foundation

Greyston is unique in its focus because it uses the skills and rewards of entrepreneurship to address issues related to the inner city. The foundation follows the creed of Greyston, which is "We don't hire people to make brownies. We make brownies to hire people." Greyston Foundation programs serve 2,200 community members every year, and it has a budget of $15 million. Greyston Foundation acquires buildings that are renovated and repaired and are offered to people in the local community who would not otherwise have any means of shelter. Greyston has developed real estate with a value of more than $8 million and is currently working on real estate projects that total another $25 million. The housing also incorporates Greyston-focused programs to help individuals both physically and spiritually. The programs are based on the five elements that are the foundation of the Zen philosophy: meditation, study, interfaith expression, work–practice, and social action. The individuals are not required to participate in religious activities, and the programs are designed for both personal and social growth. Glassman believes that breaking the cycle of homelessness is not just giving individuals temporary housing but also giving individuals the skills and confidence they need to be self-sustaining in their lives. The ultimate goal is not just to stabilize and enrich the individual's life but also to stabilize and enrich the living conditions of the local community.[6]

Greyston Foundation also focuses on a holistic approach to addressing the needs of HIV/AIDS individuals. Housing is offered to these individuals, as are specially designed health care programs addressing the unique needs of these individuals.[7]

Greyston Foundation developed training and job skills programs to successfully transfer "hard to employ" into easy to employ. The training programs are not solely designed to fill positions at the bakery but also focus on the development of general skills so the individual can also apply for employment at different businesses. Greyston Foundation also supports high-quality child and youth services for low-income people in the local community. The programs facilitate the development of the children and give the parents an opportunity to seek employment and to become financially self-sufficient.[8]

The Mistake That Saved the Business

In 1988, Ben & Jerry's Ice Cream contacted Greyston, wanting Greyston to produce a thin brownie piece that would be part of an ice cream sandwich. The first batch of extra thin brownies that arrived at Ben & Jerry's was a disaster. The brownies stuck together and created a 50-pound block of brownies. The brownies could not be used to make ice cream sandwiches, but Ben Cohen decided Ben & Jerry's needed to do something with the purchased materials. Ben & Jerry's realized that small chunks of brownies could be easily taken from the block and included in chocolate ice cream. Chocolate Fudge Brownie Ice Cream was born. Greyston also supplies the brownies for Ben & Jerry's Dave Matthew's Magic Brownies, Half-Baked, and Neapolitan Dynamite ice cream flavors. Greyston makes 11,000 pounds of brownies a day for Ben & Jerry's, which constitutes 90% of Greyston's daily production.[9]

Greyston Bakery's Guiding Principles

Greyston Bakery's vision is based on its 10 guiding principles:

- The bakery will be a model for inner-city business development that other organizations can follow.
- The bakery should remain financially sustainable to consistently achieve an operating profit.
- The bakery will continue to have an open door policy related to the hiring of workers.
- The bakery will integrate their activities with the Greyston Foundation so that bakery employees can also participate in the Greyston Foundation programs.
- The bakery must sustain profitability to continue to fund the Greyston Foundation.
- The bakery will also establish and measure the bakery's achievement on all nonfinancial goals.
- The bakery will compensate the employees fairly and move toward a living wage that will further empower the employees.
- The bakery will attempt to maintain low and stable turnover rates of employees for post-apprenticeship employees.
- The bakery will automate various aspects of the production process when those changes are fiscally appropriate.
- The bakery will support the individual growth of each employee through Greyston's PathMaking Program. The PathMaking program is based on a holistic approach to the employee by focusing not on the individual skills and abilities in a work setting but on developing and maintaining their skill sets in areas such as money management, nutrition, and parenting.[10]

Fine-Tuning the Vision

In 2000, Julius Walls Jr. became the CEO of Greyston Bakery. He previously worked at a chocolate company and tried to sell Greyston chocolate chips from his company. Greyston said no, but Walls continued to have contact with Greyston, trying to develop a relationship. Eventually, Walls was asked to join the board at Greyston as the director of marketing, which led to a job first as a consultant then as a full-time employee. This then led to his becoming CEO. Before 2000, Greyston Bakery was profitable but was still missing opportunities to increase its level of profitability. Walls implemented a more task-oriented system where the employees were much more accountable for their performance. Walls argued that this benefits both Greyston and the employee because the individual can become better at controlling his or her efforts.[11]

Walls instilled his own personal management philosophy into the culture at Greyston. His philosophy is based on three Cs: clarity, consistency, and compassion. The managers must be clear in what they expect from their employees, managers must be consistent when dealing with employees, and every action done by managers must be done with compassion. When individuals go through the apprenticeship program to become employees of Greyston, Walls focuses on the three Rs: reward, responsibility, and recognition. The employees will be rewarded if they take it upon themselves to accept personal responsibility, and those employees will also be recognized for their achievement. Based on their performance, employees can receive a bonus as their reward, and their names go up on Greyston's bulletin board if they have performed well for the company.[12]

In September 2009, Walls announced he was leaving Greyston Bakery. He was leaving to take over as the executive minister of Greater Centennial A.M.E. Zion Church in Mount Vernon, New York.[13] William Mistretta became CEO of Greyston Bakery in 2009. He had 25 years' experience in the baking, beverage, and food industries, including tenures at PepsiCo, George Weston, and Interstate Bakeries.[14]

On March 3, 2015, Greyston announced that the president of Greyston Bakery, Mike Brady, would become the president and CEO of all of Greyston, including the Greyston Foundation. Mike Brady was instrumental in increasing the revenue of the bakery operations by 50% during his tenure as well as increasing the national distribution of the bakery products through Whole Foods Market.[15]

Questions for Thought

1. The new CEO appears to have much more corporate business experience than the previous CEO. Should this be a concern for the corporation?

2. In your opinion, why has Greyston Bakery been so successful?

3. Comment on the social activism of Greyston Bakery. Why don't more companies follow suit?

4. Is it possible to continue making a profit while trying to transform employees' lives? Explain your position.

• End Notes •

Chapter 1

1. Panera Cares News Release, January 16, 2011.
2. Panera Cares News Release, January 16, 2011.
3. Jim Salter, "Pay-What-You-Want Panera Called a Success," *USA Today*, May 16, 2011.
4. Lynn Sharp Paine, *Ethics: A Basic Framework* (Boston: Harvard Business School, 2006), 2.
5. Andrew Wicks, Jared Harris, and Bidhan Parmar, *Moral Theory and Frameworks* (Charlottesville: University of Virginia, Darden Business Publishing, 2008).
6. Ibid.
7. http://www.americanrhetoric.com/MovieSpeeches/moviespeechwallstreet.html.
8. *Growing Beyond: A Place for Integrity*, 12th Global Fraud Survey (Ernst & Young, 2012).
9. Kenneth E. Goodpaster, *Ethical Frameworks for Management* (Boston: Harvard Business School, 1983), 2.
10. Ibid, 5.
11. Ibid.
12. www.britannica.com.
13. Kenneth E. Goodpaster, *Ethical Frameworks for Management* (Boston: Harvard Business School, 1983), 6.
14. Ibid.
15. Ibid., 7.
16. Ibid., 8.
17. Ibid., 8.
18. William Shakespeare, *Hamlet*, Act I, Scene iii.
19. Kenneth E. Goodpaster, *Ethical Frameworks for Management* (Boston: Harvard Business School, 1983), 9.
20. Ibid., 9–10.
21. Ibid., 11–12.
22. www.danteinferno.info.
23. Ibid.
24. Dante, *Inferno*, 5.38–39.
25. www.danteinferno.info.
26. Ibid.
27. Dante, *Inferno*, 7.42.
28. www.danteinferno.info.
29. Ibid.
30. Ibid.
31. William Grimes, "Philippe Foot, Renowned Philosopher, Dies at 90," *New York Times*, October 9, 2010.
32. Lynn Paine, Rohit Deshpande, Joshua D. Margolis, and Kim Eric Bettcher, "Up to Code: Does Your Company's Conduct Meet World-Class Standards?," *Harvard Business Review* 83, no. 12 (2005): 122–133.
33. Ibid.
34. Ibid.
35. Ibid.
36. Ibid.
37. Ibid.
38. Ibid.
39. Ibid.
40. Ibid.
41. Rob Cameron, "Premiere for Nicholas Winton Who Saved Jewish Children," *BBC News Europe*, January 20, 2011.
42. "Profile: Nicholas Winton," *BBC News*, August 28, 2009.
43. "Save the Children," *CBS News, 60 Minutes*, April 27, 2014.

Chapter 2

1. Lynnley Browning, "The Netherlands: The New Tax Shelter Hot Spot," *New York Times*, February 4, 2007, www.nytimes.com.
2. Peter Wilkinson, "Glastonbury Tax Activists Target 'Hypocritical' U2," *CNN.com*, June 24, 2011.
3. http://www.americanrhetoric.com/MovieSpeeches/moviespeechnetwork4.html.
4. Jo Becker, "U.S. Approved Business With Blacklisted Nations," *New York Times*, December 23, 2010.
5. Simon London, "Business Life: Ancient Greek Lessons on Good Life and Good Management," *Financial Times*, January 4, 2006, www.ft.com.
6. www.ethics.org.
7. Ashby Jones, "'Dead Peasant' Policies: The Next Big Thing in Insurance Litigation," *Wall Street Journal*, February 24, 2009; Ellen Schultz, "Million Dollar Check, Widow Got None," *Wall Street Journal*, February 24, 2009; Ellen Schultz, "Banks Use Life Insurance to Fund Bonuses," *Wall Street Journal,* May 20, 2009.
8. Michael Moore, Anne Moore, Rod Birleson, John Hardesty, and Jeff Gibbs, *Capitalism: A Love Story* (Hollywood, CA: Paramount Pictures, 2010).
9. http://www.businessinsurance.com/apps/pbcs.dll/article?AID=999920003331.
10. http://www.merriam-webster.com/dictionary/integrity.
11. Ethics Teaching Group, *Integrity and Management* (Boston: Harvard Business School, 1992), 1.
12. Ibid.
13. Donald G. Zauderer, "Integrity: An Essential Executive Quality," *Business Forum* (Fall 1992): 4–5.
14. Ibid.
15. Greg Smith, "Why I Am Leaving Goldman Sachs," *New York Times*, March 14, 2012.
16. Mahzarin R. Banaji, Max H. Bazerman, and Dolly Chugh, "How (Un)ethical Are You?," *Harvard Business Review* (December 2003).
17. Ibid.
18. Max H. Bazerman and Ann E. Tenbrunsel, "Ethical Breakdowns: Good People Often Let Bad Things Happen. Why?" *Harvard Business Review* (April 2011).
19. David Callahan, *The Cheating Culture: Why More Americans Are Doing Wrong to Get Ahead* (Orlando, FL: Harcourt, 2004), 13.

20. Ibid., 14.

21. Ibid., 19.

22. Ibid., 167.

23. www7.gsb.columbia.edu/honor/.

24. Leslie Wayne, "A Promise to Be Ethical in an Era of Immorality," *New York Times*, May 30, 2009.

25. Victoria Crittenden, Richard Hanna, and Robert Peterson, "The Cheating Culture: A Global Societal Phenomenon," *Business Horizons* 52 (2009): 337–346.

26. Edward Wyatt, "F.C.C. Opens an Inquiry for a Game Show on Fox," *New York Times*, February 20, 2010.

27. Amir Efrati and Joann S. Lublin, "Yahoo CEO's Downfall," *Wall Street Journal*, May 16, 2012.

28. Lauren Weber and Melissa Korn, "Yahoo's CEO Among Many Notable Resume Flaps," *Wall Street Journal*, May 7, 2012.

29. Vanessa O'Connell, "Test for Dwindling Retail Jobs Spawns a Culture of Cheating," *Wall Street Journal*, January 7, 2009.

30. Catherine Rampell, "In Law Schools, Grades Go Up, Just Like That," *New York Times*, June 21, 2010.

31. Trip Gabriel, "Under Pressure, Teachers Tamper With Tests," *New York Times*, June 10, 2010.

32. Ibid.

33. Trip Gabriel, "Plagiarism Lines Blur for Students in Digital Age," *New York Times*, August 1, 2010.

34. Brent Staples, "Cutting and Pasting: A Senior Thesis by (Insert name)," *New York Times*, July 12, 2010.

35. *Millennials, Gen X and Baby Boomers: Who's Working at Your Company and What Do They Think About Ethics?*, Supplemental Research Brief, 2009 National Business Ethics Survey (Arlington, VA: Ethics Resource Center).

36. Ibid., 6.

37. Ibid., 11.

38. Mark Weber, Deepak Malhotra, and Keith Murnigham, "The Trust Development Process,"

Rotman Magazine (2006): 37–40.

39. Pablo Cardona and Helen Wilkinson, "Building the Virtuous Circle of Trust," *IESE-Insight Magazine* (December 15, 2009): 20–27.

40. Ibid., 23.

41. Rebecca Knight, "When Faculty Meets Felony," *Financial Times*, October 31, 2010.

Chapter 3

1. Jennifer Alsever, "Fair Prices for Farmers: Simple Idea, Complex Reality," *New York Times,* March 16, 2006, http://www.nytimes.com.

2. *Fair Trade USA 2013 Almanac,* http://fairtradeusa.org/sites/default/files/2013-Fair_Trade_USA-Almanac.pdf.

3. Andrew Adam Newman, "This Wake-Up Cup Is Fair-Trade Certified," *New York Times*, September 27, 2012, http://www.nytimes.com/2012/09/28/business/media/green-mountain-coffee-begins-fair-trade-campaign-advertising.html.

4. *Fairtrade Labelling Organizations International,* http://www.fairtrade.net/who-we-are.html.

5. Jennifer Alsever, "Fair Prices for Farmers: Simple Idea, Complex Reality," *New York Times,* March 16, 2006, http://www.nytimes.com.

6. Ibid.

7. Ibid.

8. A. A. Berle, "Corporate Powers as Powers in Trust," *Harvard Law Review* 44 (1931).

9. E. Merrick Dodd, Jr., "For Whom Are Corporate Managers Trustees?," *Harvard Law Review* 45 (1932).

10. Milton Friedman, "The Social Responsibility of Business Is to Increase Its Profits," *New York Times Magazine*, September 13, 1970.

11. R. E. Freeman, *Strategic Management: A Stakeholder Approach* (Boston: Pitman, 1984).

12. Archie Carroll, "The Pyramid of Corporate Social Responsibility: Toward the Moral Management of Organizational Stakeholders," *Business Horizons* (July–August 1991): 44–47.

13. Catherine G. Page, "The Determination of Organization Stakeholder Salience in Public Health," *Journal of Public Health Management Practice* 8, no. 5 (2002): 76–84.

14. David Harrison and Patsy Lewellyn, "Russian Management Training Programs: Do Corporate Responsibility Topics Have a Place?" *Management Accounting Quarterly* (Summer 2004): 25–36.

15. Michelle Greenwood and Harry Van Buren III, "Trust and Stakeholder Theory: Trustworthiness in the Organization-Stakeholder Relationship," *Journal of Business Ethics* 95, no. 3 (2010): 425–438.

16. Diana Ingenhoff and Katharina Sommer, "Trust in Companies and in CEOs: A Comparative Study of the Main Influences," *Journal of Business Ethics* 95, no. 3 (2010): 339–355.

17. John Elkington, *Cannibals with Forks: The Triple Bottom Line of Twenty-First-Century Business* (Stony Creek, CT: New Society Publishers, 1998).

18. Graham Hubbard, "Measuring Organizational Performance: Beyond the Triple Bottom Line." *Business Strategy and the Environment* 18, no. 3 (2009): 177–191.

19. Wayne Norman and Chris MacDonald, "Getting to the Bottom of 'Triple Bottom Line,'" *Business Ethics Quarterly* 14, no. 2 (2004): 243–262.

20. CIBC, *Annual Accountability Report 2009*, https://www.cibc.com/ca/pdf/about/aar09-en.pdf.

21. Graham Hubbard, "Measuring Organizational Performance: Beyond the Triple Bottom Line," *Business Strategy and the Environment*, 18, no. 3 (2009): 177–191.

22. http://www.bcorporation.net/about.

23. Angus Loten, "With New Law, Profits Take a Back Seat," *Wall Street Journal,* January 19, 2012.

24. Marc Lifsher, "Businesses Seek State's New 'Benefit Corporation' Status," *Los Angeles Times,* January 4, 2012.

25. Angus Loten, "With New Law, Profits Take a Back Seat," *Wall Street Journal,* January 19, 2012.

26. http://www.bcorporation.net/Certification-Overview.

27. http://www.bcorporation.net

28. B Lab, *B Corporation 2011 Annual Report,* http://www.bcorporation.net/B-Media/2011-Annual-Report.

29. http://supplier.intel.com/static/ethics/.

30. "Global Comparisons: How China's Labor Conditions Stack Up Against Those of Other Low-Cost Nations," *Businessweek,* November 27, 2006, http://www.businessweek.com.

31. "Business Ethics, the Foundation of Customer Relations" (Nashville, TN: National Federation of Independent Business, October 17, 2003).

32. Debora L. Spar and Lane T. LaMure, "The Power of Activism: Assessing the Impact of NGOs on Global Business," *California Management Review* 45, no. 3 (2003): 78–101.

33. http://devstudies.wisc.edu/resources_ngo.html.

34. Lynda Applegate, *Stakeholder Analysis Tool* (Boston: Harvard Business, 2008).

35. Ibid.

36. Terry Leap and Misty Loughry, "The Stakeholder-Friendly Firm," *Business Horizons* (March–April, 2004): 27–32.

37. Ibid., 27–32.

38. H. R. Bowen, *Social Responsibilities of the Businessman* (New York: Harper & Row, 1953).

39. T. J. Zenisek, "Corporate Social Responsibility: A Conceptualization Based on Organizational Literature," *Academy of Management Review* 4 (1979): 359–368.

40. Archie Carroll, "A Three-Dimensional Conceptual Model of Corporate Performance," *Academy of Management Review* 4, no. 4 (1979): 497–505.

41. Michael Porter and Mark Kramer, "Strategy & Society: The Link Between Competitive Advantage and Corporate Social Responsibility," *Harvard Business Review* 84, no. 12 (December 2006): 78–92, 163.

42. Ibid.

43. Archie Carroll, "The Pyramid of Corporate Social Responsibility: Toward the Moral Management of Organizational Stakeholders," *Business Horizons* (July–August 1991): 40.

44. Ibid.

45. Ibid, 41.

46. Ibid.

47. Archie Carroll, "Managing Ethically with Global Stakeholders: A Present and Future Challenge," *Academy of Management Executive* 18, no. 2 (2004): 114–120.

48. Ibid.

49. Ida E. Berger, Peggy H. Cunningham, and Minette E. Drumwright, "Mainstreaming Corporate Social Responsibility: Developing Markets for Virtue," *California Management Review* 49, no. 4 (2007): 32–57.

50. Philip Mirvis, "Employee Engagement and CSR: Transactional, Relational, and Developmental Approaches," *California Management Review* 54, no. 4 (2012): 93–117.

51. Andres Martinuzzi and Barbara Krumay, "The Good, the Bad, and the Successful – How Corporate Social Responsibility Leads to Competitive Advantage and Organizational Transformation," *Journal of Change Management* 13, no. 4 (2013): 424–443.

52. Eleanor O'Higgins, "Corporations, Civil Society, and Stakeholders: An Organizational Conceptualization," *Journal of Business Ethics* 94, no. 2 (2010): 157–176.

53. Ibid., 157–176.

54. Charles Fombrun, *Reputation: Realizing Value From the Corporate Image* (Boston: Harvard Business School Press, 1996).

55. Ibid.

56. Grahame Dowling, "Corporate Reputations: Should You Compete on Yours?" *California Management Review* 46, no. 3 (Spring 2004): 20.

57. Ibid., 20–36.

58. Grahame Dowling. "Communicating Corporate Reputation Through Stories," *California Management Review* 49, no. 1 (Fall 2006): 82–100.

59. Karen Cravens and Elizabeth Oliver, "Employees: The Key Link to Corporate Reputation Management," *Business Horizons* 49, no. 4 (2006): 293.

60. http://www.filmsite.org/bestspeeches2.html.

61. Robert Williams and Douglas Barrett, "Corporate Philanthropy, Criminal Activity, and Firm Reputation: Is There a Link?" *Journal of Business Ethics* 26, no. 4 (2000): 341–350.

62. Michael Porter and Mark Kramer, "The Competitive Advantage of Corporate Philanthropy," *Harvard Business Review* (December 2002): 57–68.

63. Ibid.

64. Forbes Insights, *Corporate Philanthropy The New Paradigm: Volunteerism. Competence. Results* (New York: Author, 2011).

65. Heike Bruch and Frank Walter, "The Keys to Rethinking Corporate Philanthropy," *MIT Sloan Management Review* 47, no. 1 (Fall 2005): 49–55.

66. Ibid.

67. http://thelede.blogs.nytimes.com/2012/01/17/transcripts-of-calls-to-cruise-ship-captain-published-by-italian-media/.

68. Steven Erlanger, "Oversight of Cruise Lines at Issue After Disaster," *New York Times,* January 16, 2012.

69. Amelia Smith, *Raising the Costa Concordia* (Jacksonville, FL: Crowley Maritime Corporation, 2015).

70. Associated Press, "Costa Concordia Prosecutors Ask Court to Give Captain 26-Year Sentence," *The Guardian*, January 26, 2015.

71. Gaia Pianigiani, "Captain of Ship That Capsized off Italy in '12 Is Convicted," *New York Times*, February 11, 2015.

72. Giada Zampano, "Costa Concordia Captain Found Guilty," *The Wall Street Journal*, February 11, 2015.

Chapter 4

1. Bill Whitaker, "The Swiss Leaks," *60 Minutes,* February 8, 2015.

2. Gerard Ryle, Will Fitzgibbon, Mar Cabra, Rigoberto Carvajal, Martina Walker Guevara, Martha M. Hamilton, and Tom Stites, "Banking Giant HSBC Sheltered Murky Cash Linked to Dictators and Arms Dealers," *International Consortium of Investigative Journalists*, February 8, 2015.

3. Bill Whitaker, "The Swiss Leaks," *60 Minutes,* February 8, 2015.

4. Chad Bray, "New Claims That HSBC Aided Tax Evaders," *New York Times*, February 9, 2015.

5. http://improbable.com/ig/ ig-pastwinners.html#ig2002.

6. Tobias Smollett, *Adventures of Peregrine Pickle. Plays and Poems* (Edinburgh: Mundell, Doig & Stevenson, 1806), 332.

7. J. Hoberman, "Film: When the Nazis Became Nudniks," *New York Times*, April 15, 2001.

8. D. Gerboth, "The Conceptual Framework: Not Definitions, but Professional Values," *Accounting Horizons* (September, 1987): 6.

9. Ralph Blumenthal, "Lost Manuscript Unmasks Details of Original Ponzi," *New York Times*, May 5, 2009.

10. Ibid.

11. David Margolick, "His Last Name Is Scheme," *New York Times*, April 10, 2005.

12. "Wanted: More Dupes. Lots More," *New York Times*, December 21, 2008.

13. Lynn Sharp Paine and Christopher M. Bruner. "Background Note: Note on Insider Trading Liability" (Boston: Harvard Business, 2006), 1.

14. Ibid.

15. David Satava, Cam Caldwell, and Linda Richards, "Ethics and the Auditing Culture: Rethinking the Foundation of Accounting and Auditing," *Journal of Business Ethics* 64 (2006): 271–284.

16. Ibid., 272.

17. Brian Shapiro, "Objectivity, Relativism, and Truth in External Financial Reporting: What's Really at Stake in the Disputes?," *Accounting, Organizations, and Society* 22 (1997): 165–185.

18. David Satava, Cam Caldwell, and Linda Richards, "Ethics and the Auditing Culture: Rethinking the Foundation of Accounting and Auditing," *Journal of Business Ethics* 64 (2006): 271.

19. Arieh Goldman and Benzion Barlev, "The Auditor-Firm Conflict of Interests: Its Implications for Independence," *Accounting Review* (October, 1974): 707–718.

20. Don Moore, Philip Tetlock, Lloyd Tanlu, and Max Bazerman, "Conflicts of Interest and the Case of Auditor Independence: Moral Seduction and Strategic Issue Cycling," *Academy of Management Review* 31, no. 1 (2006): 10–29.

21. Ibid.

22. http://www.aicpa.org/about/ code/sec50.htm.

23. http://www.aicpa.org/about/ code/et_52.html.

24. http://www.aicpa.org/about/ code/et_section_53__article_ii_ the_public_interest.html.

25. http://www.aicpa.org/about/ code/et_54.html.

26. http://www.aicpa.org/about/ code/et_55.html.

27. http://www.aicpa.org/about/ code/et_56.html.

28. http://www.aicpa.org/about/ code/et_section_57__article_ vi_scope_and_nature_of_ services.html.

29. Rob Norton, "Living with an 800-Pound Law," *Corporate Board Member* (May/June, 2004): 1–10.

30. Philip Toomey, "Advising Private Companies: What You Need to Know About SOX," *Accounting Today* 19, no. 17 (2005): 19.

31. Shaker A. Zahra, Richard L. Priem, and Abdul A. Rasheed, "The Antecedents and Consequences of Top Management Fraud," *Journal of Management* 31 (2005): 803–828.

32. http://www.investorglossary .com/one-time-charge.htm.

33. http://www.investorwords .com/1121/cookie_jar_ accounting.html.

34. "Enron Accountant Admits to Raiding Reserves to Boost Earnings," *Associated Press*, March 2, 2006.

35. http://www.sec.gov.

36. Larry Bitner and Robert Dolan, "Does Smoothing Earnings Add Value?" *Management Accounting* (October, 1998): 44–47.

37. Louise Story and Landon Thomas Jr., "Tales From Lehman's Crypt," *New York Times*, September 13, 2009.

Chapter 5

1. In-Soo Nam, "Korean Air Executive Ejects Crew Member After Poor Nut Service," *The Wall Street Journal*, December 8.

2. Jeyup S. Kwaak, "Macadamia Sales Take Off After Korean Air Nut Row," *The Wall Street Journal*, December 10.

3. Choe Sang-Hun, "Korean Air Chairman Strips Daughter's Titles After Her 'Foolish' Behavior," *New York Times*, December 12, 2014.

4. Associated Press, "Korean Air to be Sanctioned for Nut Rage Cover-Up," *New York Times*, December 16.

5. Alastair Gale, "'Nut Rage' Reignites Backlash Against South Korea's Family-Run Conglomerates," *The Wall Street Journal*, January 7, 2015.

6. Jeyup S. Kwaak, "Former Korean Air Executive Indicted Over Flight Delay," *The Wall Street Journal*, January 7, 2015.

7. In-Soo Nam, "Prosecutors Seek Three-Year Sentence for Daughter of Korean Air Chairman," *The Wall Street Journal*, February 2, 2015.

8. Choe Sang-Hun, "An Instant of Nut-Fueled Rage Draws a Year in Korean Jail," *New York Times*, February 12, 2015.

9. Michael Brown, Linda Trevino, and David Harrison, "Ethical Leadership: A Social Learning Perspective for Construct Development and Testing," *Organizational Behavior and Human Decision Processes* 97, no. 2 (2005): 120.

10. Mitchell Neubert, Dawn Carlson, K. Michele Kacmar, James Roberts, and Lawrence Chonko, "The Virtuous Influence of Ethical Leadership Behavior: Evidence From the Field," *Journal of Business Ethics* 90, no. 2 (2009): 157–170.

11. David Mayer, Maribeth Kuenzi, Rebecca Greenbaum, Mary Bardes, and Rommel Salvador, "How Low Does Ethical Leadership Flow? Test of a Trickle-Down Model," *Organizational Behavior and Human Decision Processes* 108, no. 1 (2009): 1–13.

12. Annebel De Hoogh and Deanne Den Hartog, "Ethical and Despotic Leadership, Relationship With Leader's Social Responsibility, Top Management Team Effectiveness and Subordinates' Optimism: A Multi-Method Study," *Leadership Quarterly* 19, no. 9 (2008): 297–311.

13. Manuel Mendonca, "Preparing for Ethical Leadership in Organizations," *Canadian Journal of Administrative Sciences* 18, no. 4 (2001): 266–276.

14. Michael Brown, Linda Trevino, and David Harrison, "Ethical Leadership: A Social Learning Perspective for Construct Development and Testing," *Organizational Behavior and Human Decision Processes* 97, no. 2 (2005): 117–134.

15. Manuel Mendonca, "Preparing for Ethical Leadership in Organizations," *Canadian Journal of Administrative Sciences* 18, no. 4 (2001): 266–276.

16. Bernard Bass and Bruce Avolio, *Improving Organizational Effectiveness Through Transformational Leadership.* (Thousand Oaks, CA: Sage, 1993).

17. Michael Brown, Linda Trevino, and David Harrison, "Ethical Leadership: A Social Learning Perspective for Construct Development and Testing," *Organizational Behavior and Human Decision Processes* 97, no. 2 (2005): 117–134.

18. Manuel Mendonca, "Preparing for Ethical Leadership in Organizations," *Canadian Journal of Administrative Sciences* 18, no. 4 (2001): 266–276.

19. Jay Alden Conger, "Charismatic and Transformational Leadership in Organizations: An Insider's Perspective on These Developing Streams of Research," *Leadership Quarterly* 10, no. 2 (1999): 145–179.

20. Bernard Bass and Paul Steidlmeier, "Ethics, Character, and Authentic Transformational Leadership Behavior," *Leadership Quarterly* 10, no. 2 (1999): 181–218.

21. Jay Alden Conger and Rabindra Nath Kanungo, *Charismatic Leadership in Organizations* (Thousand Oaks, CA: Sage, 1998).

22. Edward Aronson, "Integrating Leadership Styles and Ethical Perspectives," *Canadian Journal of Administrative Sciences* 18, no. 4 (2001): 244–256.

23. Manuel Mendonca, "Preparing for Ethical Leadership in Organizations," *Canadian Journal of Administrative Sciences* 18, no. 4 (2001): 266–276.

24. Michael Brown, Linda Trevino, and David Harrison, "Ethical Leadership: A Social Learning Perspective for Construct Development and Testing," *Organizational Behavior and Human Decision Processes* 97, no. 2 (2005): 117–134.

25. Rabindra Nath Kanungo, "Ethical Values of Transactional and Transformational Leaders," *Canadian Journal of Administrative Sciences* 18, no. 4 (2001): 257–265.

26. LaRue Tone Hosmer, "Strategic Planning as If Ethics Mattered," *Strategic Management Journal* 15 (1994): 17–34.

27. Chester Barnard, *The Functions of the Executive* (Boston: Harvard University Press, 1938).

28. R. Edward Freeman and Daniel R. Gilbert, *Corporate Strategy and the Search for Ethics* (Englewood Cliffs, NJ: Prentice Hall, 1988).

29. LaRue Tone Hosmer, "Strategic Planning as If Ethics Mattered," *Strategic Management Journal* 15 (1994): 17–34.

30. Cam Caldwell, Linda Hayes, Ranjan Karri, and Patricia Bernal, "Ethical Stewardship: Implications for Leadership and Trust," *Journal of Business Ethics* 78, no. 1–2 (2008): 153.

31. Ibid., 153–164.

32. Linda K. Trevino, Laura P. Hartman, and M. Brown, "Moral Person and Moral Manager: How Executives Develop a Reputation for Ethical Leadership," *California Management Review* 42, no. 4 (2000).

33. Surendra Arjoon, "Corporate Governance: An Ethical Perspective," *Journal of Business Ethics* 61 (2005): 344.

34. Eugene H. Fram, "Governance Reform—It's Only Just Begun," *Business Horizons* 47 (2004): 12.

35. Mark S. Schwartz, Thomas W. Dunfee, and Michael J. Kline, "Tone at the Top: An Ethics Code for Directors?" *Journal of Business Ethics* 58 (2005): 91–94.

36. Clifton R. Wharton, Jr., Jay W. Lorsch, and Lord Hanson, "Advice and Dissent: Rating the Corporate Governance Compact," *Harvard Business Review* (November–December, 1991): 136.

37. Michael Useem, "How Well-Run Boards Make Decisions," *Harvard Business Review* (November 2006): 4.

38. David A. Nadler, "Building Better Boards," *Harvard Business Review* 82 (2004): 102–111.

39. Paula L. Rechner and Dan Dalton, "CEO Duality and Organizational Performance: A Longitudinal Analysis," *Strategic Management Journal* 12 (1991): 155–160.

40. Paul Strebel, "The Case for Contingent Governance," *MIT Sloan Management Review*, Winter, 2004.

41. Andrew J. Felo, "Ethics Programs, Board Involvement, and Potential Conflicts of Interest in Corporate Governance," *Journal of Business Ethics* 32 (2001): 205–218.

42. Peter A. Stanwick and Sarah D. Stanwick, "The Relationship Between Corporate Governance and Financial Performance: An Empirical Study," *Journal of Corporate Citizenship* 8 (2002): 35–48.

43. Peter A. Stanwick and Sarah D. Stanwick, "CEO and Ethical Reputation: Visionary or Mercenary?," *Management Decision* 41 (2003): 1050–1057.

44. M. Skapinker, "CEO: (n) Greedy Liar with Personality Disorder," *Financial Times*, July 2, 2003, 8.

45. S. Finkelstein, L. Gomez-Mejia, B. Hall, D. Hambrick, K. Murphy, and M. Wiersema, "What Should Be Done About CEO Pay?" (Paper presented at the Academy of Management Issues Forum, 2003).

46. Linda L. Carr and Moosa Valinezhad, "The Role of Ethics in Executive Compensation: Toward a Contractarian Interpretation of the Neoclassical Theory of Managerial Remuneration,"

Journal of Business Ethics 13 (1994): 84.

47. Waymond Rodgers and Susana Gago, "A Model Capturing Ethics and Executive Compensation," *Journal of Business Ethics* 48 (2003): 193–197.

48. http://www.w3.org/People/Berners-Lee/.

Chapter 6

1. Monica Langley, "Behind Citigroup Departures: A Culture Shift by CEO Prince," *Wall Street Journal*, August 24, 2005, www.wallstreetjournal.com.

2. Jeffrey Seglin, "How to Make Tough Ethical Calls," *Harvard Management Update*, April 1, 2005.

3. I. van de Poel and L. Royakkers, "The Ethical Cycle," *Journal of Business Ethics* 71 (2007): 4–7.

4. Ibid.

5. Joseph L. Badaracco Jr., "The Discipline of Building Character," *Harvard Business Review* (March–April, 1998), 115–124.

6. Ibid.

7. Nicolai Foss, "Ethics, Discovery, and Strategy," *Journal of Business Ethics* 16 (1997): 1131–1142.

8. G. Svensson, G. Wood, and M. Callaghan, "A Comparison Between Corporate and Public Sector Business Ethics in Sweden," *Business Ethics: A European Review* 13, nos. 2–3 (2004): 166–184.

9. Constance E. Bagley, "The Ethical Leader's Decision Tree," *Harvard Business Review* 81 (2003): 18–19.

10. Christopher Robertson and William Crittenden, "Mapping Moral Philosophies: Strategic Implications for Multinational Firms," *Strategic Management Journal* 24 (2003): 385–392.

11. Peter Snyder, Molly Hall, Joline Robertson, Tomasz Jasinski, and Janice Miller, "Ethical

Rationality: A Strategic Approach to Organizational Crisis," *Journal of Business Ethics* 63 (2006): 371–383.

12. Muel Kaptein and Scott Avelino, "Measuring Corporate Integrity: A Survey-Based Approach," *Corporate Governance* 5, no. 1 (2005): 45–54.

13. www.tnellen.com/ted/tc/schein.html.

14. Ibid.

15. Edgar H. Schein, "Kurt Lewin's Change Theory in the Field and in the Classroom: Notes Toward a Model of Managed Learning," *Systems Practice* 9, no. 1 (1996): 27–47.

16. William D. Hitt, *Ethics and Leadership: Putting Theory into Practice* (Columbus, OH: Battelle Press, 1990).

17. Alan B. Graf Jr., "Building Corporate Cultures," *Chief Executive* (2005): 18.

18. Deloitte & Touche, *Ethics and Corporate Compliance: The Advantages of a Values-Based Approach* (May 2003), http://www.deloitte.com/assets/Dcom-UnitedStates/Local%20Assets/Documents/us_assurance_ethicsandcompliance_112408%20.pdf.

19. Lee Anna Jackson, "The Business of Ethics," *Black Enterprise* (October 2005), http://www.blackenterprise.com/mag/the-business-of-ethics/.

20. Ibid.

21. Ethics Resource Center, "The 2011 National Business Ethics Survey," http://www.ethics.org/nbes/.

22. David Gebler, "Why Is It so Hard to Create an Ethical Culture?" (2005), http://accounting.smartpros.com/x48460.xml.

23. Susan Chandler, "Boeing CEO Resigns After Confirming Consensual Affair," *Knight Ridder Tribune Business News*, March 8, 2005, 1.

24. Lynn Sharp Paine, "Managing for Organizational Integrity," *Harvard Business Review* (March–April 1994): 106–117.

25. Ibid., 111.
26. Deloitte & Touche, *Ethics and Corporate Compliance: The Advantages of a Values-Based Approach* (May 2003), http://www.deloitte.com/assets/Dcom-UnitedStates/Local%20Assets/Documents/us_assurance_ ethicsandcompliance_112408%20.pdf.
27. Surendra Arjoon, "Corporate Governance: An Ethical Perspective," *Journal of Business Ethics* 61 (2005): 348.
28. www.businesswire.com, accessed on August 16, 2005.
29. U.S. Sentencing Commission, "An Overview of the Organizational Guidelines," http://www/USSC.gov/Guidelines/Organiational_Guidelines/ORGOVERVIEW.pdf.
30. PricewaterhouseCoopers, "Assessing Awareness and Impact of Sarbanes-Oxley Section 404 in the Global Capital Markets" (2005), http://www.pwc.com/gx/en/financial-transaction-management-strategy/pdf/brochure.pdf.
31. Deloitte, "Sarbanes-Oxley Section 404: Ten Threats to Compliance" (2004), http://www.deloitte.com/us/tenthreats.
32. KPMG, "Sarbanes-Oxley Section 404: Management's Assessment Process— Frequently Asked Questions" (2004), http://www.us.kpmg.com/microsite/attachments/aco_so404faq_040856_post.pdf.
33. Christopher J. Robertson and Andrew Watson, "Corruption and Change: The Impact of Foreign Direct Investment," *Strategic Management Journal* 25 (2004): 385–396.
34. Robert E. Kennedy and Rafael Di Tella, *Corruption in International Business (A)* (Boston: Harvard Business School, 2001).
35. Ibid., 4–5.
36. Associated Press, "I.O.C. Investigates Allegations of Black Market for Olympic Tickets," *New York Times*, June 16, 2012.

Chapter 7

1. PBS, "Triangle Fire Transcript" *American Experience*, http://www.pbs.org/wgbh/americanexperience/features/transcript/triangle-transcript/.
2. "Triangle Shirtwaist Factory Fire (1911)," *New York Times*, March 11, 2011.
3. Lawrence Kohlberg, "Moral Stages and Moralization: The Cognitive-Development Approach," in *Moral Development and Behavior: Theory, Research, and Social Issues*, edited by Thomas Lickona (New York: Holt, Rinehart and Winston, 1976).
4. Michael Wheeler and Julianna Pillemer, "Moral Decision-Making: Reason, Emotion, & Luck" (Boston: Harvard Business Publishing, 2010).
5. Ibid.
6. Stanley Milgram, "Behavioral Study of Obedience," *Journal of Abnormal and Social Psychology* 67, no. 4 (1963): 371–378.
7. Ibid.
8. Miguel Alzola, "When Urgency Matters: On Nondiscretionary Corporate Social Responsibility," *Human Systems Management* 27 (2008): 273–282.
9. www.ti.com.
10. Linda Trevino, "Ethical Decision Making in Organizations: A Person-Situation Interactionist Model," *Academy of Management Review* 11, no. 3 (1986): 601–617.
11. Ibid.
12. Thomas Jones, "Ethical Decision Making by Individuals in Organizations: An Issue-Contingent Model," *Academy of Management Review* 16, no. 2 (1991): 366–395.
13. Richard Luecke, "The Ethics of Power, Influence, and Persuasion: Points to Honor," Chapter 8 in *Power, Influence, and Persuasion: Sell Your Ideas and Make Things Happen* (Boston: Harvard Business School Press, 2005).
14. www.prisonexp.org.
15. Linda Hill, "Exercising Influence Without Formal Authority: How New Managers Can Build Power and Influence" (Boston: Harvard Business Press, December 2008).
16. "Influence: Your Mechanism for Using Power," Chapter 3 in *Power, Influence, and Persuasion: Sell Your Ideas and Make Things Happen* (Boston: Harvard Business School Press, 2005).
17. Richard Luecke, "The Ethics of Power, Influence, and Persuasion: Points to Honor," Chapter 8 in *Power, Influence, and Persuasion: Sell Your Ideas and Make Things Happen* (Boston: Harvard Business School Press, 2005).
18. Richard Christie and Florence L. Geis, *Studies in Machiavellianism* (New York: Academic Press, 1970).
19. Richard Christie, "Machiavelli Personality Test," www.Salon.com.
20. Richard Luecke, "The Ethics of Power, Influence, and Persuasion: Points to Honor," Chapter 8 in *Power, Influence, and Persuasion: Sell Your Ideas and Make Things Happen* (Boston: Harvard Business School Press, 2005), 10.
21. Charles Schwepker Jr., "Ethical Climate's Relationship to Job Satisfaction, Organizational Commitment, and Turnover Intention in the Salesforce," *Journal of Business Research* 54, no. 1 (2001): 39–52.
22. Randi Sims and K. Galen Kroeck, "The Influence of Ethical Fit on Employee Satisfaction, Commitment and Turnover," *Journal of Business Ethics* 13, no. 12 (1994): 939–947.
23. Ibid.
24. Hian Koh and El'fred Boo, "The Link Between Organizational Ethics and Job Satisfaction: A Study of Managers in Singapore," *Journal of Business Ethics* 29, no. 4 (2001): 309–324.

25. Ibid.
26. Maria Riaz Hamdani and M. Ronald Buckley, "Diversity Goals: Reframing the Debate and Enabling a Fair Evaluation," *Business Horizons* 54, no. 1 (2011): 33–40.
27. Amy Edmondson and Kathryn Roloff, "Leveraging Diversity Through Psychological Safety," *Rotman Magazine* (Fall 2009): 47–51.
28. Rose Mary Wentling and Nilda Palma-Riva, "Current Status and Future Trends of Diversity Initiatives in the Workplace: Diversity Experts' Perspective," *Human Resource Development Quarterly* 9, no. 3 (1998): 235–253.
29. Yoav Vardi and Ely Weitz, "Using the Theory of Reasoned Action to Predict Organizational Misbehavior," *Psychological Reports* 91, no. 3 (2002): 1027–1040.
30. Wendi Everton, Jeffrey Jolton, and Paul Mastrangelo, "Be Nice and Fair or Else: Understanding Reasons for Employees' Deviant Behaviors," *Journal of Management Development* 26, no. 2 (2007): 117–131.
31. Ibid.
32. Yoav Vardi, "The Effects of Organizational and Ethical Climates on Misconduct at Work," *Journal of Business Ethics* 29, no. 4 (2001): 325–337.
33. Roland Kidwell and Sean Valentine, "Positive Group Context, Work Attitudes, and Organizational Misbehavior: The Case of Withholding Job Effort," *Journal of Business Ethics* 86, no. 1 (2009): 15–28.
34. Wendi Everton, Jeffrey Jolton, and Paul Mastrangelo, "Be Nice and Fair or Else: Understanding Reasons for Employees' Deviant Behaviors," *Journal of Management Development* 26, no. 2 (2007): 117–131.
35. Jerald Greenberg, "Employee Theft as a Reaction to Underpayment Inequity: The Hidden Cost of Pay Cuts," *Journal of Applied Psychology* 75, no. 5 (1990): 561–568.

36. Brian Niehoff and Robert Paul, "Causes of Employee Theft and Strategies That HR Managers Can Use for Prevention," *Human Resource Management* 39, no. 1 (2000): 51–64.
37. Rich Russakoff and Mark Goodman, "Employee Theft: Are You Blind to It?," CBSNews.com (July 14, 2011).
38. T. Singer, "Stop Thief! Are Your Employees Robbing You Blind?," *Entrepreneur* (January 1996): 148–153.
39. Arthur Gross-Schafer, Jeff Trigilio, Jamie Negus, and Ceng-Si Ro, "Ethics Education in the Workplace: An Effective Tool to Combat Employee Theft," *Journal of Business Ethics* 26, no. 2 (2000): 89–100.
40. Ibid.
41. http://www1.eeoc.gov//eeoc/statistics/enforcement/sexual_harassment.cfm?renderforprint=1.
42. Curt Levey, "Sexual Harassment's Legal Morass," *Wall Street Journal*, November 7, 2011.
43. Hilary Stout, "Less 'He Said, She Said' in Sex Harassment Cases," *New York Times*, November 5, 2011.
44. Curt Levey, "Sexual Harassment's Legal Morass," *Wall Street Journal*, November 7, 2011.
45. Chelsea Willness, Piers Steel, and Kibeom Lee, "A Meta-Analysis of the Antecedents and Consequences of Workplace Sexual Harassment," *Personnel Psychology* 60, no. 1 (2007): 127–162.
46. Lynn Sharp Paine and Lara Adamsons, "Note on the Law of Sexual Harassment" (Boston: Harvard Business Press, 2008).
47. Ibid.
48. Inez Dekker and Julian Barling, "Personal and Organizational Predictors of Workplace Sexual Harassment of Women by Men," *Journal of Occupational Health Psychology* 3, no. 1 (1998): 7–18.
49. Chelsea Willness, Piers Steel, and Kibeom Lee, "A Meta-Analysis of the Antecedents

and Consequences of Workplace Sexual Harassment," *Personnel Psychology* 60, no. 1 (2007): 127–162.
50. David Streitfeld, "Lawsuit Shakes Foundation of a Man's World of Tech," *New York Times*, June 2, 2012.
51. Tara Parker-Pope, "When the Bully Sits in the Next Cubicle," *New York Times*, March 25, 2008.
52. Brad Stone, "Settlement Was Paid in Whitman Shoving Incident," *New York Times*, June 14, 2010.
53. Washington State Department of Labor & Industries, "Workplace Bullying and Disruptive Behavior: What Everyone Needs to Know" (Olympia: Author, April 2011).
54. Ibid.
55. www.apa.org.
56. Barry Friedman and Lisa Reed, "Workplace Privacy: Employee Relations and Legal Implications of Monitoring Employee E-Mail Use," *Employee Responsibilities and Rights Journal* 19, no. 2 (2007): 75–83.
57. Laura Petrecca, "Employers Use Myriad Ways to Monitor Employees," *USA Today*, March 17, 2010.
58. Laura Petrecca, "More Employers Use Tech to Track Workers," *USA Today*, March 17, 2010.
59. Laura Petrecca, "Employers Use Myriad Ways to Monitor Employees," *USA Today*, March 17, 2010.
60. Sylvia Ann Hewlett and Carolyn Buck Luce,"Extreme Jobs: The Dangerous Allure of the 70-Hour Workweek," *Harvard Business Review* (December 2006).
61. Sue Shellenbarger, "Companies Deal With Employees Who Refuse to Take Time Off By Requiring Vacations, Paying Them to Go," *The Wall Street Journal*, August 12, 2014.
62. Leslie Alderman, "When the Stork Carries a Pink Slip," *New York Times*, March 27, 2009; Dina Bakst, "Pregnant, and

Pushed out of a Job," *New York Times*, January 30, 2012.

Chapter 8

1. We would like to thank Olivia M. Stanwick for suggesting this topic for the opening vignette.
2. Ulla Klostier, "Now That's Something to Advertise: Agency Invents Billboard That Makes Gallons of Drinking Water out of This Air," *The Daily Mail*, August 12, 2013.
3. Duncan Geere, "Peruvian Billboard Creates Drinking Water," http://www.wired.co.uk/news/archive/2013-03/24/utec-billboard.
4. Matt Peckham, "The Billboard Sucks Pollution from the Sky and Returns Purified Air," *Time*, May 1, 2014.
5. Garrett Hardin, "The Tragedy of the Commons," *Science* 162 (1968): 1243–1248.
6. Ibid.
7. Mark Starik, "Should Trees Have Managerial Standing? Toward Stakeholder Status for Non-Human Nature," *Journal of Business Ethics* 14 (1995): 207–217.
8. David G. Woodward, "Is the Natural Environment a Stakeholder? Of Course It Is (No Matter What the Utilitarians Might Say)!" (Presented at Critical Perspectives on Accounting Conference, Baruch College: City University of New York, 2002).
9. Michael E. Porter and Claas van der Linde, "Green and Competitive: Ending the Stalemate," *Harvard Business Review* 22, no. 4 (1995): 853–886.
10. Renato J. Orsato, "Competitive Environmental Strategies: When Does It Pay to Be Green?" *California Management Review* (Winter, 2006): 127–143.
11. "1995—Shell Reverses Decision to Dump the Brent Spar," Greenpeace.org, September 13, 2011.

12. Amy Cortese, "Friend of Nature? Let's See Those Shoes," *New York Times*, March 6, 2007, www.nytimes.com.
13. Catherine A. Ramus, "Organizational Support for Employees: Encouraging Creative Ideas for Environmental Sustainability," *California Management Review* 43 (2001): 98.
14. David Lubin, Amy Longsworth, and Randall Russell, "Sustainability Strategy Transforms the Enterprise," Harvard Business Publishing, November 15, 2011.
15. Catherine A. Ramus, "Organizational Support for Employees: Encouraging Creative Ideas for Environmental Sustainability," *California Management Review* 43 (2001): 85–105.
16. www.greenpeace.org/international/about.
17. www.sierraclub.org/inside.
18. www.environmentaldefense.org/page.cfm?tagID=362.
19. "Environmental Accounting Tricks," www.foe.org/WSSD/tricks.html.
20. Sarah D. Stanwick and Peter A. Stanwick, "The Relationship Between Environmental Disclosures and Financial Performance: An Empirical Study of U.S. Firms," *Eco-Management and Auditing* 7 (2000): 155–164.
21. www.epa.gov.
22. Ibid.
23. "EPA's Commitment to Environmental Justice" (EPA mail memorandum), August 9, 2002.
24. Douglas Fischer, "Low-Income, Minority Areas Bear Brunt of Bay Area Pollution," February 18, 2007, www.insidebayarea.com.
25. Anne Grafé-Buckens and Sebastian Beloe, "Auditing and Communicating Business Sustainability," *Eco-Management and Auditing* 5 (1998): 103.
26. Stuart L. Hart, "Beyond Greening: Strategies for a Sustainable World," *Harvard Business Review* 75 (1997): 66–76.

27. Kimberly O. Packard and Forest Reinhardt, "What Every Executive Needs to Know About Global Warming," *Harvard Business Review* (July–August, 2000): 177.
28. "What Is the Kyoto Treaty?" *BBC News,* September 29, 2003, news.bbc.co.uk.
29. Ans Kolk and Jonathan Pinkse, "Business Responses to Climate Change: Identifying Emergent Strategies," *California Business Review* 47 (2005): 6–20.
30. Jonathan Lash and Fred Wellington, "Competitive Advantage on a Warming Planet," *Harvard Business Review* (March, 2007): 2–11.
31. Ibid.
32. Michael Toffel and Stephanie Van Sice, "Carbon Footprints: Methods and Calculations" (Boston: Harvard Business, June 2011), 1–16.
33. Ibid.
34. *Carbon Disclosure Project 2010 Global 500 Report,* PricewaterhouseCoopers, https://www.cdproject.net/CDPResults/CDP-2010-G500.pdf.
35. Ibid., 16.
36. Ibid., 16.
37. Somini Sengupta, "Decades Later, Toxic Sludge Torments Bhopal," *New York Times*, July 7, 2008.
38. Lydia Polgreen, "Indians, Envious of U.S. Spill Response, Seethe Over Bhopal," *New York Times*, June 24, 2010; Somini Sengupta, "Decades Later, Toxic Sludge Torments Bhopal," *New York Times*, July 7, 2008.

Chapter 9

1. Brooks Barnes and Nicole Perlroth, "As More Documents Appear, Sony Seeks to Calm Nervous Employees," *New York Times*, December 8, 2014.
2. Ben Fritz, Dan Yadron, and Erich Schwartzel, "Behind the Scenes at Sony as Hacking Crisis Unfolded," *The Wall Street Journal*, December 30, 2014.

3. Ben Fritz, "Email Claims Fresh Sony Data Released, Threatens Studio," *The Wall Street Journal*, December 8, 2014.

4. Lori Grisham, "Timeline: North Korea and the Sony Pictures Hack," *USA Today*, January 5, 2015.

5. Ben Fritz, "Sony Makes 'The Interview' Available on Cable, Satellite Systems," *The Wall Street Journal*, January 1, 2015.

6. Ben Fritz, "Amy Pascal Steps Down as Head of Sony's Film Business," *The Wall Street Journal*, February 5, 2015.

7. American Management Association/ePolicy Institute, *2007 Electronic Monitoring & Surveillance Survey*, http://www.amanet.org/training/whitepapers/2007-Electronic-Monitoring-and-Surveillance-Survey-41.aspx.

8. Ibid.

9. Ibid.

10. Ibid.

11. Ibid.

12. Ibid.

13. Mary Gentile and John J. Sviokla, *Information Technology in Organizations: Emerging Issues in Ethics and Policy* (Boston: Harvard Business School, 1990), 5.

14. Ibid, 8.

15. Ibid, 9.

16. Suzanne P. Weisband and Bruce A. Reinig, "Managing User Perceptions of Email Privacy," *Communications of the ACM* 38, no. 12 (1995): 41.

17. Mark S. Dichter and Michael S. Burkhardt, "Electronic Interaction in the Workplace: Monitoring, Retrieving, and Storing Employee Communications in the Internet Age," The American Employment Law Council Fourth Annual Conference, October 1996.

18. Thomas Hilton, "Information Systems Ethics: A Practitioner Study," *Journal of Business Ethics* 28 (2000): 279–284.

19. www.privacyrights.org.

20. Dan Frommer, "The Tell-Tale Heart," *Forbes*, February 16, 2006, www.forbes.com.

21. "U.S. Group Implants Electronic Tags in Workers," *Financial Times*, February 13, 2006.

22. W. A. Parent, "Privacy, Morality, and the Law," *Philosophy & Public Affairs* (Fall 1983).

23. http://www.dun.usda.gov/opcm/security%20guide/v2comint/cellular.htm.

24. www.cpuc.ca.gov/.

25. www.privacyrights.org.

26. Frank Buytendijk and Jay Heiser, "Confronting the Privacy and Ethical Risk of Big Data," *The Financial Times*, September 24, 2013.

27. www.ftc.gov.

28. Larry Ponemon, "The Value of Protecting Customer Privacy," *CIO Magazine*, January 15, 2006.

29. Victoria Bush, Beverly Venable, and Alan Bush, "Ethics and Marketing on the Internet: Practitioners' Perceptions of Societal, Industry, and Company Concerns," *Journal of Business Ethics* 23 (2000): 237–248.

30. L. Himmelstein, "Log on, Boxx," *Businessweek*, March 22, 1999, EB48–49.

31. Robert Berner and Adrienne Carter, "Swiping Back at Credit Card Fraud," *Businessweek*, July 11, 2005, www.businessweek.com.

32. "At Online Stores, Sniffing Out Crooks Is a Matter of Survival," http://online.wsj.com/article/SB112311786883304593.html.

33. Thomas Vartanian and Mark Fajfar, "Sarbanes-Oxley Act Underscores Importance of Information Security," *Community Banker* (June 2004): 50–51.

34. Matthew Newman, "So Many Countries, So Many Laws," *Wall Street Journal*, April 28, 2003, www.wallstreetjournal.com.

35. G. Elijah Dann and Neil Haddow, "Just Doing Business or Doing Just Business: Google, Microsoft, Yahoo! And the Business of Censoring China's Internet," *Journal of Business Ethics* 79: 219–234.

36. Kirsten Martin, "Google, Inc., in China (condensed)", *Business Roundtable Institute for Corporate Ethics* (2007), http://www.corporate-ethics.org/pdf/BRI-1004.pdf.

37. G. Elijah Dann and Neil Haddow, "Just Doing Business or Doing Just Business: Google, Microsoft, Yahoo! and the Business of Censoring China's Internet," *Journal of Business Ethics* 79: 228.

38. Ibid., 229.

39. Richard De George, *Competing With Integrity in International Business* (New York: Oxford University Press, 1993).

40. Ibid., 122.

41. Department of Justice, "Special Report on 'Phishing,'" www.usdoj.gov.

42. "Investigative Programs Cyber Investigations," http://www.fbi.gov/about-us/investigate/cyuber/cyber.

43. www.fdic.gov/consumers/consumer/fighttheft.

44. Tommie Singleton and Aaron Singleton, "Cyberterrorism: Are You at Risk?," *Journal of Corporate Accounting and Finance* 15, part 5 (2004): 3–12. www.interscience.wiley.com.

45. Gerritt Hornung, "A General Data Protection Regulation for Europe? Light and Shade in the Commission's Draft of 25 January 2012," Scripted.org 9, no. 1 (April 2012).

46. "Cyber Thieves Silently Copy Your Passwords as You Type," February 27, 2006, www.nytimes.com.

47. Uniting and Strengthening America by Providing Appropriate Tools Required to Intercept and Obstruct Terrorism (USA PATRIOT Act) Act of 2001, www.gpo.gov.

48. Ibid.

49. Jenna Wortham, "Use of Homeless as Internet Hot Spots Backfires on Marketer," *New York Times*, March 12, 2012.

50. Ibid.

Chapter 10

1. "Pepsi Apologizes for Before You Score iPhone App," *Wall Street Journal*, October 13, 2009;

Valerie Bauerlein and Suzanne Vranica, "Drink's iPhone 'App' Gets Anger Flowing," *Wall Street Journal*, October 14, 2009; Melissa Rohlin, "Pepsi's Amp App Will No Longer 'Help'" Men Seduce Women," *Los Angeles Times*, October 22, 2009.

2. Jerome McCarthy, *Basic Marketing: A Managerial Approach* (Homewood, IL: Richard D. Irwin, 1960).

3. Ken Peattie and Andrew Crane, "Green Marketing: Legend, Myth, Farce or Prophesy?," *Qualitative Market Research* 8 (2005): 357–370.

4. Jill Meredith Ginsberg and Paul Bloom, "Choosing the Right Green Marketing Strategy," *MIT Sloan Management Review* (Fall 2004): 79–84.

5. Ken Peattie, "Towards Sustainability: The Third Age of Green Marketing," *Marketing Review* 2 (2001): 129–146.

6. Ibid.

7. Jaime Rivera-Camino, "Re-Evaluating Green Marketing Strategy: A Stakeholder Perspective," *European Journal of Marketing* 41, no. 11 (2007): 1328–1358.

8. Ibid.

9. David Vinjamuri, "Ethics and the Five Deadly Sins of Social Media," *Forbes*, November 3, 2011.

10. Johannes Brinkman, "Looking at Consumer Behavior in a Moral Perspective," *Journal of Business Ethics* 51 (2004): 129–141.

11. Sarah Steenhaut and Patrick Van Kenhove, "Relationship Commitment and Ethical Consumer Behavior in a Retail Setting: The Case of Receiving Too Much Change at the Checkout," *Journal of Business Ethics* 56 (2005): 335–353.

12. Ibid.

13. http://www.brainyquote.com/ quotes/keywords/consumer .html#ixzz1n1w2Mu4U.

14. Brad Brown, Michael Chui, and Kames Manyika, "Are You Ready for the Era of 'Big

Data'?," *McKinsey Quarterly* (October, 2011): 24–35.

15. Alexandra Campbell, "Relationship Marketing in Consumer Markets: A Comparison of Managerial and Consumer Attitudes About Information Privacy," *Journal of Direct Marketing* 11 (1997): 44–57.

16. Frank V. Cespedes and H. Jeff Smith, "Database Marketing: New Rules for Policy and Practice," *Sloan Management Review* (Summer, 1993): 13.

17. George Long, Margaret Hogg, Mary Hatley, and Steven Angold, "Relationship Marketing and Privacy: Exploring the Thresholds," *Journal of Marketing Practice* 5 (1999): 4–20.

18. Lisa O'Malley, Maurice Patterson, and Martin Evans, "Intimacy or Intrusion? The Privacy Dilemma for Relationship Marketing in Consumer Markets," *Journal of Marketing Management* 13 (1997): 541–559.

19. Russell Winer, "Framework for Customer Relationship Management," *California Management Review* 43 (2001): 89–105.

20. Ibid.

21. http://www.brainyquote.com/ quotes/authors/m/mahatma_ gandhi.html.

22. Michelle Singletary, "Rage, Rage Against the Financial Sector Fuels Protest," *Washington Post*, October 8, 2011.

23. Monroe Friedman, "Consumer Boycotts in the United States, 1970–1980: Contemporary Events in Historical Perspective," *Journal of Consumer Affairs* 19 (1985): 97.

24. Jill Kein, N. Craig Smith, and Andrew John, "Why We Boycott: Consumer Motivations for Boycott Participation," *Journal of Marketing* 68 (2004): 92–109.

25. Ibid.

26. Ibid.

27. Associated Press, "Tylenol-Recall Liability Case," *New York Times*, September 18, 1986.

28. Ibid.

29. Barry Berman, "Planning for the Inevitable Product Recall," *Business Horizons* (March–April 1999): 69–78.

30. Ibid.

31. N. Craig Smith, Robert Thomas, and John Quelch, "A Strategic Approach to Managing Product Recalls," *Harvard Business Review* (September–October, 1996): 102–112.

32. Ibid.

33. Barry Berman, "Planning for the Inevitable Product Recall," *Business Horizons* (March–April, 1999): 69–78.

34. Ibid.

35. Julio Rotemberg, "Fair Pricing," NBER Working Paper Series (Cambridge, MA: National Bureau of Economic Research, November 2004).

36. Mohammed Razzaque and Tan Hwee, "Ethics and Purchasing Dilemma: A Singaporean View," *Journal of Business Ethics* 35, no. 4 (2002): 307–326.

37. Gregory Turner, Stephen Taylor, and Mark Hartley, "Ethics, Gratuities, and Professionalization of the Purchasing Function," *Journal of Business Ethics* 14 (1995): 751–760.

38. http://ethics.walmartstores .com/IntegrityIntheWorkplace/ GiftAndEntertainment.aspx.

39. Amit Saini, "Purchasing Ethics and Inter-Organizational Buyer-Supplier Relational Determinants: A Conceptual Framework," *Journal of Business Ethics* 95 (2010): 439–455.

40. Ibid.

41. http://dca.lacounty.gov/ tsfalseadvertising.htm.

42. Ibid.

43. http://www.find-laws.com/ fraud/overview-of-false-advertising.html.

44. Ibid.

45. http://dca.lacounty.gov/ tsfalseadvertising.htm.

46. Ibid.

47. Ibid.

48. Howard Schutz and Marianne Casey, "Consumer Perceptions of Advertising as Misleading,"

Journal of Consumer Affairs 15 (1981): 340–357.

49. Christopher Thompson and Neil Hume, "Big Tobacco Prepares for Plain Packaging," *Financial Times*, February 15, 2012.

50. www.youtube.com/watch?v=NAExoSozc2c.

51. John Broder, "F.T.C. Charges Joe Camel Ad Illegally Takes Aim at Minors," *New York Times*, May 29, 1997.

52. http://www.tobaccofreekids.org/.

53. Marlene Schwartz, Craig Ross, Jennifer Harris, David Jernigan, Michael Siegel, Joshua Ostroff, and Kelly Brownell, "Breakfast Cereal Industry Pledges to Self-Regulate Advertising to Youth: Will They Improve the Marketing Landscape?," *Journal of Public Health* Policy 31 (2010): 59–73.

54. Alex Molnar, David Garcia, Faith Boninger, and Bruce Merrill, "Marketing of Foods of Minimal Nutritional Value to Children in Schools," *Preventive Medicine* 47 (2008): 504–507.

55. http://www.fcc.gov/encyclopedia/childrens-educational-television-rules-and-orders.

56. Morgan Spurlock, *Super Size Me* (Culver City, CA: Columbia TriStar Home Entertainment, 2004).

57. Sharon Bernstein, "San Francisco Bans Happy Meals," *Los Angeles Times*, November 2, 2010.

58. Boyd Sinburn, Gary Sacks, Tim Lobstein, Neville Rigby, Louise Baur, Kelly Brownell, Tim Gill, Jaap Seidell, and Shiriki Kumanyika, "The 'Sydney Principles' for Reducing the Commercial Promotion of Foods and Beverages to Children," *Public Health Nutrition* 11 (2008): 881–886.

59. Brooks Barnes, "Promoting Nutrition, Disney to Restrict Junk-Food Ads," *New York Times*, June 5, 2012.

60. John Radosta, "Ford's Pinto: Some Virtues and Limitations," *New York Times*, January 24, 1971.

61. Mark Dowie, "Pinto Madness," *Mother Jones* 2, no. 8 (September/October 1977): 18–24, 28–32.

62. Gail Bauva, *Engineering Ethics: An Industrial Perspective* (Boston: Elsevier Academic Press, 2006), 45.

63. Reginald Stuart, "Ford Orders Recall of 1.5 Million Pintos for Safety Changes," *New York Times*, June 10, 1978.

Chapter 11

1. We would like to thank Olivia M. Stanwick for suggesting this topic for the opening vignette.

2. China Labor Watch, "Samsung Factory Exploiting Child Labor: Investigative Report on HEG Electronics (Huizhou) Co., Ltd. Samsung Supplier, August 7, 2012.

3. Min-Jeong Lee, "Samsung Faces New Child-Labor Allegations," *The Wall Street Journal*, July 10, 2014.

4. David Barboza, "Despite a Pledge by Samsung, Child Labor Proves Resilient," July 10, 2014.

5. David Barboza, "Samsung Contractor Suspended Over Child Labor Allegations," *New York Times*, July 14, 2014.

6. Reuters, "Samsung Electronics to Pass Fewer Orders to China Supplier in Child Labor Response," *New York Times*, August 5, 2014.

7. C. K. Prahalad, *The Fortune at the Bottom of the Pyramid: Eradicating Poverty Through Profits* (Upper Saddle River, NJ: Wharton School Publishing, 2004).

8. C. K. Prahalad and Allen Hammond, "Serving the World's Poor, Profitably," *Harvard Business Review* 80, no. 9 (September, 2002): 48–57.

9. C. K. Prahalad, *The Fortune at the Bottom of the Pyramid: Eradicating Poverty Through Profits* (Upper Saddle River, NJ: Wharton School Publishing, 2004).

10. C. K. Prahalad and Allen Hammond, "Serving the World's Poor, Profitably," *Harvard Business Review* 80, no. 9 (September, 2002): 48–57, 124.

11. Ibid.

12. V. Kasturi Rangan, Michael Chu, and Dijordjija Petkoski, "Segmenting the Base of the Pyramid," *Harvard Business Review* 89, no. 6 (June, 2011): 113–117.

13. Ibid.

14. Ashish Karamchandani, Mike Kubzansky, and Nishant Lalwani, "Is the Bottom of the Pyramid Really for You?," *Harvard Business Review* 89, no. 3 (March, 2011): 107–111.

15. Ibid.

16. Kirk Davidson, "Ethical Concerns at the Bottom of the Pyramid: Where CSR Meets BOP," *Journal of International Business Ethics* 2 (2009): 22–32.

17. Ted London and Stuart Hart, *Next Generation Business Strategies for the Base of the Pyramid: New Approaches for Building Mutual Value* (Upper Saddle River, NJ: Pearson Education).

18. Ibid.

19. Christian Seelos and Johanna Mair, "Social Entrepreneurship: Creating New Business Models to Serve the Poor," *Business Horizons* 48 (2005): 241–246.

20. Paul Tracy and Nelson Phillips, "The Distinctive Challenge of Educating Social Entrepreneurs: A Postscript and Rejoinder to the Special Issue on Entrepreneurship Education," *Academy of Management Learning & Education* 6 (2007): 264–271.

21. John Thompson, Geoff Alvy, and Ann Less, "Social Entrepreneurship: A New Look at the People and the Potential," *Management Decision* 38, no. 5 (2000): 328–338.

22. Ibid.

23. John Elkington and Pamela Hartigan, "Roots of Unreason, Sources of Power: The Social Entrepreneurs Who Are Changing the World" (Boston: Harvard Business Press, 2008).

24. Ibid.

25. Skaker Zahra, Eric Gedajlovic, Donald Nuebaum, and Joel Shulman, "A Typology of Social Entrepreneurs: Motives, Search Processes and Ethical Challenges," *Journal of Business Venturing* 24 (2009): 519–532.

26. Ibid.

27. http://www.nobelprize.org/nobel_prizes/peace/laureates/2006/yunus-lecture-en.html.

28. Muhammad Yunus and Karl Weber, *Building Social Business: The New Kind of Capitalism That Serves Humanity's Most Pressing Needs* (New York: Public Affairs, 2010).

29. Lydia Polgreen, "Microcredit Pioneer Faces an Inquiry in Bangladesh," *New York Times*, January 29, 2011.

30. http://www.grameenfoundation.org.

31. Greg Powell and Rick Aubry, "TransFair USA" (Palo Alto, CA: Stanford Graduate School of Business Case, 2004), 1.

32. "A Charter of Fair Trade Principles," World Fair Trade Organization and Fairtrade Labeling Organizations International (2009), www.befair.be.

33. *Monitoring the Scope and Benefits of FairTrade*, 3rd ed. 2011, Fairtrade Labeling Organization International e.V., www.fairtrade.net.

34. "A Charter of Fair Trade Principles," World Fair Trade Organization and Fairtrade Labeling Organizations International (2009), www.befair.be.

35. Ibid.

36. Peter Griffiths, "Ethical Objections to Fairtrade," *Journal of Business Ethics* 105 (2012): 357–373.

37. Ibid.

38. Obama Addresses the United Nations General Assembly, Speech Transcript, *Washington Post*, September 23, 2010.

39. Lynn Sharp Paine and Lara Adamson, "Business and Human Rights" (Boston: Harvard Business Publishing, 2011).

40. Ibid.

41. John Kamm, "The Role of Business Rights in Promoting Respect for Human Rights in China," 1997, www.business-ethics.org.

42. www.sa-intl.org.

43. http://www.presidency.ucsb.edu/ws/?pid=11288#axzz1lzzbFeye.

44. Roger Thurdow and Scoot Kilman, *Enough: Why the World's Poorest Starve in an Age of Plenty* (New York: Public Affairs, 2009).

45. http://www.wfp.org/hunger/stats.

46. http://www.wfp.org/hunger/causes.

47. Ibid.

48. Jenny Mead and R. Edward Freeman, "Food Versus Fuel" (Charlottesville: University of Virginia, Darden Business Publishing, 2007).

49. Ibid.

50. Jose Goldemberg, "The Challenge of Biofuels," *Energy Environmental Science* 1 (2008): 523–525.

51. Zibin Zhang, Luanne Lohr, Cesar Escalante, and Michael Wetzstein, "Food Versus Fuel: What Do Prices Tell Us?," *Energy Policy* 38 (2010): 445–451.

52. Elisabeth Rosenthal, "Rush to Use Crops as Fuel Raises Food Prices and Hunger Fears," *New York Times*, April 6, 2011.

53. Bryan Walsh, "Why Biofuels Help Push Up World Food Prices," *Time*, February 14, 2011.

54. Robert Pear, "After Three Decades, Tax Credit for Ethanol Expires," *New York Times*, January 1, 2012.

55. Song Jung-a and Christian Oliver, "Daewoo to Cultivate Madagascar Land for Free," *Financial Times*, November 19, 2008.

56. United States Census Bureau. http://www.census.gov/hhes/www/poverty/about/overview/.

57. United States Department of Health & Human Services, http://aspe.hhs.gov/poverty/14poverty.cfm.

58. Feeding America, http://www.feedingamerica.org/hunger-in-america/our-research/hunger-in-america/key-findings.html.

59. *The Millennium Development Goals Report 2011* (New York: United Nations, 2011).

60. Ibid.

61. Ibid.

62. Ibid.

63. J. D. Sachs and J. W. McArthur, "The Millennium Project: A Plan for Meeting the Millennium Development Goals," *The Lancet* 365 (January 12, 2005): 347–353, http://image.thelancet.com/extras/04art12121web.pdf.

64. Ibid.

65. UN Commission on the Private Sector & Development, "Unleashing Entrepreneurship: Making Business Work for the Poor," Report to the Secretary-General of the United Nations (New York: UN Development Programme, 2004).

66. Ibid.

67. Jane Nelson and Dave Prescott, "Business and the Millennium Development Goals: A Framework for Action," *International Business Leaders Forum* (Manila, Philippines: United Nations Development Programme, 2008).

68. Ibid.

69. Humphrey Hawksley, "India's Exploited Child Cotton Workers," BBC News, January 19, 2012.

Chapter 12

1. Eric Pillmore, "How We're Fixing Up Tyco," *Harvard Business Review* 81, no. 12 (December 2003): 96–103, 126.

2. Jang Singh, "A Comparison of the Contents of the Code of Ethics of Canada's Largest Corporations in 1992 and 2003," *Journal of Business Ethics* 64, no. 1 (2006): 17–29.

3. Patrick E. Murphy, "Developing, Communicating, and Promoting Corporate Ethics Statements:

A Longitudinal Analysis," *Journal of Business Ethics* 62 (2005): 183–189.

4. Cecily Raiborn and Dinah Payne, "Corporate Codes of Conduct: A Collective Conscience and Continuum," *Journal of Business Ethics* 9, no. 11 (1990): 879–889.

5. "The Penney Idea and Wal-Mart," *World History Blog*, http://www.worldhistoryblog.com/2006/09/penney-idea-and-wal-mart.html.

6. Enron's Code of Ethics, www.thesmokinggun.com.

7. Jeff Turner, "Business Ethics: What Would You Do?," www.refresher.com/archives44.html.

8. William A. Stimson, "A Deming-Inspired Management Code of Ethics," *Quality Progress* 38 (2005): 67–75.

9. Ibid.

10. Amy Klemm Verbos, Joseph A. Gerard, Paul R. Forshey, Charles S. Harding, and Janice S. Miller, "The Positive Ethical Organization: Enacting a Living Code of Ethics and Ethical Organizational Identity," *Journal of Business Ethics*, no. 76 (2007): 17–33.

11. Sandra Waddock and Charles Bodwell, "From TQM to TRM: Total Responsibility Management Approaches," *Journal of Corporate Citizenship* (Autumn, 2002): 113–126.

12. www.deloitte.com/us/corpgov.

13. Charles H. Calhoun and Philip Wolitzer, "Ethics as a Value-Added Service," *CPA Journal* 71 (2001).

14. www.smokinggun.com.

15. Bethany McLean, Peter Elkind, and Alex Gibney, *Enron: The Smartest Guys in the Room*, directed by Alex Gibney (New York: Magnolia Home Entertainment. 2005), DVD.

16. Krista Bondy, Dirk Matten, and Jeremy Moon, "The Adoption of Voluntary Codes of Conduct in MNCs: A Three-Country Comparative Study," *Business and Society Review* 109, no. 4 (2004): 449–477.

17. www.metlife.com.

18. www.smokinggun.com.

19. Ibid.

20. www.fdic.gov.

21. Randy Myers, "Ensuring Ethical Effectiveness," *Journal of Accountancy* (February, 2003): 28–29.

22. Sarbanes-Oxley Act of 2002, Section 406.

23. http://www.ussc.gov/Guidelines/2004_guidelines/manual/gl2004.pdf.

24. http://www.cauxroundtable.org.

25. http://www.oecd.org/daf/investment/guidelines.

26. http://www.unglobalcompact.org/AboutTheGC/index.html.

27. http://www.cauxroundtable.org/index.cfm?&menuid=8.

28. http://www.oecd.org/daf/investment/guidelines.

29. http://www.unglobalcompact.org/AboutTheGC/TheTenPrinciples/index.html.

30. Russell Boisjoly, Ellen Foster Curtis, and Eugene Mellican, "Roger Boisjoly and the *Challenger* Disaster: The Ethical Dimensions," *Journal of Business Ethics* 8 (1989): 217–230.

Chapter 13

1. "Hillsborough Disaster: Timeline to Disaster," *BBC News*. November 13, 2014.

2. "Hillsborough Disaster and its Aftermath," *BBC News*. December 19, 2012.

3. John F. Burns, "23 Years After Soccer Tragedy, an Apology and a Shift in Blame," *New York Times*, September 12, 2012.

4. Ibid.

5. PricewaterhouseCoopers, "Global Economic Crime Survey 2011," www.pwc.com/crimesurvey.

6. Ibid.

7. PricewaterhouseCoopers, "Global Economic Crime Survey 2014," http://www.pwc.com/gx/en/economic-crime-survey/downloads.jhtml

8. Ibid.

9. Ibid.

10. Ibid.

11. Gary R. Weaver, Linda K. Trevino, and Philip L. Cochran, "Corporate Ethics Programs as Control Systems: Influences of Executive Commitment and Environmental Factors," *Academy of Management Journal* 42 (1999): 41–57.

12. Debbie T. LeClair and Linda Ferrell, "Innovation in Experiential Business Ethics Training," *Journal of Business Ethics* 23 (2000): 313–322.

13. Ibid., 316.

14. http://accounting.smartpros.com/x54196.xml.

15. Pat Croce, "Don't Worry, Be Sorry," *FSB: Fortune Small Business*, February 1, 2005.

16. Gael McDonald, "Business Ethics: Practical Proposals for Organisations," *Journal of Business Ethics* 25 (2000): 169–184.

17. Kevin T. Jackson, "Globalizing Corporate Ethics Programs: Perils and Prospects," *Journal of Business Ethics* 16 (1997): 1227–1235.

18. Ibid., 1230–1232.

19. Gary Weaver, "Ethics Programs in Global Businesses: Culture's Role in Managing Ethics," *Journal of Business Ethics* 30 (2001): 3–15.

20. Ibid., 6–9.

21. http://accounting.smartpros.com/x44962.xml.

22. Muel Kaptein, "Guidelines for the Development of an Ethics Safety Net," *Journal of Business Ethics* 41 (2002): 217–234.

23. Henry Adobor, "Exploring the Role Performance of Corporate Ethics Officers," *Journal of Business Ethics* 69 (2006): 57–75.

24. Michael Allen, "The Ethics Audit: A Tool Whose Time Has Come," *Nonprofit World* (November/December 1995): 51–55.

25. John Rosthorn, "Business Ethics Auditing: More Than a Stakeholder's Toy," *Journal of Business Ethics* 27 (2000): 13.

26. Janet P. Near and Marcia P. Miceli, "Organizational Dissidence: The Case of Whistle-Blowing," *Journal of Business Ethics* 4 (1985): 5.

27. Gregory Watchman, "Sarbanes-Oxley Whistleblowers: A New

Corporate Early Warning System," Government Accountability Project (Washington, DC, November 2004), 9–10.

28. www.ethicsline.com/services/hotlines.asp.

29. Integrity Helpline FAQs, www.deloitte.com.

30. "Whistleblowers Pay a Heavy Price," August 3, 2005, www.accountingweb.com.

31. "A Global Perspective on Whistleblowing," June 1, 2005, www.business-ethics.org.

32. "Protecting the Whistleblower," *Job Safety and Health Quarterly* (Winter 2003), www.osha.gov.

33. Steven Greenhouse, "Interns, Unpaid by a Studio, File Suit," *New York Times*, September 28, 2011.

34. Steven Greenhouse, "Judge Rules That Movie Studio Should Have Been Paying Interns," *New York Times*, June 11, 2013.

Part V: Cases

Case 1

1. "Bernard L. Madoff," *New York Times*, Updated June 28, 2012. http://topics.nytimes.com/top/reference/timestopics/people/m/bernard_l_madoff/index.html

2. Jason Szep, "No Record of Madoff's Trades," *Washington Post*, January 16, 2009.

3. Jon Stempel and Christian Plumb, "Investors Scramble After Madoff Is Charged With $50B Fraud," *USA Today*, December 11, 2008.

4. Diana B. Henriques, "Wife Withdrew Millions Before Madoff's Arrest," *New York Times*, February 12, 2009.

5. Erin E. Arvedlund, "Don't Ask, Don't Tell: Bernie Madoff Attracts Skeptics in 2001." *Barron's*. May 7, 2001; http://online.barrons.com/article/SB989019667829349012.html.

6. Gregory Zuckerman, "Fee, Even Returns and Auditor All Raised Flags," *Wall Street Journal*, December 13, 2008.

7. Madoff Complaint-US Department of Justice. http://www.justice.gov/archive/usao/nys/pressreleases/December08/madoffcomplaint.pdf.

8. "Class Action Suits Begin in Madoff Case," *New York Times*, December 12, 2008.

9. Diana B. Henriques, "More Names of Note Appear on Madoff List," *New York Times*, February 6, 2009.

10. Paul Kiel, "The World's Largest Hedge Fund is a Fraud," *ProPublica*, December 18, 2008.

11. "The Madoff Affair," *PBS Frontline*, May 12, 2009.

12. "The Red Flags in the Madoff Fund's Past," *CNBC*, December 12, 2008.

13. David Glovin, Karen Freifeld and David Voreacos, "Investment Adviser Aksia Warned Clients of Madoff 'Red Flags'," *Bloomberg.com*, December 13, 2008. http://www.bloomberg.com/apps/news?pid=news archive&sid=afr_KQndJUUs.

14. Kara Scannell, "Madoff Chasers Dug for Years, to No Avail," *Wall Street Journal*, January 5, 2009.

15. Thomas A. Buckhoff and Bonita K. Peterson Kramer. Conducting Effective Ponzi Scheme Investigations. *Journal of Forensic & Investigative Accounting* 3, no. 3 (2011): 1–24.

16. David Stout, "Report Details How Madoff's Web Ensnared S.E.C.," *New York Times*, September 3, 2009.

17. David Stout, "Report Details How Madoff's Web Ensnared SEC," *New York Times*, September 2, 2009.

18. Bloomberg News, "S.E.C. Punishes 8 Workers in Errors Tied to Madoff," *New York Times*, November 11, 2011.

19. Jenny Strasburg, "Firm Touted Its Family Connections to Reassure Clients," *Wall Street Journal*, December 16, 2008.

20. Javier Hernandez, "Betrayed by Madoff, Yeshiva U. Adds a Lesson," *New York Times*, December 23, 2008.

21. Bob Minzesheimer, "Wiesel Again Rebuilds on Ruins," *USA Today*, February 17, 2009.

22. Carrick Mollenkamp, Cassell Bryan-Low, and Thomas Catan, "The Madoff Fraud Case: Fairfield Group Is Forced to Confront Its Ties," *Wall Street Journal*, December 17, 2008.

23. Chad Bray, "Madoff Now on 24-Hour Home Detention," *Wall Street Journal*, December 19, 2008.

24. Alex Berenson, "Madoff Sent 16 Watches and Jewelry," *New York Times*, January 8, 2009.

25. Andrew Ross Sorkin, "$173 Million in Madoff Checks Reportedly Found," *New York Times*, January 8, 2009.

26. Diana B. Henriques. "Madoff Will Plead Guilty: Face Life for Vast Swindle," *New York Times*, March 11, 2009.

27. Andrew Ross Sorkin, "Madoff Is Jailed After Pleading Guilty to Fraud," *New York Times*, March 12, 2009.

28. Amir Efrati, "Accountant Arrested for Shame Audits," *Wall Street Journal*, March 19, 2009.

29. Diana B. Henriques, "Madoff Is Sentenced to 150 Years for Ponzi Scheme," *New York Times*, June 30, 2009.

30. Chad Bray, "Madoff Begins 1st Day of 150 Years," *Wall Street Journal*, July 15, 2009.

31. Dionne Searcey, "Bernie Madoff, the $19 Billion Con, Makes New Friends Behind Bars," *Wall Street Journal*, December 15, 2009.

32. Diana B. Henriques, "Madoff's Accountant Pleads Guilty in Scheme," *New York Times*, November 4, 2009.

33. Diana B. Henriques, "Two Are Charged With Helping Madoff Falsify Records," *New York Times*, November 14, 2009.

34. Chad Bray and Tom Lauricella, "'All Fake': Key Madoff Executive Admits Guilt," *Wall Street Journal*, August 12, 2009.

35. Diana B. Henriques, "Another Madoff Aide Faces Fraud

Charges," *New York Times*, February 26, 2010.

36. Chad Bray and Michael Rothfeild, "Former Madoff Employees Indicted," *Wall Street Journal*, November 18, 2010.

37. Peter Lattman, "Two Women Indicted as Participants in Madoff Scheme," *New York Times*, September 19, 2010.

38. Diana B. Henriques and Al Baker, "A Madoff Son Hangs Himself on Father's Arrest Anniversary," *New York Times*, December 11, 2010.

39. Diana B. Henriques, "Madoff to Skip Son's Funeral to Protect Family Privacy," *New York Times*, December 14, 2010.

40. Chad Bray, "Judge Approves $7.2 Billion Settlement in Madoff Case," *Wall Street Journal*, January 13, 2011.

41. Diana B. Henriques and Peter Lattman, "Deal Recovers $7.2 Billion for Madoff Fraud Victims," *New York Times*, December 18, 2010.

42. Associated Press, "Madoff's Former Payroll Manager Admits Faking Records," *New York Times*, June 6, 2011.

43. Associated Press, "Madoff Associate Says Fraud Went Back to '70s," *New York Times*, November 21, 2011.

44. Peter Lattman, "Former Madoff Employee to Admit Guilt," *New York Times*, December 16, 2011.

45. Chad Bray, "Spouses of Madoff Sons Face Claims," *Wall Street Journal*, April 5, 2012.

46. Chad Bray and Michael Rothfeld, "Peter Madoff Pleads Guilty to Fraud," *The Wall Street Journal*, June 29, 2012.

47. Peter Lattman and Diana B. Henriques, "Peter Madoff Is Sentenced to 10 Years for His Role in Fraud," *New York Times*, December 20, 2012.

48. Dan Fitzpatrick, "J.P. Morgan Settles Its Madoff Tab," *The Wall Street Journal*, January 7, 2014.

49. Christopher M. Matthews, "Five Former Employees of Bernie Madoff Found Guilty of Fraud," *The Wall Street Journal*, March 25, 2014.

50. James Sterngold, "Bernard Madoff's Surviving Son Dies," *The Wall Street Journal*, September 3, 2014.

51. Christopher M. Matthews, "Bernard Madoff's Former Accountant Pleads Guilty," *The Wall Street Journal*, June 24, 2014.

52. Christopher M. Matthews, "Former Madoff Operations Director Sentenced to 10 Years in Prison," *The Wall Street Journal*, December 8, 2014.

53. Daniel Huang, "Former Madoff Portfolio Manager Sentenced to Six Years in Prison," *The Wall Street Journal*, December 9, 2014.

54. Reuters, "Payout to Madoff Victims Tops $7.2 Billion," *New York Times*, February 9, 2015.

Case 2

1. Craig Morris, "Siemens Accused of Embezzling 200 Million Euros," *Financial Times*, November 24, 2006.

2. David Crawford and Mike Esterl, "At Siemens, Witnesses Cite Pattern of Bribery," *Wall Street Journal*, January 31, 2007.

3. Ibid.

4. David Crawford and Mike Esterl, "Widening Scandal: At Siemens, Witnesses Cite Pattern of Bribery: They Call It Common: Firm Denies Impropriety by Any High Officials," *Wall Street Journal*, January 31, 2007.

5. Mike Esterl and David Crawford, "Why Siemens Bribery Probe Slogs On; Decentralization, Stonewalling Make Quick Resolution Unlikely," *Wall Street Journal*, August 16, 2007.

6. Carter Dougherty, "Ex-Siemens Executives on Trial for Bribery," *New York Times*, March 14, 2007.

7. G. Thomas Sims, "2 Former Siemens Officials Convicted for Bribery," *New York Times*, May 15, 2007.

8. Mark Landler, "Chairman to Quit Siemens, Casualty of Graft Accusations," *New York Times*, April 20, 2007.

9. G. Thomas Sims, "Siemens Chief Agrees to Quit in Scandal," *New York Times*, April 26, 2007.

10. Lionel Laurent, "Siemens Anti-Corruption Chief Canned," *Forbes*, July 2, 2007.

11. Carter Dougherty, "Chief of Siemens Pledges to Streamline Operations," *New York Times*, July 6, 2007.

12. David Crawford and Mike Esterl, "Siemens Fine Ends a Bribery Probe," *Wall Street Journal*, October 5, 2007.

13. David Crawford and Mike Esterl, "Siemens Ruling Details Bribery Across the Globe," *Wall Street Journal*, November 16, 2007.

14. Mike Esterl, "Siemens Amnesty Plan Assists Bribery Probe," *Wall Street Journal*, March 5, 2008.

15. Mike Esterl and David Crawford, "Siemens Executive Steps Down Amid Probe," *Wall Street Journal*, April 24, 2008.

16. Mike Esterl and David Crawford, "Siemens Ex-Chairman Faces Civil Proceedings," *Wall Street Journal*, May 10, 2008.

17. Carter Dougherty, "Ex-Manager Tells of Bribery at Siemens," *New York Times*, May 27, 2008.

18. Carter Dougherty, "Ex-Manager at Siemens Is Convicted in Bribe Case," *New York Times*, July 29, 2008.

19. Mike Esterl, "Siemens Trial Opens," *Wall Street Journal*, September 25, 2008.

20. Mike Esterl and David Crawford, "Ex-Siemens Manager Sentenced—Feldmayer Fined but Jail Times Is Suspended in Case Over Payments to Labor Group," *Wall Street Journal*, November 25, 2008.

21. David Crawford and Mike Esterl, "Siemens Pays Record Fine in Probe," *Wall Street Journal*, December 16, 2008.

22. Mike Esterl and David Crawford, "Siemens to Pay Huge Fine in Bribery Inquiry,"

Wall Street Journal, December 15, 2008.

23. Eric Lichtblau and Carter Dougherty, "Siemens to Pay $1.34 Billion in Fines," *New York Times*, December 16, 2008.

24. Vanessa Fuhrmans, "Siemens Settles With World Bank on Bribes—Company Will Pay $100 Million to Help Combat Corruption and Forgo Bidding on Contracts for Two Years," *Wall Street Journal*, July 3, 2009.

25. Archibald Preuschat and Matthias Karpstein, "Siemens Settles With Former CEOs," *Wall Street Journal*, December 2, 2009.

26. Edward Wyatt, "Former Siemens Executives Are Charged With Bribery," *New York Times*, December 13, 2011.

27. Reuters, "Ex-Siemens CFO Neuburger Commits Suicide," *New York Times*, February 6, 2015.

Case 3

1. *TOMS Giving Report* (2010), http://www.toms.com/giving-report.

2. Ibid.

3. Ibid.

4. Ibid.

5. Adriana Herrera, "Questioning the TOMS Shoes Model for Social Enterprise," *New York Times*, March 19, 2013.

6. http://www.cdc.gov/parasites/hookworm/.

7. http://www.isradiology.org/tropical_deseases/tmcr/chapter26/clinical19.htm.

8. http://www.digidrift.com/jiggers-chigoe-flea-the-hidden-african-killer/.

9. http://health.nytimes.com/health/guides/disease/tetanus/overview.html.

10. *TOMS Giving Report* (2010), http://www.toms.com/giving-report.

11. Ibid.

12. "TOMS to Launch Eyewear" (February 29, 2012), www.fashionunited.cu.uk/fashion-news/design/toms-to-launch-eyewear.

13. Stephanie Strom, "Turning Coffee Into Water to Expand Business Model," *New York Times,* March 11, 2014.

14. Michael J. de la Merced, "After Sale to Bain, Toms's Chief Wants to Expand Global Reach," *New York Times,* August 20, 2014.

15. Maureen Farrell, "Can Toms Shoes Sell to Bain Without Selling Out?", *The Wall Street Journal,* August 22, 2014.

16. Gillian Tan, "Jefferies Expected to Book Loss on Toms Shoes Debt," *The Wall Street Journal*, October 28, 2014.

17. https://www.toms.com/stories/giving/building-a-sustainable-shoe-industry-in-haiti.

Case 4

1. This case is dedicated to our two favorite Mouseketeers, Olivia M. Stanwick and John W. Stanwick.

2. *Disney Citizenship 2014 Performance Summary*, p. 3.

3. 2014 Global CSR Reptrak 100: Annual Corporate Social Responsibility (CSR) Reputation Ranking, Reputation Institute, December 2014.

4. *Disney Citizenship 2014 Performance Summary*, 7.

5. Ibid., 53.

6. Ibid., 54–55.

7. Ibid., 58.

8. Ibid., 66–67.

9. Ibid., 68.

10. Ibid., 71.

11. Ibid., 73.

12. Ibid., 76–77.

13. Ibid., 78.

14. Ibid., 80.

15. Ibid., 82.

16. Ibid., 25.

17. Ibid., 28–29.

18. Ibid., 32.

19. Ibid., 28–29.

20. http://forceforchange.starwars.com/

21. http://www.unicefusa.org/supporters/organizations/businesses/partners/disney.

22. *Disney Citizenship 2014 Performance Summary*, 42–43.

23. Ibid., 48–49.

24. Ibid., 50.

25. Ibid., 46–47.

26. Ibid., 97.

Case 5

1. www.wfp.org.

2. Ibid.

3. Ibid.

4. Ibid.

5. Ibid.

6. http://documents.wfp.org/stellent/groups/public/documents/communications/wfp265227.pdf.

7. Fighting Hunger Worldwide (Rome: World Food Programme, 2010).

8. Ibid.

9. www.wfp.org.

10. Ibid.

11. *Fighting Hunger Worldwide* (Rome: World Food Programme, 2010).

12. Reuters, "WFP Alarmed by Pictures of ISIS Logos on Its Syria Food Parcels," *New York Times*, February 3, 2015.

13. Ibid.

14. www.wfp.org.

15. Ibid.

16. Alison Maitland, "Project Laser Beam: Scheme Puts the Focus on Malnutrition in Children, *Financial Times*, June 22, 2011.

17. http://www.unilever.com/aboutus/foundation/wfp/laserbeam/allforone/.

18. www.wfp.org.

19. *Revolution: From Food Aid to Food Assistance* (Rome: World Food Programme, 2010).

Case 6

1. Don Van Natta Jr., Jo Becker, and Graham Bowley, "Tabloid Hack Attack on Royals, and Beyond," *New York Times*, September 1, 2010.

2. Ibid.

3. Alan Cowell, "British Police Arrest 3 Over Taps on Phones at Royal Residence," *New York Times*, August 9, 2006.

4. "Pair Jailed Over Royal Phone Taps," *BBC News,* January 26, 2007.

5. Don Van Natta Jr., Jo Becker, and Graham Bowley, "Tabloid Hack Attack on Royals, and Beyond," *New York Times*, September 1, 2010.

6. Ibid.

7. Ibid.

8. Ibid.

9. "'When the Spokesman Needs a Spokesman It's Time to Go': Cameron's Spin Doctor Andy Coulson Quits Over Phone Hacking Row," *Daily Mail*, January 22, 2011.

10. Don Van Natta Jr., Jo Becker, and Graham Bowley, "Tabloid Hack Attack on Royals, and Beyond," *New York Times*, September 1, 2010.

11. Ibid.

12. Cassell Bryan-Low, "Singer Alleges a Trade-Off to Sway News Corp. Coverage," *Wall Street Journal*, November 29, 2011.

13. Russell Adams and Jessica E. Vascellaro, "Scandal Clouds James Murdoch's Path," *Wall Street Journal*, September 14, 2011.

14. Ravi Somaiya, "New Challenge to a Murdoch Over Hacking," *New York Times*, December 13, 2011.

15. John F. Burns, "Latest Hacking Scandal Arrest Suggests Focus on Cover-Up," *New York Times*, January 7, 2012.

16. Sarah Lyall, "E-Mail on 'Rife' Hacking Deleted From James Murdoch Computer, Lawyers Say," *New York Times*, February 1, 2012.

17. John F. Burns and Amy Chozick, "James Murdoch Gives Up Role at British Unit," *New York Times*, February 29, 2012.

18. Paul Sonne, "James Murdoch Quits BSKYB Post," *Wall Street Journal*, April 3, 2012.

19. John F. Burns and Jo Becker, "Murdoch Tabloids' Targets Included Downing Street and the Crown," *New York Times*, July 11, 2011.

20. Sarah Lyall and Don Van Natta Jr., "An Arrest and Scotland Yard Resignation Roil Britain," *New York Times*, July 17, 2011.

21. Sarah Lyall, "British Tabloid Hacked Missing Girl's Voice Mail, Lawyer Says," *New York Times*, July 4, 2011.

22. Cassell Bryan-Low, "News Corp. Unit Plans to Pay $4.7 Million in Dowler Hack," *Wall Street Journal*, September 20, 2011.

23. Tim Arango, "Editor Says a Murdoch Paid to Settle on Phone Tap," *New York Times*, July 22, 2009.

24. Jeremy W. Peters and Brian Stelter, "The Murdoch Style, Under Pressure," *New York Times*, July 6, 2011.

25. John F. Burns and Alan Cowell, "Former Aide to Cameron Is Arrested in Tabloid Scandal," *New York Times*, July 7, 2011.

26. Dana Cimilluca and Alistair MacDonald, "News Corp. Caves as Support Fades," *Street Journal*, July 14, 2011.

27. Cassell Bryan-Low and Bruce Orwall, "News International CEO Brooks Resigns," *Wall Street Journal*, July 15, 2011.

28. Cassell Bryan-Low and Russell Adams, "Dow Jones CEO Resigns Over Scandal," *Wall Street Journal*, July 16, 2011.

29. Cassell Bryan-Low and Paul Sonne, "Murdochs Are Grilled," *Wall Street Journal*, July 20, 2011.

30. Sarah Lyall and Ravi Somaiya, "Murdoch Settles Suits by Dozens of Victims of Hacking," *New York Times*, January 19, 2012.

31. Jeanne Whalen, "U.K. Bribe Probe Broadens to Sun," *Wall Street Journal*, January 30, 2012.

32. Andrew Edgecliffe-Johnson, "More Senior Sun Journalists Arrested," *Financial Times*, February 11, 2012.

33. Andrew Edgecliffe-Johnson, "News Corp Hacking Costs Near $200M," *Financial Times*, February 8, 2012.

34. Andrew Edgecliffe-Johnson and Helen Warrell, "Murdoch Empire Rocked as Probe Widens," *Financial Times*, February 13, 2012.

35. Ben Fenton, "'Evidence Was Destroyed' in Newspaper Phone Scandal," *Financial Times*, February 24, 2012.

36. Paul Sonne and Cassel Bryan-Low, "Brooks Hit With Obstruction Charges," *The Wall Street Journal*, May 15, 2012.

37. Paul Sonne and Jeanne Whalen, "Hacking Charges Filed," *The Wall Street Journal*, July 24, 2012.

38. Jenny Gross and Jeannie Whalen, "Guilty Pleas Disclosed in U.K. Trail," *The Wall Street Journal*, October 30, 2013.

39. Jenny Gross, "Different Fates for Ex-Editors in U.K. Hacking Trail," *The Wall Street Journal*, June 24, 2014.

40. Alexis Flynn, "Andy Coulson Sentenced to 18 Months in Jail for Phone Hacking," *The Wall Street Journal*, July 4, 2014.

41. Jenny Gross, "Ex-News Corp Editor Pleads Guilty in U.K. Phone-Hacking Case," *The Wall Street Journal*, October 3, 2014.

42. Reuters, "Justice Department Drops News Corp Probe Related to Phone Hacking," *New York Times*, February 2, 2015.

Case 7

1. Robert Cole, "Gas Pipeline Giant Agrees to Merger," *New York Times*, May 3, 1985, www.nytimes.com.

2. C. William Thomas, "The Rise and Fall of Enron," *Journal of Accountancy*, April 2002, http://www.journalofaccountancy.com/Issues/2002/Apr/TheRiseAndFallOfEnron.htm.

3. David Barboza and John Schwartz. "Enron's Many Strands: The Transactions; The Financial Wizard Tied to Enron's Fall." *New York Times*, February 06, 2002; Allen R. Myerson, "Enron, Seeking to Be a Household Name, Plans to Start Its Campaign on Super Bowl Sunday," *New York Times*, January 14, 1997.

4. Monica Perin, "Fastow Details Enron's LJM Partnerships in First Day on Stand,"

Houston Business Journal, March 7, 2006; Tom Fowler, "Partnerships Likely Key to Fastow's Testimony," *Houston Chronicle*, March 7, 2006.

5. David Barboza and John Schwartz, "Enron's Many Strands: The Transaction; The Financial Wizard Tied to Enron's Fall," *New York Times*, February 6, 2002, www.nytimes.com.

6. Alex Berenson and Richard Oppel, "Once-Mighty Enron Strains under Scrutiny," *New York Times*, October 28, 2001, www.nytimes.com.

7. Kurt Eichenwald and Diana Henriques, "Enron Buffed Image to a Shine as It Rotted From Within," *New York Times*, February 10, 2002, www.nytimes.com.

8. Rebecca Smith and John R. Emshwiller, "Enron Replaces Fastow as Finance Chief—McMahon Takes Over Post; Moves Follows Concerns Over Partnership Deals," *Wall Street Journal*, October 25, 2001, www.wallstreetjournal.com.

9. Alan Murray, "Twelve Angry CEOs—The Ideal Enron Jury," *Wall Street Journal*, February 15, 2006, www.wallstreetjournal.com.

10. John Greenwald, "Rank and Fire," *Time*, June 11, 2001, www.time.com.

11. C. William Thomas, "The Rise and Fall of Enron," *Journal of Accountancy*, April 2002, http://www .journalofaccountancy .com/Issues/2002/Apr/ TheRiseAndFallOfEnron.htm.

12. Bethany McLean, "Is Enron Overpriced?" *Fortune*, March 5, 2001, http://money.cnn .com/magazines/fortune.

13. Kurt Eichenwald and Diana Henriques, "Enron Buffed Image to a Shine as It Rotted From Within," *New York Times*, February 10, 2002, www.nytimes.com.

14. Ibid.

15. Kurt Eichenwald and Diana Henriques, "Enron Buffed Image to a Shine as It Rotted From Within," *New York Times*, February 10, 2002, www.nytimes.com.

16. Douglas Harbrecht, "Enron's Ken Lay: 'There's No Other Shoe to Fall,'" *Businessweek*, August 24, 2001, www .businessweek.com.

17. Jonathan Friedland, "Enron Chief Executive Skilling Steps Down Citing Personal Reasons: Lay Takes Duties," *Wall Street Journal*, August 15, 2001, www .wallstreetjournal.com.

18. C. William Thomas, "The Rise and Fall of Enron," *Journal of Accountancy* (April 2002): 41–45, 47–48.

19. Andrew Hall, Joshua Chaffin, and Stephen Fidler, "Enron: Virtual Company, Virtual Profits," *Financial Times*, March 19, 2002, www.ft.com.

20. http://fl1.findlaw.com/news .findlaw.com/hdocs/docs/ enron/empltr2lay82001.pdf.

21. January 28, 2002; http:// www.forbes.com/2002/01/28/ 0128veenron.html.

22. Kurt Eichenwald and Diana Henriques, Enron's Many Strands: The Company Unravels; Enron Buffed Image to a Shine Even as It Rotted From Within," *New York Times*, February 10, 2002, www.nytimes.com.

23. John R. Emshwiller and Rebecca Smith, "Enron Posts Surprise Third-Quarter Loss After Investment, Asset Write-Downs," *Wall Street Journal*, October 17, 2001, www .wallstreetjournal.com.

24. Alex Berenson and Richard Oppel, "Once-Mighty Enron Strains Under Scrutiny," *New York Times*, October 28, 2001, www.nytimes.com.

25. Kristen Hays, "Ex-Enron CFO McMahon to pay $300,000." *Houston Chronicle*. June 20, 2007; http://www.chron .com/business/enron/article/ Ex-Enron-CFO-McMahon-to-pay-300-000-1844063.php.

26. *Enron: The Smartest Guys in the Room*. Magnolia Home Entertainment, 2002.

27. John Schwartz and Richard Oppel, "Foundation Gives Way on Lay's Big Dream," *New York Times*, November 29, 2001, www.nytimes.com.

28. Richard Oppel and Andrew Ross Sorkin, "Enron Collapses as Suitor Cancels Plans for Merger," *New York Times*, November 29, 2001, www.nytimes.com.

29. Rebecca Smith, "Enron Files for Chapter 11 Bankruptcy, Sues Dynergy—Proceeding Is Biggest Ever in the U.S., With Assets of Just Under $50 Billion," *Wall Street Journal*, December 3, 2001, www.wall streetjournal.com.

30. Alan Chernoff, "Former Enron Exec Dies in Apparent Suicide," CNN.com, January 26, 2002.

31. Robert Lear and Boris Yavitz, "Boards on Trial," *Chief Executive*, October 2000, 6.

32. Reed Abelson, "Enron's Collapse: The Directors; One Enron Inquiry Suggests Board Played Important Role," *New York Times*, January 19, 2002, www.nytimes.com.

33. Joann Lubin, "Inside, Outside Enron, Audit Panel Is Scrutinized—Links to Company of Certain Members Are Called Too Cozy," *Wall Street Journal*, February 1, 2002, www.wallstreetjournal.com.

34. Reed Abelson, "Enron's Collapse: The Directors; One Enron Inquiry Suggests Board Played Important Role," *New York Times*, January 19, 2002, www.nytimes.com.

35. Matt Andrejczak, "Will Enron's Directors Be Exonerated?" *Stanford Law School Securities Class Action Clearinghouse*, MarketWatch .com, October 10, 2002; http://securities. stanford.edu/news-archive/2002/20021010_ Headline02_Andrejczak.htm.

36. Kurt Eichenwald and Diana Henriques, "Enron Buffed Image to a Shine as It Rotted From Within," *New York Times*, February 10, 2002, www.nytimes.com.

37. Kurt Eichenwald, "Enron's Many Strands: The Accountants," *New York Times*, May 8, 2002, www.nytimes.com.

38. Luisa Beltran, "Andersen Exec: Shredding Began after E-mail," Cnnmoney.com, January 21, 2002.

39. Ken Brown, Greg Hitt, Steve Liesman, and Jonathan Weil, "Paper Trail: Andersen Fires Partner It Says Led Shredding of Enron Documents—It Claims Disposal Effort Started After SEC Asked Energy Firm for Data—Was He Following Orders?" *Wall Street Journal*, January 16, 2002, www.wallstreetjournal.com.

40. Kurt Eichenwald, "Enron's Many Strands: The Accountants," *New York Times*, May 8, 2002, www.nytimes.com.

41. Ibid.

42. Luis Beltran, Brett Gering, and Alice Martin, "Andersen Guilty," *CNNMoney*, June 16, 2002, http://money.cnn.com.

43. Jess Bravin, "Justices Overturn Criminal Verdict in Andersen Case," *Wall Street Journal*, June 1, 2005, www.wallstreetjournal.com.

44. http://www.justice.gov.opa/pr(2004)January/04_crm_079.htm.

45. U.S. Securities and Exchange Commission Litigation Release No. 18582, February 19, 2004, 1–4.

46. Alexei Barrionuevo, "Ex-Enron Chief Executive Prepares for Trial," *New York Times*, January 19, 2006, www.nytimes.com.

47. U.S. Securities and Exchange Commission, Litigation Release No. 18776, July 8, 2004, 2–5.

48. John R. Emshwiller, Deborah Solomon, Kara Scannell, and Rebecca Smith, "Lay Strikes Back as Indictment Cites Narrow Role of Enron Fraud," *Wall Street Journal*, July 9, 2004, www.wallstreetjournal.com.

49. John R. Emshwiller and John M. Biers, "Enron Prosecutors Gain New Ally," *Wall Street Journal*, December 29, 2005, www.wallstreetjournal.com.

50. Associated Press, "Executives on Trial: Enron Causey Gets Jail Term of 5½ Years," *Wall Street Journal*, November 16, 2006, www.wallstreetjournal.com.

51. John R. Emshwiller, "An Audacious Enron Defense: Company's Moves Were All Legal," *Wall Street Journal*, January 20, 2006, www.wallstreetjournal.com.

52. John R. Emshwiller and Gary McWilliams, "Lay's Lawyer Argues That Panic in Market Sank Enron, Not Fraud," *Wall Street Journal*, February 10, 2006, www.wallstreetjournal.com.

53. Gary McWilliams and Kara Scannell, "Profit Tweaking May Lose Favor After Enron Trial," *Wall Street Journal*, February 16, 2006, www.wallstreetjournal.com.

54. Gary McWilliams and John R. Emshwiller, "Skilling Team Continues Attack on U.S. Portrayal of Enron Unit," *Wall Street Journal*, February 17, 2006, www.wallstreetjournal.com.

55. Gary McWilliams and John R. Emshwiller, "Enron Witness Begins Tying in Lay," *Wall Street Journal*, February 22, 2006, www.wallstreetjournal.com.

56. Gary McWilliams and John R. Emshwiller, "Accountant Says Enron Dipped Into Reserves to Pad Earnings," *Wall Street Journal*, February 28, 2006, www.wallstreetjournal.com.

57. Alexei Barrionuevo, "Jury Is Told Chief Backed Shifts in Enron Accounting," *New York Times*, March 1, 2006, www.nytimes.com.

58. Kurt Eichenwald and Alexei Barrionuevo, "At the Enron Trial, Skilling Then Versus Skilling Now," *New York Times*, April 5, 2006, www.nytimes.com.

59. John R. Emshwiller and Gary McWilliams, "Enron's Fastow Testifies Skilling Approved Fraud: Ex-Executive Says Company Used Deals to Hide Losses, Chokes Up Over Lie to Wife," *Wall Street Journal*, March 8, 2006, www.wallstreetjournal.com.

60. John R. Emshwiller and Gary McWilliams, "Ex-Enron CFO Fastow Testifies That His Deals Masked Losses," *Wall Street Journal*, March 7, 2006, www.wallstreetjournal.com.

61. John R. Emshwiller and Gary McWilliams, "Enron's Fastow Testifies Skilling Approved Fraud: Ex-Executive Says Company Used Deals to Hide Losses, Chokes Up Over Lie to Wife," *Wall Street Journal*, March 8, 2006, www.wallstreetjournal.com.

62. Ibid.

63. Ibid.

64. Alexei Barrionuevo and Kurt Eichenwald, "In Enron Trial, a Calculated Risk," *New York Times*, April 4, 2006, www.nytimes.com.

65. John R. Emshwiller and Gary McWilliams, "Skilling Defends Enron, Himself," *Wall Street Journal*, April 11, 2006, www.wallstreetjournal.com.

66. John R. Emshwiller and Gary McWilliams, "Skilling, Denying U.S. Charges, Talks of His Dedication to Enron," *Wall Street Journal*, April 12, 2006, www.wallstreetjournal.com.

67. Alexei Barrionuevo, "Jury Hears Indignation of Skilling," *New York Times*, April 14, 2006, www.nytimes.com.

68. Alexei Barrionuevo and Vikas Bajaj, "U.S. Takes First Shots at Skilling," *New York Times*, April 18, 2006, www.nytimes.com.

69. Somin Romero, "Ex-Chairman of Enron Takes the Stand," *New York Times*, April 24, 2006, www.nytimes.com.

70. Gary McWilliams and John R. Emshwiller, "Kenneth Lay Takes the Stand at Enron

Trial in Houston," *Wall Street Journal*, April 24, 2006, www.wallstreetjournal.com.

71. John R. Emshwiller and Gary McWilliams, "Prosecutors Get First Shot at Lay," *Wall Street Journal*, April 27, 2006, www.wallstreetjournal.com.

72. John R. Emshwiller and Gary McWilliams, "Lay on Defensive at Enron Trial," *Wall Street Journal*, April 28, 2006, www.wallstreetjournal.com.

73. Gary McWilliams and John R. Emshwiller, "Lay Defends Family's Role in Selling Shares," *Wall Street Journal*, May 2, 2006, www.wallstreetjournal.com.

74. Alexei Barrionuevo, "Did Ken Lay Demonstrate Credibility?," *New York Times*, May 3, 2006, www.nytimes.com.

75. John R. Emshwiller, "Enron Judge's Jury Instructions May Raise Odds of Convictions," *Wall Street Journal*, May 10, 2006, www.wallstreetjournal.com.

76. John R. Emshwiller and Gary McWilliams, "Lay Convicted on All Counts; Skilling Guilty on Most Charges," *Wall Street Journal*, May 25, 2006, www.wallstreetjournal.com.

77. John R. Emshwiller, Gary McWilliams, and Ann Davis, "Lay, Skilling Are Convicted of Fraud," *Wall Street Journal*, May 26, 2006, 1–2.

78. "Lay, Skilling Pursued by U.S. for $183 Million," *Wall Street Journal*, July 1, 2006, www.wallstreetjournal.com.

79. John Emshwiller. In New Interview, Skilling says he hurt case by speaking up. *Wall Street Journal*, June 17, 2006.

80. Reuters, "Lay Autopsy Finds Severely Clogged Arteries," *Wall Street Journal*, July 20, 2006.

81. Ashby Jones and John R. Emshwiller, "Quirk of U.S. Law Exonerates Lay, Possibly Hindering Asset Seizure," *Wall Street Journal*, July 7, 2006, www.wallstreetjournal.com.

82. Dow Jones Newswires, "Executives on Trial: Ken Lay Estate, Agency Settle," *Wall Street Journal*, September 8, 2006, www.wallstreetjournal.com.

83. "Former Enron Official Is Sentenced to Prison," *Wall Street Journal*, September 19, 2006, www.wallstreetjournal.com.

84. Kate Murphy, Alexei Barrionuevo, and Kurt Eichenwald, "Fastow Sentenced to Six Years," *New York Times*, September 27, 2006, 1–2.

85. "Fastow Assigned to Prison," *Wall Street Journal*, November 11, 2006, www.wallstreetjournal.com.

86. "Enron Corp.: Ex-Officer Rieker's Sentence Is Lighter Than Expected," *Wall Street Journal*, October 7, 2006, www.wallstreetjournal.com.

87. Kristen Hays, "No Fanfare as Skilling Walks Into Prison Life," *Houston Chronicle*, December 14, 2006, www.chron.com.

88. John R. Emshwiller, "Skilling Gets Twenty-Four Years in Prison; Enron Ex-CEO Faced Longer Term for Fraud, Conspiracy Conviction; Victims Fund to Get $45 Million," *Wall Street Journal*, October 24, 2006, www.wallstreetjournal.com.

89. Archelle Georgiou, "Skilling Speaks: Enron CEO's Jailhouse Interview," *Fortune*, June 14, 2010.

90. Peter J. Henning, "When a Legal Victory Isn't a Victory," *New York Times*, June 1, 2011.

91. Mitchell Pacelle and Robin Sidel, "Citigroup Accord to End Enron Suit May Pressure Others," *Wall Street Journal*, June 13, 2005, www.wallstreetjournal.com.

92. Robin Sidel and Mitchell Pacelle, "J.P. Morgan Settles Enron Lawsuit," *Wall Street Journal*, June 15, 2005, www.wallstreetjournal.com.

93. Jad Mouawad, "Settlement Is Reached With Enron," *New York Times*, July 16, 2005, www.nytimes.com.

94. Jennifer Bayot, "Canadian Bank Pays $2.4 Billion to Settle With Enron Investors," *New York Times*, August 2, 2005, 1.

95. The Associated Press, "UBS Agrees to $115 Million Enron Payment," *New York Times*, June 7, 2007.

96. Reuters, "Enron Case Settled," *New York Times*, December 19, 2007.

97. Reuters, "Accountant and S.E.C. Reach Deal in Enron Case," *New York Times*, January 29, 2008.

98. Eric Dash, "Citigroup Resolves Claims That It Helped Enron Deceive Investors," *New York Times*, March 27, 2008.

99. Ben Brantley, "Titans of Tangled Finances Kick Up Their Heels Again," *New York Times*, April 28, 2010.

100. Ashby Jones, "Breaking: Jeff Skilling Loses Appeal of Criminal Conviction," *The Wall Street Journal*, April 6, 2011.

101. Tom Fowler, "Ex-Enron CEO Skilling's Sentence Cut to 14 Years," *The Wall Street Journal*, June 21, 2013.

Case 8

1. Adam Cohen, "What Google Should Roll out Next: A Privacy Upgrade," *New York Times*, November 28, 2005, www.nytimes.com.

2. Ronald Alsop, "Ranking Corporate Reputations; Tech Companies Score High in Yearly Survey as Google Makes Its Debut in Third Place; Autos, Airlines, Pharmaceuticals Lose Ground," *Wall Street Journal*, December 6, 2005, www.wallstreetjournal.com.

3. "Google Gets the Message, Launches Gmail," Google Press Release, April 1, 2004.

4. Cynthia Webb, "Google's Eyes in Your Inbox," *Washington Post*, April 2, 2004, www.washington post.com.

5. Kim Zetter, "Free E-Mail with a Steep Price?," *Wired News*, April 2, 2004, 2.

6. Amol Sharma and Kevin Delaney, "Tailoring Ads to Email Users, Google Has Some Poor Fits," *Wall Street Journal*, October 31, 2006, www.wallstreetjournal.com.

7. Cynthia Webb, "Google's Eyes in Your Inbox," *Washington Post*, April 2, 2004, www.washington post.com.

8. Kim Zetter, "Free E-Mail with a Steep Price?," *Wired News*, April 2, 2004, 2.

9. Elinor Mills, "Google Balances Privacy, Reach," CNET News, July 14, 2005, http://news.cnet.com.

10. Randall Stross, "Google Anything, So Long as It's Not Google," *New York Times*, August 28, 2005, www.nytimes.com.

11. Ben Elgin, "Google's Chinese Wall," *Businessweek*, September 30, 2004, www.businessweek.com.

12. Tom Zeller Jr., "Critics Press Companies on Internet Rights Issues," *New York Times*, November 8, 2005, www.nytimes.com.

13. Jason Dean and Kevin Delaney, "Limited Search: As Google Pushes into China, It Faces Clashes with Censors; Executives Wrestled with Issue as Others Took the Lead; Now, It's Charging Ahead; What 'Don't Be Evil' Means," *Wall Street Journal*, December 16, 2005, www.wallstreetjournal.com.

14. David Barboza, "Version of Google in China Won't Offer E-Mail or Blogs," *New York Times*, January 25, 2006, www.nytimes.com.

15. Mure Dickie, "Bloggers Quick to Condemn Google for Bowing to the Beijing Censors," *Financial Times*, January 26, 2005, 6.

16. Mure Dickie, "Internet Provider See Choice as Lesser of Two Evils," *Financial Times*, January 26, 2006, 6.

17. Joseph Kahn, "So Long, Dalai Lama: Google Adapts to China," *New York Times*, February 12, 2006, www.nytimes.com.

18. John Gapper, "Google Is Risking Its Freedom in China," *Financial Times*, January 29, 2006, www.ft.com.

19. Richard Waters, Mure Dickie, and Stephanie Kirchgaessner, "Evildoers? How the West's Net Vanguard Toils Behind the Great Firewall of China," *Financial Times*, February 15, 2006, 11.

20. Joseph Kahn, "In Rare Briefing, Chinese Official Defends Internet Controls," *New York Times*, February 14, 2006, www.nytimes.com.

21. Tom Zeller Jr., "Web Firms Are Grilled on Dealings in China," *New York Times*, February 16, 2006, www.nytimes.com.

22. Amy Schatz, "Tech Firms Defend China Web Policies," *Wall Street Journal*, February 16, 2006, www.wallstreetjournal.com.

23. Jason Dean, "China Users Have Trouble Reaching Main Google Site," *Wall Street Journal*, June 7, 2006, www.wallstreetjournal.com.

24. Jonathan Birchall and Richard Waters, "Search Engines Unite on China Rights," *Financial Times*, January 18, 2007, www.ft.com.

25. Andrew Jacobs and Miguel Helft, "Google Citing Attack, Threatens to Exit China," *New York Times*, January 13, 2010.

26. Miguel Helft and David Barboza, "Google Shuts China Site in Dispute Over Censorship," *New York Times*, March 22, 2010.

27. David Barboz and Miguel Helft, "China Renews Google's License," *New York Times*, July 9, 2010.

28. Amir Efrati and Loretta Chao, "Google Softens Tone on China," *Wall Street Journal*, January 12, 2012.

29. Kevin Delaney, "Google to Buck U.S. on Data Request," *Wall Street Journal*, January 20, 2006, www.wallstreetjournal.com.

30. Katie Hafner and Matt Richtel, "Google Resists U.S. Subpoena of Search Data," *New York Times*, January 20, 2006, www.nytimes.com.

31. Kevin Delaney, "Google to Buck U.S. on Data Request," *Wall Street Journal*, January 20, 2006, www.wallstreetjournal.com.

32. Chris Kraeuter, "Google's Gotta Give up the Goods," *Forbes*, March 14, 2006, www.forbes.com.

33. Reuters, "Google Ordered to Submit Data for Child Pornography Study," *New York Times*, March 18, 2006, www.nytimes.com.

34. David Whelan, "Google's Scan Plan Hits More Bumps," *Forbes*, May 31, 2005, www.forbes.com.

35. Edward Wyatt, "Writers Sue Google, Accusing It of Copyright Violation," *New York Times*, September 21, 2005, www.nytimes.com.

36. Edward Wyatt and Lawrence Van Gelder, "Major Publishers Sue Google," *New York Times*, October 20, 2005, www.nytimes.com.

37. "Google Inc.: Belgian Newspapers Win Lawsuit Tied to Copyright," *Wall Street Journal*, September 19, 2006, www.wallstreetjournal.com.

38. Stephanie Bodoni, "Google Loses Copyright Appeal Over Internet Links to Belgian Newspapers," *Bloomberg*, May 6, 2011; http://www.bloomberg.com/news/2011-05-06/google-loses-copyright-appeal-over-links-to-belgian-newspapers.html.

39. Kevin Delaney, "Google Looks to Boost Ads With YouTube," *Wall Street Journal*, October 10, 2006, www.wallstreetjournal.com.

40. "Google Video Is Named in Copyright Claims," *Wall Street Journal*, November 9, 2006, www.wallstreet journal.com.

41. Jason Fry, "The Revolution May Be Briefly Televised; Popular YouTube Clips' Short Shelf Life Reflects Copyright Laws Run

Amok," *Wall Street Journal*, November 15, 2006, www.wallstreetjournal.com.

42. David Glovin and Don Jeffrey, "Viacom's Copyright Suit Against Google's YouTube Reinstated," *Bloomberg*, Apr 5, 2012; http://www.bloomberg.com/news/2012-04-05/google-s-youtube-must-defend-viacom-suit-appeals-court-says-1-.html.

43. Andrew Albanese, "Publishers Settle Google Books Lawsuit." *Publisher's Weekly*, Oct 05, 2012, http://www.publishersweekly.com/pw/by-topic/digital/copyright/article/54247-publishers-settle-google-books-lawsuit.html.

44. Carolyn Kellogg, "Publishers and Google reach agreement in Google Books case." *LA Times*. October 4, 2012. http://www.latimes.com/features/books/jacketcopy/la-jc-publishers-and-google-reach-agreement-in-google-books-case-20121004,0,1677717.story.

45. David Glovin and Don Jeffrey, "Viacom's Copyright Suit Against Google's YouTube Reinstated." Apr 5, 2012, www.Bloomberg.com.

46. Sam Schiechner, "Google to Stop Publishing German Newspaper Extracts," *The Wall Street Journal*, October 2, 2014.

47. Elise Ackerman "Google Shares Its Suspicions on Click Fraud: Company Hopes Data Assures Advertisers It's Addressing Problem," *Knight Ridder/Tribune Business News*, July 26, 2006, 2.

48. Kevin Delaney, "Web Start-ups Vie to Detect 'Click Fraud,'" *Wall Street Journal*, June 9, 2005, www.wallstreetjournal.com.

49. Kevin Delaney, "Google to Settle Ad Lawsuit, Paying as Much as $90 Million," *Wall Street Journal*, March 9, 2006, www.wallstreetjournal.com.

50. Chris Nuttall, "Hefty Bill for Online Click Fraud," *Financial Times*, July 6, 2006, www.ft.com.

51. Chris Nuttall, "Google Moves to Tackle Click Fraud," *Financial Times*, July 27, 2006, www.ft.com.

52. Miguel Helft, "Critics Say Google Invades Privacy With New Service," *New York Times*, February 13, 2010, www.nytimes.com.

53. Amir Efrati, "Google Settles Privacy Lawsuit for $8.5 Million," *Wall Street Journal*, September 3, 2010.

54. Julia Angwin and Amir Efrati, "Google Settles With FTC Over Google Buzz," *Wall Street Journal*, March 30, 2011.

55. "A Fall Sweep," *Google Official Blog*, October 14, 2011.

56. Rachel Donadio, "Larger Threat Is Seen in Google Case," *New York Times*, February 24, 2010.

57. Jessica Vascellaro, "Ten Countries Ask Google to Do More to Protect Privacy," *Wall Street Journal*, April 20, 2010.

58. Kevin J. O'Brien and Brad Stone, "Anger in Europe Over Google and Privacy," *New York Times*, May 17, 2010.

59. Kevin J. O'Brien, "Wider European Scrutiny of Google on Privacy," *New York Times*, May 21, 2010.

60. Bloomberg News, "Google Toughens Privacy Controls," *New York Times*, October 22, 2010.

61. Scott Morrison and Andrew Morse. "Google Snared Emails During Data Collection," *Wall Street Journal*, October 24, 2010.

62. Eric Pfanner, "Google Faces French Fine for Breach of Privacy," *New York Times*, March 21, 2011.

63. Julia Angwin and Jennifer Valentino-Devries, "Apple, Google Collect User Data," *Wall Street Journal*, April 21, 2011.

64. Grant Gross, "NTIA to address mobile privacy at July 12 meeting," *Computerworld*, June 15, 2012; http://www.computerworld.com/s/article/9228157/NTIA_to_address_mobile_privacy_at_July_12_meeting.

65. Julia Angwin, "Google Widens Its Tracks," *Wall Street Journal*, January 25, 2012.

66. The Associated Press, "Google's New Privacy Policy Goes Into Action Today. How Will It Affect You?," *NY Daily News.com*, March 01, 2012; http://articles.nydailynews.com/2012-03-01/news/31114892_1_google-products-search-engine-privacy-policy.

67. Julia Angwin and Jennifer Valentino-Devries, "Google's iPhone Tracking," *Wall Street Journal*, February 17, 2012.

68. Jennifer Valentino-Devries, "Google to Pay $22.5 Million in FTC Settlement," *The Wall Street Journal*, August 9, 2012.

69. Frances Robinson, Sam Schiechner and Amir Mizroch, "EU Orders Google to Let Users Erase Past," *The Wall Street Journal*, May 13, 2014

70. Sam Schiechner, "Google Starts Removing Search Results Under Europe's 'Right to be Forgotten,'" *The Wall Street Journal*, June 26, 2014.

Case 9

1. "American Greed: A Wall Street Wonder Takes a Fall," *CNBC.com*, October 13, 2012.

2. United States District Court Northern District of Alabama Civil Action No. CV-03-J-0615-S. *Securities and Exchange Commission, Plaintiff, v. HealthSouth Corporation and Richard M. Scrushy, Defendants*, http://www.sec.gov/litigation/complaints/comphealths.htm.

3. "HealthSouth Corporation History," *FundingUniverse*, http://www.fundinguniverse.com/company-histories/healthsouth-corporation-history/.

4. Anita Sharpe, "HealthSouth CEO Uses Glitz To Sell Low-Cost Health Care," *Wall Street Journal*, Wednesday, December 4, 1996, http://online.wsj.com/article/SB849650392259803500.html.

5. Sherri C. Goodman, "Rebranding HealthSouth?," *The Birmingham News*, April 13, 2003, http://www.al.com/specialreport/birminghamnews/index.ssf?healthsouth/healthsouth61.html.

6. John Helyar, "The Insatiable King Richard He Started as a Nobody. He Became a Hotshot CEO. He Tried to Be a Country Star. Then It All Came Crashing Down. The Bizarre Rise and Fall of HealthSouth's Richard Scrushy," *CNNMoney*, July 7, 2003, http://money.cnn.com/magazines/fortune/fortune_archive/2003/07/07/345534/index.htm.

7. "American Greed: A Wall Street Wonder Takes a Fall," *CNBC.com*, October 13, 2012.

8. "Former HealthSouth CEO Speaks Out," *CBS News*, November 4, 2003, www.cbsnews.com.

9. "American Greed: A Wall Street Wonder Takes a Fall," *CNBC.com*, October 13, 2012.

10. Carrick Mollenkamp and Jonathan Weil, "HealthSouth Auditor Got Tip in 1998 Questioning Accounting," *Wall Street Journal*, May 22, 2003, www.wallstreetjournal.com.

11. Carrick Mollenkamp, "An Accountant Tried in Vain To Expose HealthSouth Fraud," *Wall Street Journal*, May 20, 2003, http://online.wsj.com/article/0SB10533844 7947754000,00.html.

12. Chad Terhune and Ann Carms, "HealthSouth Offered $150 Million to Settle Medical Fraud Charges, "*Wall Street Journal*, April 21, 2003, http://online.wsj.com/article/0SB105070832 344878900,00.html

13. "Former HealthSouth CEO Speaks Out," *CBS News*, November 4, 2003, www.cbsnews.com.

14. Ibid.

15. Reed Abelson, "HealthSouth Fires Chief Executive and Audit Firm," *New York Times*, April 1, 2003, http://www.nytimes.com/2003/04/01/business/healthsouth-fires-chief-executive-and-audit-firm.html

16. Ibid.

17. Ibid.

18. Ibid.

19. Ibid.

20. Ibid.

21. Vivi Abrams, "Anxiety Hits HealthSouth: Embattled Firm Plans to Cut 165 Non-Clinical Jobs," *The Birmingham News*, April 4, 2003, http://www.al.com/specialreport/birminghamnews/?healthsouth/health south39.html.

22. "American Greed: A Wall Street Wonder Takes a Fall," *CNBC.com*, October 13, 2012.

23. Associated Press, "Medicare Billed for Famous Singers," *Billboard.com*.

24. Steve Lohr, "How to Exorcise a Corporate Scandal," *New York Times*, June 4, 2005.

25. "American Greed: A Wall Street Wonder Takes a Fall," *CNBC.com*, October 13, 2012.

26. Ibid.

27. Karen Jacobs, "Trial Begins for HealthSouth's Former CEO Scrushy," *Reuters*, January 25, 2005, 1.

28. Ibid.

29. "Update 5: Former HealthSouth President Indicted," Associated Press, February 3, 2005.

30. Associated Press, "HealthSouth Says Ernst & Young Failed to Unearth Fraud at Firm," *Wall Street Journal*, April 6, 2005, www.wallstreetjournal.com.

31. Dan Morse, Chad Terhune, and Ann Carms, "HealthSouth's Scrushy Is Acquitted," *Wall Street Journal*, June 29, 2005, www.wallstreetjournal.com.

32. Ibid.

33. Ibid.

34. Bloomberg News, "Loss Doubles at HealthSouth," *New York Times*, March 30, 2006, www.nytimes.com.

35. Kyle Whitmire, "HealthSouth to Pay $3 Million in U.S. Accounting Fraud Case," *New York Times*, May 19, 2006, www.nytimes.com.

36. Valerie Bauerlein, "Scrushy Is Convicted in Bribery Case," *Wall Street Journal*, June 30, 2006, www.wallstreetjournal.com.

37. Kyle Whitmire, "Former Governor Convicted with Ex-Chief of HealthSouth," *New York Times*, June 30, 2006, www.nytimes.com.

38. "Scrushy's Prison Sentence ends," *Birmingham Business Journal*, July 25, 2012, http://www.bizjournals.com/birmingham/news/2012/07/25/scsrushys-prison-sentence-ends.html.

39. Bloomberg News, "HealthSouth Sentence Rejected Again," *New York Times*, July 12, 2006, www.nytimes.com.

40. Reuters, "HealthSouth Figure Is Sentenced Again," *New York Times*, September 13, 2006, www.nytimes.com.

41. Associated Press, "Court Orders Scrushy to Repay $47.8 Million," *Wall Street Journal*, August 26, 2006, www.wallstreetjournal.com.

42. "HealthSouth Corp.: Scrushy Settles Claims Tied to Bonuses, Legal Bills," *Wall Street Journal*, November 30, 2006, www.wallstreetjournal.com.

43. Associated Press, "Scrushy's Conviction Is Upheld by Judge," *Wall Street Journal*, October 3, 2006, www.wallstreetjournal.com.

44. Associated Press, "HealthSouth to Rejoin Big Board Next Week," *Wall Street Journal*, October 19, 2006, www.wallstreetjournal.com.

45. Kyle Whitmire, "Scrushy to Pay $81 Million to Settle S.E.C. Lawsuit," *New York Times*, April 24, 2007.

46. "Today in Business: HealthSouth Sells Headquarters," *New York Times*, June 2, 2007.

47. Kyle Whitmire, "Profits Aren't Real, but the Refund Is," *New York Times*, October 21, 2007.

48. Adam Nossiter, "Former Alabama Governor Gets 7-Year Sentence in Bribery Case," *New York Times*, June 29, 2007.

49. Adam Nossiter, "Ex-Governor of Alabama Is Ordered Released," *New York Times*, March 28, 2008.

50. Michael Muskal, "Ex-Alabama Gov. Don Siegelman Heads Back to Prison for Bribery." *Los Angeles Times*, August 3, 2012,

http://articles.latimes
.com/2012/aug/03/nation/
la-na-nn-alabama-governor-
don-siegelman-bribery-
prison-20120803.

51. Kyle Whitmire, "Openers: Suits; Did Anyone Ask About a Yacht?," *New York Times*, April 15, 2007.

52. Russell Hubbard, "CEO Puts Recovery From Fraud at $1 Billion," *Birmingham News*, March 27, 2008.

53. Valerie Bauerlein, "Scrushy Denies Role in HealthSouth Fraud," *Wall Street Journal*, May 21, 2009.

54. Valerie Bauerlein and Mike Esterl, "Judge Orders Scrushy to Pay $2.88 billion in Civil Suit," *Wall Street Journal*, June 19, 2009.

55. Mike Esterl and Valerie Bauerlein, "Big Verdict Sends Lawyers on a Treasure Hunt," *Wall Street Journal*, September 5, 2009.

56. Mike Esterl, "Scrushy Seeks to Exit Big House, Faces Much Smaller Digs Outside," *Wall Street Journal*, July 15, 2010, http://online.wsj.com/article/ SB1000142405274870383460457 5365071095621144.html.

57. Mike Esterl, "Scrushy Could Exit Prison in a Month," *Wall Street Journal*, January 25, 2012.

58. Kent Faulk, "Former HealthSouth CEO Richard Scrushy Ends Prison Sentence," A*l.com*, July 25, 2012

59. Kent Faulk, "Former HealthSouth CEO Richard Scrushy released From Federal Probation Supervision," *Al.com*, November 14, 2014

Case 10

1. http://www.un.org/peace/ africa/Diamond.html.

2. Lydia Polgreen, "Diamonds Move From Blood to Sweat and Tears," *New York Times*, March 25, 2007.

3. Alan Cowell, "Off the Shelf; Diamonds, Money and Madness in Brutal African Wars," *New York Times*, October 13, 2002.

4. Roy Maconachie and Tony Binns, "Beyond the Resource Curse? Diamond Mining, Development and Post-Conflict Reconstruction in Sierra Leone," *Resources Policy* 32 no. 3 (2007): 104–115.

5. Vanessa O'Connell, "De Beers Polishes Its Image," *Wall Street Journal*, July 7, 2008.

6. "The Kimberley Process at Risk," *Global Witness,* November 2006, http:// s3.amazonaws.com/3b 59dcdf1c4552f8d85a1 6a4808a3b38-default/ TheKimberleyProcessatRisk .pdf.

7. Bain & Company, *The Global Diamond Industry: Lifting the Veil of Mystery* (2011), 15–16, http://www.bain.com/Images/ PR_BAIN_REPORT_The_ global_diamond_industry.pdf.

8. "The Kimberley Process at Risk," *Global Witness,* November 2006.

9. Reuters, "World Briefing Africa: Congo Republic: Blood Diamonds Penalty," *New York Times*, July 14, 2004.

10. Sarah Childress and Farai Mutsaka, "Zimbabwe's Diamond Production Draws Scrutiny," *Wall Street Journal*, September 14, 2009.

11. Sarah Childress, "Diamond Trade Finds Regulatory Loophole in Mozambique," *Wall Street Journal*, November 6, 2009.

12. Celia Dugger, "Group Won't Suspend Zimbabwe on Mining Abuses," *New York Times*, November 7, 2009.

13. William MacNamara, "Founder Pulls Out of 'Failed' Kimberley Process," *Financial Times*, December 5, 2011.

14. Bain & Company, *The Global Diamond Industry: Lifting the Veil of Mystery* (2011), http:// www.bain.com/Images/PR_ BAIN_REPORT_The_global_ diamond_industry.pdf.

15. http://www.diamonds.net/ News/PrintArticle .aspx?ArticleID=39452.

16. http://www.debeersgroup .com/en/.

17. Adam Hochschild, "A Cartel Is Forever," *New York Times*, August 8, 1993.

18. Edward Jay Epstein, "U.N. Is Diamond Cartel's Best Friend," *Wall Street Journal*, August 3, 2000.

19. Barry B. Kaplan, "Forever Diamonds," *Gemnation,* n.d., http://www.gemnation.com.

20. J. Courtney Sullivan, "How Diamonds Became Forever," *New York Times,* May 3, 2013.

21. Barry B. Kaplan, "Forever Diamonds," *Gemnation,* n.d., http://www.gemnation.com.

22. Bain & Company, *The Global Diamond Industry: Lifting the Veil of Mystery* (2011), 9, http:// www.bain.com/Images/PR_ BAIN_REPORT_The_global_ diamond_industry.pdf.

23. Marc Santora, "Hollywood's Multifaceted Cause du Jour," *New York Times*, December 3, 2006, 1.

24. J. Courtney Sullivan, "How Diamonds Became Forever," *New York Times,* May 3, 2013.

25. Ibid.

26. John Donnelly, "As Peace Comes to Angola, So Do the Diamond Chasers," *Boston Globe*, February 9, 2006.

27. www.debeers.com.

28. "South Africa's DeBeers: The Most Unethical Corporation in the World," *St. Antoninus Institute*, http://www.ewtn .com/library/business/antdebrs .htm.

29. Marilyn Berger, "Harry Oppenheimer, 91, South African Industrialist, Dies," *New York Times*, August 21, 2000.

30. John Wilke, "DeBeers Is in Talks to Settle Price-Fixing Charge; Ending the Diamond Case Could Finally Give Cartel a Retail Presence in U.S.," *Wall Street Journal*, February 24, 2004.

31. Stephen Labaton and Alan Cowell, "De Beers Agrees to Guilty Plea to Re-Enter the U.S. Market," *New York Times*, July 10, 2004.

32. "Guilty Plea by De Beers," *New York Times*, July 14, 2004.

33. Dow Jones Service, "De Beers Will Pay $250 Million to Settle Diamond Pricing Suits," *New York Times*, December 1, 2005.
34. Bain & Company, *The Global Diamond Industry: Lifting the Veil of Mystery* (2011), 10, http://www.bain.com/Images/PR_BAIN_REPORT_The_global_diamond_industry.pdf.
35. Andrew England, "De Beers Warns Bumper 2011 Will Be a Hard Act to Follow," *Financial Times*, February 12, 2012.
36. Devon Maylie and John W. Miller, "Oppenheimer Family Bids Adieu to DeBeers," *The Wall Street Journal*, November 5, 2011.
37. *Anglo American 2013 Annual Report*. p. 110.

Case 11

1. http://www.interfaceglobal.com.
2. Ibid.
3. Ibid.
4. Ibid.
5. Ibid.
6. Ibid.
7. Ibid.
8. Ibid.
9. Ibid.
10. Ibid.
11. Ibid.
12. Ibid.
13. Ibid.
14. Ibid.
15. "Interface Posts Global Environmental Progress with 2005 EcoMetrics Report," Interface Press Release, April 17, 2006, 1–2.
16. "Interface Named #24 on Business Ethics Best Corporate Citizens List: Annual Survey Focuses on Corporate Social Responsibility Performance of Major U.S. Companies," Interface Press Release, May 5, 2006, 1.
17. "InterfaceFLOR Facility in Shanghai Becomes First LEED-CI Facility in China," Interface Press Release, November 15, 2006, 1.
18. "Interface FABRIC Creates Next Generation Upholstery Fabric for 2008 Ford Escape Hybrid: Soda Bottle Resin Finds New Life as Seating Fabric," Interface Press Release, November 29, 2006, 1.
19. http://www.interfaceglobal.com/ZazzSustainabilityAssetts/pdfs/Interface_pdf_summary_report.pdf.
20. Paul Vitello, "Ray Anderson, Businessman Turned Environmentalist, Dies at 77," *New York Times*, August 10, 2011.
21. http://www.interfaceglobal.com/sustainability.aspx
22. Interface Inc. 2013 Annual Report. p. 20.

Case 12

1. Paul Boutin, "Status Update: Megasuccessful," *Wall Street Journal*, June 8, 2010.
2. http://techcrunch.com/2005/09/07/85-of-college-students-use-facebook/.
3. Nancy Hass, "In Your Facebook.com," *New York Times*, January 8, 2006.
4. Alan Finder, "For Some, Online Persona Undermines a Resume," *New York Times*, June 11, 2006.
5. Warren St. John, "When Information Becomes T.M.I.," *New York Times*, September 10, 2006, http://www.nytimes.com.
6. Jamin Warren and Vauhini Vara, "New Facebook Features Have Members in an Uproar," *The Wall Street Journal*, September 7, 2006.
7. "Facebook Agrees to New Rules to Promote Safety for Youth," *New York Times*, May 12, 2009.
8. Brad Stone, "Facebook to Offer Free Classifieds," *New York Times*, May 11, 2007.
9. Facebook, "Information We Receive about You," https://www.facebook.com/about/privacy/your-info.
10. Michelle Slatalla, "'OMG My Mom Joined Facebook!!,'" *New York Times*, June 7, 2007.
11. Brad Stone, "New Scrutiny for Facebook Over Predators," *New York Times*, July 30, 2007.
12. Anne Barnard, "Facebook Agrees to More Safeguards," *New York Times*, October 17, 2007.
13. Louise Story, "Facebook Is Marketing Your Brand Preferences (With Your Permission)," *New York Times*, November 7, 2007.
14. Saul Hansell, "Are Facebook's Social Ads Illegal?," *New York Times Bits*, November 8, 2007.
15. Louise Story and Brad Stone, "Facebook Retreats on Online Tracking," *New York Times*, November 30, 2007, http://www.nytimes.com/2007/11/30/technology/30face.html.
16. Sarah Wheaton, "MoveOn Takes on Facebook," *New York Times*, November 20, 2007.
17. Sarah Wheaton, "Facebook Bows to Privacy Protest," *New York Times*, November 29, 2007.
18. Louise Story and Brad Stone, "Facebook Retreats on Online Tracking," *New York Times*, November 30, 2007.
19. 9 Tomio Geron, "Judge Approves Facebook's Privacy Settlement," *Wall Street Journal*, March 19, 2010.
20. Associated Press, "Facebook Cancels Beacon Program as Part of $9.5 Million Settlement," *NY Daily News*, September 22, 2009.
21. Brian Stelter, "Facebook's Users Ask Who Owns Information," *New York Times,* February 17, 2009.
22. Brad Stone and Brian Stelter, "Facebook Withdraws Changes in Data Use," *New York Times*, February 19, 2009.
23. Jessica Vascellaro, "Facebook's About-Face on Data," *Wall Street Journal*, February 19, 2009.
24. http://schumer.senate.gov/record.cfm?id=324226&
25. Nick Bilton, "Price of Facebook Privacy? Start Clicking," *New York Times*, May 12, 2010.
26. Ibid.
27. Ben Worthen, "Facebook Redesigns Privacy Controls," *Wall Street Journal*, May 27, 2010.
28. Emily Steel and Geoffrey Fowler, "Facebook in Privacy

Breach," *Wall Street Journal*, October 17, 2010.

29. Somini Sengupta, "F.T.C. Settles Privacy Issue at Facebook," *New York Times*, November 29, 2011.

30. Shayndi Raice, "Facebook Set Historic IPO," *Wall Street Journal*, February 2, 2012.

31. David Carr, "Facebook Now Must Balance User Experience and Investor Experience," *New York Times*, February 6, 2012.

32. Elizabeth Dwoskin, "FTC Probing Facebook's New Privacy Policy," *The Wall Street Journal*, September 11, 2013.

33. Vindu Goel, "Facebook Eases Privacy Rules for Teenagers," *New York Times*, October 16, 2013.

34. Reed Albergotti, "Facebook Gives Its Privacy Policy a Makeover," *The Wall Street Journal*, November 13, 2014.

35. Adam D. L. Kramer, Jamie E Gullory and Jeffrey T. Hancock, "Experimental Evidence of Massive-Scale Emotional Contagion Through Social Networks," *Proceeding of the National Academy of Sciences of the United States of America*, 111, no. 24 (June 17, 2014).

36. http://www.apa.org/gradpsych/2011/01/kramer.aspx.

37. https://tobacco.ucsf.edu/users/jeg258.

38. http://infosci.cornell.edu/faculty/jeffrey-hancock.

39. Tim Bradshaw, "Facebook Hit by Psychology Test Backlash," *The Financial Times*, June 29, 2014.

40. Vindu Goel, "Facebook Tinkers With Users' Emotions in News Feed Experiment, Stirring Outcry," *New York Times*, June 29, 2014.

41. Ibid.

42. Reed Albergotti, "Facebook Changes Guidelines on User Experiments," *The Wall Street Journal*, October 2, 2014.

Case 13

1. David Barboza and Louise Story, "Toymaking in China, Mattel's Way," *New York Times*, July 26, 2007.

2. Nicholas Casey, "Mattel Toys to Be Pulled Amid Lead Fears," *Wall Street Journal*, August 2, 2007.

3. "Mattel Recalls One Million Toys," *New York Times*, August 2, 2007.

4. Louise Story, "Lead Paint Prompts Mattel to Recall 967,000 Toys," *New York Times*, August 2, 2007.

5. David Barboza, "China Suspends Exports by 2 Firms Over Lead Paint," *New York Times*, August 10, 2007.

6. David Barboza, "Head of Chinese Toy Company Said to Kill Himself," *New York Times*, August 13, 2007.

7. David Barboza and Louise Story, "Mattel Issues New Recall of Toys Made in China," *New York Times*, August 14, 2007.

8. Nicholas Casey, "Mattel Issues Third Major Recall," *Wall Street Journal*, September 5, 2007.

9. http://www.rsc.org/chemistryworld/News/2007/August/21080701.asp; David Barboza, "Why Lead in Toy Paint? It's Cheaper," *New York Times*, September 11, 2007.

10. Eric Lipton, "Senators Urge More Stringent Rules for Toy Safety," *New York Times*, September 13, 2007.

11. Louise Story, "Mattel Official Delivers an Apology in China," *New York Times*, September 22, 2007.

12. Louise Story, "Disney to Test Character Toys for Lead Paint," *New York Times*, September 10, 2007.

13. Mark Landler and Ivar Ekman, "In Europe, Some Toy Makers Shun the China Label," *New York Times*, September 18, 2007.

14. Louise Story, "Pension Fund Sues Mattel on Toy Recalls," *New York Times*, October 11, 2007.

15. Lauren Pollock, "Mattel Puts Lead Probe Behind It," *Wall Street Journal*, December 16, 2008.

16. Ibid.

17. Bloomberg News, "Mattel to Pay $2.3. Million Penalty for Lead in Toys," *New York Times*, June 6, 2009.

18. Mae Andersen, "Mattel Settles Lawsuit Over High Levels of Lead in Chinese Toys," *USA Today*, October 16, 2009.

19. Deborah Crowe, "Mattel CEO Robert Eckert to Retire," *Los Angeles Business Journal*, November 21, 2011.

20. William Alden, "Former Chief Robert Ecker Joins Friedman Fleischer & Lowe," *New York Times*, September 25, 2014.

Case 14

1. Christopher Jensen, "General Motors Recalls 778,000 Small Cars for Ignition Switch Problem," *New York Times*, February 13, 2014.

2. Jeff Bennett, "GM Expands Ignition Switch Recall to 1.6 Million Cars," *The Wall Street Journal*, February 25, 2014.

3. Jeff Bennett, "Recall Is First Big Test for GM Chief Barra," *The Wall Street Journal*, March 5, 2014.

4. Joseph B. White, Jeff Bennett and Siobhan Hughes, "Regulators Twice Failed to Open GM Probes," *The Wall Street Journal*, March 31, 2014.

5. Jeff Bennett and Siobhan Hughes, "Gm's Barra Says Failure to Fix Switch 'Very Disturbing," *The Wall Street Journal*, April 1, 2014.

6. Jeff Bennett, "GM Now Says It Detected Ignition Switch Problem Back in 2001," *The Wall Street Journal*, March 12, 2014.

7. Jeff Benett and Siobhan Hughes, "New Details Emerge in GM Cobalt Recall," *The Wall Street Journal*, March 24, 2014.

8. Jeff Benett and Siobhan Hughes, "New Details Emerge in GM Cobalt Recall," *The Wall Street Journal*, March 24, 2014.

9. Jeff Bennett, "GM Recalls 971,000 More Vehicles," *The Wall Street Journal*, March 28, 2014.

10. Jeff Bennett and Joann S. Lublin, "GM Raises Recall Costs to $1.3 Billion," *The Wall Street Journal*, April 10, 2014.

11. Joann S. Lublin and Jeff Bennett, "GM Directors Ask Why Cobalt Data Didn't Reach Them," *The Wall Street Journal*, May 14, 2014.

12. Jeff Bennett and Joseph B. White, "GM Gets Record Penalty for Failing to Report Defect," The Wall Street Journal, May 16, 2014.

13. Mike Spector, Joseph B. White, Mike Ramsey and Jeff Bennett, "The 'GM Nod:' 315 Scathing Pages on General Motors' Culture," *The Wall Street Journal*, June 5, 2014.

14. Mike Spector and Jeff Bennett, "GM Dismissals Include Lawyers Lawrence Buonomo, Bill Kemp," *The Wall Street Journal*, June 5, 2014.

15. Jeff Bennett, "GM Board Forms Operational Risk Committee," *The Wall Street Journal*, June 12, 2014.

16. Jeff Bennett, "GM Recalls Nearly 600,000 More Vehicles," *The Wall Street Journal*, June 13, 2014.

17. Associated Press, "Numbers on GM Recall for Faulty Ignition Switches," *New York Times*, July 24, 2014.

18. Jeff Bennett and Mike Spector, "GM Victims Fund Claims Top 4,000," *The Wall Street Journal*, February 1, 2015.

19. Mike Spector, "GM Heads Back Into Court," *The Wall Street Journal*, February 16, 2015.

20. Associated Press, "Death Toll From General Motors Ignition Switches Rises to 57," *New York Times*, February 23, 2015.

Case 15

1. "A Dangerous Business: Two Companies, Two Visions," *Frontline*, www.PBS.org.

2. David Barstow and Lowell Bergman, "Family Profits, Wrung From Blood and Sweat," *New York Times*, January 9, 2003, www.nytimes.com.

3. Ibid.

4. Ibid.

5. "A Dangerous Business: Two Companies, Two Visions," *Frontline*, www.PBS.org.

6. Robin Stein, "Worker Is Crushed to Death at Troubled Foundry Upstate," *New York Times*, February 21, 2004, www.nytimes.com.

7. "A Dangerous Business: The Victims," *Frontline*, www.PBS.org.

8. "A Dangerous Business: Two Companies, Two Visions," *Frontline*, www.PBS.org.

9. "A Dangerous Business: Interview—Charles Jeffress," *Frontline*, www.PBS.org.

10. Ibid.

11. Ibid.

12. "A Dangerous Business: The Victims," *Frontline*, www.PBS.org.

13. "A Dangerous Business," *Frontline*, Transcript, 3, www.PBS.org

14. Ibid.

15. Ibid.

16. Ibid., 5.

17. "A Dangerous Business: The Victims," *Frontline*, www.PBS .org.

18. Ibid.

19. David Barstow and Lowell Bergman, "Family Profits, Wrung From Blood and Sweat," *New York Times*, January 9, 2003, www.nytimes.com.

20. David Barstow and Lowell Bergman, "At a Texas Foundry, an Indifference to Life," *New York Times*, January 8, 2003, www.nytimes.com.

21. Ibid.

22. Ibid.

23. Ibid.

24. David Barstow, "Officials at Foundry Face Health and Safety Charges," *New York Times*, December 16, 2003, www .nytimes.com.

25. "A Dangerous Business," *Frontline*, Transcript, 6, www.PBS.org.

26. Ibid.

27. Ibid., 7.

28. David Barstow and Lowell Bergman, "At a Texas Foundry, an Indifference to Life," *New York Times*, January 8, 2003, www.nytimes.com.

29. Ibid.

30. David Barstow and Lowell Bergman, "Family Profits, Wrung From Blood and Sweat," *New York Times*, January 9, 2003, www.nytimes.com.

31. Ibid.

32. Tom Quigley, "Atlantic States on OSHA's Risk List," *Express-Times*, April 17, 2005, www.nj.com/expresstimes.

33. "A Dangerous Business: The Victims," *Frontline*, www.PBS.org.

34. David Barstow, "Pipe Maker Will Admit to Violations of Safety Law," *New York Times*, August 30, 2005, www.nytimes.com.

35. Russell Hubbard, "McWane Cited for Thirty-Eight Violations," *Birmingham News*, February 17, 2006, 3B.

36. Katherine Torres, "McWane in Hot Water for Alleged Safety Violations," *Occupational Hazards*, March 2006, 10–11.

37. David Barstow, "Guilty Verdicts in New Jersey Worker-Safety Trial," *New York Times*, April 27, 2006.

38. Mary Fuchs, "Plant Manager Sentenced to 70 Months in Prison in Pollution, Safety Case," NJ.com, April 21, 2009.

39. "A Toxic Company: The Canadian Connection," *The Fifth Estate*, www.cbc.ca/fifth/pipes/canada.html.

40. "A Toxic Company: The McWane Story," *The Fifth Estate*, http://www.cbc.ca/fifth/pipes/canada.html.

41. "A Dangerous Business," *Frontline*, Transcript, 17, www.PBS.org.

42. David Barstow, "U.S. Brings New Set of Charges Against Pipe Manufacturer," *New York Times*, May 26, 2004, www .nytimes.com.

43. "A Dangerous Business: An Update," *Frontline*, www .PBS.org.

44. "McWane Pipe Manufacturing Facility in Texas Will Plead Guilty to Air Violations, Pay $4.5 Million," EPA Press Release, March 22, 2005, 1.

45. "A Dangerous Business: An Update," *Frontline*, 2, www.PBS .org.

46. David Barstow, "Officials at Foundry Face Health and Safety

Charges," *New York Times*, December 16, 2003, www .nytimes.com.

47. Val Walton, "McWane Inc., Execs Fined, Get Probation," *Birmingham News*, December 5, 2005, 1A.

48. Ibid.

49. Ibid., 8A.

50. Kyle Whitmire, "Pipe Maker Found Guilty of Violating Pollution Law," *New York Times*, June 11, 2005, www.nytimes .com.

51. "Pipe Company Faces Pollution Indictment," *New York Times*, November 4, 2005, www .nytimes.com.

52. Russell Hubbard, "McWane Settles Utah Pollution Charges," *Birmingham News*, February 9, 2006, www .bhamnews.com.

53. Bruce Geiselman, "More Hot Water; Ex-McWane Exec Sentenced for Clean Air Act Violations," *Waste News*, June 19, 2006, 1.

54. Joe Truini, "Jury: Pipe Maker, Workers Guilty of Enviro, Safety Abuses," *Waste News*, May 8, 2006, 1.

55. David Barstow, "Guilty Verdicts in New Jersey Worker-Safety Trial," *New York Times*, April 27, 2006, www.nytimes.com.

56. Occupational Health & Safety (OH&S), "Cast Iron Manufacturer Pays $4 Million to Resolve 400+ Violations in 14 States," Press Release, July 15, 2010.

57. "A Dangerous Business Revisited," Transcript, *Frontline*, http://www.pbs.org/wgbh/ pages/frontline/mcwane/etc/ script.html.

58. Stan Diel, "FTC Accuses McWane Inc. of Price Fixing, Company Denies Allegations," *Birmingham News*, January 4, 2012.

59. David Foster, "Sentences For Atlantic States, Former Managers Upheld," lehighvalleylive.com, September 19, 2012. On January 26, 2015, Atlantic States Cast Iron Pipe changed its name to McWane Ductile

New Jersey. Jeff Otterstedt, senior president at McWane Ductile commented that "(w)hile we have many valued and rich traditions that are unique to each of our divisions, we believe that we become stronger collectively as one distinct brand."

60. Kurt Bresswein, "Atlantic States in Phillipsburg Now McWane Ductile New Jersey," *leighvalleylive.com*, January 26, 2015.

Case 16

1. Andrew Pollack, "New Scrutiny of Drugs in Vioxx's Family," *New York Times*, October 4, 2004, www.nytimes.com.

2. "The Trials of Merck," *Wall Street Journal*, November 18, 2004, www.wallstreetjournal.com.

3. Anna Wilde Mathews and Barbara Martinez, "Warning Signs: E-Mails Suggest Merck Knew Vioxx's Dangers at Early Stage; As Heart-Risk Evidence Rose, Officials Played Hardball; Internal Message: 'Dodge'; Company Says 'Out of Context,'" *Wall Street Journal*, November 1, 2004, www .wallstreetjournal.com.

4. Ibid.

5. Barbara Martinez, Anna Wilde Mathews, Joann Lublin, and Ron Winslow, "Expiration Date: Merck Pulls Vioxx From Market After Link to Heart Problems; Stock Plunges Amid Questions About Drug Giant's Future; Loss of $2.5 Billion in Sales; Arthritis Patients' Quandary," *Wall Street Journal*, October 1, 2004, www.wallstreetjournal .com.

6. Anna Wilde Mathews and Barbara Martinez, "Warning Signs: E-Mails Suggest Merck Knew Vioxx's Dangers at Early Stage; As Heart-Risk Evidence Rose, Officials Played Hardball; Internal Message: 'Dodge'; Company Says 'Out of Context,'" *Wall Street Journal*, November 1, 2004, www .wallstreetjournal.com.

7. Barbara Martinez, "Vioxx Lawsuits May Focus on FDA Warning in 2001," *Wall Street Journal*, October 5, 2004, www .wallstreetjournal.com.

8. Anna Wilde Mathews and Barbara Martinez, "Warning Signs: E-Mails Suggest Merck Knew Vioxx's Dangers at Early Stage; As Heart-Risk Evidence Rose, Officials Played Hardball; Internal Message: 'Dodge'; Company Says 'Out of Context,'" *Wall Street Journal*, November 1, 2004, www .wallstreetjournal.com.

9. Ibid.

10. "Vioxx, in a New Investigational Study, Relieved Symptoms of Juvenile Rheumatoid Arthritis," Business Wire, October 27, 2003, www.businesswire.com.

11. "FDA Approves Vioxx for the Acute Treatment of Migraine in Adults; First and Only Cox-2 Specific Inhibitor Approved to Relieve Pain and Symptoms of Migraine Attacks," Business Wire, April 1, 2004, www .businesswire.com.

12. Barbara Martinez, Anna Wilde Mathews, Joann Lublin, and Ron Winslow, "Expiration Date: Merck Pulls Vioxx From Market After Link to Heart Problems; Stock Plunges Amid Questions About Drug Giant's Future; Loss of $2.5 Billion in Sales; Arthritis Patients' Quandary," *Wall Street Journal*, October 1, 2004, www .wallstreetjournal.com.

13. Anna Wilde Mathews and Scott Hensley, "Big HMO Reconsiders Vioxx After Study Points to Heart Risks," *Wall Street Journal*, August 26, 2004, www .wallstreetjournal.com.

14. "Merck & Co.: FDA Approves Vioxx Drug to Treat Juvenile Arthritis," *Wall Street Journal*, September 9, 2004, www .wallstreetjournal.com.

15. Leila Abboud and Geeta Anand, "Coping Without Vioxx; Recall of Merck's Pain Drug Sparks Hunt for Alternatives; Just How Safe Is Celebrex?," *Wall Street Journal*, October 1, 2004, www .wallstreetjournal.com.

16. Barbara Martinez, Anna Wilde Mathews, Joann Lublin, and Ron Winslow, "Expiration Date: Merck Pulls Vioxx From Market After Link to Heart Problems; Stock Plunges Amid Questions About Drug Giant's Future; Loss of $2.5 Billion in Sales; Arthritis Patients' Quandary," *Wall Street Journal*, October 1, 2004, www.wallstreetjournal.com.

17. Milt Freudenheim, "A Blow to Efforts to Close in on Rivals," *New York Times*, October 1, 2004, www.nytimes.com.

18. Gina Kolata, "Widely Used Arthritis Drug Is Withdrawn," *New York Times*, October 1, 2004, www.nytimes.com.

19. Barbara Martinez, "Vioxx Lawsuits May Focus on FDA Warning in 2001," *Wall Street Journal*, October 5, 2004, www.wallstreetjournal.com.

20. Scott Hensley, "Merck Faces Twin Vioxx Inquiries; U.S. Probes Deepen Crisis Faced by the Drug Maker; Potential Liability Outlined," *Wall Street Journal*, November 9, 2004, www.wallstreetjournal.com.

21. Kim Norris, "Merck Leader Says Its Recall of Vioxx Was Ethical Choice," *Detroit Free Press*, November 11, 2004, 1–2.

22. Anna Wilde Mathews and Scott Hensley, "Merck May Return Vioxx to Market; Move Depends on Whether FDA Panel Decides Risks Exist in Similar Medicines," *Wall Street Journal*, February 18, 2005, www.wallstreetjournal.com.

23. Barbara Martinez, "Merck's CEO Received Bonus of $1.4 Million," *Wall Street Journal*, March 1, 2005, www.wallstreetjournal.com.

24. Barbara Martinez and Joann Lublin, "Change of Formula: Merck Replaces Embattled CEO With Insider Richard Clark; As Gilmartin Accelerates Retirement, Drug Giant Plans Review of Strategy; Unusual Role for a Board Trio," *Wall Street Journal*, May 6, 2005, www.wallstreetjournal.com.

25. Alex Berenson, "Contrary Tales of Vioxx Role in Texan's Death," *New York Times*, July 15, 2005, www.nytimes.com.

26. Marc Kaufman, "Merck Found Liable in Vioxx Case; Texas Jury Awards Widow $253 Million," *Washington Post*, August 20, 2005.

27. Scott Hensley, Paul Davies, and Barbara Martinez, "Verdict Stokes Backlash," *Wall Street Journal*, August 22, 2005, www.wallstreetjournal.com.

28. Heather Won Tesoriero, Ilan Brat, Gary McWilliams, and Barbara Martinez, "Merck Loss Jolts Drug Giant, Industry," *Wall Street Journal*, August 22, 2005, www.wallstreetjournal.com.

29. Barbara Martinez and Heather Won Tesoriero, "Merck Eases Stance on Vioxx Suits," *Wall Street Journal*, August 26, 2005, www.wallstreetjournal.com.

30. Bloomberg News, "At Vioxx Trial, Witness Says Short-Term Use Posed a Risk," *New York Times*, September 20, 2005, 1.

31. Associated Press, "Merck Wins Second Vioxx Trial," *Forbes*, November 3, 2005, www.forbes.com.

32. Ron Winslow, Sylvia Pagan Westphal, and Heather Won Tesoriero, "Medical Journal Says Merck Study Omitted Key Data; Allegation Could Damage Company in Vioxx Trials; Third Case Goes to Jury," *Wall Street Journal*, December 9, 2005, www.wallstreetjournal.com.

33. Heather Won Tesoriero, Robert Tomsho, and Ron Winslow, "Vioxx Plaintiffs Seek Mistrial After Allegation on Merck Study," *Wall Street Journal*, December 10, 2005, www.wallstreetjournal.com.

34. Heather Won Tesoriero and Barbara Martinez, "Lone Holdout Forces Mistrial in Third Vioxx Case," *Wall Street Journal*, December 13, 2005, www.wallstreetjournal.com.

35. Heather Won Tesoriero, "Merck Wins Vioxx Decision in Vital Second Court Victory," *Wall Street Journal*, February 18, 2006, www.wallstreetjournal.com.

36. Heather Won Tesoriero, "Defending Multiple Vioxx Cases Is Costly Burden for Merck," *Wall Street Journal*, January 26, 2006, www.wallstreetjournal.com.

37. Heather Won Tesoriero, "Merck Is Handed Another Loss Over Vioxx," *Wall Street Journal*, April 22, 2006, www.wallstreetjournal.com.

38. Heather Won Tesoriero, "Texas Jury's Vioxx Finding Stands, but Plaintiff Award Is Lowered," *Wall Street Journal*, December 22, 2006, www.wallstreetjournal.com.

39. Heather Won Tesoriero, "Merck Withheld Vioxx Safety Information, Plaintiff's Lawyer Claims," *Wall Street Journal*, March 7, 2006, www.wallstreetjournal.com.

40. Alex Berenson, "A Second Loss for Merck Over Vioxx," *New York Times*, April 6, 2006, www.nytimes.com.

41. Heather Won Tesoriero, "Vioxx Jury Adds $9 Million to Damages Merck Must Pay," *Wall Street Journal*, April 11, 2006, www.wallstreetjournal.com.

42. Heather Won Tesoriero, "Vioxx 'Trial in a Box' Cuts Cost of Filing Suit," *Wall Street Journal*, April 17, 2006, www.wallstreetjournal.com.

43. Heather Won Tesoriero and Ron Winslow, "New Merck Data Suggest Risks From Vioxx Begin Earlier in Use," *Wall Street Journal*, May 18, 2006, www.wallstreetjournal.com.

44. Elena Cherney and Heather Won Tesoriero, "Study Raises Questions on Short-Term Vioxx Use," *Wall Street Journal*, May 3, 2006, www.wallstreetjournal.com.

45. Ron Windslow, Heather Won Tesoriero, and John Carreyrou, "Merck Study Finds a Vioxx Risk After Use Ended," *Wall Street Journal*, May 12, 2006, www.wallstreetjournal.com.

46. David Armstrong, "Bitter Pill: How the *New England Journal* Missed Warning Signs on Vioxx; Medical Weekly Waited Years to Report Flaws in Article That Praised Pain Drug; Merck Seen as 'Punching Bag,'" Wall Street Journal, May 15, 2006, www.wallstreetjournal.com.

47. Peter Loftus and Heather Won Tesoriero, "Latest Verdict in Vioxx Suits Is Merck Victory," *Wall Street Journal*, July 14, 2006, www.wallstreetjournal .com.

48. Andrew Simons and Heather Won Tesoriero, "Merck Wins California Vioxx Case, Widening Edge on Trial Score Card," *Wall Street Journal*, August 3, 2006, www.wallstreetjournal.com.

49. Alex Berenson, "Legal Stance May Pay off for Merck," *New York Times*, August 4, 2006, www.nytimes.com.

50. Heather Won Tesoriero, "Merck Is Dealt a Twin Blow on Vioxx; Jury Awards One Plaintiff $51 Million as Verdict in New Jersey Is Tossed Out," *Wall Street Journal*, August 18, 2006, www.wallstreetjournal.com.

51. Matthew Herper, "Vioxx Anxiety Rises," *Forbes*, August 17, 2006, www.forbes.com.

52. Heather Won Tesoriero and Darren McDermott, "Judge Calls $51 Million Award Against Merck 'Grossly Excessive,'" *Wall Street Journal*, August 31, 2006, www .wallstreetjournal.com.

53. Alex Berenson, "Merck Inquiry Backs Conduct Over Vioxx," *New York Times*, September 7, 2006, www.nytimes.com.

54. John Carreyrou and Heather Won Tesoriero, "Merck Vioxx Probe Clears Officials," *Wall Street Journal*, September 7, 2006, www.wallstreetjournal .com.

55. Peter Loftus, "Merck's Vioxx Tied to New Threat; Heart Risks Start Early in Study," *Wall Street Journal*, September 13, 2006, www.wallstreetjournal.com.

56. Associated Press and Bloomberg News, "Legal: Merck Wins Vioxx Case," *Washington Post*, September 27, 2006, www.washingtonpost.com.

57. Peter Loftus, "Number of Vioxx-Related Lawsuits Tops 22,000 as Key Deadline Nears," *Wall Street Journal*, September 29, 2006, www .wallstreetjournal.com.

58. Roger Parloff, "Nearly Final Vioxx Suit Tally: 23,800 Cases for 41,750 Plaintiffs," CNNMoney, October 20, 2006, http://money.cnn.com.

59. Bloomberg News, "Merck Is Winner in a Vioxx Lawsuit," *New York Times*, November 16, 2006, www.nytimes.com.

60. Associated Press, "Judge Rules Federal Vioxx Suits Can't Be Single Class-Action Case," *Wall Street Journal*, November 22, 2006, www.wallstreetjournal .com.

61. Reuters, "Vioxx Suit Is Won Quickly by Merck," *New York Times*, December 14, 2006, www.nytimes.com.

62. Associated Press, "Merck Scores Win in Alabama Court Over Vioxx Drug," *Wall Street Journal*, December 16, 2006, www.wallstreetjournal.com.

63. Berenson, Alex, "Plaintiffs Find Payday Elusive in Vioxx Cases," *New York Times*, August 21, 2007.

64. Associated Press, "Court Denies Class Status for Plaintiffs Against Merck," *New York Times*, September 7, 2007.

65. Berenson, Alex, "Merck Agrees to Settle Vioxx Suits for $4.85 Billion," *New York Times*, November 9, 2007.

66. Associated Press, "Vioxx Settlement on Track as 44,000 Sign Up," *New York Times*, March 4, 2008.

67. Associated Press, "Merck to Settle U.S. Claims for $671 Million," *New York Times*, February 8, 2008.

68. Stephanie Saul, "Merck Wrote Drug Studies for Doctors," *New York Times*, April 16, 2008.

69. Associated Press, "Merck Agrees to Settlement Over Vioxx Ads," *New York Times*, May 21, 2008.

70. Alex Berenson, "Courts Reject Two Major Vioxx Verdicts," *New York Times*, May 30, 2008.

71. Natasha Singer, "Merck Paid for Medical 'Journal' Without Disclosure," *New York Times*, May 14, 2009.

72. Natasha Singer, "Does Merck Agreement Pave a Road Toward Change?," *New York Times*, April 3, 2010.

73. Peter Loftus and Brent Kendall, "Merck to Pay $950 Million in Vioxx Settlement," *Wall Street Journal*, November 23, 2011; Duff Wilson, "Merck to Pay $950 Million Over Vioxx," New York Times, November 22, 2011.

74. Jonathan D. Rockoff, "Studies Shine Light on How Vioxx Raises Heart Risks," *The Wall Street Journal,* May 2, 2012.

Case 17

1. Tony Smith, "Ten Years Old: The World's First MP3 Player," Freerepublic.com, March 10, 2008.

2. Spencer Ante, "Napster's Shawn Fanning: The Teen Who Woke Up Web Music," *Businessweek*, April 12, 2000, www.businessweek.com.

3. Michael Learmonth, "Analysis: Why the RIAA Sued MP3.com," CNN.com, January 26, 2000.

4. Wylie Wong, "AOL's Nullsoft Creates Software for Swapping MP3s," Cnet.com, March 14, 2000.

5. "Computer Users Sued for Swapping Music," Associated Press, December 16, 2004, www.ap.org.

6. Anna Wilde Mathews and Nick Wingfield, "Entertainment Industry Loses File-Sharing Case," Wall Street Journal, April 28, 2003, www .wallstreetjournal.com.

7. Nicole St. Pierre, "Musicians to Congress: What About Us?" *Businessweek*, April 4, 2001, www.businessweek.com.

8. Jane Black, "After Napster, a New Net Target," *Businessweek*, June 7, 2001, www.businessweek.com.

9. Alex Salkever, "Digital Music's New Battle Hymn," *Businessweek*, June 21, 2001, www.business week.com.

10. Jane Black, "Napster's Sons: Singing a Different Tune?," *Businessweek*, February 21, 2002, www.businessweek.com.

11. Anna Wilde Mathews and Nick Wingfield, "Entertainment Industry Loses File-Sharing Case," *Wall Street Journal*, April 28, 2003, A3.

12. Mike France and Ronald Grover, "The Music Industry Strikes Back," *Businessweek*, September 29, 2003, www.businessweek.com.

13. Chris Baker, "Industry Group Sues Song Swappers; Amnesty Offer Decried as Sham," *Washington Times*, September 9, 2003.

14. David Kravets, "Judge Says First-Ever RIAA Piracy Trail May Need a Do-Over," Wired .com, May 15, 2008.

15. Joe Barrett, "Don't Stop Believing in Risk of Song Sharing," *Wall Street Journal*, November 5, 2010.

16. Arik Hesseldahl, "Grokster Loses Copyright Case," *Forbes*, June 27, 2005, www.forbes.com.

17. Wayne Arnold, "Australian Court Rules Kazaa Has Violated Copyrights," *New York Times*, September 6, 2005, www .nytimes.com.

18. Associated Press, "Kazaa Owner to Pay $115 Million to Settle Music Piracy Lawsuits," *Wall Street Journal*, July 27, 2006, www.wallstreetjournal.com.

19. Jennifer Bayot, "Grokster File-Sharing Service Shuts Down in Settlement," *New York Times*, November 7, 2005, www.nytimes.com.

20. Sarah McBride, "Music Industry Sues XM Over Replay Device," *Wall Street Journal*, May 17, 2006, www.wallstreetjournal.com.

21. Ibid.

22. Sarah McBride and Ethian Smith, "Music Industry to Abandon Mass Suits," *Wall Street Journal*, December 19, 2008; Paul Sonne and Max Colchester, "France, the U.K. Take Aim at Digital Pirates," *Wall Street Journal*, April 15, 2010.

23. Ben Sisario, "Major Record Labels Settle Suit With LimeWire," *New York Times*, May 12, 2011.

24. Kevin Allison, "The Battle for Grokster Leaves a War to Be Won," *Financial Times*, December 20, 2005, 9.

25. Andrew Dansby, "Dixie Chicks Sue Sony," Rollingstone.com, August 28, 2001.

26. Edna Gundersen, "Bye, Bye, A Piece of the Pie," *USA Today*, May 16, 2004, www.usatoday .com.

27. Edna Gundersen, "Rights Issue Rocks the Music World," *USA Today*, September 15, 2002, www.usatoday.com.

28. Steve Gorman, "Dixie Chicks Settle Sony Suit, Unveil Album Date," *Reuters*, June 17, 2002, www.reuters.com.

29. "Stars in Line for Royalties Payout," BBC News, January 17, 2002, http://news.bbc.co.uk.

30. "Music Stars Get $50M in Royalties," BBC News, May 5, 2004, http://news.bbc.co.uk.

31. Lola Ogunnaike and Leslie Eaton, "Record Labels Must Pay Shortchanged Performers," *New York Times*, May 5, 2004, www.nytimes.com.

32. Ben Sisario, "Eminem Lawsuit May Raise Pay for Older Artists," *New York Times*, March 27, 2011.

33. Jim DeRogatis, "A Cheap Trick," *Chicago Sun-Times*, May 21, 2006, www.suntimes.com.

34. Ethan Smith, "Sony BMG Is Sued by Bands Over Song-Download Royalties," *Wall Street Journal*, April 28, 2006, www.wallstreetjournal.com.

35. Tom Zeller, "The Ghost in the CD," *New York Times*, November 14, 2005, www.nytimes.com.

36. Matthew Fordhal, "Sony Patch Reveals Its Anti-Piracy Files on PCs," *Washington Post*, November 3, 2005, www.washingtonpost.com.

37. "Sony Music Issues Fix to Anti-Piracy Program," Associated Press, November 3, 2005, 2.

38. Andrew Kantor, "Sony: The Rootkit of All Evil?" *USA Today*, November 17, 2005, www .usatoday.com.

39. "Viruses Exploit Sony CD Anti-Piracy Scheme," Associated Press, November 10, 2005, 1–2.

40. Brian Krebs, "Study of Sony Anti-Piracy Software Triggers Uproar," *Washington Post*, November 2, 2005, www .washingtonpost.com.

41. "Sony BMG Pulls CD Copy-Protection Software," Associated Press, November 11, 2005, 1.

42. Tom Zeller, "The Ghost in the CD," *New York Times*, November 14, 2005, www .nytimes.com.

43. Ethan Smith, "Sony BMG Pulls Millions of CDs Amid Antipiracy-Software Flap," *Wall Street Journal*, November 17, 2005, www .wallstreetjournal.com.

44. Tom Zeller Jr., "Sony BMG Sued Over CDs With Anti-Piracy Software," *New York Times*, November 22, 2005, www.nytimes.com.

45. Ethan Smith, "Sony BMG Agrees to Settle Fifteen Suits Over CD Software," *Wall Street Journal*, December 30, 2005, www.wallstreetjournal.com.

46. "Free Downloads End Sony CD Saga," BBC News, May 23, 2006, http://news.bbc.co.uk.

47. "Sony BMG Music Entertainment: Venture Agrees to Penalties, Refunds to Settle CD Lawsuits," *Wall Street Journal*, December 20, 2006, www.wallstreetjournal.com.

48. Ohio Attorney General's Office, "Ohio, Thirty-Nine States Settle With Sony BMG Over Anti-Copying Software," *Insurance Journal*, December 28, 2006, 1.

49. Martin Fridson, *Unwarranted Intrusions: The Case Against Government Intervention in the Marketplace* (New York: Wiley, 2006).

50. Michael Cieply, "A Few Promoters Dominate Record

Business—Independents Said to Be Linked to Certain Radio Outlets," *Wall Street Journal*, April 18, 2006, www.wallstreet journal.com.

51. "Former Record Promoter Pleads Guilty to Payola," *Wall Street Journal*, May 24, 1989, www.wallstreetjournal.com.

52. Patrick Reilly, "Radio's New Spin on an Oldie; Pay-for-Play," *Wall Street Journal*, March 16, 1998, www.wallstreetjournal .com.

53. Anna Wilde Mathews and Jennifer Ordonez, "Music Labels Say It Costs too Much to Get Songs on Radio," *Wall Street Journal*, June 10, 2002, www .wallstreetjournal.com.

54. Ethan Smith, "Spitzer Probes How Music Labels Get Radio Airplay," *Wall Street Journal*, October 22, 2004, www .wallstreetjournal.com.

55. Jeff Leeds, "Sony BMG Called Close to Settlement With Spitzer," *New York Times*, July 23, 2005, www.nytimes.com.

56. "Sony Settle Payola Investigation," Office of New York State Attorney General Eliot Spitzer Press Release, July 25, 2005, 1–3.

57. Lorne Manly, "How Payola Went Corporate," *New York Times*, July 31, 2005, www .nytimes.com.

58. "Sony Settle Payola Investigation," Office of New York State Attorney General Eliot Spitzer Press Release, July 25, 2005, 1–3.

59. Ethan Smith, "Sony BMG Fires Senior Executive After Settlement," *Wall Street Journal*, July 26, 2006, www .wallstreetjournal.com.

60. Amy Schatz and Sarah McBride, "FCC Launches Bribery Probe Over Payouts for Radio Airplay," *Wall Street Journal*, August 9, 2005, www .wallstreetjournal.com.

61. Jeff Leeds, "Sony BMG Sued in Bribery Case," *New York Times*, October 19, 2005, www.nytimes.com.

62. Ethan Smith, "Spitzer Settles With Warner, Shifts Focus to Radio Operators," *Wall Street Journal*, November 23, 2005, www.wallstreetjournal.com.

63. Chick Taylor, "Hundreds of Radio Stations Marked on Payola Probe," *Billboard Radio Monitor*, February 10, 2006, 1.

64. "Radio Giant Named in Payola Lawsuit," Office of New York State Attorney General Eliot Spitzer Press Release, March 8, 2006, 1–2.

65. Jeff Leeds, "Spitzer Sues Radio Chain as Part of Music Inquiry," *New York Times*, March 9, 2006, www.ny times.com.

66. Sarah McBride and Ethan Smith, "Spitzer Sues Radio-Station Operator as Payola Probe Expands," *Wall Street Journal*, March 9, 2006, www.wallstreetjournal.com.

67. Ethan Smith, "Universal Music Settle Claims Over Radio Play," *Wall Street Journal*, May 12, 2006, www.wallstreetjournal .com.

68. Ethan Smith, "EMI Settle Spitzer's Payola Probe; Label to Pay $3.75 Million, Adhere to Tighter Rules on Securing Radio Airplay," *Wall Street Journal*, June 16, 2006, www .wallstreetjournal.com.

69. "CBS Corp: Radio Unit Resolves Probe Over Payoffs for $2 Million," *Wall Street Journal*, October 20, 2006, www .wallstreetjournal.com.

70. Hannah Karp, "Apple iTunes Sees Big Drop in Music Sales," *The Wall Street Journal*, October 24, 2014.

71. http://riaa.com/ media/1806D32F-B3DD-19D3-70A4-4C31C0217836.pdf

72. David Goldman, "Music's Lost Decade: Sales Cut in Half," http://money.cnn .com/2010/02/02/news/ companies/napster_music_ industry/

73. Hannah Karp and Sven Grundber, "Taylor Swift Pulls Her Music From Spotify," *The Wall Street Journal*, November 4, 2014.

74. Ben Sisario, "Chief Defends Spotify After Snub by Taylor Swift," *New York Times*, November 11, 2014.

75. Ben Sisario, "Sales of Taylor Swift's '1989' Intensify Streaming Debate," *New York Times*, November 5, 2014.

76. Ben Sisario, "Chief Defends Spotify After Snub by Taylor Swift," *New York Times*, November 11, 2014.

77. Ibid.

78. Keith Caulfield, "Billboard 200 Chart Moves: Taylor Swift's '1989' Hits 4 Million in U.S. Sales, *Billboard*, January 23, 2015.

Case 18

1. Charles Duhigg and Keith Bradsher, "How the U.S. Lost Out on iPhone Work," *New York Times*, January 21, 2012.

2. Ibid.

3. Charles Duhigg and David Barboza, "In China, Human Costs Are Built Into an iPad," *New York Times*, January 25, 2012.

4. Ibid.

5. "The Stark Reality of iPod's Chinese Factories," *Daily Mail*, August 18, 2006.

6. Ellen Lee, "Apple Says iPod Factory in China Treats Workers Fairly," SFGate.com, August 18, 2006.

7. Ting-I Tsai, "Employee's Suicide Puts Hon Hai, Apple in Spotlight," *Wall Street Journal*, July 23, 2009.

8. Andrew Morse and Nick Wingfield, "Apple Audits Labor Practices," *Wall Street Journal*, March 1, 2010.

9. Jason Dean, "China Worker Suicides Draw Scrutiny," *Wall Street Journal*, May 14, 2010.

10. David Barboza, "Another Death at Electronics Supplier in China," *New York Times*, May 21, 2010.

11. David Barboza, "String of Suicides Continues at Electronics Supplier in China," *New York Times*, May 25, 2010.

12. David Barboza, "Electronics Maker Promises Review After Suicides," *New York Times*, May 26, 2010.

13. Jason Dean and Ting-I Tsai, "Hon Hai to Raise Wages by 30%," *Wall Street Journal*, June 3, 2010.
14. Bloomberg News, "Foxconn Raises Worker Pay 30%," *New York Times*, June 1, 2010; David Barboza, "After Spate of Suicides, Technology Firm in China Raises Workers' Salaries," *New York Times*, June 2, 2010.
15. David Barboza, "After Suicides, Scrutiny of China's Grim Factories," *New York Times*, June 6, 2010.
16. David Barboza, "Foxconn Increases Size of Raise in Chinese Factories," *New York Times*, June 6, 2010.
17. Alex Pevzner, "Hon Hai Hands Over Management of Staff Dorms," *Wall Street Journal*, June 28, 2010.
18. David Barboza, "Foxconn Plans to Lift Pay Sharply at Factories in China," *New York Times*, February 18, 2012.
19. James Areddy and Yukari Iwatani Kane, "Explosion Kills 3 at Foxconn Plant," *Wall Street Journal*, May 21, 2011.
20. Aries Poon, Loretta Chao, and Yukari Iwatani Kane, "Factory Blast Roils Tech Supply Chain," *Wall Street Journal*, May 24, 2011.
21. Loretta Chao, "Hon Hai Says Halted Workshops Resume," *Wall Street Journal*, June 2, 2011.
22. Charles Duhigg and David Barboza, "In China, Human Costs Are Built Into an iPad," *New York Times*, January 25, 2012.
23. Nick Wingfield and Charles Duhigg, "Apple Lists Its Suppliers for 1st Time," *New York Times*, January 13, 2012.
24. *Apple Supplier Responsibility, 2012 Progress Report,* http://images.apple.com/supplierresponsibility/pdf.
25. *Apple Supplier 2014 Progress Report,* 5.
26. Ibid., p. 32.
27. Ibid.
28. Ibid., p. 5.
29. Ibid., p. 11.
30. Ibid., p. 14.
31. Ibid.
32. Ibid., p. 33.
33. Ibid.
34. Ibid., p. 37.
35. Ibid.

Case 19

1. "Company Info: Our History," www.patagonia.com.
2. Ibid.
3. Ibid.
4. Andrea Adelson, "Casual Worker-Friendly, and a Moneymaker, Too," *New York Times*, June 30, 1998.
5. www.patagonia.com.
6. Todd Henneman, "Patagonia Fills Payroll With People Who Are Passionate," *Workforce*, November 4, 2011, http://www.workforce.com/article/20111104/NEWS02/111109975/patagonia-fills-payroll-with-people-who-are-passionate.
7. Ibid.
8. www.patagonia.com.
9. Ibid.
10. Ibid.
11. Patagonia.com, "The Footprint Chronicles: Methodology for Environmental Cost Calculations," March 2009, http://www.patagonia.com/pdf/en_US/method_for_cost5.pdf
12. www.patagonia.com.
13. Yvon Chouinard, "Have a Snack, Save a Species," *Environmentalism: Essay,* Holiday 2011, http://www.patagonia.com/us/patagonia.go?assetid=66131.
14. *Patagonia Environmental & Social Initiatives 2014,* 6.
15. www.patagonia.com.
16. Ibid.
17. *Patagonia Environmental & Social Initiatives 2014,* 11.
18. Ibid., p. 18.

Case 20

1. Kenneth Chang, "Quake Moves Japan Closer to U.S. and Alters Earth's Spin," *New York Times*, March 13, 2011.
2. Phred Dvorak and Yuka Hayashi, "Fukushima Daiichi Diary: Other Problems," *Wall Street Journal*, May 18, 2011.
3. Yuka Hayashi and Phred Dvorak, "Fresh Tales of Chaos Emerge From Early in Nuclear Crisis," *Wall Street Journal*, May 18, 2011.
4. Phred Dvorak and Peter Landers, "Japanese Plant Had Barebones Risk Plan," *Wall Street Journal*, March 31, 2011.
5. Henry Fountain, "A Look at the Mechanics of a Partial Meltdown," *New York Times*, March 13, 2011.
6. "Experts Had Long Criticized Potential Weaknss in Design of Stricken Reactor," *New York Times*, March 15, 2011, http://www.nytimes.com/2011/03/16/world/asia/16contain.html?_r=0.
7. Matthew Wald, "Japan Orders Evacuation Near 2nd Nuclear Plant," *New York Times*, March 11, 2011.
8. Tom Zeller Jr., "Experts Had Long Criticized Potential Weakness in Design of Stricken Reactor," *New York Times*, March 15, 2011, http://www.nytimes.com/2011/03/16/world/asia/16contain.html?_r=0.
9. Hiroko Tabuchi, Ken Belson, and Norimitsu Onishi, "Dearth of Candor From Japan's Leadership," *New York Times*, March 16, 2011.
10. Ibid.
11. Norimitsu Onishi, "Japan Offers Little Response to U.S. Assessment," *New York Times*, March 17, 2011.
12. Henry Fountain, "Japan Raises Danger Level at Power Plant," *New York Times*, March 18, 2011.
13. Norimitsu Onishi and Martain Fackler, "In Nuclear Crisis, Crippling Mistrust," *New York Times*, June 12, 2011.
14. Hiroko Tabuchi, Ken Belson, and Norimitsu Onishi, "Dearth of Candor From Japan's Leadership," *New York Times*, March 16, 2011.
15. Norihiko Shirouzu, Phred Dvorak, Yuka Hayashi, and Andrew Morse, "Bid to 'Protect

Assets' Slowed Reactor Fight," *Wall Street Journal*, March 21, 2011.

16. John Foley and Robert Cyran, "Doing the Math on Japan Crisis," *New York Times*, March 24, 2011.

17. Rebecca Smith, Ben Casselman, and Mitsuru Obe, "Japan Plant Had Troubled History," *Wall Street Journal*, March 21, 2011.

18. Hiroko Tabuchi, Norimitsu Onishi, and Ken Belson, "Japan Extended Reactor's Life, Despite Warning," *New York Times*, March 21, 2011.

19. Norimitsu Onishi and Ken Belson, "Culture of Complicity Tied to Stricken Nuclear Plant," *New York Times*, April 26, 2011, http://www.nytimes .com/2011/04/27/world/ asia/27collusion.html?page wanted=all.

20. Norimitsu Onishi and Ken Belson, "Culture of Complicity Tied to Stricken Nuclear Plant," *New York Times*, April 26, 2011.

21. Norimitsu Onishi, Henry Fountain, and Tom Zeller Jr., "Crisis Underscores Fears About Safety of Nuclear Energy," *New York Times*, March 12, 2011.

22. David Sanger and Matt Wald, "Radioactive Releases in Japan Could Last Months, Experts Say," *New York Times*, March 13, 2011.

23. Hiroko Tabuchi and Matthew Wald, "Japanese Scramble to Avert Meltdowns as Nuclear Crisis Deepens After Quake," *New York Times*, March 12, 2011.

24. Hiriko Tabuchi and Matthew Wald, "Second Explosion at Reactor as Technicians Try to Contain Damage," *New York Times*, March 13, 2011.

25. David Sanger and Matt Wald, "Radioactive Releases in Japan Could Last Months, Experts Say," *New York Times*, March 13, 2011.

26. Hiroko Tabuchi and Keith Bradsher, "Japan Says 2nd Reactor May Have Ruptured With Radioactive Release," *New York Times*, March 15, 2011.

27. Mitsuru Obe, "Core Damaged at Three Reactors," *Wall Street Journal*, May 16, 2011.

28. Hiroko Tabuchi and Keith Bradsher, "Japan Nuclear Disaster Put on Par With Chernobyl," *New York Times*, April 11, 2011.

29. Keith Bradsher, Hiroko Tabuchi, and Andrew Pollack. "Japanese Officials on Defensive as Nuclear Alert Level Rises," *New York Times*, April 12, 2011.

30. Keith Bradsher and Andrew Pollack, "Nuclear Company to Compensate Evacuees in Japan," *New York Times*, April 15, 2011.

31. Martin Fackler, "Fatal Radiation Level Found at Japanese Plant," *New York Times*, August 1, 2011.

32. Kazunori Anzai, Nobuhiko Ban, Toshihiko Ozawa, and Shinji Tokonami, "Fukushima Daiichi Nuclear Power Plant Accident: Facts, Environmental Contamination, Possible Biological Effects, and Countermeasures," *Journal of Clinical Biochemistry and Nutrition*. 50, no. 1 (January 2012): 2–8. http://www.ncbi.nlm.nih.gov/ pmc/articles/PMC3246178/.

33. Jena McGregor, "TEPCOTEPCO TEPCOTEPCOTEPCO President Steps Down in 'Symbolic Close' to Japanese Power Company's Crisis," *Washington Post*, May 20, 2011.

34. Hiroko Tabuchi, "Japan Passes Law Supporting Stricken Nuclear Plant's Operator," *New York Times*, August 3, 2011.

35. Hiroko Tabuchi, "Tokyo Electric Posts $7.4 Billion Loss," *New York Times*, August 9, 2011.

36. Reuters, "Radiation Cleanup Will Cost at Least $13 billion, Premier Says," *New York Times*, October 21, 2011.

37. Mitsuru Obe, "'No Errors' in Nuclear Crisis," *Wall Street Journal*, December 3, 2011.

38. Mitsuru Obe and Paul Jackson, "New Leak Detected at Nuclear Facility," *Wall Street Journal*, December 5, 2011.

39. Hiroko Tabuchi, "Japan's Prime Minister Declares Fukushima Plant Stable," *New York Times*, December 16, 2011.

40. Phred Dvorak and Mitsuru Obe, "Japan Plots 40-Year Nuclear Cleanup," *Wall Street Journal*, December 22, 2011.

41. Martin Fackler, "Small Leak Is Reported at Fukushima Nuclear Plant," *New York Times*, April 7, 2013.

42. Alexander Martin, "Fukushima Watch: Former Daiichi Nuclear Power Plant Chief Dies," *The Wall Street Journal*, July 9, 2013.

43. Phred Dvorak, "Japan Races to Contain Worst Fukushima Spill Since Meltdown," *The Wall Street Journal*, August 22, 2013.

44. Hiroko Tabuchi, "Japan: No Indictments Over Fukushima Accident," *New York Times*, September 9, 2013.

45. Hiroko Tabuchi, "Unskilled and Destitute Are Hiring Targets for Fukushima Cleanup," *New York Times*, March 16, 2014.

46. Martin Fackler, "Fuel Rods Are Removed From Damaged Fukushima Reactor Building," *New York Times*, December 20, 2014.

Case 21

1. Alex Berenson, "Tyco Chief Out as Tax Inquiry Picks up Speed," *New York Times*, June 4, 2002, www.nytimes.com.

2. David Armstrong, "A Tyco Veteran Returns to Helm to Steer Firm Through Its Storm," *Wall Street Journal*, June 10, 2002, www.wallstreetjournal.com.

3. Mark Maremont, John Hechinger, Jerry Markon, and Gregory Zuckerman, "Tainted Chief: Kozlowski Quits Under a Cloud, Worsening Worries About Tyco Ex-CEO Faces Criminal Probe of New York Sales Taxes, Said to Involve Costly Art—Stock Takes a 27% Shellacking," *Wall Street Journal*, June 4, 2002, www.wallstreetjournal.com.

4. Alex Berenson and Carol Vogel, "Ex-Tyco Chief Is Indicted in Tax Case," *New York Times*, June 5, 2002, www.nytimes.com.

5. Alex Berenson and William Rashbaum, "Tyco Ex-Chief Is Said to Face Wider Inquiry Into Finances," *New York Times*, June 7, 2002, www.nytimes.com.

6. Laurie Cohen and Mark Maremont, "Tyco Relocations to Florida Are Probed," *Wall Street Journal*, June 10, 2002, www.wallstreetjournal.com.

7. www.highbeam.com/doc/1p2-771.2086.html.

8. Andrew Ross Sorkin and Susan Saulny, "Former Tyco Chief Faces New Charges," *New York Times*, June 27, 2002, www.nytimes.com.

9. Mark Maremont, "Tyco Posts $2.32 Billion Loss; Cites Downturn, CIT Spinoff," *Wall Street Journal*, July 24, 2002, www.wallstreetjournal.com.

10. Mark Maremont and Jesse Drucker, "Tyco Lures Breen From Motorola to Become CEO," *Wall Street Journal*, July 26, 2002, www.wallstreetjournal.com.

11. Andrew Ross Sorkin, "Two Top Tyco Executives Charged With $600 Million Fraud Scheme," *New York Times*, September 13, 2002, www.nytimes.com.

12. Mark Maremont and Jerry Markon, "Former Tyco Executives Are Charged—New York Prosecutors Say Ex-CEO, Finance Officer Ran 'Criminal Enterprise,'" *Wall Street Journal*, September 13, 2002, www.wallstreetjournal.com.

13. Andrew Ross Sorkin, "Tyco Details Lavish Lives of Executives," *New York Times*, September 18, 2002, www.nytimes.com.

14. www.reuters.com/article/2012/08/10/tyco-kozlowski-idUSL2E8JAJ7820120810.

15. James Bandler and Jerry Guidera, "Tyco Ex-CEO's Party for Wife Cost $2.1 Million, but Had Elvis," *Wall Street Journal*, September 17, 2002, www.wallstreetjournal.com.

16. Mark Maremont, "Next Evidence for Kozlowski Jurors: Party Video," *Wall Street Journal*, October 28, 2003, www.wallstreetjournal.com.

17. Andrew Ross Sorkin, "The Tyco Videotape Has Been Edited for Content," *New York Times*, October 28, 2003, www.nytimes.com.

18. Chad Bray, "Party in Sardinia Is Revisited in Tyco Ex-Executives' Retrial; Weeklong 2001 Celebration Is Reprised by Prosecution in Kozlowski-Swartz Case," *Wall Street Journal*, February 23, 2005, www.wallstreetjournal.com.

19. Associated Press. "Retrial of Tyco Ex-Executives to Begin Today," *Los Angeles Times*, January 18, 2005, http://articles.latimes.com/2005/jan/18/business/fi-tyco18.

20. John Hechinger and Gregory Zuckerman, "Artful Evasion: Is Clock Ticking for Tyco's Swartz?" *Wall Street Journal*, June 6, 2002, www.wallstreetjournal.com.

21. Mark Maremont and Laurie Cohen, "Tyco Finance Chief Set to Leave as New CEO Begins to Clean House," *Wall Street Journal*, August 2, 2002, www.wallstreetjournal.com.

22. Kris Maher, "Tyco Set to Name Finance Chief, a United Technologies Executive," *Wall Street Journal*, September 11, 2002, www.wallstreetjournal.com.

23. David Armstrong, "Former Executive at Tyco Is Charged With Tax Evasion," *Wall Street Journal*, February 20, 2003, www.wallstreetjournal.com.

24. Mark Maremont and Beth Demain Reigber, "Kozlowski Called Payment 'Mistake'; Former Tyco Chief Admitted $20 Million Sent to Director Needed Approval, Trial Told," *Wall Street Journal*, October 10, 2003, www.wallstreetjournal.com.

25. Mark Maremont, "Tyco Ex-Treasurer Tells of Benefits Changes," *Wall Street Journal*, October 22, 2003, www.wallstreetjournal.com.

26. Mark Maremont, "Tyco Ex-Manager Tells of Her Perks," *Wall Street Journal*, October 24, 2003, www.wallstreetjournal.com.

27. Chad Bray, "Tyco Accountant Says Kozlowski Used Company Funds as His Own," *Wall Street Journal*, November 20, 2003, www.wallstreetjournal.com.

28. Chad Bray, "Tyco Ex-Officer Tells of Fund Transfers; Company Loans Were Used for Personal Purchases, Director of Treasury Says," *Wall Street Journal*, December 3, 2003, www.wallstreetjournal.com.

29. Chad Bray, "Tyco Aide Testifies About Incidents; Cross Tells of Ring Bought With a $5 Million Loan; Tuition for Her Daughter," *Wall Street Journal*, January 6, 2004, www.wallstreetjournal.com.

30. Mark Maremont, "Tyco Lawsuit Seeks Damages From Ex-Officer," *Wall Street Journal*, April 3, 2003, www.wallstreetjournal.com.

31. William Neuman, "Apartment Prices May Be up, but Tyco Sells at a Discount," *New York Times*, September 19, 2004, www.nytimes.com.

32. Chad Bray, "Swartz Says He Didn't Notice Millions Unreported on Tax Form," *Wall Street Journal*, May 12, 2005, www.wallstreetjournal.com.

33. Alex Berenson, "Tyco Turmoil Deepens as It Fires Lawyer," *New York Times*, June 11, 2002, www.nytimes.com.

34. David Armstrong, John Hechinger, and Laurie Cohen, "Tyco Payments to Law Firm Queried—Employer of Director Got up to $2 Million a Year, Raising Some Concerns," *Wall Street Journal*, June 12, 2002, www.wallstreetjournal.com.

35. www.sec.gov/litigation/litve/eases/lrl7722.htm.

36. Laurie Cohen and John Hechinger, "Tyco Dismisses General Counsel After a Dispute—Belnick Refused to Assist Internal Probes, Boies Says; Plus, a $20 Million Question," *Wall Street Journal*, June 11, 2002, www.wallstreetjournal.com.

37. Laurie Cohen, "Tyco Former Top Lawyer Joins CEO on Hot Seat," *Wall Street Journal*,

September 13, 2002, www.wallstreetjournal.com.

38. Andrew Ross Sorkin, "New Charges in Tyco Case Involve Bonus for Ex-Counsel," *New York Times*, February 4, 2003, www.nytimes.com.

39. Chad Bray, "Tyco Lawyer Testifies Executives Got Loans to Purchase Homes," *Wall Street Journal*, May 18, 2004, www.wallstreetjournal.com.

40. Jonathan Glater and Susan Saulny, "Jury Finds Ex-Tyco Lawyer Not Guilty of All Charges," *New York Times*, July 16, 2004, www.nytimes.com.

41. Jennifer Levitz, "Former Tyco Lawyer Will Pay Fine to Settle SEC Charges Over Loans," *Wall Street Journal*, May 3, 2006, www.wallstreetjournal.com.

42. David Armstrong, James Bandler, John Hechinger, and Jerry Guidera, "Tyco Directors Involved in Deals—Investors Weren't Aware of Transactions by Pair of Board Members," *Wall Street Journal*, June 14, 2002, www.wallstreetjournal.com.

43. Dan Ackman, "The Millions Kozlowski Didn't Steal," *Forbes*, May 23, 2005, www.forbes.com.

44. Laurie Cohen and John Hechinger, "Tyco Suits Say Clandestine Pacts Led to Payments," *Wall Street Journal*, June 18, 2002, www.wallstreetjournal.com.

45. Andrew Ross Sorkin, "Tyco Figure Pays $22.5 Million in Guilty Plea," *New York Times*, December 18, 2002, www.nytimes.com.

46. Mark Maremont and John Hechinger, "Tyco Ex-CEO Invested $5 Million in Fund Run by Director of Firm," *Wall Street Journal*, October 23, 2002, www.wallstreetjournal.com.

47. Beth Demain Reigber, "Tyco Ex-Director Says Payment Without Approval Was 'Corrupt,'" *Wall Street Journal*, October 17, 2003, www.wallstreetjournal.com.

48. Michael Schroeder and John Hechinger, "SEC Reopens Tyco Investigation—Company Faces Questions About Its Accounting During Acquisition Binge," *Wall Street Journal*, June 13, 2002, www.wallstreetjournal.com.

49. Mark Maremont and Laurie Cohen, "Tyco's Internal Inquiry Concludes Questionable Accounting Was Used," *Wall Street Journal*, December 31, 2002, www.wallstreetjournal.com.

50. Andrew Ross Sorkin and Alex Berenson, "Tyco Admits Using Accounting Tricks to Inflate Earnings," *New York Times*, December 31, 2002, www.nytimes.com.

51. Mark Maremont, "Questioning the Books: Tyco Is Likely to Report New Woes," *Wall Street Journal*, April 30, 2003, www.wallstreetjournal.com.

52. Joann Lublin and Mark Maremont, "Taking Tyco by the Tail; A Tumultuous First Year, Breen Discusses His Strategy to Clean House, Restore Trust," *Wall Street Journal*, August 6, 2003, www.wallstreetjournal.com.

53. Mark Maremont, "Tyco Ex-Officer Says Swartz Made Admission on Bonuses," *Wall Street Journal*, October 30, 2003, www.wallstreetjournal.com.

54. Kevin McCoy, "Tyco Spent Millions on Exec Perks, Records Say," *USA Today*, September 16, 2002.

55. Andrew Ross Sorkin, "Court Is Told Tyco Deals Had Backing of Auditors," *New York Times*, February 8, 2003, www.nytimes.com.

56. Gretchen Morgenson, "SEC Puts Ban on Accountant Over His Work on Tyco's Books," *New York Times*, August 14, 2003, www.nytimes.com.

57. Chad Bray, "Ex-Tyco Officer Testifies Auditor Cleared Bonuses," *Wall Street Journal*, December 12, 2003, www.wallstreetjournal.com.

58. Chad Bray, "Tyco's Auditor Undercuts Bonus Defense; Scalzo Knew That Executives Got Payments but Didn't Check If Board Had Given Approval," *Wall Street Journal*, January 29, 2004, www.wallstreetjournal.com.

59. "Kozlowski: Trial Starts," CNNmoney.com, September 29, 2003.

60. Mark Maremont, "Tyco Posts Loss, Will Cut 7,200 Jobs," *Wall Street Journal*, November 5, 2003, www.wallstreetjournal.com.

61. Beth Demain Reigber, "Tyco Employees Will Be Taking an Ethics Class," *Wall Street Journal*, November 12, 2003, www.wallstreetjournal.com.

62. Mark Maremont and Colleen DeBaise, "Tyco Executives May Not Benefit From a Mistrial," *Wall Street Journal*, March 29, 2004, www.wallstreetjournal.com.

63. "Tyco Prosecutors Plan Rebuttal as Defense Rests." *New York Times*. February 27, 2004; http://www.nytimes.com/2004/02/27/business/tyco-prosecutors-plan-rebuttal-as-defense-rests.html.

64. Andrew Ross Sorkin and Contributors, "Tyco Trial Ended as a Juror Cites Outside Pressure," *New York Times*, April 3, 2004, www.nytimes.com.

65. William Neuman, "Tyco to Sell Ex-Chief's Apartment for $21 Million," *New York Times*, October 9, 2004, www.nytimes.com.

66. Chad Bray, Kara Scannell, and Mark Maremont, "Tyco Kozlowski Takes the Stand at His Retrial; Former CEO Denies Charges He Stole From Conglomerate; A $25 Million Tax Omission," *Wall Street Journal*, April 28, 2005, www.wallstreetjournal.com.

67. Andrew Ross Sorkin, "Tyco's Ex-Chief and Top Aide Are Convicted of Grand Larceny," *New York Times*, June 17, 2005, www.nytimes.com.

68. Mark Maremont and Chad Bray, "Tyco Trial Jurors Say Defendants Weren't Credible," *Wall Street Journal*, June 20, 2005, www.wallstreetjournal.com.

69. Andrew Ross Sorkin. "Ex-Tyco Executives Get 8 to 25 Years in Prison," *New York Times*. September 20, 2005. http://www.nytimes.com/2005/09/20/business/20tyco.html?pagewanted=all&_r=1&

70. Samuel Maull, "Ex-Tyco Execs Get up to Twenty-five Years in Prison," Associated Press, September 19, 2005, www.ap.org.

71. Mark Maremont, "Tyco Figures Will Be Jailed at Least Seven Years; Judge Orders Kozlowski, Swartz to Also Pay Back $240 Million; CEO 'Kleptocratic Management,'" *Wall Street Journal*, September 20, 2005, www.wallstreetjournal.com.

72. Claudia Deutsch, "Tyco Will Pay $50 Million to Settle Case With SEC," *New York Times*, April 18, 2006, www.nytimes.com.

73. Jennifer Levitz, "Former Tyco CEO to Settle Tax Case in New York State," *Wall Street Journal*, May 13, 2006, www.wallstreetjournal.com.

74. Jennifer Levitz, "Kozlowski Seeks Reimbursement," *Wall Street Journal*, June 5, 2006, www.wallstreetjournal.com.

75. Associated Press, "Tyco Ex-CEO Is Sued for Divorce by Wife Who Got $2 Million Party," *Wall Street Journal*, August 17, 2006, www.wallstreetjournal.com.

76. New York State Department of Correctional Services.

77. Chad Bray, "Tyco Ex-CEO's Sales-Tax Charges Are Dismissed," *Wall Street Journal*, December 16, 2006, www.wallstreetjournal.com.

78. Floyd Norris, "Tyco to Pay $3 Billion to Settle Investor Lawsuits," *New York Times*, May 16, 2007.

79. Chad Bray, "Former Tyco Executives Appeal Convictions to Supreme Court," *Wall Street Journal*, April 14, 2009.

80. Bloomberg, "Ex Tyco Boss' Appeal Gets Rejected," *New York Post*, June 9, 2009.

81. Bloomberg News, "S.E.C. Ends Case Against 2 at Tyco," *New York Times*, July 15, 2009.

82. Chad Bray, "Ex-Tyco CEO Ordered to Forfeit Compensation," *Wall Street Journal*, December 3, 2010.

83. Chad Bray, "Tyco, Former CEO Settle Dispute," *The Wall Street Journal*, August 10, 2012.

84. Jason Knott, "Ex-Tyco CEO Dennis Kozlowski Released from Prison," *CEPro*, January 17, 2014

85. David A. Kaplan, "Tyco's 'Piggy', Out of Prison and Living Small," *New York Times*, March 1, 2015.

Case 22

1. Jonathan Soble, "More Than a Clash of the Cultures at Olympus," *Financial Times*, October 14, 2011.

2. Hiroko Tabuchi, "In a Culture Clash, Olympus Ousts its British Chief," *New York Times*, October 14, 2011.

3. Jonathan Soble, "More Than a Clash of the Cultures at Olympus," *Financial Times*, October 14, 2011.

4. Jonathan Soble, "Olympus Acquisitions Central to Claims," *Financial Times*, October 17, 2011.

5. Jonathan Soble, "Olympus Chairman Responds to Accusations," *Financial Times*, October 18, 2011.

6. Jonathan Soble, "Olympus Admits to $687M Fee for Advisor," *Financial Times*, October 19, 2011.

7. Lindsay Whipp, "Olympus Investors Demand Answers Over Fees," *Financial Times*, October 20, 2011.

8. John Gapper, "Olympus Shows Japan's Negative Side," *Financial Times*, October 19, 2011.

9. Lindsay Whipp, "Olympus Agrees to Acquisitions Probe" *Financial Times*, October 21, 2011.

10. Jonathan Soble, "Olympus Chairman Lashes Out at Ex-CEO," *Financial Times*, October 25, 2011.

11. Louise Lucas, Jonathan Soble, and Kara Scannell, "FBI Probes Olympus Over Payment to Advisor," *Financial Times*, October 25, 2011.

12. Jonathan Soble, "Change at Top of Olympus Solves No Puzzles," *Financial Times*, October 26, 2011.

13. Hiroko Tabuche, "At Olympus, Western Questions for Old-School Ways," *New York Times*, October 26, 2011.

14. Kana Inagaki and Phred Dvorak, "Olympus Admits to Hiding Losses," *Wall Street Journal*, November 8, 2011.

15. Kana Inagaki, "Olympus Admits to Hiding Losses," *Wall Street Journal*, November 8, 2011.

16. Third Party Committee, "Investigation Report Summary," Olympus Corporation, December 6, 2011, www.olympusglobal.com/en/info/20116/if111206corpe_2.pdf.

17. Ibid.

18. Daisuke Wakabayashi and Phred Dvorak, "Panel Calls Olympus 'Rotten' at Core," *Wall Street Journal*, December 7, 2011.

19. Floyd Norris, "Deep Roots of Fraud at Olympus," *New York Times*, December 8, 2011.

20. Hiroko Tabuchi and Keith Bradsher, "The Culture Was Corrupt at Olympus, Panel Finds," *New York Times*, December 6, 2011.

21. Third Party Committee, "Investigation Report Summary," Olympus Corporation, December 6, 2011, www.olympusglobal.com/en/info/20116/if111206corpe_2.pdf.

22. Ibid.

23. Juro Osawa and Daisuke Wakabayashi, "At Olympus, Stumbles in Scandal," *Wall Street Journal*, December 21, 2011.

24. Juro Osawa, "Olympus Hotline Didn't Blow Whistle," *Wall Street Journal*, January 4, 2012.

25. Michiyo Nakamoto, "Olympus Disclosure Shakes Auditors' Reputations," *Financial Times*, November 10, 2011.

26. Jonathan Soble and Lindsay Whipp, "Olympus Accounts Deadline Exposes Auditors," *Financial Times*, December 13, 2011.

27. Hiroko Tabuchi, "Authorities Seize Documents in Raid on

Olympus in Tokyo," *New York Times*, December 21, 2011.

28. Louise Lucas and Jonathan Soble, "Woodford Abandons Bid to Lead Olympus," *Financial Times*, January 6, 2012.

29. Hiroko Tabuchi, "Olympus Sues Executives Over Cover-Up, but Does Not Dismiss Them," *New York Times*, January 10, 2012.

30. James Simms, "Japan Can Learn From Olympus Ills," *Wall Street Journal*, November 19, 2011.

31. Hiroko Tabuchi and Keith Bradsher, "Olympus Clears Auditors in an Accounting Cover-Up," *New York Times*, January 17, 2012.

32. Jonathan Soble, "Olympus Panel Finds Auditors Liable," *Financial Times*, January 17, 2012.

33. Hiroko Tabuchi, "Arrests in Olympus Scandal Point to Widening Inquiry Into a Cover-Up," *New York Times*, February 16, 2012.

34. Jonathan Soble, "Olympus Unveils New Management," *Financial Times*, February 27, 2012.

35. Kana Inagaki, "Japan Prosecutors Charge Olympus, Executives," *Wall Street Journal*, March 7, 2012.

36. Reuters, "Olympus and Ex-Executives Plead Guilty in Accounting Fraud," *New York Times*, September 25, 2012.

37. Peter Eavis, "U.S. Makes Arrest in Olympus Scandal," *New York Times*, December 20, 2012.

38. Hiroko Tabuchi, "Suspended Sentences in Olympus Fraud Case," *New York Times*, July 3, 2013.

39. Chad Bray, "Former Banking Executive Pleads Guilty to Assisting Olympus Fraud," *The Wall Street Journal*, September 18, 2013.

Case 23

1. Kortney Stringer, "Wal-Mart Is Sued by Ex-Employee Over Overtime Pay," *Wall Street Journal*, August 10, 2001, www.wallstreetjournal.com.

2. Fortune 500, "Our Annual Ranking of America's Largest Corporations," CNNMoney, http://money .cnn.com/magazines/fortune/ fortune500/2012/full_list/.

3. Walmart, "History Timeline," Wal-Mart Stores, Inc., http:// corporate.walmart.com/our-story/heritage/history-timeline.

4. Fortune 500, "Our Annual Ranking of America's Largest Corporations," CNNMoney, http://money .cnn.com/magazines/fortune/ fortune500/2012/full_list/.

5. Walmart News and Views, "Walmart CEO Says Combination of Momentum, Discipline and Investment Driving Growth, Leverage and Returns," Wal-Mart Stores, Inc., http://news.walmart .com/news-archive/2012/10/10/ walmart-ceo-says-combination-of-momentum-discipline-investment-driving-growth-leverage-returns.

6. Investor Place, "Best Department and Discount Stores for Customer Satisfaction," February 22, 2012, http://investorplace .com/2012/02/best-department-and-discount-stores-for-customer-satisfaction/.

7. Harris Interactive, Heading into Black Friday, Target Ranks as the No. 1 Customer Preferred Discount Retailer in Harris Poll Simple 7 Customer Relationship Index," November 22, 2011, http://www.harrisinteractive .com/NewsRoom/HarrisPolls/ tabid/447/ctl/ReadCustom%20 Default/mid/1508/ArticleId/920/ Default.aspx.

8. Steven Greenhouse, "Suits Say Wal-Mart Forces Workers to Toil Off the Clock," *New York Times*, June 25, 2002.

9. Ibid.

10. Steven Greenhouse, "Workers Assail Night Lock-ins by Wal-Mart," *New York Times*, January 18, 2004, www.nytimes.com.

11. Ibid.

12. Ibid.

13. Steven Greenhouse, "Altering of Worker Time Cards Spurs Growing Number of Suits," *New York Times*, April 4, 2004, www.nytimes.com.

14. Ann Zimmerman, "Big Retailers Face Overtime Suits as Bosses Do More 'Hourly' Work," *Wall Street Journal*, May 26, 2004, www.wallstreetjournal.com.

15. Ibid.

16. Steven Greenhouse, "U.S. Jury Cites Unpaid Work at Wal-Mart," *New York Times*, December 20, 2002, www .nytimes.com.

17. The Associated Press, "Wal-Mart Loses Unpaid Overtime Case," CBSNews.com, February 11, 2009, http://www.cbsnews .com/2100-201_162-533818. html.

18. Associated Press, "Jury Orders Wal-Mart to Pay at Least $78 Million for Breaking Labor Laws," *USA Today*, October 13, 2006, www.usatoday.com.

19. Steven Greenhouse, "Wal-Mart Told to Pay $78 Million," *New York Times*, October 14, 2006, www.nytimes.com.

20. Steven Greenhouse, "Wal-Mart Settles U.S. Suit About Overtime," *New York Times*, January 26, 2007, www.nytimes.com.

21. Steven Greenhouse, "Wal-Mart to Pay $54 Million to Settle Suit Over Wages," *New York Times*, December 10, 2008.

22. Steven Greenhouse and Stephanie Rosenbloom, "Wal-Mart Settles 63 Lawsuits Over Wages," *New York Times*, December 24, 2008.

23. http://m.chainstorage.com/ article/wal-mart-pay-3-million-settle-mealbreaks-claim.

24. Steven Greenhouse and Constance Hays, "Wal-Mart Sex-Bias Suit Given Class-Action Status," *New York Times*, June 23, 2004, www.nytimes.com.

25. Steven Greenhouse, "Wal-Mart Faces Lawsuit Over Sex Discrimination," *New York Times*, February 16, 2003, www.nytimes.com.

26. Constance Hays, "Social Issues Tug Wal-Mart in Differing Directions," *New York Times*, June 30, 2004, www.nytimes.com.

27. Steven Greenhouse, "Wal-Mart Gender Case Divides Court," *New York Times*, April 26, 2010.

28. Adam Liptak and Steven Greenhouse, "Supreme Court Agrees to Hear Wal-Mart Appeal," *New York Times*, December 6, 2010.

29. "Wal-Mart's Class Victory," *Wall Street Journal*, June 21, 2011.

30. Andrew Martin, "Female Wal-Mart Employees File New Bias Case," *New York Times*, October 27, 2011.

31. Bernard Wysocki and Ann Zimmerman, "Bargain Hunter: Wal-Mart Cost-Cutting Finds a Big Target in Health Benefits; Restrictions and Tough Stance on Basic Claims Keep Its Outlays Below Average; Setting Industry 'Benchmark'?," *Wall Street Journal*, September 30, 2003, www.wallstreetjournal.com.

32. Ibid.

33. Susan Chambers, "Health Plan at Wal-Mart," *New York Times*, December 12, 2003, www.nytimes.com.

34. Reed Abelson, "States Are Battling Against Wal-Mart Over Health Care," *New York Times*, November 1, 2004, www.nytimes.com.

35. Michael Barbaro, "Wal-Mart to Expand Health Plan for Workers," *New York Times*, October 24, 2005, www.nytimes.com.

36. Steven Greenhouse and Michael Barbaro, "Wal-Mart Memo Suggests Ways to Cut Employee Benefit Costs," *New York Times*, October 25, 2005, www.nytimes.com.

37. Michael Barbaro and Claudia Deutsch, "Maryland Sets a Health Cost for Wal-Mart," *New York Times*, January 13, 2006, www.nytimes.com.

38. Dylan Q. Maui, "Wal-Mart Says It Will Improve Health Benefits," *Washington Post*, February 24, 2006, www.washingtonpost.com.

39. "Wal-Mart Eases Benefits Rules for Part-Timers," *Wall Street Journal*, April 18, 2006, www.wallstreetjournal.com.

40. "The 'Wal-Mart Tax' Goes Down," *Wall Street Journal*, July 20, 2006, www.wallstreetjournal.com.

41. Michael Barbaro and Reed Abelson, "Wal-Mart Says Health Plan Is Covering More Workers," *New York Times*, January 11, 2007, www.nytimes.com.

42. Michael Barbaro "Wal-Mart Says More Than Half Its Workers Have Its Health Insurance," *New York Times*, January 23, 2008.

43. Steven Greenhouse and Reed Abelson, "Wal-Mart Cuts Some Care Benefits," *New York Times*, October 20, 2011.

44. Shelly Banjo and Stephanie Armour, "Wal-Mart to End Health Insurance for Some Part-Time Employees", *The Wall Street Journal*, October 7, 2014.

45. Steven Greenhouse, "Judge Rules against Wal-Mart on Refusal to Talk to Workers," *New York Times*, June 19, 2003, www.nytimes.com.

46. Steven Greenhouse, "Trying to Overcome Embarrassment, Labor Opens a Drive to Organize Wal-Mart," *New York Times*, November 8, 2002, www.nytimes.com.

47. "Walmart Strike Memo Reveals Confidential Management Plans," *Huffington Post Business*, October 31, 2012, http://www.huffingtonpost.com/2012/10/13/walmart-strike-memo_n_1962039.html

48. Ibid.

49. Dow Jones Newswires, "Wal-Mart to Review Quebec Union Ruling," *Wall Street Journal*, August 4, 2004, www.wallstreetjournal.com.

50. Ian Austen, "A Rarity for Wal-Mart: Talking to a Union," *New York Times*, October 26, 2004, www.nytimes.com.

51. Associated Press, "Canadian Court Backs Wal-Mart in Store Closure," *New York Times*, November 28, 2009.

52. Leslie Chang, "Wal-Mart Says It Would Allow Unions in Its Chinese Operations," *Wall Street Journal*, November 24, 2004, www.wallstreetjournal.com.

53. Elizabeth A. Harris, "Labor Panel Finds Illegal Punishments at Walmart," *New York Times*, November 18, 2013.

54. Jad Mouawad, "Walmart Is Facing Claims That It Fired Protesters," *New York Times*, January 14, 2014.

55. Steven Greenhouse, Walmart Illegally Punished Workers, Judge Rules," *New York Times*, December 10, 2014.

56. Mei Fong and Ann Zimmerman, "Red Flag: China's Union Push Leaves Wal-Mart with Hard Choice; Law Requires Foreign Firms to Allow Organized Labor; Retailer's Tough Stance; One Store's Workers Wary," *Wall Street Journal*, May 13, 2006, www.wallstreetjournal.com.

57. David Barboza, "Wal-Mart Will Unionize in All of China," *New York Times*, August 10, 2006, www.nytimes.com.

58. Mei Fong, "Wal-Mart Bends to Party Rules in China, Allowing Store Cells," *Wall Street Journal*, December 19, 2006, www.wallstreetjournal.com.

59. www.Walmartfoundation.org.

60. Steven Greenhouse, "Wal-Mart Raids by U.S. Aimed at Illegal Aliens," *New York Times*, October 24, 2003, www.nytimes.com.

61. "Nine Immigrants Sue Wal-Mart Over Pay, Tax Contributions," *Wall Street Journal*, November 10, 2003, www.wallstreetjournal.com.

62. "Immigrants File Racketeering Suit Against Wal-Mart," *Wall Street Journal*, November 12, 2003, www.wallstreetjournal.com.

63. Ann Zimmerman, "Labor Pains: After Huge Raid on Illegals, Wal-Mart Fires Back at U.S.; Retail Giant Says It Believed It Was Helping Long Probe When Agents Struck; Complex Web of Contractors," *Wall Street Journal*, December 19, 2003, www.wallstreetjournal.com.

64. Steven Greenhouse, "Wal-Mart to Pay U.S. $11 Million in Lawsuit on Immigrant

Workers," *New York Times*, March 19, 2005, www.nytimes.com.

65. Steven Greenhouse, "Wal-Mart Agrees to Pay Fine in Child Labor Cases," *New York Times*, February 12, 2005, www.nytimes.com.

66. Steven Greenhouse, "In-House Audit Says Wal-Mart Violated Labor Laws," *New York Times*, January 13, 2004, www.nytimes.com.

67. Kris Hudson, "Wal-Mart Workers Awarded $172 Million," *Wall Street Journal*, December 23, 2005, www.wallstreetjournal.com.

68. Lisa Alcalay Klug, "Jury Rules Wal-Mart Must Pay $172 Million Over Meal Breaks," *New York Times*, December 23, 2005, www.nytimes.com.

69. "Wal-Mart Stores Inc.: Group Files Suit Challenging Enforcement of Conduct Code," *Wall Street Journal*, September 14, 2005, www.wallstreetjournal.com.

70. Steven Greenhouse, "Suit Says Wal-Mart Is Lax on Labor Abuses Overseas," *New York Times*, September 14, 2005, www.nytimes.com.

71. Andrew Rosenthal, "No Comment Necessary: Walmart's Food Drive, for Employees," *New York Times*, November 18, 2013.

72. Michael Barbaro and Steven Greenhouse, "Wal-Mart Says Thank You to Workers," *New York Times*, December 4, 2006, www.nytimes.com.

73. Paul Ziobro and Eric Morath, "Wal-Mart Raising Wages as Market Gets Tighter," *The Wall Street Journal*, February 19, 2015.

Case 24

1. Deborah Solomon, "WorldCom CEO's Loans Come Due as Company's Share Price Implodes," *Wall Street Journal*, February 1, 2002, www.wallstreetjournal.com.

2. Shawn Young, "WorldCom Net Income Falls 64%; Telecom Plans $15 Billion Charge," *Wall Street Journal*, February 8, 2002, www.wallstreetjournal.com.

3. Joann Lublin and Shawn Young, "WorldCom's $341 Million Loan to CEO Is Most Generous in Recent Memory," *Wall Street Journal*, March 15, 2002, www.wallstreetjournal.com.

4. Shawn Young and Deborah Solomon, "WorldCom CEO Owes $339.7 Million for Loans He Took out to Buy Stock," *Wall Street Journal*, February 8, 2002, www.wallstreetjournal.com.

5. Yochi Dreazen, "WorldCom Suspends Executives in Order Overbooking Scandal," *Wall Street Journal*, February 14, 2002, www.wallstreetjournal.com.

6. Barnaby J. Feder, "Technology: SEC Seeks WorldCom and Qwest Documents," *New York Times*, March 12, 2002, www.nytimes.com.

7. Deborah Solomon and Shawn Young, "Qwest, WorldCom Face Scrutiny From SEC on Accounting Practices," *Wall Street Journal*, March 12, 2002, www.wallstreetjournal.com.

8. Shawn Young, "WorldCom Says Big Loan to CEO May Have Spurred SEC's Inquiry," *Wall Street Journal*, March 14, 2002, www.wallstreetjournal.com.

9. Ibid.

10. Jared Sandberg, "Bernie Ebbers Bet the Ranch—Really—on WorldCom Stock," *Wall Street Journal*, April 12, 2002, www.wallstreetjournal.com.

11. Charles Haddad and Steve Rosenbush, "Woe Is WorldCom," *Businessweek*, May 6, 2002, www.businessweek.com.

12. Shawn Young, "WorldCom Plans to Cut 3,700 Jobs From Core Data-Services Group," *Wall Street Journal*, April 4, 2002, www.wallstreetjournal.com.

13. Shawn Young, "WorldCom CEO Didn't Get Bonus: Stock Falls 33% on Sales Warning," *Wall Street Journal*, April 23, 2002, www.wallstreetjournal.com.

14. Rebecca Blumenstein and Jared Sandberg, "WorldCom's CEO Ebbers Resigns Amid Board Pressure Over Probe," *Wall Street Journal*, April 30, 2002, www.wallstreetjournal.com.

15. Shawn Young, "Credit Facility for WorldCom Faces Delay as Talks Continue," *Wall Street Journal*, June 17, 2002, www.wallstreetjournal.com.

16. Jared Sandberg, "WorldCom's New Leader Brings Sound Reputation to Shaky Helm," *Wall Street Journal*, May 1, 2002, www.wallstreetjournal.com.

17. Shawn Young and Mitchell Pacelle, "WorldCom Will Tap Its Credit Line, Indicating Possible Loan Troubles," *Wall Street Journal*, May 16, 2002, www.wallstreetjournal.com.

18. Shawn Young, "WorldCom Shares Slip Under $1 on Downgrade From Grubman," *Wall Street Journal*, June 25, 2002, www.wallstreetjournal.com.

19. Jared Sandberg, Rebecca Blumenstein, and Shawn Young, "WorldCom Internal Probe Uncovers Massive Fraud," *Wall Street Journal*, June 26, 2002, www.wallstreetjournal.com.

20. Shawn Young and Nicole Harris, "Internal Auditor at WorldCom Felt Sad About Alerting Board," *Wall Street Journal*, June 28, 2002, www.wallstreetjournal.com.

21. Susan Pulliam and Deborah Solomon, "How Three Unlikely Sleuths Exposed Fraud at WorldCom," *Wall Street Journal*, October 30, 2002, www.wallstreetjournal.com.

22. Ibid.

23. Ibid.

24. Ibid.

25. www.sec.gov/Archives/edgar/data/723527/000093176303001862/dex991.htm

26. Ibid.

27. Ibid.

28. Ibid.

29. Susan Pulliam, "WorldCom Internal Memos Reveal Sullivan's Plan to Bury Misstatement," *Wall Street*

Journal, July 9, 2002, www.wallstreetjournal.com.

30. Ibid.

31. Yochi Dreazen and Deborah Solomon, "Internal Documents Suggest WorldCom Knew of Violations," *Wall Street Journal*, July 16, 2002, www.wallstreetjournal.com.

32. Ibid.

33. Jared Sandberg, Deborah Solomon, and Rebecca Blumenstein, "Accounting Spot-Check Unearthed a Scandal in WorldCom's Books," *Wall Street Journal*, June 27, 2002, www.wallstreetjournal.com.

34. Kurt Eichenwald and Simon Romero, "Technology; Inquiry Finds Effort at Delay at WorldCom," *New York Times*, July 4, www.nytimes.com.

35. Charles Haddad, Dean Foust, and Steve Rosenbush, "WorldCom's Sorry Legacy," *Businessweek*, June 28, 2002, www.businessweek.com.

36. *SEC v. WorldCom, Inc.*, Civ. No. 02 CV 4963 (JSR), Nov. 26, 2002 (S.D.N.Y.).

37. Susan Pulliam and Deborah Solomon, "How Three Unlikely Sleuths Exposed Fraud at WorldCom," *Wall Street Journal*, October 30, 2002, www.wallstreetjournal.com.

38. Shawn Young, "WorldCom's Assets Have Plummeted, Leaving Gap Between Books, Reality," *Wall Street Journal*, July 3, 2002, www.wallstreetjournal.com.

39. Yochi J. Dreazen and Deborah Solomon, "Internal Documents Suggest WorldCom Knew of Violation." *Wall Street Journal*, July 16, 2002. www.wallstreetjournal.com.

40. Ibid.

41. Jared Sandberg, Deborah Solomon, and Nicole Harris, "WorldCom Investigations Shift Focus to Ousted CEO Ebbers," *Wall Street Journal*, July 1, 2002, www.wallstreetjournal.com.

42. "A Guide to Corporate Scandals," *The Economist*. July 15, 2002.

43. Jared Sandberg, Shawn Young, and Deborah Solomon, "WorldCom to File Chapter 11, as Cash Reserves Dwindle Fast," *Wall Street Journal*, July 19, 2002, www.wallstreetjournal.com.

44. Simon and Floyd Norris, "New Disclosures From WorldCom May Add to Accounting Scandal," *New York Times*, July 2, 2002.

45. Rebecca Blumenstein and Susan Pulliam, "Reports Say Ebbers and Others Conspired in WorldCom Fraud," *Wall Street Journal*, June 10, 2003, www.wallstreetjournal.com.

46. www.findlaw.com/news .findlaw.com/wsj/docs/ worldcom/120902cp11smot .pdf; Seth Schiesel, "Most of Board at WorldCom Resigns Posts," *New York Times*, December 18, 2002.

47. "WorldCom's Bankruptcy Crisis," *Daniels Fund Ethics Initiative*, n.d, http:// danielsethics.mgt.unm.edu.

48. Ibid.

49. Reuters, "WorldCom Company Timeline," *The Washington Post*, March 15, 2005.

50. "MCI Restates $74.4 Billion in pre-tax income," *USAToday.com*, March 12, 2004.

51. Shawn Young and Christine Nuzum, "Sullivan Says Ebbers Ducked Merger Talks to Keep Veil on Fraud," *Wall Street Journal*, February 11, 2005, www.wallstreetjournal.com.

52. Christine Nuzum, "WorldCom Ex-Controller Says Ebbers Cited His Own Difficulties," *Wall Street Journal*, January 31, 2005, www.wallstreetjournal.com.

53. Christine Nuzum, "WorldCom Ex-Controller Traces Improper Accounting Back to 1997," *Wall Street Journal*, February 2, 2005, www.wallstreetjournal.com.

54. Erin McClam, "Ex-CFO Warned About WorldCom Accounting," Associated Press, February 9, 2005, www.ap.org.

55. Ibid.

56. "Excerpts from the Ebbers's Trial," *Wall Street Journal*, March 1, 2005, www.wallstreetjournal.com.

57. Almar Latour, Shawn Young, and Li Yuan, "Ebbers Is Convicted in Massive Fraud," *Wall Street Journal*, March 16, 2005, www.wallstreetjournal.com.

58. Shelia Byrd, "WorldCom's Successor Will Pay $100 Million to State," *Associated Press*, May 9, 2005. www.ap.org.

59. Shawn Young, "Court Is Told That Andersen Ignored Red Flags at WorldCom," *Wall Street Journal*, March 30, 2005, www.wallstreetjournal.com.

60. Erin McClam, "Andersen Pays $65 Million to Settle WorldCom Claims," *Associated Press*, April 26, 2005, www.ap.org.

61. "Former WorldCom Chief to Forfeit Assets in Settlement," *Associated Press*, June 30, 2005, 1.

62. Ken Belson, "WorldCom Chief Is Given Twenty-Five Years for Huge Fraud," *New York Times*, July 14, 2005, www.nytimes.com.

63. Ken Belson, "Ex-WorldCom Executives Forfeits Florida Mansion," *New York Times*, July 27, 2005, www.nytimes.com.

64. Shawn Young, Dionne Searcey, and Nathan Koppel, "Cooperation Pays: Sullivan Gets Five Years," *Wall Street Journal*, August 12, 2005, www.wallstreetjournal.com.

65. Jonathan Weil and Robin Sidel, "WorldCom Investors Settle Lawsuits," *Wall Street Journal*, October 27, 2005, www.wallstreetjournal.com.

66. "WorldCom Ex-Officer Won't Pay a Fine," *Wall Street Journal*, July 28, 2006, www.wallstreetjournal.com.

67. Associated Press, "Former WorldCom Chief Begins Twenty-Five Years in Prison," *New York Times*, September 27, 2006, www.nytimes.com.

68. "Ebbers Seeks Presidential Pardon," *Wall Street Journal*, December 4, 2008.

69. "Former SEC Chairman Richard Breeden to Supervise Distribution of SEC's Civil Penalty Against WorldCom," U.S. Securities and Exchange Commission, Litigation Release No. 18451, November 10, 2003. http://www.sec.gov/litigation/litreleases/lr18451.htm.

70. Lynn Sharp Paine and Bridget Gurtler, *Governance Reform at MCI* (Boston: Harvard Business School Publishing, 2004).

71. Steve Rosenbush, "Five Lessons of the WorldCom Debacle," *Businessweek*, March 16, 2005, www.businessweek.com.

72. Associated Press, "Former WorldCom Chief Begins Twenty-Five Years in Prison," *New York Times*, September 27, 2006, www.nytimes.com.

73. Aaron Smith, "Enron Exec Andy Fastow Nears Prison Release," *CNN.com*, May 18, 2011. http://money.cnn.com/2011/05/18/news/companies/fastow_enron_prison.

Case 25

1. "BP Chief to Gulf Residents: 'I'm Sorry," *CNN.com*, May 30, 2010.

2. Campbell Roberson, "Search Continues After Oil Rig Blast," *New York Times*, April 21, 2010.

3. Ian Urbina and Justin Gillis, "Workers on Oil Rig Recall a Terrible Night of Blasts," *New York Times*, May 7, 2010.

4. Ian Urbina, "In Gulf, It Was Unclear Who Was in Charge of Rig," *New York Times*, June 5, 2010. http://www.nytimes.com/2010/06/06/us/06rig.html.

5. Douglas A. Blackmon, Vanessa O'Connell, Alexandra Berzon, and Ana Campoy, "There Was 'Nobody in Charge'," *Wall Street Journal*, May 28, 2010.

6. Ibid.

7. Campbell Robertson, Clifford Krauss, Jordan Flaherty, and Liz Robbins, "Oil Rig Sinks, Raising Fears of a Major Spill in the Gulf," *New York Times*, April 23, 2010.

8. "BP Doing 'Whatever Necessary' to Contain Oil Spill," *Wall Street Journal*, April 26, 2010.

9. Russell Gold, "Leaking Oil Well Lacked Safeguard Device," *Wall Street Journal*, April 28, 2010.

10. Eric Lipton and John Broder, "Regulator Deferred to Oil Industry on Rig Safety," *New York Times*, May 7, 2010, http://www.nytimes.com/2010/05/08/us/08agency.html.

11. Ian Urbina, "In Gulf, It Was Unclear Who Was in Charge of Rig," *New York Times*, June 5, 2010.

12. Russell Gold, Ben Casselman, and Guy Chazan, "Leaking Oil Well Lacked Safeguard Device," *Wall Street Journal*, April 28, 2010.

13. Gardiner Harris, "Minerals Management Service Director Resigns Over Spill," *New York Times*, May 27, 2010.

14. Sarah Lyall, Clifford Krauss, and Jad Mouawad, "In BP's Record, a History of Boldness and Costly Blunders," *New York Times*, July 12, 2010, http://www.nytimes.com/2010/07/13/business/energy-environment/13bprisk.html.

15. Jad Mouawad, Clifford Kraus, Julie Werdiger, Andrew Lehrer, and Griffin Palmer, "Fast-Growing BP Also Has a Mounting List of Spills and Safety Lapses," *New York Times*, May 9, 2010.

16. Steven Greenhouse, "BP to Pay Record Fine for Refinery," *New York Times*, August 12, 2010.

17. Sarah Lyall, Clifford Krauss, and Jad Mouawad, "In BP's Record, a History of Boldness and Costly Blunders," *New York Times*, July 12, 2010, http://www.nytimes.com/2010/07/13/business/energy-environment/13bprisk.html.

18. John M. Broder, "BP Is Fined $25 Million for '06 Spills at Pipelines," *New York Times*, May 3, 2011.

19. Ben Casselman, "Rig Owner Had Rising Talley of Accidents," *Wall Street Journal*, May 10, 2010.

20. Ibid.

21. "BP Doing 'Whatever Necessary' to Contain Oil Spill," *Wall Street Journal*, April 26, 2010.

22. Guy Chazan and Jim Carlton, "BP Wasn't Prepared for Leak, CEO Says," *Wall Street Journal*, May 14, 2010.

23. Helene Cooper and John M. Broder, "BP's Ties to Agency Are Long and Complex," *New York Times*, May 25, 2010.

24. "BP Chief to Gulf Residents: 'I'm Sorry," *CNN.com*, May 30, 2010.

25. Campbell Robertson, "Efforts to Repel Oil Spill Are Described as Chaotic," *New York Times*, June 14, 2010.

26. Jad Mouawad and Clifford Krauss, "Another Torrent BP Works to Stem: Its C.E.O.," *New York Times*, June 3, 2010.

27. Liz Robbins, "BP Chief Draws Outrage for Attending Yacht Race," *New York Times*, June 19, 2010.

28. John Broder, "BP's Chief Offers Answers, But Not to Liking of House Committee," *New York Times*, June 17, 2010.

29. Jad Mouawad and Clifford Krauss, "BP Is Expected to Replace Chief With American," *New York Times*, July 26, 2010.

30. Ben Casselman and Jennifer Levitz, "Congress Homes in on Rig's Blowout Preventer," *Wall Street Journal*, May 13, 2010.

31. Russell Gold and Neil King, "Red Flags Were Ignored Aboard Doomed Rig," *Wall Street Journal*, May 13, 2010.

32. James C. McKinley Jr., "Documents Fill in Gaps in Narrative on Oil Rig Blast," *New York Times*, September 7, 2010.

33. Ben Casselman and Russell Gold, "BP Decisions Set Stage for Disaster," *Wall Street Journal*, May 27, 2010.

34. Ian Urbina, "Documents Show Early Worries About Safety of Rig," *New York Times*, May 29, 2010.

35. Russell Gold and Ben Casselman, "Alarm Was Disabled Before BP Blast," *Wall Street Journal*, July 23, 2010.

36. Helene Cooper and Peter Baker, "U.S. Opens Criminal Inquiry Into Oil Spill," *New York Times*, June 1, 2010.

37. "Can BP Ever Get It Right?," *New York Times*, June 7, 2010.

38. Clifford Krauss, "BP Moves Chief Executive to Lesser Role in Spill Response," *New York Times*, June 18, 2010.

39. Ibid.

40. Campbell Robertson and Clifford Krauss, "Gulf Spill Is the Largest of Its Kind, Scientists Say," *New York Times*, August 2, 2010.

41. Ben Casselman and Spencer Swartz, "BP Report Pins Most of Blame on Others," *Wall Street Journal*, September 8, 2010.

42. Guy Chazan, "Well Is Sealed; Tale Isn't Over," *Wall Street Journal*, September 19, 2010.

43. Henry Fountain, "Once Well Is Fully Sealed, BP May Go Back for More," *New York Times*, September 19, 2010.

44. Russell Gold and Angel Gonzalez, "BP Sues Contractors Transocean, Cameron," *Wall Street Journal*, April 21, 2011.

45. John Schwartz, "U.S. Sues Companies for Spill Damages," *New York Times*, December 15, 2010.

46. "Mr. Feinberg and the Gulf Settlement," *New York Times*, August 29, 2010.

47. Dionne Searcey, "Death Payouts in BP Spill Start at $8 Million," *Wall Street Journal*, March 30, 2011; Guy Chazan, "BP Sues Halliburton Over Gulf Disaster," *Wall Street Journal*, April 21, 2011.

48. "BP's Spill Fund: Facts and Figures," *New York Times*, August 20, 2010.

49. *BP 2011 Sustainability Review*, http://www.bp.com/sustainability.

50. Tom Fowler, "BP, Plaintiffs Reach Settlement in Gulf Oil Case," *Wall Street Journal*, March 4, 2012. http://online.wsj.com/article/SB1000142405 2970203753704577258230885 387926.html.

51. *BP 2011 Sustainability Review*, http://www.bp.com/sustainability.

52. "Criminality in the Gulf Spill," *New York Times*, November 15, 2012.

53. John Schwartz, "Rig Owner Will Settle With U.S. in Gulf Spill," *New York Times*, January 3, 2013.

54. John Schwartz, "Judge's Ruling on Gulf Oil Spill Lowers Ceiling on the Fine BP Is Facing," *New York Times*, January 15, 2015.

Case 26

1. www.greystonbakery.com.

2. Ibid.

3. www.bcccc.net.

4. www.bcorporation.net/greystonbakery.

5. www.greystonbakery.com.

6. Elizabeth Field, "Zen Bakery Begins Training Program," *New York Times*, October 18, 1987.

7. www.greystonbakery.com.

8. www.greystonbakery.com/the-Foundation/.

9. Rebecca Leung, "Greyston Bakery: Let 'Em Eat Cake," *CBS News*, February 11, 2009.

10. *The Greyston Bakery's Guiding Principles*. http://www.greystonbakery.com/up-content/uploads/pdf/greyston-bakery-guiding-principles.pdf.

11. Julius Walls, "Next Path to My Life," *Yonkers Tribune*, September 29, 2009.

12. Julia Kennedy, "Ethics in Business: Interview With Julius Walls, Jr., CEO, Greyston Bakery," Carnegie Council's Global Ethics Forum, September 1, 2009, http://www.carnegiecouncil.org/studio/multimedia/20090903/index.html.

13. Julius Walls, "Next Path to My Life," *Yonkers Tribune*, September 29, 2009.

14. http://communityfoundationsj.org/PublicPages/summit.aspx.

15. "Greyston Names Mike Brady President & CEO," press release, March 3, 2015, http://greyston.com/wp-content/uploads/2013/09/Greyston-announces-Mike-Brady-CEO-2.pdf.

• Index •

• About the Authors •

Peter A. Stanwick is an Associate Professor in the Department of Management at Auburn University. His research has been published in various journals, including *The Journal of Business Ethics, Management Decision, The Journal of Corporate Citizenship, The Journal of Corporate Accounting and Finance, Business Strategy and the Environment, Eco-Management and Auditing, American Business Review, International Journal of Commerce and Management, Southern Business Review, International Journal of Management, Journal of Business Strategies, Journal of Organizational Change Management, Journal of Business and Economic Perspectives, Journal of Hospital Marketing,* and *The International Journal of Organizational Analysis.* In addition, Dr. Stanwick serves as a reviewer for the *Journal of Business Ethics.* He was invited to present papers in 2004 and 2011 at Oxford University. Dr. Stanwick has received two grants from the Daniel F. Breeden Endowments for Faculty Enhancement and a Pursell Ethics Grant. In 1995, Dr. Stanwick received the Graduate Faculty Member Award for Excellence by the Association of Graduate Business Students at Auburn University. Dr. Stanwick teaches strategic management at the undergraduate and graduate level, international management at the undergraduate level, and business ethics at the undergraduate and graduate levels. In addition, Dr. Stanwick is the College of Business Advisor for Sigma Iota Epsilon (The National Honorary and Professional Management Fraternity) and the Committee of 19, which addresses the social problems of hunger.

Sarah D. Stanwick is Associate Professor in the School of Accountancy at Auburn University. Her research has been published in various journals, including *The Journal of Business Ethics, Advances in Accounting, The Accounting Educators' Journal, The Journal of Corporate Accounting and Finance, the CPA Journal, The Journal of Corporate Citizenship, Business Strategy and the Environment, Eco-Management and Auditing,* and the *International Journal of Commerce and Management.* While at Auburn University, she has received two Daniel F. Breeden Endowments for Faculty Enhancement and a Pursell Ethics Grant. In addition, she received a grant from the World Resources Institute to write an instructional case on the pulp and paper industry in Alabama. She has taught financial and managerial/cost accounting at the undergraduate and graduate levels. She has also taught accounting ethics at the graduate level. Her research interests include the areas of environmental accounting, ethical issues for managers and accountants, and social responsibility issues. Currently, she is the advisor for the Auburn University chapter of Beta Gamma Sigma (the international honor society for achievement in the study of business) and the advisor for the Auburn University Women in Business Organization. She serves as co-editor for the Public Interest Section newsletter for the American Accounting Association. On campus, she serves as the College of Business Diversity Officer. She is a Certified Public Accountant.